The

OXFORD

Children's

THESAURUS

The
OXFORD

Children's

THESAURUS

Compiled by
Alan Spooner

OXFORD UNIVERSITY PRESS

Oxford University Press, Great Clarendòn Street, Oxford OX2 6DP

Oxford New York
Athens Auckland Bangkok Bogotá
Buenos Aires Calcutta Cape Town Chennai Dar es Salaam Delhi
Florence Hong Kong Istanbul Karachi
Kuala Lumpur Madrid Melbourne
Mexico City Mumbai Nairobi Paris São Paulo Singapore
Taipei Tokyo Toronto Warsaw

and associated companies in
Berlin   Ibadan

Oxford is a trade mark of Oxford University Press

© **Oxford University Press 1987**

First published 1987
Redesigned impression 1994
10

ISBN 0 19 910323 2 (Hardback–Trade Edition)
ISBN 0 19 910322 4 (Hardback–Educational Edition)
A CIP catalogue record for this book is available from the British Library

Printed in Great Britain by Cambridge University Press

Do you have a query about words, their origin, meaning, use, spelling,
pronunciation, or any other aspect of the English language? Then write to
OWLS at Oxford University Press, Great Clarendon Street, Oxford OX2 6DP

All queries will be answered using the full resources of the
Oxford Dictionary Department

Preface

I have designed this thesaurus to enable young people to make good use of the words they already know, and to help them to improve their knowledge and understanding of language generally. I hope that it is simple to use, but that at the same time it includes a wide enough vocabulary to make it interesting and thought-provoking.

Our language is an extremely complicated system. Clearly, a book of this kind cannot give all the information a young person needs in order to judge whether a word is likely to convey a particular shade of meaning, or to be appropriate to a particular spoken or written context. It will often be important, therefore, for young people to be helped in their use of the book, as in their general language development, by parents, teachers, and other experienced users of English. Indeed, I hope that teachers may find it a useful book not only for children to refer to, but also for them to work from in various kinds of language work in the classroom.

The basic vocabulary of the *Thesaurus* is the same as that of *The Oxford Children's Dictionary (Second Edition)*. This means that the two books can be used alongside each other easily and confidently. Very occasionally I have included in the *Thesaurus* a sense or form of a word different from that in the *Dictionary*: but I have done so only when I felt it would be helpful rather than confusing to do so.

I should like to record my debt to John Weston, with whom I collaborated on the two editions of *The Oxford Children's Dictionary*. Without his enthusiasm and hard work on the *Dictionary*, this *Thesaurus* would not have come about.

I should also like to thank members of the Oxford University Press: Tony Augarde and Rob Scriven for their supportive help and advice; and in particular Janette Brown who has done an enormous amount of hard and constructive work in preparing the book for publication.

AJS

Headwords

The first word of each entry (the *headword*) is printed in green so that you can find it easily.

Cross-references

If we don't have space for all the information you might want under a particular headword, we suggest that you look up another entry. This is called *cross-referencing*.

geranium SEE **flower**.

gerbil SEE **animal, pet**.

germ bacteria, (informal) bug, microbe, virus. ! *Bacteria* is a plural word.

germinate *Our seeds have germinated.* to grow, to shoot, to spring up, to sprout, to start growing.

gesture 1 action, movement, sign. **2** WAYS TO MAKE GESTURES ARE to beckon, to nod, to point, to salute, to shake your head, to shrug, to wave, to wink.

get 1 *What did you get for Christmas? What can I get for £10?* to acquire, to be given, to buy, to gain, to get hold of, to obtain, to procure, to purchase, to receive. **2** *Tell the dog to get the ball.* to bring, to fetch, to pick up, to retrieve. **3** *Did you get a prize?* to earn, to take, to win. **4** *Lucy got a cold.* to catch, to contract, to develop, to suffer from. **5** *Get Tony to do the washing-up.* to cause, to persuade. **6** *Let's get tea now.* to make ready, to prepare. **7** *I don't get what he means.* to comprehend, to follow, to grasp, to understand. **8** *What time do you get to school?* to arrive at, to reach.

Warnings

When you need to be particularly careful about how you use a word, a warning goes in brackets before the word or phrase concerned.

Notes

Occasionally, we draw your attention to some interesting fact or problem about a word. This goes at the end of an entry after a big exclamation mark.

Related words

An explanation in small capitals tells you that the words we give are not synonyms but are related in some other way.

Synonyms

Most entries give you *synonyms*, words which are similar in meaning to the headword.

Numbers

When a word has more than one meaning, or can be used in more than one way, numbers separate the main meanings or uses of a word from each other.

Examples

Phrases or sentences printed in *italics* are examples of how the headword can be used.

What is a thesaurus for?

A thesaurus helps you find the words you need to make your language more interesting and more effective in saying what you want to say. It gives you words with similar meaning to the word you look up, so that you can choose the best word for your purpose. It also helps you find words which are related in other ways: names of various foods, words to describe the weather, terms to do with medical treatment, and so on.

What will you find in this thesaurus?

Headwords
The first word of each entry (the *headword*) is printed in green so that you can find it easily. All the headwords are arranged in alphabetical order.

Numbers
When a word has more than one meaning, or can be used in more than one way, numbers separate the main meanings or uses of a word from each other.

Examples
Phrases or sentences printed in *italics* are examples of how the headword can be used.

Synonyms
Most entries give you *synonyms*, words which are similar in meaning to the headword. Synonyms hardly ever mean exactly the same, so you should think carefully about how you use them. Which is the word which gives *most exactly* the meaning you have in mind? Which words are more informal, and which more for-

mal? Which words are more old-fashioned, and which are more up-to-date?

Related words
Sometimes an explanation in small capitals tells you that the words we give are not synonyms but are related in some other way. *For example*: *to nod* and *to point* do not mean the same, but they are both ways to make gestures. So under gesture we say WAYS TO MAKE GESTURES ARE ... and *to nod* and *to point* are listed there.

Cross-references
If we don't have space for all the information you might want under a particular headword, we suggest that you look up another entry. This is called *cross-referencing*. When you look up a cross-reference you will find synonyms or related words which may help you. *For example*: if you look up geranium, it says: SEE flower. Under *flower* you will find *geranium* listed with other words to do with flowers.

Warnings

When you need to be particularly careful about how you use a word, a warning goes in brackets before the word or phrase concerned. *For example*: (informal) means that the word or phrase which comes next is usually *informal*, or more likely to be used in conversation than in writing. Similar warnings mark words which are *old-fashioned, insulting*, etc.

Notes

Occasionally, we draw your attention to some interesting fact or problem about a word. This goes at the end of an entry after a big exclamation mark.

Definitions

A thesaurus does not give definitions of words, although it helps you to understand words by putting them with other words of similar or related meaning. If you want a definition of a word, you must look it up in a dictionary. *The Oxford Children's Dictionary (Second Edition)* gives definitions of all the words in this thesaurus.

A a

abandon 1 *The weather was so bad they had to abandon their walk.* to cancel, to discard, to drop, to give up, to postpone, to scrap. 2 *Abandon ship!* to desert, to evacuate, to forsake, to leave, to quit. 3 *They abandoned Ben Gunn on Treasure Island.* to maroon, to strand.

abbey cathedral, church, monastery, priory. SEE ALSO **church**.

abdicate *to abdicate the throne.* to give up, to renounce, to resign.

abdomen belly, stomach, (informal) tummy. SEE ALSO **body**.

abduct *Terrorists abducted the millionaire's son.* to carry off, to kidnap.

abhorrent *The idea of eating meat is abhorrent to vegetarians.* disgusting, hateful, horrifying, repulsive, revolting. SEE ALSO **unpleasant**.

abide 1 (old-fashioned) to remain, to stay. 2 *Mrs Brunswick can't abide people who smoke.* to bear, to endure, to put up with, to stand, to tolerate. 3 *You must agree to abide by our rules.* to conform to, to keep to, to obey.

ability *Tony has the ability to become a good artist.* aptitude, capability, capacity, competence, gift, intelligence, knack, know-how, knowledge, power, prowess, skill, talent, training.

able 1 *Are you able to play today?* allowed, fit, free, permitted. 2 *Lucy is an able player.* capable, clever, competent, effective, experienced, gifted, intelligent, proficient, qualified, skilful, skilled, talented, trained.

abnormal *It's abnormal to have frost in the summer.* curious, exceptional, freak, funny, irregular, odd, peculiar, queer, rare, singular, strange, uncommon, unconventional, unusual.

abode (old-fashioned) *my humble abode.* dwelling, home, house, residence.

abolish *Dad wishes they would abolish income tax.* to eliminate, to end, to finish, to get rid of, to remove.

abominable *The weather was abominable: it rained all week.* appalling, awful, beastly, brutal, cruel, dreadful, hateful, horrible, nasty, odious, terrible. SEE ALSO **bad**.

abortion SEE **pregnant**.

about 1 *Is Lucy about?* around, close, near. 2 *It costs about £1.* almost, approximately, around, close to, nearly, roughly. 3 *Tony's got a book about sharks.* concerning, connected with, involving, regarding, relating to, telling of.

abridged *an abridged book.* abbreviated, condensed, cut, shortened.

abroad overseas.

abrupt 1 *The lesson came to an abrupt end when the fire bell went.* hasty, quick, sharp, sudden, unexpected. 2 *His abrupt manner made us feel uncomfortable.* blunt, curt, impolite, rude, short, unfriendly.

abscess boil, inflammation, sore. FOR OTHER AILMENTS SEE **illness**.

abscond to elope, to escape, to flee, to run away.

absent *Who's absent from school?* away, off.

absolute *Our rehearsal was absolute chaos!* complete, perfect, pure, sheer, total, unrestricted, utter.

absorb 1 to soak up. 2 *to be absorbed in your work.* to be immersed, to be interested, to be preoccupied. 3 *an absorbing hobby.* fascinating, interesting.

abstain *to abstain from voting.* to do without, to refrain from.

abstract *That maths was too abstract for me.* theoretical.

absurd *It was absurd to give the goldfish a Christmas present.* amusing, comic, crazy, farcical, foolish, funny, grotesque, illogical, irrational, laughable, ludicrous, mad, preposterous, ridiculous, senseless, silly, stupid, unreasonable, zany.

abundant *The explorers found an abundant supply of fresh water.* ample, copious, generous, liberal, plentiful, profuse.

abuse *He abused the driver who had crashed into his car.* to be rude to, to insult.

abysmal *Our team gave an abysmal performance.* appalling, awful, dreadful, worthless. SEE ALSO **bad**.

abyss chasm, crater, hole, pit.

academic *Lucy is good at games, but Tony is more academic.* brainy, clever, intellectual, intelligent, studious.

academy SEE **educate**.

accelerate to go faster, to quicken, to speed up.

accelerator SEE **vehicle**.

accent *You can tell Mr Brunswick comes from London because of his accent.* brogue, dialect, language.

accept 1 *Please accept this small gift.* to receive, to take. 2 *Most people accept that the world is round.* to acknowledge, to admit, to agree, to believe, to think.

acceptable *Flowers make an acceptable present.* adequate, appropriate, passable, pleasing, satisfactory, suitable, tolerable.

access *There is no direct access to our school from the main road.* approach, entrance, entry, way in.

accessory *accessories for an electric drill.* attachment, extension, fitting.

accident 1 *Was anyone injured in the accident?* calamity, catastrophe, crash, derailment, disaster, misadventure, misfortune, mishap. 2 *We met by accident.* chance, coincidence, fluke, luck.

accidental *We didn't mean to break the window: it was accidental.* casual, chance, fortunate, haphazard, lucky, unfortunate, unintentional, unplanned.

accommodate *The refugees were accommodated in tents.* to board, to house, to lodge, to put up.

accommodating *The people at the information office were very accommodating.* considerate, co-operative, helpful, obliging, thoughtful.

accommodation SEE **holiday**.

accompany *The headmaster accompanied our visitors to their car.* to escort, to go with.

accomplice *The two sets of fingerprints show that the burglar had an accomplice.* ally, assistant, collaborator, confederate, partner.

accomplish *We accomplished our mission successfully.* to achieve, to carry out, to complete, to do, to finish, to fulfil, to perform.

accomplished *an accomplished pianist.* brilliant, clever, experienced, gifted, masterly, skilful, talented.

accomplishment *Have you got any special accomplishments?* gift, skill, talent.

accordingly consequently, so, therefore, thus.

accordion SEE **music**.

account 1 *Can you account for your behaviour?* to explain, to make excuses. 2 *The shopkeeper gave us the account.* bill, receipt. 3 *We wrote a detailed account of our museum trip.* commentary, description, diary, explanation, log, narration, narrative, record, report, story, tale.

accountant SEE **job**.

accumulate *We accumulate a lot of rubbish in our garage.* to assemble, to bring together, to collect, to concentrate, to gather, to heap up, to hoard, to mass, to pile up, to store up.

accurate *Make sure the measurements are accurate.* correct, exact, meticulous, precise, right, true.

accuse *You should have evidence before you accuse someone of a crime.* to blame, to charge, to condemn, to incriminate, to prosecute.

accustomed *We went home by our accustomed route.* conventional, customary, habitual, normal, ordinary, regular, routine, traditional, usual.

ache 1 *an ache in a bad tooth.* discomfort, pain, pang, soreness, twinge. 2 *Lucy ached all over after running in the half marathon.* to be sore, to hurt, to sting, to throb.

achieve 1 *See what you can achieve in an hour.* to accomplish, to carry out, to complete, to do, to finish, to fulfil, to manage, to perform. 2 *Did they achieve their objective?* to gain, to get to, to reach.

achievement *It's a great achievement to get into the county team.* accomplishment, attainment, feat, success.

acid 1 SEE **chemical**. 2 *Lemons taste acid.* sharp, sour, tangy, tart. SEE ALSO **taste**.

acknowledge *Logan won't acknowledge that Lucy runs faster than he does.* to accept, to admit, to agree, to grant.

acquaintance *I don't know him well: he's just an acquaintance.* friend.

acquire *Where did Mrs Brunswick acquire that hat?* to buy, to gain, to get, to get hold of, to obtain, to procure, to purchase, to receive.

acquit *The prisoner was acquitted because of lack of evidence.* to discharge, to excuse, to free, to let off, to liberate.

acre SEE **measure**.

acrid *an acrid smell of burning.* bitter, unpleasant.

acrobat SEE **entertainment**.

act 1 *a brave act.* action, deed, exploit, feat, performance. 2 *He's only putting on an act.* deception, hoax, pretence. 3 *He's acting like a fool.* to behave, to conduct yourself, to pretend to be. 4 *Tony loved acting in the pantomime.* to appear, to perform, to play. 5 *Give the medicine time to act.* to function, to operate, to work.

action 1 *a helpful action.* act, deed, exploit, feat, performance. 2 *Lucy prefers films with plenty of action.* activity, drama, excitement, liveliness, movement. 3 *Grandad saw action in the Second World War.* battle, combat, conflict, fighting.

activate *Press that button to activate the alarm.* to set off, to start.

active 1 *Our puppy is so active he wears me out!* agile, energetic, lively, vigorous. 2 *Mum is active in charity work.* busy, employed, engaged, involved, occupied.

activity 1 *School is full of activity near Christmas.* action, excitement, liveliness, movement. 2 *What is your favourite activity?* hobby, occupation, pastime, project, task.

actor, actress SEE **entertainment, theatre**.

actual *That old oak tree isn't the actual tree Robin Hood lived in.* authentic, genuine, real, true.

acute 1 *acute pain.* extreme, intense, keen, severe, sharp, sudden. 2 *An acute angle.* pointed, sharp.

adamant *Mrs Brunswick was adamant that Lucy should not go to Logan's party.* decided, determined, firm, resolute, resolved.

adapt 1 *They adapted our minibus so that handicapped children can use it.* to adjust, to convert, to modify, to transform, to vary. 2 *Mrs Angel adapted a play by Shakespeare for us to perform.* to alter, to change, to edit, to rewrite.

add 1 *Add these numbers together.* to combine, to join, to put together, to unite. 2 *What does it all add up to?* to amount to, to come to, to make, to total. 3 *Add up what we have collected so far.* to calculate, to count, to reckon, to work out.

adder SEE **snake**.

addict *Mr Brunswick is a snooker addict.* enthusiast, fan, fanatic.

addiction custom, habit, obsession.

addition SEE **mathematics**.

additional *We need additional information.* extra, further, more, supplementary.

address 1 *Write the address clearly.* directions. **2** *The vicar addressed the school.* to speak to, to talk to.

adenoids SEE **body**.

adequate *The food was just adequate.* acceptable, enough, passable, satisfactory, sufficient, tolerable.

adhere *Limpets adhere to rocks.* to attach yourself, to cling, to fasten, to stick.

adhesive 1 *We need some adhesive to stick our work on to cards.* glue, gum, paste. **2** *adhesive tape.* gluey, gummed, sticky.

adjacent *Granny lives in the house adjacent to ours.* closest, nearest, neighbouring, next.

adjective SEE **language**.

adjourn *The teachers adjourned their meeting when the bell went.* to break off, to defer, to postpone, to put off, to suspend.

adjudicate *A famous musician adjudicated our music competition.* to arbitrate, to judge.

adjust *Tony has to adjust the saddle when he rides Lucy's bike.* to alter, to amend, to change, to modify, to put right, to vary.

administer 1 *The head administers the school.* to administrate, to command, to control, to direct, to govern, to look after, to manage, to rule, to run, to supervise. **2** *Are teachers still allowed to administer corporal punishment?* to deal out, to give, to hand out.

admirable *The actors gave an admirable performance.* creditable, excellent, (informal) fabulous, fine, marvellous, praiseworthy, wonderful. SEE ALSO **good**.

admiral SEE **sailor**.

admire 1 *We admired the firemen's courage.* to approve of, to honour, to marvel at, to praise, to respect, to revere, to value, to wonder at. **2** *We admired the view.* to appreciate, to enjoy, to like, to love.

admit 1 *Persons under sixteen are not admitted.* to allow in, to let in. **2** *Lucy admitted that she broke the window.* to accept, to acknowledge, to agree, to confess, to own up.

adolescence *People say that adolescence is a difficult time.* growing up, puberty, (informal) your teens.

adolescent 1 *adolescent behaviour.* juvenile, youthful. **2** *Most adolescents like pop music.* teenager, youngster, youth.

adopted SEE **family**.

adore *Lucy and Tony adore their grandad.* to dote on, to idolize, to love, to revere, to worship.

adorn *The table was adorned with flowers.* to decorate.

adornment decoration, ornament.

adrift *We were adrift in the middle of the lake.* afloat, drifting, floating.

adult 1 *That film is for adults only.* grown-up. **2** *Tony has some very adult ideas.* developed, grown-up, mature.

adultery infidelity, unfaithfulness.

advance 1 *As we advanced, the birds flew away.* to approach, to come near, to go on, to make headway, to move forward, to proceed. **2** *Computers have advanced a lot in recent years.* to develop, to evolve, to improve, to move on, to progress.

advanced 1 *The school is buying a more advanced computer.* modern, sophisticated, up-to-date. **2** *Tony's maths is more advanced than Logan's.* complicated, difficult, hard.

advantage *It's an advantage to be tall when you play basketball.* asset, benefit, gain, help, profit.

advantageous beneficial, good, helpful, profitable, useful.

Advent SEE **church**.

adventure *Exploring the caves was quite an adventure.* escapade, excitement, .exploit.

adventurous bold, brave, courageous, daring, enterprising, fearless, heroic, intrepid.

adverb SEE **language**.

adversary enemy, foe, opponent, opposition, rival.

adverse *adverse weather conditions.*

contrary, hostile, opposing, unfavourable.

adversity *It's good to have friends in times of adversity.* calamity, catastrophe, difficulty, disaster, distress, hardship, misfortune, trouble.

advertise *We advertised our concert in the local shops.* to make known, (informal) to plug, to promote, to publicize.

advertisement (informal) ad, (informal) advert, bill, commercial, notice, placard, (informal) plug, poster, publicity, sign.

advice *Dad gave me some advice.* help, suggestion, tip, warning.

advisable *It's advisable to wrap up warmly if you have a cold.* proper, prudent, sensible, wise.

advise 1 *They will advise us when the TV is mended.* inform, notify, tell. 2 *What medicine did the doctor advise?* prescribe, recommend, suggest.

aerobatics SEE **entertainment**.

aerobics SEE **exercise**.

aerodrome airfield, airport, airstrip, landing-strip.

aeroplane SEE **aircraft**.

affair 1 *Don't interfere: it's my affair!* business, concern, matter, thing. 2 *The robbery at the police station was a strange affair.* event, happening, incident, occasion.

affect 1 *Alcohol does affect your driving.* to alter, to change, to influence, to modify. 2 *The audience was deeply affected by the music.* to impress, to move, to stir, to touch.

affectionate attached, fond, friendly, kind, loving, tender, warm.

afflict *He was afflicted by boils.* to distress, to hurt, to torment, to torture, to trouble.

affliction ailment, blight, disease, disorder, illness, sickness. SEE ALSO **illness**.

affluent *They must be affluent to own a car like that.* prosperous, rich, wealthy, well-off, well-to-do.

afford *Can you afford a contribution to the famine appeal?* to manage, to provide, to spare.

afloat adrift, floating.

afraid apprehensive, cowed, fearful, frightened, scared, terrified.

aft SEE **vessel**.

afternoon SEE **time**.

age 1 *the Victorian age.* era, period. SEE ALSO **time**. 2 *Dad's home-made wine won't taste so horrible if he leaves it to age.* to develop, to grow older, to mature, to ripen.

aged ancient, elderly, old.

aggravate 1 *If you scratch it will aggravate the soreness.* to make worse, to worsen. 2 (informal)*Don't aggravate mum by asking for more pocket-money.* to annoy, to bother, to exasperate, to irritate. ! Some people think this is a wrong use of *aggravate*.

aggressive *Most people think lions are aggressive animals.* attacking, belligerent, hostile, militant, pugnacious, warlike.

agile *Gymnasts need to be agile.* acrobatic, active, deft, graceful, lively, nimble, quick-moving, swift.

agitate *The thunder agitated the animals.* to disturb, to excite, to stir up.

agonizing *an agonizing wound.* excruciating, painful, unbearable.

agony anguish, pain, suffering, torment, torture.

agree 1 *Lucy agreed to pay for the broken window.* to consent, to undertake. 2 *Do you agree that I was right?* to accept, to acknowledge, to admit. 3 *We agreed that Logan would play in goal.* to choose, to decide, to establish, to fix, to settle. 4 *Unfortunately, Tony's story didn't agree with Lucy's.* to coincide, to correspond, to match.

agreeable *an agreeable companion, an agreeable occasion, etc.* amiable, decent, friendly, nice. SEE ALSO **kind, pleasant**.

agreement 1 *Lucy and Tony have quarrels, but they usually end in agreement.* accord, consent, concord, harmony. 2 *After a lot of arguing, they* *reached an agreement.* alliance, arrangement, bargain, contract, deal, pact, pledge, settlement, treaty, understanding.

agriculture farming.

aground stranded.

ahead forwards, onwards.

aid 1 *Even a small contribution will aid the starving.* to assist, to back, to help, to relieve, to support. 2 *They need our aid.* assistance, backing, co-operation, help, support.

ailment *No medicine will cure all ailments.* affliction, blight, complaint, disease, disorder, infection, infirmity, malady, sickness. SEE ALSO **illness.**

aim 1 *Aim the gun at the target.* to direct, to point. 2 *He is aiming to arrive for dinner.* to intend, to plan, to try. 3 *What's your aim in life?* ambition, cause, goal, intention, object, objective, plan, purpose, target.

air 1 *They fired into the air.* atmosphere, sky. 2 *to air a room.* to dry, to freshen, to ventilate. 3 *to air your opinions.* to display, to make known, to reveal, to show.

aircraft 1 KINDS OF AIRCRAFT ARE aeroplane, air-liner, airship, balloon, biplane, bomber, fighter, glider, hang-glider, helicopter, jet, jumbo jet, jump-jet, micro-light, plane, seaplane, supersonic aircraft. 2 PARTS OF AIRCRAFT ARE fin, fuselage, jet engine, joystick, propeller, rotor, rudder, tail, undercarriage, wing.

aircraft-carrier SEE **vessel.**

airfield aerodrome, airport, airstrip, landing-strip.

air force SEE **armed services.**

airgun SEE **weapon.**

air hostess SEE **job.**

air-liner SEE **aircraft.**

airport aerodrome, airfield, airstrip, landing-strip.

airship SEE **aircraft.**

airstrip SEE **airport.**

airy *an airy room.* breezy, draughty, fresh, ventilated.

aisle SEE **church.**

akin alike, related, similar.

alarm 1 *The thunder alarmed the animals.* to dismay, to disturb, to frighten, to scare, to shock, to startle, to surprise, to terrify, to upset. 2 *Alarm spread through the town when the volcano began to erupt.* consternation, dismay, fear, fright, panic, surprise. 3 *Move quickly into the playground when you hear the alarm.* bell, fire-alarm, gong, signal, siren, warning.

albatross SEE **bird.**

album 1 SEE **book.** 2 SEE **record.**

alcohol (informal) booze, liquor, spirits. SEE ALSO **drink.**

alcoholic 1 *alcoholic drink.* intoxicating. 2 *an alcoholic.* addict, drunkard.

ale beer. SEE ALSO **drink.**

alert 1 *You must stay alert if you play in goal.* attentive, awake, careful, lively, observant, vigilant, watchful. 2 *When the floods came, they rang the church bell to alert the villagers.* to caution, to warn.

algebra SEE **mathematics.**

alien *The green women in the spacecraft were obviously alien beings.* foreign, strange, unfamiliar.

alike akin, identical, similar.

alive *Is your pet hedgehog still alive?* existing, live, living.

alkali SEE **chemical.**

Allah SEE **Islam.**

allegiance *allegiance to the king.* duty, faithfulness, loyalty.

allergy SEE **illness.**

alley SEE **road.**

alliance *an alliance between two sides.* agreement, association, combination, league, pact, treaty, union.

alligator crocodile. SEE ALSO **reptile.**

allot *We allotted half our food to the visitors.* to allow, to deal out, to distribute, to divide, to give out, to ration, to share out.

allotment SEE **garden.**

allow 1 *They allowed us to use the first team's pitch.* to authorize, to approve, to enable, to let, to license, to permit. 2 *We allowed £5 for spending money.* to allot, to give, to grant, to provide, to set aside.

alloy SEE **metal**.

all right 1 *Are you all right again after your illness?* fit, healthy, well. 2 *Is my work all right?* acceptable, adequate, passable, satisfactory, tolerable.

allude *Did mum allude to the spilt paint?* to mention, to refer to.

alluring *She wore an alluring dress.* attractive, bewitching, captivating, charming, enchanting, fascinating, fetching, glamorous. SEE ALSO **beautiful**.

ally collaborator, confederate, friend, partner.

almighty omnipotent.

almond SEE **nut**.

almost about, approximately, around, nearly, not quite, practically.

alone 1 *to be alone.* friendless, isolated, lonely, solitary. 2 *to perform alone.* solo.

alongside *Our friends parked their car alongside ours.* adjacent to, beside, next to.

aloud *to read aloud.* audibly, clearly, distinctly.

Alsatian SEE **dog**.

also additionally, besides, furthermore, moreover, too.

altar SEE **church**.

alter *Don't alter your story: it's excellent as it is.* to adapt, to adjust, to affect, to amend, to change, to convert, to edit, to modify, to transform, to vary.

alteration change, difference, modification.

alternative *The alternatives are beef or chicken.* choice, option, possibility.

altitude height.

altogether *We were not altogether satisfied.* absolutely, completely, entirely, quite, totally, utterly, wholly.

aluminium SEE **metal**.

always continually, continuously, eternally, evermore, for ever, repeatedly, unceasingly.

amalgamate *Because they had so few players, the two teams amalgamated. They amalgamated the two teams.* to combine, to come together, to integrate, to join, to merge, to put together, to unite.

amateur *an amateur player.* unpaid. ! *Amateur* is the opposite of *professional.*

amaze 1 *His speed amazed us.* to astonish, to astound, to bewilder, to confuse, to shock, to stun, to surprise. 2 *amazed*: dazed, dumbfounded, nonplussed, thunderstruck. 3 *amazing*: exceptional, extraordinary, notable, phenomenal, remarkable, special, unusual.

ambassador consul, diplomat, representative.

amber 1 SEE **colour**. 2 SEE **jewellery**.

ambiguous *When you ride your bike, don't give ambiguous signals.* confusing, uncertain, unclear, vague.

ambition 1 *You need ambition to succeed in business.* drive, enterprise, enthusiasm. 2 *Lucy's ambition is to play for the county team.* aim, desire, goal, intention, objective, wish.

amble SEE **walk**.

ambulance SEE **vehicle**.

ambush *The outlaws ambushed the travellers in the mountains.* to attack, to ensnare, to intercept, to pounce on, to swoop on, to trap.

amend *Mr Brunswick amended the wording of his letter to the newspaper.* to adapt, to adjust, to alter, to change, to improve, to modify.

amiable *The crocodile seemed quite amiable.* agreeable, friendly, goodhumoured, kind-hearted, nice, pleasant. SEE ALSO **kind**.

ammonia SEE **chemical**.

ammunition KINDS OF AMMUNITION ARE bullet, cannonball, cartridge, grenade, missile, round, shell, shrapnel. SEE ALSO **weapon**.

amnesia SEE **illness**.

amnesty pardon.

amount 1 *What did the collection amount to?* to add up to, to come to, to make, to total. **2** *Dad gave us a cheque for the full amount.* quantity, sum, total.

amphibious AMPHIBIOUS ANIMALS ARE frog, newt, toad. SEE ALSO **animal**.

ample *The spring provided an ample supply of water.* abundant, copious, generous, liberal, plentiful.

amplifier SEE **audio equipment**.

amplify *The head asked me to amplify my explanation.* to develop, to enlarge, to expand, to magnify.

amputate *to amputate a limb.* to cut off, to remove, to sever.

amuse 1 *A comedian's job is to amuse people.* to cheer up, to delight, to divert, to entertain. **2** *amusing*: SEE **funny**.

amusement *What's your favourite form of amusement?* diversion, enjoyment, fun, hobby, joke, laughter, merriment, pastime, play, pleasure, recreation. SEE ALSO **entertainment, game, sport**.

anaemia SEE **illness**.

anaesthetic SEE **medicine**.

analyse *Tomorrow we're going to analyse our traffic survey.* to examine, to study.

anarchy *There would be anarchy if we had no police.* chaos, confusion, disorder, lawlessness.

anatomy *A doctor has to know all about anatomy.* the body. SEE ALSO **body, science**.

ancestor *Mum's hobby is tracing her ancestors.* forefather, predecessor.

anchor 1 *to anchor a ship.* to berth, to moor, to tie up. **2** *to anchor something firmly.* SEE **fasten**.

anchorage harbour, haven, marina.

ancient aged, antiquated, antique, early, old, old-fashioned, prehistoric, primitive, venerable.

angel SEE **church**.

anger 1 *to be filled with anger.* exasperation, fury, rage, temper, wrath. **2** *They angered the referee with their foul play.* to aggravate, to annoy, to enrage, to exasperate, to incense, to inflame, to infuriate, to madden, to provoke, to vex.

angle bend, corner.

angler fisherman.

angling fishing.

angry 1 bad-tempered, cross, enraged, fiery, fuming, furious, incensed, indignant, infuriated, irate, livid, mad, raging, raving, vexed, wild, wrathful. **2** *to be angry*: to be in a temper, to boil, to fume, to rage, to rave, to seethe. **3** *to make someone angry*: to enrage, to incense, to infuriate, to vex.

anguish agony, distress, pain, suffering, torment, torture.

animal 1 beast, brute, creature. **2** KINDS OF ANIMAL ARE amphibious animal, bird, carnivorous animal, fish, insect, mammal, marsupial, mollusc, pet, predator, quadruped, reptile, rodent, scavenger. **3** VARIOUS SPECIES ARE antelope, ape, ass, baboon, badger, bat, bear, beaver, bison, boar, buffalo, bull, bullock, camel, cat, cattle, cheetah, chimpanzee, cow, deer, dinosaur, dog, dolphin, donkey, dormouse, dromedary, elephant, elk, ferret, fox, gerbil, giraffe, goat, gorilla, grizzly bear, guinea-pig, hamster, hare, hedgehog, hippopotamus, horse, hyena, jackal, jaguar, kangaroo, koala, leopard, lion, llama, mammoth, mastodon, mink, mole, mongoose, monkey, moose, mouse, mule, octopus, otter, ox, panda, panther, pig, platypus, polar bear, porcupine, porpoise, rabbit, rat, reindeer, rhinoceros, seal, sea-lion, sheep, shrew, skunk, squirrel, stoat, tiger, tortoise, turtle, vole, wallaby, walrus, weasel, whale, wolf, zebra. **4** SEE ALSO **amphibious, bird, fish, insect, reptile, snake**. **5** SEE ALSO **female, male, young**.

animated *an animated conversation.* boisterous, bright, brisk, cheerful, energetic, excited, exuberant, lively, quick, spirited, sprightly, vivacious.

ankle SEE **body, joint, leg.**

annexe *They built an annexe for the extra class.* extension, wing.

annihilate *Nuclear weapons can annihilate whole cities.* to destroy, to eliminate, to eradicate, to exterminate, (informal) to finish off, to kill, to slaughter, to wipe out.

anniversary birthday, jubilee.

announce 1 *The head announced that we would have an extra holiday.* to declare, to proclaim, to publish, to report, to state. 2 *Tony announced the items at the concert.* to introduce.

announcement *Watch out for a special announcement.* bulletin, communication, communiqué, declaration, message, notice, proclamation, report, statement.

annoy *Don't annoy the bull.* (informal) to aggravate, to bait, to bother, to cross, to displease, to exasperate, to irritate, to molest, to offend, to pester, to tease, to torment, to trouble, to try, to upset, to vex, to worry.

annual 1 *Sports day is an annual event.* yearly. 2 *I bought a football annual with my book token.* SEE **book.** 3 *Mrs Brunswick planted annuals in her garden.* SEE **plant.**

anonymous nameless, unidentified, unnamed.

anorak SEE **clothes.**

answer 1 *the answer to a question.* reaction, reply, response, retort. 2 *the answer to a problem.* explanation, solution, sum, total.

ant SEE **insect.**

antagonism *You could see the antagonism between the two fighters.* conflict, hostility, opposition.

Antarctic SEE **geography.**

antelope SEE **animal.**

anthem SEE **music.**

anthology SEE **book.**

anthracite SEE **fuel.**

antibiotic SEE **medicine.**

anticipate *In chess, you have to anticipate your opponent's next move.* to expect, to forecast, to foresee, to predict, to prevent. | Some people think this is a wrong use of *anticipate.*

anticyclone SEE **weather.**

antidote SEE **medicine.**

antiquated *Do you remember that antiquated car of grandpa's?* aged, old, old-fashioned, out-of-date, quaint.

antique *antique furniture.* aged, ancient, old, old-fashioned.

antiseptic SEE **medicine.**

antisocial *an antisocial person.* disagreeable, nasty, obnoxious, offensive, rude, unfriendly.

anxiety care, concern, dismay, doubt, dread, fear, misgivings, strain, stress, tension, worry.

anxious 1 *Mum was anxious about travelling by air.* apprehensive, concerned, fearful, jittery, nervous, uneasy, worried. 2 *Tony is always anxious to do his best.* eager, keen.

apart divided, separate.

apartment flat.

ape SEE **animal.**

apex *The steeplejack climbed to the apex of the spire.* crown, head, peak, tip, top.

apiary hive.

apologetic *Mrs Brunswick was apologetic about the burnt cake.* penitent, regretful, remorseful, repentant, sorry.

apologize *I apologized for being rude.* to regret, to repent, to say sorry.

apostle disciple, follower.

apostrophe SEE **punctuation.**

appal 1 *The crowd's bad behaviour appalled us.* to alarm, to disgust, to dismay, to frighten, to horrify, to shock, to terrify. 2 *What an appalling piece of work!* SEE **bad.**

apparatus appliance, device, equipment, instrument, machinery, tool.

apparent *It was apparent that Logan was lying.* blatant, clear, evident, obvious, plain, self-explanatory.

apparition *Logan claims he saw an*

apparition in the haunted tower. ghost, hallucination, illusion, phantom, spirit, (informal) spook, vision.

appeal 1 *The stranded motorist appealed for help.* to ask, to beg, to entreat, to plead, to request. 2 *I bought the picture because it appealed to me.* to attract, to fascinate, to interest. 3 *appealing:* SEE **attractive**.

appear 1 *Our visitors appeared an hour late.* to arrive, to come, to turn up. 2 *Whenever we think we've finished, another difficulty appears.* to arise, to emerge, to loom, to materialize, to show. 3 *This appears to be the coat Lucy lost.* to look, to seem. 4 *Tony appeared as Joseph in the nativity play.* to act, to perform.

appease *They offered a sacrifice to appease the gods.* to calm, to pacify, to soothe.

appendicitis SEE **illness**.

appendix SEE **body**.

appetite *an appetite for food, an appetite for adventure, etc.* craving, desire, greed, hunger, longing, lust, passion, zest.

applaud *The audience applauded our performance.* to approve of, to cheer, to clap, to commend, to praise.

apple SEE **fruit**.

appliance apparatus, device, equipment, instrument, machinery.

applicant candidate, entrant, participant.

apply 1 *to apply for a job.* to ask. 2 *to apply ointment to a wound.* to administer, to spread. 3 *to apply your strength.* to employ, to use.

appoint *Who did they appoint as captain?* to choose, to elect, to name, to nominate, to select.

appointment *I've got an appointment with a friend after tea.* date, engagement, fixture, meeting, rendezvous.

appreciate 1 *Do you appreciate classical music?* to admire, to approve of, to enjoy, to like, to prize, to respect, to value. 2 *I appreciate that you must be*

tired. to know, to realize, to see, to understand.

apprehensive *Tony was apprehensive about his music exam.* afraid, anxious, concerned, fearful, frightened, nervous, uneasy, worried.

apprentice beginner, learner, novice.

approach 1 *The approach to the school is off Church Street.* access, entrance, entry, way in. 2 *The lion approached its prey stealthily.* to come near, to draw near, to move towards. 3 *approaching: approaching traffic.* advancing, oncoming.

appropriate *an appropriate punishment, appropriate clothes.* apt, becoming, deserved, due, fit, fitting, proper, right, suitable, timely.

approve 1 *Do you approve of what we did?* to admire, to applaud, to commend, to like, to love, to praise, to value. 2 *The council approved Mr Brunswick's application to build an extension.* to allow, to authorize, to permit, to tolerate.

approximately about, around, close to, nearly, roughly.

apricot SEE **fruit**.

apron SEE **clothes**.

apt 1 *an apt pupil.* clever, quick, skilful. 2 *an apt reply.* appropriate, deserved, fitting, proper, right, suitable.

aptitude *Lucy has considerable aptitude as a gymnast.* ability, gift, knack, skill, talent.

aqueduct SEE **bridge**.

arbitrary *an arbitrary decision.* unplanned, unreasonable.

arbitrate *When the captains quarrelled, the referee had to arbitrate.* to make peace, to negotiate.

arc curve.

arcade SEE **building**.

arch 1 SEE **building**. 2 *The cat arched its back.* to bend, to curve.

archaeology SEE **subject**.

archbishop SEE **church**.

archipelago SEE **geography**.

architect SEE **art, job**.

architecture SEE **art, subject**.
arctic 1 SEE **geography**. 2 *arctic weather*. bitter, bleak, freezing, frozen, (informal) perishing. SEE ALSO **cold**.
arduous *The mountaineers faced an arduous climb*. difficult, gruelling, hard, laborious, strenuous, tough.
area 1 *The Brunswicks like the area where they live*. district, locality, neighbourhood, region, sector, territory, vicinity, zone. 2 *a large area of ice*. expanse, sheet, surface. 3 SEE **measure**.
arena *a sports arena*. field, ground, pitch, stadium.
argue 1 *to argue about politics*. to debate, to discuss, to dispute, to quarrel. 2 *to argue about the price*. to bargain, to haggle. 3 *The lawyer argued that the man was guilty*. to contend, to reason.
argument 1 *We had an argument about what to watch on TV*. controversy, debate, disagreement, dispute, quarrel. 2 *The bloody knife was the biggest argument against him*. evidence, grounds, justification, proof, reason.
arid 1 *arid desert*. barren, dry, lifeless, parched, sterile. 2 *an arid subject*. boring, dull, uninteresting.
arise *We'll deal with any problems as they arise*. to appear, to begin, to come up, to crop up, to emerge, to occur, to result, to spring up.
aristocrat lord, noble, peer. SEE ALSO **title**.
arithmetic SEE **mathematics**.
arm 1 SEE **body**. 2 *an arm of a tree*. branch, limb. 3 *They armed themselves with sticks*. to provide, to supply.
armada *an armada of ships*. convoy, fleet, navy.
armaments SEE **weapon**.
armchair SEE **furniture**.
armed services GROUPS OF FIGHTING MEN ARE air force, army, battalion, brigade, cavalry, commandos, company, corps, garrison, fleet, foreign legion, infantry, marines, mercenaries, navy, paratroops, patrol, platoon, recruits, regiment, reinforcements, squad, squadron, task-force, troop. SEE ALSO **fighter**.
armistice *The armistice ended the fighting*. pact, peace, treaty, truce.
armour *Soldiers used to wear armour in battle*. mail, protection.
armoury arsenal, weapons.
army SEE **armed services**.
aroma fragrance, odour, perfume, scent, smell, whiff.
arouse 1 *The milkman aroused us by dropping four bottles*. to awaken, to call, to rouse, to wake up. 2 *The sound of music aroused our interest*. to excite, to incite, to inspire, to provoke, to stimulate, to stir.
arrange 1 *Tony is arranging books in the library*. to classify, to distribute, to group, to put in order, to set out, to sort. 2 *We arranged an outing for Saturday*. to fix, to organize, to plan, to prepare, to settle.
arrangement *We have an arrangement to buy eggs from a local farmer*. agreement, bargain, contract, deal, pact, settlement, understanding.
arrest 1 *The police arrested the suspect*. to capture, to catch, to detain, (informal) to nab, to seize, to take prisoner. 2 *A landslide arrested our progress*. to bar, to block, to check, to halt, to hinder, to stop.
arrive 1 *We arrived at our destination*. to come to, to reach. 2 *When will granny arrive?* to appear, to come, to turn up.
arrogant *an arrogant manner*. boastful, bumptious, (informal) cocky, conceited, disdainful, haughty, insolent, pompous, presumptuous, proud, scornful, self-important, snobbish, (informal) stuck-up, vain.
arrow SEE **weapon**.
arsenal armoury. SEE ALSO **weapon**.
arson SEE **crime**.
art 1 KINDS OF ART AND CRAFT ARE architecture, carpentry, cartoons, collage, crochet, drawing, embroidery, engraving, fashion design, graphics, illustrations,

jewellery, knitting, metalwork, mobiles, modelling, mosaic, murals, needlework, origami, painting, patchwork, photography, portraits, pottery, prints, sculpture, sewing, sketching, spinning, stencils, weaving, wickerwork, woodwork. SEE ALSO **music, picture, theatre.** 2 VARIOUS ARTISTS AND CRAFTSMEN ARE architect, blacksmith, carpenter, engraver, goldsmith, painter, photographer, potter, printer, sculptor, weaver. FOR PERFORMING ARTISTS SEE **entertainment, music, theatre.** 3 *There's an art in lighting a bonfire.* craft, knack, skill, talent, technique, trick.

artery SEE **body.**

artful *People say that foxes are artful creatures.* astute, clever, crafty, cunning, ingenious, knowing, shrewd, skilful, sly, tricky, wily.

arthritis SEE **illness.**

article 1 *Have you any old articles for the jumble sale?* item, object, thing. 2 *Did you read Tony's article in the magazine?* SEE **writing.**

articulated lorry SEE **vehicle.**

artificial *an artificial beard.* bogus, faked, false, feigned, man-made, manufactured, (informal) phoney, pretended, synthetic, unnatural, unreal.

artillery SEE **weapon.**

artist SEE **art.**

artistic attractive, beautiful, creative, imaginative.

ascend 1 *We ascended the hill.* to climb, to go up, to mount, to scale. 2 *The road ascends to the church.* to rise, to slope up.

Ascension Day SEE **church.**

ash 1 *the ashes of a fire.* cinders, embers. 2 *an ash tree.* SEE **tree.**

ashamed *Logan never seems ashamed when Mrs Angel tells him off.* distressed, embarrassed, upset.

Ash Wednesday SEE **church.**

ask 1 *to ask a question, to ask for help, etc.* to beg, to demand, to enquire, to entreat, to implore, to inquire, to pose a question, to query, to question, to request. 2 *to ask someone to a party.* to invite.

asleep dormant, hibernating, inactive, resting, sleeping.

asparagus SEE **vegetable.**

aspect *There's one aspect of this affair we don't understand.* circumstance, detail, feature.

asphalt SEE **road.**

aspirin SEE **medicine.**

ass 1 SEE **animal.** 2 SEE **fool.**

assail *The defenders were assailed with missiles.* to assault, to attack, to bombard, to set on.

assassinate to murder. SEE ALSO **crime, kill.**

assault *They assaulted their victim without warning.* to assail, to attack, to bombard, to molest, to mug, to raid, to rape, to set on.

assemble 1 *A crowd assembled.* to accumulate, to collect, to come together, to congregate, to crowd together, to group, to herd, to meet, to muster, to swarm, to throng. 2 *We assembled our belongings.* to bring together, to gather, to get together, to pile up. 3 *These cars are assembled in Britain.* to build, to construct, to fit together, to make, to manufacture, to put together.

assembly *an assembly of Scouts.* conference, congress, council, gathering, meeting.

assert *He asserted that he was innocent.* to argue, to claim, to contend, to declare, to emphasize, to insist, to maintain, to proclaim, to state, to stress.

assess *The garage assessed the damage to the car.* to calculate, to estimate, to reckon, to value, to work out.

asset 1 *Good health is a great asset.* advantage, blessing, benefit. 2 *What assets have you got?* capital, funds, money, resources, savings, wealth.

assignment *Mrs Angel gave the class an assignment to be done by Monday.* job, project, task, work.

assist *Can you assist us?* to aid, to back, to help, to second, to serve, to support.

assistant accomplice, collaborator, deputy, helper, partner, second.

association *an association of youth clubs.* alliance, body, club, combination, company, group, league, organization, party, society, union.

assorted *assorted colours.* different, diverse, miscellaneous, mixed, varied, various.

assortment *Mum gave us an assortment of flowers to plant in the garden.* collection, mixture, variety.

assume *I assume you'd like some ice-cream?* to believe, to guess, to imagine, to presume, to suppose, to think.

assumed *an assumed name.* false, feigned, pretended.

assumption *My assumption is that you will be hungry.* guess, supposition, theory.

assurance *We had his assurance that the car worked properly.* guarantee, oath, pledge, promise, vow.

assure *He assured me the work would be done by Friday.* to promise, to tell, to vow.

assured *Although she was young, her manner was assured.* certain, confident, definite, positive, sure.

asteroid SEE **astronomy**.

asthma SEE **illness**.

astonish *The acrobats astonished the crowd.* to amaze, to astound, to dumbfound, to surprise.

astound *The news that the school might be closed astounded us.* to amaze, to astonish, to dumbfound, to shock, to stagger, to surprise.

astronaut cosmonaut, space-traveller.

astronomy 1 SEE **science**. 2 WORDS USED IN ASTRONOMY ARE asteroid, comet, constellation, cosmos, eclipse, galaxy, meteor, meteorite, moon, planet, satellite, shooting star, sun, universe, world.

astute *It was an astute move to bring on a*

substitute at that moment. artful, clever, crafty, cunning, ingenious, observant, perceptive, shrewd.

asylum *The refugees hoped to find asylum in a neighbouring country.* haven, refuge, retreat, safety, sanctuary, shelter.

asymmetrical lop-sided, unbalanced, uneven.

athletics 1 VARIOUS EVENTS IN ATHLETICS ARE cross-country, decathlon, discus, high jump, hurdles, javelin, long jump, marathon, pentathlon, pole-vault, relay race, running, shot, sprinting, triple jump. 2 SEE **sport**.

atlas SEE **book**.

atmosphere 1 *a stuffy atmosphere.* air. 2 *There was a happy atmosphere at the party.* feeling, mood, tone.

atom 1 molecule, particle. 2 *an atom bomb.* SEE **weapon**.

atrocious *an atrocious terrorist attack.* barbaric, evil, hateful, wicked. SEE ALSO **cruel**.

atrocity crime, outrage.

attach 1 to anchor, to bind, to connect, to fasten, to fix, to join, to link, to secure, to tie, to unite. FOR WAYS OF ATTACHING THINGS SEE **fasten**. 2 *The twins are very attached.* close, fond, friendly, loving.

attack 1 *They launched an attack at dawn.* ambush, assault, blitz, charge, counter-attack, invasion, onslaught, raid. 2 *an attack of coughing.* bout, fit, outbreak, turn. 3 *Logan's gang attacked us for no reason.* to ambush, to assail, to assault, to bombard, to charge, to mug, to raid, to set on, to storm.

attainment achievement, success.

attempt *to attempt to break a record.* to endeavour, to exert yourself, to make an effort, to strive, to try.

attend 1 *Attend to your work.* to concentrate on, to observe, to think about, to watch. 2 *Who will attend to the goldfish while we are away?* to care for, to look after. 3 *Do you attend church?* to go to, to visit.

attention 1 *Give proper attention to your work.* care, concentration, diligence, heed, notice, regard. 2 *Thank you for your attention while I was ill.* consideration, kindness, politeness, thoughtfulness.

attentive *We were attentive because it was an interesting lesson.* alert, observant, thoughtful, vigilant, watchful.

attic loft. SEE ALSO **house**.

attire clothes, clothing, costume, dress, garments.

attitude 1 *Dad didn't like Logan's attitude when he refused to wash up.* behaviour, disposition, manner. 2 *What's your attitude towards smoking?* belief, feeling, opinion, standpoint, thought.

attract 1 *Magnets attract iron.* to draw, to pull. 2 *The old steam engines attracted Mr Brunswick.* to appeal to, to captivate, to entice, to fascinate, to lure.

attractive *an attractive person, an attractive picture, an attractive dress.* alluring, appealing, artistic, bewitching, captivating, charming, (informal) cute, endearing, enticing, fascinating, fetching, good-looking, glamorous, handsome, inviting, lovable, pleasing, pretty, quaint, seductive, tempting. SEE ALSO **beautiful**.

auburn SEE **hair**.

auction SEE **sale**.

audible *an audible voice.* clear, distinct.

audience crowd, spectators.

audio equipment KINDS OF AUDIO EQUIPMENT ARE amplifier, cassette recorder, compact disc player, earphones, gramophone, headphones, hi-fi, high-fidelity equipment, juke-box, loudspeaker, microphone, music centre, pick-up, radio, recorder, record-player, stereo, stylus, tape-recorder, tuner, turntable.

aunt SEE **family**.

au revoir farewell, goodbye.

austere 1 *Dad says his grandfather was*

an austere man. forbidding, hard, harsh, severe, stern, strict. 2 *an austere dress.* plain, simple.

authentic *an authentic antique.* actual, genuine, real, true.

author composer, creator, dramatist, novelist, playwright, poet, script-writer, writer. SEE ALSO **writer**.

authority 1 *We've got the head's authority to have a party.* approval, consent, permission. 2 *The police have the authority to stop the traffic.* control, influence, power, right. 3 *Mr Brunswick is an authority on steam trains.* expert, specialist.

authorize 1 *The head authorized the purchase of a new computer.* to agree to, to allow, to approve, to consent to, to permit. 2 *You aren't authorized to buy cigarettes for your dad.* to entitle, to license.

autobiography SEE **writing**.

autograph signature.

automatic 1 *Blinking is an automatic reaction.* impulsive, involuntary, spontaneous, unconscious, unthinking, unintentional. 2 *an automatic dishwasher.* mechanical, programmed. 3 *an automatic machine*: robot. 4 *an automatic weapon.* SEE **weapon**.

automobile car, motor car. SEE ALSO **vehicle**.

auxiliary *auxiliary engines.* additional, helping, supplementary, supporting.

available *There are plenty of books available in the library.* accessible, handy, obtainable, ready.

avalanche SEE **disaster**.

avenue SEE **road**.

average *It was an average sort of day.* common, mediocre, medium, middling, normal, typical, usual. SEE ALSO **ordinary**.

aversion *Tony has an aversion to spiders.* contempt, disgust, dislike, hatred, loathing, revulsion.

avid *Tony is an avid reader.* eager, enthusiastic, fervent, greedy, keen.

avoid *Mr Brunswick will do anything to*

avoid gardening! to dodge, to elude, to escape, to evade, to fend off, to shirk.

awake *A sentry must stay awake.* alert, attentive, conscious, lively, vigilant, watchful.

awaken *The alarm awakened us.* to arouse, to call, to rouse, to wake.

award 1 *They awarded first prize to Lucy.* to give, to hand over, to present. **2** VARIOUS AWARDS ARE badge, cup, decoration, medal, prize, reward, scholarship, trophy.

aware *When cycling, be aware of the traffic.* conscious, observant.

away *away from school.* absent, off.

awe *They watched the erupting volcano with awe.* admiration, fear, respect, reverence, wonder.

awful *Murder is an awful crime.* abominable, appalling, beastly, dreadful, hateful, horrible, nasty, shocking, terrible. SEE ALSO **bad, unpleasant.**

awkward 1 *an awkward machine.* cumbersome, inconvenient, unwieldy. **2** *Tony is awkward with tools.* blundering, clumsy, gawky, ungainly, unskilful. **3** *Are you trying to be awkward?* difficult, unco-operative.

axe chopper. SEE ALSO **tool.**

axle SEE **vehicle.**

azure blue. SEE ALSO **colour.**

B b

babble SEE **talk.**

baboon SEE **animal.**

baby child, infant, toddler. SEE ALSO **person.**

babyish childish, immature, infantile.

bachelor SEE **unmarried.**

back 1 *the back of the train.* end, rear, tail. **2** *the back of the envelope.* reverse. **3** *He backed away.* to move back, to retreat, to reverse, to withdraw. **4** *Will you back our plan?* to aid, to assist, to help, to promote, to second, to sponsor, to subsidize, to support.

backbone spine. SEE ALSO **body.**

backer *We've got a new backer for our team.* promoter, sponsor, supporter.

background *Tell me the background to this affair.* circumstances, setting.

backing *If we go ahead with the plan, will you give us your backing?* aid, assistance, help, sponsorship, subsidy, support.

backside behind, bottom, buttocks, rear, rump.

backstroke SEE **swim.**

backward handicapped, retarded, slow, underdeveloped, undeveloped. ! These words may sound insulting.

bacon gammon, ham, rashers. SEE ALSO **food, meat.**

bacteria (informal) bugs, germs, microbes, viruses.

bad 1 *a bad man, a bad deed, etc.* abhorrent, base, beastly, corrupt, criminal, cruel, deplorable, detestable, evil, immoral, infamous, malevolent, malicious, malignant, mean, naughty, offensive, regrettable, reprehensible, rotten, shameful, sinful, unworthy, vicious, vile, villainous, wicked, wrong. SEE ALSO **cruel. 2** *a bad accident.* appalling, awful, calamitous, dire, dreadful, frightful, ghastly, hair-raising, hideous, horrible, nasty, serious, severe, shocking, terrible, unfortunate, unpleasant, violent. **3** *a bad performance, a bad piece of work, etc.* abominable, abysmal, appalling, awful, cheap, defective, deficient, dreadful, faulty, feeble, hopeless, imperfect, inadequate, incompetent, incorrect, ineffective, inefficient, inferior, (informal) lousy, pitiful, poor, unsound, useless, weak, worthless. **4** *bad food.* decayed, decomposing, diseased, foul, mildewed, mouldy, polluted, putrid, rotten, smelly, spoiled, tainted. **5** *a bad smell.* loathsome, nauseating, objectionable, obnoxious, odious, offensive, repellent, repulsive, revolting, sickening, vile. **6** *Smoking is bad for you.* damaging, dangerous, destructive, harmful, injurious,

unhealthy. **7** *I feel bad today.*
diseased, feeble, ill, indisposed,
(informal) poorly, queer, sick,
unwell. ! *Bad* has many shades of
meaning, and these are only some of
the other words you could use.

badge *the school badge.* crest, emblem,
medal, rosette, sign, symbol.

badger SEE **animal**.

badminton SEE **sport**.

bad-tempered angry, cross,
disgruntled, gruff, grumpy, irascible,
irritable, moody, morose, peevish,
petulant, rude, short-tempered,
snappy, sulky, sullen, testy.

baffle **1** *The police were baffled by the
strange crime.* to bewilder, to confuse,
to frustrate, to perplex, to puzzle.
2 *baffling*: inexplicable, insoluble,
mysterious.

bag basket, carrier-bag, case,
handbag. SEE ALSO **container**.

baggage *We always have a lot of
baggage when we go on holiday.* bags,
cases, luggage, suitcases, trunks.

bagpipes SEE **music**.

bait *Logan is always baiting the younger
children.* to annoy, to persecute, to
pester, to tease, to torment, to worry.

bake **1** SEE **cook**. **2** to harden, to
heat.

baker SEE **shop**.

balance **1** *He lost his balance and fell off.*
equilibrium, stability, steadiness.
2 *Balance the boat so that it doesn't lean
to one side.* to equalize, to even up, to
make steady, to make symmetrical.
3 *The chemist weighed the pills on the
balance.* scales, weighing-machine.

balcony SEE **building, theatre**.

bald bare, hairless.

balderdash (informal) *He talks a lot
of balderdash!* (informal) bilge, drivel,
gibberish, nonsense, rubbish,
(informal) tripe, (informal) twaddle.

bale *a bale of straw.* bundle.

ball **1** *a glass ball.* globe, sphere.
2 *Cinderella went to a ball.* dance,
disco, party, social.

ballad SEE **poem**.

ballerina ballet-dancer, dancer. SEE
ALSO **entertainment, theatre**.

ballet SEE **entertainment, theatre**.

balloon SEE **aircraft**.

ballot *We held a ballot to choose the
captain.* election, poll, vote.

ball-point pen. SEE ALSO **write**.

balmy *a balmy evening.* gentle, mild,
peaceful, pleasant, soothing.

balsa SEE **wood**.

bamboo FOR OTHER PLANTS SEE
plant.

ban *Some people would like to ban all
smoking.* to bar, to forbid, to make
illegal, to outlaw, to prevent, to
prohibit, to veto.

band **1** *Our football shirts have a white
band round the chest.* belt, hoop, line,
loop, ribbon, ring, strip, stripe. **2** *a
band of robbers.* company, crew, gang,
group, horde, troop. **3** *a recorder band.*
ensemble, group, orchestra. SEE
ALSO **music**.

bandage dressing, lint, plaster. SEE
ALSO **medicine**.

bandit brigand, buccaneer,
highwayman, hijacker, outlaw,
pirate, robber, thief.

bandy-legged SEE **leg**.

bang **1** *a bang on the head.* blow, hit,
knock. SEE ALSO **hit**. **2** *a loud bang.*
blast, boom, crash, explosion,
report. SEE ALSO **sound**.

banger SEE **firework**.

bangle SEE **jewellery**.

banish *They used to banish criminals as a
punishment.* to deport, to eject, to
exile, to expel, to send away.

banisters SEE **building**.

banjo SEE **music, strings**.

bank **1** *We lay on a grassy bank.*
embankment, mound, ridge, shore,
slope. **2** *Mum'll give you the money when
she's been to the bank.* SEE **shop**. **3** *The
plane banked as it turned to land.* to heel,
to incline, to lean, to list, to slant, to
slope, to tilt.

banker SEE **job**.

banner *waving banners.* colours,

ensign, flag, standard, streamer.
banquet dinner, feast, meal, spread.
bantam SEE **farm, poultry.**
banter teasing.
baptize to christen. SEE ALSO
church.
bar 1 *a wooden bar.* beam, girder, rail,
rod. **2** *a refreshment bar.* café, counter,
pub, saloon. **3** *Logan was barred from
the club because he was too young.* to ban,
to exclude, to keep out, to prohibit.
4 *A fallen tree barred their way.* to
block, to deter, to hinder, to impede,
to obstruct, to prevent, to stop.
barbarian heathen, pagan, savage.
! It is insulting to use these words to
describe people of other nations.
barbaric *a barbaric attack.* atrocious,
cruel, fierce, savage, violent. SEE
ALSO **cruel.**
barbarous *a barbarous tribe.* savage,
uncivilized.
barbecue SEE **cook, meal, party.**
barber hairdresser. SEE ALSO **job,
shop.**
bard minstrel, poet, singer. SEE ALSO
writer.
bare 1 *bare legs, a bare patch.* bald,
naked, nude, unclothed, uncovered,
undressed. **2** *a bare hillside.* barren,
bleak, desolate, windswept. **3** *a bare
room.* empty, plain, unfurnished.
4 *He is not the sort of person to bare his
private thoughts.* to betray, to disclose,
to expose, to reveal, to uncover.
barely hardly, scarcely.
bargain 1 *After some arguing, they made
a bargain.* agreement, arrangement,
contract, deal, understanding. **2** *In
the market people bargain over the prices.*
to argue, to discuss terms, to haggle,
to negotiate.
barge SEE **vessel.**
bark SEE **sound.**
barley SEE **cereal.**
barmaid, barman waiter, waitress.
SEE ALSO **job.**
bar mitzvah SEE **Jew.**
barn SEE **building, farm.**
barnacle SEE **shellfish.**

barometer SEE **weather.**
baron, baroness SEE **title.**
barracks SEE **building.**
barrage 1 gunfire. **2** *a barrage across
the river.* barrier, dam.
barrel cask, tub. SEE ALSO **container.**
barrel-organ SEE **music.**
barren *barren desert.* arid, bare, lifeless,
sterile.
barricade *a barricade across a road.*
barrier, obstacle, obstruction.
barrier 1 *We built a barrier to keep the
spectators off the pitch.* barricade, fence,
hurdle, obstacle, railings, wall.
2 *They built a barrier across the river.*
barrage, dam.
barrister SEE **job, law.**
barrow cart, wheelbarrow.
base 1 *Dad made a concrete base for the
new shed.* basis, bottom, foot,
foundation, rest, stand, support.
2 *The climbers set up a base at the foot of
the mountain.* depot, headquarters.
3 *He based his argument on what he read
in the paper.* to establish, to found, to
set up. **4** *Stealing from old people is a
base crime.* contemptible, cowardly,
depraved, evil, immoral, low, mean,
wicked.
baseball SEE **sport.**
basement cellar, crypt, vault. SEE
ALSO **building.**
bash (informal) *He bashed his head
against a beam.* to bang, to batter, to
beat, to bump, (informal) to clout, to
dash, to hammer, to knock, to
smash, to strike, to thump, to
wallop, to whack. SEE ALSO **hit.**
bashful *There's no need to be so bashful
about getting first prize!* coy, demure,
faint-hearted, modest, reserved, self-
conscious, sheepish, shy, timid,
timorous.
basic *the basic facts.* chief, elementary,
essential, foremost, fundamental,
important, main, primary, principal.
basin bowl, dish. SEE ALSO
container.
basis *What was the basis of your story?*
base, foundation, starting-point.

basket bag. SEE ALSO **container**.
basketball SEE **sport**.
bass SEE **sing**.
bassoon SEE **woodwind**.
bastard illegitimate. ! Nowadays *bastard* is often insulting, while *illegitimate* is a polite word.
bat 1 *Bats usually fly at dusk.* SEE **animal**. 2 *You hit the ball with the bat.* club, racket. SEE ALSO **sport**.
batch *Is there anything good in the latest batch of records?* bunch, collection, consignment, group, set.
bath 1 *a bath of water.* SEE **container**. 2 *to have a bath.* sauna, shower, wash.
bathe 1 *Tony only bathes when it's really warm.* to go swimming, to swim, to take a dip. 2 *Bathe the wound in clean water.* to clean, to rinse, to swill, to wash.
bathroom 1 THINGS YOU FIND IN A BATHROOM ARE bath, bath mat, bath salts, comb, cosmetics, curlers, extractor fan, flannel, foam bath, hair-drier, medicine cabinet, mirror, nail-brush, nail-scissors, pumice-stone, razor, scales, shampoo, shaver, shower, soap, sponge, taps, tiles, toilet, toilet-roll, toothbrush, towel, towel rail, tweezers, ventilator, wash-basin. 2 SEE **house**.
baton *a policeman's baton.* cane, club, rod, stick.
battalion SEE **armed services**.
batter 1 *We battered on the door.* to bang, to bash, to beat, to hammer, to knock, to pound, to strike, to thump. SEE ALSO **hit**. 2 *fish cooked in batter.* SEE **food**.
battering-ram SEE **weapon**.
battery SEE **electricity**.
battle *Many died in the battle.* action, campaign, clash, combat, conflict, confrontation, encounter, engagement, struggle. SEE ALSO **fight**.
battle-axe SEE **weapon**.
battlements SEE **building, castle**.
battleship SEE **vessel**.
bawl *Stop bawling: I'm not deaf!* to

bellow, to call, to cry, to roar, to scream, to shout, to shriek, to yell. SEE ALSO **sound**.
bay 1 *The ship sailed into a quiet bay.* cove, estuary, fiord, gulf, inlet. SEE ALSO **geography**. 2 *the baying of hounds.* SEE **sound**.
bayonet SEE **weapon**.
bay window SEE **building**.
bazaar *We held a bazaar to raise money for our camping trip.* auction, fair, jumble sale, market.
be 1 *Will I still be here in 50 years?* to continue, to exist, to live, to remain, to survive. 2 *When will the next eclipse be?* to happen, to occur, to take place.
beach *a sandy beach.* coast, sands, seaside, shore. SEE ALSO **seaside**.
beacon SEE **warning**.
bead 1 *She wore some pretty beads.* SEE **jewellery**. 2 *There were beads of sweat on her face.* blob, drip, drop.
beagle SEE **dog**.
beak SEE **bird**.
beaker *a beaker of water.* SEE **container, drink**.
beam 1 *That beam holds up the ceiling.* bar, girder, joist, rafter. 2 *a beam of light.* gleam, ray, shaft. 3 *He beamed at us happily.* to grin, to laugh, to smile.
bean SEE **food, vegetable**.
bear 1 *Will that pillar bear the weight?* to carry, to hold up, to prop up, to support. 2 *The angels bore good tidings.* to bring, to convey. 3 *Lucy's dog bore six puppies.* to give birth to, to produce. 4 *Mrs Brunswick cannot bear the smell of onions.* to abide, to cope with, to endure, to put up with, to stand, to suffer, to tolerate, to undergo. 5 SEE **animal**.
bearings *We lost our bearings in the fog.* course, direction, position, way.
beast *a wild beast.* animal, brute, creature, monster.
beastly 1 *beastly cruelty.* abominable, brutal, hateful, horrible. SEE ALSO **cruel**. 2 *beastly weather.* awful, nasty, terrible. SEE ALSO **unpleasant**.
beat 1 *They beat him mercilessly.* to batter, to cane, (informal) to clout,

to flog, to knock about, to lash, to manhandle, to pound, to scourge, to strike, to thrash, to thump, to wallop, to whack, to whip. SEE ALSO **hit**. 2 *The cook beat the mixture until it was creamy.* to agitate, to mix, to stir, to whisk. 3 *Our opponents beat us easily.* to conquer, to crush, to defeat, (informal) to lick, to master, to outdo, to overcome, to overpower, to overthrow, to overwhelm, to rout, to subdue, (informal) to thrash, to vanquish. 4 *Our car could beat yours any day!* to exceed, to excel, to outdo, to surpass, to top, to win against. 5 *This music has a good beat.* pulse, rhythm, throb.

beautiful *a beautiful bride, beautiful embroidery, beautiful scenery, beautiful weather.* admirable, alluring, appealing, artistic, attractive, bewitching, brilliant, captivating, charming, dainty, elegant, exquisite, (old-fashioned) fair, fascinating, fetching, fine, good-looking, glamorous, glorious, gorgeous, graceful, handsome, imaginative, irresistible, lovely, magnificent, neat, picturesque, pleasing, pretty, quaint, radiant, scenic, seductive, spectacular, splendid, superb, tempting. ! The word *beautiful* has many shades of meaning. The words given here are only some of the other words you could use.

beaver SEE **animal**.

beckon SEE **gesture**.

become 1 *Remember that this little puppy will become a big dog!* to change into, to grow into, to turn into. 2 *That dress becomes you.* to be appropriate for, to fit, to suit.

becoming *a becoming dress.* appropriate, apt, attractive, decent, fitting, proper, suitable.

bed 1 bedstead, berth, bunk, divan, four-poster, hammock. SEE ALSO **bedclothes, furniture**. 2 *a flower bed.* border, patch, plot. SEE ALSO **garden**. 3 *the bed of a river.* bottom, course.

bedclothes, bedding THINGS YOU

USE TO MAKE A BED ARE bedspread, blanket, bolster, continental quilt, counterpane, coverlet, duvet, eiderdown, electric blanket, mattress, pillow, pillowcase, pillowslip, quilt, sheet, sleeping-bag.

bedlam *There was absolute bedlam in the classroom by the time Mrs Angel came back.* chaos, hubbub, pandemonium, riot, rumpus, turmoil, uproar. SEE ALSO **commotion**.

bedraggled *We came in from the rain very bedraggled.* dishevelled, scruffy, untidy, wet.

bedridden *The sick woman was bedridden.* infirm. SEE ALSO **ill**.

bedroom SEE **house**.

bedspread SEE **bedclothes**.

bedtime SEE **time**.

bee SEE **insect**.

beech SEE **tree**.

beef, beefburger SEE **meat**.

beefy *The wrestler looked a beefy character.* big, brawny, burly, hefty, muscular, strong, tough.

beer SEE **drink**.

beetle SEE **insect**.

beetroot SEE **salad, vegetable**.

befall *The travellers told us what had befallen them.* to come about, to happen, to occur, to take place.

before earlier, previously, sooner.

beg 1 *It was shameful to see the poor begging for food.* to cadge, to scrounge. 2 *Granny begged us to visit her soon.* to ask, to entreat, to implore, to plead, to request.

beggar *In many countries you see beggars in the street.* destitute person, homeless person, pauper, poor person, ragamuffin, tramp, vagrant.

begin 1 *Mrs Angel always stops trouble as soon as it begins.* to arise, to commence, to start. 2 *Mr Brunswick wants to begin a new business.* to create, to embark on, to found, to initiate, to introduce, to open, to originate, to set up.

beginner apprentice, learner, novice.

beginning 1 *the beginning of life on*

earth. birth, commencement, creation, origin, start. 2 *the beginning of a book.* introduction, opening, preface, prelude, prologue.

begrudge *You don't begrudge him his pocket-money, do you?* to be bitter about, to envy, to resent.

behave *I hope you'll behave well.* to act, to conduct yourself.

behaviour *Mrs Angel said their behaviour had been excellent.* attitude, conduct, manners.

behead to decapitate. SEE ALSO **execute, kill.**

behold (old-fashioned) *He beheld a vision of a golden city.* to discern, to look at, to make out, to see, to witness.

beige SEE **colour.**

being creature.

belated *It was two weeks before we sent belated thanks.* delayed, late.

belch *The factory chimneys belched out filthy smoke.* to discharge, to emit, to erupt, to fume, to send out, to smoke, to vomit.

belfry SEE **church.**

belief *religious beliefs.* attitude, conviction, creed, faith, opinion, religion, thought, trust, view.

believe 1 *You can't believe anything Logan says.* to accept, to have confidence in, to have faith in, to rely on, to trust. 2 *I believe he cheated.* to consider, to feel, to judge, to reckon, to think. 3 *I believe it was you who finished off the chocolates?* to assume, to presume, to suppose.

bell 1 *Didn't you hear the bell?* alarm, signal. 2 VARIOUS WAYS BELLS SOUND ARE to chime, to clang, to jangle, to jingle, to peal, to ping, to ring, to tinkle, to toll.

belligerent *Logan is a belligerent fighter.* aggressive, hostile, martial, militant, pugnacious, warlike.

bellow SEE **sound.**

bellows SEE **blacksmith.**

belly abdomen, stomach, (informal) tummy. SEE ALSO **body.**

belong 1 *This book belongs to me.* to be

owned by. 2 *Do you belong to the youth club?* to be a member of.

belongings *Remember to take your belongings when you get off the train.* possessions, property, things.

beloved darling, dearest, loved.

belt 1 *She wore a belt round her waist.* girdle, loop, strap. 2 *The fox made for a belt of trees.* band, line, strip.

bench 1 *a park bench.* form, seat. 2 *a carpenter's bench.* table. SEE ALSO **furniture.**

bend 1 *The blacksmith bent an iron bar.* to arch, to buckle, to coil, to curl, to curve, to distort, to fold, to loop, to turn, to twist, to warp, to wind. 2 *We bent down to go under the low branch.* to bow, to crouch, to duck, to kneel, to stoop. 3 *a bend in the road.* angle, corner, curve, turn, twist.

benediction blessing. SEE ALSO **church.**

benefactor *The benefactor who paid for our new sports gear wants to remain anonymous.* donor, sponsor.

beneficial *They say that garlic is beneficial to your health.* advantageous, constructive, good, healthy, helpful, profitable, useful.

benefit *Clean air is one of the benefits of living in the country.* asset, advantage, blessing, gain, help, privilege, profit.

benevolent *a benevolent old gentleman.* considerate, good, helpful, humane, kindly, merciful, sympathetic, warm-hearted. SEE ALSO **kind.**

bent *a bent nail.* angled, crooked, curved, distorted, twisted, warped.

bequest *Mrs Brunswick received a small bequest from her grandmother's will.* inheritance, legacy.

bereavement *a bereavement in the family.* death, loss.

beret SEE **hat.**

berry SEE **fruit.**

berserk *The dog went berserk when the wasp stung him.* crazy, demented, frantic, frenzied, mad, violent, wild.

berth 1 *There were four berths in each cabin.* bed, bunk. 2 *The ship tied up at* *its berth.* anchorage, dock, landing-stage, moorings, pier, quay, wharf.

besides additionally, also, furthermore, moreover, too.

besiege *The Greeks besieged Troy for 10 long years.* to blockade, to cut off, to encircle, to surround.

bet 1 *People don't often gain anything by betting.* to gamble, to do the pools, to enter a lottery. 2 *How much was your bet?* stake, wager.

betray 1 *to betray someone who trusts you.* to cheat, to double-cross, to let down. 2 *to betray a secret.* to disclose, to divulge, to expose, to reveal.

betrayal disloyalty, treachery, treason.

betrothed engaged.

better *Are you better after your flu?* cured, healed, improved, recovering, recovered, well.

beverage drink. FOR VARIOUS DRINKS SEE **drink**.

bewilder 1 *The different lights bewildered the driver.* to baffle, to confuse, to distract, to muddle, to perplex, to puzzle. 2 *bewildered*: dazed, stunned.

bewitch 1 *The magical atmosphere bewitched us.* to captivate, to charm, to enchant, to fascinate. 2 *bewitched*: entranced, spellbound. 3 *bewitching*: SEE **attractive**.

biased *The referee was biased in favour of their team.* influenced, one-sided, prejudiced, unfair, unjust.

bib SEE **clothes**.

bicycle 1 (informal) bike, cycle, penny-farthing. SEE ALSO **cycle**. 2 PARTS OF A BICYCLE ARE brake, frame, gear, handlebar, pedal, saddle, spoke, wheel.

bid *What will you bid for this watch?* to offer, to propose.

bifocals glasses, spectacles.

big 1 *a big amount, a big person, a big shop, etc.* ample, bulky, colossal, considerable, enormous, extensive, fat, giant, gigantic, grand, great, hefty, high, huge, hulking, husky, immense, immeasurable, incalculable, infinite, large, lofty, mammoth, massive, mighty, monstrous, roomy, sizeable, spacious, substantial, tall, (informal) terrific, towering, tremendous, vast. 2 *a big decision, a big moment, etc.* grave, important, major, momentous, notable, serious, significant, weighty.

bike SEE **cycle**.

bikini SEE **clothes**.

bilge (informal) *Don't talk bilge!* (informal) balderdash, drivel, gibberish, nonsense, rubbish, (informal) tripe, (informal) twaddle.

bilious queasy, sick. SEE ALSO **illness**.

bill 1 *a bird's bill.* beak. SEE ALSO **bird**. 2 *Keep the bill to prove how much you paid.* account, receipt. 3 advertisement, notice, poster.

billiards SEE **game**.

billow *billowing waves.* to bulge, to rise, to swell.

billycan SEE **container, cook**.

billy-goat SEE **male**.

bin SEE **container**.

bind 1 *to bind things together.* to attach, to connect, to join, to secure, to tie. SEE ALSO **fasten**. 2 *to bind a wound.* to cover, to wrap.

bingo SEE **game**.

binoculars field-glasses. SEE ALSO **optical**.

biography SEE **writing**.

biology SEE **science**.

biplane SEE **aircraft**.

birch SEE **tree**.

bird 1 chick, cock, fledgeling, hen, nestling. 2 VARIOUS BIRDS ARE albatross, blackbird, budgerigar, bullfinch, buzzard, canary, chaffinch, chicken, coot, cormorant, crane, crow, cuckoo, curlew, dove, duck, eagle, emu, falcon, finch, flamingo, goldfinch, goose, grouse, gull, hawk, heron, jackdaw, jay, kingfisher, kiwi, lapwing, lark, magpie, nightingale, ostrich, owl, parrot, partridge, peacock, peewit, pelican, penguin, petrel, pheasant, pigeon, plover, puffin, quail, raven, robin, rook, seagull, skylark, sparrow, starling, stork, swallow, swan, swift, thrush, tit, turkey, vulture, wagtail, warbler, woodpecker, wren, yellowhammer. 3 VARIOUS PARTS OF A BIRD ARE beak, bill, claw, crest, down, feather, plumage, tail, talon, wing. 4 SEE **female, male, young.**

birth appearance, beginning, creation, origin, start. SEE ALSO **pregnant.**

biscuit cracker, wafer. FOR OTHER FOODS SEE ALSO **food.**

bishop SEE **church.**

bison SEE **animal.**

bit 1 *a bit of chocolate, a bit of stone, etc.* block, chip, chunk, crumb, dollop, fragment, grain, hunk, lump, morsel, particle, scrap, slab, speck. 2 *I don't need it all, just a bit of it.* division, fraction, helping, part, piece, portion, section, segment, share, slice.

bitch SEE **dog, female.**

bite 1 to chew, to gnaw, to munch, to nip, to snap, to sting. 2 *I'll just have a bite.* morsel, mouthful.

bitter 1 *a bitter smell.* acrid, harsh, sharp, unpleasant. SEE ALSO **taste.** 2 *a bitter experience.* distressing, painful, unhappy. 3 *bitter feelings.* cruel, embittered, envious, jealous, resentful, sour, spiteful. 4 *a bitter quarrel.* angry, vicious, violent. 5 *a bitter wind.* biting, cold, freezing, (informal) perishing, piercing, raw.

black 1 SEE **colour.** 2 *a black night.* dark, inky, pitch-black, sooty, starless, unlit. 3 *a black mood.* bad, depressing, evil, gloomy, sad, sombre, sinister.

black-beetle SEE **insect.**

blackberry bramble. SEE ALSO **fruit.**

blackbird SEE **bird.**

blacken *He blackened his face with soot.* to darken.

blackguard knave, rascal, rogue, scoundrel, villain.

blackmail SEE **crime.**

blacksmith 1 SEE **art, job.** 2 THINGS USED BY A BLACKSMITH ARE anvil, bellows, forge, hammer, tongs.

bladder SEE **body.**

blade *a sharp blade.* edge, knife, razor, sword.

blame 1 *They blamed me, but I didn't do it!* to accuse, to charge, to condemn, to criticize, to denounce, to incriminate, to rebuke, to reprimand, to scold. 2 *Tony admitted that the blame was his.* fault, guilt, responsibility.

blameless guiltless, innocent.

blancmange SEE **food.**

blank 1 *blank paper, a blank tape.* clean, empty, unmarked, unused. 2 *a blank look.* expressionless, vacant.

blanket SEE **bedclothes.**

blare *The trumpets blared.* to bray, to roar, to shriek. SEE ALSO **sound.**

blasphemous *It would be blasphemous to tear up a Bible.* irreverent, sacrilegious, sinful, wicked.

blast 1 *a blast of air.* gale, wind. 2 *a bomb blast.* bang, boom, explosion, noise, report.

blatant *a blatant mistake.* conspicuous, evident, obvious, open, unconcealed, undisguised, unmistakable.

blaze 1 *The fire blazed up.* to burn, to flame, to flare. 2 *The firemen couldn't control the blaze.* conflagration, fire, inferno.

blazer SEE **clothes.**

bleach *The sun bleached our curtains.* to discolour, to fade, to whiten.

bleak *a bleak moor.* bare, barren, cold, desolate, dismal, windswept.

bleat, bleep SEE **sound.**

blemish *There wasn't a blemish in Lucy's work.* blot, defect, fault, flaw, imperfection, mark, spot, stain.

blend *Tony blended the ingredients for his cake.* to combine, to mingle, to mix. SEE ALSO **cook.**

blessed hallowed, holy, sacred.

blessing 1 *The vicar said the blessing.* benediction, grace, prayer. 2 *The fine weather this year is a great blessing to the farmers.* advantage, asset, benefit, comfort, help.

blight affliction, ailment, disease, illness, sickness.

blind 1 sightless, unseeing. SEE ALSO **handicap**. **2** *Please close the blind.* curtain, screen, shade, shutters.

blink *blinking lights.* to flicker, to wink.

bliss *It's bliss to have a nice hot bath!* delight, ecstasy, happiness, joy, pleasure, rapture.

blister SEE **illness**.

blitz attack, onslaught, raid.

blizzard SEE **weather**.

bloated *The pictures of starving children with bloated stomachs horrified us.* distended, swollen.

blob *a blob of paint.* bead, drop, spot.

block 1 *a block of ice-cream.* brick, chunk, hunk, lump, slab. **2** *The drain was blocked with leaves.* to bung up, to clog, to fill, to jam, to stop up. **3** *An overturned lorry blocked our way.* to bar, to barricade, to deter, to hamper, to hinder, to hold back, to impede, to obstruct, to prevent, to prohibit.

blockade siege.

blockage *a blockage in a drain.* block, hindrance, impediment, obstacle, obstruction.

blockhead ass, dope, dunce, half-wit, idiot, ignoramus, imbecile, moron, nit, nitwit, twerp. ! These words are insulting.

bloke (informal) fellow, guy, man.

blond, blonde *blond hair.* fair, light. SEE ALSO **hair**. ! A man is *blond*; a woman is *blonde*.

blood SEE **body**.

bloodhound SEE **dog**.

bloodshed carnage, killing, massacre, murder, slaughter.

bloodthirsty brutal, ferocious, fierce, inhuman, murderous, pitiless, ruthless, savage, vicious, violent. SEE ALSO **cruel**.

bloody blood-stained, gory.

bloom *Most flowers bloom in summer.* to blossom, to flourish, to flower.

blossom to bloom, to flower.

blot 1 *a blot of ink.* blotch, spot, stain. **2** *a blot on the landscape.* blemish,

eyesore. **3** *Look out, you've made me blot the page!* to mar, to mark, to smudge, to spoil, to stain. **4** *The fog blotted out the view.* to conceal, to cover, to erase, to hide, to mask, to rub out, to wipe out.

blow 1 *The wind blew.* to puff, to whistle. **2** *The tyres need blowing up.* to inflate. **3** *The bomb blew up.* to burst, to detonate, to explode, to go off. **4** *The falling branch gave him a nasty blow on the head.* bang, bump, hit, knock. **5** *It was a terrible blow when she lost her purse.* bombshell, jolt, shock, surprise.

blubber *Stop blubbering and help me clear up!* to cry, to snivel, to sob, to wail, to weep.

blue 1 SEE **colour**. **2** *I'm feeling blue today.* dejected, depressed, gloomy, melancholy, unhappy.

bluebell SEE **flower**.

bluebottle SEE **insect**.

blues SEE **music**.

bluff *Don't believe Logan: he's only bluffing.* to deceive, to fool, to hoax, to hoodwink, (informal) to kid, to lie, to mislead, to pretend, to take in, to trick.

blunder 1 *to blunder about.* to stagger, to stumble. **2** *to make a blunder.* (informal) clanger, error, (informal) howler, mistake, (informal) slip-up. **3** *blundering*: awkward, bungling, clumsy, gawky, lumbering, ungainly.

blunderbuss SEE **weapon**.

blunt 1 *a blunt knife.* dull, unsharpened, worn. **2** *a blunt reply.* abrupt, candid, curt, direct, frank, honest, impolite, outspoken, plain, rude, straight, straightforward.

blurred *a blurred photograph.* cloudy, confused, dim, faint, fuzzy, hazy, indistinct, misty, unclear.

blurt SEE **talk**.

blush to colour, to flush, to glow, to redden.

blustery *blustery weather.* gusty, squally, windy. SEE ALSO **weather**.

boa-constrictor SEE **snake**.

boar SEE **animal, male.**

board 1 *wooden boards.* plank, timber. 2 *to board a ship.* to embark. 3 *He boards in a hotel.* to live, to lodge.

boarder guest, lodger, resident, tenant.

boast *People who boast are usually unpopular.* to brag, to crow, to gloat, to show off, to swank.

boastful arrogant, conceited, haughty, proud, (informal) stuck-up.

boat craft, ship. SEE ALSO **vessel.**

boat-house SEE **building.**

bobsleigh SEE **sport.**

bodice SEE **clothes.**

body 1 *Doctors have to know about the body.* anatomy. 2 *The body of the dead animal was burned.* carcass, corpse, remains. 3 *The boxer aimed blows at his opponent's body.* trunk. 4 PARTS OF YOUR BODY ARE abdomen, adenoids, ankle, appendix, arm, artery, backbone, belly, bladder, blood, bone, bowels, brain, breast, buttocks, calf, cheek, chest, chin, ear, elbow, eye, finger, foot, forehead, funny-bone, gland, gullet, gums, guts, hand, head, heart, heel, hip, intestines, jaw, kidney, knee, knee-cap, knuckle, leg, limb, lip, liver, lung, marrow, mouth, muscle, navel, neck, nerve, nipple, nose, nostril, pores, rib, saliva, scalp, shin, shoulder, shoulder-blade, skeleton, skin, skull, spine, stomach, thigh, throat, thumb, toe, tongue, tonsils, tooth, trunk, vein, vertebra, waist, windpipe, womb, wrist.

bodyguard *The President always has a bodyguard.* guard, protector.

bog *Don't get stuck in the bog.* fen, marsh, quagmire, quicksands, swamp.

bogie SEE **railway.**

bogus *a bogus £5 note.* counterfeit, faked, false, feigned, (informal) phoney, pretended.

boil 1 *It's uncomfortable to have a boil on your bottom.* abscess, inflammation, sore. SEE ALSO **illness.** 2 *Are the potatoes boiling yet?* to bubble, to seethe, to simmer, to stew. SEE ALSO **cook.**

boisterous *boisterous behaviour.* animated, disorderly, irrepressible, lively, noisy, obstreperous, rough, rowdy, unruly, wild.

bold 1 *a bold adventure, a bold explorer.* adventurous, brave, courageous, daring, enterprising, fearless, heroic, intrepid, self-confident, valiant. 2 *It was a bit bold to ask for a day off school.* brazen, cheeky, forward, impertinent, impudent, insolent, presumptuous, rude, shameless. 3 *bold writing.* big, clear, large.

bolster cushion, pillow. SEE ALSO **bedclothes.**

bolt 1 *Dad fixed a bolt on the door.* bar, catch, latch, lock. 2 *We bolt the door when we go out.* to close, to fasten, to lock, to secure. 3 *The animals have bolted!* to escape, to flee, to run away. 4 *Don't bolt your food.* to gobble, to gulp. SEE ALSO **eat.**

bomb SEE **weapon.**

bombard *They bombarded us with missiles.* to assail, to assault, to attack, to fire at, to pelt, to shell, to shoot at.

bomber SEE **aircraft.**

bombshell *The £100 prize came as a complete bombshell!* shock, surprise.

bond 1 *The prisoner couldn't undo his bonds.* chain, cord, fetters, handcuffs, rope, shackles. 2 *There is usually a strong bond between twins.* connection, link, relationship.

bondage slavery.

bone SEE **body.**

bonnet 1 *the bonnet of a car.* SEE **vehicle.** 2 *a woolly bonnet.* cap, hat. SEE ALSO **hat.**

bonus *At Christmas mum gives us a bonus on top of our normal pocket-money.* addition, extra, supplement.

boo to hoot, to jeer. SEE ALSO **sound.**

booby trap ambush, snare, trap.

book 1 publication, volume. 2 KINDS OF BOOK ARE album, annual, anthology, atlas, booklet, diary, dictionary, encyclopaedia, fiction, hardback, hymn-book, manual, manuscript, omnibus, paperback, reference book, scrap-book, scroll, textbook. SEE ALSO **magazine, writing**. 3 PARTS OF A BOOK ARE chapter, epilogue, index, introduction, preface, prologue, title. 4 *Have you booked tickets for the pantomime?* to order, to reserve.

bookcase SEE **furniture**.

booklet book, brochure, leaflet, pamphlet.

bookmaker SEE **job**.

boom bang, blast, crash, explosion. SEE ALSO **sound**.

boomerang SEE **weapon**.

boost *Winning a race boosts your morale.* to encourage, to help, to improve, to increase, to raise.

boot, bootee SEE **shoe**.

booth *a telephone booth, a voting booth.* compartment, cubicle, kiosk, stall, stand.

booty *The thieves dropped their booty as they escaped.* contraband, loot, plunder, (informal) swag, takings, trophies.

booze SEE **alcohol**.

border 1 *We showed our passports at the border.* boundary, frontier. 2 *We put a colourful border round the edge.* edging, frame, frieze, frill, fringe, hem, margin, verge. 3 *a flower border.* bed. SEE ALSO **garden**.

bore 1 *to bore a hole.* to drill, to penetrate, to perforate, to pierce. 2 *The long speech bored most of the audience.* to tire, to weary.

boring *a boring book, boring work, etc.* arid, commonplace, dreary, dry, dull, flat, long-winded, monotonous, tedious, unexciting, uninteresting, wordy.

borrow *Can I borrow your pen?* to be lent, to use.

Borstal SEE **punishment**.

bosom breast, chest, heart.

boss *Who's the boss here?* chief, controller, director, employer, foreman, governor, head, leader, manager, master, proprietor, ruler, superintendent, supervisor.

bossy *You may be captain, but don't get bossy!* dictatorial, domineering, masterful, tyrannical.

botany SEE **science**.

bother 1 *There was some bother in the playground at dinner time.* ado, commotion, disorder, disturbance, fuss, to-do. SEE ALSO **commotion**. 2 *Is the dog a bother to you?* inconvenience, nuisance, trouble, worry. 3 *Are the wasps bothering you?* to annoy, to disturb, to exasperate, to irritate, to molest, to pester, to plague, to trouble, to upset, to vex, to worry. 4 *Don't bother to wash up.* to care, to mind.

bottle SEE **container**.

bottom 1 *the bottom of a wall.* base, foot, foundation. 2 *The wasp stung me on the bottom.* backside, behind, buttocks, rear, rump. 3 *the bottom of the sea.* bed, depths.

bough *a bough of a tree.* branch, limb.

boulder *The beach was strewn with large boulders.* rock, stone.

bounce *The ball bounced over the fence.* to bound, to jump, to rebound, to recoil, to ricochet, to spring.

bound 1 *Grandpa is bound to be here soon.* certain, compelled, obliged, required, sure. 2 *The rocket was bound for the moon.* aimed at, destined for, directed towards. 3 *He bounded over the fence.* to bounce, to hop, to jump, to leap, to skip, to spring, to vault.

boundary *A fence marked the boundary.* border, circumference, edge, frontier, limit, margin, perimeter.

boundless *Lucy has boundless energy.* endless, everlasting, limitless, unlimited, unrestricted.

bounty *Millionaires are not always known for their bounty.* charity, generosity.

bouquet *a bouquet of flowers.* arrangement, bunch, posy, spray, wreath.

bout 1 *a boxing bout.* combat, contest,

fight, match, round. 2 *a bout of coughing.* attack, fit, turn.

boutique SEE **shop.**

bow 1 *bows and arrows.* SEE **weapon.** 2 *Tie it in a bow.* SEE **knot.** 3 *the bow of a ship.* SEE **vessel.** 4 *They bowed before the queen.* to bend, to curtsy, to stoop.

bowels SEE **body.**

bowl 1 *a bowl of soup.* basin. SEE ALSO **container.** 2 *He bowled a faster ball.* to fling, to hurl, to lob, to pitch, to throw, to toss.

bow-legged SEE **leg.**

bowler 1 SEE **cricket.** 2 SEE **hat.**

bowls SEE **game.**

box 1 carton, case, chest, crate. SEE ALSO **container.** 2 *boxing*: SEE **fight, sport.**

box-office SEE **theatre.**

boy (insulting) brat, lad, (insulting) urchin, youngster, youth. SEE ALSO **person.**

bra SEE **underclothes.**

brace couple, pair.

bracelet SEE **jewellery.**

braces SEE **clothes.**

bracket SEE **punctuation.**

brag *Even if you did win, don't brag about it.* to boast, to crow, to gloat, to show off, to swank.

braid *She decorated the hem of her skirt with red braid.* band, ribbon.

brain 1 SEE **body.** 2 *Use your brains!* intellect, intelligence, reason, sense, understanding, wisdom, wit.

brainwash *People can be brainwashed by advertising.* to indoctrinate.

brainwave (informal) SEE **idea.**

brainy *Tony is the brainy one in the family.* academic, bright, clever, intellectual, intelligent.

brake SEE **vehicle.**

bramble blackberry.

bran SEE **food.**

branch 1 *the branch of a tree.* arm, bough, limb. 2 *a branch of the bank.* department, part, office, section. 3 *The road branches a short distance from here.* to divide, to fork.

brand 1 *What brand of margarine do you buy?* kind, make, trademark. 2 *The farmer brands his cattle with a hot iron.* to mark, to stamp.

brandish *He brandished his umbrella to catch our attention.* to flourish, to shake, to twirl, to wave.

brandy SEE **drink.**

brass 1 *a brass door-knob.* SEE **metal.** 2 BRASS INSTRUMENTS ARE bugle, cornet, horn, trombone, trumpet, tuba. SEE ALSO **music.**

brat SEE **child.**

brave *She was brave to go back into the burning house.* adventurous, bold, courageous, daring, fearless, gallant, heroic, intrepid, noble, plucky, spirited, undaunted, valiant.

bravery *Everyone praised her bravery.* courage, daring, determination, fortitude, (informal) grit, (informal) guts, heroism, nerve, pluck, prowess, spirit, valour.

brawl *There was a brawl outside the football ground.* clash, confrontation, fight, quarrel, row, scrap, scuffle, squabble, struggle, tussle.

brawny *That weight-lifter looks a brawny fellow.* beefy, burly, muscular, strong, tough.

bray SEE **sound.**

brazen *It was brazen to march up to the prince and ask for a kiss!* bold, cheeky, forward, impertinent, impudent, insolent, rude, shameless.

breach *a breach in the sea wall.* break, crack, gap, hole, opening, space, split.

bread loaf, roll. SEE ALSO **food.**

break 1 *to break an egg, to break a leg, to break down a wall.* to burst, to chip, to crack, to crumple, to crush, to damage, to demolish, to destroy, to fracture, to knock down, to ruin, to shatter, to smash, to splinter, to split, to squash, to wreck. 2 *The sandcastle broke up.* to collapse, to crumble, to decay, to deteriorate, to disintegrate, to fall apart, to tumble down. 3 *Did he break the law?* to disobey, to disregard, to infringe, to violate. 4 *There was a break in the pipe.* breach, chink, crack, cut, gap, gash, hole, leak, opening, rift, slit, split, tear. 5 *We ran home in a break between the showers.* interlude, interval, lapse, lull, pause, respite, rest.

breaker *The breakers crashed on the shore.* surf, waves.

breakfast SEE meal.

breakneck *breakneck speed.* dangerous, hasty, headlong, suicidal.

breast bosom. SEE ALSO body.

breast-stroke SEE swim.

breathless *Lucy was breathless after her race.* exhausted, gasping, panting, tired out.

breathe *Don't breathe the fumes.* to inhale.

breech *the breech of a gun.* SEE gun.

breeches SEE clothes.

breed 1 *Lucy's mice bred rapidly.* to increase, to multiply, to produce young, to reproduce. 2 *What breed of dog is that?* kind, species, variety.

breeze *a cool breeze.* air, draught, wind.

breezy airy, draughty, fresh, windy.

brew SEE cook.

brewer SEE job.

bribe *You mustn't try to bribe the judge.* to corrupt, to entice, to influence, to pervert, to tempt.

brick block. SEE ALSO building.

bricklayer SEE job.

bride, bridegroom, bridesmaid SEE wedding.

bridge 1 KINDS OF BRIDGE ARE aqueduct, fly-over, suspension bridge, viaduct. 2 *the bridge of a ship.* SEE vessel. 3 *Can you play bridge?* SEE cards.

bridle SEE horse.

brief 1 *We paid a brief visit to granny.* little, momentary, passing, short, temporary, transient. 2 *He gave me a brief summary of the story.* abbreviated, abridged, compact, concise, condensed, terse.

briefs knickers, panties, pants, shorts, trunks, underpants. SEE ALSO underclothes.

brigade SEE armed services.

brigand bandit, buccaneer, desperado, gangster, highwayman, outlaw, pirate, robber, thief.

bright 1 *bright colours, bright lights, a bright day, etc.* brilliant, clear, flashy, gaudy, gleaming, radiant, resplendent, shining, shiny, showy, sparkling, sunny, vivid. SEE ALSO light. 2 *a bright manner, a bright voice.* animated, cheerful, happy, lively. 3 *a bright idea, a bright pupil.* brainy, clever, ingenious, intelligent, quick, shrewd, (informal) smart.

brighten *We need to brighten this gloomy place up.* to cheer up, to illuminate, to lighten, to light up.

brilliant 1 *brilliant lights.* bright, dazzling, gleaming, glittering, resplendent, shining, sparkling. SEE ALSO light. 2 *a brilliant scientist.* brainy, clever, gifted, intelligent, marvellous, outstanding, talented, wonderful. 3 (informal) *Their playing was brilliant today.* SEE excellent.

brim *The reservoir was full to the brim.* brink, edge, rim, top.

brimming full, overflowing.

bring 1 *Mrs Brunswick asked Tony to bring the shopping.* to carry, to fetch, to take. 2 *A change in the wind will bring snow.* to cause, to create, to generate, to give rise to, to induce, to lead to, to provoke. 3 *We are planning to bring out a new magazine.* to introduce, to issue, to produce, to publish, to release, to start. 4 *Parents have to bring up their children.* to care for, to educate, to look after, to raise, to rear, to train.

brink *He stood on the brink of the pool.* brim, edge, rim.

brisk *You need some brisk exercise.* animated, energetic, fast, lively, quick, rapid, speedy, sprightly.

bristle hair.

brittle *Eggshell is extremely brittle.* breakable, crisp, fragile, frail.

broad 1 *a broad path.* wide. 2 *a broad plain.* expansive, extensive, large. 3 *a broad outline of a story.* general, imprecise, indefinite, vague.

broadcast 1 *to broadcast a concert.* to relay, to send out, to transmit, to televise. 2 *broadcasting:* SEE communication.

brochure *We got a brochure from the travel agent.* booklet, catalogue, leaflet, pamphlet, prospectus.

brogue 1 SEE shoe. 2 *an Irish brogue.* accent, dialect, language.

bronchitis SEE illness.

bronze SEE metal.

brooch clasp. SEE ALSO jewellery.

brood 1 *a brood of chicks.* family, litter. SEE ALSO group. 2 *It's no use brooding about past mistakes.* to meditate, to mope, to ponder, to reflect, to sulk, to think.

brook burn, stream.

broom 1 brush. 2 SEE shrub.

broth SEE food.

brother SEE family.

brown SEE colour.

brownie SEE legend.

bruise to damage, to injure. SEE ALSO wound.

brunette SEE hair.

brush 1 broom. FOR OTHER HOUSE-HOLD TOOLS SEE house. 2 *Brush out the garage when you have finished your woodwork.* to clean, to sweep.

Brussels sprouts SEE vegetable.

brutal *a brutal murder.* atrocious, beastly, bloodthirsty, ferocious, inhuman, murderous, pitiless, ruthless, savage, vicious, violent. SEE ALSO cruel.

brute animal, beast, creature.

bubble 1 *soap bubbles.* foam, froth, lather, suds. 2 *The water was bubbling.* to boil, to fizz, to fizzle, to foam, to froth, to seethe.

bubbly *bubbly drinks.* effervescent, fizzy, foaming, sparkling.

buccaneer bandit, brigand, highwayman, marauder, outlaw, pirate, robber.

buck 1 *a buck rabbit.* SEE male. 2 (informal) *Buck up!* SEE hurry.

bucket pail. SEE ALSO container.

buckle 1 *the buckle of a belt.* clasp, fastener, fastening. 2 *The framework buckled under the heavy weight.* to bend, to collapse, to crumple, to curve, to dent, to distort, to twist, to warp.

bud SEE plant.

Buddhist SEE religion.

budge *The stubborn donkey wouldn't budge.* to move, to shift.

budgerigar SEE bird, pet.

buffalo SEE animal.

buffer SEE railway.

buffet 1 *We went to the buffet for a snack.* bar, café, cafeteria, snack-bar. 2 *Mrs Brunswick made a buffet for Lucy's party.* SEE meal.

bug (informal) 1 *There are bugs on these roses.* insect. 2 *Tony has a bug which makes him feel poorly.* SEE bacteria, illness. 3 *a bug in a computer program.* error, fault, mistake.

bugle SEE brass.

build 1 *Tony builds models.* to assemble, to construct, to erect, to make, to put together, to put up. 2 *Mr Brunswick is beginning to build up his business.* to develop, to enlarge, to expand, to increase, to strengthen.

builder SEE job.

building 1 construction, edifice, structure. 2 KINDS OF BUILDING ARE abbey, arcade, art gallery, barn, barracks, boat-house, bungalow, cabin, castle, cathedral, chapel, château, church, cinema, complex, cottage, crematorium, dovecote, factory, farmhouse, filling station, flats, garage, granary, gymnasium, hall, hotel, house, inn, library, lighthouse, mansion, mill, minaret, monastery, mosque, museum, observatory, orphanage, outhouse, pagoda, palace, pavilion, pier, pig-sty, police station, post office, power-station, prison, pub, public house, restaurant, shed, shop, silo, skyscraper, slaughterhouse, stable, studio, synagogue, temple, theatre, tower, villa, warehouse, waterworks, windmill, woodshed. SEE ALSO **house, shop.** 3 PARTS OF BUILDINGS ARE arch, balcony, banisters, basement, battlements, bay window, belfry, bow window, brickwork, buttress, ceiling, cellar, chimney, cloisters, courtyard, crypt, dome, drawbridge, dungeon, eaves, floor, foundations, foyer, gable, gallery, gateway, gutter, joist, keep, lobby, masonry, parapet, porch, portcullis, quadrangle, rafter, rampart, roof, room, sill, spire, staircase, steeple, tower, turret, vault, veranda, wall, window, window-sill. 4 MATERIALS USED IN BUILDING ARE asbestos, asphalt, brick, cement, concrete, fibreglass, glass, hardboard, metal, mortar, plaster, plastic, plywood, slate, stone, tile, timber, wood.

bulb 1 *an electric bulb.* lamp, light. 2 FLOWERS THAT GROW FROM BULBS ARE bluebell, crocus, daffodil, hyacinth, lily, snowdrop, tulip. SEE ALSO **flower, plant.**

bulge 1 *What's that bulge in the middle of the new carpet?* bump, hump, knob, lump, swelling. 2 *The shopping bag was bulging with interesting shapes.* to billow, to protrude, to stick out, to swell.

bulk *The bulk of the airship amazed us.* largeness, magnitude, size, volume.

bull SEE **cattle, farm, male.**

bulldog SEE **dog.**

bulldozer SEE **vehicle.**

bullet SEE **ammunition.**

bulletin *a news bulletin.* announce-ment, communiqué, dispatch, notice, proclamation, report, statement.

bullfight 1 *bullfighting:* SEE **sport.** 2 *a bullfighter:* matador, toreador.

bullfinch SEE **bird.**

bullock SEE **cattle, young.**

bull's-eye 1 *to hit the bull's-eye.* centre, target. 2 SEE **sweet.**

bully *Logan sometimes bullies younger children.* to frighten, to intimidate, to persecute, to terrorize, to threaten, to torment.

bumble-bee SEE **insect.**

bump 1 *Mr Brunswick had a bump in the car.* blow, collision, crash, hit, knock. 2 *How did you get that bump on the head?* bulge, hump, lump, swelling. 3 *He bumped us deliberately.* to bang, to collide with, to crash into, to jolt, to knock, to ram, to strike, to thump, to wallop. SEE ALSO **hit.**

bumper SEE **vehicle.**

bumptious *The man next door has got bumptious since he was promoted.* arrogant, boastful, cocky, conceited, officious, self-important.

bumpy *a bumpy road.* irregular, rough, uneven.

bun SEE **cake.**

bunch 1 *a bunch of carrots, a bunch of friends.* batch, bundle, clump, cluster, collection, crowd, gathering, group, pack, set. 2 *a bunch of flowers.* bouquet, posy, spray.

bundle *a bundle of waste paper.* bale, bunch, collection, package, parcel, sheaf.

bung *Who took the bung out of the barrel?* cork, plug, stopper.

bungalow SEE **building, house.**

bungle *Trust Logan to bungle the job!* to mess up, to spoil.

bunk bed, berth. SEE ALSO **furniture.**

burden 1 *to carry a burden.* load, weight. 2 *It may help to share your burdens.* problem, trouble, worry.

bureau 1 desk. SEE ALSO **furniture.** 2 *an information bureau.* office.

burglar intruder, robber, thief. SEE ALSO **criminal.**

burial SEE **funeral.**

burly *a burly figure.* beefy, big, brawny, hefty, husky, muscular, strong, tough.

burn 1 VARIOUS WAYS THINGS BURN ARE to blaze, to flame, to flare, to smoulder. 2 WAYS TO BURN THINGS ARE to char, to cremate, to ignite, to kindle, to light, to scald, to scorch, to set fire to, to singe. 3 SEE ALSO **fire.** 4 *a Scottish burn.* brook, stream.

burnished *burnished brass.* polished, shiny.

burrow 1 *a rabbit's burrow.* hole, tunnel, warren. 2 *The rabbits burrowed under the fence.* to dig, to excavate, to tunnel.

burst *The tyre burst. They burst open the door. They burst into laughter.* to blow out, to break, to erupt, to explode, to force open.

bury to conceal, to cover, to hide.

bus SEE **vehicle**.

bush SEE **shrub**.

business 1 *The new shop is doing a lot of business.* buying and selling, commerce, industry, trade. 2 *What sort of business do you want to go into?* calling, career, employment, job, occupation, profession, trade, work. 3 *Mr Brunswick worked for a sports equipment business.* company, concern, corporation, establishment, firm, organization. 4 *It's none of your business.* affair, concern, matter.

busy 1 *Mum is busy in the garden.* active, diligent, employed, engaged, industrious, involved, occupied. 2 *It's busy in town on Saturdays.* bustling, frantic, hectic, lively.

busybody *to be a busybody:* SEE **interfere**.

butane SEE **fuel**.

butcher SEE **shop**.

butler SEE **servant**.

butt 1 *a rifle butt.* SEE **gun**. 2 *a water butt.* SEE **container**. 3 *The goat butted her.* to bump, to knock, to strike, to thump. SEE ALSO **hit**. 4 *Please don't butt in.* to interfere, to interrupt, to intervene, to intrude, to meddle.

butter SEE **fat**.

buttercup SEE **flower**.

butterfingers SEE **clumsy**.

butterfly SEE **insect**.

butterscotch SEE **sweet**.

buttocks backside, behind, bottom, rear, rump.

button *Button your coat!* SEE **fasten**.

buttress SEE **building**.

buy to acquire, to gain, to get, to get on hire purchase, to obtain, to pay for, to procure, to purchase.

buzz SEE **sound**.

buzzard SEE **bird**.

by-law SEE **regulation**.

bypass SEE **road**.

bystander *The police asked the bystanders to describe the accident.* eyewitness, observer, onlooker, passer-by, spectator, witness.

C c

cab taxi. SEE ALSO **vehicle**.

cabaret SEE **entertainment**.

cabbage SEE **vegetable**.

cabin SEE **building**.

cabinet 1 *a china cabinet.* SEE **furniture**. 2 SEE **government**.

cable 1 *an anchor cable.* chain, cord, hawser, line, rope. 2 *an electric cable.* flex, lead, wire. 3 *They sent a cable to say they'd arrive tomorrow.* telegram, wire.

cable television SEE **communication**.

cache *a cache of arms.* depot, dump, hoard, stores.

cackle SEE **sound**.

cactus SEE **plant**.

cadge *The cat from next door always cadges food from us.* to beg, to scrounge.

café bar, buffet, cafeteria, canteen, restaurant, snack-bar.

cage *an animal's cage.* coop, enclosure, hutch, pen.

cagoule SEE **clothes**.

cake 1 KINDS OF CAKES ARE bun, doughnut, éclair, flan, fruit cake, gingerbread, meringue, scone, shortbread, sponge, tart. 2 SEE ALSO **food**.

caked *caked with mud.* dirty, muddy.

calamitous *Setting sail today was a calamitous mistake.* dire, disastrous, dreadful, serious, terrible, tragic, unfortunate, unlucky.

calamity *The hotel fire was a terrible calamity.* accident, catastrophe, disaster, misadventure, misfortune, mishap, tragedy.

calculate *Calculate how many sandwiches we need for the party.* to add up, to assess, to compute, to estimate, to figure out, to reckon, to total, to work out.

calendar FOR SPECIAL TIMES OF THE YEAR SEE **time**.

calf 1 *a new-born calf.* SEE **cattle, young**. 2 *My calves ache after that running.* SEE **body, leg**.

call 1 *Did you hear someone call?* to cry out, to exclaim, to shout, to yell. 2 *The head called Lucy to his office.* to summon. 3 *I couldn't call because the phone was out of order.* to dial, to phone, to ring, to telephone. 4 *When did granny call?* to drop in, to visit. 5 *On Saturdays mum calls us at nine o'clock.* to arouse, to awaken, to rouse, to wake up. 6 *What did they call the baby?* to baptize, to christen, to name. 7 *What will you call your story?* to entitle.

calling *What was grandpa's calling in life?* business, career, employment, job, occupation, profession, trade.

callous *a callous murder.* cold-blooded, hard-hearted, heartless, insensitive, merciless, pitiless, ruthless, unfeeling. SEE ALSO **cruel**.

calm 1 *calm water.* even, flat, motionless, placid, smooth, still. 2 *a calm mood.* peaceful, quiet, sedate, serene, tranquil, untroubled. 3 *Keep calm!* cool, level-headed, patient, sensible. 4 *He was upset and it took ages to calm him.* to appease, to lull, to pacify, to quieten, to soothe.

calypso SEE **music**.

camel dromedary. SEE ALSO **animal**.

camera SEE **photography**.

camouflage *We camouflaged our hideout.* to conceal, to cover up, to disguise, to hide, to mask, to screen.

camp SEE **holiday**.

campaign *We fought a campaign to save our playing-fields.* action, battle, crusade, fight, operation, struggle, war.

campus *the school campus.* grounds, site.

can 1 *a can of beans.* tin. 2 *They can most of the peas they grow at the farm.* SEE **preserve**.

canal channel, waterway.

canary SEE **bird, pet**.

cancel 1 *We cancelled the game because of the snow.* to abandon, to give up, to postpone, to scrap. 2 *They cancelled our order.* to cross out, to delete, to erase, to wipe out.

cancer SEE **illness**.

candid *Give me a candid answer.* direct, frank, honest, open, outspoken, plain, straightforward.

candidate *a candidate for an exam.* applicant, competitor, entrant.

candle SEE **light**.

candy SEE **sweet**.

cane 1 *Mrs Brunswick put up some canes for her runner beans.* rod, stick. 2 *to give someone the cane.* SEE **punishment**.

canister SEE **container**.

cannon SEE **weapon**.

canoe SEE **vessel**.

canteen *Let's have a snack in the canteen.* buffet, café, cafeteria, restaurant, snack-bar.

canter SEE **horse, move**.

canvas SEE **cloth**.

canyon *a deep canyon.* defile, gorge, pass, ravine, valley. SEE ALSO **geography**.

cap 1 *Boys don't usually wear caps these days.* SEE **hat**. 2 *Where's the cap off the ketchup bottle?* cover, covering, lid, top.

capable *Lucy is a capable organizer.* able, accomplished, clever, competent, efficient, gifted, handy, practical, proficient, skilful, skilled, talented.

capacity 1 *the capacity of a container.* size, volume. 2 *It isn't within my capacity to run one hundred metres in ten seconds.* ability, capability, competence, skill, talent.

cape SEE **clothes.**

caper *The lambs capered about the field.* to dance, to frisk, to jump, to leap, to play, to prance, to romp, to skip.

capital 1 *Paris is the capital of France.* SEE **geography. 2** *Mr Brunswick needs more capital to start his new business.* funds, money, property, riches, savings, wealth.

capitulate *The town capitulated after a long siege.* to give in, to submit, to surrender, to yield.

capsize *The boat capsized.* to overturn, to tip over, to turn over, to turn turtle.

capsule 1 *The doctor gave her some capsules for her rheumatism.* pill, tablet. SEE ALSO **medicine. 2** *a space capsule.* SEE **space.**

captain *the captain of a ship.* commander, master, skipper. SEE ALSO **chief.**

caption *Write a caption under your picture.* heading, headline, title.

captivate 1 *The kittens captivated us.* to attract, to bewitch, to charm, to delight, to enchant, to entrance, to fascinate. **2** *captivating*: SEE **attractive.**

captive *They guarded their captives closely.* convict, hostage, prisoner.

capture *Did they capture the thief?* to arrest, to catch, to corner, (informal) to nab, to seize, to take.

car automobile, motor car. SEE ALSO **vehicle.**

caravan SEE **vehicle.**

carbon SEE **chemical.**

carburettor SEE **vehicle.**

carcass *the carcass of an animal.* body, corpse, remains.

card 1 cardboard. SEE ALSO **paper.** **2** *a game of cards.* SEE **cards.**

cardigan SEE **clothes.**

cardinal SEE **church.**

cards 1 playing-cards. **2** CARD GAMES ARE bridge, patience, pontoon, rummy, snap, whist. **3** SUITS ARE club, diamond, heart, spade. **4** VALUES ARE ace, jack, joker, king, knave, number 2 to 10, queen. **5** SEE ALSO **game.**

care 1 *We should care about the starving.* to bother, to concern yourself, to mind, to trouble, to worry. **2** *He cares for his dog.* to attend to, to cherish, to guard, to keep, to look after, to mind, to mother, to protect, to tend, to watch over. **3** *Work with care.* attention, carefulness, caution, concentration, diligence, exactness, heed, pains, thoroughness. **4** *He doesn't have a care in the world!* anxiety, concern, trouble, worry. **5** *She left the baby in Lucy's care.* charge, custody, keeping, protection, safe-keeping.

career 1 *She's training for a career in industry.* business, calling, employment, job, occupation, profession, trade, work. **2** *They careered along.* to dash, to hurtle, to race, to rush, to speed, to tear, (informal) to zoom. SEE ALSO **move.**

carefree *Our dog lives a carefree life.* contented, easy, easygoing, happy, light-hearted, untroubled.

careful 1 *Be careful when you are on your bike.* alert, attentive, cautious, diligent, observant, prudent, vigilant, wary, watchful. **2** *Tony's work is always careful.* conscientious, deliberate, exhaustive, methodical, meticulous, neat, orderly, organized, painstaking, precise, scrupulous, systematic, thorough.

careless 1 *careless driving.* inattentive, inconsiderate, irresponsible, negligent, rash, reckless, uncaring. **2** *careless work.* confused, disorganized, hasty, jumbled, messy, scatterbrained, shoddy, slapdash, sloppy, slovenly, thoughtless, untidy.

caress *She caressed the baby's skin.* to fondle, to kiss, to pat, to pet, to stroke. SEE ALSO **touch.**

caretaker SEE **job.**

cargo *to transport cargo.* freight, goods, load, merchandise.

carnage *a terrible scene of carnage.* bloodshed, killing, slaughter. SEE ALSO **kill.**

carnation SEE **flower**.

carnival *We want good weather for our carnival*. celebration, fair, festival, fête, gala, jamboree, show.

carnivorous SEE **animal**.

carol SEE **music, sing**.

carp SEE **fish**.

carpenter joiner. SEE ALSO **art, job**.

carpentry woodwork.

carpet SEE **floor**.

carriage SEE **vehicle**.

carrot SEE **vegetable**.

carry **1** *Can we carry this wardrobe up the stairs?* to bring, to lift, to manhandle, to move, to remove, to take, to transfer. **2** *Aircraft carry passengers and goods*. to convey, to ferry, to ship, to transport. **3** *The foundations carry the weight of the building*. to bear, to hold up, to support. **4** *Have you carried out my orders?* to accomplish, to achieve, to complete, to do, to enforce, to execute, to finish, to perform. **5** *Shall we carry on?* to continue, to go on, to keep on, to last, to persevere, to persist, to remain, to stay, to survive.

cart barrow. SEE ALSO **vehicle**.

cart-horse SEE **horse**.

carton box, case. SEE ALSO **container**.

cartoon SEE **film, picture**.

cartridge SEE **container**.

carve SEE **cut**.

case **1** box, carton, crate. SEE ALSO **container**. **2** *It was an obvious case of favouritism*. example, illustration, instance. **3** *The detective said he'd never known a case like this one*. inquiry, investigation.

cash change, coins, money, notes.

cashier SEE **job**.

cask barrel, tub. SEE ALSO **container**.

casket SEE **container**.

casserole SEE **cook**.

cassette SEE **record**.

cassock SEE **clothes**.

cast **1** *We cast a coin into the well*. to bowl, (informal) to chuck, to fling, to hurl, to lob, to pitch, to sling, to throw, to toss. **2** *The sculptor cast his*

statue in bronze. to form, to mould, to shape.

castanets SEE **percussion**.

castaway SEE **maroon**.

castle **1** château, citadel, fort, fortress, palace. SEE ALSO **building**. **2** PARTS OF A CASTLE ARE battlements, buttress, courtyard, drawbridge, dungeon, gate, keep, magazine, moat, parapet, portcullis, rampart, tower, turret, wall.

casual **1** *a casual meeting*. accidental, chance, unexpected, unintentional, unplanned. **2** *casual clothes, a casual manner*. careless, easygoing, informal, relaxed.

casualty *Although it looked a bad accident, there were no casualties*. dead person, fatality, injured person, victim, wounded person.

cat kitten, (informal) pussy, tabby, tomcat. SEE ALSO **animal, pet**.

catalogue *a shopping catalogue, a library catalogue*. brochure, directory, index, list, register.

catamaran SEE **vessel**.

catapult SEE **weapon**.

cataract **1** *There are many cataracts along the river*. rapids, torrent, waterfall. **2** *a cataract in the eye*. SEE **illness**.

catarrh SEE **illness**.

catastrophe *The plane crash was a terrible catastrophe*. accident, calamity, disaster, misfortune, mishap, tragedy.

catch **1** *to catch a ball*. to clutch, to grab, to grasp, to hang on to, to hold, to seize, to snatch, to take. **2** *to catch a rabbit, to catch a fish*. to ensnare, to hook, to net, to trap. **3** *to catch a thief*. to arrest, to corner, to capture, (informal) to nab, to stop. **4** *to catch an illness*. to be infected by, to contract, to get. **5** *a catch on a door*. bolt, latch, lock.

catching *a catching disease*. contagious, infectious.

catchy *a catchy tune*. attractive, memorable, tuneful.

category *The cars were in categories*

depending on the size of the engine. class, group, kind, set, sort.

cater *We catered for twelve people at Christmas.* to cook, to provide.

caterer SEE **job**.

caterpillar grub, larva, maggot.

cathedral SEE **church**.

Catherine wheel SEE **firework**.

catkin SEE **flower**.

cattle bullocks, bulls, calves, cows, heifers, oxen, steers. SEE ALSO **animal, farm**.

catty *Lucy was hurt by her friend's catty remarks.* malevolent, malicious, nasty, sly, spiteful, vicious.

cauldron pot, saucepan. SEE ALSO **container, cook**.

cauliflower SEE **vegetable**.

cause 1 *What was the cause of the trouble?* grounds, occasion, origin, reason, source. 2 *We are collecting for a good cause.* aim, object, purpose. 3 *It'll cause trouble if we don't share the sweets fairly.* to bring about, to give rise to, to induce, to lead to, to provoke, to result in.

causeway SEE **road**.

caution 1 *Proceed with caution.* attentiveness, care, heed, vigilance, wariness. 2 *The police let him off with a caution.* reprimand, warning. 3 *They cautioned us about the danger of falling rocks.* to alert, to warn.

cautious *Mrs Brunswick is a cautious driver.* attentive, careful, deliberate, vigilant, wary, watchful.

cavalcade parade, procession.

cavalry SEE **armed services**.

cave cavern, cavity, grotto, hole, pothole.

caviare SEE **food**.

cavity cave, hole, hollow.

CB SEE **communication**.

cease *Cease work!* to break off, to cut off, to discontinue, to end, to finish, to stop, to terminate.

ceaseless *Logan's ceaseless chatter annoys Mrs Angel.* chronic, constant, continual, continuous, incessant, interminable, non-stop, permanent, persistent, relentless, unending.

cedar SEE **tree**.

ceiling SEE **building**.

celebrate 1 *Let's celebrate!* to be happy, to rejoice, to revel. 2 *How shall we celebrate granny's seventieth birthday?* to keep, to observe, to remember.

celebrated *a celebrated actor.* distinguished, eminent, famous, noted, popular, renowned, well-known.

celebration KINDS OF CELEBRATION ARE anniversary, banquet, birthday, carnival, feast, festival, festivity, jamboree, jubilee, party, wedding.

celery SEE **salad, vegetable**.

celestial *celestial music.* blissful, divine, heavenly.

cell 1 *a monk's cell, a prison cell.* den, prison, room. 2 *an electric cell.* battery.

cellar basement, crypt, vault.

cello SEE **music, strings**.

Celsius SEE **temperature**.

cement SEE **building**.

cemetery burial-ground, churchyard, graveyard. SEE ALSO **funeral**.

censor *They censored the violent film.* to ban, to cut, to forbid, to prohibit.

censure 1 *He deserved the referee's censure for that foul.* condemnation, criticism, disapproval, rebuke, reprimand. 2 *The referee censured him.* to reproach, to scold, (informal) to tick off.

centigrade SEE **temperature**.

centimetre SEE **measure**.

centipede SEE **insect**. | *Centipedes* are not proper insects.

central heating SEE **fire, house**.

centre *the centre of the earth, the centre of town.* core, focus, heart, hub, inside, middle, nucleus.

century SEE **time**.

cereal 1 corn, grain. 2 CEREALS GROWN BY FARMERS ARE barley, maize, oats, rice, rye, sweetcorn, wheat. 3 *breakfast cereal.* cornflakes.

ceremony 1 *They held a ceremony to*

open the sports centre. event, function, occasion. **2** *The wedding was conducted with great ceremony.* formality, grandeur, pageantry, pomp, ritual, spectacle.

certain 1 *When the brakes failed, disaster seemed certain.* destined, fated, inescapable, inevitable, sure, unavoidable. **2** *If your watch doesn't go, the shop is certain to refund your money.* bound, compelled, obliged, required, sure. **3** *Are you certain it will rain?* assured, confident, definite, positive, sure.

certificate *a certificate for swimming.* award, degree, diploma, document. SEE ALSO **qualification**.

chaffinch SEE **bird**.

chain 1 *The prisoners were in chains.* bonds, fetters. **2** *Form a chain.* column, cordon, line, row, sequence, series. **3** *The slaves were chained together.* to link, to tie. SEE ALSO **fasten**.

chair armchair, seat. SEE ALSO **furniture**.

chalet SEE **house**.

chalk SEE **rock**.

challenge 1 *The sentry challenged the intruder.* to confront. **2** *He challenged his rival to fight a duel.* to dare, to defy.

chamber room.

chamber music SEE **music**.

champagne SEE **drink**.

champion hero, victor, winner.

championship *a snooker championship.* competition, contest, tournament.

chance 1 *It happened by chance.* accident, coincidence, destiny, fate, fluke, fortune, luck, misfortune. **2** *There's a chance of rain.* danger, possibility, risk. **3** *Now it's your chance to try.* opportunity, turn. **4** *a chance meeting.* accidental, casual, lucky, unexpected, unintentional, unplanned.

chancel SEE **church**.

chancellor SEE **government**.

chancy *It's chancy driving on icy roads.* dangerous, hazardous, risky.

chandelier SEE **light**.

change 1 *to change your mind, to change the rules, etc.* to adapt, to adjust, to affect, to alter, to amend, to convert, to influence, to modify, to process, to reform, to transform, to vary. **2** *to change clothes, to change places, etc.* to exchange, to replace, to substitute, to switch, to swop. **3** *The pumpkin changed into a coach.* to become, to turn into. **4** *Have you any change?* cash, coins, money, notes.

changeable *The weather in Britain is very changeable.* erratic, fickle, inconsistent, temperamental, unpredictable, unreliable, variable.

channel 1 *We dug a channel to take away the water.* canal, dike, ditch, gully, gutter, waterway. **2** *Which channel is your programme on?* station, wavelength.

chant SEE **music, sing**.

chaos *It was chaos when Logan let off the fire-extinguisher.* anarchy, bedlam, confusion, lawlessness, shambles.

chaotic *a chaotic mess.* confused, disorderly, disorganized, haphazard, higgledy-piggledy, incoherent, jumbled, mixed up, muddled, topsy-turvy.

chapel, chaplain SEE **church**.

chapter SEE **book**.

char *charred remains.* to blacken, to burn, to scorch, to singe.

character 1 *Logan's grandfather is an interesting character.* human being, individual, person. **2** *Who was your favourite character in the pantomime?* part, role. **3** *This brand of tea has a character of its own.* characteristic, flavour, quality, taste. **4** *Tony has a nice character.* attitude, disposition, manner, nature, personality, temperament. **5** *the characters of the alphabet.* letter, sign, symbol.

characteristic *A red breast is the characteristic feature of the robin.* distinctive, essential, individual, particular, recognizable, special, unique.

charade SEE **game**.

charcoal SEE **fuel**.

charge 1 *Their charges are reasonable.*
cost, fare, fee, payment, price, rate,
terms, toll, value. 2 *They left the dog in
my charge.* care, command, control,
custody, keeping, protection, safe-
keeping. 3 *Did the police charge him?* to
accuse, to blame, to prosecute. 4 *The
cavalry charged.* to attack, to assault,
to storm.

chariot SEE **vehicle**.

charity 1 *The animals' hospital depends
on your charity.* generosity, kindness,
love. 2 *We collected for a charity.* good
cause.

charm 1 *People used to believe in the
power of charms.* enchantment, magic,
sorcery, spell, witchcraft, wizardry.
2 *He charmed us with his music.* to
attract, to bewitch, to captivate, to
enchant, to entrance, to fascinate, to
spellbind. 3 *charming*: SEE **attractive**.

chart 1 map, plan. 2 diagram, graph.

charter *We chartered a bus for our trip to
the zoo.* to hire, to rent.

chase *Our dog chased that rabbit for
miles.* to follow, to hound, to hunt, to
pursue, to track, to trail.

chasm *We nearly fell into the chasm.*
abyss, crater, hole, pit.

chaste *Holy people are expected to be
chaste.* decent, good, innocent,
modest, pure, virgin, virtuous.

chat SEE **talk**.

château castle, mansion, stately
home. SEE ALSO **building**.

chatter to gossip, to prattle. SEE ALSO
talk.

chatterbox SEE **talkative**.

chauffeur driver. SEE ALSO **servant**.

cheap 1 *You can find cheap clothes in the
sales.* cut-price, economical,
inexpensive, reasonable. 2 *It was
cheap stuff which didn't last.* inferior,
poor, shoddy, tawdry, tinny.

cheat 1 to deceive, to defraud, to
dupe, to fool, to hoax, to hoodwink,
to outwit, to swindle, to take in. SEE
ALSO **trick**. 2 *to cheat in an examination.*
to crib.

check 1 *Mrs Angel checked our answers.*
to compare, to examine, to test. 2 *A
fallen tree checked our progress.* to arrest,
to bar, to block, to curb, to delay, to
foil, to halt, to hamper, to hinder, to
impede, to stop. 3 *Mr Brunswick took
the car to the garage for a check.*
examination, investigation, test.

checkmate SEE **chess**.

cheek 1 SEE **body, head**.
2 (informal) *She's got a cheek!* nerve.

cheeky *a cheeky manner, a cheeky remark.*
arrogant, bold, discourteous,
disrespectful, forward, impertinent,
impolite, impudent, insolent,
insulting, presumptuous, rude,
saucy, shameless.

cheer 1 *The audience cheered.* to
applaud, to clap, to shout. 2 *The
clowns cheered us up.* to amuse, to
brighten, to divert, to entertain.

cheerful *a cheerful mood.* animated,
bright, delighted, elated, festive, gay,
glad, gleeful, good-humoured,
happy, jolly, jovial, joyful, laughing,
light-hearted, lively, merry,
optimistic, pleased, rapturous,
spirited, warm-hearted.

cheese SEE **food**.

cheetah SEE **animal**.

chef cook. SEE ALSO **job**.

chemical VARIOUS CHEMICALS ARE
acid, alcohol, alkali, ammonia,
arsenic, carbon, chlorine, fluoride,
litmus, sulphur.

chemist SEE **job, shop**.

chemistry SEE **science**.

cheque SEE **money**.

cherish *I shall cherish the lovely present
you gave me.* to care for, to look after,
to love, to prize, to protect, to
treasure, to value.

cherry SEE **fruit**.

chess 1 PIECES USED IN CHESS ARE
bishop, castle or rook, king, knight,
pawn, queen. 2 TERMS USED IN
CHESS ARE checkmate, mate,
stalemate. 3 SEE **game**.

chest 1 SEE **body**. 2 *a chest full of
treasure.* box, case, crate, trunk. SEE
ALSO **container**. 3 *a chest of drawers.*
SEE **furniture**.

chestnut SEE **tree**.

chew to bite, to crunch, to eat, to gnaw, to munch, to nibble. SEE ALSO **eat**.

chewing-gum SEE **sweet**.

chick SEE **bird, young**.

chicken cockerel, fowl, hen, rooster. SEE **bird, meat, poultry**.

chicken-pox SEE **illness**.

chief 1 *What was the chief lesson you learned?* basic, dominant, essential, fundamental, greatest, important, leading, main, major, outstanding, primary, prime, principal, supreme. 2 *the chief cook.* head, leading, senior. 3 *Who's the chief around here?* boss, captain, chieftain, commander, director, employer, governor, head, leader, manager, master, president, principal, ruler.

chiefly generally, mainly, mostly, predominantly, primarily, usually.

chilblain SEE **illness**.

child baby, boy, (insulting) brat, girl, infant, (informal) kid, (informal) nipper, offspring, toddler, (insulting) urchin, youngster, youth.

childish *Mrs Angel says it's childish to make rude noises.* babyish, immature, infantile, juvenile.

chill 1 *Lucy caught a chill.* SEE **illness**. 2 *to chill food.* to freeze, to refrigerate.

chilly *a chilly evening.* cold, cool, frosty, icy, (informal) nippy, raw, wintry.

chime SEE **bell, sound**.

chimney SEE **building**.

chimney-sweep SEE **job**.

chimpanzee SEE **animal**.

chin SEE **body, head**.

china earthenware, porcelain, pottery. SEE ALSO **crockery**.

chink *a chink in the curtains.* crack, gap, opening, slit, split.

chip 1 *I knocked a chip off the plate.* bit, flake, fragment, piece, scrap, slice, splinter. 2 *fish and chips.* SEE **food**. 3 *a silicon chip.* SEE **computer**. 4 *Who chipped this cup?* to break, to crack, to damage, to splinter.

chirp SEE **sound**.

chisel SEE **cut, tool**.

chivalrous *a chivalrous knight.* courteous, gallant, gentlemanly, heroic, noble, polite.

chlorine SEE **chemical**.

chocolate SEE **sweet**.

choice *Can we have a choice?* alternative, option, pick, selection.

choir chorus. SEE ALSO **music**.

choke 1 *The smoke choked us. This collar is choking me.* to smother, to stifle, to strangle, to suffocate, to throttle. 2 *The firemen choked in the smoke.* to gasp, to suffocate. 3 *The car won't start without the choke.* SEE **vehicle**.

cholera SEE **illness**.

choose *We chose a captain.* to appoint, to decide on, to draw lots, to elect, to name, to nominate, to opt for, to pick, to prefer, to select, to settle on, to vote for.

chop 1 *to chop wood.* to hack, to hew, to slash, to split. SEE ALSO **cut**. 2 *lamb chops.* SEE **meat**.

chopper axe. SEE ALSO **tool**.

chop-suey SEE **food**.

chord SEE **music**.

chores *We help with chores around the house.* drudgery, errands, jobs, tasks, work.

chorus 1 choir. SEE ALSO **music**. 2 *We joined in the chorus.* refrain.

christen *Tony was christened Antony.* to baptize, to name.

Christianity FOR WORDS TO DO WITH THE CHRISTIAN CHURCH SEE **church**.

Christmas yule, yuletide. SEE ALSO **church, time**.

chromatic scale SEE **music**.

chromium SEE **metal**.

chronic *a chronic illness.* ceaseless, constant, continual, continuous, everlasting, incessant, lifelong, permanent, persistent, unending.

chrysalis SEE **insect**.

chrysanthemum SEE **flower**.

chub SEE **fish**.

chubby *a chubby figure.* dumpy, fat, plump, podgy, portly.

chuck (informal) *Stop chucking things*

into the water. to fling, to hurl, to lob, to sling, to throw, to toss.

chuckle to giggle, to titter. SEE ALSO **laugh**.

chum companion, friend, mate.

chunk *a chunk of cheese, a chunk of wood.* bar, block, brick, dollop, hunk, lump, mass, piece, slab.

church 1 CHURCH BUILDINGS ARE abbey, cathedral, chapel, convent, monastery, parish church, priory. 2 PARTS OF A CHURCH ARE aisle, altar, belfry, buttress, chancel, chapel, cloisters, crypt, dome, gargoyle, porch, precinct, spire, steeple, tower, vestry. 3 THINGS YOU FIND IN A CHURCH ARE Bible, candle, crucifix, font, hymn-book, lectern, memorial tablet, pews, prayer book, pulpit. 4 WORDS TO DO WITH CHURCH ARE Advent, angel, Ascension Day, Ash Wednesday, baptism, benediction, christening, Christmas, communion, confirmation, Easter, Good Friday, gospel, hymn, incense, Lent, martyr, mass, Nativity, New Testament, Old Testament, Palm Sunday, patron saint, Pentecost, prayer, preaching, psalm, requiem, Resurrection, sabbath, sacrament, saint, scripture, sermon, service, Shrove Tuesday, Whitsun, worship. 5 PEOPLE CONNECTED WITH CHURCH ARE archbishop, bishop, cardinal, chaplain, choir, clergyman, congregation, curate, deacon, deaconess, dean, evangelist, friar, minister, missionary, monk, nun, parson, pastor, Pope, preacher, priest, rector, verger, vicar.

churchyard burial-ground, cemetery, graveyard.

churn SEE **container**.

chutney SEE **food**.

cider SEE **drink**.

cigar, cigarette SEE **smoke**.

cinders *the cinders of a fire.* ashes, embers.

cine-camera SEE **photography**.

cinema SEE **building, entertainment**.

circle 1 disc, hoop, ring. SEE ALSO **shape**. 2 *The plane circled before landing.* to go round, to turn, to wheel. 3 *The police circled the hide-out.* to encircle, to enclose, to ring.

circuit 1 *a racing circuit.* race-course. 2 *I completed one circuit.* circle, lap, orbit, revolution.

circulate *We circulated a notice about our sale.* to distribute, to issue, to send round.

circumference *It's a mile round the circumference of our playing-field.* boundary, edge, limit, perimeter.

circumstances *Don't jump to conclusions before you know the circumstances.* background, conditions, details, facts, position, situation.

circus WORDS TO DO WITH A CIRCUS ARE acrobat, clown, contortionist, juggler, lion-tamer, ring, tight-rope, trapeze. SEE ALSO **entertainment**.

cistern *a water cistern.* tank. SEE ALSO **container**.

citadel castle, fort, fortress, garrison.

citizen *the citizens of a town.* inhabitant, native, resident.

citrus fruit CITRUS FRUITS ARE grapefruit, lemon, lime, orange, tangerine. SEE ALSO **fruit**.

city *London is a huge city.* conurbation, town. SEE ALSO **geography**.

civil *I know you're angry, but try to be civil.* considerate, courteous, polite, respectful, well-mannered.

civilized *a civilized nation.* cultured, orderly, organized.

claim 1 *I didn't claim my pocket-money last week.* to ask for, to demand, to request, to require. 2 *Logan claims that he's stronger than Tony.* to assert, to declare, to insist, to maintain, to pretend, to state.

clam SEE **shellfish**.

clamber *We clambered up the rocks.* to climb, to crawl, to scramble.

clammy *His hands were clammy.* damp, dank, humid, moist.

clamour *The starlings always make a*

clamour. commotion, din, hubbub, noise, racket, row, screeching, shouting, uproar.

clamp SEE **fasten**.

clan family, group, tribe.

clang, clank SEE **sound**.

clap *The audience clapped*. to applaud, to cheer, to praise.

clarify *We asked Mrs Angel to clarify what she wanted us to do*. to define, to explain, to make clear.

clarinet SEE **woodwind**.

clash 1 *the clash of cymbals*. SEE **sound**. 2 *a clash between two gangs*. battle, collision, combat, conflict, confrontation, contest, fight, struggle.

clasp 1 *She wore a gold clasp*. brooch, buckle, fastener, fastening. 2 *She clasped the child in her arms*. to cling to, to embrace, to grasp, to grip, to hold, to hug, to squeeze. 3 *He clasped his hands*. to hold together, to wring.

class 1 *Whose class are you in?* form, group, set. 2 *In gymnastics Lucy's in a class of her own*. category, classification, grade, group, kind, set, sort, species, type.

classic *This book is a classic!* masterpiece.

classical *classical music*. highbrow.

classify *We classified the petals according to shape*. to arrange, to group, to put into sets, to sort.

classroom SEE **school**.

claustrophobia SEE **illness**.

claw 1 *a bird's claws*. nail, talon. 2 *The animal clawed at its attacker*. to scratch, to tear.

clay SEE **rock**.

clean 1 *a clean floor*. hygienic, spotless, washed. 2 *clean water*. clear, fresh, pure. 3 *clean paper*. blank, unmarked, untouched, unused. 4 *to clean the house, to clean yourself, etc*. to bathe, to brush, to dust, to hoover, to mop up, to rinse, to sponge down, to sweep out, to swill, to wash, to wipe.

cleaner SEE **job**.

clear 1 *clear water*. clean, colourless, pure, transparent. 2 *a clear case of*

cheating. apparent, blatant, evident, obvious, plain. 3 *clear handwriting*. bold, definite, legible, plain, simple. 4 *a clear sound*. audible, distinct. 5 *a clear picture*. focused, visible, well-defined. 6 *a clear explanation*. coherent, comprehensible, intelligible, lucid, understandable, unambiguous. 7 *a clear sky*. bright, cloudless, starlit, sunny, unclouded. 8 *a clear road*. free, open, passable, uncluttered, vacant. 9 *The fog cleared*. to disappear, to evaporate, to fade, to melt away, to vanish. 10 *Wait for the water to clear*. to become transparent, to clarify. 11 *When the alarm went, we cleared the building*. to empty, to evacuate. 12 *The horse cleared the fence*. to bound over, to jump, to leap over, to spring over, to vault. 13 *We asked Mrs Angel to clear up one point*. to clarify, to explain, to make clear.

clearing *a clearing in the forest*. gap, space.

clef SEE **music**.

clench *to clench your teeth*. to clamp up, to close, to grit.

clergyman SEE **church, preacher**.

clerk office worker, secretary, typist. SEE ALSO **job**.

clever *a clever child, a clever idea, etc*. able, academic, accomplished, apt, artful, artistic, astute, brainy, bright, brilliant, crafty, cunning, cute, deft, expert, gifted, handy, imaginative, ingenious, intellectual, intelligent, quick, quick-witted, sharp, shrewd, skilful, skilled, slick, smart, talented, wily, wise.

click SEE **sound**.

client *a client of the bank*. customer.

cliff SEE **seaside**.

climate SEE **geography, weather**.

climax *The music built up to a climax*. crisis, highlight, peak.

climb *to climb a ladder*. to ascend, to clamber up, to go up, to mount, to scale.

climber CLIMBING PLANTS ARE honeysuckle, hops, ivy, vine.

cling 1 *Ivy clings to the wall.* to adhere, to stick. 2 *The baby clung to its mother.* to clutch, to clasp, to grasp, to hug.

clinic health centre, infirmary. SEE ALSO **medicine**.

clink SEE **sound**.

clip 1 *a paper-clip.* fastener. SEE ALSO **fasten**. 2 *a clip from a film.* excerpt, extract. 3 *to clip a hedge.* to crop, to shear, to snip, to trim. SEE ALSO **cut**.

clipper SEE **vessel**.

cloak SEE **clothes**.

cloakroom SEE **house**.

clock KINDS OF CLOCK ARE alarm clock, digital clock, grandfather clock, hour- glass, pendulum clock, stop-watch, sundial, watch.

clog 1 SEE **shoe**. 2 *Don't clog the drain with all that paper.* to block, to bung up, to jam, to obstruct, to stop up.

cloisters SEE **building, church**.

close 1 *Close the door.* to bolt, to fasten, to lock, to seal, to secure, to shut. 2 *They closed the road.* to bar, to barricade, to block, to stop up. 3 *We closed the concert with a song.* to conclude, to end, to finish, to stop, to terminate. 4 *Our house is close to the park.* adjacent, near, neighbouring. 5 *The twins are close to each other.* affectionate, attached, familiar, fond, friendly, intimate, loving. 6 *It's close in here: open a window.* airless, humid, muggy, oppressive, stifling, stuffy, sultry, warm. 7 *He's close with his money.* mean, mingy, miserly, stingy.

clot *a clot of blood.* lump.

cloth 1 *Mrs Brunswick bought some cloth to make curtains.* fabric, material, stuff, textile. 2 KINDS OF CLOTH ARE canvas, corduroy, cotton, denim, elastic, felt, flannel, gauze, lace, linen, muslin, nylon, patchwork, polyester, rayon, sacking, satin, silk, taffeta, tapestry, tartan, tweed, velvet, wool, worsted.

clothes 1 attire, costume, dress, garments, outfit. 2 VARIOUS GARMENTS ARE anorak, apron, bib, bikini, blazer, blouse, bra, braces, breeches, briefs, cagoule, cape, cardigan, cassock, cloak, coat, corset, drawers, dress, dressing-gown, duffle coat, dungarees, frock, garter, gauntlet, girdle, glove, gown, jacket, jeans, jersey, jodhpurs, jumper, kilt, knickers, leg-warmers, leotard, lingerie, livery, mackintosh, miniskirt, mitten, muffler, night-dress, oilskins, overalls, overcoat, panties, pants, panty-hose, parka, petticoat, pinafore, poncho, pullover, pyjamas, raincoat, rompers, sari, scarf, shawl, shirt, shorts, singlet, skirt, slacks, slip, smock, sock, sou'wester, stockings, suit, surplice, sweater, tie, tights, trunks, T-shirt, tunic, underpants, uniform, vest, waistcoat, wet-suit, wind-cheater, yashmak. SEE ALSO **hat, shoe**. 3 PARTS OF A GARMENT ARE bodice, button, button-hole, collar, cuff, hem, lapel, pocket, sleeve.

cloud SEE **weather**.

cloudless *a cloudless sky.* bright, clear, starlit, sunny, unclouded.

cloudy 1 *a cloudy sky.* dull, gloomy, grey, overcast. 2 *The windows are cloudy.* blurred, dim, milky, misty, murky, opaque, steamy, unclear.

clout (informal) *She clouted her brother with the newspaper.* to bang, (informal) to bash, to drive, to hammer, to knock, to punch, to slam, to slog, to smash, to strike, to swipe, to thump, to wallop, to whack. SEE ALSO **hit**.

clown 1 fool, jester. 2 SEE ALSO **circus, entertainment**.

club 1 *to hit someone with a club.* baton, cudgel, stick. 2 *to hit a ball with a club.* bat. 3 *a football club, a book club.* association, league, organization, party, society, union. 4 *the ace of clubs.* SEE **cards**.

cluck SEE **sound**.

clue *Give me a clue what I'm getting for Christmas.* hint, indication, inkling, key, sign, suggestion.

clump *Look at that clump of daffodils.* bunch, cluster, collection, group, tuft. SEE ALSO **group**.

clumsy 1 awkward, blundering, fumbling, gawky, hulking, lumbering, ungainly, unskilful. 2 *to be clumsy*: to be a butterfingers.

cluster *a cluster of trees, people, etc.* bunch, clump, collection, crowd, gathering, group. SEE ALSO **group**.

clutch 1 *He clutched the rope.* to clasp, to cling to, to grab, to grasp, to grip, to hold on to, to seize, to snatch. 2 *The driver had his foot on the clutch.* SEE **vehicle**. 3 *a clutch of eggs.* SEE **group**.

clutter *Please get rid of the clutter in your bedroom.* confusion, jumble, junk, litter, mess, muddle.

coach 1 *We travelled by coach.* SEE **vehicle**. 2 *to coach a football team.* to instruct, to teach, to train.

coal SEE **fuel**.

coarse 1 *coarse cloth.* hairy, harsh, rough, scratchy. 2 *coarse language.* blasphemous, common, crude, foul, impolite, improper, indecent, offensive, rude, uncouth, vulgar.

coast 1 *In summer we sometimes go to the coast.* beach, sea-shore, seaside, shore. 2 *Lucy coasted down the hill on her bike.* to drift, to free-wheel, to glide.

coat 1 SEE **clothes**. 2 *a coat of paint.* coating, cover, covering, film.

coax *We coaxed the animal back into its cage.* to entice, to induce, to persuade, to tempt.

cobble 1 pebble, stone. 2 FOR OTHER SURFACES SEE **road**.

cobbler shoemaker. SEE ALSO **job**.

cobra SEE **snake**.

cock SEE **bird, male**.

cockerel SEE **chicken, poultry**.

cockle SEE **shellfish**.

cockroach SEE **insect**.

cocktail SEE **drink**.

cocky (informal) *Don't get cocky just because she said your work was the best.* arrogant, boastful, bumptious, cheeky, conceited, impudent, insolent, rude, self-satisfied.

cocoa SEE **drink**.

coconut SEE **nut**.

cod SEE **fish**.

code 1 *The Highway Code.* laws, regulations, rules. 2 *A message in code was sent to the government spy.* language, signs, signals.

coeducational SEE **school**.

coffee SEE **drink**.

coffin SEE **funeral**.

coherent *a coherent argument, a coherent story.* clear, convincing, logical, reasonable, sound.

coil *to coil a rope.* to bend, to curl, to entwine, to loop, to turn, to twist, to wind.

coin cash, change, money.

coincide *Fortunately, our opinions about holidays coincide.* to agree, to correspond, to match.

coincidence *We met by coincidence.* accident, chance, luck.

coke SEE **fuel**.

cold 1 *cold weather, cold hands, etc.* Arctic, biting, bitter, bleak, chill, chilly, cool, freezing, frosty, frozen, icy, (informal) nippy, (informal) perishing, raw, shivery, wintry. 2 *cold feelings, a cold heart.* callous, cold-blooded, cool, cruel, half-hearted, hard, hard-hearted, heartless, indifferent, insensitive, uncaring, unconcerned, unfeeling, unfriendly, unkind. 3 *to have a cold*: to cough, to sneeze. SEE ALSO **illness**.

cold-blooded *a cold-blooded killing.* callous, cruel, hard-hearted, heartless, insensitive, merciless, pitiless, ruthless, unfeeling.

colic SEE **illness**.

collaborate *We were allowed to collaborate on the project.* to co-operate, to work together.

collaborator accomplice, ally, assistant, partner.

collage SEE **picture**.

collapse 1 *Several people collapsed in the heat.* to drop, to faint, to fall down. 2 *The building collapsed in the earth-quake.* to buckle, to fall in, to fold up, to tumble down. 3 *The earthquake caused the collapse of many old buildings.* destruction, downfall, end, fall, ruin.

collapsible *a collapsible chair.* folding.

collar SEE **clothes**.

collect 1 *Squirrels collect nuts. A crowd collected to watch the fire.* to accumulate, to assemble, to bring together, to cluster, to come together, to crowd, to gather, to group, to hoard, to muster, to pile up, to store. **2** *Please collect the bread from the baker's.* to bring, to fetch, to get, to obtain.

collection *a collection of stamps.* accumulation, assortment, batch, crowd, gathering, hoard, mass, pile, set, stack. SEE ALSO **group**.

college polytechnic, university. SEE ALSO **educate**.

collide *The car collided with the gatepost.* to bump into, to crash into, to knock, to run into, to slam into, to smash into, to strike. SEE ALSO **hit** .

collie SEE **dog**.

collision *There was a collision at the end of the road.* accident, bump, crash, impact, knock, smash.

colon SEE **punctuation**.

colonel SEE **rank**.

colony 1 settlement. **2** *a colony of ants.* SEE **group**.

colossal *A colossal statue towered above us.* enormous, giant, gigantic, huge, immense, mammoth, massive, mighty, monstrous, towering, vast. SEE ALSO **big**.

colour 1 dye, hue, shade, tinge, tint, tone. **2** VARIOUS COLOURS ARE amber, azure, beige, black, blue, bronze, brown, cream, crimson, fawn, gilt, gold, golden, green, grey, indigo, ivory, jet-black, khaki, lavender, maroon, mauve, navy blue, orange, pink, purple, red, rosy, sandy, scarlet, tan, tawny, turquoise, vermilion, violet, white, yellow. **3** *I'm colouring a picture.* to dye, to paint, to stain, to tinge, to tint. **4** *Tony's fair skin colours easily.* to blush, to flush, to redden, to tan. **5** *The regiment was carrying its colours.* banner, ensign, flag, standard.

colourful *colourful flowers.* bright, brilliant, flashy, gaudy, showy, vivid.

colourless *a colourless scene.* dingy, dismal, dowdy, drab, dreary, dull, grey, shabby.

colt SEE **horse**.

column 1 pile, pillar, pole, post, prop, shaft, support. **2** *a column of soldiers.* file, line, procession, queue, rank, row.

coma SEE **illness**.

comb *I've combed the house and still can't find my pen.* to ransack, to rummage through, to scour, to search.

combat *a fierce combat.* action, battle, bout, conflict, contest, duel, fight, struggle.

combination alliance, blend, compound, mixture, union.

combine 1 *We'll have enough players if we combine the first and second teams.* to add together, to amalgamate, to couple, to join, to merge, to put together, to unite. **2** *Combine the ingredients in a bowl.* to blend, to integrate, to mingle, to mix.

combine harvester SEE **farm**.

come 1 *Our visitors have come.* to appear, to arrive. **2** *Tell me when we come to my station.* to arrive at, to get to, to reach. **3** *There are some dark clouds coming.* to advance, to approach, to draw near. **4** FOR OTHER WORDS WHICH YOU CAN USE SEE **move**.

comedian, comedy SEE **entertainment**.

comet SEE **astronomy**.

comfort 1 *to live in comfort.* ease, luxury, relaxation. **2** *His dog died yesterday, so try to give him some comfort.* consolation, relief, sympathy. **3** *He was upset, so we tried to comfort him.* to calm, to console, to ease, to relieve, to soothe, to sympathize with.

comfortable *a comfortable chair.* cosy, easy, luxurious, relaxing, restful, snug, soft.

comic 1 absurd, amusing, comical, facetious, farcical, funny, humorous, hysterical, laughable, ludicrous, (informal) priceless, ridiculous, silly, uproarious, witty. 2 *A comic sang some songs and made us laugh.* comedian, fool, jester, wit. 3 *Tony bought a comic to read on the train.* SEE **magazine**.

comma SEE **punctuation**.

command 1 *The general issued a command that all fighting should stop.* decree, instruction, order. 2 *He commanded that all fighting should stop.* to decree, to demand, to direct, to instruct, to order, to require, to rule. 3 *A captain commands his ship.* to administer, to be in charge of, to control, to direct, to govern, to head, to lead, to manage, to rule, to supervise.

commander captain, head, leader. SEE ALSO **chief**.

commando SEE **armed services, soldier**.

commence *We're ready to commence.* to begin, to embark on, to initiate, to open, to start, to take the initiative.

commend *The head commended our efforts.* to applaud, to approve of, to praise, to recommend.

comment 1 *Did mum make any comment about your dirty clothes?* mention, observation, opinion, reference, remark, statement. 2 *He commented that the weather had been bad.* to explain, to mention, to observe, to remark, to say.

commentary *They broadcast a commentary on the big match.* account, description, report.

commentator SEE **job**.

commerce *A country depends on commerce to keep going.* business, buying and selling, trade, traffic.

commercial 1 *commercial affairs.* business, economic, financial. 2 *a TV commercial.* advertisement, (informal) plug.

commit *to commit a crime.* to carry out, to do, to perform.

committee *a school committee.* council.

common 1 *The school committee discusses our common problems.* communal, general, joint, mutual, shared. 2 *It's common to have turkey at Christmas. Our car is a common make.* commonplace, conventional, customary, everyday, familiar, frequent, habitual, normal, ordinary, prevalent, regular, typical, usual, well-known, widespread. 3 *Don't use common language!* coarse, crude, rude, vulgar. 4 *We play football on the common.* heath, park.

commonplace *a commonplace event.* boring, common, everyday, indifferent, mediocre, normal, ordinary, unexciting, usual.

commotion *There was a commotion when a dog attacked the sheep.* ado, bedlam, bother, chaos, clamour, confusion, din, disorder, disturbance, fuss, hubbub, hullabaloo, noise, pandemonium, racket, riot, row, rumpus, tumult, turbulence, turmoil, unrest, upheaval, uproar.

communal *Most schools have communal washing facilities.* common, joint, mutual, shared.

communicate 1 *to communicate with other people.* to contact, to correspond with, to get in touch with, to speak to, to talk to. 2 *to communicate our thoughts.* to convey, to express, to indicate, to say, to show, to speak, to write.

communication 1 *to send a communication.* announcement, information, message, report, statement. 2 KINDS OF COMMUNICATION ARE advertising, broadcasting, cable, cable television, CB, correspondence, intercom, letter, the media, newspaper, note, the press, radar, radio, telecommunications, telegram, telephone, television, walkie-talkie, wire, wireless. 3 SEE **language**.

communicative *a communicative person.* chatty, talkative.

communion SEE **church**.

communiqué announcement, bulletin, dispatch, message, report, statement.

Communist SEE **politics**.

community nation, public, society.

compact 1 *a compact set of instructions.* brief, compressed, concise, condensed, short. 2 *a compact typewriter.* neat, portable, small.

compact disc SEE **record.**

companion *Who was your companion this morning?* chum, comrade, escort, friend, mate, partner.

company 1 *We enjoy other people's company.* companionship, fellowship, friendship, society. 2 *a company of rebels.* band, crew, gang, troop. SEE ALSO **armed services.** 3 *a theatrical company.* association, club, group, society. 4 *a shipping company.* business, concern, firm, organization, union.

compare 1 *Compare your answers with your neighbour's.* to check against, to contrast with, to set against. 2 *Their team cannot compare with ours.* to compete with, to match, to rival.

comparison *Look at the comparison between your work and Tony's.* contrast, difference, similarity.

compartment 1 *The box has compartments for nails of different sizes.* division, section. 2 *At the baths there are compartments where you can change.* booth, cubicle.

compass SEE **mathematics, navigate.**

compassion *The muggers showed no compassion for their victim.* feeling, mercy, pity, sympathy.

compel 1 *You can't compel me to play for your side.* to drive, to force, to oblige, to order, to press, to require, to urge. 2 *compelled: They'll be compelled to use the motorway if they want to get here for tea.* bound, certain, obliged, sure.

compensate *Will the insurance compensate us for what we lost in the fire?* to make up, to recompense, to repay.

compère SEE **entertainment.**

compete 1 *We competed against a good side in the final.* to conflict, to contend, to contest, to oppose, to rival, to struggle. 2 *How many runners are*

competing in this race? to enter, to participate, to take part.

competent *Mr Brunswick needs a competent bricklayer to build his extension.* able, capable, effective, efficient, experienced, handy, practical, proficient, qualified, skilful, skilled, trained.

competition 1 *a darts competition.* championship, contest, event, game, match, tournament. 2 *The competition between the teams was intense.* competitiveness, rivalry. 3 SEE **game, sport.**

competitor *competitors in a quiz.* candidate, contestant, entrant, opponent, participant, rival.

compile *We compiled a magazine.* to arrange, to compose, to edit, to put together.

complacent *Lucy knew she mustn't be complacent after winning the gold cup.* self-righteous, self-satisfied, smug.

complain *We complained about the awful food.* to grouse, to grumble, to moan, to object, to protest.

complaint 1 *We had a complaint about the food.* grievance, objection, protest. 2 *Flu is a common complaint in winter.* affliction, ailment, disease, disorder, infection, malady, sickness. SEE ALSO **illness.**

complete 1 *When will you complete the work?* to accomplish, to achieve, to carry out, to conclude, to do, to end, to finish, to fulfil, to perform, to round off. 2 *We've got the complete story on video.* entire, full, intact, total, unabridged, whole. 3 *His story was complete rubbish.* absolute, perfect, pure, sheer, total, utter.

complex *A computer is a complex machine.* complicated, elaborate, intricate, involved, sophisticated.

complexion 1 *The colour of your dress suits your complexion.* colour, skin, texture. 2 WORDS USED TO DESCRIBE PEOPLE'S COMPLEXION ARE black, brown, dark, fair, freckled, pasty, ruddy, swarthy, tanned, white.

complicated *The instructions were too*

complicated to understand. complex, difficult, elaborate, hard, intricate, involved, sophisticated.

complication *We thought we had no problems, but then we discovered a complication.* difficulty, problem, setback, snag.

compliment *It's nice to get compliments.* appreciation, congratulations, flattery, praise, tribute.

complimentary *People made complimentary remarks about Lucy's gymnastics.* admiring, appreciative, approving, flattering.

component *The garage got the components needed to mend the car.* bit, element, part, unit.

compose 1 *The team is composed of good players.* to compile, to constitute, to make up, to put together. 2 *to compose music.* to create, to write.

composer, composition SEE **music**.

compost SEE **garden**.

compound 1 *The chemist made up a nasty-looking compound.* blend, combination, mixture. 2 *The animals were kept in a compound overnight.* enclosure, pen, run.

comprehend *I can't comprehend how terrible it must be to experience an earthquake.* to appreciate, to follow, to grasp, to know, to realize, to see, to understand.

comprehensive SEE **school**.

compress 1 *to compress something into a small space.* to crush, to press, to squash, to squeeze. 2 *compressed*: compact, concise, condensed.

comprise *This album comprises the best hits of the year.* to consist of, to contain, to include.

compulsion *Taking drugs can become a compulsion.* addiction, habit.

compulsory *At our school it's compulsory to have a shower after games.* necessary, required, unavoidable.

compute *It would be interesting to compute how many hours Lucy trains in a year.* to add up, to calculate, to count, to reckon, to total, to work out.

computer WORDS TO DO WITH COMPUTING ARE chip, cursor, data, disc, disc drive, floppy disc, hardware, interface, joystick, keyboard, micro, microchip, microcomputer, micro-processor, monitor, printer, print-out, program, software, terminal, VDU, word-processor.

comrade chum, companion, friend, mate, partner.

conceal *to conceal a mistake, to conceal the truth, etc.* to blot out, to bury, to camouflage, to cover up, to disguise, to envelop, to hide, to hush up, to keep quiet, to mask.

conceited *Logan was so conceited when his poem went in the magazine!* arrogant, boastful, bumptious, (informal) cocky, proud, self-important, (informal) stuck-up.

conceive 1 *to conceive a baby.* SEE **pregnant**. 2 *to conceive an idea.* to create, to imagine, to invent, to plan, to think up.

concentrate 1 *Concentrate on your work.* to attend to, to think about. 2 *Their supporters concentrated on the far side of the field.* to accumulate, to collect, to gather, to mass. 3 *to concentrate a liquid.* to condense, to reduce, to thicken.

concept *When dad was a boy, space travel was a strange concept.* belief, idea, notion, thought.

concern 1 *Some people don't show any concern for the starving.* care, interest, responsibility. 2 *They think it's no concern of theirs.* affair, business, matter. 3 *Uncle Graham has a job with a business concern.* company, firm, organization. 4 *Paying her gas bill is a great concern to granny.* anxiety, cause of distress, fear, worry. 5 *Road safety concerns us all.* to affect, to be important to, to interest, to involve, to matter to. 6 *concerned*: anxious, bothered, caring, distressed, fearful, troubled, worried. 7 *concerning*: about, involving, regarding, relating to.

concert SEE **entertainment**.

concerto SEE **music**.

concise *a concise dictionary, a concise account, etc.* brief, compact, condensed, short, small, terse.

conclude 1 *We concluded the concert with a song.* to close, to complete, to end, to finish, to round off, to stop, to terminate. **2** *When you didn't arrive, we concluded that the car had broken down.* to decide, to gather, to judge.

conclusion 1 *We were tired at the conclusion of the journey.* close, end, finish. **2** *You have heard the evidence, so what is your conclusion?* decision, judgement, opinion.

concoct *Logan concocts all sorts of excuses.* to counterfeit, to devise, to feign, to invent, to make up, to put together, to think up.

concord *It would be nice if everyone lived in concord.* agreement, harmony, peace.

concrete SEE **building**.

concussion SEE **illness**.

condemn 1 *The head condemned the vandals who broke the windows.* to blame, to denounce, to disapprove of, to rebuke. **2** *The judge condemned the muggers to a spell in prison.* to convict, to punish, to sentence.

condense 1 *to condense a book.* to abbreviate, to abridge, to compress, to shorten. **2** *to condense a liquid.* to concentrate, to reduce, to thicken.

condition 1 *The lavatories were in a bad condition.* order, situation, state. **2** *An athlete has to keep in condition.* fitness, health.

conduct 1 *We were praised for our good conduct.* attitude, behaviour, manners. **2** *The curator conducted us round the museum.* to escort, to guide, to lead, to pilot. **3** *Mrs Angel conducts the school choir.* to be in charge of, to direct, to lead. **4** *Everyone conducted themselves well.* to act, to behave.

conductor 1 *a bus conductor.* SEE **job**. **2** *the conductor of an orchestra.* SEE **music**.

cone SEE **shape**.

conference *Mrs Angel went to a teachers' conference.* assembly, committee, congress, debate, gathering, meeting.

confess *Logan confessed that he broke the window.* to acknowledge, to admit, to own up.

confetti SEE **wedding**.

confide *to confide in:* to tell secrets to, to trust.

confidence *We have confidence in our goalie.* belief, faith, hope, trust.

confident 1 *I'm confident that you'll succeed.* certain, hopeful, optimistic, positive, sure. **2** *a confident person.* assertive, assured, definite.

confidential *Mrs Brunswick keeps her confidential papers locked in a box.* intimate, personal, private, secret.

confine *Battery hens are confined in a very small space.* to cramp, to curb, to detain, to enclose, to gaol, to imprison, to intern, to limit, to restrict, to shut in.

confirm *Our experiments confirmed that plants need light to grow.* to demonstrate, to establish, to prove, to show, to verify.

confirmation SEE **church**.

confiscate *Mrs Angel confiscated my catapult.* to seize, to take away.

conflagration *Three fire-engines came to deal with the conflagration.* blaze, fire, inferno.

conflict 1 *an angry conflict.* antagonism, confrontation, discord, hostility, opposition. **2** *Many men died in the conflict.* action, battle, clash, combat, encounter, fight, struggle, war, warfare. **3** *The twins' views seldom conflict.* to clash, to compete, to contend, to oppose each other.

conform *Conform to the rules.* to abide by, to keep to, to fit in with, to obey.

confront 1 *Even Logan won't confront the headmaster.* to argue with, to attack, to challenge, to defy, to face up to, to resist, to stand up to. **2** *We went the wrong way and suddenly confronted a 'no entry' sign.* to encounter, to face, to meet.

confuse 1 *The complicated rules confused us.* to baffle, to bewilder, to distract,

to mislead, to perplex, to puzzle.
2 *Don't confuse those two packs of cards.*
to jumble, to mix up, to muddle.
3 *confused*: chaotic, disjointed,
disorganized, flustered, fuddled,
garbled, higgledy-piggledy,
incoherent, jumbled, mixed up,
muddled, rambling, topsy-turvy,
unclear.

confusion *There was terrible confusion
when the animals escaped.* ado, anarchy,
bedlam, bother, chaos, clutter,
commotion, confusion, din, disorder,
disturbance, fuss, hubbub,
hullabaloo, jumble, mess, muddle,
pandemonium, racket, riot, rumpus,
shambles, tumult, turbulence,
turmoil, uproar.

congested *The roads are congested at
rush hour.* blocked, full, jammed,
overcrowded.

congratulate *Everyone congratulated
Lucy when she won the gold cup.* to
applaud, to commend, to praise.

congregate *On summer evenings, we
congregate outside the sweet shop.* to
assemble, to come together, to
cluster, to collect, to crowd, to
gather, to get together, to group, to
mass, to meet, to muster, to swarm,
to throng.

congregation SEE **church**.

congress assembly, conference,
gathering, meeting.

conifer SEE **tree**.

conjunction SEE **language**.

conjurer SEE **entertainment**.

conjuring *The magician did some
conjuring.* illusions, magic, tricks.

connect *Connect these two bits of rope.* to
attach, to fasten, to fix, to join, to
link, to relate, to tie.

connection bond, link, relationship.

conquer to beat, to crush, to defeat,
(informal) to lick, to master, to
overcome, to overpower, to
overthrow, to overwhelm, to rout, to
subdue, to succeed against, to
suppress, (informal) to thrash, to
vanquish.

conquest capture, occupation,
victory, win.

conscientious *a conscientious worker.*
careful, diligent, dutiful, hard-
working, honest, scrupulous, serious,
thorough.

conscious 1 *In spite of the knock on the
head, he remained conscious.* alert,
awake, aware. 2 *It was a conscious foul.*
deliberate, intended, intentional,
premeditated.

consecrated *The churchyard is
consecrated ground.* blessed, hallowed,
holy, religious, sacred.

consent *We wondered if mum and dad
would consent to a party.* to agree to, to
allow, to approve of, to authorize, to
permit.

consequence *The floods were a
consequence of all that snow.* effect, end,
issue, outcome, result, sequel.

conservation *the conservation of the
countryside.* preservation.

Conservative SEE **politics**.

conservatory SEE **house**.

consider 1 *He considered the problem for
a long time.* to contemplate, to
discuss, to meditate on, to ponder, to
reflect on, to study, to think about.
.2 *Do you consider he was telling the truth?*
to believe, to judge, to reckon.

considerable *a considerable amount of
rain.* big, biggish, noticeable,
significant, sizeable, substantial,
worthwhile.

considerate *It was considerate of you to
lend granny your umbrella.* attentive,
friendly, helpful, kind, kind-hearted,
obliging, polite, sympathetic,
thoughtful, unselfish.

consignment *a fresh consignment of
strawberries.* batch, delivery.

consist *What does this fruit salad consist
of?* to be composed of, to contain, to
include.

consistent 1 *Tony is a very consistent
chess-player.* dependable, faithful,
regular, reliable, steady. 2 *That is not
consistent with what you said yesterday.*
compatible with, in accordance with.

console *to console someone who is*

unhappy. to comfort, to ease, to soothe, to sympathize with.

consort SEE **royal**.

conspicuous *a conspicuous landmark, a conspicuous case of cheating.* blatant, impressive, notable, noticeable, obvious, prominent, pronounced, showy, striking, unconcealed, unmistakable, visible.

conspiracy *a conspiracy against the government.* intrigue, plot, scheme.

constable (informal) cop or copper, officer, policeman, policewoman.

constant 1 *a constant cough, a constant rhythm.* ceaseless, chronic, continual, everlasting, incessant, invariable, non-stop, permanent, persistent, repeated, unending. 2 *a constant friend.* dedicated, dependable, devoted, faithful, firm, loyal, reliable, steady, trustworthy, unchanging.

constellation SEE **astronomy**.

constipation SEE **illness**.

constituency SEE **government**.

constitute *In soccer, eleven players constitute a team.* to compose, to form, to make up.

constitution SEE **government**.

construct *We constructed a den out of old planks.* to assemble, to build, to erect, to fit together, to make, to put together.

constructive *a constructive suggestion.* beneficial, co-operative, helpful, positive, useful.

consul ambassador, diplomat, representative.

consult *I consulted the doctor about my cough.* to discuss with, to refer to.

consume 1 *We consumed an enormous amount of food.* to devour, to digest, to eat, to gobble up, to swallow. 2 *If we buy a video, it'll consume all our savings.* to exhaust, to use up.

contact 1 *Mrs Brunswick contacted the police about her lost brooch.* to communicate with, to correspond with, to get in touch with, to speak to, to talk to. 2 *The wires must contact*

each other before the electric current will flow. to connect with, to touch.

contagious *a contagious disease.* catching, infectious.

contain 1 *What does this cake contain?* to be composed of, to consist of, to incorporate. 2 *What does this box contain?* to hold, to include.

container 1 receptacle. 2 VARIOUS CONTAINERS ARE bag, barrel, basin, basket, bath, beaker, billycan, bin, bottle, box, bucket, butt, can, canister, carton, cartridge, case, cask, casket, casserole, cauldron, chest, churn, cistern, coffin, cup, dish, drum, dustbin, envelope, flask, glass, goblet, hamper, handbag, haversack, hold-all, holster, jar, jug, keg, kettle, knapsack, money-box, mould, mug, pail, pan, pannier, pitcher, pot, pouch, purse, rucksack, sack, satchel, saucepan, suitcase, tank, tankard, teapot, test tube, Thermos, tin, trough, trunk, tub, tumbler, urn, vacuum-flask, vase, vat, wallet, watering-can, wineglass.

contaminate *The fish died because the water was contaminated by chemicals.* to defile, to infect, to poison, to pollute, to soil.

contemplate 1 *We contemplated the lovely view.* to eye, to gaze at, to look at, to observe, to regard, to stare at, to view, to watch. 2 *We contemplated what to do next.* to consider, to meditate, to plan, to ponder, to reflect on, to study, to think about.

contemporary 1 *contemporary events.* current, simultaneous, topical. 2 *contemporary music.* fashionable, modern, newest, (informal) trendy, up-to-date.

contempt disgust, dislike, disrespect, loathing, scorn.

contemptible *The judge said that the muggers were contemptible.* despicable, detestable, hateful, pitiful, worthless.

contemptuous *Don't be contemptuous: we did our best.* disdainful, scornful, sneering.

contend 1 *We contended against strong*

opposition. to compete, to contest, to dispute, to fight, to oppose, to rival, to struggle. 2 *Tony contended that he put the oven on at the right time.* to argue, to assert, to claim, to declare, to maintain.

content *The cat looks content after his dinner.* carefree, comfortable, happy, relaxed, satisfied.

contest 1 *to contest a title.* to compete for, to contend for, to fight for, to struggle for. 2 *to contest a decision.* to argue against, to challenge, to oppose, to resist. 3 *a sporting contest.* bout, championship, combat, competition, conflict, duel, fight, game, match, struggle.

contestant competitor, participant.

continent SEE geography.

continental quilt SEE bedclothes.

continual *Stop your continual chattering!* ceaseless, chronic, constant, continuous, endless, eternal, everlasting, frequent, incessant, interminable, lasting, limitless, non-stop, permanent, perpetual, persistent, recurrent, relentless, repeated, unending, uninterrupted.

continue 1 *How long will the fine weather continue?* to carry on, to endure, to go on, to keep on, to last, to linger, to live on, to persist, to remain, to stay, to survive. 2 *Please continue with your work.* to carry on, to persevere, to proceed, to resume.

continuous SEE continual.

contortionist SEE circus, entertainment.

contour SEE geography.

contraband *The smugglers hid their contraband.* booty, loot.

contract 1 *Our team has signed a contract with a new goalkeeper.* agreement, bargain, deal, pact, settlement, treaty. 2 *Most substances contract as they get colder.* to decrease, to diminish, to dwindle, to lessen, to reduce, to shrink.

contradict *Are you contradicting me?* to oppose, to speak against.

contradictory *We heard contradictory* reports *about the match.* conflicting, incompatible, inconsistent, opposite.

contralto SEE sing.

contraption *What do you use that contraption for?* contrivance, device, gadget, invention, machine.

contrary 1 *In our debate, Tony spoke for the proposal, and Lucy put the contrary view.* opposite, reverse. 2 *contrary winds.* adverse, hostile, opposing, unfavourable. 3 *a contrary child.* defiant, disobedient, obstinate, perverse, rebellious, stubborn.

contrast 1 *Mrs Angel contrasted Logan's work with Tony's.* to compare, to set against. 2 *The colours of the two dresses contrasted.* to differ. 3 *There was an obvious contrast between them.* comparison, difference, distinction.

contribute *Everyone contributed something to eat.* to donate, to give, to provide, to supply.

contribution *Please make a contribution to the school fund.* fee, gift, offering, payment, subscription.

contrivance *I invented a contrivance for sweeping the snow away.* contraption, device, gadget, invention.

control 1 *Mrs Angel controls the class well.* to administer, to command, to cope with, to deal with, to direct, to dominate, to govern, to handle, to look after, to manage, to manipulate, to master, to regulate, to rule, to supervise. 2 *They built a dam to control the floods.* to check, to curb, to hold back, to restrain. 3 *Who is in control here?* charge, command, management, rule. 4 *Mrs Angel has good control over the class.* authority, discipline, influence, power.

controversy *There is a controversy about whether they should build a bypass.* argument, debate, disagreement, dispute, issue, quarrel.

conundrum riddle.

conurbation SEE geography.

convalescent *Granny is convalescent in hospital after her operation.* getting better, improving, recovering, recuperating.

convector SEE **fire**.

convenient *There's a convenient shop round the corner.* accessible, available, handy, suitable, useful.

convent SEE **church**.

convention *It's a convention to give presents at Christmas.* custom, formality, rule, tradition.

conventional *'How are you?' is a conventional way to greet people.* accustomed, common, commonplace, customary, everyday, habitual, normal, ordinary, orthodox, regular, traditional, usual.

converge *The motorways converge in a mile.* to come together, to intersect, to join, to meet, to merge.

conversation chat, chatter, dialogue, discussion, talk.

convert *We converted the attic into a games room.* to adapt, to alter, to amend, to change, to modify, to process, to transform, to turn.

convey 1 *Please convey our best wishes to your father.* to bear, to carry, to deliver, to send, to take. **2** *Lorries convey goods all over the country.* to carry, to take, to transfer, to transport. **3** *Does that signal convey anything to you?* to communicate, to indicate, to mean.

convict 1 *The convicts were forced to work hard all day.* captive, criminal, prisoner. **2** *He was convicted for murder.* to condemn, to sentence.

conviction *religious convictions.* belief, creed, faith, opinion, view.

convince *He tried to convince the jury that he was innocent.* to persuade, to win over.

convoy *a convoy of ships.* armada, fleet. SEE ALSO **group**.

convulsion fit, seizure, spasm. SEE ALSO **illness**.

coo SEE **sound**.

cook 1 WAYS TO COOK ARE to bake, to barbecue, to boil, to brew, to fry, to grill, to pickle, to poach, to roast, to simmer, to steam, to stew, to toast. **2** OTHER THINGS YOU DO IN COOKING ARE to blend, to chop, to grate, to freeze, to knead, to mix, to peel, to sieve, to sift, to stir, to whisk. **3** CONTAINERS USED TO COOK IN ARE basin, billycan, casserole, cauldron, dish, frying-pan, kettle, pan, percolator, pot, saucepan. **4** SEE ALSO **kitchen**. **5** *Would you like to be a cook?* SEE **job**.

cool 1 *cool weather.* chilly, cold. **2** *Keep cool!* calm, level-headed, sensible, unflustered. **3** *When he asked her to go out with him, she was rather cool.* distant, half-hearted, indifferent, reserved, unconcerned, unenthusiastic, unfriendly. **4** *to cool food.* to chill, to freeze, to refrigerate.

coop *a chicken coop.* cage, enclosure, pen.

co-operate *Logan wouldn't co-operate with Tony.* to aid, to assist, to collaborate with, to help, to support, to work together with.

co-operative *The dealer was co-operative when the TV went wrong.* accommodating, constructive, helpful, willing.

coot SEE **bird**.

cop SEE **police**.

cope *Can you cope with the housework?* to control, to deal with, to endure, to handle, to look after, to manage, to suffer, to tolerate, to withstand.

copious *copious supplies of food.* abundant, ample, generous, lavish, liberal, plentiful, profuse.

copper SEE **metal**.

coppice, copse *a coppice of birch trees.* grove, thicket, wood.

copulate *Animals copulate when the time is right for them to have young ones.* to couple, to have sexual intercourse, to mate.

copy 1 *a copy of a painting, a copy of Stevenson's Rocket, etc.* double, duplicate, fake, forgery, imitation, likeness, model, photocopy, print, replica, reproduction, twin. **2** *to copy a picture, to copy someone's work, etc.* to counterfeit, to crib, to duplicate, to forge, to imitate, to photocopy, to print, to reproduce. **3** *to copy someone's* *voice.* to imitate, to impersonate, to mimic.

coral SEE **jewellery**.

cord *a length of cord.* cable, lace, line, rope, string, twine.

cordial 1 *a cordial welcome.* friendly, genial, kind, warm, warm-hearted. **2** *lime cordial.* SEE **drink**.

cordon *a cordon of policemen.* chain, line, row.

corduroy SEE **cloth**.

core *the core of an apple, the core of the earth, etc.* centre, heart, inside, middle, nucleus.

cork *Put the cork back in the bottle.* bung, plug, stopper.

corkscrew SEE **kitchen**.

cormorant SEE **bird**.

corn 1 cereal, grain. SEE ALSO **cereal**. **2** *corns on your feet.* SEE **illness**.

corner 1 *the corner of the room.* angle, nook. **2** *the corner of the road.* bend, crossroads, intersection, junction, turn. **3** *After a chase, they cornered him.* to capture, to catch, to trap.

cornet SEE **brass**.

cornflakes SEE **cereal, food**.

cornflour SEE **food**.

cornflower SEE **flower**.

coronation crowning. SEE ALSO **royal**.

coroner SEE **law**.

coronet crown, diadem. SEE ALSO **hat**.

corporal SEE **rank**.

corporal punishment SEE **punishment**.

corporation 1 *the town corporation.* council. **2** *a business corporation.* organization.

corps SEE **armed services**.

corpse body, carcass, remains.

correct 1 *Can the garage correct the fault in the car?* to cure, to put right, to rectify, to remedy, to repair. **2** *Mrs Angel corrected our maths.* to assess, to mark. **3** *Is that the correct time?* accurate, exact, faultless, precise, right, true.

correspond 1 *Tony corresponds with a girl in Paris.* to communicate with, to send letters to, to write to. **2** *Tony's answer doesn't correspond with Logan's.* to agree with, to coincide with, to match.

correspondent *a newspaper correspondent.* journalist, reporter. SEE ALSO **writer**.

corridor hall, passage. SEE ALSO **house**.

corrode *Chemicals corroded the metal.* to eat away, to erode, to rot, to rust.

corrupt 1 *You don't expect a judge to be corrupt.* criminal, crooked, depraved, dishonest, evil, immoral, low, untrustworthy, wicked. **2** *You'd get into serious trouble if you tried to corrupt a judge.* to bribe, to influence, to pervert, to tempt.

corset SEE **underclothes**.

cosmetics 1 make-up. **2** VARIOUS COSMETICS ARE cream, deodorant, eye-shadow, lipstick, lotion, nail varnish, perfume, scent, talcum powder.

cosmonaut astronaut, space-traveller.

cosmos universe.

cost *What's the cost of a return ticket?* charge, expense, fare, payment, price, value.

costly *costly jewels.* dear, exorbitant, expensive, precious, priceless, (informal) pricey, valuable.

costume *The actors wore weird costumes.* attire, clothing, dress, garments, outfit. SEE ALSO **clothes**.

cosy *a cosy room, a cosy atmosphere, etc.* comfortable, relaxing, restful, secure, snug, soft, warm.

cot cradle. SEE ALSO **furniture**.

cottage SEE **house**.

cotton 1 SEE **cloth**. **2** *If you find some cotton, I'll sew your button on.* thread.

couch SEE **furniture**.

cough SEE **illness**.

council 1 *We held a council to decide what to do.* assembly, committee, conference. **2** *the town council.* corporation.

council-house SEE **house**.

count 1 *It's amazing how quickly the bank clerk counts the money.* to add up, to calculate, to compute, to figure out, to number, to reckon, to total, to work out. **2** *You can count on Tony to do his best.* to bank on, to depend on, to rely on, to trust.

count, countess SEE **title**.

countenance *His countenance shows that he's had bad news.* appearance, expression, face, features, look.

counter 1 *You play ludo with counters.* disc, token. **2** *You can buy a drink at the counter.* bar, table.

counterfeit 1 *They were put in prison for counterfeiting £5 notes.* to copy, to fake, to forge, to imitate. **2** *They weren't really ill, only counterfeiting.* to pretend, to sham.

counterpane SEE **bedclothes**.

countless *There are countless stars in the sky.* frequent, innumerable, many, numberless, numerous, untold.

country 1 *the countries of the world.* land, nation, state. **2** KINDS OF COUNTRY ARE democracy, dictatorship, kingdom, monarchy, realm, republic. **3** *There's some lovely country near here.* countryside, landscape, rural surroundings, scenery. **4** SEE **geography**.

county SEE **geography**.

couple 1 *a couple of rabbits.* brace, pair. **2** *They coupled the wagons to the locomotive.* to combine, to join, to link, to unite.

coupon *If you save ten coupons you get a free mug.* ticket, token, voucher.

courage *We admired the firemen's courage.* bravery, daring, determination, fortitude, (informal) grit, (informal) guts, heroism, nerve, (informal) pluck, prowess, spirit, valour.

courageous bold, brave, daring, determined, fearless, heroic, intrepid, plucky, valiant.

courier SEE **job**.

course 1 *The pilot checked the air-liner's course.* bearings, direction, route, way. **2** *a course of driving lessons.* series.

3 *a race-course.* SEE **sport**. **4** *We had beef for the main course.* SEE **meal**.

court 1 *The court decided that he was guilty.* court martial, lawcourt. SEE ALSO **law**. **2** *a tennis court.* SEE **sport**. **3** *to court someone.* to go out with, to make love to, to woo.

courteous *Granny says that her paperboy is a courteous young man.* chivalrous, civil, considerate, gallant, gracious, polite, respectful, well-mannered.

courtesy good manners, politeness.

courtyard enclosure, quadrangle, yard. SEE ALSO **building**.

cousin SEE **family**.

cove *a sandy cove.* bay, inlet.

cover 1 *Fog covered the town.* to blot out, to bury, to camouflage, to clothe, to conceal, to enclose, to envelop, to hide, to mask, to obscure, to plaster, to protect, to shroud. **2** *An encyclopaedia covers many subjects.* to deal with, to include, to incorporate. **3** *a jam-pot cover, a cover to keep the rain off, etc.* cap, coat, covering, envelope, folder, lid, protection, roof, top, wrapper. **4** *The animals searched for cover in the bad weather.* hiding-place, protection, refuge, shelter.

covering *a light covering of snow.* cap, coating, layer, skin.

coverlet SEE **bedclothes**.

cow SEE **animal, farm, female**.

cowardly *a cowardly person, a cowardly action.* base, faint-hearted, fearful, spineless, timid, unheroic, (informal) yellow.

cowed *Logan seemed cowed in front of our famous visitor.* afraid, fearful, frightened, scared, terrified.

cower *The terrified dog cowered in a corner.* to cringe, to crouch, to grovel, to hide, to quail, to shrink.

cowslip SEE **flower**.

cox SEE **sailor**.

coy *Don't be coy: come and be introduced.* bashful, modest, self-conscious, sheepish, shy, timid.

crab SEE **shellfish**.

crab-apple SEE **fruit**.

crack 1 *a crack in the wall.* break, chink, cranny, crevice, flaw, fracture, gap, opening, rift, split. 2 *He cracked a bone in his leg.* to break, to chip, to fracture, to snap, to splinter, to split. 3 *the crack of a rifle.* SEE **sound**.

cracker 1 SEE **firework**. 2 biscuit. SEE ALSO **food**.

crackle SEE **sound**.

cradle cot. SEE ALSO **furniture**.

craft 1 *Few people know the craft of thatching.* handicraft, skill, technique, trade. FOR VARIOUS CRAFTS SEE **art**. 2 *There were many kinds of craft in the harbour.* boat, ship. SEE ALSO **vessel**.

craftsman SEE **art**.

crafty *They say the fox is a crafty creature.* artful, astute, clever, cunning, deceitful, ingenious, knowing, skilful, sly, sneaky, tricky, wily.

crag *The climb up the crag was dangerous.* cliff, precipice, rock.

cram 1 *The room was crammed with people.* to crowd, to fill, to jam, to pack. 2 *Don't cram any more in your mouth!* to squeeze, to stuff.

cramp 1 *cramp in the leg.* SEE **illness**. 2 clamp. SEE ALSO **tool**. 3 *I'm sorry you are so cramped in this little room.* to confine, to enclose, to restrict.

crane 1 SEE **bird**. 2 derrick.

crane-fly SEE **insect**.

cranky (informal) *It seems a bit cranky to have jam with scrambled egg.* eccentric, odd, unconventional, weird, zany.

cranny *a cranny in a rock.* crack, gap, split.

crash 1 *The car crashed into the wall.* to bump, to collide, to knock, to smash. SEE ALSO **hit**. 2 *We heard a crash.* SEE **sound**. 3 *Did you see the crash?* accident, bump, collision, derailment, impact, knock, smash.

crash-helmet SEE **hat**.

crate box, carton, case. SEE ALSO **container**.

crater *The explosion left a deep crater.* abyss, chasm, hole, pit.

crawl 1 *He crawled along a narrow ledge.* to clamber, to creep, to edge, to worm. 2 SEE **swim**.

crayon SEE **write**.

craze *the latest craze.* diversion, enthusiasm, fashion, mania, pastime.

crazy 1 *The dog went crazy when it was stung by a wasp.* berserk, delirious, demented, deranged, frantic, frenzied, hysterical, insane, lunatic, mad, (informal) potty, unhinged, wild. 2 *a crazy comedy.* absurd, farcical, illogical, irrational, ludicrous, preposterous, ridiculous, silly, stupid, unreasonable, zany.

creak SEE **sound**.

cream SEE **colour, food**.

crease *to crease a piece of paper.* to crinkle, to crumple, to fold, to furrow, to pleat, to wrinkle.

create *to create something beautiful, to create trouble, etc.* to begin, to breed, to bring about, to compose, to conceive, to construct, to establish, to form, to found, to generate, to initiate, to invent, to make, to originate, to produce, to think up.

creation *the creation of the world.* beginning, birth, construction, invention, origin.

creative *Artists are creative people.* artistic, imaginative, inventive, original, resourceful.

creator author, discoverer, inventor, maker, painter.

creature being. SEE ALSO **animal, bird, fish, insect, reptile, snake**.

crèche nursery.

credible *No one thought the story about Martians was credible.* believable, plausible, reasonable.

credit *Lucy's win brought credit to the school.* honour, merit, reputation.

creditable *Tony gave a creditable performance in the swimming gala.* admirable, commendable, honourable, praiseworthy, respectable, worthy.

credit card SEE **money**.

creed *a religious creed.* belief, conviction, faith.

creek inlet. SEE ALSO **geography**.

creep *to creep along the ground.* to crawl, to edge, to slink, to slither, to worm. SEE·ALSO **move**.

creepy *I don't like creepy noises in the dark.* eerie, frightening, ghostly, scary, spooky, uncanny, weird.

cremate SEE **burn**.

cremation SEE **funeral**.

crescent *a crescent moon.* curved.

cress SEE **salad**.

crest *the school crest.* badge, emblem, seal, sign, symbol.

crestfallen *Logan was crestfallen when he didn't win.* dejected, disappointed, discouraged, downcast, down-hearted, forlorn, glum, miserable, wretched. SEE ALSO **sad**.

crevice *a crevice in the rock.* crack, cranny, gap, split.

crew *a ship's crew.* company, team. SEE ALSO **group**.

crib *to crib in a test.* to cheat, to copy.

cricket 1 WORDS TO DO WITH CRICKET ARE batsman, boundary, bowler, fielder, innings, lbw, maiden over, over, pads, slips, stumps, test match, wicket, wicket- keeper. 2 SEE **sport**. 3 *A cricket chirped in the grass.* SEE **insect**.

crime 1 dishonesty, misdeed, offence, racket, sin, wrongdoing. 2 VARIOUS CRIMES ARE abduction, arson, assassination, assault, blackmail, burglary, hijacking, hold-up, kidnapping, manslaughter, mugging, murder, pilfering, poaching, rape, robbery, shoplifting, smuggling, stealing, theft.

criminal 1 convict, crook, culprit, delinquent, hooligan, malefactor, offender, outlaw, thug, wrongdoer. SEE ALSO **rogue, ruffian**. 2 VARIOUS KINDS OF CRIMINAL ARE assassin, bandit, blackmailer, brigand, buccaneer, burglar, desperado, gangster, gunman, highwayman, hijacker, kidnapper, mugger, murderer, outlaw, pickpocket, pirate, poacher, robber, shop-lifter, smuggler, terrorist, thief, vandal.

crimson SEE **colour**.

cringe *The frightened dog cringed in his kennel.* to cower, to crouch, to flinch, to grovel, to quail, to wince.

crippled 1 *a crippled person.* disabled, handicapped, hurt, injured, lame, maimed, mutilated. 2 *a crippled vehicle.* damaged, immobilized.

crisis *We had a crisis when we found a gas leak.* danger, emergency.

crisp 1 *crisp biscuits.* brittle, crackly, fragile, hard and dry. 2 *potato crisps.* SEE **food**.

criticism *The head's criticism of our behaviour was unfair.* censure, disapproval, reprimand, reproach.

criticize *Mrs Angel criticized us for being noisy.* to find fault with, to judge, to rebuke, to scold.

croak SEE **sound**.

crochet SEE **art**.

crockery 1 china, earthenware, porcelain, pottery. 2 VARIOUS ITEMS OF CROCKERY ARE basin, bowl, cup, dish, jug, plate, pot, saucer, teapot.

crocodile alligator. SEE ALSO **reptile**.

crocus SEE **bulb, flower**.

croft farm. SEE ALSO **building**.

crook delinquent, gangster, offender, wrongdoer. SEE ALSO **criminal**.

crooked 1 *a crooked road.* angled, bent, twisted, twisty, zigzag. 2 *a crooked salesman.* corrupt, criminal, dishonest, untrustworthy.

croon SEE **sing**.

crop 1 *to crop the grass.* to clip, to shear, to trim. SEE ALSO **cut**. 2 *A difficulty has cropped up.* to arise, to come up, to emerge, to occur, to spring up, to turn up. 3 *The corn crop is good this year.* harvest, produce, yield. 4 *He hit the horse with his crop.* lash, whip.

croquet SEE **sport**.

cross 1 *The road crosses the river.* to go across, to intersect with, to pass over, to span. 2 *The trains crossed at high speed.* to pass. 3 *They crossed out my name.* to cancel, to delete, to erase, to wipe out. 4 *Mrs Brunswick was cross when Lucy trod on her plants.* angry, annoyed, bad-tempered, grumpy, indignant, irate, irritated, short-tempered, upset, vexed.

crossbow SEE **weapon**.

cross-country SEE **athletics**.

cross-examine *to cross-examine a witness.* to examine, to question.

cross-eyed squinting.

crossroads interchange, intersection, junction.

crossword SEE **game**.

crotchet SEE **music**.

crouch *They crouched in the low tunnel.* to bend, to bow, to cower, to duck, to kneel, to stoop.

crow 1 SEE **bird**. 2 *The cock crows every morning.* SEE **sound**. 3 *Logan was crowing about the goal he scored.* to boast, to brag, to show off, (informal) to swank.

crowbar SEE **tool**.

crowd 1 *There was a crowd round the ambulance.* bunch, cluster, collection, crush, gathering, horde, host, mob, multitude, pack, rabble, swarm, throng. SEE ALSO **group**. 2 *The crowd cheered.* audience, spectators. 3 *We crowded round when we heard there was free food.* to assemble, to congregate, to flock, to gather, to herd, to swarm, to throng. 4 *They crowded us into a small room.* to cram, to crush, to huddle, to overcrowd, to pack, to press, to push, to shove, to squeeze.

crown 1 coronet, diadem. SEE ALSO **hat, royal**. 2 *the crown of a hill.* apex, head, top.

crow's nest SEE **vessel**.

crucifix SEE **church**.

crucify SEE **execute**.

crude 1 *crude oil.* natural, raw, unprocessed, unrefined. 2 *We made a crude table out of planks.* clumsy, primitive, rough, unskilful. 3 *crude language.* coarse, common, improper, indecent, rude, vulgar.

cruel *a cruel action, a cruel person.* atrocious, barbaric, beastly, blood-thirsty, bloody, brutal, callous, cold-blooded, ferocious, fierce, hard, hard-hearted, harsh, heartless, inhuman, merciless, murderous, pitiless, relentless, ruthless, sadistic, savage, severe, stern, tyrannical, unfeeling, unjust, unkind, vicious, violent.

cruise *to go on a cruise.* holiday, journey, sail, voyage. SEE ALSO **travel**.

cruiser SEE **vessel**.

crumb *a crumb of bread.* bit, fragment, particle, scrap, speck.

crumble *The road surface is crumbling.* to break up, to disintegrate.

crumple *Don't crumple the clothes I've just ironed!* to crease, to crush, to dent, to fold, to wrinkle.

crunch 1 *The monster crunched his victim in his massive jaws.* to break, to chew, to crush, to munch, to smash, to squash. 2 *We heard the crunch of their feet on the gravel.* SEE **sound**.

crusade *a crusade against drinking and driving.* campaign, struggle, war.

crush 1 *He crushed his finger in the door.* to break, to crumple, to crunch, to grind, to jam, to mangle, to mash, to pound, to press, to pulp, to smash, to squash, to squeeze. 2 *We crushed their best team.* to conquer, to defeat, to overcome, to overpower, to overthrow, to overwhelm, to rout, to subdue, (informal) to thrash.

crust *the crust of a loaf, the crust of the earth.* outside, rind, skin.

crutch *The lame man needed a crutch.* prop, support.

cry 1 *Baby cries when she's tired.* to blubber, to grizzle, to shed tears, to snivel, to sob, to wail, to weep. 2 *Who cried out?* to bawl, to call, to exclaim, to scream, to shout, to yell.

crypt *the church crypt.* basement, cellar, vault. SEE ALSO **church**.

crystal *a crystal ball.* glass.

cub SEE **young**.

cube SEE **shape**.

cubicle *Do you know if there are any changing cubicles at the swimming-baths?* booth, compartment, kiosk.

cuckoo SEE **bird**.

cucumber SEE **salad, vegetable**.

cuddle *Baby loves to cuddle her mother.* to caress, to embrace, to fondle, to huddle against, to hug, to kiss, to nestle against, to snuggle against.

cudgel *The bandits were armed with cudgels.* baton, cane, club, stick.

cue *In our nativity play, Logan missed the cue for him to come on.* reminder, sign, signal.

cuff 1 (informal) to clout, to knock, to slap, to smack, to swipe. SEE ALSO **hit**. **2** *the cuffs of a shirt.* SEE **clothes**.

cul-de-sac SEE **road**.

culprit *Have they caught the culprit yet?* offender, trouble-maker, wrongdoer. SEE ALSO **criminal**.

cultivate *to cultivate the land, to cultivate crops.* to farm, to grow, to produce, to raise.

cultivated *a cultivated person.* courteous, cultured, educated, well-bred. SEE ALSO **polite**.

cultivation agriculture, farming, gardening.

cultural *cultural pursuits.* civilizing, educational, high-brow, improving, intellectual.

culture *a nation's culture.* art, background, education, learning.

cultured *a cultured person.* civilized, cultivated, educated, well-bred.

cumbersome *a cumbersome machine.* awkward, heavy, unwieldy.

cunning *a cunning trick.* artful, astute, clever, crafty, ingenious, knowing, skilful, sly, tricky, wily.

cup 1 SEE **drink**. **2** *Lucy won a cup on sports day.* award, prize, trophy.

cupboard SEE **furniture**.

cup-tie SEE **sport**.

cur dog, mongrel.

curate SEE **church**.

curator SEE **job**.

curb *I don't want to curb your enthusiasm, but please be a little quieter.* to check, to control, to hamper, to hinder, to hold back, to limit, to restrain.

curdle *curdled milk.* to clot, to go sour.

cure 1 *Can they cure arthritis?* to heal, to remedy. **2** *Dad cured that nasty noise in the car.* to correct, to put right, to rectify. **3** *Is there a cure for the common cold?* medicine, remedy, therapy, treatment. **4** SEE **medicine**.

curious 1 *Our cat was curious about the puppy.* inquisitive, interested, nosey, prying. **2** *There's a curious smell in here.* abnormal, odd, peculiar, queer, strange, unusual.

curl to bend, to coil, to loop, to turn, to twist, to wind.

curlew SEE **bird**.

currant SEE **fruit**.

currency SEE **money**.

current 1 *Beware of currents in the water.* flow, stream, tide, undertow. **2** *What do you think of current fashions?* contemporary, fashionable, modern, present, prevailing, up-to-date.

curry SEE **food**.

curse 1 *He let out a curse.* exclamation, oath, swear-word. **2** *Logan's dad cursed us for waking him.* to damn, to swear at.

cursor SEE **computer**.

cursory *The mechanic only gave the car a cursory inspection.* hasty, hurried, quick.

curt *His curt answer showed he was in a bad mood.* abrupt, rude, short.

curtail *They had to curtail their holiday when Mrs Brunswick was ill.* to break off, to cut, to shorten.

curtain *Close the curtains.* blind, drape, screen.

curtsy *She curtsied to acknowledge the applause.* to bend, to bow.

curve 1 arc, arch, bend, curl, loop, turn, twist. **2** *curved:* arched, bowed, crescent, curled, looped, twisted.

cushion bolster, pillow. SEE ALSO **furniture**.

custard SEE **food**.

custodian *the custodian of the museum.* guardian, keeper, warder.

custom *It's our custom to take flowers when we visit friends.* convention, habit, institution, practice, routine, tradition.

customary *Every Friday, the Brunswicks have their customary fish and chips.* accustomed, common, conventional, habitual, normal, ordinary, regular, traditional.

customer buyer, client.

customs *customs duty.* duty, tax.

cut 1 VARIOUS WAYS TO CUT THINGS ARE to amputate, to carve, to chisel, to chop, to clip, to crop, to gash, to grate, to guillotine, to hack, to hew, to lop, to mince, to mow, to nick, to prune, to saw, to scalp, to sever, to shave, to shear, to shred, to slash, to slice, to slit, to snip, to split, to stab, to trim. **2** *Mrs Angel cut the story as it was too long.* to abbreviate, to abridge, to censor, to shorten. **3** *I was talking to granny on the phone, but we were cut off.* to interrupt, to stop, to terminate. **4** *a cut on the finger.* gash, injury, nick, notch, slash, slit, tear, wound.

cute SEE **attractive, clever.**

cutlass SEE **weapon.**

cutlery 1 ITEMS OF CUTLERY ARE bread-knife, carving knife, dessert-spoon, fork, knife, ladle, spoon, tablespoon, teaspoon. **2** SEE **kitchen.**

cutlet SEE **meat.**

cut-price cheap, inexpensive.

cutter SEE **vessel.**

cutting 1 *a railway cutting.* SEE **railway. 2** *plant cuttings.* SEE **plant.**

cycle 1 KINDS OF CYCLE ARE bicycle, (informal) bike, moped, (informal) motor bike, motor cycle, penny-farthing, scooter, tandem, tricycle. SEE ALSO **travel, vehicle. 2** *a cycle of events.* sequence, series.

cyclone hurricane, storm, tempest, tornado, typhoon. SEE ALSO **weather.**

cygnet SEE **young.**

cylinder SEE **shape.**

cymbal SEE **percussion.**

cypress SEE **tree.**

D d

dab SEE **touch.**

dachshund SEE **dog.**

daddy-long-legs SEE **insect.**

daffodil SEE **bulb, flower.**

dagger SEE **weapon.**

dainty *dainty embroidery.* delicate, exquisite, fine, neat, pretty.

dairy SEE **shop.**

daisy SEE **flower.**

dale *Yorkshire Dales.* glen, valley.

dally *Don't dally: we must move on.* to dawdle, to hang about, to linger, to loaf, to loiter.

Dalmatian SEE **dog.**

dam *They built a dam across the stream.* bank, barrage, barrier, dike, embankment, wall, weir.

damage 1 *Did it cause any damage?* destruction, devastation, havoc, injury, sabotage. **2** *Did the accident damage the car?* to break, to chip, to cripple, to dent, to destroy, to harm, to hurt, to immobilize, to injure, to mar, to scratch, to spoil, to strain, to wound.

dame 1 SEE **woman. 2** SEE **title.**

damn to condemn, to curse.

damp *The spare room feels damp.* clammy, dank, humid, moist.

dampen to moisten.

damson SEE **fruit.**

dance 1 *We danced for joy.* to caper, to jig about, to jump about, to leap, to prance, to skip. **2** KINDS OF DANCING ARE disco dancing, hornpipe, jig, limbo dancing, minuet, reel, tap-dancing, waltz. **3** *Lucy went to a dance.* ball, disco, party, social.

dancer SEE **entertainment.**

dandelion SEE **flower.**

dandruff SEE **illness.**

danger 1 *There's a danger of catching cold in this weather.* chance, possibility, risk, threat. **2** *Astronauts are always facing danger.* crisis, distress, hazard, peril, pitfall, trouble.

dangerous 1 *a dangerous journey.* chancy, hazardous, perilous, precarious, risky, unsafe. 2 *a dangerous lion.* destructive, harmful, treacherous. 3 *a dangerous criminal.* desperate, violent.

dangle *The rope dangled just above his head.* to be suspended, to droop, to hang, to sway, to swing.

dank clammy, damp, moist.

dare 1 *Would you dare to jump off that rock?* to risk, to venture. 2 *Logan dared Tony to eat four ice-creams.* to challenge, to defy.

daring *a daring explorer, a daring feat, etc.* adventurous, bold, brave, fearless, intrepid.

dark 1 *a dark place, a dark sky, etc.* black, dim, gloomy, murky, shadowy, shady, sombre, starless, sunless, unlit. 2 *dark hair.* black, brown, brunette. 3 *a dark complexion.* swarthy, tanned.

darken *The sky darkened.* to blacken.

darling beloved, dear, love, sweetheart.

darn *Tony darned the hole in his jumper.* to mend, to patch, to repair, to sew, to stitch.

dart 1 *to play darts.* SEE **game**. 2 *to dart about.* SEE **move**.

dash 1 *He dashed his foot against a rock.* to beat, to smash, to strike. SEE ALSO **hit**. 2 *Lucy dashed home.* to hasten, to hurry, to run, to rush, to speed, (informal) to zoom. SEE ALSO **move**.

data *Feed the data into the computer.* evidence, facts, information, statistics.

date 1 SEE **time**. 2 *Lucy has a date with a friend.* appointment, engagement, fixture, meeting, rendezvous. 3 *Do you like dates?* SEE **fruit**.

daughter SEE **family**.

daunt *The steepness of the climb daunted us.* to discourage, to dishearten, to dismay, to frighten, to intimidate, to put off.

dawdle *Don't dawdle: we haven't got all day.* to be slow, to dally, to hang about, to lag behind, to linger, to straggle.

dawn day-break, sunrise.

day SEE **time**.

day-break dawn, sunrise.

day-dream dream, fantasy, illusion, reverie.

daylight SEE **light**.

dazed *The blow dazed him.* amazed, bewildered, confused, shocked, stunned.

dazzle SEE **light**.

deacon, deaconess SEE **church**.

dead 1 *the dead king.* deceased, late. 2 *Is that fish dead?* killed, lifeless. 3 *It's so cold my fingers are dead.* deadened, numb, paralysed.

deaden *The silencer deadens the noise of the engine.* to muffle, to quieten, to soften, to stifle, to suppress.

deadly *a deadly illness.* fatal, lethal, mortal, terminal.

deaf SEE **handicap**.

deafening *a deafening roar.* loud, noisy.

deal 1 *Deal the cards.* to allot, to distribute, to divide, to give out, to share out. 2 *Mrs Angel dealt with the problem.* to attend to, to control, to cope with, to grapple with, to handle, to look after, to manage, to sort out, to tackle. 3 *I want a book that deals with insects.* to be concerned with, to cover. 4 *Dad made a deal with the garage about his new car.* agreement, bargain, contract, pact, settlement, understanding. 5 *They went to a great deal of trouble.* amount, quantity, volume.

dealer *If you have a complaint, take the goods back to your dealer.* merchant, retailer, shopkeeper, stockist, supplier, trader.

dean SEE **church**.

dear 1 *dear friends.* beloved, darling, loved. 2 *dear goods.* costly, expensive, (informal) pricey.

death decease, end, passing. SEE ALSO **funeral, kill**.

debate 1 *We debated whether to go to the*

pictures. to argue, to discuss, to dispute. 2 *We had a debate about cruelty to animals.* argument, conference, controversy, discussion, dispute.

debris *The debris of the aircraft was scattered over a wide area.* fragments, remains, rubble, ruins, wreckage.

decade SEE **time.**

decapitate to behead. SEE ALSO **kill.**

decathlon SEE **athletics.**

decay *Meat decays quickly in warm weather.* to decompose, to deteriorate, to disintegrate, to go bad, to perish, to rot, to spoil.

deceased *the deceased king.* dead, late.

deceit *We saw through his deceit.* deception, dishonesty, fraud, hoax, pretence, ruse, trickery, untruthfulness.

deceitful *a deceitful person.* dishonest, false, furtive, lying, secretive, shifty, sneaky, treacherous, unfaithful, untrustworthy.

deceive *He tried to deceive us, but we discovered the truth.* to be an impostor, to bluff, to cheat, to defraud, to dupe, to fool, to hoax, to hoodwink, to kid, to lie, to mislead, to outwit, to pretend, to swindle, to take in, to trick.

decent 1 *decent behaviour.* becoming, chaste, good, honourable, law-abiding, modest, proper, respectable. 2 *a decent meal.* agreeable, nice, pleasant, satisfactory.

deception *We soon discovered the deception.* deceit, dishonesty, fraud, hoax, pretence, ruse, trickery.

deceptive *When you look into the pool, you get a deceptive impression of the depth.* deceiving, false, misleading, unreliable.

decide 1 *Have you decided what to say?* to conclude, to fix on, to resolve, to settle. 2 *We decided on fish and chips.* to choose, to elect, to opt for, to pick, to select.

decided *He is very decided in his opinions.* adamant, determined, firm, resolute.

deciduous SEE **tree.**

decimal *decimal scales.* metric.

decipher *I can't decipher his writing.* to decode, to interpret, to make out, to read, to understand.

decision *After all that talking, what was your decision?* conclusion, judgement, outcome, result.

deck *the deck of a ship.* floor, level. SEE ALSO **vessel.**

declare *He declared that he would never play again.* to announce, to assert, to contend, to emphasize, to insist, to maintain, to proclaim, to pronounce, to report, to reveal, to state, to testify.

decline 1 *Logan declined the invitation to Tony's party.* to refuse, to reject, to turn down. 2 *Their enthusiasm declined after a while.* to decrease, to degenerate, to deteriorate, to die, to diminish, to fail, to flag, to lessen, to sink, to weaken, to wilt, to worsen.

decode *We tried to decode their signal.* to decipher, to explain, to interpret, to understand.

decompose *The dead bird had begun to decompose.* to decay, to disintegrate, to go bad, to perish, to rot.

decorate 1 *We decorated the church with flowers.* to adorn, to make beautiful. 2 *Mr Brunswick decorated Tony's room.* to paint, to paper. 3 *The soldier was decorated for bravery.* to honour, to reward.

decoration 1 *Christmas decorations.* adornment, ornament. 2 *a decoration for bravery.* award, badge, medal.

decorator painter. SEE ALSO **job.**

decoy *We had to decoy Logan away from the sweet stall.* to bait, to entice, to lure, to tempt.

decrease 1 *They ought to decrease the bus fares for a change.* to cut, to lessen, to lower, to reduce. 2 *The number of children in our school decreased this term.* to contract, to decline, to diminish, to dwindle, to fall, to lessen, to shrink, to wane.

decree 1 *an official decree.* command, declaration, order, proclamation. 2 *The government decreed that income tax would go up.* to command, to declare, to direct, to order, to proclaim.

decrepit *a decrepit old building.* broken down, derelict, dilapidated, old, ramshackle, worn out.

dedicated 1 *Mrs Brunswick was a dedicated fan of the Beatles.* devoted, faithful, loyal. 2 *This part of the church is dedicated to private prayer.* devoted to, set aside for.

deduct *Mr Brunswick threatened to deduct £1 from Lucy's pocket-money.* to subtract, to take away.

deed 1 *a heroic deed.* act, action, adventure, exploit, feat. 2 *the deeds of a house.* documents, papers, records.

deep 1 *deep feelings.* earnest, intense, profound, serious, sincere. 2 *a deep conversation.* intellectual, learned, thoughtful. 3 *a deep colour.* dark, strong. 4 *a deep note.* base, low. 5 *deep snow.* thick.

deer SEE **animal**.

deface *Vandals defaced the statue.* to disfigure, to mar, to spoil.

defeat *to defeat an enemy.* to beat, to conquer, to crush, to destroy, (informal) to flatten, (informal) to lick, to master, to outdo, to overcome, to overpower, to overthrow, to overwhelm, to rout, to subdue, to suppress, to thrash, to triumph over, to vanquish.

defect 1 *a defect in a piece of work, a defect in a person's character.* blemish, failing, fault, flaw, imperfection, mark, spot, stain, weakness. 2 *The traitor defected to the enemy's side.* to desert, to go over.

defective *Our TV set was defective.* faulty, imperfect, out of order.

defence 1 *When you accused him, what was his defence?* excuse, explanation, justification. 2 *We built a defence against the cold wind.* guard, protection, shelter, shield.

defend 1 *They did what they could to defend their homes from the hurricane.* to fortify, to guard, to keep safe, to protect, to safeguard, to shelter, to shield. 2 *He defended himself before the*

judge. to speak up for, to stand up for, to support.

defer *We deferred the match until the weather got better.* to adjourn, to delay, to postpone, to put off.

defiant *Logan was defiant when Mrs Angel told him to clear up.* disobedient, mutinous, obstinate, rebellious, unyielding.

deficient *Their diet is deficient in vitamins.* lacking, scarce, short.

defile 1 *We thought the sewage works might defile our water supply.* to contaminate, to corrupt, to infect, to poison, to pollute, to soil. 2 *The horsemen rode down the steep path into the defile.* canyon, gorge, pass, ravine, valley.

define *A thesaurus simply lists words, whereas a dictionary defines them.* to clarify, to explain.

definite 1 *Mrs Brunswick has definite views about where to go on holiday.* assured, certain, confident, fixed, positive, settled, sure. 2 *We saw a definite improvement in granny's health.* clear, distinct, noticeable, obvious, plain, pronounced.

deformed *a deformed tree.* disfigured, distorted, grotesque, mis-shapen, twisted, ugly, warped.

defraud *He's in court because he tried to defraud the bank.* to cheat, to dupe, to swindle, to trick.

defrost to de-ice, to unfreeze.

deft *deft movements.* agile, clever, nimble, quick, skilful.

defy 1 *It isn't wise to defy the head.* to confront, to disobey, to face up to, to resist, to stand up to. 2 *I defy you to come any further.* to challenge, to dare.

degenerate *The sick man's condition degenerated.* to decline, to deteriorate, to sink, to weaken, to worsen.

degree 1 SEE **measure**. 2 *Lucy's cousin got a degree at Trent Polytechnic.* SEE **qualification**.

dehydrated *dehydrated food.* dried, dry.

de-ice *to de-ice the fridge.* to defrost, to unfreeze.

deity *Ancient tribes worshipped many deities.* divinity, god, goddess.

dejected *Tony was dejected when he didn't get into the swimming team.* crestfallen, depressed, discouraged, downcast, down-hearted, gloomy, melancholy, unhappy. SEE ALSO **sad**.

delay 1 *The snow delayed the traffic.* to detain, to hinder, to hold up, to keep, to obstruct, to slow down. 2 *We delayed the start of our journey.* to defer, to postpone, to put off. 3 *Don't delay if you want to catch that bus.* to hang back, to hesitate, to pause, to stall, to wait.

delete *Lucy was away ill, so we deleted her name from the list.* to cancel, to cross out, to erase, to remove, to wipe out.

deliberate 1 *a deliberate insult.* calculated, conscious, intentional, planned, premeditated, wilful. 2 *deliberate planning.* careful, cautious, methodical, painstaking, slow.

deliberately *He hit me deliberately.* intentionally, purposely.

delicacy SEE **food**.

delicate 1 *delicate material.* dainty, exquisite, fine, flimsy, fragile, frail, soft, tender. 2 *delicate health.* feeble, sickly, unhealthy, weak. 3 *delicate machinery.* intricate, sensitive. 4 *a delicate flavour.* faint, gentle, mild, subtle.

delicatessen SEE **shop**.

delicious appetizing, luscious, tasty. SEE ALSO **taste**.

delight 1 *The play delighted the children.* to amuse, to captivate, to charm, to enchant, to entertain, to entrance, to fascinate, to please, to thrill. 2 *Mum's greatest delight is a nice hot bath.* bliss, ecstasy, enjoyment, joy, pleasure, rapture.

delinquent *a juvenile delinquent.* criminal, culprit, hooligan, offender, wrongdoer.

delirious *Lucy was delirious with joy when she got in the county team.* crazy, demented, excited, frantic, frenzied, hysterical, mad, wild.

deliver *to deliver letters.* to convey, to distribute, to give out, to hand over, to present, to take round.

delivery *The greengrocer has a fresh delivery of vegetables each day.* batch, consignment.

delta SEE **geography**.

delude *Logan deliberately tried to delude us.* to deceive, to fool, to hoax, to mislead.

deluge *We got soaked in the deluge.* downpour, flood, rainstorm.

delusion *The boy who said he met a Martian must have suffered a delusion.* hallucination, illusion.

demand *He demanded to have his money back.* to ask, to beg, to claim, to command, to order, to request, to require.

demented *The dog was demented when the wasp stung him.* berserk, crazy, delirious, deranged, frantic, frenzied, insane, lunatic, mad, wild.

demerara SEE **sugar**.

democracy SEE **country, government**.

Democrat SEE **politics**.

demolish *They demolished a block of old flats.* to destroy, to dismantle, to knock down, to raze.

demon devil, imp, spirit.

demonstrate 1 *The local garage demonstrated a new car.* to display, to exhibit, to show. 2 *She demonstrated how to make a cake.* to describe, to explain, to illustrate, to show. 3 *They demonstrated that smoking does affect your health.* to establish, to prove. 4 *We demonstrated against experiments on live animals.* to march, to protest.

demonstration 1 *a cookery demonstration.* display, exhibition, presentation, show. 2 *a political demonstration.* demo, march, protest, rally.

demure *a demure expression.* bashful, coy, modest, quiet, retiring, shy.

den *We made a den in the garden.* hideout, hiding-place, lair.

denim SEE **cloth**.

denounce *At the end of the play, the detective denounced the murderer.* to accuse, to blame, to complain about, to condemn, to inform against, to report, to reveal, to tell of.

dense 1 *dense fog.* heavy, impenetrable, thick. **2** *a dense crowd.* packed, solid. **3** *a dense pupil.* dim, dull, foolish, obtuse, slow, stupid, (informal) thick, unintelligent.

dent *Dad dented the wing of the car.* to bend, to buckle, to crumple, to knock in.

dentist SEE **job, medicine**.

denture SEE **tooth**.

deny 1 *Do you deny the accusation?* to contradict, to disclaim, to dispute, to reject. **2** *Within reason, grandad doesn't deny us anything.* to deprive of, to refuse.

deodorant SEE **cosmetics**.

depart *Are you ready to depart?* to embark, to emigrate, to go away, to leave, to quit, to set off, to set out.

department branch, part, section.

depend *Lucy depends on dad to drive her to the gym.* to bank on, to count on, to need, to rely on, to trust.

dependable *a dependable bus service, a dependable friend.* consistent, faithful, regular, reliable, safe, sound, steady, true, trustworthy.

depict *We depicted a snowy scene.* to describe, to draw, to illustrate, to paint, to picture, to portray, to represent, to show.

deplorable *deplorable behaviour.* regrettable, reprehensible, unfortunate. SEE ALSO **bad**.

deport *They used to deport people for stealing.* to banish, to exile, to expel, to send away.

depose *to depose a monarch.* to get rid of, to remove.

deposit 1 *Deposit your dirty plates by the hatch.* to leave, to place, to put down, to set down. **2** *I deposited some money in the building society.* to pay in, to save. **3** *There's a dirty deposit in the bottom of the cup.* dregs, sediment.

depot *The climbers established a depot at the foot of the mountain.* base, cache, dump, headquarters, hoard, store.

depraved *Only a depraved person would torture a fellow human being.* base, corrupt, evil, immoral, vicious, wicked. SEE ALSO **bad**.

depress 1 *His dog's death depressed him.* to dishearten, to grieve, to sadden. **2** *depressed*: dejected, desolate, despondent, disconsolate, gloomy, heart-broken, low, melancholy, miserable, mournful, unhappy, wretched. SEE ALSO **sad**. **3** *depressing*: black, discouraging, disheartening, dismal, gloomy, sombre, tragic. **4** SEE **sad**.

depression 1 *a mood of depression.* despair, gloom, hopelessness, melancholy, sadness. **2** SEE **weather**. **3** *a depression in the ground.* dent, dip, hollow.

deprive *Would a vegetarian deprive a dog of his bone?* to deny, to refuse, to rob, to take away.

deputy *The mayor was ill, so he sent a deputy.* assistant, replacement, reserve, representative, stand-in, substitute.

derailment accident, crash.

deranged *He was so odd that we thought he was deranged.* crazy, demented, insane, (informal) loony, lunatic, mad.

derelict *a derelict farmhouse.* abandoned, broken down, decrepit, deserted, dilapidated, forsaken, ruined, tumbledown.

derive *Grandpa derives a lot of pleasure from his garden.* to acquire, to get, to obtain, to procure, to receive.

dermatitis SEE **illness**.

derrick crane.

descant SEE **sing**.

descend to come doxwn, to climb down, to drop, to fall, to move down, to sink.

descendants heirs, offspring, posterity.

describe *An eyewitness described what happened.* to depict, to explain, to express, to narrate, to portray, to recount, to relate, to represent, to tell.

description account, commentary, depiction, narration, portrait, representation, sketch, story.

desert 1 *The camels crossed the desert.* wasteland, wilderness. 2 *a desert island.* barren, uninhabited, wild. 3 *Don't desert your friends.* to abandon, to forsake, to leave. 4 *They deserted him on an island.* to maroon, to strand. 5 *The soldiers deserted.* to defect, to run away.

deserter fugitive, outlaw, renegade, traitor.

deserve *Does he deserve a prize?* to earn, to merit.

design 1 *a design for a dress.* drawing, pattern, plan, sketch. 2 *Our car is an old design.* model, type, version. 3 *An architect designs buildings.* to draw, to plan, to plot, to scheme, to sketch.

designer SEE **job**.

desire 1 *What do you desire most?* to fancy, to hanker after, to long for, to want, to wish for, to yearn for. 2 *He stole because of his desire for money.* ambition, appetite, craving, hunger, itch, longing, love, lust, passion, thirst, urge, wish.

desk SEE **furniture**.

desolate 1 *The desolate house was haunted.* bleak, barren, deserted, dreary, empty, isolated, lonely, remote, windswept. 2 *He was desolate after his dog died.* depressed, forlorn, forsaken, neglected, unhappy, wretched. SEE ALSO **sad**.

despair *a state of despair.* depression, desperation, hopelessness.

desperado brigand, criminal, crook, gangster, gunman, ruffian.

desperate 1 *The shipwrecked sailors were desperate.* despairing, hopeless. 2 *a desperate situation.* bad, serious. 3 *a desperate criminal.* dangerous, reckless, violent.

despicable *a despicable crime.* base, contemptible, detestable, hateful.

despise *We sometimes despise people who can't do what we can.* to be contemptuous of, to detest, to disdain, to dislike, to hate, to look down on, to scorn, to sneer at.

despondent *Tony was despondent when he didn't get into the swimming team.* depressed, desolate, gloomy, melancholy, unhappy. SEE ALSO `sad`.

dessert SEE **meal**.

dessert-spoon SEE **cutlery**.

destination *This train's destination is London.* terminus.

destined *Logan's resolutions were destined to fail.* doomed, fated, intended.

destiny chance, doom, fate, fortune, luck, providence.

destitute 1 *destitute beggars.* deprived, homeless, impoverished, needy, penniless, poor, poverty-stricken. 2 *the destitute:* beggars, paupers, tramps, vagrants.

destroy WAYS TO DESTROY THINGS ARE to abolish, to annihilate, to crush, to demolish, to devastate, to dismantle, to eliminate, to end, to eradicate, to exterminate, to finish off, to flatten, to get rid of, to knock down, to raze, to ruin, to stamp out, to uproot, to wipe out, to wreck. SEE ALSO **defeat, kill**.

destroyer SEE **vessel**.

destruction *a scene of destruction.* damage, devastation, havoc.

destructive *destructive animals.* dangerous, harmful, violent.

detach *We helped dad detach the caravan from the car.* to disconnect, to divide, to part, to remove, to separate, to undo, to unfasten.

detached 1 *a detached house.* separate. 2 *a detached attitude.* disinterested, impartial, neutral, unbiased, unemotional, uninvolved, unprejudiced.

detail *The policeman noticed every detail.* circumstance, fact, feature, particular.

detain 1 *What detained you?* to delay, to hold up, to keep. 2 *The police detained* *the suspect.* to arrest, to capture, to confine, to gaol, to hold, to imprison.

detect *Did the garage detect anything wrong with the car?* to diagnose, to discern, to discover, to find, to identify, to notice, to observe, to sense.

detective SEE job, police.

detention SEE punishment.

deter *We put up a scarecrow to deter the birds.* to daunt, to discourage, to dismay, to hinder, to impede, to obstruct, to prevent.

detergent soap. SEE ALSO wash.

deteriorate *His health deteriorated in the winter.* to decay, to decline, to degenerate, to disintegrate, to get worse, to weaken, to worsen.

determination *Marathon runners show great determination.* courage, (informal) grit, (informal) guts, spirit, will.

determined *He was determined that he would succeed.* adamant, firm, resolute, resolved, strenuous.

detest *Our dog detests snow.* to despise, to dislike, to hate, to loathe.

detestable *a detestable crime.* contemptible, despicable, hateful, horrible, loathsome, odious. SEE ALSO unpleasant.

detonate *to detonate a bomb.* to blow up, to discharge, to explode, to fire, to let off, to set off.

detour diversion.

devastate *The hurricane devastated the town.* to demolish, to destroy, to flatten, to ravage, to wreck.

develop 1 *Lucy's technique in gymnastics is developing well.* to advance, to evolve, to improve, to move on, to progress. 2 *The local shop plans to develop next year.* to build up, to expand, to grow, to increase. 3 *Leave the apples on the tree to develop.* to age, to mature, to ripen. 4 *Your story starts well: you ought to develop it.* to amplify, to enlarge, to strengthen.

device *That tin-opener is a clever device.* appliance, contraption, contrivance,

gadget, implement, instrument, invention, machine, tool, utensil.

devil demon, fiend, imp, spirit.

devious 1 *We came home by a devious route.* indirect, roundabout. 2 *You can't always trust Logan: he can be very devious.* deceitful, dishonest, sly, sneaky, wily.

devise *Logan says he's devising a scheme to make lots of money!* to concoct, to design, to invent, to make up, to plan, to think up.

devoted *That dog is Tony's devoted companion.* constant, dedicated, devout, enthusiastic, faithful, loving, loyal, reliable.

devour *The lions devoured the meat greedily.* to consume, to gobble, to gulp. SEE ALSO eat.

devout *a devout worshipper.* committed, dedicated, devoted, genuine, religious, sincere.

dew SEE weather.

dhow SEE vessel.

diabetes SEE illness.

diabolical *diabolical behaviour.* devilish, fiendish, hellish.

diadem coronet, crown. SEE ALSO hat.

diagnose *The doctor diagnosed mumps.* to detect, to find, to identify.

diagram chart, graph, figure, plan, outline, sketch.

dial *Did you dial the right number?* to call, to phone, to ring, to telephone.

dialect *a London dialect, a northern dialect.* accent, brogue, language.

dialogue *The play contained a funny dialogue between a giant and an elf.* conversation, discussion, talk.

diamond 1 *a diamond ring.* SEE jewellery. 2 SEE shape. 3 *the ace of diamonds.* SEE cards.

diarrhoea SEE illness.

diary *Lucy writes a diary every day.* journal, log, record. SEE ALSO book.

dice SEE game.

dictator SEE ruler.

dictatorial *He's very dictatorial and*

won't let us say anything. bossy, domineering, tyrannical.

dictatorship SEE **country, government.**

dictionary SEE **book.**

die 1 *All mortal creatures must die.* to expire, to pass away, to perish. **2** *Our enthusiasm began to die after a while.* to decline, to decrease, to fail, to lessen, to stop, to weaken.

diesel SEE **engine.**

diet *You need a good diet to keep healthy.* food, nourishment.

differ 1 *I wonder how our school differs from the one granny went to?* to contrast with. **2** *We often differ about what to watch on TV.* to argue, to disagree, to quarrel.

difference 1 *What's the difference between the cheap jeans and the expensive ones?* comparison, contrast, distinction. **2** *We told Logan to stop messing about, but it didn't make any difference.* alteration, change, modification. **3** *There was a difference between Tony and Lucy about what to watch on TV.* argument, disagreement, quarrel.

different 1 *Have the chocolates got different centres?* assorted, contrasting, dissimilar, miscellaneous, mixed, unlike, varied, various. **2** *Everyone's handwriting is different.* distinct, particular, personal, separate, special, specific, unique. **3** *Tony and Lucy have different views about music.* conflicting, contradictory, incompatible, opposite.

difficult 1 *a difficult problem.* advanced, complicated, hard, thorny, ticklish, tricky. **2** *a difficult climb.* arduous, laborious, strenuous, tough.

difficulty *Have you got a difficulty?* adversity, complication, dilemma, fix, hardship, hindrance, jam, obstacle, plight, predicament, problem, snag, trouble.

dig *to dig a hole.* to burrow, to excavate, to gouge out, to hollow out, to mine, to scoop, to tunnel.

digest SEE **eat.**

digit figure, integer, number, numeral.

dignified *a dignified ceremony.* calm, elegant, formal, grave, noble, proper, sedate, serious, sober, solemn, stately, tasteful.

dike 1 *They dug a dike across the marsh.* channel, ditch. **2** *They built a dike as a defence against flooding.* dam, embankment.

dilapidated *a dilapidated old building.* broken down, decrepit, derelict, ramshackle, rickety, ruined, tumbledown.

dilemma *Tony was in a dilemma because he was invited to two parties on the same day.* difficulty, fix, jam, plight, predicament, problem.

diligent *a diligent worker.* careful, conscientious, earnest, hardworking, persevering, scrupulous, thorough.

dilute *You dilute orange squash with water.* to thin, to water down, to weaken.

dim 1 *We saw a dim outline in the mist.* blurred, cloudy, dark, faint, gloomy, hazy, indistinct, misty, murky, obscure, shadowy, unclear. **2** (informal) *You are dim if you can't understand that!* dense, dull, foolish, obtuse, slow, stupid, (informal) thick.

dimensions *If you're having a new carpet, we need to know the dimensions of your bedroom.* magnitude, measurements, proportions, size, volume.

diminish *Our supply of sweets diminished rather quickly.* to contract, to decline, to reduce, to shrink, to subside.

diminutive *We saw a diminutive figure in the distance.* little, miniature, minute, short, small, (informal) teeny, tiny, undersized, wee.

din *We were deafened by the din.* bedlam, clamour, commotion, hubbub, hullabaloo, noise, pandemonium, racket, row, rumpus, shouting, tumult, uproar.

dine SEE **eat.**

dinghy SEE **vessel.**

dingy *This room is dingy: it needs*

decorating. depressing, dirty, dismal, drab, dull, gloomy, grimy.

dining-room SEE **house**.

dinner banquet, feast. SEE ALSO **meal**.

dinosaur SEE **animal**.

dip 1 *to dip in water.* to dive, to drop, to immerse, to lower, to plunge, to submerge. 2 *a dip in the sea.* plunge, swim. 3 *a dip in the ground.* dent, depression, hollow.

diphtheria SEE **illness**.

diploma *Tony got a diploma in the swimming gala.* award, certificate. SEE ALSO **qualification**.

diplomat ambassador, consul, representative.

diplomatic *Lucy was diplomatic about not wanting to go to granny's.* discreet, polite, tactful.

dire *a dire calamity.* appalling, awful, calamitous, dreadful, serious, terrible. SEE ALSO **bad**.

direct 1 *a direct line.* straight, unswerving. 2 *a direct answer.* blunt, candid, frank, honest, outspoken, plain, straight, straightforward, uncomplicated. 3 *Can you direct me to the station?* to guide, to indicate, to show. 4 *Their guns were directed at us.* to aim, to point, to turn. 5 *The head directed us to come in.* to command, to instruct, to order, to tell. 6 *The fireman directed the rescue.* to administer, to command, to control, to govern, to manage, to regulate, to supervise.

director *the director of a business.* administrator, boss, captain, controller, executive, governor, head, manager, overseer, ruler, supervisor.

directory *a telephone directory.* catalogue, index, list, register.

dirge SEE **music**.

dirt dust, filth, grime, (informal) muck, mud, pollution.

dirty 1 *a dirty room, dirty shoes, etc.* dingy, dusty, filthy, foul, grimy, grubby, messy, (informal) mucky, muddy, soiled, sooty, sordid, squalid, unclean. 2 *dirty language.*

coarse, crude, improper, indecent, obscene, offensive, rude, smutty, vulgar.

disable 1 to damage, to weaken. 2 *disabled*: crippled, handicapped, lame, maimed.

disadvantage *It's a disadvantage to be short if you play basketball.* drawback, handicap, hindrance, inconvenience.

disagree *Logan disagrees with nearly everything we say.* to argue, to differ, to quarrel.

disagreeable *a disagreeable remark, a disagreeable smell, etc.* distasteful, nasty, offensive, rude, unfriendly. SEE ALSO **unpleasant**.

disagreement *Was there any disagreement about Tony playing in goal?* argument, controversy, debate, dispute, opposition, quarrel.

disappear *The fog disappeared quickly.* to clear, to dwindle, to evaporate, to fade, to melt away, to pass, to vanish.

disappointed *We were disappointed when our team lost.* crestfallen, dejected, discontented, dissatisfied, downcast, down-hearted, let down, unhappy. SEE ALSO **sad**.

disapproval *Mrs Angel showed her disapproval of our behaviour.* censure, condemnation, criticism, dissatisfaction, reprimand, reproach.

disaster 1 *We had a disaster when our water pipes burst last winter.* accident, calamity, catastrophe, fiasco, mishap. 2 VARIOUS DISASTERS ARE air crash, avalanche, derailment, earthquake, flood, landslide, road accident, shipwreck, tidal wave, volcanic eruption.

disbelieving *Dad was disbelieving when I said I didn't want any pocket-money.* incredulous, sceptical.

disc 1 circle, counter, token. 2 *Do you buy discs or cassettes?* album, LP, single. SEE ALSO **record**. 3 *a disc drive.* SEE **computer**.

discard *It's time we discarded these old comics.* to dispose of, to dump, to eliminate, to get rid of, to reject, to scrap, to shed, to throw away.

discern *We discerned a change in the weather.* to detect, to distinguish, to mark, to notice, to observe, to perceive, to recognize, to see, to spy, to understand.

discharge 1 *The judge discharged him.* to acquit, to excuse, to free, to let off, to liberate. 2 *His boss discharged him because he was lazy.* to dismiss, to fire, to sack. 3 *to discharge a gun.* to detonate, to fire, to shoot. 4 *The chimney discharged black smoke.* to belch, to eject, to emit, to expel, to give out, to release, to send out.

disciple admirer, apostle, follower.

discipline *Usually the discipline in our class is good.* control, management, obedience, order, system.

disclaim *Everyone disclaimed responsibility for the broken window.* to deny, to disown, to renounce.

disclose *Whatever you do, don't disclose our secret to anyone!* to bare, to betray, to divulge, to expose, to make known, to reveal, to uncover.

disco SEE **entertainment**.

discolour *The spilt acid discoloured the table.* to bleach, to stain, to tarnish, to tinge.

discomfort *Tony hates the discomfort of wearing new shoes.* ache, distress, pain, soreness, uncomfortableness, uneasiness.

disconsolate *Tony was disconsolate when his dog disappeared.* desolate, despondent, gloomy, melancholy, unhappy. SEE ALSO **sad**.

discontented *How can we cheer up this discontented crowd?* disappointed, disgruntled, displeased, dissatisfied, miserable, unhappy. SEE ALSO **sad**.

discontinue *They discontinued the Sunday bus service.* to cease, to end, to finish, to stop, to terminate.

discord 1 *Was there any discord, or did you all agree?* argument, conflict, disagreement, dispute, quarrelling. 2 SEE **music**.

discount *Did you pay the full price, or did they give you a discount?* concession, reduction.

discourage *The climbers were discouraged by the bad weather.* to daunt, to deter, to dishearten, to dismay, to dissuade, to frighten, to intimidate, to put off, to scare.

discourteous *It was discourteous to go into Mrs Wilson's garden without asking.* bad-mannered, cheeky, disrespectful, impertinent, impolite, impudent, insolent, rude, uncouth.

discover *We were in the library seeing what we could discover about dinosaurs.* to come across, to detect, to explore, to find out, to identify, to learn, to locate, to notice, to observe, to perceive, to reveal, to search out, to track down, to uncover, to unearth.

discoverer creator, explorer, inventor.

discreet *Could you ask a few discreet questions about what mum wants for her birthday?* careful, diplomatic, polite, prudent, tactful.

discretion *You showed great discretion in choosing those nice colours.* good sense, judgement.

discriminate 1 *Can you discriminate between instant coffee and ground coffee?* to distinguish, to tell apart. 2 *It is wrong to discriminate against people because of their religion or colour or sex.* to be biased, to be intolerant, to be prejudiced, to show favouritism.

discrimination *racial discrimination.* bias, favouritism, intolerance, prejudice, racialism, racism.

discus SEE **athletics**.

discuss *Let's discuss the problem.* to argue about, to consider, to debate, to examine, to talk about.

discussion argument, conversation, debate, dialogue, talk.

disdain *That cat's too fussy: he disdains everything we give him.* to despise, to dislike, to look down on, to scorn, to snub.

disdainful *a disdainful smile.* arrogant, contemptuous, haughty, proud, scornful, snobbish, stuck-up.

disease *to suffer from a disease.*
affliction, ailment, blight, (informal)
bug, complaint, disorder, infection,
infirmity, malady, sickness. SEE
ALSO **illness**.

disembark *to disembark from a ship.* to
go ashore, to land.

disentangle *to disentangle a piece of
string.* to untie, to untwist.

disfigured *He was disfigured in the fire.*
defaced, deformed, scarred.

disgrace 1 *If you do something wrong,
you suffer the disgrace of being punished.*
dishonour, embarrassment,
humiliation, shame. 2 *The way that
man treats his dog is a disgrace!* outrage,
scandal.

disgraceful *disgraceful behaviour.*
dishonourable, embarrassing,
humiliating, shameful.

disgruntled *A disgruntled old gentleman
complained about the food.* bad-
tempered, cross, discontented,
dissatisfied, grumpy.

disguise 1 *The bird-watchers disguised
their hide-out.* to camouflage, to
conceal, to cover up, to hide, to
mask. 2 *to disguise yourself as*: to
counterfeit, to dress up as, to pretend
to be.

disgust 1 *He couldn't hide his disgust for
the rotten food.* aversion, contempt,
dislike, hatred, loathing, revulsion.
2 *The rotten food disgusted him.* to
appal, to horrify, to nauseate, to
offend, to repel, to revolt, to shock, to
sicken. 3 *disgusting*: SEE **unpleasant**.

dish basin, bowl, plate. SEE ALSO
container.

dishearten *They were disheartened by
losing four games in a row.* to depress,
to deter, to discourage, to dismay, to
put off, to sadden.

dishevelled *dishevelled hair.*
bedraggled, messy, scruffy, tangled,
uncombed, unkempt, untidy.

dishonest cheating, corrupt, criminal, crooked, deceitful, deceptive,
false, fraudulent, insincere, lying,
misleading, underhand,
unscrupulous, untrustworthy.

dishonour disgrace, shame.

dishwasher SEE **kitchen**.

disinclined *As we couldn't see any shops,
we were disinclined to walk any further.*
hesitant, reluctant, unwilling.

disinfect *When Lucy had measles, Mrs
Brunswick disinfected all her things.* to
purify, to sterilize.

disintegrate *The wrecked ship soon
disintegrated.* to break up, to crumble,
to decay, to degenerate, to
deteriorate, to fall apart, to shatter,
to smash up.

disinterested *A referee is supposed to be
disinterested.* detached, impartial,
neutral, unbiased, uninvolved,
unprejudiced.

disjointed *I didn't like that programme:
the story seemed disjointed.* broken up,
confused, incoherent, jumbled,
mixed up, muddled.

dislike 1 *I dislike shopping.* to despise,
to detest, to hate, to loathe, to scorn.
2 *He couldn't hide his dislike.* aversion,
contempt, disgust, distaste, hatred,
loathing, revulsion.

disloyal *a disloyal friend.* treacherous,
unfaithful.

disloyalty *We found it hard to forgive his
disloyalty.* betrayal, infidelity,
treachery, treason, unfaithfulness.

dismal *Our garden looks dismal in the
winter.* bleak, cheerless, depressing,
dingy, dreary, gloomy, sombre. SEE
ALSO **sad**.

dismantle *They dismantled the old
factory chimney.* to demolish, to take
down.

dismay 1 *He realized with dismay that
the brakes were not working.* alarm,
anxiety, consternation, dread, fear,
horror. 2 *They were dismayed to see a
rhinoceros charging towards them.* to
alarm, to appal, to daunt, to
discourage, to disgust, to dishearten,
to distress, to frighten, to horrify, to
scare, to shock, to terrify.

dismiss 1 *The head dismissed us at the
end of the lesson.* to let go, to release, to
send away. 2 *The boss dismissed him
because he was lazy.* to discharge, to

dissatisfied

fire, to sack. 3 *We dismissed the idea of going abroad because it was too expensive.* to discard, to disregard, to get rid of, to reject, to set aside.

disobedient *disobedient children, a disobedient crew.* contrary, defiant, insubordinate, mutinous, obstinate, perverse, rebellious, stubborn, troublesome, unmanageable, unruly.

disobey 1 *to disobey an order.* to defy, to disregard, to ignore. 2 *to disobey a rule.* to break, to infringe, to violate. 3 *to disobey your leader.* to mutiny, to rebel, to revolt.

disorder 1 *The police wanted to prevent disorder in the streets.* anarchy, chaos, confusion, lawlessness, rioting, unrest. 2 *The burglars left the house in great disorder.* mess, muddle, shambles. 3 *There was a bit of disorder in the playground when Logan started a fight.* commotion, disturbance, fuss, rumpus, turmoil.

disorderly 1 *That disorderly class next door is making a lot of noise!* badly-behaved, boisterous, lawless, noisy, obstreperous, riotous, rough, rowdy, turbulent, undisciplined, unruly, wild. 2 *Your work is very disorderly.* SEE **disorganized**.

disorganized *Your work is very disorganized.* careless, chaotic, confused, disorderly, haphazard, jumbled, messy, muddled, scatter-brained, slapdash, sloppy, slovenly, unsystematic, untidy.

disown *Tony disowned his dog when it misbehaved.* to renounce.

disparaging *disparaging remarks.* insulting, mocking, rude, uncomplimentary.

dispatch 1 *Have you dispatched that parcel yet?* to convey, to post, to send, to transmit. 2 *They decided they would have to dispatch the wounded animal.* (informal) to finish off, to put an end to. SEE ALSO **kill**. 3 *A messenger arrived with important dispatches.* bulletin, communiqué, letter, message, report.

dispensary SEE **medicine**.

dispense 1 *The chemist is qualified to dispense medicine.* to distribute, to give out, to provide. 2 *It's time we dispensed with that old bike in the garage.* to do without, to get rid of, to remove.

disperse *The crowd dispersed when it rained.* to scatter, to spread out.

display 1 *a gymnastics display.* demonstration, exhibition, presentation, show. 2 *to display your knowledge.* to air, to demonstrate, to exhibit, to present, to produce, to reveal, to show.

displease *Our noise displeased Mrs Angel.* to annoy, to exasperate, to irritate, to offend, to trouble, to upset, to vex, to worry.

dispose 1 *Can we dispose of that old bike?* to discard, to dump, to get rid of, to give away, to sell, to throw away. 2 *Do you think dad's disposed to give me a new bike?* to be inclined to, to be liable to, to be likely to, to be ready to, to be willing to.

disposition *Our dog has a friendly disposition.* attitude, character, manner, mood, nature, personality, temperament.

dispute 1 *There was a dispute between Tony and Logan.* argument, debate, quarrel. 2 *No one disputed the referee's decision.* to argue against, to contradict, to deny, to oppose, to question.

disregard 1 *Tony usually disregards Lucy's advice.* to dismiss, to disobey, to forget, to ignore, to neglect, to overlook, to reject. 2 *Logan disregarded the hard sums.* to leave out, to miss out, to omit, to skip.

disreputable *a disreputable-looking character.* dubious, shady, suspicious, untrustworthy.

disrespectful *Logan is sometimes disrespectful to the teachers.* cheeky, discourteous, impertinent, impolite, impudent, insolent, rude.

disrupt *The arrival of the visitors disrupted our work.* to break up, to interrupt, to upset.

dissatisfied *a dissatisfied customer.*

disappointed, discontented, displeased.

dissimilar *The teams need to wear dissimilar colours.* contrasting, different, distinct, unalike.

dissolve *Sugar dissolves in tea.* to disappear, to melt.

dissuade *Lucy dissuaded Tony from buying the record she hated.* to advise against, to discourage.

distance *What's the distance between us and the moon?* gap, interval, length, space, stretch. SEE ALSO **measure**.

distant 1 *distant places.* far, far-away, outlying, remote. **2** *a distant manner.* cool, reserved, unenthusiastic, unfriendly.

distasteful *The job of clearing up when the cat was sick was distasteful.* disagreeable, horrid, nasty, objectionable, repellent, revolting. SEE ALSO **unpleasant**.

distended bloated, bulging, swollen.

distinct 1 *We saw distinct footprints in the mud.* clear, definite, obvious, plain. **2** *Tony's handwriting is distinct from Lucy's.* contrasting, different, dissimilar, separate. **3** *Tony has a distinct kind of handwriting.* individual, special.

distinction 1 *Is there any distinction between different brands of soap powder?* contrast, difference. **2** *Lucy has the distinction of being in the county team.* excellence, fame, honour, importance, renown.

distinctive *Mrs Angel has distinctive handwriting.* characteristic, different, distinct, individual, personal, special, typical, unique.

distinguish 1 *Can you distinguish butter from margarine?* to discriminate, to tell apart. **2** *In the dark we couldn't distinguish who the visitor was.* to discern, to make out, to perceive, to recognize, to see. **3** *distinguished: a distinguished actor.* celebrated, eminent, famous, foremost, great, important, leading, notable, noted, outstanding, prominent, renowned, well-known.

distort *to distort the truth.* to bend, to deform, to twist, to warp.

distract *The flashing lights distracted us.* to bewilder, to confuse, to divert, to trouble, to worry.

distress 1 *The trapped animal was in distress.* agony, anguish, discomfort, pain, suffering, torment, torture. **2** *The phones by the motorway are for the use of motorists in distress.* adversity, danger, difficulty, trouble. **3** *The news of the disaster distressed us.* to afflict, to alarm, to dismay, to frighten, to grieve, to hurt, to perturb, to scare, to shake, to shock, to terrify, to torment, to torture, to trouble, to upset, to worry.

distribute *Mrs Angel asked Tony to distribute the papers.* to allot, to circulate, to deal out, to deliver, to dispense, to divide, to give out, to hand round, to issue, to share out.

district *There are plenty of shops in our district.* area, locality, neighbourhood, region, vicinity, zone.

distrust *I distrust dogs that bark.* to doubt, to mistrust, to suspect.

disturb 1 *Don't disturb granny.* to annoy, to bother, to interrupt, to worry. **2** *A fox disturbed the chickens.* to agitate, to alarm, to excite, to frighten, to perturb, to scare, to stir up, to upset.

disused *a disused railway line.* abandoned, obsolete.

ditch channel, dike, drain, gutter, trench.

divan SEE **bed**.

dive *to dive into the water.* to dip, to go under, to nosedive, to plunge, to sink, to submerge, to subside, to swoop.

diver frogman. SEE ALSO **job**.

diverge *The motorways diverge.* to branch, to divide, to fork, to separate, to split.

diverse *a diverse collection of things.* assorted, different, miscellaneous, mixed, varied, various.

diversion 1 *a traffic diversion.* detour. **2** *Can you organize some diversions for the* *guests?* amusement, entertainment, game, hobby, pastime, recreation.

divert 1 *Because of the fog they diverted the plane to another airport.* to change direction. **2** *Dad diverted us with funny stories.* to amuse, to cheer up, to distract, to entertain.

divide 1 *The road divides: which way do we go?* to branch, to diverge, to fork, to separate. **2** *How shall we divide these sweets?* to allot, to deal out, to distribute, to give out, to halve, to share out. **3** *We'll divide the class into two.* to part, to separate, to split.

dividers SEE **mathematics**.

divine celestial, god-like, heavenly, holy, religious, sacred.

division 1 *The box has divisions for different tools.* compartment, part, section, segment. **2** *a division of a business.* branch, department.

divorce to separate, to split up.

divulge *Don't divulge our secret, will you?* to betray, to disclose, to expose, to make known, to publish, to reveal, to tell.

DIY SEE **shop**.

dizzy *I feel dizzy when I look down from a height.* confused, faint, giddy, reeling, unsteady.

DJ SEE **entertainment**.

do 1 *Have you done your work?* to accomplish, to achieve, to carry out, to commit, to complete, to execute, to finish, to perform. **2** *Will you do the potatoes?* to attend to, to cope with, to deal with, to handle, to look after, to manage. **3** *Will four big potatoes do?* to be enough, to be satisfactory, to be sufficient, to be suitable. ! *Do* can mean many things. The words given here are only some of the other words you can use.

docile *a docile animal.* gentle, meek, obedient, patient, tame.

dock 1 *The ship came in to the dock.* berth, dockyard, harbour, haven, jetty, landing-stage, pier, port, quay, wharf. **2** *The prisoner stood in the dock.* SEE **law**.

docker SEE **job**.

doctor SEE **job, medicine**.

document VARIOUS DOCUMENTS ARE certificate, deed, form, licence, paper, passport, records, visa, warrant, will.

documentary SEE **film**.

dodder SEE **walk**.

dodge 1 *I dodged out of the way of the snowball.* to avoid, to duck, to elude, to evade, to swerve, to turn, to veer. **2** *I know a dodge for opening lemonade bottles.* knack, trick.

dodgems SEE **fun-fair**.

doe SEE **female**.

dog 1 bitch, cur, hound, mongrel, pedigree, puppy. **2** VARIOUS BREEDS ARE Alsatian, beagle, bloodhound, bulldog, collie, dachshund, Dalmatian, foxhound, greyhound, husky, Labrador, mastiff, Pekingese, poodle, pug, retriever, sheepdog, spaniel, terrier, whippet. **3** SEE **animal, pet**.

dogged *dogged persistence.* determined, firm, obstinate, persistent, resolute, stubborn, unwavering, wilful.

dole 1 social security, unemployment benefit. **2** *to be on the dole*: to be out of work, to be unemployed.

doleful *a doleful expression.* dismal, gloomy, sorrowful, unhappy. SEE ALSO **sad**.

doll SEE **toy**.

dollop *a dollop of ice-cream.* chunk, hunk, lump, mass.

dolphin SEE **animal**.

dome SEE **building**.

domestic *domestic animals.* domesticated, house-trained, tame.

dominant 1 *The teacher is usually the dominant influence in a class.* chief, main, outstanding, prevailing, principal, ruling. **2** *The church is the dominant feature in the landscape.* biggest, highest, largest, tallest.

dominate *Their captain dominated the game.* to control, to govern, to influence, to manage, to rule.

domineering *a domineering personality.* bossy, dictatorial, tyrannical.

dominoes SEE **game**.

donate *A local business donated £100 to keep the team going*. to contribute, to give, to grant, to provide, to supply.

donation *a donation to OXFAM*. contribution, gift, offering, present.

donkey SEE **animal**.

donor *The donors were very generous when we raised money for cancer research*. benefactor, contributor, giver, provider, sponsor.

doodle *I wasn't drawing properly, just doodling*. to jot, to scribble. SEE ALSO **picture**.

doom 1 *We shall never know the doom of the missing ship*. destiny, fate. 2 *The dying woman faced her doom bravely*. death, end.

door doorway, entrance, entry, exit, French windows, gate. SEE ALSO **house**.

dope 1 *to take dope*. SEE **drug**. 2 *You're a dope!* SEE **fool**.

dormant *Many plants are dormant in winter*. asleep, hibernating, inactive, resting, sleeping.

dormitory SEE **school**.

dormouse SEE **animal**.

dot mark, point, speck, spot.

dote *Tony dotes on his dog*. to adore, to idolize, to love, to worship.

dotty (informal) *That was a dotty thing to do*. SEE **mad**.

double 1 dual, twice. 2 *I saw Tony's double in town*. copy, duplicate, twin.

double-bass SEE **strings**.

double-cross to betray, to cheat.

double-decker bus. SEE ALSO **vehicle**.

doubt 1 *Have you any doubt about whether we can trust him?* anxiety, hesitation, misgiving, qualm, suspicion, uncertainty, worry. 2 *Do you doubt my word?* to distrust, to mistrust, to question, to suspect.

doubtful *The weather made us doubtful about our picnic*. dubious, hesitant, uncertain, undecided, unsure.

doughnut SEE **cake**.

dove SEE **bird**.

dowdy *dowdy clothes*. colourless, drab, dull, shabby, sloppy, unattractive.

down *a pillow filled with down*. feathers.

downcast *We were downcast after losing 12-0*. dejected, depressed, downhearted, unhappy. SEE ALSO **sad**.

downpour *Tony got soaked in the downpour*. deluge, rainstorm, shower.

downs fells, hills, moors. SEE ALSO **geography**.

downtrodden *downtrodden slaves*. exploited, oppressed.

downy *The jacket was made of downy material*. feathery, fleecy, furry, fuzzy, soft, woolly.

doze *Dad often dozes in the evening*. to nod off, to sleep, to snooze, to take a nap.

dozen SEE **number**.

drab *drab colours*. cheerless, colourless, dingy, dismal, dowdy, dreary, dull, grimy, shabby, sombre, unattractive.

drag 1 *The tractor dragged a load of logs*. to draw, to haul, to lug, to pull, to tow, to tug. 2 *Time drags when you are bored*. to crawl, to creep, to pass slowly.

dragon SEE **legend**.

dragon-fly SEE **insect**.

drain 1 *They are repairing the drains*. ditch, drainage, gutter, pipe, sanitation, sewer. 2 *Mr Brunswick drained the oil out of his engine*. to clear, to draw off, to empty, to take off. 3 *The long game drained our energy*. to consume, to exhaust, to sap, to spend, to use up. SEE ALSO **exhaust**.

drake SEE **male**.

drama 1 *Drama is one of our favourite lessons*. acting, improvisation, plays, the stage, theatre. SEE ALSO **entertainment, theatre**. 2 *We had a drama today when Logan fell off the roof*. action, excitement, suspense.

dramatist SEE **author, writer**.

draper SEE **shop**.

drastic *It would be drastic to have all your teeth out*. extreme, severe.

draught breeze, wind.

draughts *a game of draughts.* SEE **game**.

draw 1 *to draw with crayons.* to depict, to portray, to represent, to sketch. SEE ALSO **picture**. 2 *The locomotive was drawing eleven coaches.* to drag, to haul, to lug, to pull, to tow, to tug. 3 *The dentist drew two of my teeth.* to extract, to remove, to take out. 4 *The show drew a big crowd.* to attract, to bring in, to entice, to lure. 5 *Even after extra time they still drew.* to be equal, to tie. 6 *Lucy draws out her chewing-gum like a bit of string.* to elongate, to extend, to lengthen, to prolong, to stretch. 7 *The bus drew up.* to halt, to pull up, to stop. 8 *a prize draw.* competition, lottery, raffle.

drawback *Being tall can be a drawback when you are exploring caves.* disadvantage, handicap, hindrance, inconvenience.

drawbridge SEE **castle**.

drawer SEE **furniture**.

drawers SEE **underclothes**.

drawing design, pattern, sketch. SEE ALSO **picture**.

drawing-room living-room, lounge, sitting-room. SEE ALSO **house**.

dread 1 *These days, there's no need to dread going to the dentist.* to be afraid of, to fear. 2 *Tony has a dread of spiders.* anxiety, fear, horror, terror.

dreadful 1 *a dreadful accident.* alarming, appalling, awful, fearful, frightening, frightful, ghastly, grisly, horrifying, monstrous, shocking, terrible, tragic. 2 *Logan's work is dreadful!* SEE **bad**.

dream 1 *Extraordinary things happen in dreams.* day-dream, fantasy, hallucination, illusion, nightmare, reverie, vision. 2 *She dreamed that she was flying.* to fancy, to imagine.

dreary *dreary weather.* boring, cheerless, depressing, dismal, drab, dull, gloomy, joyless, melancholy, sombre, unhappy. SEE ALSO **sad**.

dredger SEE **vessel**.

dregs *the dregs at the bottom of a bottle.* deposit, remains, sediment.

drench *The rainstorm drenched us.* to saturate, to soak, to wet.

dress 1 frock, gown. SEE ALSO **clothes**. 2 *Can a man's dress tell you the sort of person he is?* attire, clothes, clothing, costume, garments. 3 *You must dress when you come in from the beach.* to clothe yourself, to cover yourself, to wear clothes. 4 *A nurse dressed my wound.* to attend to, to bandage, to care for, to treat.

dresser SEE **furniture**.

dressing 1 *a dressing on a wound.* SEE **medicine**. 2 *salad dressing.* SEE **food, sauce**.

dressing-gown SEE **clothes**.

dribble *Blood dribbled down his face.* to drip, to flow, to leak, to ooze, to run, to seep, to trickle.

drift 1 *The boat drifted down the river.* to float. 2 *We had nowhere special to go, so we drifted about.* to ramble, to wander.

drill 1 *an electric drill.* SEE **tool**. 2 *to drill through something.* to bore, to penetrate, to pierce.

drink 1 WAYS TO DRINK ARE to gulp, to guzzle, to lap, to sip, to swallow, (informal) to swig. 2 VARIOUS DRINKS ARE alcohol, ale, beer, brandy, champagne, cider, cocktail, cocoa, coffee, cordial, gin, juice, lager, lemonade, lime-juice, milk, mineral water, nectar, orangeade, pop, port, punch, rum, shandy, sherbet, sherry, soda-water, squash, tea, vodka, water, whisky, wine. 3 CONTAINERS YOU DRINK FROM ARE beaker, cup, glass, goblet, mug, tankard, tumbler, wineglass.

drip 1 *The water dripped onto the floor.* to dribble, to leak, to sprinkle, to trickle. 2 *I felt a few drips of rain.* bead, drop.

dripping SEE **fat**.

drive 1 *The starving people were driven to stealing.* to compel, to force, to oblige, to press. 2 *The dog drove the sheep into a pen.* to propel, to push, to urge. 3 *Is it easy to drive a car?* to control, to operate, to pilot, to steer. 4 *He drove the ball over the boundary.* to hit, to

strike. 5 *We went for a drive in the car.*
excursion, journey, outing, trip.
6 *Park the car in the drive.* SEE **road**.
7 *Lucy does well because she's got lots of
drive.* ambition, determination,
energy, enthusiasm, keenness, zeal.

drivel *Don't talk drivel!* (informal)
balderdash, (informal) bilge,
gibberish, nonsense, rubbish,
(informal) tripe, (informal) twaddle.

driver chauffeur. SEE ALSO **job**.

drizzle mist, rain. SEE ALSO **weather**.

dromedary camel. SEE ALSO
animal.

drone 1 *a drone bee.* SEE **male**.
2 *a droning noise.* SEE **sound**.

droop *The flag drooped in the windless air.*
to be limp, to dangle, to flop, to
hang, to sag, to wilt.

drop 1 *a drop of liquid.* bead, drip, tear.
2 *to drop to the ground.* to collapse, to
descend, to dip, to dive, to fall, to
lower, to plunge. 3 *They dropped
Logan from the team.* to eliminate, to
exclude, to leave out, to omit. 4 *It
isn't nice when a friend drops you.* to
abandon, to desert, to dump, to
forsake, to leave. 5 *We dropped our
plan when we knew what it would cost.* to
give up, to scrap. 6 *Some trees drop
their leaves in autumn.* to discard, to
shed.

drought SEE **weather**.

drown 1 SEE **kill**. 2 *The floods drowned
everything for miles around.* to engulf, to
flood, to immerse, to inundate, to
overwhelm, to sink, to submerge, to
swamp. 3 *The music drowned our voices.*
to overpower, to overwhelm.

drowsy *Go to bed: you look drowsy.*
sleepy, tired, weary.

drudgery *Rich people used to have
servants to do all their drudgery.* chores,
labour, toil, work.

drug 1 ADDICTIVE DRUGS ARE
(informal) dope, heroin, marijuana,
narcotic, nicotine, opium. 2 *Doctors
use drugs to cure illnesses.* cure, remedy,
treatment. SEE ALSO **medicine**.

drum 1 SEE **percussion**. 2 *an oil drum.*
barrel. SEE ALSO **container**.

drunk *He sounded drunk.* fuddled,
intoxicated, (informal) tight.

drunkard alcoholic.

dry 1 *In the desert everything is dry.* arid,
dehydrated, parched, thirsty.
2 *a dry book.* boring, dull, tedious,
uninteresting. 3 *The flowers dried up.*
to shrivel, to wither.

dual *a dual carriageway.* double.

dubious 1 *Mrs Brunswick looked
dubious when Lucy offered to wash up.*
disbelieving, doubtful, incredulous,
sceptical, uncertain, unconvinced.
2 *Tony saw a dubious character loitering
about.* shady, suspicious, unreliable,
untrustworthy.

duchess SEE **title**.

duck 1 drake, duckling. SEE ALSO
bird, poultry. 2 *We ducked under the
low branches.* to bend, to crouch, to
dodge, to stoop, to swerve.

duckling SEE **young**.

dud (informal) *a dud battery.* unusable,
useless, worthless.

due 1 *Your club subscription is due.*
outstanding, owed, owing, unpaid.
2 *I gave the matter due consideration.*
appropriate, decent, fitting, proper,
right, suitable. 3 *Is the bus due?*
expected, scheduled.

duel *to fight a duel.* bout, combat,
contest, fight.

duet SEE **music**.

duffle coat SEE **clothes**.

duke SEE **title**.

dull 1 *a dull pupil.* dense, dim, obtuse,
slow, stupid, (informal) thick,
unintelligent. 2 *a dull film.* boring,
dry, stodgy, tame, tedious,
uninteresting. 3 *a dull sky.* cloudy,
grey, overcast, sunless. 4 *dull colours.*
dingy, dowdy, drab, gloomy,
shabby, sombre. 5 *a dull sound.*
deadened, indistinct, muffled.

dumb mute, silent, speechless,
tongue-tied. SEE ALSO **handicap**.

dumbfounded *When we heard we had
won £1000 we were dumbfounded.*
amazed, astonished, astounded,
nonplussed, speechless, stunned,
thunderstruck.

dummy 1 *a dummy revolver.* imitation, model. 2 *a ventriloquist's dummy.* doll, puppet.

dump 1 *a rubbish dump.* rubbish-heap, tip. 2 *an ammunition dump.* cache, depot, hoard, store. 3 *We dumped that old bike.* to discard, to dispose of, to get rid of, to reject, to scrap, to throw away. 4 *Just dump your things on the table.* to drop, to place, to throw down, to unload.

dumpling SEE **food.**

dumpy *a dumpy figure.* chubby, fat, plump, podgy, portly, short, squat, stocky.

dunce ass, blockhead, dope, fool, half-wit, idiot, ignoramus, imbecile, moron. ! These words are usually insulting.

dune SEE **seaside.**

dung manure, muck.

dungarees SEE **clothes.**

dungeon gaol, prison. SEE ALSO **castle.**

dupe *Logan duped me into buying a dud radio.* to cheat, to deceive, to defraud, to fool, to hoax, to hoodwink, to swindle, to take in, to trick.

duplicate 1 *a duplicate of the original painting.* copy, double, imitation, likeness, replica, reproduction, twin. 2 *Mrs Angel duplicated our poems so that we could take them home.* to copy, to photocopy, to print, to reproduce.

durable *durable shoes.* hard-wearing, indestructible, lasting, strong, sturdy, tough, unbreakable, well-made.

dusk evening, gloom, sunset, twilight. SEE ALSO **time.**

dust 1 *Wipe the dust off the shelf.* dirt, grit, powder, sawdust. 2 *I dusted the shelf.* to clean, to wipe.

dustbin SEE **container.**

dustcart SEE **vehicle.**

dustman SEE **job.**

dusty *The spare room is dusty.* dirty, filthy, grimy, gritty, grubby, (informal) mucky, sooty.

dutiful *a dutiful worker.* conscientious, diligent, faithful, hard-working, loyal, reliable, responsible, scrupulous, thorough, trustworthy.

duty 1 *a sense of duty towards your country.* allegiance, faithfulness, loyalty, obligation, responsibility. 2 *When we go camping, we each have a special duty.* assignment, function, job, task. 3 *customs duty:* customs, tax.

dwarf midget, pigmy. ! These words may be insulting.

dwell to inhabit, to live in, to occupy, to reside in.

dwelling abode, home, house, residence.

dwindle *Our stock of sweets seems to have dwindled.* to contract, to decrease, to diminish, to disappear, to fade, to lessen, to shrink, to shrivel, to subside, to wane.

dye to colour, to paint, to stain, to tint. SEE ALSO **colour.**

dynamic *The team's new manager is a dynamic person.* active, energetic, forceful, powerful, vigorous.

dynamite SEE **explosive.**

dynamo SEE **electricity.**

dysentery SEE **illness.**

E e

eager *an eager pupil.* anxious, avid, earnest, enthusiastic, excited, fervent, impatient, intent, interested, keen, passionate, zealous.

eagle SEE **bird.**

ear SEE **body, head.**

earache SEE **illness.**

earl SEE **title.**

early 1 *an early motor car.* ancient, antiquated, old, primitive. 2 *The baby was born early.* prematurely. 3 *earlier:* before, previously. 4 *earliest: the earliest motor car.* first, initial, original.

earn 1 *Lucy earned her success with hard training.* to deserve, to merit. 2 *How much do you earn doing a paper round?* to clear, to gain, to get, to make, to receive, to take home.

earnest *an earnest worker.*
conscientious, determined, diligent, grave, hard-working, industrious, serious, sincere, solemn, zealous.

earnings income, pay, salary, wages.

earphone SEE **audio equipment**.

ear-ring SEE **jewellery**.

earth 1 *We live on the earth.* globe, world. 2 *Plants grow in the earth.* ground, land, loam, soil.

earthenware china, crockery, porcelain, pottery.

earthquake *The earthquake rocked the town.* shock, tremor. SEE ALSO **disaster**.

earwig SEE **insect**.

ease 1 *Grandad hopes for a life of ease when he retires!* comfort, leisure, luxury, relaxation, repose, rest. 2 *Take an aspirin to ease the pain.* to calm, to comfort, to lessen, to quieten, to relieve, to soothe. 3 *Ease the tension in the guy ropes.* to relax, to slacken.

easel SEE **furniture**.

east SEE **geography**.

Easter SEE **church, time**.

easy 1 *easy work.* effortless, elementary, light, painless. 2 *easy to use.* foolproof, simple, straightforward, uncomplicated. 3 *an easy life.* carefree, comfortable, contented, cosy, leisurely, peaceful, relaxed, relaxing, restful, soft, tranquil, untroubled.

easygoing *Our teacher last year was easygoing, but Mrs Angel is strict.* carefree, casual, genial, indulgent, informal, lenient, liberal, patient, relaxed, tolerant, unexcitable.

eat 1 WAYS TO EAT THINGS ARE to bite, to bolt, to chew, to consume, to devour, to digest, to dine, to feast, to feed on, to gnaw, to gobble, to graze, to gulp, to gorge, to guzzle, to live on, to munch, to nibble, to peck, to swallow, to taste, (informal) to tuck in. 2 SEE ALSO **food, meal**. 3 *Acid can eat into metal.* to corrode, to rot, to rust. 4 *The river ate the bank away.* to erode, to wear away.

eatable *Is the food eatable?* edible.

eaves SEE **building**.

eavesdrop *It isn't polite to eavesdrop on other people's conversations.* to listen, to overhear.

ebb *When the tide ebbed we walked out onto the beach.* to flow back, to go down, to recede, to retreat.

ebony SEE **wood**.

eccentric *eccentric behaviour.* cranky, odd, peculiar, strange, unconventional, weird, zany.

echo 1 *The sound echoed back across the valley.* to resound, to reverberate. 2 *The parrot echoed everything I said.* to imitate, to mimic.

éclair SEE **cake**.

eclipse SEE **astronomy**.

ecology SEE **subject**.

economical 1 *It's more economical to walk than to go by bus.* careful with money, sparing, thrifty. 2 *Mum buys economical kinds of meat.* cheap, inexpensive, reasonable.

ecstasy *Lucy's idea of ecstasy is to lie in a hot bath.* bliss, delight, happiness, joy, pleasure, rapture.

ecstatic *They gave their heroes an ecstatic welcome.* delighted, elated, exultant, gleeful, joyful, overjoyed, rapturous. SEE ALSO **happy**.

eddy *an eddy in the water.* swirl, whirl, whirlpool.

edge 1 *the edge of a field.* border, boundary. 2 *the edge of the road.* side, verge. 3 *the edge of a crowd.* fringe. 4 *the edge of a picture.* frame, margin. 5 *the edge of a cup.* brim, brink, lip, rim. 6 *We edged cautiously away.* to creep, to slink.

edgy *The dog seems edgy: will he bite?* highly-strung, jittery, jumpy, irritable, nervous, tense, touchy, (informal) uptight.

edible *I don't think conkers are edible.* digestible, eatable.

edifice building, structure.

edit *We edited our articles for the magazine.* to adapt, to alter, to compile, to revise, to rewrite.

edition *When will the next edition of the magazine be ready?* issue, number, publication.

editor SEE **job, writer**.

editorial SEE **writing**.

educate 1 to bring up, to coach, to indoctrinate, to inform, to instruct, to lecture, to teach, to train. 2 *educated: an educated person.* cultivated, cultured, knowledgeable, learned, literate, well-bred. 3 PLACES WHERE YOU CAN BE EDUCATED ARE academy, college, kindergarten, play-group, polytechnic, SEE **school**, university. 4 PEOPLE WHO EDUCATE US ARE coach, guru, instructor, lecturer, professor, SEE **teacher**, trainer, tutor.

eel SEE **fish**.

eerie *The castle looked eerie in the moonlight.* creepy, frightening, ghostly, scary, spooky, uncanny, unearthly, weird.

effect 1 *Did the head's warning have any effect?* consequence, impact, influence, outcome, result, sequel. 2 *The new wallpaper in the bathroom gives a nice effect.* impression.

effective *an effective goalkeeper, an effective cure for colds, etc.* capable, competent, efficient, powerful, productive, proficient, strong, successful.

effervescent *effervescent drinks.* bubbling, bubbly, fermenting, fizzy, foaming, sparkling.

efficient *an efficient worker.* capable, competent, effective, productive, proficient, useful.

effort 1 *You deserve a rest after all that effort.* exertion, labour, struggle, toil, trouble, work. 2 *We made a real effort to win.* attempt, endeavour, try.

effortless *Lucy makes gymnastics look effortless.* easy, painless, simple.

egg 1 *a hen's egg.* SEE **food**. 2 (informal) *to egg someone on.* to encourage, to inspire, to prompt, to urge.

eiderdown SEE **bedclothes**.

eject *Logan was ejected from the youth club because of his behaviour.* to banish, to discharge, to dismiss, to evict, to expel, (informal) to kick out, to send out, to throw out.

elaborate 1 *an elaborate plan.* complex, complicated, detailed, intricate, involved. 2 *elaborate embroidery.* decorated, fancy, intricate, showy.

elapse *A lot of time has elapsed since we met.* to go by, to pass.

elastic *an elastic band.* springy, stretching.

elated *We were elated by our win.* delighted, ecstatic, joyful, overjoyed. SEE ALSO **happy**.

elbow SEE **body, joint**.

elder SEE **tree**.

elderly aged, old.

elect *The gymnastics team elected Lucy as captain.* to appoint, to choose, to name, to nominate, to pick, to select, to vote for.

election *We had an election to choose a captain.* ballot, poll, vote.

electrician SEE **job**.

electricity 1 WORDS TO DO WITH ELECTRICITY ARE adaptor, battery, bell, bulb, cable, charger, circuit, dynamo, element, flex, fuse, generator, insulation, lead, meter, negative, plug, positive, power-point, power-station, pylon, socket, switch, terminal, torch, transformer, volt, watt, wire, wiring. 2 SEE **fuel**.

electrifying *an electrifying performance.* exciting, stimulating, thrilling.

electrocute SEE **kill**.

electronics SEE **science**.

elegant *an elegant palace, an elegant dance, etc.* dignified, graceful, handsome, noble, (informal) posh, refined, stately, tasteful. SEE ALSO **beautiful, splendid**.

element 1 *the main elements of a subject.* component, ingredient, part. 2 *The explorers battled against the elements.* weather.

elementary *an elementary problem.*

basic, easy, fundamental, simple, uncomplicated.

elephant SEE **animal**.

elevate 1 *The gunners elevated the angle of the big guns.* to lift, to raise. **2** *elevated: an elevated position.* high, raised.

elf SEE **legend**.

eligible *Tony won't be eligible to swim in the junior race after his next birthday.* acceptable, allowed, authorized, qualified, suitable.

eliminate 1 *How can Mrs Brunswick eliminate the ants from her garden?* to abolish, to annihilate, to destroy, to end, to eradicate, to exterminate, to finish off, to get rid of, to remove, to stamp out. **2** *Our team was eliminated in the first round.* to knock out. **3** *I was eliminated because I wasn't fit.* to drop, to leave out, to omit, to reject.

elk SEE **animal**.

ellipse SEE **shape**.

elm SEE **tree**.

elongated *Lucy described an ellipse as an elongated circle.* drawn out, extended, lengthened, stretched.

eloquent *an eloquent speaker.* fluent, persuasive.

elude *The thieves couldn't elude the police.* to avoid, to dodge, to escape, to evade.

emaciated *The refugees were terribly emaciated.* bony, gaunt, scraggy, skinny, thin, wasted away.

emancipate *to emancipate slaves.* to free, to liberate.

embankment bank, dam.

embark 1 *The sailors embarked at high tide.* to board, to depart, to go, to leave, to set out. **2** *Mr Brunswick embarked on the building of his extension.* to begin, to commence, to start, to undertake.

embarrass 1 *Tony was embarrassed when mum bought him pink underwear.* to disgrace, to distress, to humiliate. **2** *embarrassing:* humiliating, shameful. **3** *embarrassed:* ashamed, distressed, flustered, humiliated, self-conscious, shy, upset.

embedded *My wellingtons were embedded in the mud.* fixed, set.

embers ashes, cinders.

embittered *Tony was not embittered by being beaten in the last race.* bitter, envious, resentful, sour.

emblem badge, crest, seal, sign, symbol.

embrace *They embraced each other lovingly.* to clasp, to cling to, to cuddle, to fondle, to grasp, to hold, to hug, to kiss.

embroidery needlework, sewing. SEE ALSO **art**.

embryo foetus.

emerald SEE **jewellery**.

emerge *It's nice to see the flowers emerge in the spring.* to appear, to come out, to evolve, to issue, to materialize, to show, to surface.

emergency *We knew there was an emergency when we heard the fire-engine.* crisis, danger, predicament.

emigrate *Many people emigrated from Europe to America.* to depart, to leave, to quit.

eminent *an eminent TV personality.* celebrated, distinguished, famous, great, important, notable, outstanding, prominent, renowned, well-known.

emit *The exhaust of your car emits a lot of smoke. That fire emits a lot of heat.* to belch, to discharge, to expel, to give out, to radiate, to send out, to transmit.

emotion feeling, passion, sentiment.

emotional *Saying goodbye was an emotional moment.* moving, passionate, romantic, sentimental, touching.

emperor SEE **ruler**.

emphasize *Mrs Angel emphasized that we must not wander off.* to assert, to insist, to stress, to underline.

employ 1 *The school employs a special teacher to teach music.* to give work to, to pay. **2** *Our doctor employs the most modern methods.* to apply, to use, to utilize. **3** *to be employed in something:* to be active, to be busy, to be engaged, to be involved, to be occupied.

employer boss, chief, head, manager, owner.

employment *Tony's uncle is looking for employment.* business, job, occupation, profession, trade, work.

empty 1 *an empty space.* hollow, unfilled, void. 2 *an empty room.* bare, unfurnished. 3 *an empty house.* deserted, desolate, forsaken, uninhabited, unoccupied, vacant. 4 *an empty page.* blank, clean, unused. 5 *Empty the cup. Empty the room.* to clear, to drain, to evacuate.

emu SEE **bird**.

emulsion SEE **paint**.

enable 1 *A little more money will enable us to have a really good time.* to aid, to assist, to help. 2 *A passport enables you to travel to certain countries.* to allow, to authorize, to entitle, to permit.

enamel SEE **paint**.

enchant 1 *The ballet enchanted us.* to allure, to bewitch, to captivate, to charm, to delight, to entrance, to fascinate. 2 *enchanted*: spellbound.

enchantment *The witch's enchantment held them in its power.* charm, magic, spell, witchcraft, wizardry.

encircle *We encircled the area where the tortoise was last seen.* to besiege, to circle, to enclose, to ring, to surround.

enclose *The lions were enclosed behind a high fence.* to confine, to encircle, to envelop, to fence in, to hedge in, to hem in, to imprison, to pen, to restrict, to ring, to shut in, to surround, to wall in.

enclosure *an enclosure for animals.* cage, compound, corral, courtyard, farmyard, fold, pen, run.

encounter 1 *a violent encounter.* battle, clash, confrontation, fight, meeting, struggle. 2 *The plan to close the school encountered fierce opposition.* to clash with, to confront, to face, to meet, to run into.

encourage 1 *The supporters encouraged their team.* to cheer up, (informal) to egg on, to inspire, to reassure, to support. 2 *Advertising encourages sales.* to boost, to help, to promote. 3 *Encourage people to pay their subscriptions.* to invite, to prompt, to urge. 4 *encouraging*: favourable, hopeful, promising, reassuring. SEE ALSO **kind**.

encouragement *The team needs encouragement.* boost, incentive, reassurance, support.

encyclopaedia SEE **book**.

end 1 *the end of a film.* close, conclusion, ending, finale, finish. 2 *the end of an ambition.* collapse, death, destruction, downfall, fall, passing, ruin. 3 *the end of a train.* back, rear, tail. 4 *the end of a pin.* point, tip. 5 *What was the end of all your efforts?* consequence, effect, outcome, result. 6 *What end did you have in mind when you started?* aim, intention, objective, purpose. 7 *When does your club membership end?* to cease, to close, to expire, to finish, to stop. 8 *Do you want to end your club membership?* to discontinue, to terminate. 9 *Please end your work now.* to break off, to cut off, to halt, to round off. 10 *We have the power to end all life on earth.* to abolish, to destroy, to eliminate, to get rid of, to kill.

endanger *If you don't keep your bike in good condition, you could endanger your life.* to threaten.

endearing *an endearing puppy.* appealing, attractive, charming, lovable.

endeavour *Logan endeavoured to behave.* to attempt, to exert yourself, to make an effort, to strain, to strive, to try.

endless 1 *an endless journey into space.* boundless, eternal, immeasurable, infinite, limitless, unlimited. 2 *We are sick of Logan's endless chattering.* ceaseless, constant, continual, everlasting, incessant, interminable, persistent, unending.

endure 1 *Some people have to endure a lot of pain.* to abide, to bear, to cope with, to experience, to put up with, to stand, (informal) to stick, to suffer, to tolerate, to undergo, to withstand. 2 *We hope that life on earth will endure for a long time yet.* to carry on, to continue, to exist, to last, to live on, to remain, to stay, to survive.

enemy adversary, antagonist, attacker, foe, opponent, opposition, rival.

energetic *an energetic player.* active, animated, brisk, dynamic, enthusiastic, forceful, hard-working, lively, powerful, spirited, sprightly, vigorous.

energy *The winning team played with tremendous energy.* force, liveliness, might, power, strength, vigour, vitality, zeal, zest.

enforce *The referee enforces the rules.* to carry out, to impose, to inflict, to insist on.

engaged 1 *an engaged couple.* betrothed. 2 *What are you engaged in?* busy, employed, involved, occupied.

engagement 1 *I can't come because I have another engagement.* appointment, date, fixture, meeting. 2 *a fierce engagement between two armies.* battle, clash, encounter, fight, struggle.

engine 1 KINDS OF ENGINE ARE diesel engine, electric motor, internal combustion engine, jet engine, outboard motor, steam engine, turbine. 2 *a railway engine.* locomotive.

engineer SEE **job**.

engraving SEE **picture**.

engulf *A tidal wave engulfed the town.* to flood, to inundate, to overwhelm, to submerge, to swallow up, to swamp.

enjoy *Do you enjoy snooker?* to admire, to appreciate, to be pleased by, to delight in, to like, to love, to relish, to revel in.

enjoyable agreeable, amusing, delightful, diverting, entertaining, likeable, pleasant, satisfying.

enjoyment *They ate the food with great enjoyment.* appreciation, delight, pleasure, satisfaction, zest.

enlarge *Tony is enlarging his collection of records.* to amplify, to build up, to develop, to expand, to extend, to fill out, to increase, to inflate, to lengthen, to magnify, to swell, to widen.

enlargement SEE **photograph**.

enlist *to enlist in the army.* to enrol, to join up, to register, to sign on, to volunteer.

enormous *an enormous elephant.* gigantic, gross, huge, immense, mammoth, massive, mighty, monstrous, towering, tremendous, vast. SEE ALSO **big**.

enough *Was there enough food?* adequate, sufficient.

enquire WAYS TO ENQUIRE ARE to ask, to beg, to demand, to entreat, to implore, to inquire, to query, to question, to request.

enrage *Logan's silly questions enrage us.* to anger, to exasperate, to incense, to inflame, to infuriate, to madden, to provoke, to vex. SEE ALSO **angry**.

enrol 1 *to enrol in the army.* to enlist, to join up, to register, to sign on, to volunteer. 2 *How many people have we enrolled for the youth club outing?* to accept, to recruit, to sign up, to take on.

ensemble *a recorder ensemble.* band, group, orchestra. SEE ALSO **music**.

ensign *a ship's ensign.* banner, colours, flag, standard.

ensnare *to ensnare animals.* to ambush, to capture, to catch, to entangle, to trap.

ensure *Will you ensure that the goldfish gets fed?* to guarantee, to make certain, to secure. ! This is not the same word as *insure.*

enter *to enter a cave.* to come in, to go in, to penetrate.

enterprising *Several enterprising children organized a sponsored walk.* adventurous, ambitious, bold, courageous, daring, energetic, enthusiastic, hard-working, industrious, intrepid, keen, resourceful.

entertain 1 *The comedian entertained the audience.* to amuse, to delight, to divert, to please. 2 *We usually entertain some friends at Christmas.* to cater for, to give hospitality to, to greet, to receive, to welcome.

entertainment 1 amusement, diversion, enjoyment, fun, recreation. **2** KINDS OF ENTERTAINMENT ARE aerobatics, ballet, cabaret, casino, cinema, circus, comedy, concert, dance, disco, drama, fair, gymkhana, musical, night-club, night-life, opera, pageant, pantomime, play, recital, recitation, radio, rodeo, show, tap-dancing, tattoo, television, variety show, waxworks, zoo. **3** VARIOUS ENTERTAINERS ARE acrobat, actor, actress, ballerina, broadcaster, clown, comedian, comic, compère, conjurer, contortionist, dancer, DJ, jester, juggler, lion-tamer, magician, matador, minstrel, musician, question-master, singer, star, stunt man, superstar, toreador, trapeze artist, ventriloquist. SEE ALSO **music, theatre**.

enthusiasm 1 *You need plenty of enthusiasm to succeed in sport.* ambition, drive, eagerness, excitement, fervour, keenness, zeal. **2** *Mr Brunswick's enthusiasms include water-skiing.* craze, diversion, pastime.

enthusiast *Logan is a pop music enthusiast.* addict, fan, fanatic, supporter.

enthusiastic *The team needs an enthusiastic new manager.* avid, eager, energetic, fervent, keen, lively, passionate, spirited.

entice *I enticed the rabbit into the hutch with a carrot.* to attract, to bribe, to coax, to lure, to tempt.

entire *Did you read the entire book?* complete, full, intact, total, unbroken, whole.

entitle 1 *Grandad's bus pass entitles him to travel free of charge.* to allow, to authorize, to enable, to permit. **2** *What did you entitle your story?* to call, to name.

entrance 1 *You pay at the entrance.* access, door, entry, gate, opening, turnstile, way in. **2** *The ballet entranced everyone.* to bewitch, to captivate, to

charm, to delight, to enchant, to fascinate, to spellbind.

entrant *How many entrants are there for the swimming gala?* applicant, candidate, competitor, contestant, participant, rival.

entreat *The captain entreated the passengers to remain calm.* to appeal to, to ask, to beg, to implore, to plead, to request.

entry access, door, entrance, gate, opening, turnstile, way in.

entwine *The wires became entwined.* to coil, to entangle, to tangle, to twist, to wind.

envelop *Fog enveloped the town.* to conceal, to cover, to encircle, to enclose, to surround, to wrap up.

envelope cover, wrapper. SEE ALSO **container**.

envious bitter, grudging, jealous, resentful.

environment *What kind of environment do you live in?* surroundings.

envy *Tony doesn't envy Lucy's success.* to begrudge, to resent.

epic SEE **poem, writing**.

epidemic *an epidemic of measles.* outbreak, plague.

epilepsy SEE **illness**.

epilogue SEE **book**.

episode *What happened in the last episode?* instalment, passage, scene, section.

epistle letter.

epitaph *an epitaph on a tombstone.* inscription.

equal *equal amounts.* equivalent, even, identical, level, matching, the same.

equalize *to equalize the scores.* to balance, to even up.

equator SEE **geography**.

equilateral SEE **mathematics**.

equilibrium *to keep your equilibrium.* balance, poise, stability, steadiness.

equip *They equipped the hall with new lighting.* to furnish, to provide, to supply.

equipment *Mr Brunswick has a lot of decorating equipment.* apparatus, furnishings, gear, hardware, instruments, kit, machinery, outfit, paraphernalia, supplies, tackle.

equivalent *They'll refund the money or give you something of equivalent value.* equal, matching, the same.

era *The Roman era.* age, period, time.

eradicate *Mrs Brunswick wants to eradicate those ants!* to abolish, to annihilate, to destroy, to eliminate, to end, to exterminate, to get rid of, to remove, to uproot.

erase *It's easy to erase mistakes when you're using a word-processor.* to blot out, to cancel, to delete, to remove, to rub out, to wipe out.

erect 1 *to erect a tent.* to build, to construct, to pitch, to put up, to raise, to set up. **2** *Human beings stand erect.* upright, vertical.

erode *The river is eroding the bank.* to corrode, to eat away, to grind down, to wear away.

err *It is better to err by arriving early than by arriving late.* to do wrong, to go wrong, to misbehave, to miscalculate.

errand *She sent Tony on an errand to the shops.* job, mission, task.

erratic *The team's performance has been erratic lately.* changeable, fickle, inconsistent, irregular, unpredictable, variable.

error *Mrs Angel corrected the errors in Logan's work.* blunder, fallacy, fault, (informal) howler, inaccuracy, miscalculation, misconception, mistake, misunderstanding, oversight, (informal) slip-up.

erupt *A flow of lava erupted from the volcano.* to be discharged, to be emitted, to belch, to burst out, to gush, to issue, to pour out.

eruption *an eruption of laughter, a volcanic eruption.* explosion, outburst.

escalate *The trouble escalated as more people joined in.* to become worse, to increase, to multiply, to step up.

escalator lift, staircase, stairs.

escapade *Don't get involved in any escapades!* adventure, mischief, prank, scrape.

escape 1 *The prisoner escaped.* to abscond, to bolt, to elope, to flee, to run away, to slip away. **2** *Lucy always escapes the washing-up.* to avoid, to dodge, to elude, to evade, to get away from, to shirk. **3** *His escape wasn't noticed until the morning.* getaway, flight, retreat, running away.

escort 1 *The security man has an escort if he's carrying a lot of money.* companion, guard, guide, protector. **2** *Dad escorted the little ones home after the party.* to accompany, to conduct, to see.

espionage intelligence, spying.

esplanade SEE **seaside**.

essay SEE **writing**.

essential 1 *the essential facts.* basic, chief, fundamental, important, indispensable, main, primary, principal. **2** *It's essential that you come.* imperative, necessary, vital.

establish 1 *Mr Brunswick established a new business.* to base, to begin, to construct, to create, to found, to initiate, to install, to introduce, to originate, to set up. **2** *We must establish what to do first.* to agree, to decide, to fix, to settle. **3** *Can you establish where you were last night?* to confirm, to demonstrate, to prove, to show, to verify.

establishment *What sort of establishment does uncle run?* business, company, concern, factory, firm, institution, office, organization, shop.

estate 1 *a housing estate.* area, development. **2** *a family estate.* fortune, inheritance, possessions, property, wealth.

estate agent SEE **job**.

estate car SEE **vehicle**.

estimate *We estimated how many sandwiches we needed for the party.* to assess, to calculate, to guess, to reckon, to work out.

estuary SEE **geography**.

eternal 1 *eternal life.* endless,

everlasting, immortal, infinite, limitless, timeless, unending. 2 *I'm tired of your eternal quarrelling.* ceaseless, constant, continual, frequent, incessant, interminable, non-stop, perennial, permanent, perpetual, persistent, recurrent, relentless, repeated.

ethnic *ethnic music.* national, racial.

eucalyptus SEE **tree**.

evacuate 1 *The police evacuated everyone from the area.* to clear, to move out, to remove. 2 *The family had to evacuate the blazing house.* to abandon, to desert, to forsake, to leave, to quit.

evade *Lucy tries to evade the washing-up.* to avoid, to dodge, to elude, to escape from, to shirk.

evangelist SEE **church, preacher**.

evaporate *The dew evaporates during the morning.* to disappear, to dry up, to vaporize.

even 1 *even ground.* flat, level, smooth. 2 *an even temper.* calm, placid, serene, steady. 3 *the even ticking of the clock.* consistent, regular. 4 *even scores.* balanced, equal, identical, level, the same. 5 *Logan played for the opposition to even up the teams.* to balance, to equalize. 6 *We evened out the wrinkled carpet.* to flatten, to level.

evening dusk, sunset, twilight. SEE ALSO **time**.

event 1 *a special event.* affair, ceremony, entertainment, experience, function, happening, incident, occasion, occurrence, proceedings. 2 *a sporting event.* championship, competition, contest, match, meeting, tournament.

eventually finally, ultimately.

evergreen SEE **tree**.

everlasting 1 *everlasting life.* endless, eternal, immortal, infinite, limitless, timeless, unending. 2 *We get tired of their everlasting quarrelling.* ceaseless, constant, continual, frequent, incessant, interminable, non-stop, perennial, permanent, perpetual, persistent, recurrent, relentless, repeated.

evermore always, eternally, for ever, unceasingly.

everyday *an everyday happening.* accustomed, common, commonplace, conventional, customary, familiar, habitual, normal, ordinary, orthodox, regular, routine, standard, typical, usual.

evict *The landlord evicted them for not paying the rent.* to eject, to expel, (informal) to kick out, to remove, to throw out, to turn out.

evidence *The judge examined the evidence.* data, facts, grounds, information, proof, sign, statistics, testimony.

evident *It is evident that Logan doesn't like work.* apparent, clear, obvious, plain, self-explanatory, unmistakable.

evil *an evil deed, an evil person.* atrocious, base, foul, hateful, immoral, infamous, malevolent, sinful, sinister, vicious, villainous, wicked, wrong. SEE ALSO **bad**.

evolve *Animals have evolved over millions of years.* to emerge, to develop, to grow, to improve, to progress.

ewe lamb, sheep. SEE ALSO **female**.

exact *the exact time.* accurate, correct, precise, right, specific, true.

exaggerate to overdo it.

examination 1 *a school examination.* exam, test. 2 *a medical examination.* check-up, inspection, investigation, scrutiny.

examine 1 *We examined the evidence.* to analyse, to check, to inquire into, to inspect, to investigate, to probe, to study, to test. 2 *The police examined the witness.* to cross-examine, to interrogate, to question.

example 1 *Give an example of what you mean.* case, illustration, instance, sample, specimen. 2 *Can we have an example to copy?* model, pattern, prototype.

exasperate *Logan exasperated the head by dropping sweets all over the floor.* (informal) to aggravate, to anger, to annoy, to bother, to enrage, to incense, to infuriate, to irritate, to provoke, to vex. SEE ALSO **anger**.

excavate *to excavate a hole.* to burrow, to dig, to mine, to scoop, to tunnel, to uncover, to unearth.

exceed *to exceed a target.* to beat, to excel, to go over, to outdo, to outnumber, to surpass, to top.

exceedingly *This is exceedingly good cake: can I have some more?* exceptionally, extremely, outstandingly, specially, unusually, very.

excel *Our team excelled theirs in nearly every event.* to beat, to exceed, to outdo, to surpass, to top.

excellent *excellent advice, excellent food, etc.* admirable, brilliant, esteemed, exceptional, (informal) fabulous, fantastic, fine, first-class, gorgeous, great, impressive, magnificent, marvellous, outstanding, (informal) super, superb, (informal) terrific, tremendous, wonderful.

except *Everyone behaved well, except Logan.* besides, excluding.

exceptional 1 *exceptional weather.* abnormal, extraordinary, peculiar, rare, remarkable, special, uncommon, unusual. 2 *an exceptional performance.* SEE **excellent**.

excerpt *an excerpt from 'Treasure Island'.* clip, extract, quotation.

excessive 1 *excessive prices.* exorbitant, extreme, high, uncalled-for, unreasonable. 2 *an excessive amount of food.* extravagant, superfluous, unnecessary.

exchange *Tony exchanged his old bike for some roller-skates.* to change, to replace, to substitute, to swop, to trade, to trade in.

exchequer SEE **government**.

excite 1 *The smell of blood excited the tiger.* to agitate, to arouse, to disturb, to electrify, to move, to provoke, to rouse, to stimulate, to stir, to thrill. 2 *excited*: animated, boisterous, delirious, exuberant, frenzied, hysterical, lively, spirited, vivacious, wild.

excitement action, activity,

adventure, drama, (informal) kicks, stimulation, suspense, thrill.

exclaim to call, to cry out, to shout, to yell. SEE ALSO **talk**.

exclamation mark SEE **punctuation**.

exclude *Mrs Angel excluded Logan because he was rude.* to ban, to bar, to keep out, to omit, to prohibit, to shut out.

excruciating *excruciating pain.* agonizing, painful, unbearable.

excursion *an excursion to the seaside.* expedition, jaunt, outing, tour, trip.

excuse 1 *Have you any excuse for what you did?* explanation, defence, justification, pretext, reason. 2 *After hearing the facts, the judge excused him.* to forgive, to free, to let off, to overlook, to pardon.

execute 1 *The pilot executed a difficult manoeuvre.* to accomplish, to carry out, to complete, to do, to perform. 2 *to execute a criminal.* to put to death. 3 WAYS TO EXECUTE PEOPLE ARE to behead, to crucify, to decapitate, to electrocute, to gas, to guillotine, to hang, to lynch, to shoot, to stone. SEE ALSO **punishment**.

executive *an executive in big business.* administrator, director, manager. SEE ALSO **chief, job**.

exercise 1 *Exercise helps to keep you fit.* activity, aerobics, games, gymnastics, PE, sport. 2 *army exercises.* drill, manoeuvres, training. 3 *Mr Brunswick likes to exercise several times a week.* to jog, to keep fit, to practise, to train. 4 *Please exercise a little more self-control.* to display, to employ, to show, to use, to wield.

exercise book jotter, notebook, pad.

exert *to exert yourself*: to attempt, to endeavour, to strain, to strive, to try.

exertion *The exertion made us sweat.* effort, energy, labour, toil, work.

exhaust 1 *The car gives out a lot of exhaust.* fumes, gases, smoke. 2 *We exhausted our money.* to consume, to spend, to use up. 3 *Don't exhaust yourselves.* to drain, to sap, to strain,

to tire, to weaken, to wear out, to
weary. 4 *exhausted*: breathless,
(informal) done in, drained, gasping,
panting, tired out, weary, worn out.
5 *exhausting*: arduous, gruelling,
hard, laborious, strenuous, tiring.

exhaustive *an exhaustive search.*
careful, complete, meticulous,
thorough.

exhibit *We exhibited our art work.* to
demonstrate, to display, to present,
to produce, to show.

exhibition *an exhibition of paintings.*
demonstration, display,
presentation, show.

exile 1 *to exile someone from his country.* to
banish, to deport, to eject, to expel,
to send away. 2 *An exile longs to be
back in her own country.* outcast,
refugee, wanderer.

exist 1 *Do dragons exist?* to be, to occur.
2 *We can't exist without water.* to
endure, to keep going, to live, to
remain, to survive.

exit door, outlet, way out.

exorbitant *exorbitant prices.* excessive,
high, unreasonable.

expand *Mr Brunswick hopes his business
will expand. Can you expand your story?*
to amplify, to build up, to enlarge, to
fill out, to grow, to increase, to
lengthen, to swell, to widen.

expanse *an expanse of water.* area,
sheet, surface.

expect 1 *We are expecting snow.* to
anticipate, to forecast, to foresee, to
hope for, to wait for. 2 *expecting a
baby*: expectant, pregnant.

expedition *a hunting expedition.*
excursion, exploration, journey,
mission, outing, safari, tour, trek,
trip, voyage. SEE ALSO **travel**.

expel *to expel someone from the country.* to
banish, to deport, to discharge, to
dismiss, to eject, to evict, to exile,
(informal) to kick out, to send away,
to throw out.

expense cost, expenditure, payment,
price.

expensive *expensive jewellery.* costly,
dear, exorbitant, extravagant,
lavish, luxurious, precious, priceless,
(informal) pricey, valuable.

experience 1 *He has a lot of experience.*
knowledge, wisdom. 2 *Flying in a
helicopter is an exciting experience.* event,
happening, incident, occurrence.
3 *to experience pain.* to endure, to feel,
to go through, to know, to live
through, to see, to suffer, to undergo.

experienced *an experienced craftsman.*
accomplished, competent, expert,
knowledgeable, proficient, qualified,
skilled, trained.

experiment *a scientific experiment.* test,
trial.

expert 1 *an expert mechanic.* clever,
experienced, knowledgeable, professional, proficient, qualified, skilful,
skilled, talented, trained. 2 *Ask an
expert.* authority, professional,
specialist.

expire 1 *My club membership expires this
month.* to cease, to end, to finish, to
run out, to stop, to terminate. 2 *The
wounded animal expired.* to die, to pass
away, to perish.

explain *Can you explain how a computer
works?* to account for, to analyse, to
clarify, to define, to demonstrate, to
describe, to illustrate, to interpret, to
justify, to make clear, to show.

explanation *Do you believe his
explanation?* account, answer,
definition, description, excuse,
justification, reason, theory.

explode to blow up, to burst, to
detonate, to go off, to set off.

exploit 1 *the exploits of King Arthur.* act,
adventure, deed, feat. 2 *The owners
exploited the slaves.* to take advantage
of, to use, to utilize. 3 *exploited*:
downtrodden, oppressed.

explore 1 *We explored the woods.* to
discover, to look around, to travel
about. 2 *We explored the problem.* to
examine, to inquire into, to
investigate, to probe.

explorer discoverer, pioneer,
prospector.

explosion bang, blast, eruption,
outburst, report.

explosive KINDS OF EXPLOSIVE ARE dynamite, gelignite, gunpowder, TNT.

expose *to expose a secret.* to bare, to disclose, to display, to divulge, to make known, to reveal, to show, to uncover.

express *We expressed our thanks.* to communicate, to describe, to make known, to put into words, to say, to speak, to talk, to utter.

expression 1 *Her expression shows she's had bad news.* countenance, face, look. 2 EXPRESSIONS ON PEOPLE'S FACES ARE beam, frown, glare, glower, grimace, grin, laugh, leer, pout, scowl, smile, smirk, sneer, wince, yawn. 3 *We learned a few French expressions before we went abroad.* phrase, remark, saying, statement, word.

expressionless *an expressionless face.* blank, vacant.

exquisite *an exquisite piece of jewellery.* beautiful, dainty, delicate, elegant, fine, lovely, perfect.

extend 1 *The pier extends into the sea.* to project, to reach out, to stick out, to stretch out. 2 *You can extend this ladder to twice its length.* to draw out, to elongate, to enlarge, to lengthen, to prolong, to stretch. 3 *We extend a warm welcome to all.* to give, to offer.

extension *an extension to a house.* addition, annexe, enlargement, wing.

extensive 1 *an extensive forest.* broad, large, vast, wide. 2 *extensive damage.* general, wholesale, widespread.

extent *the extent of a person's wealth, the extent of a piece of land.* amount, area, breadth, degree, dimensions, distance, length, limit, magnitude, measure, measurement, range, reach, scope, size.

exterior *the exterior of a house.* outside, shell, skin, surface.

exterminate *Dad exterminated an ant's nest.* to annihilate, to destroy, to eliminate, to eradicate, (informal) to finish off, to kill, to slaughter, to wipe out.

external *The external appearance of the house was attractive.* exterior, outer, outside, outward.

extinct *Dinosaurs are extinct.* dead, died out.

extinguish *to extinguish a candle.* to put out, to quench, to snuff.

extra 1 *We need extra milk for the weekend.* additional, further, more, spare, supplementary. 2 *When Mrs Brunswick grows more beans than she can use, she puts the extra in the freezer.* excess, remainder, surplus.

extract 1 *The dentist extracted the bad tooth.* to draw out, to pull out, to remove, to take out. 2 *Mrs Angel read an extract from 'Oliver Twist'.* clip, excerpt, passage, quotation.

extraordinary *We hardly believed his extraordinary story.* abnormal, amazing, curious, exceptional, fantastic, funny, incredible, miraculous, notable, odd, peculiar, phenomenal, queer, rare, remarkable, singular, special, strange, stupendous, unbelievable, uncommon, unusual.

extravagant *It was extravagant to buy the biggest ice-creams.* excessive, expensive, lavish, prodigal, wasteful.

extreme 1 *the extreme end of the runway.* farthest, furthest, furthermost, ultimate. 2 *extreme difficulties.* acute, drastic, excessive, great, intense, severe. 3 *This unsettled weather goes from one extreme to the other.* end, limit, maximum, opposite.

exuberant *The winning team was in an exuberant mood.* animated, boisterous, cheerful, energetic, excited, lively, spirited, sprightly.

exultant *Lucy was exultant when she won the cup.* delighted, ecstatic, elated, gleeful, joyful, overjoyed, rapturous. SEE ALSO **happy**.

eye SEE **body, head**.

eye-shadow SEE **cosmetics**.

eyesore *The quarry is an eyesore.* blemish, blot.

eyewitness *The police asked the eyewitnesses to describe the accident.* bystander, observer, onlooker, spectator, witness.

eyrie *an eagle's eyrie.* nest.

F f

fable SEE **writing**.

fabric cloth, material, textile. SEE ALSO **cloth**.

fabulous 1 *fabulous monsters.* fictional, imaginary, legendary, mythical, non-existent. 2 FOR FABULOUS CREATURES SEE **legend**. 3 (informal) *a fabulous record.* SEE **excellent**.

face 1 *He made a funny face.* countenance, features, look. SEE ALSO **expression**. 2 *A cube has six faces.* front, side, surface. 3 *Our house faces the pie factory.* to look at, to overlook. 4 *The explorers faced many dangers.* to confront, to encounter, to meet.

facetious *Mrs Angel hates Logan's facetious remarks.* amusing, comic, funny, humorous, joking, witty.

fact *I want the full facts.* circumstances, data, details, evidence, information, reality, statistics, truth.

factory 1 VARIOUS PLACES WHERE THINGS ARE MADE ARE forge, foundry, manufacturing plant, mill, refinery, workshop. 2 SEE **building**.

fade 1 *The sun faded the curtains.* to bleach, to discolour, to whiten. 2 *The light faded.* to decline, to diminish, to disappear, to dwindle, to fail, to melt away, to vanish, to wane, to weaken.

fail 1 *His attempt to beat the record failed.* to be unsuccessful, to fall through. 2 *The old man's health was failing.* to decline, to diminish, to disappear, to dwindle, to fade, to melt away, to vanish, to wane, to weaken. 3 *Don't fail to phone us!* to neglect, to omit.

failing *Lucy's main failing is that she is untidy.* defect, fault, imperfection, shortcoming, vice, weakness.

failure *Our attempt to cook a cake was a failure.* disaster, fiasco.

faint 1 *a faint picture.* blurred, dim, faded, hazy, indistinct, misty, pale, shadowy, unclear, weak. 2 *a faint smell.* delicate, slight. 3 *a faint sound.* low, soft. 4 *to feel faint.* dizzy, exhausted, giddy, unsteady, weak. 5 *to faint*: to become unconscious, to collapse.

faint-hearted *He made a faint-hearted attempt to stop the thieves.* cowardly, fearful, shy, spineless, timid, timorous, unheroic.

fair 1 carnival, fun-fair. SEE ALSO **entertainment**. 2 *a Christmas fair.* bazaar, exhibition, festival, fête, market, sale. 3 *fair hair.* blond, light. 4 *a fair referee, a fair decision.* honest, impartial, just, proper, right, unbiased, unprejudiced. 5 *a fair performance.* indifferent, mediocre, middling, moderate, ordinary, reasonable, satisfactory. 6 *fair weather.* bright, cloudless, fine, pleasant, sunny. SEE ALSO **weather**. 7 (old-fashioned) *a fair maiden.* attractive, beautiful, pretty.

fairly moderately, (informal) pretty, rather.

fairy SEE **legend**.

fairy-tale SEE **writing**.

faith 1 *Your dog has faith in you.* belief, confidence, trust. 2 *a religious faith.* conviction, creed, religion.

faithful *The dog is his faithful companion.* consistent, constant, dependable, devoted, dutiful, loyal, reliable, true, trustworthy.

fake 1 *He faked her signature.* to copy, to counterfeit, to feign, to forge, to imitate, to pretend, to reproduce. 2 *faked*: artificial, bogus, false, (informal) phoney, synthetic, unreal. 3 *The £5 note was a fake.* copy, counterfeit, duplicate, forgery, fraud, hoax, imitation, replica, reproduction.

falcon SEE **bird**.

fall 1 *He fell into the river.* to collapse, to drop, to overbalance, to plunge, to tumble. 2 *The temperature falls at night.* to decrease, to decline, to diminish, to lessen. 3 *Millions fell in the First World War.* to be killed, to die, to perish.

fallacy *There's a fallacy in your reasoning.* error, inaccuracy, misconception, mistake, misunderstanding.

false 1 *a false idea.* deceptive, inaccurate, incorrect, misleading, mistaken, untrue, wrong. 2 *a false friend.* deceitful, dishonest, disloyal, lying, treacherous, unfaithful. 3 *a false £5 note.* artificial, bogus, counterfeit, fake, imitation, (informal) phoney, synthetic. 4 *a false name, a false story.* assumed, fictitious, made up, unreal.

falsehood (informal) fib, lie, untruth.

falter *He faltered when he saw the lion coming towards him.* to flinch, to hesitate, to quail, to stagger, to stumble, to totter.

fame *A superstar's fame spreads everywhere.* distinction, glory, importance, prestige, renown, reputation.

familiar 1 *a familiar sight.* common, everyday, normal, regular, usual, well-known. SEE ALSO **ordinary**. 2 *a familiar companion.* close, friendly, intimate. 3 *to be familiar with*: to be acquainted with, to know about.

family 1 brood, clan, generation, kin, kinsmen, litter, relations, relatives, tribe. 2 MEMBERS OF A FAMILY ARE adopted child, ancestor, aunt, brother, cousin, daughter, descendant, divorcee, father, fiancé, fiancée, forefather, foster-child, foster-parent, godchild, godparent, grandchild, grandparent, guardian, husband, mother, nephew, niece, orphan, parent, quadruplet, quintuplet, sextuplet, sister, son, stepchild, stepparent, triplet, twin, uncle, ward, widow, widower, wife.

famine *Why is there famine in the world when we have plenty to eat?* hunger, malnutrition, starvation.

famished *We were famished after our long walk.* hungry, (informal) peckish, ravenous, starving.

famous *a famous person.* celebrated, distinguished, eminent, great, historic, important, legendary, notable, noted, outstanding, prominent, renowned, well-known.

fan *Mrs Brunswick was a Beatles fan.* addict, enthusiast, fanatic, follower, supporter.

fanatic *She was a Beatles fanatic.* addict, enthusiast, fan.

fanciful *We had a fanciful plan to sail to America.* fantastic, imaginary, make-believe, pretended, unreal.

fancy 1 *Mr Brunswick put fancy patterns on Lucy's birthday cake.* decorated, elaborate, ornamental. 2 *I fancied I saw a pink elephant.* to dream, to imagine. 3 *What do you fancy to eat?* to desire, to hanker after, to like, to long for, to prefer, to wish for.

fanfare SEE **music**.

fang *an animal's fang.* tooth.

fantastic 1 *a fantastic story about dragons and wizards.* amazing, extraordinary, fabulous, grotesque, incredible, odd, remarkable, strange, unbelievable, unreal, weird. 2 (informal) *We had a fantastic time.* fabulous, great, marvellous, sensational, wonderful. SEE ALSO **good**.

fantasy *Alice's adventures in Wonderland were a fantasy.* day-dream, dream, illusion, make-believe, reverie.

far far-away, distant, remote.

farce SEE **theatre**.

fare *How much is the fare to London?* charge, cost, payment, price.

farewell au revoir, goodbye.

far-fetched *The story about a singing dog is a bit far-fetched.* improbable, incredible, unbelievable, unconvincing, unlikely.

farm 1 croft, ranch. 2 CROPS GROWN ON FARMS ARE barley, cereals, corn, fodder, fruit, maize, oats, rye, sugar beet, sweetcorn, vegetables, wheat. SEE ALSO **fruit, vegetable.**

3 ANIMALS KEPT ON FARMS ARE bantam, bull, bullock, calf, cattle, chicken, cow, duck, goat, goose, hen, horse, lamb, livestock, pig, poultry, pullet, sheep, turkey. **4** FARM BUILDINGS ARE barn, cow-shed, farmhouse, farmyard, granary, haystack, outhouse, pigsty, rick, shed, silo, stable, sty. **5** KINDS OF FARM EQUIPMENT ARE baler, combine harvester, cultivator, harrow, harvester, mower, pitchfork, planter, plough, scythe, tractor, trailer.

fascinate 1 *Snakes fascinate some people.* to attract, to bewitch, to captivate, to charm, to enchant, to entice, to entrance, to interest, to spellbind. **2** *fascinating*: alluring, attractive, glamorous.

fashion 1 *the latest fashion.* craze, style, taste, trend, vogue. **2** *The headmaster acts in a business-like fashion.* manner, method, mode, style, way.

fashionable *fashionable clothes.* contemporary, modern, smart, sophisticated, stylish, tasteful, (informal) trendy, up-to-date.

fast 1 *a fast pace.* brisk, (informal) nippy, quick, rapid, smart, speedy, swift. **2** *fast colours.* fixed, indelible, permanent. **3** *The ship was fast on the rocks.* firm, immobile, immovable, secure. **4** *In some religions you fast on certain days.* to go without food, to starve.

fasten 1 WAYS OF FASTENING THINGS ARE to adhere, to attach, to bind, to cling, to close, to connect, to fix, to hitch, to join, to knot, to lash, to link, to lock, to moor, to seal, to secure, to stick, to tether, to tie, to unite, to weld. **2** THINGS USED TO FASTEN ARE anchor, bolt, buckle, button, cement, chain, clamp, clasp, clip, glue, hook, knot, lock, nail, padlock, paste, peg, pin, rivet, rope, safety-pin, screw, sellotape, solder, staple, strap, string, tack, tape, wedge, zip.

fastidious *Our cat is fastidious about his food.* (informal) choosey, finicky, funny, particular, squeamish.

fat 1 KINDS OF FAT ARE butter, dripping, grease, lard, margarine, oil, suet. SEE ALSO **food. 2** *a fat person.* chubby, dumpy, flabby, gross, heavy, overweight, plump, podgy, portly, squat, stocky, stout, tubby. **3** *a fat book.* thick. **4** *fat meat.* fatty, greasy, oily.

fatal *a fatal illness.* deadly, lethal, mortal, terminal.

fatality *There were no fatalities in the accident.* casualty, death.

fate *Fate was kind to him.* chance, destiny, doom, fortune, luck, providence.

fated *He believes he was fated to miss that train.* destined, doomed, intended.

father dad, daddy. SEE ALSO **family.**

fathom SEE **measure.**

fatigue exhaustion, tiredness, weakness, weariness.

fault 1 *It was Logan's fault that Lucy fell.* blame, guilt, responsibility. **2** *Look for any faults in your own work.* blemish, defect, error, failing, fallacy, flaw, imperfection, inaccuracy, mistake, shortcoming, slip, vice, weakness.

faulty *Take the faulty goods back.* defective, imperfect, out of order.

favour *Will you do me a favour?* good deed, kindness, service.

favourable 1 *a favourable wind.* beneficial, helpful. **2** *a favourable comment.* approving, encouraging, friendly, generous, kind, sympathetic.

favourite 1 *a favourite toy.* best, chosen, popular, preferred, well-liked. **2** *She's her mother's favourite.* darling, pet.

fawn 1 SEE **young. 2** SEE **colour.**

fear alarm, anxiety, awe, dread, fright, horror, panic, terror.

fearful 1 *He's fearful of spiders.* afraid, anxious, apprehensive, cowardly, cowed, frightened, scared, terrified. **2** *The volcano was a fearful sight.* alarming, appalling, awful, fearsome, frightening, frightful, horrifying, shocking, terrible, terrific, tremendous.

fearless *The fearless rescuer leapt into the sea.* adventurous, bold, brave, courageous, daring, heroic, intrepid, valiant.

feasible *Is the plan to build a twenty-mile bridge feasible?* possible, practicable, realistic, viable, workable.

feast banquet, dinner. SEE ALSO **meal**.

feat *The rescue of the wrecked sailors was a daring feat.* achievement, act, action, deed, exploit, performance.

feathers down, plumage, plumes.

feathery downy, fluffy, light.

feature 1 *One feature of the crime puzzled us.* aspect, characteristic, circumstance, detail. 2 *a person's features.* countenance, expression, face. 3 *a feature film.* SEE **film**.

fee *a fee of £1.* charge, cost, fare, payment, price, subscription, toll.

feeble 1 *I felt feeble after my illness.* delicate, frail, helpless, ill, listless, (informal) poorly, sickly, (informal) weedy. 2 *He put up a feeble defence.* puny, spineless, weak. 3 *She made some feeble excuse.* flimsy, lame, poor, tame, weak.

feed to nourish, to strengthen. SEE ALSO **eat**.

feel 1 *Feel this lovely velvet.* to finger, to handle, to manipulate, to stroke, to touch. 2 *Can you feel your way in the dark?* to grope. 3 *It feels colder today.* to seem. 4 *Do you feel the cold?* to detect, to experience, to know, to notice, to perceive, to sense, to suffer. 5 *I feel it's time to go home.* to believe, to consider, to think.

feeling 1 *What were your feelings when you won?* emotion, passion, sensation, sentiment. 2 *Lucy's feeling was that we ought to invite granny for dinner.* attitude, belief, impression, opinion, thought. 3 *There was a happy feeling at the party.* atmosphere, mood, tone. 4 *I have a feeling I'm going to be lucky.* guess, hunch, instinct, intuition.

feign *Logan feigned a cold to avoid going out.* to act, to concoct, to counterfeit, to fake, to forge, to invent, to pretend.

fell 1 down, hill. SEE ALSO **geography**. 2 *A lumberjack fells trees.* to cut down, to knock down.

fellow (informal) bloke, chap, (informal) guy, man.

fellowship *Most people enjoy the fellowship of others.* companionship, company, friendship, society.

felt *a felt hat.* SEE **cloth**.

female FEMALE CREATURES ARE bitch, cow, doe, ewe, hen, lioness, mare, nanny-goat, sow, tigress, vixen.

feminine *feminine clothes.* female, girlish, ladylike, womanly.

fen bog, marsh, swamp. SEE ALSO **geography**.

fence 1 *a garden fence.* barrier, hedge, hurdle, obstacle, paling, palisade, railing, stockade, wall. 2 *We fenced in the animals.* to enclose, to encircle, to hedge in, to pen, to surround, to wall in.

fend *The boxer fended off his opponent's blows.* to keep off, to parry, to push away, to repel, to repulse, to ward off.

ferment *Mr Brunswick's wine is fermenting.* to bubble, to effervesce, to fizz, to foam.

fern SEE **plant**.

ferocious *a ferocious attack.* barbaric, barbarous, bloodthirsty, bloody, brutal, cruel, fierce, inhuman, merciless, murderous, pitiless, ruthless, sadistic, savage, vicious, violent.

ferret SEE **animal, pet**.

ferry 1 *The ship ferried us to the island.* to carry, to convey, to take, to transfer, to transport. 2 SEE **vessel**.

fertile *a fertile garden.* flourishing, fruitful, lush, productive.

fertilizer compost, manure.

fervent *Tony is a fervent follower of the local team.* avid, eager, enthusiastic, keen, passionate, zealous.

festering *a festering wound.* infected, inflamed, poisoned, putrid.

festival carnival, celebration, fair, feast, festivity, fête, gala, jamboree, jubilee.

festive *Christmas is supposed to be a festive occasion.* cheerful, gay, gleeful, happy, joyful, joyous, light-hearted, merry.

fetch *Our dog fetches the newspaper.* to bring, to carry, to collect, to get, to obtain, to retrieve.

fetching *a fetching dress.* appealing, attractive, charming, lovely, pretty. SEE ALSO **beautiful**.

fête carnival, fair, festival, gala, jamboree.

fetters *The prisoner was in fetters.* bonds, chains, handcuffs, irons, shackles.

feud *There was a bitter feud between the two families.* dispute, quarrel, strife, vendetta.

fever SEE **illness**.

fiancé, fiancée SEE **family**.
! A *fiancé* is a man; a *fiancée* is a woman.

fiasco *Our play was a fiasco.* disaster, failure, (informal) flop, (informal) mess-up.

fib SEE **lie**.

fibre strand, thread.

fibreglass SEE **material**.

fickle *Our weather is so fickle that you never know what clothes to wear.* changeable, erratic, inconsistent, unpredictable, unreliable, variable.

fiction SEE **book**.

fictional, fictitious *His story was fictitious.* fabulous, false, fanciful, imaginary, invented, legendary, made-up, mythical, unreal.

fiddle 1 violin. SEE ALSO **music, strings**. 2 *Please don't fiddle with the knobs on the TV.* to fidget, to twiddle.

fidelity faithfulness, honesty, integrity.

fidget *It irritates other people when you fidget all the time!* to be restless, to fiddle, to jerk, to twiddle, to twitch.

fidgety *The horses became fidgety as the storm approached.* impatient, jittery, jumpy, nervous, restless.

field 1 *Cows grazed in the field.* enclosure, meadow, paddock, pasture. 2 *a games field.* arena, ground, pitch, stadium.

field-glasses binoculars. SEE ALSO **optical**.

fiend demon, devil, imp, spirit.

fierce *a fierce attack, a fierce animal, etc.* angry, barbaric, bloodthirsty, brutal, cruel, ferocious, merciless, murderous, savage, vicious, violent.

fiery 1 *a fiery furnace.* blazing, burning, flaming, hot, red, red-hot. 2 *a fiery temper.* angry, furious, livid, mad, raging.

fig SEE **fruit**.

fight KINDS OF FIGHT ARE action, attack, battle, bout, boxing-match, brawl, clash, combat, competition, confrontation, conflict, contest, counter-attack, duel, encounter, engagement, feud, hostilities, joust, quarrel, raid, rivalry, row, scramble, scrap, scuffle, squabble, strife, struggle, tussle, vendetta, war, wrestling.

fighter VARIOUS FIGHTERS ARE archer, boxer, gladiator, guerrilla, gunman, knight, marine, mercenary, paratrooper, partisan, SEE **soldier**, troops, warrior, wrestler.

figure 1 *Write down the figures 1 to 10.* digit, integer, number, numeral. 2 *Ask Tony to add it up: he's good at figures.* mathematics, sums, statistics. 3 *He has a plump figure.* form, outline, shape. 4 *In the temple was a bronze figure of the goddess.* carving, image, statue. 5 *Figure out how much we owe.* to add up, to calculate, to compute, to reckon, to total, to work out.

file 1 SEE **tool**. 2 *Stand in single file.* column, line, queue, rank, row. 3 *Keep your papers in a file.* folder.

fill 1 *Fill the box with sweets.* to cram, to crowd, to load up, to pack, to occupy. 2 *The drain was filled with muck.* to block up, to jam, to obstruct, to plug, to stop up. **3** *Mrs Brunswick tells us not to pick the peas until the pods fill out.* to enlarge, to expand, to swell.

filling station SEE **building**.

film 1 VARIOUS CINEMA OR TV FILMS ARE cartoon, documentary, feature, movie, western. **2** *a film of oil.* coating, covering, layer, sheet, skin.

filter *You filter the liquid to remove the solid bits.* to sieve, to strain.

filth dirt, grime, (informal) muck, mud, pollution.

filthy 1 *filthy shoes, a filthy room, etc.* caked, dirty, dusty, foul, grimy, grubby, messy, (informal) mucky, muddy, soiled, sooty, sordid, squalid. **2** *filthy language.* coarse, crude, improper, indecent, offensive, rude, smutty, vulgar.

fin SEE **aircraft, fish**.

final *the final moments of the game.* closing, concluding, last, ultimate.

finally eventually, ultimately.

finch SEE **bird**.

find 1 *Where do you find fossils?* to come across, to discover, to dig up, to locate, to uncover, to unearth. **2** *Did mum find her handbag?* to get back, to recover, to regain, to retrieve, to trace. **3** *Did you find your friends?* to encounter, to meet. **4** *Did the garage find the fault in the car?* to detect, to diagnose, to identify, to notice, to observe.

fine 1 *a parking fine.* charge, penalty. SEE ALSO **punishment**. **2** *fine weather.* bright, cloudless, fair, pleasant, sunny. **3** *a fine thread.* narrow, slender, slim, thin. **4** *fine sand.* minute, powdered, powdery. **5** *fine embroidery.* beautiful, dainty, delicate, exquisite. **6** *a fine performance.* admirable, excellent, first-class. SEE ALSO **good**.

finger 1 SEE **body, hand**. **2** *Please don't finger the food.* to feel, to handle, to stroke, to touch.

finicky *Our cat's finicky about food.* (informal) choosey, fastidious, fussy, particular.

finish 1 *Finish your work.* to accomplish, to complete, to conclude, to end, to round off, to stop, to terminate. **2** *Did we finish that box of sweets?* to consume, to exhaust, (informal) to polish off, to use up. **3** *When did they finish dinner?* to break off, to cease, to discontinue, to halt. **4** (informal) *to finish off:* to destroy, to dispatch, to exterminate. SEE ALSO **kill**.

fiord inlet. SEE ALSO **geography**.

fir SEE **tree**.

fire 1 blaze, bonfire, conflagration, inferno. **2** *Modern houses don't always have a fire in the lounge.* fireplace, grate, hearth. **3** OTHER KINDS OF HEATING APPARATUS ARE boiler, central heating, convector, electric fire, forge, furnace, gas fire, heater, immersion heater, incinerator, kiln, oven, stove. **4** *The vandals fired a barn.* to burn, to ignite, to kindle, to light, to set fire to. **5** *to fire a gun.* to detonate, to discharge, to explode, to let off. **6** *The gunners fired at the ship.* to bombard, to shell. **7** *His boss fired him.* to dismiss, to sack.

firearms 1 guns. **2** VARIOUS FIREARMS ARE machine-gun, pistol, revolver, rifle, shotgun, sub-machine-gun. SEE ALSO **weapon**.

fire-engine SEE **vehicle**.

fireman SEE **job**.

fireplace fire, grate, hearth.

firework VARIOUS FIREWORKS ARE banger, Catherine wheel, cracker, rocket, sparkler, squib.

firm 1 *Is the ice firm?* hard, rigid, solid, stable, stiff, unyielding. **2** *Is the nail firm?* fast, fixed, immovable, secure, steady, tight. **3** *She was quite firm that she didn't want to play.* adamant, decided, determined, dogged, obstinate, persistent, resolute, unwavering. **4** *a firm arrangement.* agreed, settled, unchangeable. **5** *a firm friend.* constant, dependable, devoted, faithful, loyal, reliable. **6** *Mr Brunswick wants to be boss of his own firm.* business, company, concern, corporation, establishment, organization.

first 1 *Who was the first to arrive?* earliest, soonest. **2** *Who made the first aeroplane?* initial, original. **3** *Who is your first choice?* foremost, leading, prime.

first-class SEE **excellent**.

fish 1 VARIOUS FISH ARE carp, chub, cod, eel, goldfish, haddock, herring, mackerel, minnow, perch, pike, pilchard, plaice, salmon, sardine, shark, sole, stickleback, tiddler, trout. SEE ALSO **shellfish**. **2** PARTS OF A FISH ARE dorsal fin, fin, gills, roe, scales, tail. **3** *fishing:* angling, trawling.

fishmonger SEE **shop**.

fist hand, knuckles.

fit 1 *Is that old house fit to live in?* appropriate, fitting, proper, right, suitable. **2** *Will Lucy be fit for the gymnastics display?* able, capable, healthy, prepared, ready, strong, well. **3** *Do casual clothes fit the occasion?* to become, to suit. **4** *Can you fit the pieces together?* to assemble, to build, to construct, to put together. **5** *She had a fit of coughing.* attack, bout, convulsion, outbreak, seizure, spasm. SEE ALSO **illness**.

fitting *Lucy waited for a fitting moment to mention the broken window.* appropriate, apt, due, proper, right, suitable, timely.

fix 1 *to fix something into place, to fix things together.* to attach, to bind, to join, to link, to make firm, to secure. SEE ALSO **fasten**. **2** *to fix a price for something.* to agree, to arrange, to decide, to establish, to settle. **3** *to fix a broken window.* to mend, to put right, to repair. **4** *to get into a fix.* difficulty, dilemma, jam, plight, predicament, problem.

fixture *Our team has a fixture at home this week.* appointment, engagement, meeting.

fizz to bubble, to effervesce, to fizzle, to foam, to froth.

fizzy *fizzy drinks.* bubbly, effervescent, foaming, sparkling.

flabby *a flabby tummy.* fat, feeble, overweight, out of condition, weak.

flag 1 *decorated with flags.* banner, colours, ensign, streamer. **2** *After two hours our interest flagged.* to decline, to flop, to sink, to weaken, to wilt, to worsen.

flake *flakes of old paint, flakes of flint.* bit, chip, scale, slice, splinter.

flame to blaze, to flare. SEE ALSO **burn**.

flamingo SEE **bird**.

flan SEE **cake**.

flannel SEE **cloth**.

flap *The flag flapped in the wind.* to flutter, to swing, to wave.

flare to blaze, to flame. SEE ALSO **burn**.

flash SEE **light**.

flashy *flashy clothes.* bright, elaborate, fancy, gaudy, showy.

flask bottle. SEE ALSO **container**.

flat 1 *a flat surface.* even, horizontal, level, smooth. **2** *a flat sea.* calm. **3** *to lie in a flat position.* prone, spread out. **4** *a flat voice.* boring, dull, monotonous, unexciting, uninteresting. **5** *to live in a flat.* SEE **house**.

flatten 1 *We must flatten the lawn if we want to play cricket on it.* to even out, to iron out, to level, to press, to roll, to smooth. **2** *The hurricane flattened the town.* to crush, to demolish, to destroy, to devastate, to knock down. **3** *Tony flattened Mrs Brunswick's geraniums.* to run over, to trample. **4** *We flattened the opposition.* SEE **defeat**.

flatter 1 to humour. **2** *flattering: a flattering remark.* complimentary.

flavour 1 SEE **taste**. **2** *Mrs Angel read an extract to give us the flavour of the book.* character, characteristic, quality.

flaw *a flaw in a piece of work.* blemish, crack, defect, error, fault, imperfection, inaccuracy, mistake, shortcoming, weakness.

flea SEE **insect**.

fledgeling SEE **bird, young**.

flee *We fled when the lion roared.* to abscond, to escape, to run away.

fleet *a fleet of ships.* armada, convoy, navy, squadron. SEE ALSO **group**.

flesh meat, muscle.

flex *The flex for our iron needs replacing.* cable, lead, wire. SEE ALSO **electricity**.

flexible bendable, (informal) bendy, floppy, pliable, soft, springy, supple.

flick to flip. SEE ALSO **hit**.

flicker *The candles flickered.* to blink, to flutter, to glimmer, to quiver, to tremble, to twinkle, to waver. SEE ALSO **light**.

flight 1 SEE **travel**. 2 escape, getaway, retreat, running away.

flimsy *A butterfly's wings seem so flimsy.* brittle, delicate, feeble, frail, fragile, rickety, shaky, slight, thin, weak.

flinch *Tony flinched when the dog rushed at him.* to cringe, to falter, to jerk away, to quail, to recoil, to shrink back, to wince.

fling *I flung a coin into the well.* to cast, (informal) to chuck, to hurl, to lob, to sling, to throw, to toss.

flint SEE **rock**.

flip to flick. SEE ALSO **hit**.

flipper SEE **limb**.

flit *Bats flitted about.* to dart, to fly, to skim. SEE ALSO **move**.

float 1 *to float on water.* to drift, to sail, to swim. 2 *to float in the air.* to drift, to hang, to hover. 3 *We're ready to float our raft.* to launch. 4 *a milk-float.* SEE **vehicle**.

flock *a flock of birds.* SEE **group**.

floe ice, iceberg.

flog 1 to beat, to cane, to lash, to scourge, to thrash, to wallop, to whip. SEE ALSO **hit**. 2 *flogging:* SEE **punishment**.

flood 1 *When the dam burst a flood of water swept through the valley.* deluge, inundation, spate, torrent. SEE ALSO **disaster**. 2 *The water flooded the whole town.* to drown, to engulf, to inundate, to overflow, to submerge, to swamp.

floodlights SEE **light**.

floor 1 SEE **building**. 2 VARIOUS FLOOR COVERINGS ARE carpet, lino, mat, matting, rug, tiles. 3 *The bedrooms are on the top floor.* deck, level, storey.

flop *The seedlings we forgot to water began to flop.* to collapse, to dangle, to droop, to drop, to fall, to flag, to sag, to wilt.

floppy *The cabbage seedlings have gone floppy.* bendable, (informal) bendy, flexible, limp, pliable.

floppy disc SEE **computer**.

florist SEE **shop**.

flounder *We floundered about in the mud.* to struggle, to wallow.

flour SEE **food**.

flourish 1 *Mrs Brunswick's plants are flourishing now that we've had some rain.* to be fruitful, to be successful, to bloom, to blossom, to flower, to grow, to prosper, to strengthen, to succeed, to thrive. 2 *He flourished his umbrella to attract our attention.* to brandish, to shake, to twirl, to wave.

flow WAYS IN WHICH LIQUIDS FLOW ARE to dribble, to drip, to ebb, to gush, to leak, to move in a current, to ooze, to pour, to run, to seep, to stream, to trickle.

flower 1 *There are flowers in the garden.* bloom, blossom, petal. 2 *a bunch of flowers:* arrangement, bouquet, garland, posy, spray, wreath. 3 VARIOUS FLOWERS ARE bluebell, buttercup, carnation, catkin, chrysanthemum, cornflower, cowslip, crocus, daffodil, daisy, dandelion, forget-me-not, foxglove, geranium, hollyhock, hyacinth, iris, lilac, lily, lupin, marigold, orchid, pansy, peony, pink, poppy, primrose, rhododendron, rose, snowdrop, sunflower, tulip, violet, wallflower, water-lily.

flu SEE **illness**.

fluent *a fluent speaker of French.* eloquent, flowing, unhesitating.

fluffy *fluffy toys.* downy, feathery, fleecy, furry, fuzzy, woolly.

fluid *a fluid substance.* flowing, liquid, runny, sloppy, watery.

fluke *It was only a fluke that you scored.* accident, chance, luck.

flush 1 *to flush the lavatory.* to rinse out, to wash out. 2 *Mrs Angel flushed with embarrassment.* to blush, to colour, to glow, to redden.

flustered *Keep calm: don't get flustered.* confused, distressed, embarrassed, nervous.

flute SEE **woodwind**.

flutter *The leaves fluttered in the wind.* to flap, to flicker, to quiver, to tremble.

fly 1 *Most birds fly.* to flit, to glide, to hover, to rise, to soar, to swoop. 2 *A flag was flying.* to flap, to flutter, to wave. 3 SEE **move**. 4 *A lot of flies were buzzing about.* SEE **insect**.

fly-over SEE **road**.

foal SEE **horse, young**.

foam 1 froth, lather, scum, suds. 2 *What makes the water foam?* to bubble, to effervesce, to fizz, to froth, to lather.

fo'c'sle SEE **vessel**.

focus 1 SEE **photography**. 2 *Let's focus on the main problem.* to concentrate on, to look at, to think about. 3 *The market square is the main focus of the town.* centre, core, heart, hub.

fodder hay, silage.

foe adversary, antagonist, attacker, enemy, opponent, opposition, rival.

foetus embryo.

fog cloud, haze, mist. SEE ALSO **weather**.

foil 1 *The security officer foiled the thieves.* to block, to frustrate, to halt, to hamper, to hinder, to obstruct, to prevent, to stop. 2 *to fight with foils.* sword. SEE ALSO **weapon**.

fold 1 *Fold the paper.* to bend, to crease, to double over. 2 *My umbrella folds up.* to collapse. 3 *The curtains hung in folds.* crease, pleat, wrinkle. 4 *The dog drove the sheep into the fold.* compound, enclosure, pen.

folder *a folder to keep papers in.* cover, file.

foliage *We want some foliage to put with the flowers.* greenery, leaves.

folk human beings, humanity, people. SEE ALSO **person**.

folk-song SEE **sing**.

folk-tale SEE **writing**.

follow 1 *Follow the car in front!* to chase, to hound, to hunt, to pursue, to shadow, to stalk, to tag on to, to tail, to track, to trail. 2 *Another bus follows this one in a few minutes.* to come after, to replace, to succeed. 3 *Follow the instructions.* to heed, to keep to, to obey, to observe, to take notice of. 4 *Did you follow what he said?* to comprehend, to grasp, to understand. 5 *Do you follow football?* to be interested in, to know about, to support.

follower admirer, apostle, disciple, fan, supporter.

fond *a fond kiss.* affectionate, attached, loving, partial, tender.

fondle *He fondled the dog's ears.* to caress, to kiss, to pat, to pet, to stroke, to touch.

font SEE **church**.

food 1 delicacy, diet, fodder, (informal) grub, nourishment, protein, provisions, recipe, refreshments, swill, vitamins. SEE ALSO **drink, meal**. 2 KINDS OF FOOD ARE batter, beans, SEE **biscuit**, blancmange, bran, bread, broth, SEE **cake**, caviare, SEE **cereal**, cheese, chips, chop suey, cornflakes, cornflour, cream, crisps, curry, custard, dumplings, egg, SEE **fat**, SEE **fish**, flour, fritter, SEE **fruit**, glucose, goulash, greens, haggis, hash, health foods, honey, hot-pot, ice-cream, icing, jam, jelly, junket, kipper, kosher food, lasagne, macaroni, malt, marmalade, SEE **meat**, milk, mincemeat, mince pie, mousse, noodles, SEE **nut**, oatmeal, omelette, pancake, pasta, pastry, pasty, pâté, pie, pizza, porridge, pudding, quiche, rice, risotto, rissole, rusk, SEE **salad**, sandwich, sausage, sausage-roll, scampi, seafood, semolina, soufflé, soup, soya beans, spaghetti, stew, stock, stuffing,

syrup, tart, toast, treacle, trifle, SEE **vegetable**, vegetarian food, wholemeal flour, yeast, yogurt.
3 THINGS YOU ADD TO FOOD ARE chutney, colouring, dressing, garlic, gravy, herbs, ketchup, mayonnaise, mustard, pepper, pickle, preservative, salt, sauce, seasoning, spice, sugar, vanilla, vinegar.

fool 1 ass, blockhead, booby, dope, dunce, half-wit, idiot, ignoramus, imbecile, moron, nit, nitwit, twerp.
! These words are mostly used informally and are often insulting. 2 *the king's fool.* clown, entertainer, jester. 3 *Logan fooled us by saying he'd won a prize.* to bluff, to cheat, to deceive, to dupe, to hoax, to hoodwink, to kid, to mislead, to swindle, to take in, to trick.

foolish *It was foolish of Logan to try to trick the headmaster.* absurd, crazy, frivolous, idiotic, irrational, ludicrous, misguided, ridiculous, silly, stupid, unwise.

foot 1 hoof, paw. SEE ALSO **body, leg.** 2 PARTS OF A FOOT ARE ankle, heel, instep, sole, toe. 3 *There are 12 inches in one foot.* SEE **measure.**

football 1 soccer. SEE ALSO **sport.** 2 WORDS USED IN FOOTBALL ARE ball, corner, cup tie, defender, draw, forward, foul, goal, goalkeeper, linesman, match, offside, penalty, pitch, referee, striker, touch-line.

footlights SEE **theatre.**

footman SEE **servant.**

footpath SEE **road.**

footplate SEE **railway.**

forbid *Mrs Brunswick forbids smoking in the house.* to ban, to bar, to deter, to outlaw, to prohibit, to veto.

forbidding *forbidding storm-clouds.* gloomy, grim, menacing, ominous, stern, threatening, unfriendly.

force 1 *We used all our force to open the door.* energy, might, power, pressure, strength, vigour. 2 *You can't force me to play with you.* to compel, to drive, to make, to oblige, to order. 3 *We had to force the door because it was locked.* to

break open, to burst open, to wrench.

forceful *a forceful leader.* dynamic, energetic, enthusiastic, masterful, powerful, strong, vigorous.

forceps SEE **medicine.**

ford SEE **road.**

foreboding *I had a foreboding that something nasty would happen.* omen, premonition, warning.

forecast 1 *They forecast rain.* to foresee, to foretell, to predict, to prophesy. 2 *the weather forecast.* outlook, prediction, prophecy.

forecastle SEE **vessel.**

forefather ancestor, predecessor. SEE ALSO **family.**

forehead SEE **body, head.**

foreign 1 *a foreign country.* alien, strange, unfamiliar. 2 *foreign goods.* imported.

foreigner *Many foreigners pass through the airport.* alien, immigrant, outsider, visitor.

foreman boss, controller, head, superintendent, supervisor. SEE ALSO **chief.**

foresee *Do they foresee any improvement in the weather?* to anticipate, to expect, to forecast, to foretell, to predict, to prophesy.

forethought planning.

forfeit *to pay a forfeit.* fine, penalty.

forge 1 *a blacksmith's forge.* furnace. 2 *to forge £5 notes.* to copy, to counterfeit, to fake, to imitate.

forgery copy, fake, fraud, imitation, replica, reproduction.

forget 1 *We almost forgot Mother's Day last year.* to disregard, to ignore, to leave out, to miss out, to neglect, to overlook, to skip. 2 *Logan forgot his money as usual.* to leave behind.

forgetful absent-minded, careless, inattentive, negligent, scatter-brained, thoughtless.

forget-me-not SEE **flower.**

forgive *Mrs Brunswick never forgave Tony for trampling on her geraniums.* to excuse, to pardon, to spare.

fork SEE **cutlery, garden.**
forked *a forked stick.* branched, divided, V-shaped.
forlorn *Lucy looked forlorn when the doctor said she couldn't play.* dejected, depressed, desolate, miserable, neglected, unhappy, wistful, wretched. SEE ALSO **sad.**
form 1 *a human form.* figure, outline, shape. 2 *What form of exercise do you like best?* kind, sort, type, variety. 3 *Tony is in Mrs Angel's form.* class, group, set. 4 *We sat on a form.* bench, seat. 5 *If you want a bus pass, you fill in a form.* document, paper. 6 *Tony formed the clay into a ball.* to cast, to mould, to shape. 7 *These players form an excellent team.* to compose, to constitute, to create, to make up, to produce. 8 *In cold weather, icicles form under the bridge.* to appear, to develop, to grow, to take shape.
formal *prize-giving was a formal occasion.* ceremonial, dignified, official, (informal) posh, proper, solemn, stately.
forsake *The dog never forsook his master.* to abandon, to desert, to evacuate, to give up, to leave, to quit, to renounce.
fort castle, citadel, fortress, garrison, stronghold.
forthwith directly, immediately, instantly, promptly.
fortify *We fortified our den against Logan's gang.* to defend, to protect, to reinforce, to strengthen.
fortitude *Lucy endured the pain with fortitude.* bravery, courage, heroism, patience, (informal) pluck, valour.
fortnight SEE **time.**
fortress castle, citadel, fort, garrison, stronghold.
fortunate *a fortunate accident.* favourable, happy, lucky.
fortune 1 *good fortune, bad fortune.* chance, destiny, fate, luck, providence. 2 *The duke lost his fortune by gambling.* estate, inheritance, possessions, property, wealth.
fortune-teller prophet.

forward *It was forward of you to yell 'Happy Christmas' at the headmaster.* bold, brazen, cheeky, impudent, insolent, shameless.
forwards ahead, onwards.
foster SEE **family.**
foul 1 *a foul mess.* dirty, disgusting, filthy, nasty, nauseating, obnoxious, repulsive, revolting. SEE ALSO **unpleasant.** 2 *foul weather.* rainy, rough, stormy, violent, windy. SEE ALSO **weather.** 3 *foul language.* blasphemous, coarse, common, crude, improper, indecent, offensive, rude, uncouth, vulgar. 4 *a foul crime.* atrocious, cruel, evil, monstrous, vicious, vile, villainous, wicked. 5 *foul air.* contaminated, impure, infected, polluted, smelly, unclean. 6 *a foul stroke.* illegal, prohibited.
found 1 *Mr Brunswick's dad founded a business in the High Street.* to begin, to create, to establish, to set up. 2 *They founded the castle on solid rock.* to base, to build, to construct, to erect.
foundation *the foundations of a building.* base, basis, bottom, foot.
foundry SEE **factory.**
fountain *a fountain of water.* jet, spray.
fountain pen SEE **write.**
four-poster SEE **bed.**
fowl bird, chicken, hen.
fox SEE **animal.**
foxglove SEE **flower.**
foxhound SEE **dog.**
foyer entrance, hall, lobby. SEE ALSO **theatre.**
fraction 1 *Only a fraction of the crowd could hear what was going on.* part, portion, section. 2 *to divide something into fractions.* shares.
fracture *to fracture a leg.* to break, to crack. SEE ALSO **wound.**
fragile *Eggshell is fragile.* breakable, brittle, delicate, frail, thin.
fragments 1 *Tony smashed granny's teapot into fragments.* atoms, bits, particles, smithereens. 2 *Please sweep up the fragments.* chips, crumbs, debris, pieces, remnants, scraps, snippets, specks.

frail 1 *As you get old, you get more frail.* delicate, feeble, infirm, unsteady, weak, (insulting) weedy.2 *The first aircraft were frail machines.* brittle, flimsy, fragile, rickety.

frame 1 *a frame for a tent.* framework, skeleton.2 *a frame for a picture.* border, edge, edging.3 *Tony framed his picture in a coloured border.* to enclose, to mount, to surround.

framework frame, outline, plan, skeleton, structure.

frank *a frank reply.* candid, direct, honest, open, outspoken, plain, sincere, straightforward.

frantic *Dad went frantic when he lost his wallet.* berserk, crazy, demented, deranged, frenzied, hectic, hysterical, mad, wild.

fraud 1 *He was put in prison for fraud.* deceit, deception, dishonesty.2 *The so-called magic was a fraud.* cheat, counterfeit, fake, hoax, ruse, sham, trick.

fraudulent cheating, crooked, deceitful, dishonest, false, lying, underhand, unscrupulous.

frayed *a frayed collar.* ragged, tattered, (informal) tatty, worn.

freak *freak weather conditions.* abnormal, exceptional, peculiar, queer, unusual.

freckle SEE **complexion**.

free 1 *Are you free to come?* able, allowed, permitted.2 *The slaves wanted to be free.* emancipated, liberated, released.3 *Uncle George is free with his money.* bounteous, generous, lavish, liberal.4 *Is the lavatory free?* available, open, unoccupied.5 *The judge freed him.* to acquit, to discharge, to let off, to let go, to pardon, to spare.6 *Robin Hood freed his friends from the castle.* to liberate, to release, to rescue, to save, to set free.

freedom *The slaves wanted their freedom.* independence, liberty.

free-wheel *Tony free-wheeled downhill.* to coast, to drift, to glide.

freeze 1 *to freeze food.* to chill, to ice, to refrigerate.2 *Will it freeze tonight?* SEE **weather**.

freezer SEE **kitchen**.

freight *Some aircraft carry passengers and some carry freight.* cargo, goods, load, merchandise.

frenzied *The frenzied fans screamed.* berserk, crazy, delirious, demented, frantic, hysterical, mad, wild.

frenzy *a frenzy of excitement.* hysteria, insanity, madness, mania.

frequent 1 *frequent bouts of illness, frequent trains.* constant, continual, countless, many, numerous, persistent, recurrent.2 *The cuckoo is a frequent visitor to Britain.* common, habitual, regular.

fresh 1 *The detectives looked for fresh clues.* different, new, recent, up-to-date.2 *We put fresh sheets on the bed.* airy, clean, unused, untouched. 3 *You feel fresh after a shower.* energetic, healthy, invigorated, lively, perky, rested.4 *fresh water.* pure, unpolluted.

fret *The dog fretted while his master was away.* to grieve, to worry.

fretsaw SEE **tool**.

friar SEE **church**.

fridge SEE **kitchen**.

friend acquaintance, ally, chum, companion, comrade, (informal) mate, (informal) pal, partner, pen-friend.

friendly *a friendly girl, a friendly welcome, etc.* affectionate, agreeable, amiable, attached, close, familiar, good-natured, favourable, gracious, helpful, hospitable, intimate, kind, kind-hearted, loving, sociable, sympathetic, tender, warm, welcoming.

frieze *a decorative frieze.* border, edging.

frigate SEE **vessel**.

fright alarm, dread, fear, horror, panic, terror.

frighten 1 *Logan frightened the cat.* to alarm, to appal, to bully, to daunt, to dismay, to horrify, to intimidate, to make afraid, to menace, to

persecute, to petrify, to scare, to shake, to shock, to startle, to terrify, to terrorize, to threaten. 2 *frightened*: afraid, apprehensive, fearful.
3 *frightening*: creepy, eerie, ghostly, hair-raising, scary, sinister, spooky, uncanny, weird.

frightful *a frightful accident*. appalling, awful, dreadful, fearful, fearsome, ghastly, grisly, hideous, horrible, horrid, horrifying, shocking, terrible. SEE ALSO **unpleasant**.

frill *a curtain with a frill round the bottom*. border, edging, fringe.

fringe 1 *a fringe round the bottom of a curtain*. border, edging, frill. 2 *the fringe of a town*. edge, outskirts.

frisk *Lambs were frisking in the field*. to caper, to dance, to jump about, to leap, to prance, to romp, to skip.

frisky jaunty, lively, perky, playful, spirited, sprightly.

fritter 1 SEE **food**. 2 *to fritter away your money*. to misuse, to squander, to waste.

frivolous *Mrs Angel hates Logan's frivolous questions*. foolish, ridiculous, silly, stupid, trivial, unimportant, worthless.

frock dress, gown. SEE ALSO **clothes**.

frog SEE **amphibious**.

frogman diver.

front *the front of an aircraft, the front of a house*. face, head, nose.

frontier *the frontier between two countries*. border, boundary.

frost, frosty SEE **cold, weather**.

frostbite SEE **illness**.

froth bubbles, foam, lather, scum, suds.

frown to glower, to scowl. SEE ALSO **expression**.

fruit VARIOUS FRUITS ARE apple, apricot, banana, berry, blackberry, cherry, citrus fruit, coconut, crab-apple, currant, damson, date, fig, gooseberry, grape, grapefruit, greengage, hip, lemon, lime, melon, olive, orange, peach, pear, pineapple, plum, prune, raisin, raspberry, rhubarb, strawberry, sultana, tangerine, tomato.

fruitful 1 *a fruitful search*. profitable, successful. 2 *a fruitful garden*. fertile, flourishing, lush, productive.

fruitless *a fruitless search*. futile, pointless, unsuccessful, useless.

frustrate *The police frustrated an attempted robbery*. to foil, to halt, to hinder, to prevent, to stop.

fry SEE **cook**.

frying-pan SEE **cook, kitchen**.

fuddled 1 *I'm always fuddled when I wake up*. confused, flustered, mixed up, muddled. 2 *fuddled with alcohol*. drunk, intoxicated.

fudge SEE **sweet**.

fuel KINDS OF FUEL ARE anthracite, butane, charcoal, coal, coke, electricity, gas, gasoline, logs, methylated spirit, nuclear fuel, oil, paraffin, peat, petrol, propane.

fugitive deserter, refugee, renegade.

fulfil 1 *I wonder if Lucy will fulfil her ambition to compete in the Olympics?* to accomplish, to achieve, to carry out, to complete, to perform. 2 *Did the shop fulfil your requirements?* to meet, to satisfy.

full 1 *The shops are full at Christmas*. bursting, congested, crammed, crowded, filled, jammed, packed, stuffed. 2 *My cup is full*. brimming, overflowing. 3 *Tell us the full story*. complete, entire, total, whole. 4 *She ran at full speed*. greatest, highest, maximum.

full stop SEE **punctuation**.

fumble *He fumbled the ball*. to grope at, to mishandle.

fume 1 *fuming chimneys*. to smoke. 2 *He was fuming because his money had been stolen*. SEE **angry**.

fumes exhaust, gases, smoke, vapour.

fun amusement, jokes, laughter, merriment, pastimes, play, pleasure, recreation. SEE ALSO **entertainment, game**.

function 1 *The function of the police is to keep order*. aim, duty, job, purpose, task, use. 2 *Uncle Rick's wedding was a happy function*. ceremony, event, gathering, occasion, party, reception. **3** *This computer isn't functioning properly*. to act, to behave, to operate, to perform, to work.

fundamental *Lucy learned the fundamental skills of windsurfing*. basic, elementary, essential, important, main, primary, principal.

funds *Mr Brunswick needs more funds to start his business*. capital, money, resources, savings, wealth.

funeral 1 burial, cremation. **2** WORDS TO DO WITH FUNERALS ARE cemetery, coffin, crematorium, grave, graveyard, hearse, memorial, mortuary, mourner, tomb, undertaker, wreath.

fun-fair SOME ENTERTAINMENTS AT A FUN-FAIR ARE dodgems, merry-go-round, roundabout, side-show.

fungus mushroom, toadstool. SEE ALSO **plant**.

funny 1 *a funny joke*. absurd, amusing, comic, crazy, facetious, farcical, hilarious, humorous, hysterical, laughable, ludicrous, (informal) priceless, ridiculous, uproarious, witty, zany. **2** *Tony had a funny pain in his stomach*. abnormal, curious, odd, peculiar, queer, strange, unusual.

funny-bone SEE **body**.

fur 1 *Many animals are covered in fur*. bristles, down, fleece, hair. **2** *Primitive people used to dress in furs*. hide, skin.

furious *a furious bull*. angry, cross, enraged, fuming, incensed, indignant, infuriated, irate, livid, mad, raging.

furlong SEE **measure**.

furnace SEE **fire**.

furnish *Mr Brunswick has a workshop furnished with the latest gadgets*. to equip, to fit up, to provide, to supply.

furniture KINDS OF FURNITURE ARE antique, armchair, bed, bench, bookcase, bunk, bureau, cabinet, chair, chest of drawers, cot, couch, cradle, cupboard, cushion, deck-

chair, desk, divan, drawer, dresser, easel, fender, fireplace, mantelpiece, pew, pouffe, rocking-chair, settee, sideboard, sofa, stool, suite, table, trestle table, wardrobe, workbench.

furrow crease, groove, rut, wrinkle.

furry *furry animals*. bristly, downy, feathery, fleecy, fuzzy, hairy, woolly.

further *We'd like further information*. additional, extra, more, supplementary.

furthermore additionally, also, besides, moreover, too.

furtive *The shopkeeper didn't like the furtive way Logan was looking round the shop*. crafty, deceitful, mysterious, secretive, shifty, sly, sneaky, stealthy, tricky, untrustworthy, wily.

fury *We were frightened by the fury of the storm*. anger, rage, violence, wrath.

fuse SEE **electricity**.

fuselage SEE **aircraft**.

fuss *Logan made a fuss when he didn't win*. ado, bother, commotion, excitement, to-do, trouble, turmoil, uproar.

fussy *fussy about food*. (informal) choosey, fastidious, finicky, particular.

futile *It's futile to complain if you've lost the receipt*. fruitless, ineffective, pointless, unsuccessful, useless, vain, worthless.

future *future events*. approaching, coming.

fuzzy 1 *a fuzzy beard*. downy, feathery, fleecy, woolly. **2** *We get a fuzzy picture on our TV*. blurred, cloudy, dim, faint, hazy, indistinct, misty, unclear.

G g

gabble *I can't understand what you say if you gabble*. to babble, to jabber, to mutter. SEE ALSO **talk**.

gable SEE **building**.

gadget *a gadget for opening lemonade bottles*. contraption, contrivance, device, implement, instrument, invention, machine, tool, utensil.

gag 1 *The comedian told some old gags.* jest, joke. 2 *The gang tied him up and gagged him.* to silence.

gain 1 *What did they gain by fighting a terrible war?* to acquire, to earn, to get, to obtain, to procure, to receive, to win. 2 *The explorers gained their objective.* to achieve, to get to, to reach. 3 *At the end of the day we added up our gains.* advantage, asset, benefit, profit.

gala carnival, fair, festival, fête.

galaxy SEE **astronomy, group**.

gale *The gale blew our TV aerial down.* blast, wind. SEE ALSO **weather**.

gallant *a gallant knight.* brave, chivalrous, courageous, fearless, gentlemanly, heroic, noble, polite, valiant.

galleon SEE **vessel**.

gallery SEE **theatre**.

galley SEE **vessel**.

gallon SEE **measure**.

gallop to race, to run, to rush. SEE ALSO **horse, move**.

gallows *to be hanged on a gallows.* scaffold.

galvanized iron SEE **metal**.

gamble 1 WAYS OF GAMBLING ARE betting, bingo, cards, dice, drawing lots, lottery, pools, raffle, wager. 2 *She gambled her life to save the drowning man.* to risk, to venture.

game 1 *What's your favourite game?* amusement, entertainment, fun, joke, pastime, playing, sport. 2 *Let's have another game of chess.* competition, contest, match, tournament. 3 VARIOUS GAMES ARE billiards, bingo, SEE **cards**, charades, chess, crossword puzzle, darts, dice, dominoes, draughts, hide-and-seek, hopscotch, jigsaw puzzle, leap-frog, ludo, marbles, pool, skittles, snooker, table-tennis, tiddlywinks. 4 FOR MORE ACTIVE GAMES SEE **sport**.

gamekeeper SEE **job**.

gammon bacon, ham. SEE ALSO **meat**.

gander SEE **male**.

gang *a gang of workmen.* band, company, crew, horde. SEE ALSO **group**.

gangster brigand, criminal, crook, desperado, gunman, robber, ruffian.

gaol 1 dungeon, prison. SEE ALSO **punishment**. 2 *He was gaoled for fraud.* to confine, to detain, to imprison, to intern, to shut up.

gap 1 *a gap in the fence.* break, hole. SEE ALSO **opening**. 2 *a gap between lessons.* interval, lapse, lull, pause, respite, rest. 3 *Is the gap between the posts wide enough for the car?* distance, space.

gape to gaze, to stare. SEE ALSO **look**.

garage SEE **building**.

garbage *Put the garbage in the dustbin.* junk, litter, refuse, rubbish, trash, waste.

garbled *a garbled message.* confused, incoherent, jumbled, misleading, mixed up.

garden 1 *Mrs Brunswick loves her garden.* allotment, patch, plot. 2 THINGS FOUND IN A GARDEN ARE bed, border, butt, compost heap, flagstones, SEE **flower**, SEE **fruit**, hedge, lawn, orchard, path, patio, pond, rockery, rock garden, shrubbery, terrace, SEE **tree**, trellis, turf, SEE **vegetable**, window-box. 3 GARDEN TOOLS ARE broom, cultivator, fork, hoe, rake, riddle, secateurs, shears, shovel, sieve, spade, trowel, watering-can. 4 SUBSTANCES USED IN A GARDEN ARE compost, fertilizer, insecticide, manure, peat, pesticide, weed-killer.

gardener SEE **job**.

gargle SEE **medicine**.

gargoyle SEE **church**.

garland SEE **flower**.

garlic SEE **food**.

garment attire, clothing, costume, dress. FOR VARIOUS GARMENTS SEE **clothes**.

garrison citadel, fort, fortress.

garter SEE **clothes**.

gas 1 *A car engine gives off poisonous gas.* exhaust, fumes, vapour. **2** VARIOUS GASES ARE hydrogen, nitrogen, oxygen, tear gas. **3** SEE **fuel**.

gash *The broken bottle made a gash in Tony's foot.* cut, slash, slit, wound. SEE ALSO **cut, opening**.

gasoline petrol. SEE ALSO **fuel**.

gasp 1 *The smoke made them gasp.* to choke, to pant, to puff, to wheeze. **2** *gasping*: breathless, exhausted, puffed, tired out.

gastric flu SEE **illness**.

gate door, entrance, entry, exit, gateway, turnstile.

gather 1 *A crowd gathered. We gathered our belongings. Gather your team together.* to accumulate, to assemble, to bring together, to cluster, to collect, to come together, to concentrate, to congregate, to crowd, to get together, to group, to herd, to hoard, to mass, to meet, to mobilize, to muster, to pile up, to round up, to store up, to swarm, to throng. **2** *We gathered strawberries.* to harvest, to pick, to pluck. **3** *I gather you've been ill.* to conclude, to learn, to understand.

gathering 1 *a gathering of people.* bunch, company, congregation, crowd, mass, swarm, throng. SEE ALSO **group**. **2** *The grown-ups are having some sort of gathering at Christmas.* assembly, function, meeting, party, social.

gaudy *gaudy colours.* bright, colourful, flashy, lurid, showy, tawdry.

gauge *a narrow gauge railway.* measurement, size.

gaunt *The old man looked gaunt after his illness.* bony, emaciated, lean, skinny, starving, thin, wasted away.

gauntlet glove. SEE ALSO **clothes**.

gauze SEE **cloth**.

gawky *The ostrich looked a gawky bird.* awkward, blundering, clumsy, ungainly.

gay 1 *gay colours, gay laughter.* bright, cheerful, joyful, light-hearted,

merry. SEE ALSO **happy**. **2** homosexual, (impolite) queer.

gaze *We gazed at the sunset.* to contemplate, to eye, to observe, to regard, to stare at, to view, to watch. SEE ALSO **look**.

gear 1 *to change gear.* SEE **vehicle**. **2** *camping gear.* apparatus, equipment, instruments, kit, paraphernalia, rig, tackle.

gelignite SEE **explosive**.

gem jewel, precious stone. SEE ALSO **jewellery**.

general 1 *The bad weather is general this year.* common, communal, global, shared, universal, widespread. **2** *Smoking used to be more general than it is now.* customary, everyday, familiar, habitual, regular, usual. **3** *He only gave us a general idea of where we were going.* broad, indefinite, unclear, vague.

generally chiefly, mainly, mostly, predominantly, usually.

generate *to generate electricity, to generate business, etc.* to breed, to bring about, to create, to make, to produce.

generation SEE **family**.

generator SEE **electricity**.

generous 1 *a generous sponsor.* bounteous, charitable, free, kind, lavish, liberal, public-spirited, unselfish. **2** *generous portions of food.* abundant, ample, copious, large, liberal, plentiful, sizeable.

genial *Our friends gave us a genial welcome.* cheerful, cordial, easy-going, friendly, pleasant, relaxed, warm-hearted. SEE ALSO **kind**.

genius 1 *He is a mathematical genius.* expert, know-all, master-mind. **2** *He has a genius for maths.* gift, intellect, talent.

gentle 1 *a gentle person.* good-tempered, kindly, merciful, mild, pleasant, soft-hearted, tender. **2** *gentle music.* peaceful, quiet, relaxing, soft, soothing. **3** *a gentle dog.* docile, manageable, meek, obedient, tame. **4** *a gentle wind.* balmy, delicate, faint, light. **5** *a gentle hint.* indirect, subtle. **6** *a gentle hill.* gradual, moderate, steady.

gentleman SEE **person.**

genuine 1 *a genuine £5 note.* actual, authentic, real. **2** *genuine feelings.* devout, honest, sincere, true.

geo-board SEE **mathematics.**

geography 1 SOME GEOGRAPHICAL WORDS ARE Antarctic, archipelago, Arctic, bay, borough, canyon, cape, capital, city, climate, continent, contour, conurbation, country, county, creek, dale, delta, downs, east, equator, estate, estuary, fells, fen, fiord, geyser, glacier, glen, gulf, hamlet, heath, hemisphere, highlands, hill, industry, inlet, island, isthmus, lagoon, lake, land, latitude, longitude, mainland, nation, north, oasis, parish, pass, peninsula, plain, plateau, pole, prairie, province, reef, relief map, river, sea, south, strait, suburb, tide, town, tributary, tropics, valley, village, volcano, west, world. **2** SEE **subject.**

geology SEE **science.**

geometry SEE **mathematics.**

geranium SEE **flower.**

gerbil SEE **animal, pet.**

germ bacteria, (informal) bug, microbe, virus. ! *Bacteria* is a plural word.

germinate *Our seeds have germinated.* to grow, to shoot, to spring up, to sprout, to start growing.

gesture 1 action, movement, sign. **2** WAYS TO MAKE GESTURES ARE to beckon, to nod, to point, to salute, to shake your head, to shrug, to wave, to wink.

get 1 *What did you get for Christmas? What can I get for £10?* to acquire, to be given, to buy, to gain, to get hold of, to obtain, to procure, to purchase, to receive. **2** *Tell the dog to get the ball.* to bring, to fetch, to pick up, to retrieve. **3** *Did you get a prize?* to earn, to take, to win. **4** *Lucy got a cold.* to catch, to contract, to develop, to

suffer from. **5** *Get Tony to do the washing-up.* to cause, to persuade. **6** *Let's get tea now.* to make ready, to prepare. **7** *I don't get what he means.* to comprehend, to follow, to grasp, to understand. **8** *What time do you get to school?* to arrive at, to reach. **9** *How do you get to school?* to go, to travel. **10** *It's getting cold.* to become, to grow, to turn. ! *Get* can mean many things. The words given here are only some of the other words you could use.

getaway *They made their getaway in a fast car.* escape, flight, retreat.

geyser SEE **geography.**

ghastly *a ghastly disaster.* appalling, awful, dreadful, fearful, frightful, grim, grisly, horrible, horrifying, shocking, terrible.

ghetto SEE **town.**

ghost apparition, hallucination, illusion, phantom, poltergeist, spectre, spirit, (informal) spook, vision.

ghostly *Tony heard a ghostly noise in the churchyard.* creepy, eerie, frightening, scary, spooky, uncanny, unearthly, weird.

giant 1 monster, ogre. **2** *a giant statue.* colossal, enormous, gigantic, huge, immense, massive, mighty, monstrous, vast.

gibberish (informal) balderdash, drivel, nonsense, rubbish, (informal) tripe, (informal) twaddle.

giddy *Heights make me feel giddy.* dizzy, faint, reeling, unsteady.

gift 1 *Mrs Brunswick sent some beans as a gift for the harvest festival.* contribution, donation, offering, present. **2** *Lucy has a gift for gymnastics.* ability, genius, knack, talent.

gifted *a gifted musician.* able, accomplished, brilliant, clever, masterly, skilful, skilled, talented, versatile.

gigantic *a gigantic monster.* colossal, enormous, giant, huge, immense, mammoth, massive, mighty, monstrous, vast. SEE ALSO **big.**

giggle to snigger, to titter. SEE ALSO **laugh**.

gill SEE **fish**.

gilt SEE **colour**.

gin SEE **drink**.

ginger SEE **spice**.

gingerbread SEE **cake**.

giraffe SEE **animal**.

girder *a framework of girders.* bar, beam, joist, rafter.

girdle belt. SEE ALSO **underclothes**.

girl lass. OLD-FASHIONED WORDS ARE damsel, maid, maiden, virgin. SEE ALSO **person**.

girth SEE **horse**.

give 1 *The headmaster gave Lucy her prize.* to award, to hand over, to offer, to pass, to present. **2** *How much did she give to you?* to allot, to allow, to contribute, to donate, to deal out, to distribute, to grant, to pay, to provide, to ration out, to supply. **3** *Give me the facts.* to display, to reveal, to show, to tell. **4** *Be careful: the roof might give.* to buckle, to collapse, to fall in, to fold up, to yield.

glacier SEE **geography**.

glad *We were glad to hear your good news.* delighted, joyful, pleased. SEE ALSO **happy**.

gladiator SEE **fighter**.

glamorous 1 *a glamorous TV star.* alluring, attractive, beautiful, good-looking, gorgeous, lovely. **2** *a glamorous place for a holiday.* colourful, exciting, fascinating.

glance SEE **look**.

gland SEE **body**.

glare 1 *glaring:* bright, dazzling, harsh. SEE ALSO **light**. **2** *an angry glare.* SEE **expression**.

glass 1 pane, plate-glass. **2** *a glass ball.* crystal. **3** *a glass of water.* tumbler, wine-glass. SEE ALSO **container, drink**.

glasses bifocals, goggles, spectacles, sun-glasses. SEE ALSO **optical**.

glasshouse greenhouse.

glass-paper sandpaper. SEE ALSO **tool**.

glazier SEE **job**.

gleam 1 *a gleam of light.* beam, flash, glimmer, glow, ray. SEE ALSO **light**. **2** *gleaming:* bright, brilliant, shining, shiny, sparkling.

gleeful *Lucy was gleeful when she beat her nearest rival.* delighted, ecstatic, exultant, joyful, merry, overjoyed, pleased. SEE ALSO **happy**.

glen dale, valley. SEE ALSO **geography**.

glide *to glide across the ice.* to coast, to drift, to fly, to skid, to slide, to slip. SEE ALSO **move**.

glider SEE **aircraft**.

glimmer *A distant light glimmered in the darkness.* to flicker, to gleam, to glow, to twinkle. SEE ALSO **light**.

glimpse *We glimpsed someone moving between the trees.* to discern, to distinguish, to make out, to notice, to observe, to see, to sight, to spot. SEE ALSO **look**.

glint *The light glinted on the bright metal.* to flash, to sparkle. SEE ALSO **light**.

glisten *The lights glistened on the wet road.* to gleam, to shine. SEE ALSO **light**.

glitter 1 *The diamond necklace glittered.* to flash, to sparkle, to twinkle. SEE ALSO **light**. **2** *glittering: The grand banquet was a glittering occasion.* brilliant, colourful, glamorous, resplendent, sparkling. SEE ALSO **splendid**.

gloat *Logan gloats when he wins.* to boast, to brag, to show off.

global *Do you think there's any danger of a global war?* general, universal, wholesale, widespread, worldwide.

globe 1 *the shape of a globe.* ball, sphere. **2** *the globe we live on.* earth, world.

glockenspiel SEE **percussion**.

gloom *We could hardly see in the gloom.* dimness, dusk, twilight.

gloomy 1 *a gloomy house, gloomy weather.* cheerless, cloudy, dark, depressing, dingy, dismal, dull, heavy, murky, overcast, shadowy, sombre. 2 *a gloomy person.* depressed, down-hearted, glum, grave, lugubrious, melancholy, miserable, morbid, unhappy. SEE ALSO **sad**.

glorious 1 *glorious scenery, glorious weather, etc.* beautiful, brilliant, excellent, gorgeous, grand, impressive, lovely, magnificent, majestic, marvellous, resplendent, spectacular, splendid, super, superb, wonderful. 2 *a glorious victory.* celebrated, distinguished, famous, heroic, noble.

gloss *We polished the table until we got a good gloss.* brightness, lustre, polish, sheen, shine.

glossy *glossy paint.* bright, gleaming, shiny, sleek.

glove gauntlet. SEE ALSO **clothes**.

glow 1 *A fire glowed in the hearth.* to gleam, to glimmer, to radiate, to shine. SEE ALSO **light**. 2 *We enjoyed the glow from the fire.* brightness, colour, redness, heat, warmth.

glower to frown, to scowl. SEE ALSO **expression**.

glow-worm SEE **insect**.

glucose SEE **food**.

glue 1 *We need some glue to stick the pictures onto card.* adhesive, gum, paste. 2 *Can we glue the broken bits together?* to paste, to stick. SEE ALSO **fasten**.

gluey adhesive, gummed, sticky, tacky.

glum *The defeated team looked glum.* depressed, down-hearted, gloomy, lugubrious, melancholy, miserable, unhappy. SEE ALSO **sad**.

gluttonous greedy.

gnarled *a gnarled old tree.* distorted, knobbly, lumpy, rough, twisted.

gnat SEE **insect**.

gnaw *The dog gnawed a bone.* to bite, to chew, to munch. SEE ALSO **eat**.

gnome dwarf, goblin. SEE ALSO **legend**.

go 1 *Let's go!* to advance, to begin, to be off, to commence, to depart, to disappear, to embark, to get away, to leave, to proceed, to retire, to retreat, to set out, to start, to withdraw. SEE ALSO **move**. 2 *I'd love to go to America.* to journey to, to travel to, to visit. SEE ALSO **travel**. 3 *This road goes to the rubbish dump.* to extend to, to lead to, to reach, to stretch to. 4 *The car won't go.* to act, to function, to operate, to perform, to run, to work. 5 *A holiday always goes quickly.* to elapse, to pass. 6 *Is he going mad?* to become, to grow, to turn. 7 *The bomb went off.* to blow up, to detonate, to explode. 8 *How long can you go on running?* to carry on, to continue, to keep on, to last, to persevere, to persist. 9 *She has gone through a serious illness.* to endure, to experience, to undergo. 10 *Who'll go with me to the shops?* to accompany, to escort. ! *Go* can be used in many ways. The words given here are just some of the other words you can use.

goal 1 SEE **sport**. 2 *to have a goal in life.* aim, ambition, objective, purpose, target.

goalkeeper SEE **football**.

goat billy-goat, kid, nanny-goat. SEE ALSO **animal**.

gobble *She gobbled her food greedily.* to bolt, to devour, to gulp, to guzzle. SEE ALSO **eat**.

goblet beaker, cup. SEE ALSO **drink**.

goblin brownie. SEE ALSO **legend**.

god deity, divinity.

godparent SEE **family**.

goggles glasses, spectacles.

go-kart SEE **vehicle**.

gold SEE **colour, jewellery, metal**.

goldfinch SEE **bird**.

goldfish SEE **fish, pet**.

goldsmith SEE **art**.

golf, golf-course SEE **sport**.

gondola SEE **vessel**.

gong SEE **percussion**.

good 1 *a good deed, a good person.* admirable, appropriate, benevolent, caring, commendable, considerate, creditable, dutiful, esteemed, fair, great, helpful, holy, honest, honourable, humane, innocent, just,

kind, kind-hearted, law-abiding, marvellous, moral, noble, obedient, outstanding, praiseworthy, proper, reliable, religious, right, righteous, saintly, thoughtful, upright, virtuous, well-behaved, wonderful, worthy. 2 *a good musician, a good worker.* able, accomplished, capable, clever, conscientious, creditable, efficient, (informal) fabulous, gifted, proficient, skilful, skilled, talented, thorough. 3 *a good holiday, good weather.* agreeable, delightful, enjoyable, excellent, fine, heavenly, lovely, nice, pleasant, pleasing, satisfactory, (informal) terrific.
! *Good* can mean many different things. The words given here are only some of the other words you could use.

goodbye au revoir, farewell.

good-humoured amiable, cheerful, friendly, genial, kind, likeable, sympathetic, warm-hearted. SEE ALSO **happy**.

good-looking attractive, handsome, lovely, pretty. SEE ALSO **beautiful**.

good-natured friendly, helpful, kind-hearted, sympathetic. SEE ALSO **kind**.

goods *a train carrying goods.* cargo, freight, merchandise.

good-tempered gentle, mild, nice. SEE ALSO **kind**.

goose gander, gosling. SEE ALSO **bird, poultry**.

gooseberry SEE **fruit**.

gore *gored by a bull.* SEE **wound**.

gorge 1 *Logan was sick after gorging himself on ice-cream.* to feast, to gobble, to guzzle. SEE ALSO **eat**. 2 *A river runs along the gorge.* canyon, defile, pass, ravine, valley.

gorgeous *a gorgeous dress, a gorgeous view.* colourful, glorious, lovely, magnificent. SEE ALSO **beautiful, splendid**.

gorilla SEE **animal**.

gorse SEE **shrub**.

gory *a gory battle.* blood-stained, bloody, grisly, gruesome.

gosling goose. SEE ALSO **young**.

gospel SEE **church**.

gossip 1 *Don't gossip while I'm reading to you!* to chatter, to prattle. SEE ALSO **talk**. 2 *Don't listen to unkind gossip.* rumour, scandal.

gouge *to gouge out a hole.* to dig, to scoop.

goulash SEE **food**.

govern *to govern a country.* to administer, to be in charge of, to command, to control, to direct, to guide, to head, to look after, to manage, to master, to regulate, to rule, to run, to supervise.

government WORDS CONNECTED WITH GOVERNMENT ARE administration, ambassador, cabinet, chancellor, civil service, commonwealth, constituency, constitution, consul, councillor, democracy, dictatorship, diplomat, embassy, empire, exchequer, kingdom, mayor, member of parliament, minister, ministry, monarchy, parliament, politician, politics, premier, president, prime minister, republic, statesman. SEE ALSO **politics**.

governor *Who is the governor here?* boss, chief, controller, director, head, manager, ruler, supervisor.

gown dress, frock. SEE ALSO **clothes**.

grab *Grab the end of that rope!* to catch, to clutch, to grasp, to hold, to pluck, to seize, to snatch.

grace 1 *God's grace.* forgiveness, goodness, mercy. 2 *grace before dinner.* blessing, prayer.

graceful 1 *A gymnast's movements are very graceful.* agile, deft, flowing, nimble, supple. 2 *She has a graceful figure.* attractive, beautiful, dignified, elegant, slim, slender.

gracious *a gracious lady.* agreeable, courteous, friendly, good-natured, kind, polite.

grade *Our butcher sells top grade meat.* category, class, quality, standard.

gradient *a steep gradient.* ascent, hill, incline, slope.

gradual *They say there will be a gradual improvement in the weather.* gentle, moderate, slow, steady.

graffiti SEE **picture.**

grain 1 *Many farmers grow grain.* corn. SEE ALSO **cereal.** 2 *a grain of sand.* bit, granule, particle, speck.

gram SEE **measure.**

grammar SEE **language.**

gramophone SEE **audio equipment.**

granary SEE **building.**

grand *The opening of the new stadium was a grand occasion.* big, great, important, imposing, impressive, lordly, magnificent, majestic, noble, (informal) posh, regal, royal, stately. SEE ALSO **splendid.**

grandchild, grandparent SEE **family.**

grandstand SEE **sport.**

granite SEE **rock.**

grant 1 *a grant of money.* allowance, donation, expenses, loan, scholarship. 2 *The insurance company granted them the full value of the wrecked car.* to allow, to allot, to donate, to give, to pay, to provide. 3 *In the end he granted that I was right.* to acknowledge, to accept, to admit, to agree.

grape, grapefruit SEE **fruit.**

graph chart, diagram.

graphics SEE **art.**

grapple 1 *The police grappled with the intruder.* to struggle, to wrestle. 2 *Tony grappled with his maths.* to attend to, to cope with, to deal with, to handle, to manage.

grasp 1 *Grasp the bat firmly.* to catch, to clasp, to clutch, to grab, to grip, to hang on to, to hold, to seize. 2 *Lucy didn't grasp how to do her maths.* to comprehend, to follow, to learn, to master, to realize, to understand.

grasping *a grasping miser.* greedy, miserly, selfish, worldly.

grass 1 *Tony helped Mrs Brunswick cut the grass.* green, lawn. 2 PLANTS RELATED TO GRASS ARE bamboo, pampas grass, sugar-cane. 3 SEE **plant.**

grasshopper SEE **insect.**

grass-snake SEE **snake.**

grate 1 *There's a fire in the grate.* fireplace, hearth. SEE ALSO **fire.** 2 *to grate cheese.* to shred. SEE ALSO **cut.** 3 *a grating noise.* SEE **sound.**

grateful *He was grateful for the gift.* appreciative, thankful.

grave 1 *She looked grave when she heard the bad news.* dignified, earnest, gloomy, pensive, sedate, serious, sober, solemn, subdued, thoughtful. SEE ALSO **sad.** 2 *Stealing is a grave offence.* important, momentous, serious, weighty. 3 *There are some old graves in the churchyard.* burial-place, gravestone, memorial, tomb. SEE ALSO **funeral.**

gravel grit, pebbles, shingle, stones.

graveyard cemetery, churchyard. SEE ALSO **funeral.**

gravy SEE **food, sauce.**

graze *grazing cattle.* to feed.

grease oil. SEE ALSO **fat.**

greasy fatty, oily.

great 1 *a great mountain.* enormous, huge, immense, large, tremendous. SEE ALSO **big.** 2 *great pain.* acute, excessive, extreme, intense, severe. 3 *a great event.* grand, important, large-scale, momentous, serious, significant, spectacular. SEE ALSO **splendid.** 4 *a great piece of music.* brilliant, classic, excellent, (informal) fabulous, famous, (informal) fantastic, fine, outstanding, wonderful. 5 *a great composer.* celebrated, distinguished, eminent, gifted, notable, noted, prominent, renowned, talented, well-known. 6 *a great friend.* chief, close, main, valued.

greedy 1 *That greedy crowd ate everything before we arrived!* avid, eager, famished, gluttonous, hungry, ravenous, starving. 2 *Don't be greedy: share things with the others.* grasping, miserly, selfish, worldly.

green SEE **colour.**

greenery foliage, leaves.

greengage SEE **fruit.**

greengrocer SEE **shop**.

greenhouse glasshouse.

greens SEE **food, vegetable**.

greet *We greeted our visitors at the door.* to receive, to welcome.

grenade SEE **weapon**.

grey SEE **colour**.

greyhound SEE **dog**.

grief misery, regret, remorse, sadness, sorrow, unhappiness.

grievance *If you have a grievance, see the manager.* complaint.

grieve 1 *He grieved terribly when his dog died.* to fret, to lament, to mope, to mourn, to weep. **2** *It grieved us to see how cruelly the animal had been treated.* to depress, to distress, to hurt, to sadden.

grill SEE **cook, kitchen**.

grim *a grim expression, grim weather, etc.* bad-tempered, cruel, forbidding, frightful, ghastly, gloomy, grisly, gruesome, harsh, horrible, menacing, ominous, severe, stern, terrible, threatening, unfriendly.

grimace *to make a grimace.* face, look. SEE ALSO **expression**.

grimy *grimy windows.* dirty, dusty, filthy, grubby, sooty.

grin to beam, to smile. SEE ALSO **expression, laugh**.

grind 1 *to grind corn.* to crush, to pound, to powder. **2** *to grind a knife.* to polish, to sharpen. **3** *to grind something away.* to eat away, to erode, to wear away.

grip *He gripped her hand.* to clasp, to clutch, to grab, to grasp, to hold, to seize.

grisly *a grisly accident.* appalling, dreadful, frightful, ghastly, gory, grim, gruesome, hideous, horrible, terrible. SEE ALSO **bad**.

gristly *gristly meat.* leathery, rubbery, tough.

grit 1 *I had some grit in my eye.* dust, gravel, sand. **2** (informal) *You need grit to climb that mountain.* bravery, courage, determination, (informal)

guts, (informal) pluck, spirit. **3** *to grit your teeth.* to clench.

grizzle *The baby grizzled.* to cry, to weep, to whimper.

grizzly bear SEE **animal**.

groan to moan, to wail. SEE ALSO **sound**.

grocer SEE **shop**.

groom 1 *The groom looks after the horses.* SEE **job**. **2** bridegroom. SEE ALSO **wedding**.

groove cut, furrow, scratch, slot.

grope *We groped about in the dark.* to feel about, to fumble.

gross 1 SEE **number**. **2** *He was gross: he never stopped eating.* enormous, fat, flabby, huge, monstrous, overweight, ugly.

grotesque *grotesque carvings.* absurd, deformed, distorted, fantastic, misshapen, ugly, weird.

grotto cave, cavern.

ground 1 *We buried it in the ground.* earth, loam, soil. **2** *We showed our visitors round the grounds.* campus, estate, gardens, playing-fields, surroundings. **3** *Whose ground are we playing on next week?* arena, field, pitch, stadium. **4** *Have you any grounds for accusing her?* argument, cause, evidence, proof, reason.

groundsheet SEE **tent**.

groundsman SEE **job**.

group 1 *We formed a group for railway enthusiasts.* alliance, association, body, club, combination, company, league, organization, party, society, union. **2** OTHER GROUPS ARE accumulation, assortment, band, batch, brood, bunch, bundle, category, clan, class, clump, cluster, clutch, collection, colony, company, congregation, convoy, crew, crowd, fleet, flock, galaxy, gang, gathering, herd, hoard, horde, host, litter, mass, mob, multitude, pack, party, picket, posse, pride, rabble, school, set, shoal, swarm, team, throng, troop. **3** *Group the specimens according to size.* to arrange, to assemble, to bring together, to classify, to collect, to set out, to sort.

grouse 1 SEE **bird**. **2** *Logan grouses even when little things go wrong.* to complain, to grumble, to moan.

grove *a grove of small trees.* coppice, copse, forest, thicket, wood.

grovel *Stand up for yourself: don't grovel!* to cower, to cringe, to be too humble, to snivel.

grow 1 *The seeds have started to grow.* to emerge, to germinate, to spring up, to sprout. **2** *Many plants won't grow in cold weather.* to flourish, to live, to prosper, to survive, to thrive. **3** *Trees grow slowly.* to become longer, to become taller, to enlarge, to expand, to fill out, to increase in size, to lengthen, to swell. **4** *Her confidence grew when she started training seriously.* to build up, to develop, to improve, to increase. **5** *Mrs Brunswick grows lovely beans.* to cultivate, to produce, to raise.

growl SEE **sound**.

grown-up adult, mature, well-developed.

grub *There's a grub in this apple!* caterpillar, larva, maggot.

grubby *You need to wash that grubby shirt.* dirty, grimy, (informal) mucky, soiled.

grudging *Logan was grudging about Tony's success.* envious, jealous, resentful, ungracious, unkind.

gruelling *a gruelling climb.* arduous, exhausting, hard, laborious, stiff, strenuous, tiring, tough.

gruesome *a gruesome accident.* bloody, disgusting, grim, grisly, hideous, horrible, ghastly, gory, revolting, sickening.

gruff 1 *a gruff voice.* harsh, hoarse, husky, rough. **2** *a gruff answer.* bad-tempered, grumpy, surly, unfriendly.

grumble to complain, to grouse, to moan.

grumpy *He's grumpy because he's got toothache.* bad-tempered, cross, gruff,

irascible, irritable, peevish, snappy, surly, testy.

grunt SEE **sound**.

guarantee 1 *He gave us his guarantee that it worked.* assurance, pledge, promise. **2** *He guarantees that it works.* to pledge, to promise, to swear, to vow. **3** *This ticket guarantees you a seat.* to ensure, to secure.

guard 1 *A mother always guards her young.* to care for, to defend, to keep safe, to look after, to preserve, to protect, to safeguard, to shelter, to shield, to tend. **2** *The sentry guarded the prisoners.* to prevent from escaping, to watch. **3** *A guard watched over the prisoner.* escort, look-out, patrol, sentinel, sentry, warder, watchman. **4** *a guard on a train.* SEE **railway**.

guardian 1 SEE **family**. **2** *The guardian of the treasure was a fierce dragon.* custodian, keeper, protector, warder.

guerrilla SEE **fighter**.

guess 1 *Make a guess.* assumption, estimate, guesswork, opinion, supposition, theory. **2** *I guess it will cost about £1.* to assume, to estimate, to suppose.

guest 1 *We had guests on Sunday.* caller, visitor. **2** *How many guests stay in this hotel?* boarder, customer, lodger, resident, tenant.

guest-house SEE **holiday**.

guide 1 *We need a guide to show us the way.* escort, pilot. **2** *Harris knows how to guide us out of the maze.* to conduct, to direct, to escort, to lead, to manoeuvre, to navigate, to pilot, to steer.

guillotine SEE **cut, execute**.

guilt *The evidence proved his guilt.* blame, fault, responsibility.

guilty 1 *The jury declared him guilty.* at fault, responsible. **2** *He looked guilty.* ashamed, regretful, remorseful, sheepish.

guinea-pig SEE **animal, pet**.

guitar SEE **music, strings**.

gulf bay. SEE ALSO **geography**.

gull SEE **bird**.

gullet throat. SEE ALSO **body**.

gulp *We gulped our food as fast as we could.* to bolt, to devour, to gobble. SEE ALSO **drink, eat**.

gum 1 *a pot of gum.* adhesive, glue, paste. 2 *We need healthy gums and healthy teeth.* SEE **body, head**.

gumboot SEE **shoe**.

gummed *gummed paper.* adhesive, gluey, sticky.

gumption (informal) *Haven't you any gumption?* judgement, sense, wisdom.

gum-tree SEE **tree**.

gun 1 VARIOUS GUNS ARE airgun, artillery, automatic, blunderbuss, cannon, machine-gun, mortar, musket, pistol, revolver, rifle, shotgun, small arms, sub-machine-gun. 2 PARTS OF A GUN ARE barrel, breech, butt, magazine, muzzle, sight, trigger.

gunboat SEE **vessel**.

gunman SEE **criminal, fighter**.

gunner SEE **soldier**.

gunpowder SEE **explosive**.

gurgle SEE **sound**.

guru leader, teacher.

gush 1 *Oil gushed out of the pipe.* to flow, to pour, to run, to spout, to spurt, to squirt, to stream. 2 *to come in a gush.* flood, jet, rush, stream.

gusty *gusty weather.* blustery, squally, windy. SEE ALSO **weather**.

guts 1 SEE **body**. 2 (informal) *They had guts to take the lifeboat out in that storm.* bravery, courage, determination, (informal) grit, nerve, (informal) pluck, spirit.

gutter *The water flows along the gutter.* channel, ditch, drain, sewer.

guy rope SEE **tent**.

guzzle *It's not polite to guzzle your food.* to bolt, to gobble, to gulp. SEE ALSO **drink, eat**.

gymkhana SEE **entertainment, horse**.

gymnasium SEE **building, sport**.

gymnastics SEE **sport**.

gypsy nomad, traveller.

H h

habit 1 *Don't let smoking become a habit!* addiction, compulsion. 2 *In our family, it's our habit to open presents on Christmas Eve.* custom, practice, routine.

habitual *We went home by our habitual route.* accustomed, conventional, common, customary, normal, ordinary, regular, routine, traditional, usual.

hack *We hacked down the undergrowth.* to chop, to hew, to slash. SEE ALSO **cut**.

hack-saw SEE **tool**.

haddock SEE **fish**.

haggis SEE **food**.

haggle *If you haggle with the man in the market, he'll knock a pound off the price.* to argue, to bargain, to discuss terms, to negotiate.

haiku SEE **poem**.

hail SEE **weather**.

hair 1 *Most animals have hairs on their skins.* bristles, fur. 2 *Does your mum do your hair?* curls, locks, tresses. 3 WAYS OF DOING HAIR ARE permanent wave, pigtail, plait, pony-tail. 4 WORDS TO DESCRIBE THE COLOUR OF HAIR ARE auburn, blond or blonde, brunette, dark, fair.

hairdresser barber. SEE ALSO **job, shop**.

hairless bald, bare.

hair-raising *The drive over the mountain road was hair-raising.* appalling, frightening, horrifying, scary, terrifying.

hairy *hairy skin.* bristly, downy, feathery, fleecy, fuzzy, shaggy, woolly.

half-hearted 1 *He made a half-hearted shot at goal.* feeble, ineffective, weak. 2 *She seems half-hearted about the party.* cool, indifferent, unenthusiastic.

half-wit blockhead, (informal) dope, dunce, fool, idiot, imbecile, moron. ! These words are usually insulting.

hall 1 *Wipe your feet before you come into the hall.* corridor, foyer, lobby, passage. 2 *We do the nativity play in the hall.* assembly hall, concert hall, theatre.

hallowed *hallowed ground.* blessed, consecrated, holy, sacred.

Hallowe'en SEE **time.**

hallucination apparition, delusion, dream, illusion, mirage, vision.

halt 1 *A red light halts the traffic.* to arrest, to block, to check, to stop. 2 *The traffic halts when the lights turn red.* to come to a standstill, to draw up, to pull up, to stop. 3 *All activity halted when the whistle went.* to break off, to cease, to end, to terminate.

halter SEE **horse.**

halve 1 *The two explorers halved their rations.* to divide, to share. 2 *Dad threatened to halve my pocket-money.* to cut, to decrease, to lessen, to reduce.

ham, hamburger SEE **meat.**

hamlet settlement, village. SEE ALSO **geography.**

hammer 1 *He hammered on the door.* to bash, to batter, to beat, to knock, to strike. SEE ALSO **hit.** 2 SEE **tool.**

hammock SEE **bed.**

hamper *Work on the Brunswicks' extension was hampered by bad weather.* to curb, to foil, to frustrate, to hinder, to hold back, to obstruct.

hamster SEE **animal, pet.**

hand 1 *She hit me with her hand.* fist. SEE ALSO **body.** 2 PARTS OF A HAND ARE finger, fingernail, index finger, knuckle, palm, thumb, wrist. 3 *to hand in, to hand over*: to deliver, to give, to present, to submit. 4 *to hand round*: to circulate, to deal out, to distribute, to give out, to pass round, to share.

handbag bag, purse. SEE ALSO **container.**

handicap 1 *It's a handicap to run a race in wellington boots!* disadvantage, drawback, hindrance, impediment, inconvenience, obstacle. 2 WAYS IN WHICH PEOPLE MAY BE PERMANENTLY HANDICAPPED ARE to be backward, blind, crippled, deaf, deformed, disabled, disfigured, dumb, lame, limbless, maimed, mute, paralysed, paraplegic, retarded, slow, spastic, to have a speech impediment. ! These words may seem insulting if you use them carelessly.

handicraft art, craft, workmanship.

handkerchief tissue.

handle 1 *Hold it by the handle.* grip, hilt, knob. 2 *You must handle small animals carefully.* to feel, to finger, to stroke, to touch. 3 *Mrs Angel handled the rowdy class firmly.* to control, to cope with, to deal with, to look after, to manage, to manipulate.

handsome 1 *a handsome man.* attractive, good-looking. 2 *a handsome piece of furniture.* beautiful, elegant, tasteful. 3 *a handsome present.* big, generous, sizeable, valuable.

handy 1 *Dad always has his tools handy.* accessible, available, close at hand, convenient, easy to reach, ready. 2 *Mum is handy at mending the car.* capable, clever, competent, helpful, practical, proficient, skilful.

hang 1 *Hang the washing on the line.* to dangle, to suspend. 2 *The smoke hung in the still air.* to drift, to float, to hover. 3 *Don't hang about.* to dally, to dawdle, to linger, to loiter. 4 *Come on, there's no need to hang back.* to hesitate, to pause, to wait. 5 *Hang on to the rope!* to catch, to grasp, to hold, to keep, to retain, to seize. 6 *They used to hang murderers.* SEE **execute.**

hangar SEE **building.**

hang-glider SEE **aircraft.**

hangman executioner.

hanker *In winter we hanker after warm sunshine.* to desire, to fancy, to long for, to want, to wish for.

haphazard *The organization of the jumble sale was a bit haphazard.* accidental, chance, chaotic, confused, disorganized, random, unplanned, unsystematic.

happen *Did anything interesting happen to Emma?* to befall, to come about, to occur, to take place.

happening event, incident, occasion, occurrence, phenomenon.

happy 1 *a happy bride, a happy event, etc.* blissful, cheerful, contented, delighted, ecstatic, elated, exultant, festive, gay, glad, gleeful, good-humoured, joyful, joyous, laughing, light-hearted, lively, merry, overjoyed, pleased, proud, radiant, rapturous. **2** *a happy accident.* favourable, fortunate, lucky.

harass *The dogs harassed the sheep.* to annoy, to bother, to disturb, to molest, to pester, to plague, to trouble, to worry.

harbour 1 *The ships tied up in the harbour.* anchorage, dock, haven, jetty, landing-stage, marina, moorings, pier, port, quay, wharf. **2** *I'd be in trouble if I harboured a criminal.* to give asylum to, to give refuge to, to protect, to shelter.

hard 1 *hard concrete.* firm, inflexible, rigid, solid, unyielding. **2** *a hard climb.* arduous, difficult, exhausting, gruelling, harsh, heavy, laborious, stiff, strenuous, tough. **3** *a hard problem.* baffling, complicated, confusing, difficult, involved, puzzling. **4** *a hard heart.* cruel, harsh, heartless, merciless, pitiless, ruthless, severe, stern, strict, unfeeling. **5** *a hard knock.* forceful, heavy, powerful, strong, violent. **6** *hard up:* SEE **poor**.

hardly barely, only just, scarcely, with difficulty.

hardship *They suffered great hardship when their father died.* adversity, difficulty, misery, suffering, trouble, unhappiness.

hardware equipment, instruments, machinery, tools.

hard-wearing *You need hard-wearing shoes for walking in the hills.* durable, lasting, strong, sturdy, tough, well-made.

hare SEE **animal**.

harm to damage, to hurt, to injure, to misuse, to spoil, to wound.

harmful *Eating stale food can be harmful.* bad, damaging, dangerous, destructive, injurious, unhealthy.

harmless *Don't you know that grass-snakes are harmless?* innocent, innocuous, inoffensive, mild, safe.

harmonica, harmonium SEE **music**.

harmony 1 *Wouldn't it be nice if we could all live in harmony?* agreement, concord, friendliness, peace. **2** SEE **music**.

harness SEE **horse**.

harp SEE **music, talk**.

harpoon SEE **weapon**.

harpsichord SEE **keyboard**.

harrow SEE **farm**.

harsh 1 *a harsh noise.* grating, jarring, raucous, shrill. **2** *harsh light, harsh colours.* bright, brilliant, dazzling, gaudy, glaring, lurid. **3** *a harsh smell.* acrid, bitter, unpleasant. **4** *harsh conditions.* arduous, austere, difficult, hard, severe, tough. **5** *a harsh texture.* bristly, coarse, hairy, rough, scratchy. **6** *a harsh judge.* cruel, stern, strict, unkind.

harvest 1 *The farmers hope for a good harvest.* crop, produce, yield. **2** *They harvest the corn in the summer.* to gather, to reap.

hash goulash, stew. SEE ALSO **food**.

hasty 1 *a hasty decision.* abrupt, hurried, impetuous, impulsive, quick, rash, reckless, speedy, sudden. **2** *hasty work.* brief, careless, cursory, hurried, slapdash.

hat KINDS OF HEAD-DRESS ARE beret, bonnet, bowler, cap, coronet, crash-helmet, crown, diadem, helmet, hood, sou'wester, turban, wig. SEE ALSO **clothes**.

hatch 1 *to hatch eggs.* to brood, to incubate. **2** *to hatch a plot.* to concoct, to devise, to plan.

hatchet SEE **tool**.

hate *Logan hates cabbage.* to despise, to detest, to dislike, to loathe, to scorn.

hateful SEE **unpleasant**.

hatred *Logan made his hatred of vegetarian food quite obvious.* aversion, contempt, dislike, loathing, revulsion.

haughty *a haughty manner.* arrogant, boastful, bumptious, (informal) cocky, conceited, disdainful, proud, self-important, (informal) stuck-up.

haul *The explorers had dogs to haul the sledge.* to drag, to draw, to lug, to pull, to tow, to tug.

haunt *Tony and his friends haunt the area near the sweet shop most evenings.* to hang around, to loiter about, to visit.

have 1 *Lucy has her own radio.* to own, to possess. 2 *Our house has six rooms.* to consist of, to contain, to hold, to include, to incorporate, to involve. 3 *What did you have for Christmas?* to acquire, to be given, to gain, to get, to obtain, to receive. 4 *Who had the last biscuit?* to consume, to eat, to remove, to take. 5 *Did you have fun? Did you have any pain?* to endure, to enjoy, to experience, to feel, to go through, to know, to live through, to suffer, to undergo. ! *Have* has many meanings. These are only some of the other words you can use.

haven 1 *The ship reached the haven before the storm broke.* anchorage, harbour, port. 2 *The climbers found haven in a mountain hut.* asylum, refuge, retreat, safety, shelter.

haversack knapsack, rucksack. SEE ALSO **container**.

havoc *The storm created havoc along the coast.* damage, destruction, devastation.

hawk SEE **bird**.

hawser cable, cord, line, rope.

hawthorn SEE **tree**.

hay fodder.

hay fever SEE **illness**.

haystack rick. SEE ALSO **farm**.

hazard *Fog is one of the worst hazards for traffic.* danger, peril, risk, threat, trouble.

hazardous *Crossing the sea in a rowing boat is hazardous.* chancy, dangerous, perilous, risky, unsafe.

haze fog, mist. SEE ALSO **weather**.

hazel SEE **nut, tree**.

hazy *The view was hazy.* blurred, dim, faint, misty, unclear.

H-bomb SEE **weapon**.

head 1 PARTS OF YOUR HEAD ARE brain, cheek, chin, ear, eye, forehead, gums, hair, jaw, lip, mouth, nose, nostril, scalp, skull, teeth, tongue. SEE ALSO **body**. 2 *the head of a mountain.* apex, crown, top. 3 *the head of an organization.* boss, director, employer, leader, manager, ruler. SEE ALSO **chief**. 4 *the head of a school.* headmaster, headmistress, headteacher, principal. SEE ALSO **school**. 5 *Captain Scott headed an expedition to the South Pole.* to be in charge of, to command, to govern, to lead, to manage, to rule, to supervise. 6 *Tony headed the ball into the net.* SEE **hit**. 7 *the head waiter.* chief, leading, most important, senior.

headache SEE **illness**.

head-dress SEE **hat**.

heading *Mrs Angel told us to write the heading in big letters.* caption, headline, title.

headlight SEE **light, vehicle**.

headline *a newspaper headline.* caption, heading, title.

headlong *a headlong dash.* breakneck, hurried, impetuous, impulsive, reckless.

headphones SEE **audio equipment**.

headquarters 1 *the headquarters of an expedition.* base, depot. 2 *the headquarters of a business.* head office, main office.

heal 1 *They claim that this ointment heals cuts.* to cure, to make better, to remedy. 2 *Wounds heal in time.* to get better, to mend, to recover.

health 1 *We'd all like to have good health.* condition, fitness, strength, vigour. 2 SEE **medicine**.

healthy 1 *a healthy animal.* hearty, lively, perky, robust, sound, strong, vigorous, well. 2 *healthy surroundings.* hygienic, sanitary, wholesome.

heap 1 *a heap of rubbish.* mass, mound, pile, stack. 2 *We heaped up the rubbish.*

to accumulate, to collect, to mass, to pile up, to stack up.

hear 1 *Have you heard this new single?* to listen to. 2 *Have you heard the news about Logan?* to discover, to find out, to gather, to learn.

hearse SEE **funeral, vehicle**.

heart 1 SEE **body**. 2 *the heart of the forest, the heart of the problem.* centre, core, focus, hub, middle.

heart-broken SEE **sad**.

hearth fireplace, grate.

heartless *heartless behaviour.* SEE **cruel**.

hearty 1 *a hearty welcome.* enthusiastic, sincere, warm. 2 *a hearty appetite.* big, healthy, robust.

heat 1 *the heat of a fire.* glow, hotness, warmth. 2 WORDS FOR HEATING THINGS OR FOR BEING HOT ARE to bake, to blister, to boil, to burn, to cook, to fry, to grill, to melt, to roast, to scald, to scorch, to simmer, to sizzle, to smoulder, to steam, to stew, to swelter, to toast. 3 *the heats for a race.* SEE **race**.

heath moor, moorland. SEE ALSO **geography**.

heathen atheist, barbarian, pagan, savage. ! These words are often insulting.

heather SEE **shrub**.

heave *They heaved the sacks onto the lorry.* to drag, to draw, to haul, to hoist, to lift, to lug, to pull, to raise, to throw, to tow, to tug.

heaven 1 paradise. 2 (informal) *Mum says it's heaven to have a hot bath.* bliss, ecstasy, happiness, rapture.

heavenly (informal) *What's that heavenly smell?* blissful, celestial, divine. SEE ALSO **pleasant**.

heavy 1 *a heavy load.* burdensome, massive, ponderous, weighty. 2 *heavy work.* arduous, difficult, hard, exhausting, laborious, strenuous, tough. 3 *heavy rain.* concentrated, considerable, severe, torrential. 4 *a heavy heart.* depressed, gloomy, miserable. SEE ALSO **sad**.

hectare SEE **measure**.

hectic *We had a hectic time doing the Christmas shopping.* active, bustling, busy, excited, frantic, lively, mad, wild.

hedge 1 fence, hedgerow. 2 *to hedge in*: to encircle, to enclose, to fence in, to hem in, to pen, to surround.

hedgehog SEE **animal**.

heed *If you're wise, you'll heed his warning.* to attend to, to follow, to keep to, to listen to, to mark, to mind, to note, to notice, to obey, to observe, to take notice of.

heel 1 SEE **body, foot**. 2 *The dinghy heeled over in the wind.* to lean, to list, to slope, to tilt.

hefty *a hefty man.* beefy, big, brawny, burly, mighty, muscular, strong, tough.

heifer SEE **cattle, young**.

height *the height of a mountain.* altitude, tallness.

heir inheritor, successor.

helicopter SEE **aircraft**.

hell underworld.

hellish diabolical, dreadful, ghastly. SEE ALSO **unpleasant**. ! *Hellish* is often used as slang.

helm SEE **vessel**.

helmet SEE **hat**.

help 1 *You can help each other if you want.* to aid, to assist, to back, to boost, to collaborate with, to co-operate with, to side with, to support. 2 *Give Logan a bit of help.* aid, assistance, backing, boost, co-operation, relief, support.

helpful 1 *a helpful person.* accommodating, benevolent, considerate, constructive, co-operative, neighbourly, obliging, thoughtful, willing. SEE ALSO **kind**. 2 *a helpful tool.* convenient, handy, useful. 3 *a helpful suggestion.* advantageous, informative, instructive, profitable, valuable.

helping *a helping of pudding.* portion, share.

helpless 1 *a helpless invalid.* feeble, impotent, incapable, weak, (informal) weedy. 2 *a helpless ship.*

aground, disabled, drifting, stranded.

hem 1 *the hem of a skirt.* border, edge. **2** *to hem in:* to encircle, to enclose, to hedge in, to surround.

hemisphere SEE **geography, shape.**

hen 1 chicken, fowl. SEE ALSO **poultry. 2** SEE **bird, female.**

herald announcer, messenger, town-crier.

herb 1 KINDS OF HERB ARE mint, parsley, sage. **2** SEE **plant.**

herd 1 *a herd of cattle.* SEE **group. 2** *to herd together.* to assemble, to congregate, to crowd, to flock, to gather, to swarm, to throng.

hereditary *a hereditary disease.* handed down, inherited, passed on.

hero, heroine champion, idol, star, superstar, victor, winner.

heroic *a heroic rescue.* bold, brave, chivalrous, courageous, daring, fearless, gallant, intrepid, noble, valiant.

heroin SEE **drug.**

heron SEE **bird.**

herring SEE **fish.**

hesitate *I hesitated before jumping into the cold water.* to delay, to falter, to hang back, to pause, to think twice, to wait, to waver.

hew *to hew down a tree.* to chop, to saw. SEE ALSO **cut.**

hexagon SEE **shape.**

hibernating *a hibernating animal.* asleep, dormant, inactive.

hide 1 *Hide the sweets when Logan's around!* to bury, to conceal, to cover, to put away. **2** *The mist hid the view.* to blot out, to camouflage, to cloak, to mask, to obscure, to screen, to shroud. **3** *The runaway hid in an old warehouse.* to lie low, to lurk. **4** *an animal's hide.* fur, leather, skin.

hide-and-seek SEE **game.**

hideous *a hideous wound.* frightful, ghastly, grisly, gruesome, repulsive, ugly, unsightly. SEE ALSO **unpleasant.**

hide-out den, hiding-place, lair.

hiding *to give someone a hiding.* SEE **punishment.**

hieroglyphics SEE **writing.**

hi-fi SEE **audio equipment.**

high 1 *a high building.* lofty, tall, towering. **2** *a high look-out.* elevated, raised. **3** *high prices.* excessive, exorbitant, unreasonable. **4** *a high rank in the army.* eminent, important, leading, powerful, prominent, top. **5** *a high wind.* great, intense, stormy, strong. **6** *a high reputation.* favourable, good, respected. **7** *a high sound.* piercing, sharp, shrill. **8** *a high school.* SEE **school.**

highbrow 1 *highbrow music.* classical. **2** *a highbrow book.* cultural, educational, improving, intellectual.

high-fidelity SEE **audio equipment.**

highlight *The highlight of our day out was a flight in a helicopter.* best moment, climax, peak.

highly-strung *Our dog yaps because he's highly-strung.* edgy, jittery, nervous, tense, touchy, (informal) uptight.

Highness SEE **royal.**

high tea SEE **meal.**

highway SEE **road.**

highwayman bandit, brigand, robber, thief. SEE ALSO **criminal.**

hijacking SEE **crime.**

hike *We hiked across the moors.* to ramble, to tramp, to trek. SEE ALSO **walk.**

hilarious *a hilarious joke.* amusing, comic, funny, hysterical, laughable, ridiculous, silly, uproarious, witty.

hill 1 *I climbed the hill.* mountain, peak, rise, summit. **2** *an area of hills:* downs, fells, highlands. **3** SEE **geography.**

hinder *Deep snowdrifts hindered our progress.* to bar, to check, to curb, to delay, to deter, to hamper, to impede, to obstruct, to prevent, to stop.

hindrance *Our heavy rucksacks were a hindrance.* difficulty, disadvantage, handicap, impediment, inconvenience, obstacle.

Hindu SEE **religion**.

hint 1 *I don't know the answer: give me a hint.* clue, implication, indication, inkling, suggestion, tip. **2** *Dad hinted that we might have a trip to London.* to imply, to indicate, to suggest.

hip 1 *Mum's got a pain in her hip.* SEE **body, joint**. **2** *rose hips.* SEE **fruit**.

hippopotamus SEE **animal**.

hire 1 *We hired a bus.* to charter, to rent. **2** *to hire out:* to let.

hiss SEE **sound**.

historic *a historic battle.* celebrated, eminent, famous, important, notable, renowned, well-known.

history SEE **subject**.

hit 1 *Logan's jokes were a hit at the concert.* success, triumph. **2** *I got a hit on the head.* blow, bump, knock. **3** VARIOUS WAYS TO HIT THINGS ARE to bang, (informal) to bash, to batter, to beat, to bump, to butt, to cane, to clout, to collide with, to cuff, to dash, to drive, to flick, to flip, to flog, to hammer, to head, to jab, to jar, to jog, to kick, to knock, to lash, to pat, to poke, to pound, to prod, to punch, to putt, to ram, to rap, to scourge, to slam, to slap, to slog, to smack, to smash, to spank, to strike, to stub, to swat, to swipe, to tap, to thrash, to thump, to wallop, to whack, to whip.

hitch-hike SEE **travel**.

hive apiary.

hoard *Squirrels hoard nuts.* to accumulate, to collect, to gather, to keep, to mass, to pile up, to save, to store, to treasure.

hoarse *a hoarse voice.* croaking, grating, gruff, harsh, husky, rasping, raucous, rough.

hoax 1 *The firemen were angry when they heard that the emergency call was a hoax.* deception, fake, fraud, practical joke, trick. **2** *They realized that someone had hoaxed them.* to bluff, to deceive, to delude, to fool, to hoodwink, to mislead, to take in, to trick.

hobble to limp. SEE ALSO **walk**.

hobby *Mr Brunswick's hobby is water-skiing.* interest, pastime, pursuit, relaxation.

hockey SEE **sport**.

hoe SEE **garden**.

hog SEE **male, pig**.

Hogmanay SEE **time**.

hoist *The crane hoisted the boxes onto the deck.* to heave, to lift, to pull up, to raise.

hold 1 *Hold this rope!* to catch, to clutch, to grasp, to grip, to hang on to, to keep, to retain, to seize. **2** *He held the baby.* to bear, to carry, to clasp, to embrace, to hug, to support, to take. **3** *Uncle George held an important position in the bank.* to have, to occupy, to possess. **4** *The suitcase held all our things.* to contain, to enclose, to include. **5** *The lock gates hold back the water.* to block, to check, to control, to curb, to halt, to keep back, to retain, to stop. **6** *The police are holding a suspect.* to arrest, to confine, to detain, to keep. **7** *Hold that pose while I put a film in the camera!* to keep up, to maintain, to preserve, to retain. **8** *The church holds services every week.* to conduct, to have. **9** *I wonder how long this heat-wave will hold?* to carry on, to continue, to endure, to keep on, to last, to persist, to stay. **10** *to hold out: Hold out your hand.* to extend, to reach out, to stick out, to stretch out. **11** *to hold up: The traffic jam held up our journey.* to delay, to hinder, to obstruct, to slow down.

hold-all SEE **container**.

hold-up 1 *There was a hold-up at the bank.* SEE **crime**. **2** *My train was late because of a hold-up on the line.* delay, pause, postponement, wait.

hole 1 *a hole in the ground.* abyss, burrow, cave, chasm, crater, excavation, pit, pothole, tunnel. **2** *a hole in a fence, a hole in a tyre, etc.* breach, break, chink, crack, cut, gap, gash, leak, opening, puncture, slit, split, tear, vent.

holiday 1 *a holiday from school.* day off, leave, rest, time off. **2** VARIOUS kinds of holiday are camping, cruise, honeymoon, safari, seaside holiday, tour, trip, vacation, youth-hostelling. **3** KINDS OF HOLIDAY ACCOMMODATION ARE apartment, boarding-house, campsite, flat, guest-house, hostel, hotel, inn, motel, self-catering, villa, youth hostel.

hollow 1 *a hollow space.* empty, unfilled. **2** *a hollow in the ground.* dent, depression, dip, hole, valley. **3** *Lucy hollowed out a pumpkin to make a lantern.* to dig, to gouge, to scoop.

holly SEE **tree**.

hollyhock SEE **flower**.

holster SEE **container**.

holy *The temple is a holy place.* blessed, consecrated, divine, hallowed, heavenly, religious, sacred, saintly.

homage *to pay homage to*: to honour, to praise, to respect, to worship.

home abode, dwelling, residence. SEE ALSO **house**.

homeless *homeless people*: beggars, the destitute, tramps, vagrants. SEE ALSO **poor**.

homework SEE **school**.

homosexual gay, (impolite) queer.

honest 1 *an honest worker.* conscientious, honourable, law-abiding, moral, trustworthy, upright. **2** *an honest answer.* blunt, candid, direct, frank, genuine, open, sincere, straightforward, truthful. **3** *an honest judgement.* fair, impartial, just, unbiased, unprejudiced.

honey SEE **food**.

honeymoon SEE **holiday, wedding**.

honeysuckle SEE **climber**.

honour 1 *Tony had the honour of presenting a bouquet to our visitor.* distinction, fame, importance, renown, respect. **2** *If Logan had any honour, he would own up.* decency, honesty, integrity, loyalty, nobility, principle, sincerity, virtue. **3** *On Remembrance Day we honour those who died in war.* to admire, to pay homage

to, to pay tribute to, to praise, to respect, to show respect to.

honourable *It was the honourable thing to hand over the money you found.* admirable, decent, good, honest, law-abiding, loyal, noble, respectable, upright, virtuous, worthy.

hood SEE **hat**.

hoodwink *Logan was silly to try to hoodwink the head.* to bluff, to cheat, to deceive, to dupe, to fool, to hoax, (informal) to kid, to mislead, to swindle, to take in, to trick.

hoof foot.

hook 1 *to hook a fish.* to capture, to catch, to take. **2** *to hook a wagon on to a train.* SEE **fasten**.

hooligan delinquent, mugger, ruffian, thug, trouble-maker, vandal. SEE ALSO **criminal**.

hoop band, circle, ring.

hoot SEE **sound**.

Hoover SEE **house**.

hop to bound, to jump, to leap, to skip, to spring.

hope 1 *Is there any hope of better weather?* likelihood, prospect. **2** *We hope that we'll win.* to have confidence, to have faith, to trust.

hopeful 1 *We're hopeful that we can win.* confident, optimistic. **2** *There are hopeful signs that we can do well.* encouraging, favourable, promising, reassuring.

hopefully 1 *The cat looked hopefully at the scraps left from dinner.* confidently, expectantly, optimistically. **2** (informal) *Hopefully, I'll be fit to play tomorrow.* all being well, probably. ! Many people think that this is a wrong use of *hopefully*.

hopeless 1 *a hopeless situation.* desperate, impossible, incurable. **2** *a hopeless footballer.* feeble, incompetent, inefficient, poor, useless, weak, worthless. SEE ALSO **bad**.

hopscotch SEE **game**.

horde *a horde of children from the other school.* band, crowd, gang, mob, swarm, tribe. SEE ALSO **group**.

horizontal *Is the snooker table*

horizontal? flat, level. ❘ *Horizontal* is the opposite of *vertical*.

horn SEE **brass, music.**

hornet SEE **insect.**

hornpipe SEE **dance.**

horrible *horrible weather, horrible food, etc.* awful, beastly, dreadful, ghastly, horrid, nasty, terrible. SEE ALSO **unpleasant.**

horrific *a horrific accident.* appalling, dreadful, frightful, gruesome, hair-raising, horrifying, shocking. ❘ You often use *horrible* to describe things that aren't important, but you use *horrific* to describe things that really horrify you.

horrify *The accident horrified us.* to appal, to frighten, to scare, to shock, to terrify.

horror dismay, dread, fear, terror.

horse 1 bronco, cart-horse, colt, foal, mare, mount, mule, nag, piebald, race-horse, stallion, steed. **2** ITEMS OF EQUIPMENT FOR HORSES ARE bridle, collar, girth, halter, harness, horseshoe, rein, saddle, spur, stirrups. **3** WAYS TO RIDE A HORSE ARE to amble, to canter, to gallop, to trot. **4** HORSE-RIDING EVENTS ARE gymkhana, hunting, pony-trekking, racing, riding, show-jumping, steeplechase.

horse-box SEE **vehicle.**

horse-chestnut SEE **tree.**

hose *a water hose.* pipe, tube.

hospitable *The people we stayed with were very hospitable.* friendly, kind, sociable, welcoming.

hospital SEE **medicine.**

hostage captive, prisoner.

hostel SEE **holiday.**

hostile 1 *a hostile crowd.* aggressive, attacking, belligerent, pugnacious, unfriendly, warlike. **2** *hostile weather conditions.* adverse, contrary, opposing, unfavourable.

hot 1 *hot weather, a hot iron, etc.* baking, blistering, boiling, burning, fiery, red-hot, roasting, scalding, scorching, sizzling, sweltering, warm. **2** *a hot temper.* angry, fierce,

passionate, violent. **3** *a hot taste.* gingery, peppery, spicy. SEE ALSO **taste.**

hotel SEE **building, holiday.**

hot-pot SEE **food.**

hound 1 SEE **dog. 2** *The wanted man was hounded by the police.* to chase, to hunt, to pursue, to track down.

hour SEE **time.**

house 1 *Come to my house.* abode, dwelling, home, lodgings, place, quarters, residence. **2** KINDS OF HOUSE ARE apartments, bungalow, chalet, cottage, council-house, croft, detached house, farmhouse, flats, hovel, lodge, manor, manse, mansion, prefab, rectory, semi-detached house, shack, shanty, terrace house, thatched house, vicarage, villa. SEE ALSO **building.** **3** ROOMS IN A HOUSE ARE attic, bathroom, bedroom, cloakroom, conservatory, corridor, dining-room, drawing room, hall, kitchen, landing, larder, lavatory, living-room, loft, lounge, outhouse, pantry, parlour, passage, porch, scullery, sitting-room, study, toilet, WC. **4** ITEMS OF EQUIPMENT IN A HOUSE ARE air-conditioning, barometer, boiler, brush, central heating, clock, double-glazing, duster, fire, fire-extinguisher, freezer, Hoover, immersion heater, incinerator, iron, ironing-board, lighter, mangle, meter, mop, phone, plumbing, radiator, sanitation, scissors, spin-drier, step-ladder, thermometer, thermostat, tray, tumble-drier, vacuum-cleaner, washing-machine, wiring. FOR OTHER HOUSEHOLD EQUIPMENT SEE ALSO **bathroom, furniture, kitchen, tool. 5** *to house someone.* to accommodate, to board, to lodge, to put up, to shelter.

house-boat SEE **vessel.**

house-trained *a house-trained dog.* clean in the house, domesticated.

hovel cottage, hut, shack, shanty. SEE ALSO **house.**

hover 1 *The hawk hovered over its prey.* to float, to fly, to hang in the air. **2** *After* *the party, people hovered about for a while.* to hang about, to linger, to loiter, to wait about.

hovercraft SEE **vessel**.

howl SEE **sound**.

howler (informal) *to make a howler.* blunder, (informal) clanger, error, mistake, (informal) slip-up.

hubbub *The head could hardly be heard above the hubbub.* clamour, commotion, din, hullabaloo, noise, pandemonium, racket, row, rumpus, uproar.

huddle 1 *The sheep huddled in the corner of the field.* to cluster, to crowd, to flock, to gather, to herd, to press, to squeeze, to swarm, to throng. **2** *The children huddled together to keep warm.* to cuddle, to curl up, to nestle, to snuggle.

hue colour, shade, tinge, tint, tone.

hug *Dad hugged the baby.* to clasp, to cling to, to crush, to cuddle, to embrace, to hold, to snuggle, to squeeze.

huge *Elephants are huge animals.* colossal, enormous, gigantic, great, immense, large, mammoth, vast. SEE ALSO **big**.

hulking *The hulking wrestler towered above us.* bulky, clumsy, heavy, massive. SEE ALSO **big**.

hull SEE **vessel**.

hum SEE **sing, sound**.

human beings folk, humanity, mankind, mortals. SEE ALSO **person**.

humane *Is it humane to kill animals for food?* benevolent, kind, kind-hearted, merciful, sympathetic, unselfish, warm-hearted.

humble 1 *humble behaviour.* lowly, meek, modest, unassuming. **2** *to humble someone.* to bring down, to disgrace, to humiliate, to shame.

humbug SEE **sweet**.

humid *humid weather.* clammy, damp, dank, moist, muggy, steamy, sultry.

humiliate *They humiliated us by winning 14-0.* to disgrace, to humble, to make ashamed.

humorous *a humorous story.* amusing, comic, facetious, funny, hilarious, laughable, ridiculous, silly, witty.

humour *You seem to be in a good humour!* mood, state of mind, temper.

hump bulge, bump, lump, swelling.

hunch *I have a hunch that Lucy broke that window.* feeling, guess, intuition.

hundredweight SEE **measure**.

hunger 1 *Did that meal satisfy your hunger?* appetite, desire, greed, longing. **2** *Hunger kills millions of people.* famine, malnutrition, starvation.

hungry *Logan's always hungry!* famished, greedy, (informal) peckish, ravenous, starved, starving, underfed.

hunk *a hunk of cheese.* block, chunk, lump, mass, piece.

hunt 1 *to hunt animals.* to chase, to hound, to poach, to pursue, to stalk, to track down. **2** *We hunted for mum's keys.* to look for, to search for, to seek. **3** *Does the fox enjoy the hunt as much as the hounds do?* chase, pursuit, quest, search.

hunter predator.

hurdle barrier, fence, obstacle.

hurl *He hurled the sword into the lake.* to cast, to chuck, to fling, to pitch, to sling, to throw, to toss.

hurricane cyclone, storm, tempest, tornado, typhoon. SEE ALSO **weather**.

hurried *a hurried decision, hurried work, etc.* careless, cursory, hasty, impetuous, quick, rushed, speedy.

hurry 1 *I hurried home.* to dash, to hasten, to hurtle, to hustle, to rush, to speed, (informal) to zoom. SEE ALSO **move**. **2** *If you want to finish you must hurry.* to accelerate, (informal) to buck up, to quicken, to work faster.

hurt 1 *That wasp sting hurts!* to ache, to be painful, to be sore, to smart, to sting, to throb. **2** *Did the attackers hurt her?* to afflict, to cripple, to damage, to disable, to distress, to harm, to injure, to maim, to misuse, to pain, to torment, to torture, to wound.

hurtle to dash, to race, to rush, to speed, (informal) to zoom. SEE ALSO **move.**

husband SEE **family, marriage.**

hush 1 be quiet! be silent! shut up! **2** *We tried to hush it up, but everyone found out.* to conceal, to hide, to keep it quiet, to keep it secret.

husk covering, shell.

husky 1 *a husky voice.* croaking, gruff, harsh, hoarse, rasping, rough. **2** *a big, husky fellow.* beefy, big, brawny, bulky, burly, hefty, hulking, muscular, strong. **3** *a team of huskies.* SEE **dog.**

hustle 1 *The gang hustled their victim into a car.* to jostle, to push, to shove. **2** *As we were late, they hustled us to our seats.* to hurry, to rush.

hut hovel, shack, shanty, shed, shelter.

hutch cage, coop, pen.

hyacinth SEE **bulb, flower.**

hydrofoil SEE **vessel.**

hydrogen SEE **gas.**

hyena SEE **animal.**

hygienic *You need hygienic conditions in hospital.* clean, disinfected, germ-free, healthy, sanitary, sterilized, unpolluted.

hymn SEE **church, sing.**

hyphen SEE **punctuation.**

hypocritical *Is it hypocritical for a vegetarian to wear leather shoes?* false, inconsistent, insincere.

hypodermic SEE **medicine.**

hysteria frenzy, madness, mania, panic.

hysterical 1 *The fans became hysterical when the group appeared.* delirious, demented, frantic, frenzied, mad, uncontrollable, wild. **2** *a hysterical joke.* comic, funny, hilarious, laughable, ridiculous, uproarious.

I i

ice 1 KINDS OF ICE ARE black ice, floe, glacier, iceberg, icicle. **2** SEE **weather.**

ice-breaker SEE **vessel.**

ice-cream SEE **food.**

ice-hockey, ice-rink SEE **sport.**

icing SEE **food.**

icy 1 *icy weather.* bitter, cold, freezing, frosty, wintry. **2** *icy roads.* frozen, slippery.

idea 1 *I have an idea.* (informal) brainwave, concept, notion, plan, point, proposal, suggestion, thought. **2** *Have you any idea who will win?* attitude, belief, impression, inkling, opinion, view.

ideal *ideal conditions.* excellent, faultless, perfect, suitable.

identical *identical twins.* alike, equal, indistinguishable.

identify *Did the vet identify what was wrong with the cat?* to detect, to diagnose, to discover, to name, to recognize.

identity *Did you discover his identity?* name.

idiot ass, blockhead, booby, dope, dunce, fool, half-wit, ignoramus, imbecile, moron, nitwit, twerp. ! These words are mostly used informally and are often insulting.

idiotic *an idiotic mistake.* absurd, crazy, foolish, irrational, ludicrous, ridiculous, silly, stupid, unwise.

idle 1 *The machines were idle during the holiday.* inactive, not working, unemployed, unoccupied, unused. **2** *He lost his job because he was so idle.* lazy, slow, sluggish.

idol 1 *a pagan idol.* god, image, statue. **2** *a pop idol.* hero, star, superstar.

idolize *The children idolize their grandfather.* to adore, to love, to revere, to worship.

ignite 1 *The gas fire won't ignite.* to burn, to catch fire, to fire. **2** *I ignited the fire with a match.* to kindle, to light, to set fire to.

ignition SEE **vehicle**.

ignoramus SEE **idiot**.

ignorant 1 *We were ignorant of the facts.* unaware, uninformed. 2 *You'd be ignorant if you didn't go to school.* illiterate, uneducated. 3 (insulting) *He's just plain ignorant!* foolish, stupid, unintelligent.

ignore *He ignored the 'stop' sign.* to disobey, to disregard, to leave out, to miss out, to neglect, to omit, to overlook, to skip, to take no notice of.

ill 1 bedridden, diseased, feeble, indisposed, infirm, pasty, (informal) poorly, queer, sick, unhealthy, unwell. SEE ALSO **illness**. 2 ILL PEOPLE ARE invalid, out-patient, patient, sufferer, victim. 3 *ill effects.* bad, evil, harmful, unfavourable.

illegal *Cycling after dark without lights is illegal.* banned, criminal, forbidden, irregular, unauthorized, unlawful.

illegible *an illegible signature.* indecipherable, unreadable.

illegitimate *an illegitimate child*: bastard. ! Nowadays *bastard* is usually insulting.

illiterate *He was illiterate because he never went to school.* ignorant, uneducated.

illness 1 *to suffer from an illness.* ailment, affliction, attack, blight, (informal) bug, complaint, disease, disorder, infection, infirmity, injury, malady, sickness, wound. 2 VARIOUS ILLNESSES OR COMPLAINTS ARE abscess, allergy, amnesia, anaemia, appendicitis, arthritis, asthma, bilious attack, blister, boil, bronchitis, cancer, cataract, catarrh, chicken-pox, chilblain, chill, cholera, claustrophobia, cold, colic, coma, concussion, constipation, convulsion, corns, cough, cramp, dandruff, dermatitis, diabetes, diarrhoea, diphtheria, dysentery, earache, epilepsy, fever, fits, flu, frostbite, gastric flu, hay fever, headache, impetigo, indigestion, inflammation, influenza, insomnia, jaundice, leprosy, leukaemia, lumbago, malaria, measles, migraine, mumps, neuralgia, paralysis, phobia, plague, pneumonia, polio or poliomyelitis, rabies, rheumatism, scarlet fever, scurvy, seasickness, smallpox, spina bifida, stroke, sty, sunstroke, tonsilitis, toothache, tuberculosis, typhoid, typhus, ulcer, verruca, wart, whooping-cough.

illogical *an illogical argument.* irrational, unreasonable.

illuminate to light up.

illusion *It didn't really happen: it was just an illusion.* conjuring trick, delusion, dream, fantasy, hallucination.

illustrate *The pictures illustrate how to do it.* to demonstrate, to depict, to explain, to picture, to portray, to show.

illustration 1 diagram, drawing, picture. 2 *This thesaurus gives illustrations of how words can be used.* case, example, instance.

image 1 *You can see your image in the mirror.* imitation, likeness, picture, reflection. 2 *The temple contained the god's image.* carving, figure, representation, statue.

imaginary *The unicorn is an imaginary beast.* fanciful, fictitious, invented, legendary, made-up, mythical, non-existent, unreal.

imaginative *Tony's stories are very imaginative.* artistic, attractive, beautiful, clever, creative, ingenious, inspired, inventive, resourceful.

imagine 1 *Can you imagine what life was like 1000 years ago?* to conceive, to create, to dream up, to invent, to picture, to see, to think up, to visualize. 2 *I imagine you'd like something to eat.* to assume, to believe, to guess, to presume, to suppose, to think.

imbecile SEE **idiot**.

imitate *Tony can imitate animal sounds.* to copy, to counterfeit, to echo, to duplicate, to impersonate, to mimic, to reproduce.

imitation *It isn't real: it's an imitation.*

copy, counterfeit, dummy, duplicate, fake, forgery, likeness, replica, reproduction.

immature *immature behaviour.* babyish, childish, inexperienced, infantile, juvenile, young, youthful.

immediate 1 *I took immediate action to end the crisis.* instant, instantaneous, prompt, quick, speedy, swift. 2 *Mrs Brunswick talks to her immediate neighbour over the fence.* adjacent, closest, nearest, next.

immediately directly, forthwith, instantly, promptly.

immense colossal, enormous, gigantic, great, huge, large, massive, vast. SEE ALSO big.

immerse 1 *to immerse something in water.* to dip, to drench, to drown, to lower, to plunge, to submerge. 2 *immersed: immersed in your work.* absorbed, interested, preoccupied.

immersion heater SEE fire.

immigrate to settle.

immobile *The car was immobile in the mud.* fast, firm, fixed, immobilized, immovable, motionless, paralysed, secure, static, stationary.

immobilize *to immobilize a vehicle.* to cripple, to damage, to put out of action, to stop.

immoral *Everyone disapproved of his immoral behaviour.* base, corrupt, depraved, evil, sinful, villainous, wicked. SEE ALSO bad.

immortal *Some people believe that your soul is immortal.* endless, eternal, everlasting, undying.

immovable SEE immobile.

immunization SEE medicine.

imp *a mischievous imp.* demon, devil, rascal, rogue, scamp, spirit.

impact 1 *Was the car damaged in the impact?* bump, collision, crash, smash. 2 *The pictures of the famine made a strong impact on us.* effect, impression, influence, shock.

impale SEE wound.

impartial *an impartial referee.* detached, disinterested, fair, just,

neutral, unbiased, uninvolved, unprejudiced.

impatient 1 *We were impatient to start.* anxious, eager. 2 *The horses were impatient.* edgy, fidgety, restless.

impede *A fallen tree impeded our progress.* to block, to check, to delay, to deter, to hinder, to obstruct, to slow down.

impediment SEE handicap.

impenetrable *impenetrable forest.* dense, thick.

imperceptible *an imperceptible movement.* insignificant, invisible, microscopic, minute, negligible, slight, small, tiny, undetectable.

imperfect *If the goods are imperfect, take them back to the shop.* defective, faulty, incomplete, unfinished.

imperfection *Lucy corrected the imperfections in her gymnastic routine.* blemish, defect, flaw, shortcoming, weakness.

impersonate *We laughed when Logan impersonated the vicar.* to copy, to imitate, to mimic, to pose as, to pretend to be.

impertinent *Mrs Angel said it was impertinent to mimic the vicar.* cheeky, discourteous, disrespectful, impolite, impudent, insolent, insulting, rude, saucy.

impetigo SEE illness.

impetuous *Logan's impetuous dash across the road almost caused an accident.* hasty, headlong, impulsive, quick, rash, reckless, speedy.

implement *gardening implements.* device, gadget, instrument, tool, utensil.

implore *Granny implored us to stay for tea.* to ask, to beg, to entreat, to plead, to request.

imply *Dad implied that we might have a treat at the weekend.* to hint, to indicate, to suggest.

impolite *It's impolite to talk with your mouth full.* discourteous, disrespectful, insulting, loutish, rude. SEE ALSO impertinent.

important 1 *important facts, an*

important event, etc. basic, big, chief, essential, fundamental, main, major, momentous, notable, pressing, primary, principal, serious, significant, urgent, weighty. 2 *an important person.* celebrated, distinguished, eminent, famous, great, influential, leading, notable, outstanding, prominent, renowned, well-known. 3 *to be important*: to matter.

impose *to impose a penalty.* to enforce, to inflict, to insist on.

imposing *an imposing castle.* big, grand, great, important, impressive, magnificent, majestic, stately, striking. SEE ALSO **splendid**.

impossible *It'd be impossible to swim the Atlantic.* impracticable, impractical, inconceivable, unimaginable.

impostor SEE **deceive**.

impotent *I was impotent to help the dying creature.* helpless, powerless, weak.

impoverished *an impoverished family.* destitute, needy, penniless, poor, poverty-stricken.

impregnable *an impregnable castle.* invincible, strong, unconquerable.

impress *Did the film impress you?* to affect, to influence, to move.

impression 1 *I had the impression you were bored.* feeling, idea, opinion, view. 2 *The film made a big impression on Tony.* effect, impact, mark. 3 *Granny has clear impressions of her childhood.* memory, recollection.

impressive *an impressive occasion.* grand, great, imposing, magnificent, majestic, moving, splendid, stately, striking.

imprison *to imprison a criminal.* to confine, to detain, to gaol, to intern, to lock up, to shut up.

improbable *an improbable story.* far-fetched, incredible, unbelievable, unconvincing, unlikely.

impromptu *an impromptu concert.* spontaneous, unplanned, unprepared, unrehearsed.

improper *improper language.* coarse,

crude, inappropriate, indecent, rude, unbecoming, unsuitable, vulgar, wrong.

improve 1 *Lucy's work has improved lately.* to advance, to develop, to move on, to progress. 2 *Has granny improved since her illness?* to get better, to recover. 3 *Has Logan improved his behaviour?* to reform, to revise. 4 *Mr Brunswick wants to improve his house.* to make better, to modernize, to rebuild, to reform, to renovate, to touch up, to upgrade.

improvise 1 *We improvised a play.* to concoct, to invent, to make up. 2 *I didn't have all the ingredients, so I had to improvise.* to make do.

impudent bold, cheeky, disrespectful, impertinent, impolite, insolent, insulting, presumptuous, rude, saucy.

impulsive *When he thought about it, he regretted his impulsive action.* automatic, hasty, impetuous, impromptu, involuntary, rash, spontaneous, sudden, unconscious, unplanned, unthinking.

impure *impure water.* contaminated, dirty, filthy, foul, infected, polluted, unclean.

inaccessible *The South Pole is an inaccessible spot.* cut off, isolated, remote, unreachable.

inaccuracy error, fault, miscalculation, mistake, (informal) slip-up.

inaccurate *It was silly to give an inaccurate statement to the police.* false, incorrect, mistaken, untrue, wrong.

inactive *Hedgehogs are inactive in winter.* asleep, dormant, hibernating.

inadequate *an inadequate supply of food.* insufficient, unsatisfactory.

inanimate lifeless.

inappropriate *an inappropriate gift.* improper, incongruous, irrelevant, unsuitable, wrong.

incendiary bomb SEE **weapon**.

incense 1 SEE **church**. 2 *Logan's bad behaviour incensed her.* to anger, to enrage, to inflame, to infuriate, to madden, to provoke, to vex.

incentive *Mrs Angel doesn't offer us sweets as an incentive to work.* encouragement, stimulus.

incessant *The insects kept up an incessant buzzing.* ceaseless, chronic, constant, continual, continuous, everlasting, interminable, permanent, persistent, relentless, unending.

inch SEE **measure**.

incident *The crash at the crossroads was a nasty incident.* affair, event, happening, occasion, occurrence.

incinerator SEE **fire**.

incite *Some trouble-makers incited the crowd to start fighting.* to arouse, to encourage, to excite, to provoke, to rouse, to stimulate, to stir up, to urge.

inclination *Grandad has an inclination to doze in the evening.* habit, instinct, leaning, readiness, tendency, trend.

incline 1 *That pillar inclines to the right.* to lean, to slant, to slope, to tilt, to tip. 2 *inclined to*: disposed to, liable to.

include *The packet includes everything you need to make a trifle.* to consist of, to contain, to cover, to incorporate, to involve.

incoherent *an incoherent message.* confused, disjointed, disorganized, garbled, jumbled, mixed up, muddled, rambling, unclear.

income earnings, pay, pension, salary, wages.

incompatible *What Logan said today is incompatible with what he said yesterday.* conflicting, contradictory, inconsistent.

incompetent *an incompetent workman.* bad, helpless, (informal) hopeless, incapable, inefficient, unqualified, untrained, useless.

incomplete *Logan's work was still incomplete when the bell went.* imperfect, unfinished.

inconceivable *It's inconceivable that anyone could swim the Atlantic.* impossible, unimaginable.

incongruous *Granny thinks it might look incongruous if she wore a miniskirt.* inappropriate, odd, out of place, unsuitable.

inconsiderate *It is inconsiderate of them to park in front of our gate.* careless, negligent, rude, tactless, thoughtless, uncaring, unkind.

inconsistent 1 *Our team's performance has been inconsistent this season.* changeable, erratic, fickle, patchy, unpredictable, variable. 2 *What he does is inconsistent with what he says.* conflicting, contradictory, incompatible.

inconvenient awkward, bothersome, troublesome.

incorporate *Our book incorporates the stories we wrote last week.* to consist of, to contain, to include.

incorrect *an incorrect answer.* false, inaccurate, mistaken, untrue, wrong.

increase 1 *They've increased the number of traffic wardens.* to add to, to boost, to build up, to enlarge, to expand, to strengthen, to swell. 2 *The traffic jam increased our journey by an hour.* to extend, to lengthen, to prolong. 3 *Dad increased my pocket-money.* to improve, to raise, to step up. 4 *The price of food seems to increase every day.* to escalate, to go up, to grow, to multiply, to rise.

incredible *an incredible story.* extra-ordinary, far-fetched, improbable, miraculous, unbelievable, unconvincing, unlikely.

incredulous *Mrs Brunswick was incredulous when Lucy won the competition.* disbelieving, dubious, sceptical, unconvinced.

incriminate *Logan incriminated Tony to avoid taking all the blame.* to accuse, to blame, to involve.

incubate *The hen was incubating her eggs.* to brood, to hatch.

incurable *an incurable illness.* hopeless.

indecent *indecent language.* coarse, crude, dirty, foul, improper, obscene, offensive, rude, smutty, vulgar.

indecipherable *indecipherable handwriting.* illegible, unreadable.

indefinite *He was indefinite about how much it would cost.* confused, general, neutral, uncertain, unclear, undecided, unsure, vague.

indelible *indelible ink.* fast, fixed, permanent.

independence *Do animals in the zoo miss their independence?* freedom, liberty.

independent *Mr Brunswick wants to run an independent business instead of working for other people.* free, private, self-governing.

indestructible *Some plastics are indestructible.* durable, everlasting, unbreakable.

index *an index of library books.* alphabetical list, catalogue, directory, register.

indicate 1 *Indicate which way you are turning.* to make known, to point out, to register, to show. **2** *A red light indicates danger.* to be a sign of, to convey, to communicate, to mean, to stand for, to symbolize.

indication *The spots are an indication of measles.* clue, hint, omen, sign, signal, symptom, token, warning.

indifferent 1 *He seemed indifferent about the result.* cold, cool, half-hearted, unconcerned, uninterested. **2** *The food was indifferent.* commonplace, fair, mediocre, middling, moderate, ordinary, unexciting.

indigestion SEE **illness**.

indignant angry, cross, furious, infuriated, irate, irritated, scornful, upset, vexed.

indigo SEE **colour**.

indirect *an indirect route.* devious, rambling, roundabout.

indispensable *A fishing rod is indispensable to an angler.* essential, necessary, vital.

indisposed *Mrs Angel wasn't here yesterday because she was indisposed.* ill, (informal) poorly, sick, unwell.

indistinct 1 *an indistinct picture.* blurred, confused, dim, faint, fuzzy, hazy, misty, obscure, unclear. **2** *indistinct sounds.* deadened, dull, muffled.

indistinguishable *The twins are indistinguishable.* alike, identical.

individual 1 *Lucy has her own individual style in gymnastics.* characteristic, different, distinct, distinctive, particular, peculiar, personal, private, separate, special, specific, unique. **2** *Who was that individual I saw you with?* SEE **person**.

indoctrinate to brainwash, to instruct, to teach, to train.

induce 1 *We couldn't induce granny to come to the disco.* to coax, to persuade, to tempt. **2** *What induced your cold?* to bring on, to cause, to lead to, to produce, to provoke.

indulgent *Mrs Brunswick says that grandpa is too indulgent.* easygoing, forgiving, genial, kind, lenient, patient, tolerant.

industrial *an industrial area.* industrialized, manufacturing.

industrious *an industrious worker.* busy, conscientious, diligent, earnest, enterprising, hard-working, involved, keen.

industry *Is there much industry in this town?* business, commerce, manufacturing, trade.

inedible *inedible food.* uneatable.

ineffective *Tony made an ineffective attempt to score.* feeble, futile, unsuccessful, useless.

inefficient 1 *an inefficient workman.* (informal) hopeless, incapable, incompetent. **2** *an inefficient use of resources.* extravagant, wasteful.

inevitable *Disaster was inevitable when the brakes failed.* certain, inescapable, sure, unavoidable.

inexcusable unforgivable, wrong.

inexhaustible never-ending.

inexpensive cheap, cut-price, economical, reasonable.

inexplicable *an inexplicable mystery.* baffling, insoluble, mysterious, puzzling, unaccountable.

infamous *an infamous crime.*
disgraceful, evil, notorious,
outrageous, scandalous, shocking,
wicked. SEE ALSO **bad**.

infant 1 baby, child. SEE ALSO
person. 2 *an infant school.* SEE
school.

infantile *infantile games.* babyish,
childish, immature.

infantry SEE **armed services**.

infatuation love, obsession, passion.

infect 1 *People asked if the spilled acid
would infect the water supply.* to
contaminate, to poison, to pollute.
2 *infected: an infected wound.* festering,
inflamed, poisoned, putrid, septic.

infection *to catch an infection.* ailment,
(informal) bug, blight, disease. SEE
ALSO **illness**.

infectious *an infectious disease.*
catching, contagious.

inferior 1 *inferior rank.* junior, lower,
subordinate. 2 *inferior quality.* cheap,
poor-quality, shoddy, tawdry, tinny.
SEE ALSO **bad**.

inferno blaze, conflagration, fire.

infested *infested with mice.* overrun,
swarming.

infidelity 1 *infidelity to your team.*
disloyalty, treachery, treason.
2 *infidelity to a wife or husband.*
adultery, unfaithfulness.

infinite *Space is infinite.* boundless,
endless, everlasting, immeasurable,
interminable, limitless, unending,
unlimited.

infirm bedridden, elderly, frail, ill,
old, (informal) poorly, senile,
unwell, weak.

infirmary clinic, health centre,
hospital. SEE ALSO **medicine**.

infirmity SEE **illness**.

inflame 1 *to inflame someone's anger.* to
arouse, to enrage, to excite, to
incense, to infuriate, to madden, to
provoke. 2 *inflamed: an inflamed wound.*
festering, infected, poisoned.

inflammation abscess, boil, sore.
SEE ALSO **illness**.

inflate *to inflate a tyre.* to blow up, to
pump up.

inflexible 1 *an inflexible framework.*
firm, hard, rigid, solid, unbending,
unyielding. 2 *an inflexible attitude.*
obstinate, strict, stubborn.

inflict *to inflict a punishment.* to
administer, to impose.

influence 1 *Did the weather have any
influence on the game?* effect, impact.
2 *Parents have influence over their
children.* authority, control, power.
3 *Does TV violence influence you?* to
affect, to control, to dominate, to
impress, to modify, to move, to stir.
4 *Don't try to influence the referee.* to
bribe, to persuade.

influential 1 *an influential person.*
important, powerful. 2 *an influential
idea.* convincing, persuasive.

influenza SEE **illness**.

inform 1 *The shop will inform us of the
cost.* to advise, to notify, to tell. 2 *to
inform against*: to complain about, to
denounce, to report, to spy on, to tell
of. 3 SEE **educate**.

informal 1 *informal clothes.* casual,
comfortable. 2 *an informal party.*
easygoing, friendly, relaxed.

information 1 *Is there any information
about our outing?* announcement,
communication, message, news,
report, statement. 2 *The police are
collecting information.* data, evidence,
facts, knowledge, statistics.

informer spy, tell-tale.

infrequent *The golden eagle is an
infrequent sight in Britain.* occasional,
rare, uncommon, unusual.

infringe *to infringe the law.* to break, to
disobey, to disregard, to violate.

infuriate *Logan often infuriates Mrs
Angel.* to anger, to enrage, to
exasperate, to incense, to madden, to
provoke, to vex.

ingenious *an ingenious plan.* artful,
clever, crafty, cunning, imaginative,
inventive, resourceful, shrewd,
skilful.

ingot *a gold ingot.* lump, nugget.

ingredient component, element,
part.

inhabit *We inhabit a council flat.* to

dwell in, to live in, to occupy, to populate, to reside in.

inhabitant citizen, native, occupant, population, resident, tenant.

inhale *to inhale smoke.* to breathe in.

inheritance *He got a small inheritance from his uncle's will.* bequest, estate, fortune, legacy.

inherited *an inherited title.* hereditary.

inheritor heir.

inhospitable *an inhospitable welcome.* unfriendly, unwelcoming.

inhuman *inhuman cruelty.* bestial, bloodthirsty, cruel, heartless, merciless, pitiless, ruthless, savage, unfeeling.

initial *If you buy this on hire-purchase, the initial payment is £10.* earliest, first, opening, original, starting.

initiate *to initiate negotiations.* to begin, to commence, to embark on, to launch, to open, to start.

initiative *to take the initiative*: to begin, to commence, to open, to start.

injection SEE **medicine**.

injure to damage, to harm, to hurt. SEE ALSO **wound**.

ink SEE **write**.

inkling *I'd no inkling he was coming.* clue, hint, idea, indication.

inlet bay, creek, fiord. SEE ALSO **geography**.

inn hotel, pub, tavern. SEE ALSO **building, holiday**.

innings SEE **cricket**.

innocent 1 *The trial proved he was innocent.* blameless, guiltless. 2 *Sleeping babies look innocent.* angelic, chaste, harmless, inoffensive, pure, virtuous.

innocuous *Grass-snakes are innocuous.* harmless, innocent, inoffensive, mild, safe.

innumerable *innumerable stars.* countless, numberless, untold.

inoffensive SEE **innocuous**.

inquest inquiry.

inquire to ask, to beg, to demand, to enquire, to entreat, to implore, to query, to question, to request.

inquiry inquest, investigation.

inquisitive *It's rude to be inquisitive.* curious, interested, nosey, prying.

insane *an insane idea, an insane person, etc.* crazy, demented, deranged, (informal) dotty, (informal) loony, lunatic, mad, unhinged.

insanitary dirty, unhealthy.

inscribe SEE **write**.

insect 1 VARIOUS INSECTS ARE ant, bee, beetle, blackbeetle, bluebottle, bumble-bee, butterfly, cockroach, crane-fly, cricket, daddy-long-legs, dragon-fly, drone, earwig, fly, glow-worm, gnat, grasshopper, hornet, ladybird, locust, louse, midge, mosquito, moth, nit, tsetse fly, wasp, woodworm. 2 OTHER FORMS OF AN INSECT ARE caterpillar, chrysalis, grub, larva, maggot. 3 OTHER CRAWLING CREATURES ARE centipede, earthworm, slug, snail, spider, wood-louse, worm. These creatures are not proper insects. 4 SEE ALSO **animal**.

insecticide pesticide. SEE ALSO **garden, poison**.

insecure *an insecure foothold.* loose, precarious, rocky, shaky, unsafe, unsteady, wobbly.

insensible *I was insensible for a moment after the accident.* knocked out, senseless, unconscious.

insensitive *It was insensitive to joke about granny's operation.* callous, cruel, hard-hearted, heartless, tactless, thoughtless, unfeeling.

insert *Insert a coin.* to push in, to put in, to tuck in.

inside centre, core, heart, middle.

insignificant *an insignificant improvement.* imperceptible, minor, minute, negligible, small, trifling, trivial, unimportant.

insincere *an insincere compliment.* deceitful, dishonest, false, hypocritical.

insist 1 *Mrs Angel insists on the importance of neatness.* to assert, to emphasize, to maintain, to state, to stress. 2 *They insisted that I went to the police station.* to command, to demand, to enforce, to require.

insolent *an insolent stare.* arrogant, bold, cheeky, disrespectful, impertinent, impolite, impudent, insulting, presumptuous, rude.

insoluble *an insoluble problem.* baffling, inexplicable, mysterious, puzzling, unanswerable.

insomnia SEE **illness**.

inspect *We inspected the damage.* to check, to examine, to investigate.

inspection check-up, examination, investigation, scrutiny.

inspector SEE **police**.

inspire *The big crowd inspired us to play well.* to arouse, (informal) to egg on, to encourage, to prompt, to reassure, to stimulate, to support.

install *New central heating has been installed.* to establish, to put in, to set up.

instalment 1 *Have you paid all the instalments?* payment, rent. 2 *Did you see last week's instalment?* episode.

instance *Give me an instance of what you mean.* case, example, illustration, sample.

instant 1 *an instant reply.* immediate, instantaneous, prompt, quick, speedy, swift. 2 *The shooting star was gone in an instant.* flash, moment, second.

instantaneous immediate, instant.

instep SEE **foot**.

instinct *Animals have an instinct to look after their young.* feeling, inclination, intuition, tendency.

institution 1 *Sunday dinner is a regular institution for the Brunswicks.* custom, habit, practice, routine. 2 *an institution for blind people.* establishment, organization.

instruct 1 to coach, to lecture, to teach, to train. SEE ALSO **educate**. 2 *He instructed us to wait.* to command, to direct, to order.

instructive *an instructive book.* educational, helpful, informative.

instructor coach, teacher, trainer.

instrument 1 *an instrument for measuring rainfall.* apparatus, device, equipment, gadget, implement, machine, tool, utensil. 2 *musical instruments.* SEE **music**.

insubordinate *The insubordinate soldier was punished.* defiant, disobedient, mutinous, rebellious.

insufficient *insufficient food.* inadequate, meagre, scanty, unsatisfactory.

insulate *to insulate pipes.* to lag.

insult 1 *Logan's continual chatter was an insult to our visitor.* cheek, impudence, rudeness. 2 *He didn't mean to insult her.* to abuse, to be rude, to mock, to offend, to snub.

intact *Did the glasses arrive intact?* complete, entire, perfect, undamaged, untouched, whole.

integer digit, figure, number.

integrate *So many players were ill that we had to integrate two teams.* to amalgamate, to combine, to join, to merge, to put together, to unite.

integrity *You can trust his complete integrity.* fidelity, honesty, honour, principle, sincerity, virtue.

intellect ability, brains, cleverness, genius, intelligence, mind, reason, sense, understanding.

intellectual 1 *an intellectual student.* SEE **intelligent**. 2 *an intellectual book.* cultural, deep, educational, highbrow, improving.

intelligence 1 SEE **intellect**. 2 *Our intelligence discovered some enemy secrets.* espionage, spying.

intelligent *an intelligent student.* brainy, bright, clever, intellectual, wise.

intelligible *an intelligible message.* clear, comprehensible, logical, lucid, unambiguous, understandable.

intend *What do you intend to do?* to aim, to contemplate, to design, to mean, to plan, to plot, to propose, to scheme.

intense 1 *intense pain.* acute, extreme, keen, severe, sharp, strong, violent. 2 *intense feelings.* burning, deep, eager, earnest, passionate, profound, serious, vehement.

intent *intent on what you're doing.* absorbed, determined, eager, keen.

intention *What is your intention?* aim, ambition, goal, object, objective, plan, point, purpose, target.

intentional *an intentional foul.* conscious, deliberate, intended, premeditated, wilful.

intercept *We intercepted Logan's gang before they got near our den.* to ambush, to attack, to cut off, to head off, to stop, to trap.

interchange *a motorway interchange.* crossroads, intersection, junction.

intercom SEE **communication.**

intercourse SEE **mate.**

interest 1 *Did he show any interest?* attention, concern, curiosity, notice. 2 *What are your main interests?* hobby, pastime, pursuit. 3 *Astronomy interests me.* to appeal to, to attract, to fascinate, to intrigue. 4 *interested*: absorbed, curious, preoccupied.

interface SEE **computer.**

interfere *Logan always interferes in our games.* to be a busybody, to butt in, to interrupt, to intervene, to intrude, to meddle, to molest, to pry, to snoop, to tamper.

interlude *There will be an interlude before Part 2.* break, gap, intermission, interval, lull, pause.

intermediate *an intermediate position.* half-way, middle, neutral.

interminable *Logan asks interminable questions.* ceaseless, constant, continual, continuous, everlasting, incessant, persistent, unending.

intermission SEE **interlude.**

intermittent *My computer has an intermittent fault.* occasional, on and off, spasmodic.

intern *Many foreigners were interned when the war started.* to confine, to gaol, to imprison.

internal inner, inside, interior.

interpret *Can you interpret this old writing?* to decipher, to decode, to explain, to make clear, to translate.

interpreter SEE **job.**

interrogate *The police interrogated him.* to ask questions, to cross-examine, to examine, to question.

interrupt 1 *Please interrupt if you have any questions.* to break in, to butt in, to cut in, to intervene, to intrude. 2 *A fire alarm interrupted the lesson.* to break off, to disrupt, to disturb, to interfere with.

interruption break, gap, pause.

intersect *Two motorways intersect.* to converge, to cross, to divide, to pass across.

intersection crossroads, interchange, junction.

interval 1 *an interval in time or space.* break, distance, gap, lapse, lull, opening, pause, respite, rest, space. 2 *We had an ice-cream in the interval.* break, interlude, intermission.

intervene *Mrs Angel intervened when Logan started quarrelling with Tony.* to butt in, to come between, to interfere, to interrupt, to intrude.

interview 1 *A reporter interviewed the eyewitness.* to ask questions, to question. 2 SEE **television.**

intestines SEE **body.**

intimate 1 *an intimate relationship.* affectionate, close, familiar, friendly, loving. 2 *intimate details.* confidential, personal, private, secret.

intimidate *Logan was in trouble for intimidating the infants.* to bully, to frighten, to make afraid, to menace, to persecute, to scare, to terrify, to terrorize, to threaten.

intolerable unbearable.

intolerant narrow-minded, prejudiced.

intoxicate 1 *intoxicated*: drunk, fuddled. 2 *intoxicating*: alcoholic.

intrepid *intrepid explorers.* bold, brave, courageous, daring, fearless, heroic, valiant.

intricate *intricate machinery.* complex, complicated, delicate, detailed, elaborate, involved.

intrigue 1 *Guy Fawkes took part in an intrigue against parliament.* conspiracy, plot, scheme. 2 *The parrot's swear-words intrigued us.* to appeal to, to arouse the curiosity of, to attract, to fascinate, to interest.

introduce 1 *Dad introduced me to his friend.* to make known, to present. 2 *The DJ introduced the next disc.* to announce. 3 *They introduced a new bus service.* to begin, to bring out, to create, to establish, to initiate, to set up, to start.

introduction *an introduction to a book.* preface, prelude, prologue.

intrude *Please don't intrude during the staff meeting.* to butt in, to interfere, to interrupt, to intervene.

intruder *The intruder ran away when the burglar alarm went off.* burglar, prowler, robber, thief, trespasser.

intuition *I had an intuition that you'd come.* feeling, instinct.

inundate *A tidal wave inundated the town.* to drown, to engulf, to flood, to submerge, to swamp.

invade *A flock of pigeons invaded Mrs Brunswick's cabbage patch.* to attack, to march into, to occupy, to overrun, to raid.

invalid 1 *He's an invalid who spends most of the time in bed.* patient, sufferer. 2 *an invalid passport.* out-of-date, unacceptable, unusable.

invaluable *Your help was invaluable.* precious, useful.

invariable *an invariable rule.* constant, reliable, unchangeable, unchanging, unvarying.

invasion attack, onslaught, raid.

invent *Who first invented a computer?* to conceive, to concoct, to contrive, to create, to devise, to discover, to make up, to plan, to put together, to think up.

invention *a useful invention.* contraption, contrivance, device, discovery.

inventive *Mrs Angel likes Tony's work because it is so inventive.* creative, enterprising, imaginative, ingenious, resourceful.

inventor creator, discoverer, originator.

invest *to invest money.* to save.

investigate *to investigate a topic.* to examine, to explore, to inquire into, to study.

investigation *an investigation into a crime.* examination, inquiry, inspection, research, scrutiny.

invigorating *an invigorating shower.* healthy, refreshing, stimulating.

invincible *We never scored: their defence was invincible.* impregnable, strong, unbeatable, unconquerable.

invisible *an invisible repair.* concealed, covered, hidden, imperceptible, inconspicuous, obscured, undetectable, unseen.

invite 1 *We invite you to join in.* to ask, to encourage, to request, to urge. 2 *inviting*: SEE **attractive**.

involuntary *Blinking is usually an involuntary movement.* automatic, impulsive, spontaneous, uncon-scious, unintentional, unthinking.

involve 1 *What does a policeman's job involve?* to contain, to include. 2 *The problem of feeding the world involves us all.* to affect, to concern, to interest. 3 *Logan tried to involve Tony in the crime.* to incriminate, to mix up. 4 *involved*: *involved in your work.* active, busy, employed, occupied. 5 *an involved story.* complex, complicated, confusing, elaborate, intricate.

iodine SEE **medicine**.

irascible *an irascible old gentleman.* bad-tempered, cross, grumpy, irritable, short-tempered, snappy.

irate angry, cross, enraged, fuming, furious, indignant, infuriated, mad, raging, vexed.

iris SEE **flower**.

iron 1 SEE **metal**. 2 *They put convicts in irons.* chains, fetters, shackles. 3 *to iron clothes.* to flatten, to press, to smooth.

ironmonger SEE **shop**.

irrational *an irrational argument.* crazy, illogical, unreasonable.

irregular 1 *an irregular surface.* bumpy, rough, uneven. 2 *irregular intervals.* erratic, random, unequal, variable.

3 *It's irregular for this train to stop here.* abnormal, illegal, odd, peculiar, unauthorized, unusual.

irrelevant *Leave out the irrelevant details.* inappropriate, pointless, unconnected.

irrepressible *Our puppy is irrepressible.* boisterous, lively, uncontrollable.

irresistible *The advertisements say that this scent is irresistible.* alluring, attractive, overpowering.

irresponsible *It is irresponsible to light fires during the dry weather.* careless, inconsiderate, negligent, reckless, unthinking, untrustworthy, wanton.

irreverent *We don't allow irreverent behaviour in church.* blasphemous, disrespectful, sacrilegious.

irrigate to water.

irritable bad-tempered, edgy, grumpy, irrascible, peevish, petulant, short-tempered, snappy, testy, touchy.

irritate 1 *Loud music irritates grandad.* (informal) to aggravate, to anger, to annoy, to bother, to exasperate, to make cross, to pester, to provoke, to upset, to vex, to worry. **2** *Cigarette smoke irritates my eyes.* to cause discomfort to, to cause itching in, to tickle.

Islam WORDS TO DO WITH ISLAM ARE Allah, imam, Koran, minaret, mosque, Muhammadan, Muslim, Ramadan. SEE ALSO **religion**.

island isle. SEE ALSO **geography**.

isolate 1 *They have to isolate the home supporters from the visitors.* to cut off, to segregate, to separate, to set apart. **2** *isolated: an isolated farmhouse.* desolate, inaccessible, lonely, private, remote, secluded, solitary.

issue 1 *Smoke issued from the chimney.* to appear, to come out, to emerge, to erupt, to flow out, to gush. **2** *The Post Office issued a special set of stamps.* to bring out, to circulate, to distribute, to give out, to print, to publish, to release, to send out. **3** *a political issue.* controversy, dispute, matter, problem, question, subject. **4** *an issue*

of a magazine. edition, number, publication.

isthmus SEE **geography**.

italics SEE **writing**.

itch 1 *I've an itch inside my shoe.* irritation, tickle, tingle. **2** *Logan had an itch to be naughty.* desire, longing, urge, wish, yearning.

item *Have you any items for the jumble sale?* article, object, piece, thing.

ivory SEE **colour, jewellery**.

ivy SEE **climber**.

J j

jab to poke, to prod, to stab. SEE ALSO **hit**.

jabber SEE **sound, talk**.

jack SEE **tool**.

jackal SEE **animal**.

jackdaw SEE **bird**.

jacket SEE **clothes**.

jackpot *to win the jackpot.* prize.

jade SEE **jewellery**.

jaded *By the end of the day the class seemed jaded.* bored, (informal) done in, exhausted, tired out, weary.

jagged *a jagged edge.* rough, sharp, uneven.

jaguar SEE **animal**.

jam 1 *It's illegal to jam so many people into a minibus.* to cram, to crowd, to crush, to pack, to squeeze. **2** *Cars jammed the street.* to block, to bung up, to congest, to fill, to obstruct, to overcrowd, to stop up. **3** *Jam the door open.* to stick, to wedge. **4** *Help me out of a jam!* difficulty, dilemma, plight, predicament, trouble. **5** *bread and jam.* SEE **food**.

jamboree carnival, celebration, festival, fête, party.

jangle SEE **sound**.

jar 1 *The collision jarred me.* to jerk, to jolt, to shake, to shock. SEE ALSO **hit**. **2** *jarring: a jarring noise.* grating, harsh, raucous, unpleasant. **3** *a glass jar.* SEE **container**.

jaundice SEE **illness**.

jaunt *to go on a jaunt.* excursion, expedition, outing, tour, trip.

jaunty *a jaunty tune.* alert, bright, frisky, lively, perky, sprightly.

javelin lance, spear. SEE ALSO **athletics, weapon**.

jaw SEE **body, head**.

jay SEE **bird**.

jazz SEE **music**.

jealous *He's jealous because I won.* bitter, envious, grudging, resentful.

jeans SEE **clothes**.

jeep SEE **vehicle**.

jeer *It was unkind to jeer at the losers.* to laugh at, to make fun of, to mock, to ridicule, to scoff at, to sneer at, to taunt. SEE ALSO **talk**.

jelly SEE **food**.

jellyfish SEE **fish**.

jerk *If you jerk the lid it may come off.* to jolt, to pull, to tug, to twist, to twitch, to wrench.

jersey SEE **clothes**.

jest to joke.

jester *the king's jester.* clown, comic, fool, wit. SEE ALSO **entertainment**.

jet 1 *a jet brooch.* SEE **jewellery**. **2** *a jet of water.* fountain, gush, spray, spurt, squirt, stream. **3** *to fly by jet.* SEE **aircraft**. **4** *jet-black*: SEE **colour**.

jetty *A boat tied up at the jetty.* landing-stage, pier, quay, wharf.

Jew WORDS TO DO WITH THE JEWISH RELIGION ARE bar mitzvah, kosher food, Passover, rabbi, sabbath, scripture, synagogue, Yom Kippur. SEE ALSO **religion**.

jewel gem, precious stone.

jeweller SEE **shop**.

jewellery 1 KINDS OF JEWELLERY ARE bangle, beads, bracelet, brooch, chain, clasp, ear-rings, locket, necklace, pendant, ring. **2** THINGS USED TO MAKE JEWELLERY ARE amber, coral, diamond, emerald, gold, ivory, jade, jet, opal, pearl, platinum, ruby, sapphire, silver.

jig SEE **dance**.

jigsaw SEE **tool**.

jigsaw puzzle SEE **game**.

jingle SEE **sound**.

jittery *Tony gets jittery before an important race.* anxious, edgy, fidgety, jumpy, nervous, touchy, (informal) uptight.

job 1 *Has your brother found a job yet?* employment, occupation, position, post, profession, trade, work. **2** *Tony does jobs in the house.* assignment, chore, duty, errand, function, task. **3** VARIOUS JOBS ARE accountant, air hostess, architect, artist (SEE **art**), astronaut, astronomer, banker, barber, barmaid or barman, barrister, blacksmith, bookmaker, brewer, bricklayer, builder, butler, caretaker, carpenter, cashier, caterer, chauffeur, chef, chemist, chimney-sweep, cleaner, clergyman, clerk, cobbler, commentator, composer, conductor, constable, cook, courier, curator, decorator, dentist, designer, detective, driver, docker, doctor, dustman, editor, electrician, engineer, entertainer (SEE **entertainment**), estate agent, executive, farmer, fireman, forester, gamekeeper, gardener, glazier, groom, groundsman, hairdresser, interpreter, joiner, journalist, labourer, lawyer, lecturer, librarian, life-guard, linguist, mannequin, manufacturer, mason, mechanic, midwife, milkman, miller, model, naturalist, night-watchman, nurse, optician, parson, photographer, physiotherapist, pilot, plasterer, plumber, policeman, politician, porter, postman, printer, probation officer, professor, programmer, publisher, radiographer, receptionist, reporter, salesman, saleswoman, scientist (SEE **science**), secretary, shepherd, shoemaker, SEE **shopkeeper**, signalman, social worker, solicitor, steeplejack, stunt man, surgeon, tailor, teacher, technician, test pilot, traffic warden, translator, typist, undertaker, usher or usherette, vet, waiter or waitress, warder, woodman.

jockey horseman, horsewoman, rider.

jodhpurs SEE **clothes**.

jog 1 *to jog someone's elbow.* to jolt, to knock, to nudge. SEE ALSO **hit**. 2 *to jog someone's memory.* to prompt, to refresh. 3 *to jog round the park.* to exercise, to run.

join 1 *to join things together.* to add, to amalgamate, to attach, to combine, to couple, to fasten, to fix, to link, to put together. 2 *Two rivers join here.* to come together, to converge, to merge. 3 *Are you going to join the youth club?* to enlist in, to enrol in, to participate in, to register for, to sign on for, to volunteer for. 4 *I can't see the join.* connection, joint, knot, link, mend, seam.

joiner carpenter. SEE ALSO **job**.

joint 1 JOINTS IN YOUR BODY ARE ankle, elbow, hip, knee, knuckle, shoulder, vertebra, wrist. 2 *We had a lamb joint for dinner.* SEE **meat**. 3 *It was a joint effort: everyone helped.* common, communal, general, shared.

joist beam, girder, rafter.

joke 1 *I told a joke.* gag, jest, pun. 2 *I was joking.* to be facetious, to jest.

jolly *a jolly party.* bright, cheerful, happy, jovial, joyful, merry.

jolt 1 *The car jolted over the rough track.* to bounce, to bump, to jar, to jerk, to shake, to twitch. 2 *The shout jolted us into action.* to shock, to startle.

jostle *The big crowd jostled us.* to hustle, to push, to shove.

jot *I jotted down her phone number.* to note, to scribble, to write.

jotter exercise book, notebook, pad.

journal 1 *You find interesting journals in the library.* magazine, newspaper, paper, periodical. 2 *The captain wrote a journal describing the voyage.* account, diary, log, record.

journalist correspondent, reporter. SEE ALSO **job, writer**.

journey KINDS OF JOURNEY ARE cruise, drive, excursion, expedition, flight, hike, mission, outing, pilgrimage, ride, safari, sail, tour, trek, trip, voyage, walk.

joust SEE **fight**.

jovial *a jovial man.* bright, cheerful, happy, jolly, joyful, merry.

joy bliss, delight, ecstasy, happiness, mirth, pleasure, rapture.

joyful cheerful, elated, exultant, glad, jolly, jovial, merry, overjoyed. SEE ALSO **happy**.

joystick SEE **aircraft, computer**.

jubilee anniversary, celebration.

judge 1 *The headmaster is the chief judge at sports day.* adjudicator, arbitrator, referee, umpire. 2 *The judge passed sentence.* SEE **law**. 3 *The referee judged that the ball was out.* to adjudicate, to conclude, to decide, to pass judgement, to rule. 4 *He was judged in a court of law.* to condemn, to convict, to punish, to sentence. 5 *Logan likes judging others.* to criticize, to rebuke, to scold. 6 *I judged that the eggs were cooked.* to believe, to consider, to guess, to reckon, to suppose.

judgement *Use your judgement.* discretion, good sense, reason, wisdom.

judo SEE **martial**.

jug SEE **container**.

juggernaut SEE **vehicle**.

juggler SEE **entertainment**.

juice SEE **drink**.

juke-box SEE **audio equipment**.

jumble 1 *Don't jumble those papers I've just sorted.* to confuse, to mix up, to muddle, to shuffle. 2 *Lucy's room is full of jumble.* chaos, clutter, confusion, disorder, mess, muddle. 3 *a jumble sale.* SEE **sale**.

jumbo SEE **aircraft**.

jump 1 to bounce, to bound, to hop, to leap, to pounce, to skip, to spring. 2 *to jump a fence.* to clear, to vault. 3 *to jump about.* to caper, to dance, to frisk, to prance. 4 *The bang made me jump.* to flinch, to jerk, to start.

jumper SEE **clothes**.

jump-jet SEE **aircraft**.

jumpy *Why are you so jumpy?* edgy, fidgety, jittery, nervous, restless, tense.

junction *a road junction.* corner, crossroads, interchange, intersection.

jungle forest, undergrowth, woods.

junior 1 *junior rank.* inferior, lower, subordinate, younger. 2 *a junior school.* SEE **school**.

junk 1 *Throw away this junk.* garbage, litter, lumber, odds and ends, refuse, rubbish, scrap, trash, waste. 2 *a Chinese junk.* SEE **vessel**.

junket SEE **food**.

juror, jury SEE **law**.

just *The decision to send him off was just.* fair, honest, impartial, lawful, legal, proper, rightful, right-minded, unbiased, unprejudiced.

justice fairness, the law, punishment, retribution, vengeance.

justify *Can you justify what you did?* to defend, to excuse, to explain, to support.

jut *A shelf juts out from the wall.* to overhang, to project, to protrude, to stick out.

juvenile 1 *juvenile behaviour.* childish, immature. 2 *juvenile novels.* adolescent, young, youthful.

K k

kale SEE **vegetable**.

kaleidoscope SEE **toy**.

kangaroo SEE **animal**.

karate SEE **martial**.

kayak SEE **vessel**.

keel SEE **vessel**.

keen 1 *He's keen to do well.* anxious, avid, eager, enthusiastic, fervent, interested. 2 *a keen pupil.* bright, clever, intelligent, quick, shrewd. 3 *keen eyesight.* acute, sharp. 4 *a keen frost.* extreme, intense, severe.

keep 1 *Keep it safe. Keep it for later.* to hang on to, to hold, to preserve, to put away, to retain, to save, to store, to stow away, to withhold. 2 *The farmer keeps sheep.* to care for, to cherish, to guard, to look after, to mind, to protect, to safeguard, to tend. 3 *Keep going!* to carry on, to continue, to persevere, to persist. 4 *Keep where you are!* to linger, to remain, to stay. 5 *How much does it cost to keep a family?* to feed, to maintain, to pay for, to provide for, to support. 6 *I won't keep you.* to delay, to detain, to hinder, to hold up, to obstruct. 7 *Keep to the rules!* to abide by, to be ruled by, to conform to, to obey, to submit to. 8 *How long will this milk keep?* to be usable, to last. 9 *the keep of a castle.* SEE **castle**.

keeper *a keeper in a zoo.* custodian, guard, guardian, warder.

keg SEE **container**.

kernel nut.

kestrel SEE **bird**.

ketchup SEE **food, sauce**.

kettle SEE **container**.

kettledrum SEE **percussion**.

key 1 *the key of C major.* SEE **music**. 2 *the key to a problem.* clue.

keyboard 1 SEE **computer**. 2 KEYBOARD INSTRUMENTS ARE harmonium, harpsichord, organ, piano. SEE ALSO **music**.

khaki SEE **colour**.

kick 1 to boot, to punt. SEE ALSO **hit**. 2 (informal) *to get a kick out of something.* adventure, excitement, stimulation, thrill.

kid 1 SEE **goat, young**. 2 (informal) child, youngster. 3 (informal) *Don't try to kid me!* to bluff, to fool, to hoodwink, to lie to. SEE ALSO **deceive**.

kidnap 1 to abduct, to carry off. 2 *kidnapping:* SEE **crime**.

kidney SEE **body**.

kill 1 to annihilate, to assassinate, to bump off, to destroy, to dispatch, to execute, to exterminate, to finish off, to martyr, to massacre, to murder, to put down, to put to death, to slaughter, to slay. 2 WAYS TO KILL ARE to behead, to choke, to crucify, to decapitate, to drown, to electrocute, to gas, to guillotine, to hang, to knife, to lynch, to poison, to shoot, to smother, to stab, to starve, to stifle, to stone, to strangle, to suffocate, to throttle. 3 *killing*: assassination, bloodshed, carnage, execution, homicide, manslaughter, massacre, murder, slaughter, suicide.

kiln SEE **fire.**

kilogram, kilometre SEE **measure.**

kilt SEE **clothes.**

kin SEE **family.**

kind 1 *a kind of dog, a kind of butter, etc.* brand, breed, category, class, form, make, nature, set, sort, species, type, variety. 2 *a kind action, a kind person, etc.* affectionate, agreeable, amiable, attentive, benevolent, compassionate, considerate, encouraging, favourable, friendly, generous, genial, gentle, good-natured, good-tempered, helpful, humane, kind-hearted, kindly, merciful, mild, motherly, neighbourly, nice, obliging, pleasant, polite, public-spirited, soft-hearted, sympathetic, tender, thoughtful, unselfish, warm-hearted.

kindergarten SEE **school.**

kindle to burn, to fire, to ignite, to light, to set fire to.

king SEE **royal, ruler.**

kingdom monarchy, realm. SEE ALSO **country, government.**

kingfisher SEE **bird.**

kink *a kink in a rope.* loop, tangle, twist.

kiosk booth, stall, telephone-box.

kipper SEE **food.**

kiss to caress, to embrace. SEE ALSO **touch.**

kit *games kit.* equipment, gear, rig, tackle.

kitchen THINGS YOU FIND IN A KITCHEN ARE baking tin, basin, blender, bowl, breadboard, bread-knife, carving-knife, casserole, chip pan, cooker, corkscrew, SEE **crockery**, SEE **cutlery**, dish, dish-rack, dishwasher, draining-board, extractor fan, freezer, fridge, frying-pan, glass, grill, jug, kettle, ladle,

larder, lighter, microwave oven, mincer, mixer, oven, pan, pantry, paper towel, percolator, pot, range, refrigerator, rolling-pin, salt-cellar, saucepan, scales, sink, skewer, stove, strainer, table-cloth, tea-cloth, teapot, thermos, tin-opener, toaster, tray, vacuum flask, whisk. SEE ALSO **food, house.**

kite SEE **toy.**

kitten SEE **cat, young.**

knack *You need a special knack to flush our toilet.* art, gift, skill, talent.

knapsack haversack, rucksack. SEE ALSO **container.**

knave (old-fashioned) blackguard, rascal, rogue, scoundrel, villain.

knead SEE **cook.**

knee, kneecap SEE **body, leg.**

kneel *He knelt to tie his shoe.* to bend, to bow, to crouch, to stoop.

knickers briefs, panties, pants, shorts, trunks, underpants. SEE ALSO **underclothes.**

knife 1 carving-knife, penknife, scalpel. SEE ALSO **cutlery, kitchen.** 2 *to knife someone.* SEE **kill.**

knight 1 warrior. SEE ALSO **fighter.** 2 SEE **chess.**

knitting SEE **art.**

knob 1 *a brass knob on his walking-stick.* handle. 2 bulge, bump, lump, swelling.

knock 1 *to knock against something.* (informal) to bash, to bump, to rap, to strike, to tap. SEE ALSO **hit.** 2 *knocked out*: insensible, unconscious.

knot 1 VARIOUS KNOTS ARE bow, granny-knot, reef-knot. 2 *to knot ropes together.* to bind, to join, to lash, to tie. SEE **fasten.**

know 1 *Do you know who he is?* to discern, to distinguish, to perceive, to realize, to recognize, to remember, to see. 2 *Logan says he knows a TV actor.* to be acquainted with, to be familiar with, to be a friend of. 3 *Do you know any French?* to appreciate, to comprehend, to understand.

know-all expert, genius, master-mind.

know-how *Have you got the know-how to sail a boat on your own?* ability, competence, knowledge, skill, talent, technique, training.

knowing *a knowing smile.* artful, crafty, cunning, sly, wily.

knowledge 1 *You need a lot of knowledge to do well in a quiz.* education, experience, facts, learning, wisdom. 2 *We've no knowledge of what happened to Uncle Fred.* information, news.

knowledgeable educated, learned, well-informed.

knuckle SEE **body, hand, joint**.

koala SEE **animal**.

Koran SEE **Islam**.

kosher food SEE **food, Jew**.

kung fu SEE **martial**.

L l

label *Put a label on your suitcase.* sticker, tag, ticket.

laboratory SEE **school**.

laborious *a laborious climb.* arduous, difficult, exhausting, gruelling, hard, stiff, strenuous, tough, uphill.

labour *You deserve a reward for your labour.* drudgery, effort, exertion, slavery, toil, work.

labourer SEE **job**.

Labrador SEE **dog**.

labyrinth *I got lost in a labyrinth of corridors.* maze.

lace 1 *a lace handkerchief.* SEE **cloth**. 2 *black shoes with red laces.* cord, string.

lack 1 *The game lacked excitement.* to be deficient in, to be short of, to need, to require, to want. 2 *They are dying for lack of food.* absence, need, scarcity, shortage, want.

lacquer SEE **paint**.

lad boy, youngster, youth.

ladder fire-escape.

laden *laden with shopping.* burdened, loaded, weighed down.

ladle SEE **kitchen**.

lady woman. SEE ALSO **person**.

ladybird SEE **insect**.

ladylike *ladylike behaviour.* (informal) posh, refined. SEE ALSO **polite**.

lag 1 *We won't wait if you lag behind.* to dally, to dawdle, to fall behind, to hang about, to linger, to loiter, to straggle. 2 *Mr Brunswick lagged his hot water pipes.* to insulate, to wrap up.

lager SEE **drink**.

lagoon SEE **geography**.

lair *an animal's lair.* den, hide-out, hiding-place.

lake pond, reservoir. SEE ALSO **geography**.

lamb SEE **sheep, young**.

lame 1 *The lame man used a walking-stick.* crippled, disabled, limping, maimed. SEE ALSO **handicap**. 2 *a lame excuse.* feeble, flimsy, poor, tame, unconvincing, weak.

lamp SEE **light**.

lamp-post SEE **road**.

lance javelin, spear. SEE ALSO **weapon**.

land 1 *The refugees had to leave their own land.* country, nation, state, territory. SEE ALSO **geography**. 2 *The farmer ploughed the land.* earth, soil. 3 *He bought some land.* estate, ground. 4 *The ship reached land.* mainland. 5 *The plane landed.* to come down, to touch down. 6 *The sailors landed.* to disembark, to go ashore.

landing-stage berth, dock, harbour, jetty, port, quay, wharf.

landing-strip aerodrome, airfield, airstrip, runway.

landlady, landlord owner.

landscape *a painting of the landscape.* countryside, panorama, scene, scenery, view, vista.

landslide SEE **disaster**.

lane SEE **road**.

language 1 *a foreign language.* tongue. 2 *a computer language.* code. 3 WORDS TO DO WITH LANGUAGE ARE accent, adjective, adverb, brogue, conjunction, consonant, dialect, grammar, informal language, noun, paragraph, phrase, plural, prefix, preposition, pronoun, SEE **punctuation**, sentence, singular, slang, suffix, swear-word, spelling, syllable, synonym, verb, vocabulary, vowel, word.

lanky *a lanky figure.* bony, long, lean, scraggy, skinny, tall, thin.

lantern SEE **light**.

lap 1 *a lap of a race-track.* circuit. 2 SEE **drink**.

lapel SEE **clothes**.

lapse *We started training again after a lapse during the holidays.* break, gap, interval, pause.

lapwing SEE **bird**.

larch SEE **tree**.

lard SEE **fat**.

larder food cupboard, pantry. SEE ALSO **house**.

large *a large building, large helpings, a large sum of money, etc.* ample, big, bold, broad, bulky, colossal, considerable, enormous, extensive, fat, giant, gigantic, grand, great, hefty, high, huge, hulking, immeasurable, immense, incalculable, infinite, large, lofty, long, massive, mighty, monstrous, roomy, sizeable, spacious, substantial, tall, thick, towering, tremendous, vast, wide.

lark SEE **bird**.

larva caterpillar, grub, maggot. SEE ALSO **insect**.

lasagne SEE **food**.

lash 1 *to lash someone with a whip.* to cane, to flog, to scourge, to thrash, to whip. SEE ALSO **hit**. 2 *to lash things together with string.* SEE **fasten**.

lass girl, (old-fashioned) damsel, (old-fashioned) maiden, youngster.

last 1 *This is your last chance.* closing, concluding, final, ultimate. 2 *Will this fine weather last?* to carry on, to continue, to keep on, to persist, to remain, to stay. 3 *When our dog was ill, the vet didn't think he'd last the night.* to endure, to linger, to live, to

survive. 4 *lasting: a lasting friendship.* continuing, durable, permanent, stable.

latch *the latch on a door.* bolt, catch, fastening, lock.

late 1 *The bus is late.* behindhand, belated, delayed, overdue, slow, unpunctual. 2 *We had a memorial service for the late headmaster.* dead, deceased.

lather *This soap makes a lot of lather.* bubbles, foam, froth, suds.

Latin SEE **subject**.

latitude SEE **geography**.

laugh 1 WAYS TO LAUGH ARE to beam, to chuckle, to giggle, to grin, to smile, to snigger, to titter. 2 *to laugh at:* to jeer, to mock, to ridicule, to scoff at, to smirk, to sneer at, to taunt, to tease. 3 FOR WORDS TO DESCRIBE THINGS THAT MAKE YOU LAUGH SEE **funny**.

laughter hysterics, laughing, mirth.

launch 1 SEE **vessel**. 2 *to launch a ship.* to float. 3 *to launch a rocket.* to fire, to set off. 4 *to launch a new business.* to begin, to embark on, to found, to initiate, to open, to set up, to start.

launderette SEE **shop**.

laundry *to do the laundry.* washing.

lava SEE **rock**.

lavatory (informal) loo, toilet, water-closet, WC. SEE ALSO **house**.

lavender SEE **colour, shrub**.

lavish *a lavish supply of food.* copious, extravagant, generous, liberal, luxurious, plentiful, sumptuous.

law 1 *the laws of a country, the laws of a game.* code, commandment, order, regulation, rule. 2 *a court of law.* justice. 3 WORDS TO DO WITH THE LAW ARE accusation, arrest, barrister, case, charge, coroner, court, court martial, defence, dock, evidence, inquest, judge, judgement, juror, jury, lawcourt, lawyer, magistrate, police, prosecution, prosecutor, SEE **punishment**, sentence, sheriff, solicitor, to sue, summons, trial, verdict, witness.

law-abiding *Tony doesn't get into*

trouble: *he's law-abiding.* decent, honest, obedient, orderly, respectable, well-behaved. SEE ALSO **good**.

lawful 1 *It isn't lawful to steal.* allowed, authorized, just, permissible, permitted. 2 *Who is the lawful owner of this car?* legal, legitimate, proper, rightful, valid.

lawless *a lawless mob.* disorderly, riotous, rowdy, turbulent, undisciplined, unruly, wild.

lawlessness *The police try to stop lawlessness.* anarchy, chaos, disorder, rioting.

lawn SEE **garden**.

lawyer SEE **job, law**.

lay 1 *Lay your work on the table.* to deposit, to leave, to place, to position, to put down, to rest, to set down, to spread. 2 *We lay down to sleep.* SEE **lie**.

lay-by SEE **road**.

layer 1 *a layer of ice.* coating, film, sheet, skin. 2 *a layer of rock.* seam, stratum, thickness.

lazy idle, listless, slack, sluggish.

lbw SEE **cricket**.

lead 1 *as heavy as lead.* SEE **metal**. 2 *It's marvellous how the dog leads that blind person.* to conduct, to escort, to guide, to pilot, to steer. 3 *It's the captain's job to lead her team.* to be in charge of, to command, to direct, to head, to manage, to rule, to supervise. 4 *Who took the lead for my radio?* cable, flex, wire. 5 *a dog's lead.* leash.

leaf 1 *the leaves of a tree.* foliage, greenery. 2 *the leaves of a book.* page, sheet.

leaflet *an advertising leaflet.* booklet, brochure, pamphlet.

league *We combined with other chess teams to form a league.* alliance, association, club, group, society, union.

leak 1 *There's a leak in the bucket.* hole, opening, puncture. 2 *The water leaked out.* to drip, to escape, to ooze, to seep, to trickle.

lean 1 *a lean figure.* bony, gaunt, lanky, skinny, slender, slim, thin, wiry. 2 *The ship leaned dangerously to one side.* to bank, to heel over, to incline, to list, to slant, to slope, to tilt. 3 *I leaned against the fence.* to prop yourself, to rest, to support yourself.

leaning *Tony has a leaning towards subjects like maths.* inclination, instinct, readiness, tendency, trend.

leap 1 *The cat leapt into my lap.* to bound, to jump, to pounce, to spring, to vault. 2 *We leapt about for joy.* to caper, to dance, to frisk, to hop, to prance.

leap-frog SEE **game**.

learn 1 *Where did Logan learn those rude words?* to discover, to find out, to gather, to grasp, to master, to memorize. 2 *We go to school to learn.* to be educated. SEE ALSO **educate**.

learner apprentice, beginner, L-driver.

leash *a dog's leash.* lead.

least slightest, smallest, tiniest.

leather hide, skin, suede.

leathery rubbery, tough.

leave 1 *The captain left his sinking ship.* to abandon, to desert, to evacuate, to forsake. 2 *We're ready to leave.* to depart, to go, to set off. 3 *Mr Brunswick left his old job last summer.* to quit, to retire from, to withdraw from. 4 *Leave the empty milk bottles by the front door.* to deposit, to place, to position, to put down, to set down. 5 *to leave out: Logan was annoyed when we left him out of the team.* to drop, to eliminate, to omit, to reject. 6 *Dad's taking some leave during the school holiday.* holiday, time off, vacation.

lectern SEE **church**.

lecture 1 *The head gave us a lecture.* speech, talk. 2 SEE **educate**.

lecturer instructor, professor, speaker, teacher, tutor. SEE ALSO **educate, job**.

ledge shelf, window-sill.

leek SEE **vegetable**.

leer SEE **expression**.

leg 1 SEE **body**. 2 PARTS OF YOUR LEG ARE ankle, calf, SEE **foot**, knee, kneecap, shin, thigh. 3 WORDS TO DESCRIBE PEOPLE'S LEGS ARE bandy-legged, bow-legged, knock-kneed.

legacy *Mrs Brunswick received a legacy from her grandmother's will.* bequest, inheritance.

legal 1 *It isn't legal to print your own £5 notes.* allowed, just, lawful, permitted, permissible. 2 *Who's the legal owner of this car?* authorized, legitimate, proper, rightful, valid.

legend 1 SEE **writing.** 2 CREATURES YOU READ ABOUT IN LEGENDS ARE brownie, dragon, dwarf, elf, fairy, giant, gnome, goblin, imp, mermaid, monster, nymph, ogre, troll, unicorn, vampire, witch, wizard.

legendary 1 *The unicorn is a legendary beast.* fictitious, invented, made-up, mythical. 2 *Presley is a legendary name for all pop fans.* celebrated, famous, historic, notable, renowned, well-known.

legible *legible handwriting.* clear, neat, plain, readable.

legitimate 1 *It isn't legitimate to copy someone's work.* allowed, just, permissible, permitted. 2 *Who is the legitimate owner of this car?* authorized, lawful, legal, proper, rightful.

leg-warmers SEE **clothes.**

leisure *Most people enjoy their leisure.* ease, recreation, relaxation, rest.

leisurely *a leisurely journey.* easy, peaceful, relaxing, slow, unhurried.

lemon SEE **fruit.**

lemonade SEE **drink.**

lend *Can you lend me a pen?* to loan.

length distance, measurement.

lengthen *The days lengthen in the spring. You can lengthen this ladder if you need to.* to draw out, to enlarge, to elongate, to extend, to get longer, to increase, to prolong, to stretch.

lengthy SEE **long.**

lenient *a lenient teacher.* easy-going, forgiving, indulgent, merciful, (informal) soft, tolerant.

lens SEE **optical.**

Lent SEE **church.**

leopard SEE **animal.**

leotard SEE **clothes.**

leprosy SEE **illness.**

lessen 1 *Please lessen the noise!* to cut, to reduce, to tone down. 2 *The noise lessened when Logan went home.* to decrease, to decline, to die, to slacken, to subside, to tail off.

lesson 1 lecture. SEE ALSO **school.** 2 *This story teaches a lesson.* moral.

let 1 *Let the dog in.* to allow, to permit. 2 *The judge let him off.* to acquit, to excuse, to free, to liberate. 3 *There's a houseboat to let on the canal.* to hire, to rent.

lethal *a lethal dose.* deadly, fatal, mortal, poisonous.

letter 1 *the letters of the alphabet.* character. 2 *to send someone a letter.* communication, correspondence, epistle, message, note, postcard. 3 *Have the letters come yet?* mail, post.

letter-box pillar-box, postbox.

lettuce SEE **salad.**

leukaemia SEE **illness.**

level 1 *a level surface.* even, flat, horizontal, smooth. 2 *level scores.* even, equal. 3 *The lift takes you to the level you want.* floor, height, storey. 4 *Lucy has reached a high level in gymnastics.* standard. 5 *We levelled the field to make a new pitch.* to even out, to flatten, to smooth. 6 *The earthquake levelled the whole town.* to demolish, to destroy, to knock down.

level-headed *You need a level-headed person to deal with a crisis.* calm, cool, reasonable, reliable, sedate, sensible.

lever 1 SEE **tool.** 2 *We had to lever open the jammed door.* to prize, to wrench.

liable *Logan is liable to do silly things.* disposed, inclined, likely, prone, willing.

liar (informal) fibber.

liberal 1 *a liberal supply of food.* abundant, ample, copious, generous, plentiful. 2 *a liberal attitude.* broad-minded, easygoing, fair, lenient, tolerant, unprejudiced. 3 *a Liberal.* SEE **politics.**

liberate *The prisoners were liberated.* to

discharge, to emancipate, to free, to let out, to loose, to release, to rescue, to save, to set free, to untie.

liberty *to give people their liberty.* freedom, independence.

librarian SEE **job**.

library SEE **building**.

licence permit. SEE ALSO **document**.

license *Our local shop is licensed to sell tobacco.* to allow, to authorize, to permit.

lichen SEE **plant**.

lick 1 *to lick a lollipop.* to suck. **2** (informal) *We licked the opposition last week.* SEE **defeat**.

lid *Where's the lid for the jam?* cap, cover, covering, top.

lie 1 *to tell a lie.* falsehood, (informal) fib, untruth. **2** *You can usually tell when Logan is lying.* to bluff, (informal) to fib, (informal) to kid. SEE ALSO **deceive**. **3** *Lie on the sofa.* to lean back, to recline, to sprawl. **4** *The house lies in a valley.* to be, to be located, to be situated.

lieutenant SEE **rank**.

life 1 *I wonder when life on earth began?* being, existence. **2** *Our dog is full of life.* energy, liveliness, sprightliness, vigour, vitality, zest. **3** *Have you read the life of Elvis Presley?* autobiography, biography.

lifeboat SEE **vessel**.

life-guard SEE **job**.

lifeless 1 *a lifeless body.* dead, deceased, killed, motionless. **2** *a lifeless substance.* inanimate. **3** *a lifeless desert.* arid, barren, sterile.

lifelike *a lifelike statue.* authentic, natural, realistic.

lifelong 1 *a lifelong friendship.* constant, everlasting, permanent, steady, unchanging, unending. **2** *a lifelong illness.* chronic, persistent.

lift 1 *We need some strong people to lift the piano.* to carry, to elevate, to hoist, to jack up, to manhandle, to pick up, to pull up, to raise. **2** *The plane lifted off the ground.* to ascend, to rise, to soar.

light 1 KINDS OF LIGHT ARE beacon, bulb, candle, chandelier, daylight, electric light, floodlight, headlight, illuminations, lamp, lantern, moonlight, neon light, pilot-light, searchlight, spotlight, standard lamp, starlight, street light, sunlight, torch. **2** WAYS IN WHICH LIGHTS SHINE ARE to be bright, to be luminous, to be phosphorescent, to blaze, to blink, to burn, to dazzle, to flash, to flicker, to glare, to gleam, to glimmer, to glint, to glisten, to glitter, to glow, to shine, to spark, to sparkle, to twinkle, to wink. **3** *to light a fire.* to fire, to ignite, to kindle, to set fire to. **4** *The bonfire lit up the sky.* to brighten, to illuminate, to lighten. **5** *The big box was surprisingly light.* portable. **6** *My sponge cake was beautifully light.* feathery. **7** *Since his illness he can only do light work.* easy, effortless, painless.

light-hearted *We felt light-hearted on the last day of term.* bright, carefree, cheerful, glad, jolly, merry, untroubled. SEE ALSO **happy**.

lighthouse SEE **building**.

lightning SEE **weather**.

lightship SEE **vessel**.

light-year SEE **measure**.

like 1 *Most of the class like Mrs Angel.* to admire, to approve of, to appreciate, to be fond of, to love. **2** *Do you like ice-cream?* to enjoy, to be partial to. **3** *Would you like some ice-cream?* to fancy, to want, to wish for. **4** *How do you like this record?* to rate, to regard.

likelihood *Is there any likelihood of a change in the weather?* hope, possibility, probability, prospect.

likely 1 *It's likely that Tony will win.* plausible, possible, probable. **2** *Lucy is a likely person to be captain.* appropriate, fitting, suitable. **3** *Logan is likely to laugh at us.* disposed to, inclined to, liable to, willing to.

likeness *The painting is a good likeness of the headmaster.* copy, image, picture, portrait, resemblance, similarity.

lilac SEE **flower, shrub**.

lily SEE **flower**.

limb VARIOUS LIMBS ARE arm, bough, flipper, leg. SEE ALSO **body**.
limbo dancing SEE **dance**.
lime SEE **fruit, tree**.
lime-juice SEE **drink**.
limerick SEE **poem**.
limestone SEE **rock**.
limit 1 *the limit of a territory.* boundary, edge, frontier. 2 *the limit of your strength.* end, extreme, maximum. 3 *to limit someone's freedom.* to confine, to curb, to restrict.
limp 1 to be lame, to hobble. SEE ALSO **walk**. 2 *Mrs Brunswick was upset when her plants went limp.* bendy, drooping, flabby, flexible, floppy, sagging, soft, wilting.
limpet SEE **shellfish**.
linctus SEE **medicine**.
line 1 *Hold the end of this line.* cable, cord, flex, hawser, lead, rope, string, thread, wire. 2 *The water left a dirty line round the bath.* band, dash, mark, streak, strip, stripe. 3 *There were lines on the old man's face.* crease, furrow, wrinkle. 4 *a line of police, a line of cars, etc.* chain, column, cordon, file, procession, queue, rank, row, series. 5 *a railway line.* route, service, track. 6 *Please line up.* to form a line, to queue.
linen SEE **cloth**.
liner SEE **vessel**.
linesman SEE **football, sport**.
linger 1 *The smell of burning lingered long after the fire was out.* to continue, to hang about, to last, to persist, to remain, to stay. 2 *Don't linger outside in this cold weather.* to dally, to delay, to hang about, to hover, to lag, to loiter, to stay behind, to wait about.
lingerie SEE **underclothes**.
link 1 *a link between two things.* bond, connection, join, joint, relationship. 2 *Can we link your computer to mine?* to attach, to connect, to couple, to join, to unite. SEE ALSO **fasten**. 3 *The police are linking this robbery with the one last week.* to compare, to connect, to relate.
links SEE **sport**.

lino SEE **floor**.
lint SEE **medicine**.
lion SEE **animal**.
lip 1 SEE **body, head**. 2 *the lip of a cup.* brim, brink, edge, rim.
lipstick SEE **cosmetics**.
liquid *a liquid substance.* flowing, fluid, runny.
liquor alcohol, alcoholic drink. SEE ALSO **drink**.
liquorice SEE **sweet**.
lisp SEE **talk**.
list 1 *a list of names.* catalogue, register. 2 *The ship listed to one side.* to heel, to lean, to slope, to tilt.
listen *Did you listen to what I said?* to hear, to eavesdrop, to overhear.
listless *It was a hot day, and everyone seemed listless.* feeble, lazy, poorly, sluggish, tired, uninterested, weak, weary.
literate SEE **educate**.
literature FOR VARIOUS KINDS OF LITERATURE SEE **writing**.
litmus SEE **chemical**.
litre SEE **measure**.
litter 1 *Clear up the litter.* clutter, garbage, jumble, junk, refuse, rubbish, trash, waste. 2 *a litter of puppies.* family. SEE ALSO **group**.
little 1 *a little book, a little dog, a little house, etc.* compact, concise, diminutive, miniature, minute, small, (informal) teeny, tiny, undersized, wee. 2 *We had a little chat.* brief, momentary, passing, short, temporary, transient. 3 *I only had a little bit to eat.* inadequate, meagre, measly, scanty, stingy. 4 *There has been little improvement in granny's health.* imperceptible, insignificant, negligible, slight. 5 *We had a little argument.* minor, petty, trifling, trivial, unimportant.
live 1 *It'd be amazing if we found a live dinosaur.* active, alive, existing, living. 2 *I wonder if our goldfish will live through the winter?* to continue, to exist, to remain, to survive. 3 *Which flat do you live in?* to dwell in, to inhabit, to occupy, to reside in.

4 *What do polar bears live on?* to eat, to feed on.

lively 1 *a lively baby, a lively game, etc.* active, agile, alert, energetic, frisky, jaunty, perky, playful, sprightly, vivacious. **2** *a lively party.* cheerful, gay, jolly, merry. SEE ALSO **happy.** **3** *a lively argument.* animated, enthusiastic, spirited.

liver SEE **body.**

livery uniform. SEE ALSO **clothes.**

livestock SEE **farm.**

livid *Mrs Brunswick was livid when the cat misbehaved on the carpet.* angry, enraged, fuming, furious, incensed, infuriated, irate, mad, raging, raving, wrathful.

living-room drawing-room, lounge, sitting-room. SEE ALSO **house.**

lizard SEE **reptile.**

llama SEE **animal.**

load 1 *a heavy load.* burden, weight. **2** *The plane carried a load of medical supplies.* cargo, freight. **3** *We helped to load the car.* to fill, to pack. **4** *loaded: loaded with gifts.* burdened, laden, weighed down.

loaf 1 bread. **2** *to loaf about.* to loiter, to lounge.

loam *Mrs Brunswick plants her seeds in good loam.* earth, ground, soil.

loan *Can you loan me 10p?* to lend.

loathe *Our dog loathes the snow.* to despise, to detest, to dislike, to hate.

loathsome *Some people find spiders loathsome.* detestable, disgusting, foul, obnoxious, odious, revolting. SEE ALSO **unpleasant.**

lob *Lob the ball to Tony.* to bowl, to cast, (informal) to chuck, to fling, to pitch, to sling, to throw, to toss.

lobby *Wait for me in the lobby.* entrance hall, foyer, hall. SEE ALSO **building.**

lobster SEE **shellfish.**

local 1 *Tony and Lucy go to their local school.* near, nearby, neighbouring, neighbourhood. **2** (informal) *Mrs Brunswick occasionally goes to the local for a drink.* SEE **pub.**

locality *There are several good shops in our* locality. area, district, neighbourhood, region, vicinity, zone.

locate 1 *Did you locate the book you wanted in the library?* to discover, to find, to search out, to track down, to unearth. **2** *They located the post office in the middle of town.* to place, to position, to situate, to station.

location 1 *Can you find our location on the map?* place, point, position, site, situation, spot. **2** *The best thing about the film was the beautiful locations.* scene, setting.

lock 1 *a lock on a door.* bolt, catch, latch, padlock. **2** *Please lock the door.* to bolt, to secure. SEE ALSO **fasten.** **3** *They locked him up as a punishment.* to confine, to gaol, to imprison, to shut in.

locket SEE **jewellery.**

locomotive engine. SEE ALSO **railway.**

locust SEE **insect.**

lodge 1 SEE **house. 2** *They lodged the homeless families in a hostel.* to accommodate, to board, to house, to put up, to quarter. **3** *We lodged in a motel.* to reside, to stay. **4** *lodgings:* boarding house, quarters.

lodger *The lodgers were only allowed to stay for a few days.* boarder, guest, resident, tenant.

loft attic. SEE ALSO **house.**

lofty *a lofty spire.* high, tall, towering.

log 1 timber, wood. SEE ALSO **fuel.** **2** *The captain kept a log of the voyage.* diary, journal, record.

logical *Tony's arguments are always logical.* clear, coherent, intelligent, rational, reasonable, sensible.

loiter *You'll get left behind if you loiter.* to dally, to dawdle, to hang about, to linger, to loaf, to mess about, to straggle.

lollipop SEE **sweet.**

lonely 1 *Lucy was lonely when her friends were away on holiday.* alone, desolate, forlorn, forsaken, friendless, neglected, solitary. **2** *a lonely farmhouse.* isolated, remote, secluded.

long 1 *a long journey.* endless,

extended, interminable, lengthy, prolonged, slow, unending. 2 *Lucy longs for warmer weather.* to desire, to fancy, to hanker after, to pine for, to want, to wish for, to yearn for. 3 *Who was it who had a longing for toasted cheese?* appetite, craving, hunger, urge, wish, yearning.

long-bow SEE **weapon.**

longitude SEE **geography.**

long-playing record album, LP. SEE ALSO **record.**

long-winded *Logan fell asleep during the head's long-winded talk.* boring, dreary, dry, lengthy, long, tedious, uninteresting, wordy.

look 1 WAYS TO LOOK AT THINGS ARE to behold, to contemplate, to examine, to eye, to gape, to gaze, to glance, to glimpse, to observe, to peep, to peer, to regard, to scan, to see, to squint, to stare, to study, to survey, to view, to watch. 2 *Our house looks south.* to face, to overlook. 3 *You look pleased.* to appear, to seem. 4 *to look after something.* to attend to, to care for, to guard, to keep, to mind, to protect, to tend. 5 *to look down on someone.* to despise, to dislike, to scorn. 6 *to look for something.* to hunt, to nose about, to search, to seek. 7 *Give me a look.* sight. 8 *He has a friendly look.* appearance, countenance, expression, face.

looking-glass mirror.

look-out guard, sentinel, sentry, watchman.

loom *A castle loomed on the skyline.* to arise, to appear, to emerge, to stand out, to stick up, to tower.

loony (informal) SEE **mad.**

loop 1 *a loop of rope.* noose. 2 *Loop the rope round the post.* to coil, to curl, to entwine, to turn, to twist, to wind.

loose 1 *loose stones, loose tiles.* insecure, movable, shaky, unsteady, wobbly. 2 *That rope is loose.* not tight, slack, unfastened, untied. 3 *The bull's loose!* free, unconfined. 4 *Someone loosed the bull.* to free, to let go, to liberate, to release, to set free, to untie.

loosen *Who loosened these guy ropes?* to ease off, to free, to loose, to relax, to release, to slacken, to undo, to unfasten, to untie.

loot 1 *The robbers ran off with their loot.* booty, contraband, plunder, (informal) swag, takings. 2 *The rioters looted the shops.* to plunder, to ransack, to rob, to steal from.

lop *to lop off a branch.* to chop, to sever. SEE ALSO **cut.**

lop-sided *The lop-sided load on the lorry looked dangerous.* asymmetrical, unbalanced, uneven.

lord aristocrat, noble, peer. SEE ALSO **title.**

lorry SEE **vehicle.**

lose 1 *Lucy lost her watch.* to mislay. 2 *Tony lost his way in the dark.* to miss, to stray from. 3 *Our team lost.* to be defeated, to fail.

lot 1 *a lot of: a lot of friends, a lot of money.* many, much, plenty of. 2 *to draw lots:* SEE **choose, gamble.**

lotion ointment. SEE **cosmetics, medicine.**

lottery SEE **gamble.**

loud *a loud noise.* deafening, noisy, piercing, raucous, shrill. FOR WAYS OF MAKING NOISE SEE ALSO **sound.**

loudspeaker SEE **audio equipment.**

lounge 1 drawing room, living-room, sitting-room. SEE ALSO **house.** 2 *We were lounging about.* to be idle, to be lazy, to loaf, to loiter, to relax, to slouch, to sprawl.

louse SEE **insect.**

lousy (informal) *What lousy weather!* dreadful, nasty, rotten, terrible, unpleasant. SEE ALSO **bad.**

loutish *We get sick of Logan's loutish behaviour.* bad-mannered, coarse, common, crude, discourteous, impolite, rude, uncouth, vulgar.

lovable *Teddy-bears are lovable toys.* appealing, attractive, charming, endearing, lovely.

love 1 *Giving flowers is a nice way to show your love for someone.* admiration, affection, desire, fondness, infatuation, passion. 2 *They love each other*. to admire, to adore, to be fond of, to cherish, to dote on, to idolize, to treasure, to value, to worship. 3 *to make love*: to court, to woo. SEE ALSO **mate**. 4 *loving*: affectionate, fond, friendly, kind, tender, warm.

lovely *a lovely day, a lovely view*. appealing, attractive, charming, enjoyable, fine, nice, pretty. SEE ALSO **beautiful, pleasant**.

lover beloved, boy-friend, darling, fiancé or fiancée, girl-friend, suitor, sweetheart, wooer.

low 1 *a low position*. inferior. 2 *a low whisper*. quiet, soft. 3 *a low note*. bass, deep. 4 *low spirits*. SEE **sad**. 5 *That was a low trick!* base, cowardly, mean, nasty, wicked. 6 *The cows were lowing*. SEE **sound**.

lower 1 *We lowered our flag*. to dip, to drop, to let down, to take down. 2 *They lowered their prices*. to cut, to decrease, to lessen, to reduce. 3 *Lower your voice*. to quieten, to turn down.

lowly *a lowly position in life*. humble, meek, modest. ! *Lowly* usually sounds old-fashioned.

loyal *a loyal supporter*. constant, dependable, devoted, dutiful, faithful, patriotic, reliable, trustworthy.

lozenge SEE **medicine**.

LP album, disc, long-playing record. SEE ALSO **record**.

lubricate to grease, to oil.

lucid *a lucid explanation*. clear, coherent, comprehensible, intelligible, understandable.

luck *Lucy found her watch by luck*. accident, chance, coincidence, destiny, fate, fluke, fortune.

lucky 1 *a lucky discovery*. accidental, chance, happy, unintentional, unplanned. 2 *a lucky person*. fortunate.

ludicrous absurd, comic, crazy, foolish, funny, laughable, preposterous, ridiculous, silly, zany.

ludo SEE **game**.

lug *How far have we got to lug this box?* to carry, to drag, to haul, to pull, to tug.

luggage baggage, bags, boxes, cases, suitcases, trunks.

lukewarm tepid, warm.

lull 1 *The song lulled him to sleep*. to calm, to pacify, to quieten, to soothe. 2 *a lull in a storm*. break, gap, interval, pause, respite, rest.

lullaby SEE **sing**.

lumbago SEE **illness**.

lumber 1 *The rhinoceros lumbered towards them*. to blunder, to move clumsily, to trudge. 2 *They are cutting lumber in the forest*. timber, wood. 3 *We cleared the lumber out of the garage*. junk, odds and ends, rubbish, trash.

luminous *a luminous clock*. glowing, phosphorescent, shining. SEE ALSO **light**.

lump 1 *a lump of chocolate, a lump of metal, etc*. bar, bit, block, chunk, clot, dollop, hunk, ingot, mass, nugget, piece, slab. 2 *a lump on the head*. bulge, bump, hump, knob, swelling.

lunatic madman, maniac. SEE ALSO **mad**.

lunch, luncheon SEE **meal**.

lunge *to lunge with a sword*. to stab, to thrust.

lupin SEE **flower**.

lurch *He lurched from side to side*. to lean, to pitch, to roll, to stagger, to totter. SEE ALSO **move, walk**.

lure *The poacher lured the animal into a trap*. to attract, to bait, to coax, to decoy, to entice, to persuade, to tempt.

lurid 1 *lurid colours*. bright, gaudy, startling, vivid. 2 *lurid details*. sensational, shocking, unpleasant, violent.

lurk *I imagined ogres lurking in the woods*. to hide, to lie low, to wait.

luscious *luscious peaches*. appetizing, delicious, juicy, sweet. SEE ALSO **taste**.

lust *a lust for power*. appetite, desire, greed, hunger, longing, passion.

lute SEE **music, strings.**
luxurious *a luxurious palace, a luxurious banquet.* costly, expensive, grand, lavish, rich, sumptuous. SEE ALSO **splendid.**
luxury *a life of luxury.* comfort, ease, enjoyment, pleasure, relaxation.
lynch SEE **execute, kill.**
lyre SEE **music, strings.**
lyric SEE **poem.**

M m

macaroni SEE food.
machine apparatus, device, instrument, machinery, mechanism, tool.
machine-gun SEE **weapon.**
machinery equipment, machines, plant.
mackerel SEE **fish.**
mackintosh (informal) mac, sou'wester, waterproof. SEE ALSO **clothes.**
mad 1 *mad behaviour.* berserk, crazy, delirious, demented, deranged, (informal) dotty, frantic, frenzied, hysterical, insane, (informal) loony, (informal) mental, (informal) potty, unbalanced, unhinged, wild. 2 *a mad person*: lunatic, madman, maniac. 3 *a mad sense of humour.* SEE **absurd.** 4 *mad with rage.* SEE **angry.**
madden *The noise maddened him.* to aggravate, to anger, to enrage, to exasperate, to incense, to inflame, to infuriate, to provoke, to vex.
madman SEE **mad.**
magazine comic, journal, newspaper, paper, periodical.
maggot caterpillar, grub, larva. SEE ALSO **insect.**
magic 1 *Can witches do magic?* charm, enchantment, sorcery, spell, witchcraft, wizardry. 2 *A conjuror did some magic.* conjuring, illusions, trickery, tricks. 3 PEOPLE WHO ARE SUPPOSED TO DO MAGIC ARE

conjuror, magician, sorcerer, witch, witch-doctor, wizard.
magician SEE **entertainment, magic.**
magistrate SEE **law.**
magnificent *magnificent mountain scenery.* glorious, gorgeous, grand, impressive, majestic, marvellous, noble, superb, wonderful. SEE ALSO **beautiful, splendid.**
magnify to amplify, to enlarge, to exaggerate.
magnitude bulk, extent, importance, largeness, size, volume.
magpie SEE **bird.**
mahogany SEE **wood.**
maid SEE **girl, servant.**
maiden SEE **girl.**
mail 1 *The knight wore chain-mail.* armour, protection. 2 *The postman brought the mail.* letters, parcels, post. 3 *The shop mailed the book to me.* to dispatch, to post, to send.
maim *He was maimed in an accident.* to cripple, to disable, to handicap, to injure, to mutilate.
main *the main ingredient, the main reason.* basic, chief, essential, foremost, fundamental, important, major, prevailing, primary, principal.
mainland SEE **geography.**
mainly chiefly, generally, mostly, predominantly, primarily, usually.
maintain 1 *Mr Brunswick maintains his car in good order.* to keep, to preserve, to service, to take care of. 2 *How long can you maintain this speed?* to continue, to keep up. 3 *He maintained that he was innocent.* to assert, to claim, to declare, to insist, to proclaim, to state.
maize SEE **cereal.**
majestic *a majestic palace.* grand, imposing, impressive, lordly, magnificent, noble, regal, royal, stately. SEE ALSO **splendid.**
majesty SEE **royal.**
major 1 *a major in the army.* SEE **rank.** 2 *Birmingham is one of England's major*

cities. chief, greater, important, larger, principal.

make 1 to create, to form, to invent, to originate, to produce, to shape, to think up. **2** VARIOUS WAYS OF MAKING THINGS ARE to assemble, to bake, to brew, to build, to carve, to cast, to compose, to construct, to cook, to cut, to erect, to knit, to manufacture, to mass-produce, to model, to mould, to sew, to weave, to write. **3** *Don't make trouble*. to bring about, to cause, to provoke, to result in. **4** *You can't make me do it*. to compel, to force, to oblige, to order, to require. **5** *The head made a speech*. to deliver, to pronounce, to speak, to utter. **6** *It's easy to make a P into a B*. to alter, to change, to convert, to modify, to transform, to turn. **7** *How can I make a fortune?* to earn, to gain, to get, to obtain, to receive. **8** *Logan would make a good player if he tried*. to become, to change into, to grow into, to turn into. **9** *Will I make the first team?* to achieve, to get to, to reach. **10** *Everyone knows that 2 and 2 make 4*. to add up to, to amount to, to come to, to total. **11** *I made an appointment*. to agree, to arrange, to decide on, to fix. **12** *Can you make out what is happening?* to decipher, to follow, to hear, to perceive, to see, to understand. **13** *Logan made up an excuse*. to concoct, to devise, to improvise, to invent, to plan, to think up. **14** *What make is your car?* brand, kind, sort.

make-believe *a make-believe story*. fanciful, fantasy, feigned, imaginary, pretended, unreal.

make-up SEE **cosmetics**.

malady affliction, ailment, complaint, disease, disorder, infection, infirmity, sickness. SEE ALSO **illness**.

malaria SEE **illness**.

male MALE CREATURES ARE billy-goat, boar, buck, cock, cockerel, drake, drone, gander, hog, ram, rooster, stag, stallion, tom-cat.

malefactor convict, criminal, crook, culprit, delinquent, offender, wrongdoer.

malevolent *a malevolent stare*. evil, malicious, nasty, revengeful, spiteful, vicious, villainous, wicked. SEE ALSO **bad, unpleasant**.

malicious *He hurt her with his malicious remarks*. bitter, catty, evil, malevolent, nasty, revengeful, sly, spiteful, vicious, vindictive. SEE ALSO **bad, unpleasant**.

malignant *a malignant disease*. dangerous, harmful, poisonous, spreading.

mallet SEE **tool**.

malnutrition famine, hunger, starvation.

malt SEE **food**.

mammal SEE **animal**.

mammoth SEE **animal**.

man bachelor, (informal) bloke, fellow, gentleman, (informal) guy, husband, widower. SEE ALSO **person**.

manage 1 *The head teacher manages the school*. to administer, to be in charge of, to command, to control, to direct, to govern, to lead, to look after, to regulate, to rule, to run, to supervise. **2** *If £10 is too much, what can you manage?* to afford, to spare. **3** *Could you manage a lively horse like that?* to cope with, to deal with, to handle, to manipulate. **4** *See how much work you can manage before dinner*. to accomplish, to achieve, to carry out, to complete, to do, to finish, to perform, to succeed in, to undertake.

manager administrator, boss, chief, controller, director, governor, head, overseer, proprietor, ruler, supervisor.

mangle *He was off work because he mangled his hand in a machine*. to crush, to cut, to damage, to injure, to mutilate, to squash. SEE ALSO **wound**.

manhandle 1 *They had to manhandle the piano up the stairs*. to carry, to lift, to move. **2** *The muggers manhandled* *him brutally.* to beat up, to knock about, to treat roughly.

mania craze, enthusiasm, frenzy, hysteria, insanity, madness, obsession.

maniac lunatic, madman. SEE ALSO **mad**.

manipulate 1 *A good speaker can manipulate an audience.* to control, to feel, to handle, to manage. **2** *The trainer manipulated the injured player's leg.* to massage, to rub.

mankind human beings, men and women. SEE ALSO **person**.

manly masculine, virile.

man-made *Plastics are man-made substances.* artificial, manufactured, synthetic.

mannequin model. SEE ALSO **job**.

manner 1 *Mr Brunswick does jobs in a professional manner.* fashion, means, method, mode, style, way. **2** *Mrs Angel didn't like Logan's cheeky manner.* attitude, behaviour, character, conduct, disposition.

manners *It's time he learned some manners.* good behaviour, civility, courtesy, politeness.

manoeuvre 1 *army manoeuvres.* exercise, operation, training. **2** *It was a clever manoeuvre to take his bishop.* move, plan, scheme, strategy, tactics, trick. **3** *He manoeuvred the van through the gate.* to guide, to move, to pilot, to steer.

manor, manse SEE **house**.

mansion château, stately home. SEE ALSO **house**.

manslaughter SEE **kill**.

mantelpiece SEE **furniture**.

manual *an instruction manual.* SEE **book**.

manufacture 1 *What does this factory manufacture?* to assemble, to make, to mass-produce. **2** *manufacturing: a manufacturing town.* industrial. **3** *manufactured:* artificial, man-made, synthetic.

manufacturer SEE **job**.

manure compost, dung, fertilizer, muck.

manuscript document, papers. SEE ALSO **book**.

many countless, frequent, innumerable, numberless, numerous, untold.

map 1 chart, diagram, plan. **2** *a book of maps:* atlas.

maple SEE **tree**.

mar *Logan marred his picture by spilling paint on it.* to blot, to damage, to deface, to disfigure, to spoil, to stain.

marathon SEE **athletics**.

marauder buccaneer, invader, pirate, raider.

marble 1 *to play marbles.* SEE **game**. **2** *a statue made of marble.* SEE **rock**.

march 1 *The soldiers marched into town.* to parade, to troop. **2** *The band played a march.* SEE **music**.

mare SEE **female, horse**.

margarine SEE **fat**.

margin border, edge, frieze, verge.

marigold SEE **flower**.

marijuana SEE **drug**.

marina *a marina for sailing-boats.* anchorage, harbour.

marine 1 SEE **sea**. **2** SEE **fighter**.

mariner sailor, seaman.

mark 1 *There's a dirty mark on your dress.* blemish, blot, dot, smear, spot, stain, streak, trace. **2** WAYS TO MARK SOMETHING ARE to brand, to bruise, to deface, to disfigure, to draw on, to mar, to scar, to scratch, to spot, to stain, to stamp, to streak, to tattoo, to write on. **3** *Has Mrs Angel marked our maths yet?* to assess, to correct. **4** *Mark what I say.* to attend to, to heed, to note, to notice, to observe, to take note of.

market 1 auction, bazaar, fair, sale. FOR VARIOUS BUSINESSES SEE ALSO **shop**. **2** *Mr Brunswick's firm markets furniture.* to retail, to sell, to trade.

marmalade SEE **food**.

maroon 1 SEE **colour**. **2** *They marooned Ben Gunn on Treasure Island.* to abandon, to desert, to forsake, to leave, to strand. **3** *a marooned person:* castaway.

marquee tent.

marriage 1 *Granny and grandad have enjoyed 40 years of marriage.* matrimony. 2 *Today is the anniversary of their marriage.* SEE **wedding**. 3 *a married person:* husband, wife. SEE ALSO **unmarried**.

marrow SEE **vegetable**.

marsh bog, fen, quagmire, quicksands, swamp.

marsupial SEE **animal**.

martial 1 *a martial figure.* belligerent, militant, pugnacious, war-like. 2 *martial law.* military. 3 *the martial arts:* judo, karate, kung fu.

martyr SEE **church**, **kill**.

marvel *We marvelled at the strange sight.* to admire, to be amazed by, to gape at, to wonder at.

marvellous 1 *The museum has some marvellous things.* admirable, excellent, fabulous, glorious, miraculous, sensational, splendid, wonderful. 2 *We had a marvellous time.* SEE **good**.

Marxist SEE **politics**.

marzipan SEE **sweet**.

masculine male, manly, virile.

mash to crush, to grind, to mangle, to pound, to pulp, to smash, to squash.

mask *We planted a tree to mask the ugly building at the back.* to blot out, to camouflage, to cloak, to conceal, to cover, to disguise, to hide, to screen, to shroud.

mason SEE **job**.

masonry brickwork, stonework.

mass 1 *a mass of food.* chunk, dollop, heap, hunk, lump, mound, pile, quantity, stack. 2 *a mass of people.* crowd, large number, multitude, throng. SEE ALSO **group**. 3 *Do you go to mass on Sundays?* communion, service, worship. SEE ALSO **church**.

massacre bloodshed, carnage, slaughter. SEE ALSO **kill**.

massage *The trainer massaged the injured player's leg.* to knead, to manipulate, to rub.

massive colossal, enormous, gigantic, heavy, huge, immense, mammoth, mighty, towering, vast, weighty. SEE ALSO **big**.

mast SEE **vessel**.

master 1 boss, captain, chief, head, ruler. 2 *a schoolmaster:* SEE **teacher**. 3 *a master at chess.* expert, genius, master-mind. 4 *Have you mastered the rules?* to grasp, to learn, to understand. 5 *You need courage to master a wild horse.* to conquer, to control, to govern, to overcome, to overpower, to quell, to subdue, to suppress.

masterful *a masterful personality.* bossy, domineering, forceful, strong.

masterly *I admire his masterly control of the ball.* accomplished, brilliant, clever, gifted, skilful, talented.

master-mind expert, genius, master.

masterpiece *That piece of music is a masterpiece.* classic.

mastiff SEE **dog**.

mastodon SEE **animal**.

mat carpet, matting, rug. SEE **floor**.

matador bullfighter, toreador.

match 1 *a boxing match.* bout, competition, contest, game, tie, tournament. 2 *Do these colours match?* to agree, to coincide, to compare, to correspond.

mate 1 *Logan went out with his mates.* chum, companion, comrade, friend, partner. 2 *Some birds take a mate for life.* husband, wife. 3 *Many birds mate in the springtime.* to copulate, to couple, to have intercourse, to make love, to unite. 4 SEE **chess**.

material 1 *Mr Brunswick bought the materials he needs to build his extension.* matter, stuff, substance. 2 MATERIALS USED IN BUILDING, ETC., ARE asbestos, asphalt, brick, cement, concrete, creosote, fibreglass, glass, hardboard, lime, metal, mortar, nylon, paint, perspex, plaster, plastic, plywood, polystyrene, polythene, putty, PVC, rubber, slate, stone, tar, tiles, timber, veneer, vinyl, wood. 3 *Lucy*

bought some material to make a skirt.
fabric, textile. SEE ALSO **cloth.**

materialize *A shape materialized out of the fog.* to appear, to come into existence, to emerge, to turn up.

maternal *maternal feeling.* motherly.

maternity motherhood, pregnancy.

mathematics, maths 1 WORDS USED IN MATHEMATICS ARE addition, algebra, angle, arithmetic, binary system, diagonal, diameter, division, equilateral, geometry, minus, multiplication, negative number, parallel, percentage, perpendicular, plus, positive number, radius, ratio, right angle, SEE **shape**, subtraction, sum, symmetry, tessellation, times. 2 MATHEMATICAL INSTRUMENTS ARE compasses, dividers, geo-board, protractor, ruler, set-square. 3 SEE **subject.**

matinée SEE **theatre.**

matrimony marriage.

matted *matted hair.* tangled.

matter 1 *We scooped a lot of filthy matter out of the drain.* material, stuff, substance. 2 *The headmaster will deal with this matter.* affair, business, concern, subject, thing, topic. 3 *What is the matter with the car?* difficulty, problem, trouble. 4 *Will it matter if I'm a bit late?* to be important.

matting carpet, mat, rug. SEE ALSO **floor.**

mattress SEE **bedclothes.**

mature 1 *Lucy is mature for her age.* adult, advanced, grown-up. 2 *mature fruit.* mellow, ready, ripe.

maul *The keeper was mauled by a lion.* to injure, to mangle, to mutilate. SEE ALSO **wound.**

mauve SEE **colour.**

maximum *maximum speed.* full, greatest, highest, most, top.

maybe perhaps, possibly.

mayonnaise SEE **food.**

maze *a maze of corridors.* labyrinth.

meadow field, pasture.

meagre *I got a meagre helping of*

pudding. inadequate, mean, (informal) measly, (informal) mingy, scanty, small, sparse, stingy, thin.

meal 1 VARIOUS MEALS ARE banquet, barbecue, breakfast, buffet, dinner, feast, high tea, lunch, luncheon, picnic, snack, (informal) spread, supper, tea. 2 PARTS OF A MEAL ARE (informal) afters, course, dessert, main course, pudding, starter, sweet.

mean 1 *What does this sign mean?* to communicate, to convey, to express, to imply, to indicate, to say, to stand for, to suggest, to symbolize. 2 *What do you mean to do?* to intend, to plan, to propose. 3 *He's too mean to give a donation.* close, (informal) mingy, miserly, sparing, stingy. 4 *It was mean to take her last sweet.* base, cruel, nasty, sneaky, unkind.

meaning *What's the meaning of this word?* sense, significance.

means *What's the best means of getting to London?* fashion, manner, method, way.

measles SEE **illness.**

measly (informal) *I got a measly spoonful of semolina.* meagre, mean, (informal) mingy, scanty, small, stingy, worthless.

measure 1 UNITS OF BREADTH, DEPTH, DISTANCE, GAUGE, HEIGHT, LENGTH OR WIDTH ARE centimetre, fathom, foot, furlong, inch, kilometre, light-year, metre, mile, millimetre, yard. 2 UNITS OF AREA ARE acre, hectare, square centimetres, etc. 3 UNITS OF TIME ARE day, hour, minute, month, second, week, year. 4 UNITS OF CAPACITY OR VOLUME ARE cubic centimetres, etc., gallon, litre, millilitre, pint, quart. 5 UNITS OF WEIGHT ARE gram, hundredweight, kilogram, milligram, ounce, pound, stone, ton, tonne. 6 UNITS OF SPEED OR VELOCITY ARE kilometre per hour, knot, mach number, mile per hour, (informal) ton. 7 UNITS OF QUANTITY ARE century, dozen, gross, score. 8 SCALES FOR measuring temperature are Celsius, centigrade, Fahrenheit. THE UNIT IS degree. 9 INFORMAL MEASUREMENTS ARE armful, cupful, handful, mouthful, pinch, plateful, spoonful.

measurement *the measurements of a room.* dimensions, extent, size.

meat 1 flesh. 2 KINDS OF MEAT ARE bacon, beef, chicken, corned beef, game, gammon, ham, lamb, mutton, oxtail, pork, poultry, tripe, turkey, veal, venison. 3 WAYS OF SERVING MEAT ARE AS beefburger, chops, cutlets, hamburger, joint, mince, sausage, steak, stew. 4 SEE **food**.

mechanic *a motor mechanic.* engineer, technician.

mechanism apparatus, device, instrument, machine, machinery.

medal award, decoration, prize.

medallist winner.

meddle *Don't meddle in my affairs.* to butt in, to interfere, to intervene, to intrude, to pry, to snoop, to tamper.

media *the media*: magazines, newspapers, the press, radio, television. ! *Media* is a plural word, so you should talk about *the media*, not *a media*.

medicine 1 *We got some medicine from the chemist's.* cure, dose, drug, prescription, remedy, treatment. 2 *Have you taken your medicine?* capsule, pastille, pellet, pill, tablet. 3 VARIOUS MEDICINES AND TREATMENTS ARE anaesthetic, antibiotic, antidote, antiseptic, aspirin, gargle, herbs, iodine, linctus, lotion, lozenge, morphia, narcotic, ointment, penicillin, the pill, sedative, tonic, tranquillizer. 4 PEOPLE WHO LOOK AFTER OUR HEALTH ARE dentist, doctor, midwife, nurse, oculist, optician, osteopath, physician, physiotherapist, psychiatrist, radiographer, sister, surgeon. 5 PLACES WHERE YOU GET MEDICAL TREATMENT ARE clinic, dispensary, health centre, hospital, infirmary, intensive care unit, nursing home,

operating theatre, out-patients' department, surgery, ward. 6 OTHER WORDS TO DO WITH MEDICAL TREATMENT ARE bandage, dressing, first aid, forceps, hypodermic syringe, immunization, injection, inoculation, lint, plaster, plastic surgery, poultice, radiotherapy, scalpel, sling, splint, stethoscope, stretcher, syringe, therapy, thermometer, transfusion, transplant, tweezers, X-ray.

mediocre *There isn't much to say about a mediocre game.* commonplace, fair, middling, moderate, ordinary, passable, second-rate, unexciting.

meditate *I meditated quietly on what I had learned.* to brood, to consider, to contemplate, to ponder, to reflect, to think.

medium *Tony is medium height for his age.* average, middle, middling, moderate, normal, ordinary, usual.

meek docile, gentle, humble, lowly, modest, obedient, patient, tame, unassuming.

meet 1 *The two roads meet here.* to come together, to converge, to intersect, to join, to merge. 2 *Lucy met Logan in town.* to come across, to confront, to encounter, to face, to run into, to see. 3 *We all met in the hall.* to assemble, to come together, to congregate, to gather.

meeting 1 *a business meeting.* assembly, conference, congress, council, gathering. 2 *an unexpected meeting.* confrontation, encounter. 3 *We've arranged a meeting.* appointment, date, rendezvous.

melancholy dejected, depressed, gloomy, unhappy. SEE ALSO **sad**.

mellow *a mellow taste.* mature, pleasant, rich, ripe, soft. SEE ALSO **taste**.

melodious musical, tuneful.

melody air, theme, tune. SEE ALSO **music**.

melon SEE **fruit**.

melt 1 *The sun melts the snow.* to soften, to thaw. 2 *The crowd melted away.* to disappear, to dissolve, to fade, to vanish.

member *to be a member*: to belong.

memorable unforgettable.

memorial monument. SEE ALSO **funeral**.

memorize to learn, to remember.

memory *We've got happy memories of our holiday*. impression, recollection, reminder, souvenir.

menace *He shook his fist in a menacing gesture*. to frighten, to intimidate, to scare, to threaten.

mend 1 *The garage mended the car*. to fix, to put right, to renovate, to repair, to restore, to touch up. **2** *Tony mended his jeans*. to darn, to patch, to sew up, to stitch.

mental 1 SEE **mind**. **2** SEE **mad**.

mention 1 *Did mum mention the broken window?* to allude to, to comment on, to refer to, to speak about. **2** *Dad mentioned that he might go out*. to observe, to remark, to say.

mercenary SEE **fighter**.

merchant 1 *a timber merchant*. dealer, retailer, salesman, shopkeeper, stockist, supplier, trader. **2** *a merchant ship*: SEE **vessel**.

merciful benevolent, compassionate, forgiving, humane, lenient, sympathetic, tolerant. SEE ALSO **kind**.

merciless callous, hard-hearted, heartless, inhumane, pitiless, ruthless, savage, unfeeling, vicious. SEE ALSO **cruel**.

mercury quicksilver. SEE ALSO **metal**.

mercy *The attackers showed no mercy*. clemency, compassion, forgiveness, grace, kindness, pity, sympathy.

merge 1 *Our school merged with the one down the road*. to amalgamate, to combine, to come together, to unite. **2** *The motorways merge here*. to converge, to join, to meet.

meringue SEE **cake**.

merit 1 *Do you think my painting has any merit?* importance, quality, value, worth. **2** *a certificate of merit*. credit,

distinction. **3** *Lucy's performance merited first prize*. to be entitled to, to deserve, to earn.

mermaid SEE **legend**.

merry *a merry tune*. bright, cheerful, glad, jolly, jovial, joyful, spirited. SEE ALSO **happy**.

mesh net, netting, network, web.

mess 1 *Clear up this mess!* clutter, confusion, jumble, muddle, shambles, untidiness. **2** (informal) *You messed up this job!* to bungle, to spoil. **3** (informal) *We were messing about*. to loaf, to loiter, to play about.

message announcement, bulletin, communication, communiqué, dispatch, letter, note, notice, report, statement.

messenger dispatch-rider, herald, postman, runner.

messy *messy work*. careless, dirty, disorderly, filthy, (informal) mucky, slapdash, sloppy, slovenly, untidy.

metal 1 VARIOUS METALS ARE alloy, aluminium, brass, bronze, chromium, copper, galvanized iron, gold, iron, lead, mercury, nickel, pewter, platinum, quicksilver, silver, solder, stainless steel, tin, uranium, zinc. **2** *a lump of metal*: ingot, nugget.

meteor, meteorite SEE **astronomy**.

meteorology SEE **science, weather**.

method fashion, knack, manner, means, mode, procedure, process, routine, style, system, technique, trick, way.

methodical *a methodical worker*. businesslike, careful, deliberate, meticulous, orderly, organized, painstaking, systematic.

metre SEE **measure**.

metric *the metric system*. decimal.

metro SEE **travel**.

micro SEE **computer**.

microbe bacteria, (informal) bug, germ, virus. ! *Bacteria* is a plural word.

microchip, microcomputer SEE **computer**.

micro-light SEE **aircraft**.

microphone SEE **audio equipment**.

microprocessor SEE **computer**.

microscope SEE **optical**.

microscopic imperceptible, minute, tiny. SEE ALSO **small**.

microwave SEE **kitchen**.

midday SEE **time**.

middle 1 *the middle of the earth.* centre, core, heart, hub, inside, nucleus. 2 *the middle stump.* central, half-way, inner, intermediate, mid-way, neutral.

middling *She gave just a middling performance.* average, fair, indifferent, mediocre, ordinary.

midge SEE **insect**.

midget dwarf, pigmy. ! These words are often insulting.

midnight, midsummer SEE **time**.

midwife SEE **medicine**.

might *We banged at the door with all our might.* energy, force, power, strength, vigour.

mighty *He gave a mighty blow with his axe.* big, enormous, great, hefty, huge, powerful, strong.

migraine SEE **illness**.

migrate *Some birds migrate to other lands.* to travel. SEE ALSO **move**.

mild 1 *mild weather.* balmy, calm, peaceful, pleasant, soothing, warm. 2 *a mild flavour.* delicate, faint, subtle. 3 *a mild person.* gentle, good-tempered, harmless, kind.

mildew mould.

mile SEE **measure**.

militant *a militant attitude.* aggressive, attacking, belligerent, hostile, pugnacious, warlike.

milk 1 KINDS OF MILK ARE condensed, evaporated, pasteurized. 2 SEE ALSO **drink, food**.

milkman SEE **job**.

milky *a milky liquid.* cloudy, misty, unclear, whitish.

mill SEE **building**.

miller SEE **job**.

milligram, millilitre, millimetre SEE **measure**.

mime SEE **theatre**.

mimic *The parrot mimicked me.* to copy, to echo, to imitate, to impersonate.

minaret SEE **building**.

mince 1 *to mince up food.* SEE **cut**. 2 *savoury mince.* SEE **meat**.

mincemeat, mince pie SEE **food**.

mind 1 *Use your mind!* brain, cleverness, intellect, intelligence, mental power, sense, understanding. 2 *Mind the step.* to heed, to look out for, to note, to remember, to take notice of. 3 *Tony won't mind if I use his pen.* to bother, to care, to complain, to grumble, to object, to worry.

mine 1 *a coal-mine.* pit, quarry, shaft, working. 2 *a land-mine.* SEE **weapon**. 3 *to mine for gold.* to dig, to excavate.

mineral 1 MINERALS FROM THE GROUND INCLUDE metal, ore, rock. 2 *mineral water.* SEE **drink**.

mingle *Everyone mingled happily at the carnival.* to blend, to combine, to mix.

mingy (informal) *He's mingy with his money.* close, mean, miserly, stingy.

miniature diminutive, little, microscopic, minute, tiny. SEE ALSO **small**.

minibus SEE **travel**.

minim SEE **music**.

minimum *the minimum price.* bottom, least, lowest, smallest.

miniskirt SEE **clothes**.

minister SEE **church, government**.

mink SEE **animal**.

minnow SEE **fish**.

minor *a minor accident.* insignificant, little, petty, small, trivial, unimportant.

minstrel bard, singer. SEE ALSO **entertainment**.

mint 1 SEE **herb, sweet**. 2 *in mint condition.* new, perfect, unmarked, unused.

minuet SEE **dance**.

minute 1 *I'll see you in five minutes.* SEE **measure**. 2 *The baby's toes are minute.* diminutive, little, microscopic, miniature, tiny, undersized. SEE ALSO **small**.

miracle marvel, mystery, wonder.
miraculous *a miraculous cure.*
extraordinary, incredible,
marvellous, mysterious,
supernatural, unbelievable.
mirage *The travellers thought they saw an
oasis, but it was a mirage.* delusion,
hallucination, illusion, vision.
mirror looking-glass.
mirth gaiety, happiness, jollity, joy,
laughter.
misadventure accident, calamity,
mischance, misfortune, mishap.
misbehave to behave badly, to
disobey, to err, to play up.
misbehaviour disobedience,
mischief, misconduct, naughtiness.
miscalculate to err, to go wrong, to
misjudge.
miscalculation error, inaccuracy,
mistake, slip-up.
miscarriage SEE **pregnant**.
miscellaneous *miscellaneous odds and
ends.* assorted, different, diverse,
mixed, varied, various.
mischief *What mischief has that puppy
been up to?* escapade, misbehaviour,
misconduct, naughtiness, prank,
scrape.
miser hoarder, miserly person.
miserable dejected, depressed,
despondent, down-hearted, gloomy,
heart-broken, melancholy, moping,
unfortunate, unhappy, unlucky,
wretched. SEE ALSO **sad**.
miserly close, mean, (informal)
mingy, stingy.
misery distress, grief, hardship,
sorrow, suffering, unhappiness.
misfortune *We had the misfortune of
breaking down.* accident, adversity,
affliction, bad luck, calamity,
disaster, mischance, mishap.
misgiving *I had misgivings about
lending Logan my money.* anxiety,
doubt, qualm, uncertainty, worry.
misguided *I was misguided to lend him
money.* foolish, mistaken, unwise.
mishap *We had a mishap on the
motorway.* accident, difficulty,

misadventure, mischance,
misfortune.
mislay *Mum mislaid her bag.* to lose.
mislead 1 *Don't try to mislead us!* to
bluff, to confuse, to deceive, to
delude, to fool, to hoax, to hoodwink,
to kid, to lie to, to muddle, to puzzle,
to take in, to trick. 2 *misleading*:
deceitful, deceptive, dishonest,
unreliable.
miss 1 *We missed the bus.* to let go, to
lose. 2 *Did we miss anything out?* to
disregard, to forget, to ignore, to
leave out, to neglect, to omit, to
overlook, to skip. 3 *We missed mum
while she was away.* to long for, to
need, to pine for, to want.
misshapen deformed, disfigured,
distorted, grotesque, twisted, ugly,
warped.
missile SEE **ammunition, weapon**.
mission expedition, exploration,
journey.
missionary SEE **church, preacher**.
mist fog, haze. SEE ALSO **weather**.
mistake 1 *I made a mistake.* blunder,
error, (informal) howler,
miscalculation, oversight, slip-up.
2 *I mistook your message.* to confuse, to
misjudge, to misunderstand, to mix
up.
mistrust *Tony mistrusted Logan's
promise.* to disbelieve, to distrust.
misty *misty windows.* blurred, clouded,
dim, faint, fuzzy, hazy, indistinct,
shadowy, steamy, unclear.
misunderstand *I misunderstood your
message.* to misjudge, to mistake.
misunderstanding blunder, error,
misconception, mistake.
misuse 1 *Someone has misused my tape-
recorder.* to damage, to harm, to hurt,
to injure. 2 *Lucy is careful not to misuse
her money.* to fritter, to squander, to
waste.
mite SEE **insect**.
mitten SEE **clothes**.
mix 1 *Mix the ingredients together.* to
blend, to combine, to integrate, to
mingle, to put together. 2 *I get things
mixed up.* to confuse, to jumble, to

muddle, to shuffle. 3 *mixed*: assorted, different, diverse, miscellaneous, varied, various.

mixture alloy, assortment, blend, collection, combination, compound, jumble, medley, variety.

moan 1 (informal) *Logan moaned about the food.* to complain, to grouse, to grumble. 2 SEE **sound**.

moat SEE **castle**.

mob *an angry mob.* bunch, crowd, horde, pack, rabble, swarm, throng. SEE ALSO **group**.

mobile *a mobile caravan.* movable, moving, travelling.

mobilize *to mobilize an army.* to assemble, to gather, to muster, to organize.

mock 1 to be sarcastic, to be satirical, to insult, to jeer, to laugh at, to make fun of, to ridicule, to scoff, to sneer, to taunt, to tease. 2 *mocking*: disparaging, rude, uncomplimentary.

model 1 *a model aircraft.* copy, dummy, imitation, replica, representation, toy. 2 *Our car is an old model.* design, type, version. 3 *We used Tony's design as a model.* example, pattern, prototype. 4 *The models showed off the latest fashions.* mannequin. SEE ALSO **job**.

moderate 1 *moderate prices.* average, fair, middle, middling, normal, ordinary, reasonable, usual. 2 *a moderate wind.* gentle, light, mild.

moderately fairly, pretty, rather.

modern *modern music, a modern house.* contemporary, current, fashionable, new, present, recent, stylish, (informal) trendy, up-to-date.

modernize *Mr Brunswick modernized his bathroom.* to improve, to rebuild, to renovate, to update.

modest 1 *a modest person.* bashful, coy, demure, humble, lowly, meek, shy, unassuming. 2 *a modest dress.* chaste, decent, plain, simple.

modify *After his model crashed, Tony modified the design.* to adapt, to adjust, to alter, to change, to convert, to transform, to vary.

moist clammy, damp, dank, humid, muggy, steamy, wet.

moisten to dampen.

mole 1 SEE **animal**. 2 (informal) *A mole must have discovered our secret plan.* secret agent, spy.

molest *The ruffians molested an old man.* to annoy, to assault, to attack, to bother, to harass, to interfere with, to pester, to set on.

mollusc SEE **animal**.

molten *molten metal.* liquid, melted.

moment 1 *It was over in a moment.* flash, instant, second. 2 *This was an important moment.* occasion, opportunity, time.

momentary *A momentary loss of concentration caused the accident.* brief, passing, short, temporary, transient.

momentous *Going to a new school is a momentous step.* grave, important, serious, weighty.

monarch SEE **royal, ruler**.

monarchy kingdom, realm.

monastery abbey. SEE ALSO **church**.

money 1 *Have you any money?* cash, change, cheque, coins, coppers, credit card, (informal) dough, notes, pocket-money, silver. 2 FORMS IN WHICH YOU MAY OWN OR EXCHANGE MONEY ARE assets, capital, currency, dowry, earnings, estate, funds, income, interest, investments, pay, pension, proceeds, profits, resources, revenue, riches, salary, savings, takings, taxes, wages, wealth, winnings.

money-box piggy-bank, safe, till. SEE ALSO **container**.

mongoose SEE **animal**.

mongrel SEE **dog**.

monitor SEE **computer**.

monk SEE **church**.

monkey SEE **animal**.

mono SEE **record**.

monorail SEE **travel**.

monotonous boring, dreary, dull, flat, tedious, unexciting, uninteresting, wearisome.

monsoon SEE **weather**.

monster beast, brute, giant, ogre.
SEE ALSO **legend**.

monstrous 1 *monstrous helpings of
food*. colossal, enormous, gigantic,
huge, hulking, immense, mighty. SEE
ALSO **big**. 2 *a monstrous crime*.
dreadful, evil, gross, hideous,
horrible, outrageous, repulsive,
shocking, terrible, wicked.

month SEE **time**.

monument memorial.

moo SEE **sound**.

mood 1 *Is she in a good mood?*
disposition, humour, state of mind,
temper. 2 FOR WORDS TO DESCRIBE
VARIOUS MOODS SEE **angry, happy,
sad**.

moody bad-tempered, cross,
depressed, disgruntled, gloomy,
grumpy, irritable, melancholy,
morose, snappy, sulky, sullen.

moon 1 SEE **astronomy**. 2 *to do with
the moon*: lunar.

moor 1 *a windswept moor*. heath. 2 *to
moor a boat*. to anchor, to berth, to tie
up. SEE ALSO **fasten**.

moorings SEE **harbour**.

moose SEE **animal**.

mop *to mop up*. SEE **clean**.

mope *He moped because he wasn't invited
to the party*. to be unhappy, to brood,
to grieve, to pine, to sulk. SEE ALSO
sad.

moped SEE **cycle**.

moral 1 *a moral person*. chaste, good,
honest, honourable, just, law-
abiding, pure, right, trustworthy,
truthful, upright, virtuous. 2 *a story
with a moral*. lesson.

morale *The team's morale is good*.
cheerfulness, confidence, spirit.

morbid *a morbid story about death*.
brooding, gloomy, morose,
pessimistic, unhappy, unhealthy.

more additional, extra, further.

moreover also, besides, furthermore,
too.

morning SEE **time**.

moron SEE **idiot**.

morose *a morose expression*. bad-

tempered, depressed, gloomy,
moody, sullen, unhappy. SEE ALSO
sad.

morphia SEE **medicine**.

morsel *a morsel of food*. bite, mouthful,
piece, taste, titbit.

mortal 1 *We are mortals*. human. SEE
ALSO **person**. 2 *a mortal sickness*.
deadly, fatal, lethal, terminal.

mortar 1 *bricks and mortar*. SEE
material. 2 *mortar fire*. SEE **gun**.

mosaic SEE **picture**.

mosque SEE **building, Islam**.

mosquito SEE **insect**.

moss SEE **plant**.

mostly chiefly, generally, mainly,
predominantly, primarily, usually.

motel SEE **holiday**.

moth SEE **insect**.

mother 1 mum, mummy. SEE ALSO
family. 2 *Lucy likes to mother the
toddlers*. to care for, to cherish, to fuss
over, to love, to nurse.

motherly *a motherly person*. kind,
loving, maternal.

motion movement.

motionless calm, immobile, lifeless,
peaceful, stationary, still, unmoving.

motive *What was the motive for the
crime?* purpose, reason.

motor 1 *an electric motor*. engine. 2 *We
motored into town*. to drive, to go by
car. SEE ALSO **travel**.

motor boat SEE **vessel**.

motor car automobile, car. SEE ALSO
vehicle..

motor cycle SEE **cycle**.

motorway SEE **road**.

mottled *The snake had mottled skin*.
blotchy, dotted, speckled, spotty.

motto proverb, saying, slogan.

mould 1 *There's mould on the cheese*.
fungus, mildew. 2 *a jelly mould*. SEE
container. 3 *Tony moulded the clay to
look like a face*. to cast, to form, to
shape.

mouldy mildewed, musty.

mound *a mound of rubbish*. bank, heap,
hill, pile, stack.

mount 1 *to mount upwards*. to ascend,

to climb, to go up, to rise, to soar.
2 *My savings have mounted up.* to grow,
to increase. 3 *to mount a picture.* to
frame. 4 *to mount a display.* to install,
to set up.

mountain hill, peak, range, summit,
volcano. SEE ALSO **geography**.

mountaineer 1 climber.
2 *mountaineering.* SEE **sport**.

mourn *He mourned for his dead dog.* to
fret, to grieve, to lament, to mope, to
pine, to weep.

mourner SEE **funeral**.

mournful SEE **sad**.

mouse SEE **animal, pet**.

mousse SEE **food**.

moustache whiskers.

mouth 1 SEE **body, head**. 2 *the mouth
of a river.* opening, outlet.

mouthful bite, morsel.

mouth-organ SEE **music**.

move 1 *to move along:* to come, to
cruise, to fly, to go, to jog, to journey,
to make headway, to march, to pass,
to proceed, to tour, to travel, to walk.
2 *to move along quickly:* to bolt, to
canter, to career, to dart, to dash, to
fly, to gallop, to hasten, to hurry, to
hurtle, to hustle, (informal) to nip, to
race, to run, to rush, to shoot, to
speed, to stampede, to streak, to
tear, (informal) to zoom. 3 *to move
along slowly:* to amble, to crawl, to
dawdle, to drift, to stroll. 4 *to move
along gracefully:* to dance, to flow, to
glide, to skate, to skim, to slide, to
slip, to sweep. 5 *to move along
awkwardly:* to dodder, to falter, to
flounder, to lumber, to lurch, to
pitch, to shuffle, to stagger, to
stumble, to sway, to totter, to trip, to
trundle. 6 *to move along stealthily:* to
crawl, to creep, to edge, to slink, to
slither. 7 *to move away:* to budge, to
depart, to leave, to migrate, to quit.
8 *to move back:* to reverse, to
withdraw. 9 *to move down:* to descend,
to drop, to fall, to lower, to sink, to
swoop. 10 *to move in:* to enter, to
penetrate. 11 *to move round:* to
circulate, to revolve, to roll, to

rotate, to spin, to turn, to twirl, to
twist, to wheel, to whirl. 12 *to move
towards:* to advance, to approach, to
proceed, to progress. 13 *to move up:* to
arise, to ascend, to climb, to mount,
to rise. 14 *to move restlessly:* to be
agitated, to fidget, to flap, to roll, to
shake, to stir, to swing, to toss, to
tremble, to turn, to twist, to twitch,
to wag, to waggle, to wave, to wiggle.
15 *to move things.* to carry, to shift, to
ship, to transfer, to transport, to
transplant. 16 *to move someone's
feelings.* to affect, to influence, to stir,
to touch. 17 *What will her next move
be?* act, action, movement, shift.
18 *It's your move next.* chance,
opportunity, turn.

movement action, activity, motion.

movie SEE **film**.

mow *to mow the grass.* to clip, to trim.
SEE ALSO **cut**.

muck dirt, dung, filth, grime,
manure, mud, rubbish, slime.

mucky (informal) *mucky shoes, a mucky
room.* dirty, filthy, foul, grimy,
grubby, messy, muddy, soiled,
sordid, squalid.

mud dirt, (informal) muck, slime.

muddy caked, dirty, filthy, messy,
(informal) mucky, soiled.

muddle 1 *Lucy's room is in a muddle.*
clutter, confusion, jumble, mess,
shambles. 2 *You'll muddle me if you
talk so fast.* to bewilder, to confuse, to
mislead, to perplex, to puzzle.
3 *Don't muddle the library books.* to
jumble, to mix up.

muffle 1 *Muffle yourself up in this icy
weather.* to cover, to wrap up. 2 *I tried
to muffle my sneeze.* to deaden, to
quieten, to soften, to stifle, to
suppress.

muffler SEE **clothes**.

mug 1 beaker, cup. SEE ALSO
container, drink. 2 to assault, to
attack, to molest, to rob, to set on.
SEE ALSO **crime**.

mugger hooligan, robber, ruffian,
thief, thug. SEE ALSO **criminal**.

muggy *muggy weather.* close, humid,

oppressive, steamy, stuffy, sultry, warm.

Muhammadan SEE **Islam**.

mule SEE **animal**.

multiply 1 SEE **mathematics.2** *Mice multiply quickly*. to breed, to increase, to reproduce.

multitude *I have a multitude of things to do*. host, large number, mass. SEE ALSO **crowd**.

mumble SEE **talk**.

mumps SEE **illness**.

munch to bite, to chew, to crunch, to gnaw. SEE ALSO **eat**.

mural SEE **picture**.

murder assassination, homicide. SEE ALSO **kill**.

murderer assassin, killer.

murderous *murderous bandits*. bloodthirsty, brutal, cruel, fierce, pitiless, ruthless, savage, vicious, violent.

murky *We couldn't see anything in the murky water*. cloudy, dark, dim, foggy, gloomy, sombre.

murmur SEE **sound, talk**.

muscle SEE **body**.

muscular *a muscular wrestler*. beefy, brawny, burly, strong, tough.

museum SEE **building**.

mushroom SEE **fungus**.

music 1 KINDS OF MUSICAL COMPOSITION ARE anthem, ballad, blues, calypso, carol, chamber music, chant, choral music, classical music, concerto, dirge, disco music, fanfare, folk music, hymn, improvisation, jazz, lullaby, march, opera, overture, pop music, reggae, rock, shanty, song, soul, spiritual, symphony. SEE ALSO **dance, sing**. **2** FOR FAMILIES OF MUSICAL INSTRUMENTS SEE **brass, keyboard, percussion, strings, woodwind**. **3** VARIOUS INSTRUMENTS ARE accordion, bagpipes, banjo, barrel-organ, bassoon, bugle, castanets, cello, clarinet, cornet, cymbals, double-bass, drum, fiddle, flute, glockenspiel, gong, guitar,

harmonica, harmonium, harp, harpsichord, horn, kettledrum, lute, lyre, mouth-organ, oboe, organ, piano, piccolo, recorder, saxophone, sitar, tambourine, timpani, tom-tom, triangle, trombone, trumpet, tuba, tubular bells, tuning fork, viola, violin, xylophone, zither. **4** VARIOUS MUSICIANS ARE bass, bugler, cellist, clarinettist, composer, conductor, contralto, drummer, fiddler, flautist, guitarist, harpist, instrumentalist, oboist, organist, percussionist, performer, pianist, piper, player, soloist, soprano, tenor, timpanist, treble, trombonist, trumpeter, violinist, virtuoso, vocalist. **5** GROUPS OF MUSICIANS ARE band, choir, chorus, duet, ensemble, group, orchestra, quartet, quintet, trio. **6** OTHER MUSICAL WORDS ARE baton, chord, chromatic scale, clef, crotchet, discord, flat, harmony, key, melody, minim, natural, note, octave, pitch, quaver, scale, semibreve, semiquaver, sharp, stave, tempo, theme, tone, tune, unison.

musical *We performed a musical at Christmas*. SEE **entertainment**.

music centre SEE **audio equipment**.

musician SEE **music**.

musket SEE **weapon**.

Muslim SEE **Islam**.

muslin SEE **cloth**.

mussel SEE **shellfish**.

mustard 1 SEE **food**. **2** *mustard and cress*. SEE **salad**.

muster *Can we muster a team for Saturday?* to assemble, to collect, to gather, to get together, to mobilize, to round up.

musty *The musty room needed airing*. damp, mildewed, mouldy, stale.

mute dumb, silent, speechless, tongue-tied. SEE ALSO **handicap**.

mutilate *The soldier was horribly mutilated in the explosion*. to cripple, to damage, to maim, to mangle. SEE ALSO **wound**.

mutinous *a mutinous crew*. defiant, disobedient, insubordinate, rebellious, unruly.

mutiny 1 *The starving crew organized a mutiny*. rebellion, revolt, rising. **2** *The crew mutinied*. to disobey, to rebel, to revolt, to rise up.

mutter SEE **talk**.

mutton SEE **meat**.

mutual *Friends usually have mutual interests*. common, joint, shared.

mysterious *a mysterious illness*. baffling, inexplicable, insoluble, puzzling, strange, unknown.

mystery 1 *Granny's sudden recovery was a mystery*. miracle. **2** *Maths is a mystery to Logan*. problem, puzzle, riddle.

myth SEE **writing**.

mythical *mythical monsters*. fabulous, fictional, imaginary, legendary, non-existent.

N n

nab (informal) *The head nabbed Logan before he could escape*. to arrest, to capture, to catch, to seize.

nag 1 SEE **horse**. **2** *Mum nags me about the washing-up*. to keep complaining, to pester, to scold.

nail SEE **fasten**.

nail varnish SEE **cosmetics**.

naked bare, nude, unclothed, uncovered, undressed.

name 1 *What's your name?* Christian name, first name, identity, nickname, surname, title. **2** *His parents named him Antony*. to baptize, to call, to christen. **3** *What did you name your story?* to entitle. **4** *They named Tony as captain*. to appoint, to choose, to elect, to nominate.

nameless anonymous, unnamed.

nanny *a child's nanny*. nurse.

nanny-goat SEE **female, goat**.

nap *to take a nap*: to doze, to nod off, to rest, to sleep, to snooze.

napalm SEE **weapon**.

narcotic SEE **drug**.

narrate *to narrate a story*. to describe, to recount, to relate, to tell.

narration *Whose voice was doing the narration?* account, commentary, description, speaking, story-telling.

narrative *an exciting narrative*. account, story, tale, yarn.

narrow fine, slender, slim, thin.

narrow-minded intolerant, old-fashioned, prejudiced, prim, prudish.

nasty ! The word *nasty* has many meanings. For some of the other words you can use SEE **unpleasant**.

nation *the nations of the world*. civilization, community, country, land, people, race, society, state. SEE ALSO **geography**.

national *national customs*. ethnic, racial.

nationalist SEE **politics**.

native 1 *I am a native of England*. citizen, inhabitant, resident. **2** *The early invaders fought the natives*. aboriginal, original inhabitant. ! Do not use *native* to mean *savage* or *uncivilized person*.

Nativity SEE **church**.

natural 1 *Many people say it's healthier to eat natural foods*. crude, raw, unprocessed, unrefined. **2** *a natural gift for music*. hereditary, inherited. **3** *a natural reaction*. normal, ordinary, regular, spontaneous. **4** *a natural pose*. authentic, realistic.

naturalist SEE **job**.

nature 1 *A naturalist loves nature*. natural environment, wildlife. **2** *He has a kind nature*. character, disposition, manner, personality, temperament. **3** *I collect coins, medals, and things of that nature*. kind, sort, type, variety.

naughty disobedient, impish, mischievous, troublesome, unruly. SEE ALSO **bad**.

nauseating *a nauseating mess*. disgusting, foul, revolting, sickening. SEE ALSO **unpleasant**.

nautical *nautical dress.* marine, naval, seafaring, sea-going.

navel SEE **body**.

navigate 1 *The captain navigated his ship through the strait.* to direct, to guide, to pilot, to sail, to steer. 2 INSTRUMENTS USED IN NAVIGATION ARE compass, sextant.

navy 1 armada, convoy, fleet. 2 FOR PEOPLE WHO WORK ON SHIPS SEE **sailor**.

navy blue SEE **colour**.

near adjacent to, close to.

nearly about, almost, around, not quite, practically.

neat 1 *a neat person.* clean, house-proud, tidy. 2 *a neat room.* orderly, shipshape, straight. 3 *neat clothes.* dainty, pretty, smart, spruce, trim.

necessary essential, important, indispensible, needed, required, unavoidable, vital.

neck SEE **body**.

necklace SEE **jewellery**.

need 1 *There's no need to shout.* necessity, obligation, requirement. 2 *The TV pictures made us aware of the need of the refugees.* poverty, suffering, want. 3 *What do you need?* to be short of, to lack, to require, to want. 4 *We need Logan to play in goal.* to depend on, to rely on.

needlework embroidery, sewing. SEE ALSO **art**.

needy *How can we help the needy?* destitute, deprived, impoverished, penniless, poor, poverty-stricken.

negative SEE **electricity, mathematics, photograph**. ! *Negative* is the opposite of *positive*.

neglect *Don't neglect your homework.* to disregard, to forget, to ignore, to miss, to overlook, to shirk, to skip.

negligent *negligent work.* careless, inattentive, reckless, sloppy, slovenly, thoughtless, uncaring.

negligible *a negligible amount of rain.* imperceptible, insignificant, slight, tiny, trifling, trivial, unimportant.

negotiate *to negotiate a price.* to arbitrate, to bargain, to discuss terms, to haggle.

neigh to whinny. SEE ALSO **sound**.

neighbourhood area, district, locality, place, region, vicinity, zone.

neighbouring adjacent, close, closest, near, nearest.

neighbourly *The people next door are a neighbourly crowd.* friendly, helpful, obliging. SEE ALSO **kind**.

neon light SEE **light**.

nephew SEE **family**.

nerve 1 SEE **body**. 2 *That steeplejack has some nerve!* bravery, courage, daring, (informal) guts, (informal) pluck, self-confidence. 3 (informal) *She's got a nerve, taking my pen!* cheek.

nervous *Tony gets nervous before an important race.* anxious, apprehensive, edgy, fearful, fidgety, flustered, highly-strung, jittery, jumpy, shy, strained, tense, timid, uneasy, (informal) uptight, worried.

nestle *The baby nestled up to his mother.* to cuddle, to lie comfortably, to snuggle.

nestling SEE **bird, young**.

net 1 criss-cross pattern, mesh, netting, network, web. 2 *to net a fish.* SEE **catch**.

netball SEE **sport**.

nettle SEE **weed**.

network 1 SEE **net**. 2 *a railway network.* organization, system.

neuralgia SEE **illness**.

neutral 1 *a neutral referee.* detached, disinterested, impartial, not involved, unbiased, unprejudiced. 2 *neutral colours.* indefinite, intermediate, middle.

new 1 *a new £5 note.* brand-new, clean, fresh, in mint condition, unused. 2 *a new invention.* modern, novel, recent, up-to-date.

news announcement, bulletin, communiqué, dispatch, information, message, notice, proclamation, report, statement, (old-fashioned) tidings.

newsagent SEE **shop**.

newspaper journal, paper, the press.

newt SEE **amphibious**.

next 1 *the next street*. adjacent, closest, nearest. 2 *the next bus*. following, subsequent, succeeding.

nibble SEE **eat**.

nice ! The word *nice* has many meanings. For some of the other words you can use SEE **beautiful, good, pleasant**.

nick 1 *I nicked my finger*. SEE **cut**. 2 (informal) *Logan nicked some ice-cream out of the fridge*. to pilfer, (informal) to pinch, to steal, to take.

nickel SEE **metal**.

nickname SEE **name**.

nicotine SEE **drug**.

niece SEE **family**.

night SEE **time**.

night-club SEE **entertainment**.

night-dress SEE **clothes**.

nightingale SEE **bird**.

nightmare SEE **dream**.

night-watchman SEE **job**.

nil SEE **nothing**.

nimble *nimble movements*. acrobatic, agile, deft, lively, quick-moving, swift.

nip 1 *A dog nipped my leg*. to bite, to pinch, to snap at, to squeeze, to sting. 2 (informal) *I nipped round to the shops*. SEE **move**.

nipper SEE **child**.

nipple SEE **body**.

nippy (informal) 1 *a nippy car*. fast, quick, rapid, speedy. 2 *nippy weather*. bitter, chilly, cold, frosty, icy, (informal) perishing, raw, wintry. SEE ALSO **weather**.

nit SEE **insect**.

nitrogen SEE **gas**.

noble 1 *a noble family*. aristocratic, high-born, princely, royal, titled. SEE ALSO **title**. 2 *a noble deed*. brave, chivalrous, courageous, gallant, glorious, heroic, honourable, virtuous, worthy. 3 *a noble building*. dignified, elegant, grand, imposing,

majestic, stately. SEE ALSO **splendid**.

nod 1 SEE **gesture**. 2 *to nod off*: to doze, to sleep, to snooze, to take a nap.

noise bedlam, clamour, commotion, din, hubbub, hullabaloo, pandemonium, racket, row, rumpus, uproar. FOR VARIOUS NOISES SEE **sound**.

noisy *a noisy class*. boisterous, deafening, loud, rowdy, uproarious.

nomad *nomads in the desert*. gypsy, traveller, wanderer.

nominate *We nominated Tony as captain*. to appoint, to choose, to elect, to name, to select.

nondescript SEE **ordinary**.

non-existent *Unicorns are non-existent*. fictitious, imaginary, made-up.

nonplussed *The head was nonplussed when we cheered him*. amazed, dumbfounded, speechless, stumped, stunned, thunderstruck.

nonsense balderdash, bilge, drivel, gibberish, rubbish, tripe, twaddle. ! These words are usually used informally.

non-stop *Logan talks non-stop*. ceaselessly, constantly, continually, continuously, persistently.

noodles SEE **food**.

noon midday. SEE ALSO **time**.

noose *a noose in a rope*. loop.

normal *normal temperature*. accustomed, average, common, conventional, customary, habitual, ordinary, regular, routine, typical, usual.

north SEE **geography**.

nose 1 SEE **body, head**. 2 *the nose of a plane*. bow, front. 3 *to nose about*. to look, to pry, to search.

nosey curious, inquisitive, prying.

nostalgic romantic, sentimental.

nostril SEE **body, head**.

notable 1 *a notable mistake*. conspicuous, extraordinary, noticeable, obvious, remarkable, striking. 2 *a notable visitor*. celebrated, distinguished, eminent, famous, important, noted, outstanding, prominent, renowned, well-known.

notch *a notch in a stick.* cut, nick.

note 1 *Write her a note.* communication, letter, message. **2** *a musical note.* SEE **music**. **3** *an angry note in her voice.* feeling, sound, tone. **4** *£5 notes.* SEE **money**. **5** *Did you note what she was wearing?* to heed, to mark, to mind, to notice, to observe, to remark, to take notice of. **6** *Note this in your book.* to jot, to record, to scribble, to write.

notebook exercise book, jotter.

nothing nought, zero. *In cricket*: duck. *In tennis*: love. *In football*: nil.

notice 1 *Did you notice what we've got for dinner?* to detect, to discern, to discover, to feel, to find, to mark, to observe, to see, to spy. **2** *Did you see the notice on the door?* advertisement, announcement, leaflet, message, placard, poster, sign, warning. **3** *Logan didn't take any notice.* attention, heed, regard.

noticeable *a noticeable improvement in the weather.* detectable, evident, obvious, perceptible, pronounced, unmistakable.

notify *If you see anything suspicious, notify the police.* to advise, to inform, to tell, to warn.

notion *I had a notion that Father Christmas kept reindeer.* belief, concept, idea, opinion, theory, thought.

notorious *a notorious thief.* infamous, scandalous, well-known, wicked.

nougat SEE **sweet**.

nought SEE **nothing**.

noun SEE **language**.

nourish 1 *Food nourishes us.* to feed, to strengthen. **2** *nourishing*: good for you, nutritious, wholesome.

nourishment SEE **food**.

novel 1 *That's a novel way of doing it!* different, new, original, strange, uncommon, unusual. **2** *Tony likes reading novels.* SEE **writing**.

novelist author. SEE ALSO **writer**.

novice apprentice, beginner, learner.

nozzle spout.

nuclear SEE **fuel, weapon**.

nucleus centre, core, heart, middle.

nude bare, naked, unclothed, uncovered.

nugget *a gold nugget.* ingot, lump.

nuisance *Don't let the dog be a nuisance to you.* annoyance, bother, inconvenience, irritation, pest, trouble, worry.

numb *The cold numbed our fingers.* to deaden, to paralyse.

number 1 digit, figure, integer, numeral. **2** VARIOUS NUMBERS ARE century, dozen, gross, score. **3** *a large number.* amount, quantity, sum, total. **4** *a musical number.* item, piece, song. **5** *a number of a magazine.* edition, issue, publication. **6** *The crowd numbered a thousand.* to add up to, to total, to work out at.

numeral digit, figure, integer, number.

numerous countless, innumerable, many, numberless, plentiful, plenty of, untold.

nun SEE **church**.

nurse 1 *a hospital nurse.* SEE **job, medicine**. **2** *a child's nurse*: nanny. **3** *to nurse a sick person.* to care for, to cherish, to look after, to mother, to tend. **4** *to nurse a baby.* to feed.

nursery crèche.

nursery school SEE **school**.

nursing home SEE **medicine**.

nut 1 kernel. **2** KINDS OF NUT ARE almond, chestnut, coconut, hazel, peanut, walnut. **3** SEE **food**.

nutritious good for you, nourishing, wholesome.

nuzzle SEE **touch**.

nylon SEE **cloth, material**.

nymph SEE **legend**.

O o

oak SEE **tree**.

oar SEE **vessel**.

oasis SEE **geography**.

oath 1 *He gave us his oath that he was telling the truth.* assurance, guarantee, pledge, promise, vow. 2 *He uttered some terrible oaths.* curse, exclamation, swear-word.

oats SEE **cereal**.

obedient *an obedient dog.* disciplined, docile, dutiful, law-abiding, well-behaved.

obey *Obey the rules.* to abide by, to be ruled by, to carry out, to conform to, to keep to, to submit to.

object 1 *What's that object you've found?* article, item, thing. 2 *What is the object of this exercise?* aim, goal, intention, objective, point, purpose, target. 3 *Mum objected because I got my feet wet.* to complain, to disapprove, to grouse, to grumble, to mind, to moan, to protest.

objection outcry, protest.

objectionable foul, nasty, offensive. SEE ALSO **unpleasant**.

objective 1 *The objective is to get the ball in the net.* aim, intention, object, purpose. 2 *Our objective was the top of the hill.* destination, goal, target.

obligation *You have an obligation to feed your pet.* duty, responsibility.

oblige 1 *obliged*: bound, certain, compelled, forced, required, sure. 2 *obliging*: accommodating, considerate, co-operative, helpful, kind, neighbourly, polite, thoughtful.

oblong rectangle. SEE ALSO **shape**.

obnoxious *an obnoxious taste.* disgusting, foul, loathsome, nasty, nauseating. SEE ALSO **unpleasant**.

oboe SEE **woodwind**.

obscene *obscene language.* coarse, crude, dirty, filthy, foul, improper, indecent, offensive, rude, smutty, vulgar.

obscure 1 *For some obscure reason he ran away.* dim, hidden, indistinct, puzzling, unclear, unheard of, unimportant, unknown. 2 *Mist obscured the view.* to cover, to conceal, to envelop, to hide, to mask, to shroud.

observant alert, astute, attentive, aware, careful, perceptive, shrewd, vigilant, watchful.

observation *Have you any observations?* comment, opinion, remark, statement.

observatory SEE **building**.

observe 1 *We observed the eclipse.* to contemplate, to detect, to follow, to look at, to note, to notice, to see, to spy, to stare at, to view, to watch. 2 *I observed that it was a nice day.* to comment, to explain, to remark, to say. 3 *Do you observe Christmas?* to celebrate, to keep, to remember.

observer bystander, eyewitness, onlooker, spectator, witness.

obsession *Motor bikes are Logan's latest obsession.* infatuation, mania, passion.

obsolete *an obsolete type of car.* antiquated, disused, old-fashioned, out-of-date.

obstacle *She put an obstacle in my way.* barricade, barrier, blockage, difficulty, hindrance, impediment, obstruction, problem, snag.

obstinate *Logan can be obstinate when he sets his heart on something.* defiant, dogged, inflexible, perverse, stubborn, unyielding, wilful.

obstreperous *We were rather obstreperous on the last day of term.* boisterous, disorderly, irrepressible, noisy, rough, rowdy, unruly.

obstruct *A fallen tree obstructed our progress.* to bar, to block, to deter, to halt, to hamper, to hinder, to impede, to interfere with, to stop.

obstruction barricade, barrier, blockage, obstacle.

obtain to acquire, to be given, to bring, to buy, to gain, to get, to get hold of, to procure, to purchase, to receive.

obtuse *Tony thought Lucy was being obtuse when she didn't understand.* dense, (informal) dim, dull, foolish, slow, stupid, (informal) thick.

obvious *Mr Brunswick has an obvious London accent.* clear, evident, notable, plain, prominent, pronounced, undisputed, unmistakable.

occasion 1 *A party is the occasion for a bit of fun.* chance, moment, opportunity, time. 2 *The wedding was a happy occasion.* ceremony, event, happening, incident, occurrence.

occasional *occasional showers.* infrequent, intermittent, rare, spasmodic, uncommon.

occupation activity, business, calling, employment, job, pastime, profession, trade, work.

occupy 1 *They won't allow six people to occupy a tiny flat like this.* to dwell in, to inhabit, to live in, to reside in. 2 *How do you occupy your time?* to fill, to take up, to use. 3 *The troops occupied the town.* to capture, to conquer, to invade, to take possession of. 4 *occupied*: active, busy, engaged.

occur 1 *When did the accident occur?* to befall, to come about, to happen, to take place. 2 *The same spelling mistake occurs throughout your story.* to arise, to appear, to be found, to crop up, to exist.

occurrence event, happening, incident, occasion, phenomenon.

ocean sea.

octagon SEE **shape**.

octave SEE **music**.

octopus SEE **animal**.

oculist SEE **medicine**.

odd 1 *odd behaviour.* abnormal, (informal) cranky, curious, freak, funny, incongruous, irregular, peculiar, queer, strange, uncommon, weird. 2 *an odd sock.* left over, remaining, single, spare.

ode SEE **poem**.

odious *We agreed that Nero was an odious person.* abominable, detestable, disgusting, hateful, loathsome, nasty, offensive, repulsive, revolting. SEE ALSO **unpleasant**.

odour SEE **smell**.

offence *a criminal offence.* crime, misdeed, sin, wrongdoing.

offend 1 *Tony offended granny by not writing.* to anger, to annoy, to displease, to insult, to irritate, to upset, to vex. 2 *to be offended*: to take umbrage.

offender criminal, delinquent, malefactor, wrongdoer.

offensive *offensive behaviour, offensive language, etc.* antisocial, coarse, disagreeable, disgusting, disrespectful, foul, improper, indecent, nasty, objectionable, rude, vulgar. SEE ALSO **unpleasant**.

offer 1 *He offered me a cup of tea.* to extend, to give, to present. 2 *He offered to come with me.* to propose, to suggest. 3 *Mr Brunswick made the garage an offer for the car.* bid, proposal, suggestion.

offering contribution, donation, gift, sacrifice.

office 1 bureau. 2 THINGS YOU FIND IN AN OFFICE ARE calculator, computer, copier, desk, diary, duplicator, enquiry desk, file, form, intercom, photocopier, stapler, stationery, switchboard, telephone, typewriter, word-processor. 3 PEOPLE WHO WORK IN AN OFFICE ARE cashier, clerk, receptionist, secretary, telephonist, typist.

officer 1 *an army officer.* SEE **rank**. 2 *an administrative officer.* SEE **official**. 3 *a police officer.* SEE **police**.

official 1 *an official document.* authorized, formal, proper. 2 *We spoke to an official.* authorized person, officer, responsible person.

officious *Dad hates that officious car-park attendant!* bumptious, (informal) cocky, interfering, self-important.

off-licence SEE **shop**.

offspring baby, child, descendant, family, young.

often again and again, constantly, frequently, regularly, repeatedly.

ogre giant, monster. SEE ALSO **legend**.

oil 1 SEE **fat, fuel**. 2 *Tony oiled his bike.* to grease, to lubricate.

oil-colour SEE **paint**.

oil-painting SEE **picture**.

oilskins SEE **clothes**.

oil-tanker SEE **vessel**.

oily *oily food.* fat, fatty, greasy.

ointment lotion. SEE ALSO **medicine**.

old 1 *old exhibits in a museum.* ancient, antiquated, antique, early, prehistoric, primitive, venerable. 2 *old people.* aged, elderly. 3 *old ruins.* decrepit, dilapidated. 4 *an old style.* former, old-fashioned, out-of-date. 5 *old bread.* stale.

old-fashioned 1 SEE **old**. 2 *old-fashioned ideas.* narrow-minded, prim, proper, prudish.

olive SEE **fruit, tree**.

omelette SEE **food**.

omen *They thought the thunder was an omen of some terrible event.* indication, premonition, sign, warning.

ominous *an ominous sound of thunder.* forbidding, grim, menacing, sinister, threatening, unlucky.

omit 1 *Why was Logan omitted from the team?* to drop, to eliminate, to exclude, to ignore, to leave out, to reject. 2 *Don't omit to sign your passport.* to fail, to neglect, to overlook, to skip.

omnibus SEE **book, vehicle**.

omnipotent almighty.

oncoming *oncoming cars.* approaching.

one-sided 1 *a one-sided referee.* biased, prejudiced, unfair. 2 *a one-sided match.* unbalanced, unequal, uneven.

onion SEE **vegetable**.

onlooker *The accident horrified the onlookers.* bystander, eyewitness, observer, spectator, witness.

onslaught *a fierce onslaught.* assault, attack, blitz, bombardment, charge.

ooze *Oil oozed out of the crack.* to dribble, to leak, to seep, to trickle.

opal SEE **jewellery**.

opaque *The muddy water was opaque.* cloudy, dark, murky, unclear.

open 1 *an open door.* ajar, unfastened, unlocked. 2 *an open space.* broad, empty, extensive, unfenced, wide, yawning. 3 *an open book.* spread out, unfolded. 4 *an open reply.* candid, frank, honest, outspoken, sincere, straightforward. 5 *an open insult.* blatant, obvious, unconcealed, undisguised. 6 *Open the door.* to undo, to unfasten, to unfold, to unlock, to unseal. 7 *The football season opens this week.* to begin, to commence, to start.

opening 1 *an opening in the fence.* breach, break, chink, crack, cut, gap, gash, hole, leak, mouth, outlet, rift, slit, slot, split, tear, vent. 2 *the opening of a concert.* beginning, commencement, start.

opera SEE **music, theatre**.

operate 1 *Do trains operate on Christmas Day?* to act, to function, to perform, to run. 2 *Can you operate this mowing-machine?* to deal with, to manage, to use, to work.

operation 1 *Granny had an operation.* surgery. SEE ALSO **medicine**. 2 *a military operation.* action, campaign, manoeuvre.

opinion *The detective had his own opinion about who was guilty.* attitude, belief, comment, conclusion, conviction, guess, idea, judgement, thought, view.

opium SEE **drug**.

opponent adversary, competitor, enemy, foe, opposition, rival.

opportunity *The weekend is a good opportunity to do some shopping.* chance, moment, occasion, time.

oppose to compete against, to contest, to contradict, to defy, to fight, to resist, to rival, to stand up to, to withstand.

opposite 1 *the opposite side of the road.* facing. 2 *opposite opinions.* conflicting, contradictory, different, incompatible, opposing.

oppress 1 *The owners oppressed the slaves.* to afflict, to depress, to exploit, to persecute, to trouble, to worry. 2 *oppressed*: downtrodden.

oppressive 1 *an oppressive ruler.* cruel, harsh, severe, tyrannical, unjust.

2 *oppressive weather.* close, hot, humid, muggy, stifling, sultry.

opt *Tony opted for rounders, and Lucy opted for cricket.* to choose, to pick, to select, to settle on, to vote for.

optical OPTICAL INSTRUMENTS ARE bifocals, binoculars, field-glasses, glasses, lens, magnifying glass, microscope, periscope, spectacles, sun-glasses, telescope.

optician SEE **job, medicine.**

optimistic *We were optimistic about our chances.* cheerful, confident, expectant, hopeful. !*Optimistic* is the opposite of *pessimistic.*

option *We had the option of beans or peas.* alternative, choice.

optional voluntary.

oral *Instead of writing, we gave an oral report.* by mouth, spoken.

orange SEE **colour, fruit.**

orangeade SEE **drink.**

orbit *The spacecraft made an orbit of the earth.* circuit, revolution.

orchard SEE **garden.**

orchestra band. SEE ALSO **music.**

orchid SEE **flower.**

ordeal *The long trek across the ice was a terrible ordeal.* difficulty, suffering, test, trial.

order **1** *The boss gives the orders.* command, decree, instruction. **2** *The head restored order.* calm, control, discipline, good behaviour, law and order, obedience, peace. **3** *Is your bike in good order?* condition, state. **4** *Put the library books in order.* arrangement, sequence, series, tidiness. **5** *Mrs Angel ordered us to be quiet.* to command, to compel, to direct, to instruct, to require. **6** *Tony ordered a new magazine.* to book, to reserve.

orderly **1** *orderly work.* careful, methodical, neat, organized, systematic, tidy, well-organized. **2** *orderly behaviour.* civilized, disciplined, law-abiding, well-behaved.

ordinary *ordinary people, ordinary things, etc.* accustomed, common, commonplace, conventional, customary, everyday, familiar, habitual, indifferent, mediocre, medium, middling, moderate, nondescript, normal, orthodox, plain, reasonable, regular, routine, satisfactory, standard, typical, undistinguished, unexciting, uninteresting, usual, well-known.

ore SEE **rock.**

organ **1** FOR ORGANS OF THE BODY SEE **body. 2** *a church organ.* SEE **music.**

organism **1** creature, living thing. **2** FOR NAMES OF VARIOUS ORGANISMS SEE **animal, plant.**

organization *a business organization.* alliance, association, body, business, club, company, corporation, firm, group, league, network, party, society, union.

organize **1** *We organized the library books.* to arrange, to classify, to group, to put in order, to sort. **2** *We organized an American football team.* to create, to establish, to mobilize, to set up. **3** *organized:* careful, civilized, methodical, orderly, scientific, systematic.

orgy party, revelry.

orienteering SEE **sport.**

origami SEE **art.**

origin *We discussed the origin of life on earth.* beginning, birth, cause, commencement, creation, source, start.

original **1** *the original inhabitants of a country.* earliest, first, initial. **2** *an original idea, an original story.* creative, fresh, imaginative, inventive, new, novel, unique, unusual.

originate *How did the name 'America' originate?* to arise, to begin, to commence, to emerge, to start.

ornament adornment, decoration.

ornamental decorative, fancy.

ornithology bird-watching. FOR OTHER SUBJECTS TO STUDY SEE **subject.**

orphan SEE **family.**

orthodox *Scientists are always questioning orthodox ideas.* accepted, conventional, official, ordinary, standard, traditional, usual.

osteopath SEE **medicine**.

ostrich SEE **bird**.

otter SEE **animal**.

ounce SEE **measure**.

outboard motor SEE **engine**.

outbreak *an outbreak of measles.* epidemic, plague.

outburst *an outburst of laughter.* eruption, explosion.

outcast exile, outlaw, refugee.

outcome *What was the outcome of your visit to the doctor?* consequence, effect, result, sequel.

outcry *There was an outcry when they stopped our bus service.* clamour, objection, protest.

outdo *Lucy can outdo anyone at gymnastics.* to beat, to exceed, to excel, to surpass, to top.

outfit *a skin-diving outfit.* apparatus, clothing, costume, equipment, gear, kit, rig.

outhouse shed. SEE ALSO **building**.

outing *an outing to the sea.* excursion, expedition, jaunt, tour, trip.

outlaw 1 *The outlaws hid in the mountains.* bandit, criminal, deserter, desperado, fugitive, outcast, renegade. 2 *Smoking has been outlawed in many places.* to ban, to forbid, to prohibit.

outlet exit, mouth, opening, way out.

outline 1 *I sketched a quick outline.* diagram, drawing, framework, sketch, summary. 2 *We saw the outline of someone passing the window.* figure, form, profile, shadow, shape.

outlook 1 *My window has a pleasant outlook.* prospect, scene, sight, view. 2 *The outlook for tomorrow is good.* forecast, prediction.

outlying *They travel by bus from outlying areas.* distant, remote.

outrage atrocity, crime, disgrace, scandal, sensation.

outrageous *outrageous behaviour.* disgraceful, infamous, monstrous, notorious, offensive, scandalous, shocking, wicked.

outside covering, exterior, shell, skin, surface.

outsider *Make outsiders feel welcome.* alien, foreigner, immigrant, visitor.

outskirts *the outskirts of the town.* edge, fringe, suburbs.

outspoken *Our trainer was outspoken about our terrible performance.* blunt, candid, direct, frank, honest, plain, straightforward.

outstanding 1 *an outstanding player.* conspicuous, distinguished, dominant, eminent, excellent, exceptional, great, notable, prominent, well-known. 2 *outstanding bills.* due, overdue, owing, unpaid.

outward *outward appearances.* external, exterior, outer, outside.

outwit *I was glad that the fox outwitted the hounds!* to cheat, to dupe, to fool, to hoodwink, to take in, to trick. SEE ALSO **deceive**.

oval SEE **shape**.

oven SEE **kitchen**.

overalls SEE **clothes**.

overcast cloudy, dull, gloomy. SEE ALSO **weather**.

overcoat SEE **clothes**.

overcome to beat, to conquer, to master, to overthrow, to overwhelm, to quell, to subdue, to suppress. SEE ALSO **defeat**.

overcrowd *The room was overcrowded.* to cram, to crush, to fill.

overdue 1 *The bus is overdue.* belated, delayed, late, unpunctual. 2 *The gas bill is overdue.* outstanding, owing, unpaid.

overflow *The lavatory cistern overflowed.* to brim over, to flood, to pour over, to run over, to spill.

overgrown *an overgrown garden.* tangled, uncut, unkempt, untidy, untrimmed, wild.

overhang *My book-shelf overhangs my bed.* to jut out, to project, to protrude, to stick out.

overhaul 1 *The garage overhauled Mr*

Brunswick's car. to renovate, to repair, to service. 2 *The fast train overhauled a goods train.* to catch up with, to overtake, to pass.

overhear *Logan overheard our conversation.* to eavesdrop, to listen in.

overjoyed delighted, ecstatic, elated, joyful. SEE ALSO **happy**.

overlook 1 *We mustn't overlook Logan when we do our Christmas cards.* to disregard, to forget, to ignore, to leave out, to miss, to neglect, to omit, to pay no attention to. 2 *My window overlooks the pie factory.* to face, to look at.

overpower 1 *She overpowered her attacker.* to beat, to keep off, to master, to overcome, to overwhelm. SEE ALSO **defeat**. 2 *overpowering*: irresistible.

overrun *A plague of mice overran the farm.* to infest, to invade, to march into, to occupy, to swarm over, to take over.

overseas abroad.

oversight *It wasn't deliberate, just an oversight.* blunder, error, mistake, slip-up.

overtake to catch up with, to overhaul, to pass.

overthrow SEE **overcome**.

overture SEE **music**.

overturn 1 *The boat overturned.* to capsize, to turn over, to turn turtle. 2 *The cat overturned the milk.* to spill, to tip over, to topple, to upset.

overweight chubby, dumpy, fat, flabby, gross, heavy, plump, podgy, portly, stout, tubby.

overwhelm 1 *We overwhelmed the opposition.* to beat, to conquer, to crush, to overcome, to overpower, to overthrow, to rout. SEE ALSO **defeat**. 2 *A tidal wave overwhelmed the town.* to drown, to engulf, to inundate, to submerge, to swamp.

owing 1 *You must pay whatever is owing.* due, outstanding, overdue, unpaid. 2 *owing to*: because of, thanks to.

owl SEE **bird**.

own 1 *Who owns a catapult?* to have, to

hold, to possess. 2 *Logan owned up.* to acknowledge, to admit, to confess.

owner 1 *the owner of a dog.* possessor. 2 *the owner of a business.* boss, proprietor.

oxen SEE **cattle**.

oxtail SEE **meat**.

oxygen SEE **gas**.

oyster SEE **shellfish**.

P p

pace 1 *Move forward two paces.* step, stride. 2 *The front runner set a quick pace.* movement, rate, speed, velocity. 3 SEE **walk**.

pacify *We pacified the baby by giving him some toys.* to appease, to calm, to quieten, to soothe.

pack 1 *a pack of biscuits.* box, bundle, package, packet, parcel. 2 *a pack of wolves.* SEE **group**. 3 *Pack your things in a box.* to fill, to load, to put, to stow. 4 *They packed us into the minibus.* to cram, to crowd, to huddle, to jam, to squeeze, to stuff.

package bale, bundle, pack, packet, parcel.

pact *We made a pact with our rivals.* agreement, alliance, armistice, bargain, contract, deal, peace, settlement, treaty, truce, understanding.

pad 1 *a pad to kneel on.* cushion, padding, wad. 2 *a writing pad.* jotter, notebook. 3 *We padded the seat with soft material.* to cover, to fill, to protect, to stuff. 4 *padding*: upholstery.

paddle *We paddled in the sea.* to wade. SEE ALSO **walk**.

paddle-steamer SEE **vessel**.

paddock field, meadow, pasture.

padlock lock. SEE ALSO **fasten**.

pagan atheist, heathen. ! *Pagan* and *heathen* often sound insulting.

page 1 *a page of a book.* leaf, sheet. 2 *a page-boy*: SEE **servant**.

pageant parade, procession.

pageantry *The royal wedding was conducted with great pageantry.* ceremony, formality, grandeur, pomp, ritual, spectacle.

pagoda SEE **building**.

pail bucket. SEE ALSO **container**.

pain ache, agony, anguish, hurt, ordeal, pang, soreness, spasm, sting, suffering, throb, torment, torture, twinge.

painful 1 *a painful wound.* agonizing, excruciating, inflamed, raw, sore. 2 *to be painful:* to ache, to hurt, to smart, to sting, to throb.

painless *My visit to the dentist was quite painless.* comfortable, easy, effortless.

paint 1 KINDS OF PAINT ARE emulsion, enamel, gloss paint, lacquer, matt paint, oil-colour, pastel, varnish, water-colour, whitewash. 2 *Mr Brunswick painted the front room.* to decorate. 3 SEE **picture**.

painter SEE **art**.

painting SEE **picture**.

pair brace, couple.

pal (informal) *Be a good pal and lend me £1!* chum, friend, (informal) mate.

palace castle, château, mansion, stately home. SEE ALSO **building**.

pale 1 *a pale face.* colourless, pasty, wan, whitish. 2 *pale colours.* dim, faint, light.

paling fence, railing, stockade.

palm 1 *the palm of your hand.* SEE **hand**. 2 *a palm-tree.* SEE **tree**.

Palm Sunday SEE **church**.

pampas-grass SEE **grass**.

pamper *Tony pampers his dog.* to humour, to indulge, to spoil.

pamphlet *a pamphlet about road safety.* booklet, brochure, catalogue, leaflet.

pan SEE **container, cook, kitchen**.

pancake SEE **food**.

panda SEE **animal**.

panda car police car. SEE ALSO **vehicle**.

pandemonium *There was pandemonium when Logan's rats escaped.* bedlam, chaos, commotion, confusion, disorder, hubbub, hullabaloo, racket, riot, row, rumpus, tumult, turmoil, uproar.

pane glass, window.

panel *a panel of experts.* committee, group, jury, team.

pang *a pang of toothache.* ache, throb, twinge. SEE ALSO **pain**.

panic *If a fire starts, we don't want any panic!* alarm, fear, horror, hysteria, stampede, terror.

pannier SEE **container**.

panorama *We saw a beautiful panorama from the top of the hill.* landscape, prospect, scene, view, vista.

pansy SEE **flower**.

pant 1 to gasp, to puff, to wheeze. 2 *panting:* breathless, exhausted, puffed, tired out.

panther SEE **animal**.

panties briefs, knickers, pants. SEE ALSO **underclothes**.

pantomime SEE **theatre**.

pantry food cupboard, larder. SEE ALSO **house**.

pants briefs, knickers, panties, shorts, trousers, trunks, underpants. SEE ALSO **underclothes**.

paper 1 KINDS OF PAPER ARE card, cardboard, newspaper, notepaper, papyrus, parchment, postcard, stationery, tissue-paper, toilet-paper, wallpaper, wrapping-paper, writing-paper. 2 *Mrs Angel keeps important papers in a file.* certificates, deeds, documents, forms, records. 3 *Mr Brunswick papered the front room.* to decorate.

paperback SEE **book**.

papyrus SEE **paper**.

parable SEE **writing**.

parade *a fancy dress parade.* cavalcade, march, pageant, procession.

paradise heaven.

paraffin SEE **fuel**.

paragraph SEE **language**.

parallel SEE **mathematics**.

paralyse 1 *The shock paralysed him.* to deaden, to numb, to petrify.

2 *paralysed*: immobile, immovable, rigid. SEE ALSO **handicap**.

paralysis SEE **illness**.

parapet SEE **castle**.

paraphernalia equipment, gear, tackle.

paraplegic SEE **handicap**.

paratroops SEE **armed services**.

parcel bale, bundle, package, packet.

parched 1 *Plants won't grow in parched ground*. arid, barren, dry, lifeless, sterile. 2 (informal) *I'm parched!* (informal) gasping, thirsty.

parchment SEE **paper**.

pardon 1 *The government issued a pardon for all prisoners*. amnesty, reprieve. 2 *The judge pardoned him*. to excuse, to forgive, to let off, to overlook, to reprieve, to set free, to spare.

parent SEE **family**.

parish SEE **church, geography**.

park KINDS OF PARK ARE car-park, gardens, recreation ground, safari park. SEE ALSO **town**.

parka SEE **clothes**.

parliament SEE **government**.

parlour SEE **house**.

parrot SEE **bird, pet**.

parry *to parry a blow*. to fend off, to push away, to repel, to repulse, to ward off.

parsley SEE **herb**.

parsnip SEE **vegetable**.

parson clergyman, minister, pastor, preacher, priest, vicar. SEE ALSO **church, job**.

part 1 *Which part of the chicken do you prefer?* bit, fraction, fragment, particle, piece, portion, share. 2 *They sell computers in another part of the shop*. branch, department, division, section, sector. 3 *Did the garage get the parts for the car?* component, unit. 4 *Which part of the country do you come from?* area, district, region. 5 *It would be terrible if the caravan parted from the car*. to detach, to disconnect, to divide, to separate, to split.

partial 1 *Our play was only a partial success*. imperfect, incomplete, unfinished. 2 *to be partial to*: to be fond of, to enjoy, to like.

participate *to participate in a game*. to be involved, to join, to share, to take part.

particle *a particle of dust*. atom, bit, crumb, fraction, fragment, grain, piece, scrap, shred, speck.

particular 1 *Logan has a particular way of writing*. distinct, individual, personal, special, specific. 2 *Our cat's particular about food*. (informal) choosey, fastidious, finicky, fussy. 3 *in particular*: *Are you writing to anyone in particular?* important, notable, outstanding. 4 *particulars*: *Give me the particulars*. details, facts, information.

partisan SEE **fighter**.

partition panel, room-divider, screen, wall.

partner accomplice, ally, assistant, collaborator, confederate.

partridge SEE **bird**.

party 1 KINDS OF PARTY ARE ball, banquet, barbecue, birthday party, celebration, Christmas party, dance, disco, feast, function, gathering, orgy, picnic, reception, social, wedding. 2 SEE **group**.

pass 1 *We watched the traffic pass*. to go by, to move along, to proceed. 2 *We passed a lot of other cars*. to cross, to overhaul, to overtake. 3 *The time passed*. to elapse. 4 *The pain soon passed*. to disappear, to fade, to vanish. 5 *Please pass the books round*. to circulate, to deal out, to deliver, to give, to hand over, to offer, to present, to share, to submit, to supply. 6 *a mountain pass*. defile, gorge, ravine, valley. SEE ALSO **geography**. 7 *a bus pass*. permit, ticket.

passable 1 *The food was passable*. acceptable, adequate, all right, mediocre, ordinary, satisfactory, tolerable. 2 *The snow has gone and the road is passable again*. clear, open.

passage 1 corridor, hall. SEE ALSO **house**. 2 *a secret passage*. tunnel. 3 *We read an exciting passage from the* *book.* episode, extract, piece, quotation, scene, section.

passenger traveller.

passer-by bystander.

passion *a passion for adventure, sexual passion.* appetite, desire, emotion, enthusiasm, infatuation, love, lust, thirst, urge.

passionate 1 *passionate love.* burning, emotional, fervent, hot, intense, lustful, sexy. 2 *a passionate interest in something.* avid, eager, enthusiastic.

Passover SEE **Jew, time.**

passport SEE **document.**

pasta SEE **food.**

paste adhesive, glue, gum. SEE ALSO **fasten.**

pastel SEE **paint.**

pastille SEE **medicine, sweet.**

pastime *Mr Brunswick's favourite pastime is water-skiing.* activity, amusement, diversion, entertainment, game, hobby, occupation, recreation.

pastor SEE **parson.**

pastry SEE **food.**

pasture field, meadow, paddock.

pasty 1 *Lucy looked pasty after having flu.* anaemic, colourless, ill, pale, (informal) poorly, unwell, wan. 2 *a meat pasty.* SEE **food.**

pat to caress, to dab, to slap, to stroke. SEE ALSO **hit, touch.**

patch *Tony patched a hole in his jeans.* to darn, to mend, to repair, to sew up, to stitch up.

patchwork SEE **art, cloth.**

patchy *The fog was patchy.* changeable, erratic, inconsistent, uneven, unpredictable, variable.

pâté SEE **food.**

paternal fatherly.

path alley, footpath, pathway, pavement, towpath, track. SEE ALSO **road.**

pathetic *It was pathetic to see how badly the dog had been treated.* moving, piteous, pitiful, touching, tragic. SEE ALSO **sad.**

patience 1 *The people in the queue showed great patience.* calmness, endurance, restraint, self-control. 2 *a game of patience.* SEE **cards.**

patient 1 *a patient animal.* calm, docile, easygoing, quiet, serene, tolerant. 2 *a patient worker.* determined, persevering, persistent, untiring. 3 *a patient at a hospital.* out-patient, sufferer. SEE ALSO **medicine.**

patio terrace. SEE ALSO **garden.**

patrol 1 guard, look-out, sentinel, sentry, watchmen. SEE ALSO **armed services.** 2 *patrol car:* SEE **vehicle.**

patron saint SEE **church.**

patter SEE **sound.**

pattern 1 *Is there a pattern I can copy?* example, guide, model, prototype. 2 *There are nice patterns in my wallpaper.* decoration, design, figure, shape.

pauper beggar, tramp, vagrant. SEE ALSO **poor.**

pause 1 *We had a pause for a drink.* break, delay, gap, interruption, interval, lull, rest, stop. 2 *We paused for a drink.* to halt, to hang back, to hesitate, to rest, to stop, to wait.

pavement SEE **path.**

pavilion SEE **building, sport.**

paw 1 foot. 2 *to paw the ground.* SEE **touch.**

pawn SEE **chess.**

pawnbroker SEE **shop.**

pay 1 *How much did you pay?* to give, to hand over, to spend. 2 *Did Logan pay his dad for the broken window?* to compensate, to recompense, to repay. 3 *How much pay do you get?* earnings, income, salary, wages.

payment *We make a payment to the wildlife fund every month.* contribution, cost, deposit, expenditure, fee, instalment, subscription, toll.

pea SEE **vegetable.**

peace 1 *After the war there was a period of peace.* agreement, concord, friendliness, harmony, order. 2 *The two sides agreed on terms for peace.* alliance, armistice, pact, treaty, truce. 3 *We enjoy the peace of the* *countryside.* calmness, quiet, serenity, stillness, tranquillity.

peaceful *a peaceful evening, peaceful music.* balmy, calm, easy, gentle, placid, pleasant, quiet, serene, soothing, still, tranquil, untroubled.

peach SEE **fruit.**

peacock SEE **bird.**

peak 1 *snowy peaks.* hill, mountain, summit, tip, top. 2 *The music rose to a peak.* climax, crisis, height, pinnacle.

peal SEE **bell, sound.**

peanut SEE **nut.**

pear SEE **fruit.**

pearl SEE **jewellery.**

peasant farm worker, labourer.
! *Peasant* refers to a poor worker in certain countries.

peat SEE **fuel, garden.**

pebbles cobbles, gravel, stones.

peck SEE **eat.**

peckish (informal) *I'm feeling peckish.* hungry, famished, ravenous, starving.

peculiar *Logan has a peculiar way of writing.* abnormal, curious, different, distinctive, funny, individual, odd, particular, queer, special, strange, uncommon, unique, unusual, weird.

pedal SEE **bicycle, travel.**

pedestrian walker. SEE ALSO **travel.**

pedigree *Do you know the dog's pedigree?* ancestry, family history.

peel 1 *orange peel.* rind, skin. 2 *to peel the covering off something.* to skin, to strip.

peep SEE **look.**

peer 1 SEE **look.** 2 aristocrat, lord, noble, nobleman, noblewoman, peeress. SEE ALSO **title.**

peevish *a peevish mood.* bad-tempered, cross, grumpy, irritable, petulant, snappy, testy.

peewit SEE **bird.**

peg SEE **fasten.**

Pekingese SEE **dog.**

pelican SEE **bird.**

pellet ball, pill.

pelt 1 *The monkeys pelted us with peanuts.*

to bombard. 2 *They pelted peanuts at us.* SEE **throw.**

pen 1 ball-point, felt-tipped pen, fountain pen. SEE ALSO **write.** 2 *a pen for animals.* cage, compound, coop, enclosure, fold, run.

penalize *He was penalized for a foul.* to punish.

penalty *We have to pay the penalty for doing wrong.* fine, forfeit, punishment.

pencil SEE **write.**

pendant SEE **jewellery.**

pendulum SEE **clock.**

penetrate *Dad's drill couldn't penetrate the concrete.* to bore through, to enter, to pierce, to probe, to puncture.

penguin SEE **bird.**

penicillin SEE **medicine.**

peninsula SEE **geography.**

penitent *Lucy was penitent after breaking the window.* apologetic, regretful, remorseful, repentant, sorry.

penknife SEE **tool.**

penniless *a penniless beggar.* destitute, impoverished, needy, poor, poverty-stricken.

penny-farthing SEE **cycle.**

pension SEE **money.**

pensive *You look pensive: what are you thinking about?* dreamy, grave, philosophical, reflective, serious, thoughtful.

pentagon SEE **shape.**

pentathlon SEE **athletics.**

Pentecost SEE **church.**

peony SEE **flower.**

people folk, human beings, humanity, individuals, mankind, mortals, persons. SEE ALSO **person.**

pepper SEE **spice.**

peppermint SEE **sweet.**

peppery SEE **taste.**

perceive 1 *We perceived a dim shape on the horizon.* to detect, to discern, to notice, to recognize, to see. 2 *At last I began to perceive what she meant.* to feel, to know, to sense, to understand.

percentage SEE **mathematics.**

perceptible *a perceptible drop in temperature.* noticeable.

perceptive *Mrs Angel is a perceptive judge of character.* astute, clever, observant, shrewd.

perch 1 SEE **fish**. 2 *a bird's perch.* roost.

percolator SEE **kitchen**.

percussion PERCUSSION INSTRUMENTS ARE castanets, cymbal, drum, glockenspiel, gong, kettledrum, tambourine, timpani, tom-tom, triangle, tubular bells, xylophone. SEE ALSO **music**.

perennial SEE **plant**.

perfect 1 *a perfect performance.* excellent, faultless, ideal. 2 *a perfect example.* in mint condition, pure, undamaged. 3 *a perfect fit.* accurate, correct, exact, precise. 4 (informal) *perfect chaos.* absolute, complete.

perforate *If you perforate a groundsheet the damp comes through.* to bore through, to pierce, to penetrate, to puncture.

perform 1 *to perform your duty.* to accomplish, to achieve, to carry out, to commit, to complete, to do, to execute, to finish. 2 *to perform on the stage.* to act, to appear, to dance, to play, to present, to produce, to sing.

performance 1 *We did a special performance for the parents.* ballet, concert, matinée, opera, play, première, preview, production, show. SEE ALSO **theatre**. 2 *Logan isn't ill: he's only putting on a performance.* act, deception, pretence.

performer FOR VARIOUS PERFORMERS SEE **entertainment, music, theatre**.

perfume 1 aroma, fragrance, odour, scent, smell, whiff. 2 SEE **cosmetics**.

perhaps maybe, possibly.

peril *Sailors face the perils of the sea.* danger, hazard, risk, threat.

perimeter *the perimeter of a field.* border, boundary, circumference, edge.

period age, era, interval, phase, season, session, spell, stretch, term, while. SEE ALSO **time**.

periodical journal, magazine, paper.

periscope SEE **optical**.

perish 1 *Many birds perish in the cold weather.* to die, to expire, to fall, to pass away. 2 *Soft fruit perishes if it isn't used quickly.* to decay, to decompose, to disintegrate, to go bad, to rot.

perky *I felt perky again after I had a sleep.* alert, animated, frisky, jaunty, lively, playful, sprightly, vivacious.

permanent *The unfortunate woman suffers from a permanent headache.* chronic, constant, continual, continuous, enduring, everlasting, incessant, lasting, lifelong, perpetual, persistent, stable, unending.

permissible *Did he have a permissible excuse?* allowable, lawful, legal, permitted, proper, right, valid.

permission *We had Mrs Angel's permission to go home.* authority, approval, consent.

permit 1 *Have you got a permit to fish here?* authorization, licence, pass, permission, ticket, warrant. 2 *Dad never permits smoking in the house.* to agree to, to allow, to approve of, to authorize, to consent to, to license, to tolerate.

perpendicular SEE **mathematics**.

perpetual *Mrs Angel hates Logan's perpetual chattering.* ceaseless, chronic, constant, continual, continuous, endless, eternal, everlasting, incessant, interminable, non-stop, permanent, persistent, recurrent, unending.

perplex *The mystery of the missing money perplexed us.* to baffle, to bewilder, to confuse, to muddle, to puzzle, to stump.

persecute *People are sometimes persecuted for their religious beliefs.* to bully, to intimidate, to oppress, to terrorize, to torment, to victimize.

persevere *You'll succeed in the end if you persevere.* to be diligent, to be patient, to carry on, to continue, to endure, to persist.

persist 1 *You'll succeed in the end if you*

persist. SEE **persevere.** 2 *How long is this snow going to persist?* to go on, to keep on, to last.

persistent 1 *a persistent cold.* ceaseless, chronic, constant, continuous, endless, eternal, everlasting, incessant, interminable, lasting, permanent, perpetual, recurrent, unending. 2 *a persistent worker.* determined, dogged, patient, resolute, stubborn, unwavering.

person adolescent, adult, baby, boy, child, gentleman, girl, human being, individual, infant, lad, lady, lass, man, mortal, teenager, toddler, woman, youngster, youth. SEE ALSO **people.**

personal 1 *personal characteristics.* distinct, distinctive, individual, particular, private, special, unique. 2 *personal details.* confidential, intimate, private, secret.

personnel *The boss issued an announcement for all personnel in the factory.* employees, people, workers.

perspire to sweat.

persuade 1 *We persuaded Logan to play in goal.* to coax, to entice, to induce, to tempt, to urge. 2 *She persuaded me that she was right.* to convince, to win over.

persuasion *It took a lot of persuasion to convince him.* argument, brain-washing, conditioning, propaganda.

persuasive *a persuasive argument.* convincing, eloquent, influential.

perturb *The bad news perturbed us.* to alarm, to distress, to disturb, to excite, to frighten, to scare, to shake, to upset, to worry.

perverse *It's perverse of Logan to buy hot dogs when we want ice-cream.* contrary, disobedient, obstinate, rebellious, stubborn, tiresome, unreasonable.

pervert *He was accused of trying to pervert a witness.* to bribe, to corrupt, to lead astray.

pessimistic *I'm afraid I'm pessimistic about our chances.* despairing, gloomy, hopeless, morbid, unhappy. SEE

ALSO **sad.** *Pessimistic* is the opposite of *optimistic.*

pest 1 *Ants can be a pest in the garden.* annoyance, nuisance. 2 *pests:* vermin.

pester *Don't pester me while I'm busy!* to annoy, to bait, to bother, to harass, to molest, to nag, to plague, to torment, to trouble, to worry.

pesticide SEE **garden, poison.**

pet 1 CREATURES COMMONLY KEPT AS PETS ARE budgerigar, canary, cat, dog, ferret, fish, gerbil, goldfish, guinea-pig, hamster, mouse, parrot, pigeon, rabbit, rat, tortoise. SEE ALSO **animal, bird.** 2 *Who's teacher's pet, then?* darling, favourite. 3 *The dog loves you to pet him.* to caress, to fondle, to stroke. SEE ALSO **touch.**

petal SEE **plant.**

petition *We organized a petition against the ending of our bus service.* appeal, entreaty, plea, request.

petrel SEE **bird.**

petrify *The scream petrified me!* to appal, to paralyse, to scare stiff, to terrify. SEE ALSO **frighten.**

petrol (informal) gas, gasoline. SEE ALSO **fuel.**

petticoat SEE **clothes.**

petty *5p is a petty amount to quarrel over!* insignificant, minor, small, trifling, trivial, unimportant.

petulant *a petulant mood.* bad-tempered, cross, grumpy, irritable, peevish, snappy, sulky, sullen, testy.

pew SEE **furniture.**

pewter SEE **metal.**

phantom *I don't believe you saw phantoms in the graveyard!* apparition, ghost, hallucination, illusion, poltergeist, spectre, spirit, (informal) spook, vision.

phase period, stage, step, time.

pheasant SEE **bird.**

phenomenal *The winner of the quiz had a phenomenal memory.* amazing, exceptional, extraordinary, fantastic, incredible, notable, remarkable, singular, unbelievable.

phenomenon *An eclipse is a rare phenomenon.* happening, event, occurrence.

philosophical *Mrs Brunswick was philosophical about losing her purse.* calm, patient, reasonable, resigned, thoughtful.

philosophy SEE **subject**.

phobia SEE **illness**.

phone *I phoned granny.* to call, to dial, to ring, to telephone.

phoney (informal) *He had a phoney Welsh accent.* artificial, bogus, faked, false, synthetic, unreal.

phosphorescent glowing, luminous, shining. SEE ALSO **light**.

photocopier SEE **office**.

photocopy to copy, to duplicate, to print, to reproduce.

photograph KINDS OF PHOTOGRAPH ARE enlargement, film, negative, photo, print, slide, snap, snapshot, transparency. SEE ALSO **picture**.

photographer SEE **job**.

photography WORDS TO DO WITH PHOTOGRAPHY ARE camera, cine-camera, to develop, exposure, to focus, SEE **photograph**, Polaroid, to print, reflex camera, telephoto lens, zoom lens.

phrase SEE **language**.

physical 1 *Do ghosts have a physical existence?* solid, tangible. 2 *physical exercise.* bodily.

physician doctor. SEE ALSO **medicine**.

physics SEE **science**.

physiotherapist SEE **job, medicine**.

piano SEE **keyboard, music**.

piccolo SEE **woodwind**.

pick 1 *to dig with a pick.* SEE **tool**. 2 *Pick a partner.* to choose, to decide on, to elect, to name, to nominate, to opt for, to prefer, to select, to settle on, to vote for. 3 *to pick flowers, to pick strawberries.* to collect, to cut, to gather, to harvest, to pull off, to take.

pickaxe SEE **tool**.

picket SEE **group**.

pickle 1 SEE **food**. 2 *to pickle onions.* to preserve. SEE ALSO **cook**.

pickpocket SEE **criminal**.

pick-up SEE **audio equipment, vehicle**.

picnic SEE **meal**.

picture 1 KINDS OF PICTURE ARE cartoon, collage, drawing, doodle, engraving, graffiti, illustration, landscape, likeness, mosaic, mural, oil-painting, painting, photograph, portrait, print, self-portrait, sketch, slide, transfer, transparency. 2 WAYS OF MAKING A PICTURE ARE to depict, to draw, to illustrate, to paint, to photograph, to portray, to represent, to sketch. 3 *Can you picture what the world will be like in 100 years?* to conceive, to dream up, to imagine, to think up, to visualize.

picturesque *picturesque scenery.* attractive, charming, pretty, quaint. SEE ALSO **beautiful**.

pie SEE **food**.

piebald SEE **horse**.

piece 1 *a piece of cake, a piece of wood, etc.* bar, bit, bite, block, chip, chunk, crumb, division, dollop, fraction, fragment, grain, helping, hunk, lump, morsel, part, particle, portion, scrap, section, segment, share, slab, slice, snippet, speck, stick, tablet. 2 *a piece of a machine.* component, element, unit. 3 *a piece of good news.* case, example, instance, specimen. 4 *a piece of music.* composition, item, number, passage, work.

pier jetty, landing-stage. SEE ALSO **dock, seaside**.

pierce 1 *The needle pierced the skin.* to bore, to drill, to go through, to perforate, to penetrate, to prick, to puncture, to stab. 2 *piercing: a piercing scream.* deafening, loud, sharp, shrill.

pig hog, sow, swine. SEE ALSO **farm**.

pigeon SEE **bird, pet**.

piggy-bank money-box.

pigmy dwarf, midget. !These words sometimes sound insulting.

pigsty SEE **farm**.

pigtail SEE **hair**.

pike SEE **fish, weapon**.

pilchard SEE **fish**.

pile 1 *a pile of rubbish.* heap, mass, mound, stack. 2 *Pile everything in the corner.* to accumulate, to assemble, to bring together, to collect, to gather, to heap up, to mass, to stack up.

pilfer *He was caught pilfering goods from a shop.* (informal) to nick, (informal) to pinch, to steal, to take. SEE ALSO **crime**.

pilgrim traveller.

pilgrimage SEE **journey**.

pill capsule, pellet. SEE ALSO **medicine**.

pillar column, pile, post, prop, shaft, support.

pillar-box letter-box, postbox.

pillow bolster. SEE ALSO **bedclothes**.

pilot 1 DIFFERENT KINDS OF PILOT ARE airman, coxswain, guide, helmsman. SEE ALSO **job**. 2 *He piloted us back to safety.* to drive, to guide, to fly, to navigate, to steer.

pilot-light SEE **light**.

pimples boils, rash, spots.

pin SEE **fasten**.

pinafore apron. SEE ALSO **clothes**.

pincers SEE **tool**.

pinch 1 *You hurt me when you pinched my arm.* to nip, to squeeze. 2 (informal) *Who pinched my pencil?* SEE **steal**.

pine 1 SEE **tree**. 2 *The dog pined when his master died.* to mope, to mourn, to waste away. 3 *In the winter I pine for some warm sunshine!* to hanker after, to long for, to miss, to yearn for.

pineapple SEE **fruit**.

ping SEE **sound**.

ping-pong SEE **sport**.

pink 1 SEE **colour**. 2 SEE **flower**.

pinnacle *the pinnacle of his career.* climax, height, peak, summit, top.

pint SEE **measure**.

pioneer discoverer, explorer, settler.

pip *an orange pip.* seed, stone.

pipe 1 *a water pipe.* hose, pipeline, tube. 2 SEE **smoke**.

piper SEE **music**.

pirate buccaneer. SEE ALSO **criminal**.

pistol SEE **weapon**.

piston SEE **vehicle**.

pit 1 *a deep pit.* abyss, chasm, crater, hole. 2 *The miners work in a pit.* mine, quarry, shaft, working.

pitch 1 tar. 2 *pitch-black*: SEE **black**. 3 *musical pitch.* SEE **music**. 4 *a football pitch.* SEE **sport**. 5 *to pitch a tent.* to erect, to put up, to set up. 6 *I pitched a stone into the pond.* to bowl, to cast, (informal) to chuck, to fling, to hurl, to lob, to sling, to throw, to toss. 7 *The boat pitched about in the storm.* to lurch, to plunge, to rock, to roll, to toss about.

pitcher SEE **container**.

pitchfork SEE **farm**.

piteous SEE **pitiful**.

pitfall danger, trap.

pitiful 1 *The injured animal was a pitiful sight.* heart-breaking, pathetic, piteous, touching. SEE ALSO **sad**. 2 *Logan made a pitiful attempt to stop the ball.* contemptible, miserable, useless, worthless.

pitiless *a pitiless attack.* bloodthirsty, callous, heartless, relentless, ruthless. SEE ALSO **cruel**.

pity *The muggers showed no pity.* compassion, feeling, kindness, mercy, sympathy.

pizza SEE **food**.

placard *an advertising placard.* bill, notice, poster, sign.

place 1 *Mark the place on the map.* location, point, position, site, situation, spot. 2 *What is your favourite place for a holiday?* area, country, district, locality, neighbourhood, region, town. SEE ALSO **geography**. 3 *Let's meet at your place.* SEE **house**. 4 *The hall has places for 90 people.* chair, seat. 5 *Place your things on the table.* to arrange, to deposit, to lay, to locate, to position, to put down, to rest, to set down, to situate, to stand, to station.

placid 1 *a placid lake.* calm, peaceful, quiet, tranquil, untroubled. 2 *a placid character*. cool, level-headed, mild, sensible, unexcitable.

plague 1 epidemic, outbreak. SEE ALSO **illness**. 2 *The flies plagued us*. to annoy, to bother, to disturb, to irritate, to molest, to pester, to trouble, to vex, to worry.

plaice SEE **fish**.

plain 1 *She gave a plain signal*. apparent, certain, clear, definite, distinct, evident, obvious, unmistakable. 2 *She wore a plain dress*. austere, simple, undecorated. 3 *She looked quite plain until she smiled*. ordinary, unattractive. 4 *He did some plain speaking*. blunt, candid, direct, frank, honest, outspoken, straightforward. 5 *We travelled across a wide plain*. SEE **geography**.

plaintive *a plaintive tune*. doleful, melancholy, mournful, sorrowful. SEE ALSO **sad**.

plait SEE **hair**.

plan 1 *Our plan was to buy food for a picnic*. aim, idea, intention, method, plot, policy, project, proposal, scheme, strategy. 2 *We drew a plan of the town*. chart, design, diagram, map. 3 *We planned to go to the seaside*. to aim, to contemplate, to intend. 4 *We planned a way to defeat the opposition*. to arrange, to design, to devise, to organize, to plot, to prepare, to think up. 5 *planned*: premeditated. 6 *planning*: forethought.

plane 1 SEE **aircraft**. 2 SEE **tool**. 3 SEE **tree**.

planet SEE **astronomy**.

plank board, timber. SEE ALSO **wood**.

plant 1 *plants*: greenery, growth, undergrowth, vegetation. 2 KINDS OF PLANT ARE annual, SEE **bulb**, cactus, SEE **cereal**, SEE **climber**, cutting, fern, SEE **flower**, SEE **fungus**, grass, SEE **herb**, lichen, moss, perennial, seedling, SEE **shrub**, SEE **tree**, SEE **vegetable**, SEE **water plant**, SEE **weed**. 3 PARTS OF A PLANT ARE bloom, blossom, bud, flower, leaf, petal, pod, root, seed,

shoot, stalk, stem, trunk, twig. 4 *Mrs Brunswick planted her beans early*. to set out, to sow.

plaster SEE **material, medicine**.

plasterer SEE **job**.

plastic SEE **material**.

plastic surgery SEE **medicine**.

plate SEE **crockery**.

plateau SEE **geography**.

plate-glass glass, pane, window.

platform 1 SEE **railway**. 2 stage.

platinum SEE **metal**.

platoon SEE **armed services**.

platypus SEE **animal**.

plausible *a plausible excuse*. believable, credible, likely, reasonable.

play 1 *The children played happily*. to amuse yourself, to caper, to frisk, to have fun, to mess about, to romp. 2 *Can you play on Saturday?* to join in, to take part. 3 *Who are we playing on Saturday?* to compete against, to oppose. 4 *Lucy played Mary in the nativity play*. to act, to pretend to be. 5 *Tony plays the piano*. to perform on. 6 *We were punished for playing up*. to be disobedient, to be naughty, to misbehave. 7 *We saw a good play on TV*. drama, production. SEE ALSO **theatre**.

play-back SEE **record**.

player 1 competitor, contestant, sportsman, sportswoman. 2 actor, musician, performer.

playful *a playful puppy*. active, frisky, lively, spirited, sprightly, vivacious.

playground, play-group SEE **school**.

playing-card SEE **cards**.

playing-field recreation ground. SEE ALSO **sport**.

playwright SEE **writer**.

plea *a plea for mercy*. appeal, entreaty, petition, request.

plead *He pleaded to be let off*. to appeal, to beg, to entreat, to implore, to request.

pleasant *pleasant food, pleasant weather, etc*. agreeable, amiable, attractive, balmy, charming, decent, delicious, delightful, enjoyable, excellent, fine, friendly, genial, gentle, good, heavenly, hospitable, kind, likeable, lovely, mellow, mild, nice, peaceful, pleasing, pretty, relaxed, satisfying, soothing, sympathetic, warm, welcome. |*Pleasant* has many meanings. The words given here are only some of the other words you can use. SEE ALSO **beautiful, good,** etc.

please 1 *Did the present please her?* to amuse, to content, to delight, to entertain, to make happy, to satisfy. **2** *pleased: You look pleased!* complacent, content, grateful, satisfied, thankful. SEE ALSO **happy**. **3** *pleasing:* SEE **pleasant**.

pleasure 1 *He smiled with pleasure.* bliss, delight, ecstasy, enjoyment, gladness, happiness, joy, rapture, satisfaction. **2** *What are your favourite pleasures?* amusement, diversion, entertainment, fun, luxury, recreation.

pleat crease, fold.

pledge 1 *He gave me his pledge that he would do what I wanted.* assurance, guarantee, oath, pact, promise, vow, word. **2** *She pledged her support.* to agree, to promise, to swear, to vow.

plentiful *a plentiful supply of food.* abundant, ample, bountiful, copious, generous, lavish, liberal, profuse.

pliable *pliable wire.* bendable, flexible, springy, supple.

pliers SEE **tool**.

plight *We were in a terrible plight when we lost our money.* condition, difficulty, dilemma, jam, predicament, problem, situation, state.

plimsoll SEE **shoe**.

plod SEE **walk**.

plop SEE **sound**.

plot 1 *Guy Fawkes led a plot to blow up Parliament.* conspiracy, intrigue, plan, scheme. **2** *This novel has a complicated plot.* narrative, outline, story. **3** *a vegetable plot.* allotment, garden, patch. **4** *We plotted to ambush*

Logan's gang. to conspire, to design, to plan, to scheme.

plough SEE **farm**.

plover SEE **bird**.

pluck 1 (informal) *She's got a lot of pluck.* SEE **courage**. **2** *to pluck fruit.* to gather, to harvest, to pick, to pull off. **3** *The mugger plucked the handbag out of her hand.* to grab, to seize, to snatch.

plug 1 *Put a plug in the hole!* bung, cork, stopper. **2** *an electric plug.* SEE **electricity**. **3** *a sparking-plug:* SEE **vehicle**. **4** *Logan plugged the leak with chewing-gum.* to block up, to close, to fill, to jam, to seal, to stop up. **5** (informal) *They keep on plugging that record on the radio.* to advertise, to mention frequently, to promote.

plum SEE **fruit**.

plumage feathers, plumes. SEE **bird**.

plumbing SEE **house**.

plump *a plump figure.* chubby, dumpy, fat, overweight, podgy, portly, squat, stout, tubby.

plunder 1 *The rioters plundered the shops.* to loot, to raid, to ransack, to ravage, to rob, to steal. **2** *They ran off with their plunder.* booty, contraband, loot, (informal) swag, takings.

plunge 1 *She plunged into the water.* to dive, to drop, to fall, to leap, to pitch. **2** *He plunged the red-hot steel into water.* to dip, to lower, to immerse, to submerge. **3** *He plunged the spear into the animal's side.* to force, to push, to thrust.

plural SEE **language**. |*Plural* is the opposite of *singular*.

plus SEE **mathematics**.

plywood SEE **material**.

pneumatic SEE **tyre**.

pneumonia SEE **illness**.

poach 1 *poached egg.* SEE **cook**. **2** *He was arrested for poaching.* to hunt, to steal. SEE ALSO **crime**.

pocket SEE **clothes**.

pocket-knife SEE **tool**.

pocket-money allowance. SEE ALSO **money**.

pod *a pea pod.* shell.

podgy *a podgy figure.* chubby, dumpy, fat, plump, portly, squat.

poem 1 poetry, rhyme, verse.
2 KINDS OF POEM ARE ballad, epic, haiku, limerick, lyric, nursery-rhyme, ode. SEE ALSO **writing**.
3 WORDS TO DO WITH POETRY ARE line, rhyme, rhythm, stanza.

poet bard. SEE ALSO **writer**.

poetry SEE **poem**.

point 1 *the point of a spear.* prong, spike, tip. **2** *a decimal point.* dot, spot. **3** *Mark the exact point on the map.* location, place, position, situation. **4** *What is the point of this game?* aim, idea, intention, object, purpose. **5** *The train's late because the points were frozen.* SEE **railway**. **6** *She pointed out the way.* to indicate, to show. **7** *Can you point us in the right direction for the castle?* to aim, to direct, to guide, to lead, to steer.

pointless 1 *As the train had gone, it was pointless to wait.* fruitless, futile, inappropriate, irrelevant. **2** *a pointless remark.* meaningless, senseless, useless, worthless.

poise *A gymnast needs poise.* balance, calmness, equilibrium, self-confidence, self-control, steadiness.

poison 1 venom. **2** KINDS OF POISON ARE arsenic, insecticide, pesticide. **3** SEE **kill**. **4** *The chemicals poisoned the lake.* to contaminate, to infect, to pollute. **5** *poisoned: a poisoned wound.* festering, infected, septic.

poisonous *a poisonous snake-bite.* deadly, fatal, lethal, mortal, toxic, venomous.

poke 1 *He poked me in the ribs.* to dig, to jab, to prod. SEE ALSO **hit**. **2** *I poked a bit of wood into the hole.* to stick, to thrust.

polar bear SEE **animal**.

Polaroid SEE **photograph**.

pole 1 *the North Pole, the South Pole.* SEE **geography**. **2** *a long pole.* column, post, rod, stick.

pole-vault SEE **athletics**.

police constable, (informal) cop or copper, detective, inspector, officer, policeman, policewoman.

policy *Our school's policy is to let us have two trips out each year.* plan, procedure, strategy, tactics.

polio, poliomyelitis SEE **illness**.

polish 1 *That table's got a lovely polish!* brightness, gloss, lustre, sheen, shine, smoothness. **2** *polished:* bright, burnished, gleaming, shiny.

polite *polite behaviour, a polite person.* attentive, chivalrous, civil, considerate, courteous, cultivated, diplomatic, gallant, gentlemanly, ladylike, (informal) posh, refined, respectful, thoughtful, well-bred, well-mannered.

politics 1 PEOPLE WITH VARIOUS POLITICAL VIEWS ARE anarchist, Communist, Conservative, Democrat, Liberal, Labour supporter, Marxist, monarchist, nationalist, Nazi, Republican, SDP supporter, Socialist, Tory. **2** SEE **government**.

poll 1 *to go to the polls.* ballot, election, vote. **2** *an opinion poll.* census, referendum, survey.

pollen SEE **plant**.

pollute *Refuse pollutes the beach.* to contaminate, to defile, to dirty, to foul, to infect, to poison, to soil.

polo SEE **sport**.

poltergeist SEE **ghost**.

polyester SEE **cloth**.

polystyrene SEE **material**.

polytechnic SEE **educate**.

polythene SEE **material**.

pomp *The coronation was conducted with great pomp.* ceremony, grandeur, magnificence, pageantry, ritual, solemnity, spectacle.

pompous *Important people don't have to be pompous.* arrogant, haughty, self-important, showy, snobbish, (informal) stuck-up.

poncho SEE **clothes**.

pond *a fish pond.* lake, pool.

ponder *We pondered about the difficulty.* to brood, to consider, to contemplate, to meditate, to reflect, to study, to think.

ponderous *a ponderous load.* bulky, burdensome, heavy, massive, unwieldy, weighty.

pontoon SEE **cards, vessel**.

pony SEE **animal**.

poodle SEE **dog**.

pool 1 lake, pond, puddle, swimming-pool. 2 SEE **game**.

pools SEE **gamble**.

poop SEE **vessel**.

poor 1 *The poor woman couldn't afford any food.* bankrupt, destitute, hard up, homeless, needy, penniless, poverty-stricken, underpaid. 2 *a poor person:* beggar, pauper, tramp, vagrant. 3 *poor quality.* cheap, faulty, feeble, inadequate, inferior, useless, worthless. SEE ALSO **bad**. 4 *We were sorry for the poor animals.* luckless, miserable, pathetic, pitiable, unfortunate, unhappy. SEE ALSO **sad**.

poorly (informal) *I felt poorly.* feeble, frail, ill, indisposed, infirm, queer, sick, unwell, wan, weak.

pop 1 *The cork popped.* SEE **sound**. 2 *a bottle of pop.* SEE **drink**. 3 *pop music.* SEE **music**.

poplar SEE **tree**.

poppy SEE **flower**.

popular *a popular performer.* celebrated, famous, favourite, renowned, well-known, well-liked.

population citizens, inhabitants, occupants, residents.

porcelain china, earthenware, pottery. SEE ALSO **crockery**.

porch SEE **church, house**.

porcupine SEE **animal**.

pore SEE **body**.

pork SEE **meat**.

porpoise SEE **animal**.

porridge SEE **food**.

port 1 *The ship entered port.* dockyard, harbour. SEE ALSO **dock**. 2 *the port side of a ship.* SEE **vessel**. ! *Port* is the opposite of *starboard*. 3 *a glass of port.* SEE **drink**.

portable *a portable tool-box.* compact, convenient, handy, light, small.

portcullis SEE **castle**.

porter SEE **job**.

porthole SEE **vessel**.

portion *Can I have a small portion of pie?* bit, fraction, helping, quota, section, segment, share, slice. SEE ALSO **piece**.

portly *a portly figure.* chubby, dumpy, fat, overweight, plump, podgy, stout, tubby.

portrait likeness, representation, self-portrait. SEE ALSO **picture**.

portray *The book portrays what life was like 1000 years ago.* to depict, to illustrate, to represent, to show. SEE ALSO **picture**.

pose 1 *to pose for a photograph.* to model. 2 *Logan is always posing.* to show off. 3 *The burglar posed as a gas man.* to impersonate, to pretend to be. 4 *to pose a question.* to ask, to put forward, to suggest.

posh (informal) *a posh party.* elegant, formal, smart, snobbish, stylish.

position 1 *Their house is in a nice position.* locality, location, place, point, site, situation, spot. 2 *I was in an awkward position because I had no money.* circumstances, condition, state. 3 *A referee takes a neutral position.* attitude, opinion, standpoint, view. 4 *Mrs Brunswick has a responsible position in the firm.* employment, job, rank, status, title. 5 *The captain positioned her players.* to arrange, to locate, to place, to situate, to station.

positive 1 *He was positive that he could come.* assured, certain, confident, convinced, definite, sure. 2 *The policeman gave some positive advice.* beneficial, constructive, helpful, practical, useful. 3 SEE **electricity, mathematics**. ! *Positive* is the opposite of *negative*.

posse SEE **group**.

possess 1 *Do you possess a dishwasher?* to have, to own. 2 *Foreign invaders possessed the country.* to control, to dominate, to govern, to occupy, to rule.

possession *I have few possessions.* belongings, fortune, goods, property, wealth.

possible 1 *Would it be possible to swim the Atlantic?* conceivable, feasible, imaginable, practicable, viable, workable. 2 *Logan is a possible goalkeeper.* likely, potential.

possibility *There's a possibility of rain.* chance, danger, likelihood, risk.

possibly maybe, perhaps.

post 1 *Concrete posts support the fence.* column, pile, pillar, pole, prop, shaft, support. 2 *Mrs Brunswick has a post in a local business.* employment, occupation, position, work. 3 *Has the post come?* airmail, letter, mail, packet, parcel, postcard. 4 *Did you post my letter?* to dispatch, to mail, to send.

post-box letter-box, pillar-box.

poster *We put up a poster about sports day.* advertisement, bill, notice, placard, sign.

posterity descendants, heirs, offspring.

postman SEE **job**.

post office SEE **shop**.

postpone *We postponed the match because of the snow.* to adjourn, to defer, to delay, to put off. ! Compare *postpone* with *cancel*.

posy *a posy of flowers.* bouquet, bunch, spray.

pot *a cooking pot.* casserole, cauldron, pan, saucepan. SEE ALSO **container, kitchen**.

potato SEE **vegetable**.

potent *a potent smell.* overpowering, powerful, strong.

potential *I think Lucy is a potential Olympic gymnast.* likely, possible.

pot-hole cave, cavern, hole.

pot-holing SEE **sport**.

potter SEE **art**.

pottery china, earthenware, porcelain. SEE ALSO **crockery**.

potty SEE **mad**.

pouch SEE **container**.

pouffe SEE **furniture**.

poultice SEE **medicine**.

poultry KINDS OF POULTRY ARE bantam, chicken, cock, cockerel, duck, goose, hen, pullet, rooster, turkey. SEE ALSO **farm**.

pounce *The cat pounced on the mouse.* to ambush, to jump, to leap, to spring, to swoop.

pound 1 *a pound of jam.* SEE **measure**. 2 *Can you lend me a pound?* SEE **money**. 3 *We pounded the clay until it was soft.* to batter, to beat, to crush, to grind, to mash, to pulp. SEE ALSO **hit**.

pour *Water poured through the hole.* to flow, to gush, to run, to stream.

pout SEE **expression**.

poverty *The refugees lived in terrible poverty.* beggary, need, want.

powder 1 dust. 2 *powdered: powdered coffee.* ground.

power 1 *We have the power to win.* ability, competence, skill, talent. 2 *The referee has the power to send him off.* authority, control, influence, right. 3 *The waves have the power to knock you over.* energy, force, might, strength, vigour.

power-boat SEE **vessel**.

powerful *a powerful machine, a powerful player.* dynamic, forceful, influential, mighty, potent, strong.

powerless *We were powerless against Logan's gang.* feeble, helpless, impotent, weak.

practicable *a practicable plan.* feasible, possible, practical, realistic, sensible, viable, workable.

practical 1 *a practical worker.* businesslike, capable, competent, efficient. 2 *a practical tool.* handy, usable, useful. 3 *a practical plan.* SEE **practicable**. 4 *a practical joke:* hoax, prank, trick.

practically almost, close to, nearly.

practice 1 *It's our practice to end the day with a story.* custom, habit, routine. 2 *We need more practice before we perform* *in public.* preparation, rehearsal, training.

practise *We must keep on practising.* to exercise, to rehearse, to train.
! Notice the different spellings of *practice* (noun) and *practise* (verb).

prairie SEE **geography**.

praise 1 *Everyone praised Tony for raising so much money.* to admire, to applaud, to commend, to congratulate, to honour, to marvel at, to pay tribute to. 2 *Praise God!* to adore, to worship.

praiseworthy *a praiseworthy effort.* admirable, commendable, creditable, deserving, worthy. SEE ALSO **good**.

pram push-chair.

prance *to prance about.* to caper, to dance, to frisk, to jump, to leap, to play, to romp, to skip.

prank *Logan is always up to some prank or other.* escapade, mischief, practical joke, scrape.

prattle to chatter. SEE ALSO **talk**.

prawn SEE **shellfish**.

prayer SEE **church**.

preach SEE **talk**.

preacher clergyman, evangelist, minister, missionary, parson, pastor, priest, vicar. SEE ALSO **church**.

precarious *The climber stood on a precarious ledge.* dangerous, insecure, perilous, rocky, shaky, unsafe, unsteady, wobbly.

precaution *What precautions can you take against flu?* defence, protection, safeguard.

precede *Christmas precedes Boxing Day.* to come before, to go before.

precious *precious jewels.* costly, dear, expensive, invaluable, priceless, valuable.

precipice *The climber fell down a precipice.* cliff, crag, rock.

precipitous *a precipitous drop.* sharp, sheer, steep, vertical.

precise 1 *the precise time.* accurate, correct, definite, exact, right, specific. 2 *precise work.* careful, meticulous.

predator hunter. SEE ALSO **animal**.

predecessor ancestor, forefather.

predicament *How did they get out of that predicament?* difficulty, dilemma, emergency, jam, plight.

predict *She predicted that I would win.* to forecast, to foretell, to prophesy, to tell fortunes.

predominantly *The people at the party were predominantly grown-ups.* chiefly, generally, mainly, mostly, primarily.

prefab SEE **house**.

preface introduction, prelude, prologue. SEE ALSO **book**.

prefect SEE **school**.

prefer *Which flavour do you prefer?* to choose, to fancy, to like better, to pick out.

prefix SEE **language**. ! The opposite of *prefix* is *suffix*.

pregnant 1 *a pregnant woman.* expectant, expecting. 2 WORDS TO DO WITH PREGNANCY ARE abortion, birth, to conceive, conception, miscarriage, premature birth.

prehistoric *prehistoric remains.* ancient, early, old, primitive.

prejudice 1 *A referee is not supposed to show prejudice to either side.* bias, discrimination, favouritism, intolerance, unfairness. 2 *racial prejudice*: racialism, racism. 3 *prejudiced*: biased, intolerant, unfair.

preliminary *the preliminary rounds in a championship.* early, introductory, opening.

prelude *The first match was an exciting prelude to the series.* beginning, introduction, opening, preface, preparation, prologue.

premature *a premature baby.* early, too early, too soon.

premeditated *a premeditated crime.* calculated, deliberate, intentional, planned, wilful.

premier SEE **government**.

première SEE **theatre**.

premonition *I had a premonition that*

something nasty would happen. foreboding, indication, omen, warning.

preoccupied *Tony is preoccupied with plans for his holiday.* absorbed in, immersed in, interested in.

prepare 1 *to prepare a display.* to arrange, to get ready, to organize, to plan, to process. **2** *to prepare food.* SEE **cook**.

preposition SEE **language**.

preposterous *The clown wore a preposterous costume.* absurd, farcical, grotesque, ludicrous, ridiculous, stupid, unconventional, weird, zany.

prep school SEE **school**.

prescribe *What did the doctor prescribe?* to advise, to recommend, to suggest.

prescription SEE **medicine**.

present 1 *Is everyone present?* here. **2** *Who's the present champion?* current, existing. **3** *She gave me a present.* contribution, donation, gift, offering. **4** *Who presented the cups?* to award, to give, to hand over, to offer. **5** *We presented our work to the parents.* to demonstrate, to display, to exhibit, to reveal, to show. **6** *Let me present our guest.* to introduce, to make known. **7** *We presented a play.* to act, to perform, to put on.

presentable *Is your room presentable?* acceptable, clean, decent, proper, respectable, tidy, worthy.

presently shortly, soon.

preservative SEE **food**.

preserve 1 *We all want to preserve peace.* to defend, to guard, to keep, to look after, to maintain, to protect, to safeguard, to save. **2** WAYS TO PRESERVE FOOD ARE to can, to cure, to dehydrate, to dry, to freeze, to pickle, to refrigerate, to salt, to tin.

president SEE **government**.

press 1 *If I press the clothes down I can close the suitcase.* to compress, to crowd, to crush, to push, to shove, to squash, to squeeze. **2** *Tony pressed his trousers.* to flatten, to iron, to smooth. **3** *They pressed me to stay.* to compel, to order, to persuade, to require, to

urge. **4** *the press:* newspapers, magazines. SEE ALSO **media**.

pressing *pressing business.* essential, important, urgent.

pressure *the pressure in a tyre.* compression, force, might, power, stress.

prestige *If we lose again, our prestige will suffer.* fame, glory, good name, honour, renown, reputation.

presume 1 *I presume you'd like something to eat.* to assume, to believe, to guess, to imagine, to suppose, to think. **2** *Logan presumed to contradict Mrs Angel.* to dare, to venture.

presumptuous *It was presumptuous to ask for more.* arrogant, bold, cheeky, forward, impertinent, impudent, insolent, shameless.

pretend 1 WAYS OF PRETENDING ARE to act, to bluff, to conjure, to counterfeit, to deceive, to disguise, to fake, to feign, to fool, to hoax, to hoodwink, to imitate, to impersonate, (informal) to kid, to lie, to make believe, to mislead, to perform, to play a part, to put on, to sham, to take someone in, to trick. **2** *I don't pretend that I play well.* to believe, to claim, to fancy, to imagine, to maintain, to suppose.

pretty 1 *a pretty dress, pretty flowers.* appealing, attractive, charming, dainty, lovely, pleasing. SEE ALSO **beautiful**. **2** (informal) *That's pretty good!* fairly, moderately, rather, somewhat.

prevailing *What's the prevailing colour in this year's fashions?* chief, current, dominant, main, normal, principal, usual.

prevalent *What's the prevalent opinion?* common, general.

prevent *The snow prevented us from travelling.* to check, to curb, to deter, to hamper, to hinder, to impede, to obstruct, to stop.

preview SEE **theatre**.

previously before, earlier.

prey 1 *The lion killed its prey.* victim.

2 *Owls prey on small animals.* to eat, to feed on, to hunt, to kill.

price *a reasonable price.* amount, charge, cost, fare, fee, payment, rate, sum, terms, toll, value.

priceless 1 *priceless jewels.* costly, dear, expensive, invaluable, precious, (informal) pricey, valuable. 2 (informal) *a priceless joke.* SEE **funny.**

prick *to prick your finger.* to pierce, to puncture.

prickly *a prickly bush.* spiky, thorny.

pride 1 *It injured his pride when he let in three goals.* arrogance, conceit, self-importance, self-satisfaction, vanity. 2 *The new car is her pride and joy.* happiness, pleasure, satisfaction. 3 *a pride of lions.* SEE **group.**

priest clergyman, minister, parson, preacher, vicar. SEE ALSO **church, religion.**

prim *She's too prim to enjoy rude jokes!* narrow-minded, old-fashioned, proper, prudish.

primarily *Amusement arcades are used primarily by young people.* chiefly, firstly, generally, mainly, mostly, predominantly.

primary 1 *In soccer, the primary aim is to score goals!* SEE **principal.** 2 *a primary school:* SEE **school.**

prime 1 *In soccer, the prime aim is to score goals!* SEE **principal.** 2 *prime grade meat.* best, top. 3 *the Prime Minister.* SEE **government.** 4 *to prime a pump.* to get ready, to prepare.

primer SEE **paint.**

primitive 1 *primitive tribes.* ancient, early, prehistoric, uncivilized, undeveloped. 2 *a primitive machine.* crude, rough, simple.

primrose SEE **flower.**

prince, princess SEE **royal.**

principal 1 *In soccer, the principal aim is to score goals!* basic, chief, dominant, first, foremost, fundamental, greatest, important, leading, main, major, outstanding, primary, prime, supreme. 2 *the Principal of a college.* SEE **head.**

principle 1 *Can you teach me the principles of chess?* law, rule, science, theory. 2 *He is a man of principle.* honesty, honour, integrity, standards, virtue.

print 1 *to print a book.* to issue, to publish. 2 *Print your name clearly.* SEE **write.** 3 *We saw the prints of huge feet in the sand.* mark, stamp. 4 *It's not an original painting: it's a print.* copy, duplicate, reproduction.

printer SEE **job.**

print-out SEE **computer.**

priory abbey, monastery. SEE ALSO **church.**

prism SEE **shape.**

prison Borstal, cell, detention centre, dungeon, gaol.

prisoner captive, convict, hostage.

private 1 *a private in the army.* SEE **rank.** 2 *private property.* individual, personal, special. 3 *private information.* confidential, intimate, secret. 4 *a private hide-out.* hidden, isolated, quiet, secluded.

privet SEE **shrub.**

privilege *Club members enjoy the privilege of cheap refreshments.* advantage, benefit, right.

prize 1 *I never win a prize!* award, jackpot, reward. 2 *Lucy prizes the ring she got from granny.* to appreciate, to approve of, to cherish, to esteem, to like, to rate, to regard, to value. 3 *I lost the key so I had to prize the lid off.* to lever, to wrench.

probable likely, possible.

probation SEE **punishment.**

probe *The police probed deeply into the problem.* to examine, to explore, to inquire into, to investigate, to penetrate.

problem 1 *Mrs Angel sets us interesting problems.* conundrum, mystery, puzzle, question, riddle. 2 *Mr Brunswick had problems when he built his extension.* burden, complication, difficulty, dilemma, predicament, set-back, snag, trouble, worry.

procedure *Mrs Brunswick explained the*

procedure for freezing beans. method, process, system, technique.

proceed *After a break, we proceeded on our way*. to advance, to carry on, to continue, to go on, to move forward, to progress.

proceedings events, happenings.

proceeds *What were the proceeds from our OXFAM collection?* income, profit, takings. SEE ALSO **money**.

process 1 *a manufacturing process*. method, procedure, system, technique. 2 *They have to process crude oil to make petrol*. to change, to convert, to prepare, to refine, to transform, to treat.

procession *a procession of soldiers*. cavalcade, line, march, pageant, parade.

proclaim *The head proclaimed that we would have an extra holiday*. to announce, to assert, to declare, to decree, to make known, to pronounce.

procure *How did you procure tickets for the Cup Final?* to acquire, to buy, to get, to get hold of, to obtain, to purchase.

prod *He prodded me in the back*. to dig, to jab, to poke, to push. SEE ALSO **hit**.

prodigal *The banquet was a prodigal waste of money*. extravagant, lavish, wasteful.

produce 1 *Mrs Brunswick gets a lot of produce from her garden*. crop, harvest, output, yield. 2 WAYS TO PRODUCE THINGS ARE to bear, to breed, to cause, to compose, to create, to cultivate, to form, to generate, to give birth to, to grow, to invent, to make, to manufacture, to originate, to provoke, to raise, to rear, to think up, to yield. 3 *The conjuror produced a rabbit from a hat*. to bring out, to disclose, to display, to exhibit, to present, to reveal, to show.

producer, production SEE **theatre**.

productive 1 *a productive factory*. busy, creative, effective, profitable, useful.

2 *a productive garden*. fertile, fruitful, lush, prolific.

profession *Nursing is an important profession*. business, calling, career, employment, job, occupation, trade, work.

professional 1 *professional advice*. expert, qualified, skilled, trained. 2 *a professional player*. paid. | *Professional* is the opposite of *amateur*.

professor lecturer, tutor. SEE ALSO **educate, job**.

proficient *a proficient worker*. able, capable, competent, effective, qualified, skilled, trained.

profile outline, shape.

profit 1 *Did you make any profit?* advantage, benefit, gain. 2 *Did you profit from the sale?* to earn, to gain, to make money. 3 SEE **money**.

profitable *Did you have a profitable shopping trip?* advantageous, beneficial, fruitful, productive, rewarding, useful, worthwhile.

profound 1 *profound sympathy*. deep, sincere. 2 *a profound discussion*. intellectual, learned, serious, thoughtful, wise.

profuse *profuse apologies*. abundant, ample, copious, plentiful.

program SEE **computer**.

programme 1 *We printed a programme for sports day*. plan, schedule, timetable. 2 *a television programme*. SEE **television**.

programmer SEE **job**.

progress 1 *Tony has made progress with his swimming this year*. development, improvement. 2 *The plans for our holiday are progressing*. to advance, to develop, to improve, to make headway, to move forward, to proceed.

progression *We had a progression of disasters!* row, series, sequence, string, succession.

prohibit *They prohibit smoking in food shops*. to ban, to bar, to censor, to forbid, to make illegal, to outlaw, to prevent, to veto.

project 1 *The shelf projects from the wall*.

to extend, to jut out, to overhang, to protrude, to stick out. 2 *The candle projected a flickering light.* to cast, to throw. 3 *We did a history project at school.* activity, assignment, task, work. 4 *There is a project to build a bypass.* plan, proposal, scheme.

prolific *Mrs Brunswick's beans are prolific this year.* fertile, fruitful, productive.

prologue beginning, introduction, preface, prelude.

prolong *The game was prolonged by a number of injuries.* to draw out, to extend, to increase, to lengthen, to make longer, to stretch out.

promenade SEE **seaside**.

prominent 1 *prominent teeth.* bulging, jutting out, large, protruding, sticking out. 2 *a prominent landmark.* conspicuous, noticeable, obvious, pronounced. 3 *a prominent politician.* celebrated, distinguished, eminent, famous, outstanding, renowned, well-known.

promise 1 *She gave me her promise.* assurance, guarantee, oath, pledge, vow. 2 *You promised me that you would pay.* to agree, to assure, to consent, to give your word, to guarantee, to pledge, to swear, to undertake, to vow.

promote 1 *Mrs Brunswick was promoted to a more responsible job.* to move up, to raise. 2 *A local firm promoted our sports festival.* to back, to boost, to encourage, to help, to sponsor, to support. 3 *We saw some posters promoting the new film.* to advertise, to make known, (informal) to plug.

prompt 1 *a prompt reply.* immediate, instantaneous, on time, punctual, quick, speedy, swift. 2 *She prompted me to join the youth club.* to egg on, to encourage, to inspire, to stimulate, to urge. 3 *Logan forgot his lines until Tony prompted him.* to jog the memory, to remind.

prone *He lay prone on the floor.* face down, flat.

prong *the prong of a fork.* point, spike.

pronoun SEE **language**.

pronounce 1 *How do you pronounce this word?* to say, to speak, to utter. 2 *The doctor pronounced me fit again.* to announce, to declare, to make known, to proclaim. 3 *pronounced:* conspicuous, definite, distinct, noticeable, obvious, prominent.

proof *The police have proof of his guilt.* evidence, facts, grounds, testimony.

prop 1 crutch, post, support. 2 *She propped her bike against the wall.* to lean, to rest, to stand. 3 *The wall was propped up by some big timbers.* to hold up, to reinforce, to support.

propane SEE **fuel**.

propel *The games teacher propelled Logan into the shower.* to drive, to force, to push, to spur, to urge.

propeller SEE **aircraft, vessel**.

proper 1 *We always use proper language when auntie is here.* becoming, decent, dignified, formal, grave, modest, polite, respectable, serious, solemn, tasteful. 2 *I think £5 is the proper price.* advisable, appropriate, correct, deserved, fair, fitting, just, lawful, legal, right, suitable, valid.

property *I don't own much property.* belongings, estate, fortune, possessions, wealth.

prophecy *Her prophecy came true.* forecast, prediction.

prophesy *She prophesied that Lucy would win a gold cup.* to forecast, to foresee, to foretell, to predict, to tell fortunes. ! Notice the difference in spelling between *prophecy* (noun) and *prophesy* (verb).

prophet 1 SEE **religion**. 2 forecaster, fortune-teller.

proportion 1 *What is the proportion of girls to boys in your class?* balance, ratio. 2 *A large proportion of the audience cheered.* fraction, part, piece, quota, section, share. 3 *She's a lady of large proportions.* dimensions, measurements, size.

proposal *A big firm made a proposal to build a supermarket.* bid, offer, plan, project, scheme, suggestion.

propose *They propose to visit us on*

Saturday. to aim, to intend, to offer, to plan, to suggest.

proprietor *the proprietor of a shop*. boss, manager, owner.

prose SEE **writing**.

prosecute *They prosecuted him for dangerous driving*. to accuse, to charge, to sue.

prosecution, prosecutor SEE **law**.

prospect 1 *There's a lovely prospect from the top of the hill*. outlook, panorama, scene, sight, view, vista. **2** *to prospect for gold*. to explore, to search.

prospectus *The school sent us their prospectus*. brochure, leaflet, pamphlet.

prosper *Mr Brunswick is happy now that his business is prospering*. to be successful, to do well, to flourish, to grow, to strengthen, to succeed, to thrive.

prosperous *He must be prosperous with a big car like that!* affluent, prospering, rich, successful, thriving, well-off, well-to-do.

protect 1 *Parents protect their young*. to care for, to cherish, to look after, to mind, to watch over. **2** *The police protected her when the crowd surged forward*. to defend, to escort, to guard, to harbour, to keep safe. **3** *Mrs Brunswick put up a screen to protect her tender plants*. to safeguard, to screen, to shield.

protein SEE **food**.

protest 1 *We made a protest against the referee's decision*. complaint, objection, outcry. **2** *There was a big protest in the square*. (informal) demo, demonstration, march, rally. **3** *Why don't you protest?* to complain, to demonstrate, to grouse, to grumble, to march, to moan, to object.

protractor SEE **mathematics**.

protrude *His teeth protrude*. to bulge, to jut out, to stick out, to swell.

proud 1 *Mr Brunswick was proud of Lucy when she won*. delighted with, happy with, pleased with. **2** *She was too proud to ask for help*. dignified, honourable, self-respecting. **3** *Don't get too proud of*

yourself! arrogant, boastful, bumptious, (informal) cocky, conceited, disdainful, haughty, (informal) stuck-up, vain.

prove *We did an experiment to prove that plants need light*. to confirm, to demonstrate, to establish, to explain, to show, to verify.

proverb motto, saying.

provide *We'll provide the food if you provide the camping gear*. to afford, to allot, to allow, to contribute, to donate, to equip, to furnish, to give, to grant, to lay on, to spare, to supply.

province SEE **geography**.

provisions food, rations, stores, supplies.

provoke 1 *Logan provoked Mrs Angel with his stupidity*. (informal) to aggravate, to anger, to annoy, to enrage, to exasperate, to incense, to infuriate, to irritate, to tease, to torment, to upset, to vex, to worry. **2** *Our play provoked a lot of laughter*. to arouse, to bring about, to cause, to excite, to incite, to produce, to stimulate, to stir up.

prow SEE **vessel**.

prowess 1 *prowess in battle*. bravery, courage, spirit, valour. **2** *The dancers showed off their prowess*. ability, accomplishment, cleverness, competence, skill, talent.

prowl SEE **walk**.

prowler intruder.

prudent *It's prudent to keep some money in the bank*. advisable, careful, discreet, proper, sensible, thoughtful, wise.

prudish *Granny isn't at all prudish*. easily shocked, narrow-minded, old-fashioned, prim, strict.

prune 1 SEE **fruit**. **2** *to prune a rose bush*. SEE **cut**.

pry 1 *Don't pry into my affairs*. to interfere, to meddle, to nose about, to snoop. **2** *prying*: curious, inquisitive, nosey.

psalm SEE **church**.

psychiatrist SEE **medicine**.

psychic *Do you believe that some people have psychic powers?* supernatural, telepathic.

psychology SEE **subject**.

pub bar, inn, (informal) local, public house, saloon, tavern.

puberty *You reach puberty in your teens.* adolescence, growing-up.

public 1 *a public place.* common, general, open, shared. 2 *public knowledge.* familiar, known, unconcealed. 3 *the public*: the community, people, society.

publication FOR KINDS OF PUBLICATION SEE **book, magazine, record**.

publicity 1 SEE **advertisement**. 2 *TV stars get a lot of publicity.* attention, fame, notoriety.

public school SEE **school**.

public-spirited *Some public-spirited person tidied up the classroom.* generous, kind, unselfish.

publish 1 *to publish a magazine.* to bring out, to issue, to print, to produce, to release. 2 *When will they publish details of the new season?* to announce, to broadcast, to declare, to disclose, to divulge, to make known, to proclaim, to reveal.

publisher SEE **job**.

pudding SEE **food, meal**.

puddle pool.

puff 1 *a puff of wind.* blast, gust. 2 *By the end of the race I was puffing.* to blow, to gasp, to pant, to wheeze. 3 *The sails puffed out.* to rise, to swell.

puffin SEE **bird**.

pug SEE **dog**.

pugnacious *a pugnacious expression.* aggressive, belligerent, hostile, militant, warlike.

pull 1 *A locomotive pulls a train.* to drag, to draw, to haul, to lug, to tow, to trail. 2 *You nearly pulled my arm off!* to jerk, to tug, to wrench. 3 *to pull up*: to draw up, to halt, to stop.

pullet SEE **poultry**.

pullover SEE **clothes**.

pulp *Mrs Brunswick pulps her soft fruit before it goes in the freezer.* to crush, to mash, to pound, to smash, to squash.

pulpit SEE **church**.

pulse *a regular pulse.* beat, throb.

pumice-stone SEE **rock**.

pump *The fire brigade pumped the water out of the cellar.* to empty, to force, to raise.

pumpkin SEE **vegetable**.

pun double meaning, joke.

punch 1 SEE **drink**. 2 *He punched me.* to beat, (informal) to clout, to cuff, to jab, to poke, to prod, to slog, to strike, to thump. SEE ALSO **hit**.

punctual *The bus is punctual today.* on time, prompt.

punctuation PUNCTUATION MARKS ARE apostrophe, asterisk, brackets, colon, comma, dash, exclamation mark, full stop, hyphen, question mark, quotation marks or speech marks, semicolon.

puncture *A nail punctured my tyre.* to penetrate, to pierce, to prick.

punish to penalize.

punishment VARIOUS PUNISHMENTS ARE Borstal, the cane, capital punishment, confiscation, corporal punishment, detention, SEE **execute**, fine, flogging, forfeit, gaol, a hiding, imposition, penalty, prison, probation, the stocks, torture, whipping.

punt 1 SEE **vessel**. 2 *to punt a ball.* to boot, to kick.

puny *a puny child.* feeble, frail, (informal) poorly, sickly, tiny, weak, (informal) weedy.

pupil learner, scholar, schoolboy, schoolchild, schoolgirl, student. SEE ALSO **school**.

puppet dummy.

puppy SEE **dog, young**.

purchase to acquire, to buy, to get, to obtain, to pay for.

pure 1 *a pure person.* chaste, good, innocent, modest, virtuous. 2 *pure water.* clean, clear, undiluted, unpolluted. 3 *pure nonsense.* absolute, complete, perfect, sheer, total, utter.

purify *We purified the water before we drank it.* to clean, to disinfect, to refine, to sterilize.

purple SEE **colour**.

purpose *Have you a particular purpose in mind?* aim, goal, intention, motive, object, objective, plan.

purposely deliberately, intentionally.

purr SEE **sound**.

purse handbag, wallet. SEE ALSO **container**.

pursue *How far did they pursue the robbers?* to chase, to follow, to hound, to hunt, to seek, to shadow, to tail, to track down.

pursuit 1 *The hounds dashed off in pursuit of the fox.* chase, hunt. **2** *What are your favourite pursuits?* hobby, interest, pastime.

push 1 *The gangsters pushed him into a car.* to drive, to force, to press, to propel, to thrust. **2** *Push everything into a suitcase.* to cram, to crush, to pack, to squeeze. **3** *The mob pushed forward.* to crowd, to force a way, to hustle, to jostle, to shove. **4** *Push a coin in the slot.* to insert, to put in.

push-chair pram.

put 1 *Put the books on the shelf.* to arrange, to deposit, to hang, to lay, to leave, to locate, to place, to position, to rest, to set down, to situate, to stand, to station. **2** *Put your question politely.* to express, to say. **3** *Dad put in new sparking-plugs.* to insert, to install. **4** *We put off our visit.* to adjourn, to defer, to delay. **5** *They put out the fire.* to extinguish, to quench. **6** *Can granny put us up?* to accommodate, to house, to lodge, to quarter. **7** *We put up the tent.* to build, to construct, to erect, to pitch, to raise, to set up. **8** *They put up their prices.* to increase, to raise, to step up.

putrid *putrid flesh.* bad, decayed, decomposing, festering, foul, rotten, smelly, tainted.

putt SEE **hit**.

putty SEE **material**.

puzzle 1 *Can you solve this puzzle?* conundrum, dilemma, mystery, problem, question, riddle. **2** *His bad mood puzzled us.* to baffle, to bewilder, to confuse, to nonplus, to perplex, to stump. **3** *puzzling:* inexplicable, insoluble, mysterious, strange, unanswerable.

pyjamas SEE **clothes**.

pylon SEE **electricity**.

pyramid SEE **shape**.

python SEE **snake**.

Q q

quack SEE **sound**.

quadrangle courtyard. SEE ALSO **building**.

quadrilateral SEE **shape**.

quadruped SEE **animal**.

quadruplet SEE **family**.

quagmire *My wellingtons got stuck in the quagmire.* bog, fen, marsh, quicksand, swamp.

quail 1 SEE **bird**. **2** *I quailed when I heard the monster roar!* to cower, to cringe, to flinch, to show fear, to shrink, to tremble, to wince.

quaint *a quaint thatched cottage.* antiquated, charming, old-fashioned, picturesque, unusual.

quake *to quake with fear.* to quaver, to quiver, to shake, to shudder, to tremble.

qualifications 1 *Has she got proper qualifications?* certificate, degree, diploma, examinations. **2** *Has she got any qualifications?* ability, experience, knowledge, skill.

qualify 1 *Tony qualifies for the senior race next birthday.* to be eligible. **2** *qualified:* equipped, skilled, trained.

quality 1 *Our butcher sells best-quality meat.* class, grade, standard, value. **2** *What qualities do you look for in a captain?* characteristic, feature.

qualm *Have you any qualms about climbing?* anxiety, doubt, hesitation, misgiving, uncertainty, worry.

quantity *a large quantity, a small*

quantity. amount, measurement, number, sum, total, volume.

quarantine isolation.

quarrel 1 *Tony had a quarrel with Logan*. argument, controversy, disagreement, dispute, feud, scene, vendetta. 2 *They often quarrel*. to argue, to differ, to disagree, to fall out, to fight, to squabble.

quarry mine, working.

quart SEE **measure**.

quarter 1 *The troops were quartered in the town*. to lodge, to put up. 2 *quarters*: boarding house, lodgings. SEE ALSO **house**.

quartet SEE **music**.

quaver 1 SEE **music**. 2 *He quavered when he heard an angry shout*. to quake, to quiver, to shake, to shudder, to tremble, to waver.

quay berth, dock, jetty, landing-stage, pier, wharf.

queasy *I felt queasy on the ship*. bilious, sick.

queen SEE **royal**.

queer 1 *a queer shape, a queer smell*. abnormal, curious, funny, odd, peculiar, strange, uncommon, unusual, weird. 2 *I felt queer after six ice-creams*. ill, poorly, sick, unwell.

quell *The police quelled the riot*. to control, to master, to overcome, to subdue, to suppress.

quench 1 *to quench your thirst*. to satisfy. 2 *to quench a fire*. to extinguish, to put out.

query *Logan queried the referee's decision*. to ask about, to dispute, to doubt, to enquire or inquire about, to question.

quest *a quest for treasure*. hunt, search.

question 1 *Can you answer this question?* conundrum, enquiry, problem, puzzle, query, riddle. 2 *There is some question about whether he is fit*. doubt, uncertainty. 3 *The police questioned me about the accident*. to ask, to cross-examine, to examine, to interrogate, to interview. 4 *Logan questioned the referee's decision*. SEE **query**. 5 *question mark*: SEE **punctuation**.

queue 1 *a queue of cars*. column, file, line, row. 2 *Please queue at the door*. to line up.

quiche SEE **food**.

quick 1 *a quick journey*. fast, (informal) nippy, rapid, speedy, swift. 2 *quick movements*. agile, animated, brisk, deft, lively, nimble. 3 *a quick end*. abrupt, hasty, immediate, instant, prompt, sudden. 4 *a quick pupil*. apt, bright, clever, intelligent, quick-witted, sharp, shrewd, smart.

quicken to accelerate, to hasten, to go faster, to speed up.

quicksand *He sank into the quicksand!* bog, marsh, quagmire, swamp.

quicksilver mercury.

quiet 1 *a quiet engine*. noiseless, silent, soundless. 2 *a quiet voice*. low, soft. 3 *a quiet evening*. calm, peaceful, placid, serene, tranquil, untroubled.

quieten 1 *Please quieten the baby!* to calm, to hush, to pacify, to silence, to soothe, to subdue. 2 *A silencer quietens the noise of the engine*. to deaden, to muffle, to soften, to stifle, to suppress, to tone down.

quilt SEE **bedclothes**.

quintet SEE **music**.

quintuplet SEE **family**.

quit 1 *to quit your job*. to abandon, to depart from, to desert, to forsake, to leave, to resign from. 2 (informal) *Quit pushing!* to cease, to give up, to stop.

quite 1 *Yes, I have quite finished*. absolutely, altogether, completely, entirely, totally, utterly, wholly. 2 *It was quite good, but nothing special*. fairly, moderately, (informal) pretty, rather. ! Take care how you use *quite*, as the two meanings are almost opposite.

quiver *He quivered with cold*. to quake, to shake, to shudder, to tremble.

quiz competition, test.

quoits SEE **sport**.

quota *The explorers shared out their daily quota of food*. portion, proportion, ration, share.

quotation 1 *a quotation from a book*.

excerpt, extract, reference.
2 *quotation marks*: SEE **punctuation**.
quote *Granny often quotes what her father used to say.* to mention, to refer to, to repeat.

R r

rabbi SEE **Jew**.
rabbit SEE **animal, pet**.
rabble *a noisy rabble.* crowd, horde, gang, mob, swarm. SEE ALSO **group**.
rabies SEE **illness**.
race 1 *a race of people.* breed, nation, people, tribe. **2** COMPETITIVE RACES ARE cross-country, heat, horse-race, hurdles, marathon, motor-race, regatta, relay race, rowing, scramble, speedway, sprinting, steeplechase, stock car race, swimming. SEE ALSO **sport**. **3** *to race along.* SEE **move**.
race-course, race-track circuit, lap. SEE ALSO **sport**.
racial *racial characteristics.* ethnic.
racialism, racism bias, discrimination, intolerance, prejudice.
rack *a plate rack.* stand, support.
racket 1 *I couldn't sleep because of the racket!* clamour, commotion, din, hubbub, hullabaloo, noise, pandemonium, row, rumpus, uproar. **2** *a tennis racket.* SEE **sport**. **3** (informal) *Their business is a racket!* crime, dishonest business.
radar SEE **communication**.
radiant bright, brilliant, gleaming, shining. SEE ALSO **beautiful, happy**.
radiate *The fire radiates heat.* to emit, to give out, to glow, to send out, to transmit.
radiator SEE **house, vehicle**.
radio set, transistor, wireless. SEE ALSO **audio equipment, communication**.
radiographer, radiotherapy SEE **medicine**.

radish SEE **vegetable**.
radius SEE **mathematics**.
raffle SEE **gamble**.
raft SEE **vessel**.
rafter beam, girder, joist.
rag *rags*: bits and pieces, cloths, scraps, shreds, tatters.
rage 1 *She couldn't hide her rage.* anger, exasperation, fury, tantrum, temper, wrath. **2** *She shouted and raged for ages.* to be angry, to be violent, to fume, to lose your temper, to rave, to seethe.
ragged *ragged clothes.* frayed, old, patched, shabby, tattered, tatty, torn, worn out.
raid 1 *We planned a raid on Logan's hide-out.* assault, attack, blitz, invasion, onslaught. **2** *We raided Logan's hide-out.* to attack, to invade, to plunder, to pounce, to ravage, to storm, to swoop down on.
rail bar, railing, rod.
railings barrier, fence.
railway WORDS TO DO WITH RAILWAYS ARE bogies, booking-office, buffers, buffet, carriage, coach, corridor, coupling, cutting, departure, diesel, driver, electric train, engine, express, fireman, footplate, freight, gauge, goods, guard, level-crossing, locomotive, passenger, platform, points, porter, rails, shunter, siding, signals, signal-box, signalman, sleeper, sleeping-car, station, steam-engine, tender, terminus, ticket-office, timetable, track, train, wagon, waiting-room. SEE ALSO **travel**.
rain 1 *We had some rain.* deluge, downpour, drizzle, raindrops, shower. **2** *It's raining.* to drizzle, to pour, to teem. **3** SEE **weather**.
rainbow SEE **weather**.
raincoat SEE **clothes**.
raise 1 *A crane raised the wreck.* to elevate, to erect, to heave, to hoist, to lift, to pick up, to put up. **2** *A farmer raises animals and crops.* to breed, to cultivate, to grow, to produce, to rear. **3** *The forecast raised our hopes of a fine day.* to arouse, to boost, to build

up, to enlarge, to excite, to improve, to increase, to stimulate. **4** *He raised £15 for charity.* to collect, to get, to make, to receive.

raisin SEE **fruit.**

rake SEE **garden.**

rally 1 *Granny rallied after her illness.* to get better, to recover, to revive. **2** *a political rally.* (informal) demo, demonstration, march, meeting, protest.

ram 1 SEE **male, sheep. 2** *The car rammed the garage door.* to bump, to collide with, to smash into, to strike. SEE ALSO **hit.**

Ramadan SEE **Islam.**

ramble to amble, to hike, to roam, to rove, to stroll, to wander. SEE ALSO **walk.**

ramp slope.

rampage *Hooligans rampaged through the town.* to go berserk, to rush about, to go wild.

rampart SEE **castle.**

ramshackle *a ramshackle old hut.* broken down, decrepit, dilapidated, rickety, ruined, shaky, tumbledown.

ranch farm.

rancid SEE **taste.**

random *a random selection.* accidental, chance, haphazard, irregular, unplanned.

range 1 *a range of mountains.* chain, line, series. **2** *The shop stocks a wide range of goods.* selection, variety. **3** *I'm afraid that's outside my range.* area, field, limit, reach, scope. **4** (old-fashioned) *a kitchen range.* cooker, oven, stove. **5** *Prices range between £10 and £15.* to differ, to vary. **6** *The sheep range over the hills.* to roam, to rove, to stray, to travel, to wander.

rank 1 *The soldiers lined up in three ranks.* column, file, line, row. **2** *to have a high or low rank.* class, grade, level, position, status, title. **3** OFFICERS AND OTHER RANKS IN THE ARMY ARE brigadier, captain, colonel, corporal, lieutenant, major, private, sergeant.

ransack 1 *We ransacked the house looking for mum's keys.* to comb, to rummage through, to scour, to search. **2** *Rioters ransacked the shop.* to loot, to plunder, to ravage, to rob, to wreck.

rap *I rapped on the door.* to knock, to strike, to tap. SEE ALSO **hit.**

rape assault. SEE ALSO **crime.**

rapid brisk, fast, (informal) nippy, quick, speedy, swift.

rapids cataract, waterfall.

rapier SEE **weapon.**

rapture *The dog greeted us with rapture.* bliss, delight, ecstasy, happiness, joy, pleasure.

rapturous SEE **happy.**

rare *A white blackbird is a rare sight!* abnormal, curious, exceptional, infrequent, occasional, odd, peculiar, scarce, singular, special, strange, uncommon, unusual.

rascal blackguard, imp, knave, rogue, scamp, scoundrel, trouble-maker, villain.

rash 1 *a rash decision.* careless, hasty, impetuous, impulsive, incautious, reckless, thoughtless. **2** *a rash on your skin.* spots.

rasher *a rasher of bacon.* slice.

raspberry SEE **fruit.**

rasping *a rasping voice.* croaking, grating, harsh, hoarse, husky, rough.

rat SEE **animal, pet.**

rate 1 *We started at a fast rate.* pace, speed, velocity. **2** *The hotel charges reasonable rates.* amount, charge, cost, fare, fee, payment, price. **3** *How did you rate the game on Saturday?* to like, to prize, to regard, to value.

rather 1 *I was rather ill.* fairly, moderately, (informal) pretty, quite, somewhat. **2** *I'd rather have an apple than an orange.* preferably, sooner.

ratio proportion. SEE ALSO **mathematics.**

ration 1 *He ate my ration of sweets!* allowance, portion, quota, share. **2** *rations:* food, provisions, stores, supplies. **3** *We rationed out the sweets.* to allot, to distribute fairly, to share out.

rational *You can't have a rational discussion with Logan!* intelligent, logical, reasonable, sane, sensible.

rattle SEE **sound**.

rattlesnake SEE **snake**.

raucous *raucous laughter.* harsh, grating, jarring, shrill.

ravage *The army ravaged the countryside.* to damage, to destroy, to devastate, to loot, to plunder, to raid, to ransack, to ruin, to wreck.

rave 1 *The head raved about our bad behaviour.* to be mad, to fume, to rage. SEE ALSO **angry, talk**. 2 *Lucy raves about her new record.* to be enthusiastic.

raven SEE **bird**.

ravenous *The ravenous crowd ate everything on the table!* famished, greedy, hungry, starved, starving.

ravine *a deep ravine.* canyon, defile, gorge, pass, valley.

raw 1 *raw food.* uncooked. 2 *raw materials.* crude, natural, unprocessed, unrefined. 3 *a raw wind.* SEE **cold**. 4 *a raw place on your skin.* grazed, inflamed, red, sore.

ray *a ray of light.* beam, shaft.

rayon SEE **cloth**.

raze *Vandals razed the building to the ground.* to demolish, to destroy, to dismantle, to knock down.

razor SEE **bathroom**.

reach 1 *Reach out your hand.* to extend, to stretch. 2 *Can you reach the handle?* to grasp, to get hold of, to touch. 3 *Have we reached the end?* to achieve, to arrive at, to get to. 4 *The shops are in easy reach.* distance, range, scope.

react *How did dad react when you asked for £10?* to answer, to reply, to respond, to retort.

read 1 *Can I read your story?* to glance at, to scan, to skim, to study. 2 *Can you read grandpa's handwriting?* to decipher, to interpret, to make out, to understand.

readable 1 *a readable story.* enjoyable, interesting, well-written. 2 *readable handwriting.* clear, legible, plain, understandable.

ready 1 *Are you ready for your holiday?* prepared, organized. 2 *Tony is always ready to help people.* disposed, eager, inclined, liable, likely, willing. 3 *Logan usually has a ready reply.* immediate, prompt, quick, speedy. 4 *Keep your tickets ready.* available, handy, obtainable.

real 1 *a real diamond.* actual, authentic, genuine. 2 *a real story.* factual, true. 3 *a real friend.* honest, sincere, trustworthy.

realistic 1 *a realistic statue.* authentic, lifelike, natural. 2 *a realistic plan.* feasible, possible, practicable, practical, viable, workable.

realize *Do you realize how expensive clothes are?* to appreciate, to comprehend, to grasp, to know, to see, to sense, to understand.

really *Was he really sorry?* actually, certainly, genuinely, honestly, truly.

realm country, kingdom, monarchy.

reap *to reap corn.* to gather in, to harvest, to mow.

rear 1 *the rear of the train.* back, end. 2 *Our dog nipped the intruder in the rear.* backside, behind, bottom, rump. 3 *Birds rear their chicks.* to bring up, to care for, to feed. 4 *Farmers rear cattle.* to breed, to produce, to raise.

reason 1 *Did he have a good reason for his behaviour?* argument, cause, excuse, explanation, grounds, justification, motive, occasion, pretext. 2 *Use your reason!* intelligence, judgement, sense, understanding, wit. 3 *Tony reasoned it out for himself.* to consider, to judge, to think, to work out. 4 *I tried to reason with her.* to argue, to debate, to discuss.

reasonable 1 *a reasonable person.* intelligent, logical, rational, sane, sensible. 2 *a reasonable price.* cheap, fair, moderate, ordinary.

reassure 1 *Tony reassured Lucy when she was worried.* to comfort, to encourage. 2 *reassuring:* favourable, hopeful, promising.

rebel *The workers rebelled because of their bad conditions.* to disobey, to mutiny, to revolt, to rise up.

rebellion mutiny, revolt, revolution, rising.

rebellious *Mrs Angel dealt quickly with Logan's rebellious gang.* defiant, disobedient, insubordinate, mutinous, quarrelsome, unruly.

rebound *The ball rebounded off the goal-post.* to bounce, to ricochet.

rebuild *They rebuilt the rooms which were damaged in the fire.* to modernize, to reconstruct, to renovate, to transform.

rebuke *The referee rebuked Logan for arguing.* to blame, to censure, to criticize, to reprimand, to reproach, to scold, (informal) to tell off, (informal) to tick off.

recall 1 *The garage recalled the faulty cars.* to call back, to withdraw. 2 *Do you recall what happened?* to recollect, to remember.

recede *The flood gradually receded.* to ebb, to go back, to retreat.

receipt *Did the shopkeeper give you a receipt?* account, bill.

receive 1 *We received lots of goods for the jumble sale.* to acquire, to get, to obtain. 2 *I received £1 for washing the car.* to accept, to earn, to take. 3 *We got ready to receive our visitors.* to entertain, to greet, to meet, to welcome.

recent *Have you got any recent records?* contemporary, fresh, modern, new, up-to-date.

receptacle SEE **container**.

reception 1 *They gave us a friendly reception.* greeting, welcome. 2 *a wedding reception.* SEE **party**.

receptionist SEE **job**.

recipe SEE **food**.

recital concert. SEE ALSO **entertainment**.

recite *to recite a poem.* to deliver, to perform, to repeat, to speak. SEE ALSO **talk**.

reckless 1 *reckless driving.* careless, inattentive, irresponsible, rash, thoughtless. 2 *reckless criminals.* desperate, violent, wild.

reckon 1 *Tony reckoned up how much Logan owed him.* to assess, to calculate, to compute, to count, to estimate, to figure out, to total, to work out. 2 *I reckon it's going to rain.* to believe, to consider, to judge, to think.

reclaim *They reclaimed some derelict land and made a nature reserve.* to recover, to restore.

recline *to recline on a sofa.* to lean back, to lie, to rest, to sprawl.

recognize 1 *I hardly recognized you.* to identify, to know, to recall, to recollect, to remember. 2 *We recognized a familiar landmark.* to discern, to distinguish, to perceive, to see. 3 *I recognize that you've been working hard.* to accept, to acknowledge, to be aware, to understand.

recoil *I recoiled when I saw the blood.* to flinch, to jerk back, to shrink, to spring back, to wince.

recollect *Do you recollect that I lent you £5?* to recall, to remember.

recommend *I recommend that film.* to approve of, to commend, to praise.

recompense *Did she recompense you for the trouble you took to find her dog?* to compensate, to pay back, to refund, to repay, to reward.

reconcile *Tony and Lucy quarrelled, but Mrs Brunswick reconciled them.* to bring together, to reunite.

reconstruct *They reconstructed the remains of the dinosaur.* to rebuild, to repair.

record 1 *We recorded what we saw in our books.* to note, to register, to write down. 2 *We kept a record of what we saw.* account, description, document, diary, narrative, note, register, report. 3 *recording*: KINDS OF RECORDING ARE album, cassette, compact disc, digital recording, disc, long-playing record, LP, mono recording, single, stereo recording, tape, video, videotape. SEE ALSO **audio equipment**.

recorder 1 SEE **audio equipment**. 2 SEE **music**.

record-player SEE **audio equipment**.

recount *He recounted his adventures.* to describe, to narrate, to relate, to tell.

recover 1 *Granny recovered slowly after her illness.* to get better, to heal, to improve, to mend, to pull through, to rally, to recuperate. 2 *I never recovered my lost watch.* to find, to get back, to reclaim, to regain, to retrieve, to salvage, to trace, to track down.

recreation 1 *You deserve a bit of recreation after working so hard.* amusement, diversion, enjoyment, entertainment, fun, games, hobby, leisure, pastime, play. 2 *recreation ground*: park, playing-field.

recruit SEE **armed services**.

rectangle oblong. SEE ALSO **shape**.

rectify *Mum rectified the fault in the car.* to correct, to cure, to put right, to remedy, to repair.

rector SEE **church**.

rectory SEE **house**.

recuperate 1 *Granny took a long time to recuperate after her operation.* to get better, to heal, to improve, to recover. 2 *recuperating*: convalescent.

recur *This problem keeps recurring.* to come again, to reappear, to return.

recurrent *recurrent illness.* chronic, constant, frequent, incessant, perpetual, persistent, repeated, unending. SEE ALSO **continual**.

recycle to use again.

red SEE **colour**.

redden to blush, to colour, to flush, to glow.

red-hot fiery.

reduce 1 *Reduce the quantity.* to cut, to decrease, to diminish, to halve, to lessen. 2 *Our supplies gradually reduced.* to contract, to dwindle, to shrink. 3 *Reduce the liquid by boiling.* to concentrate, to condense, to thicken.

reduction *You get a reduction if you're under 16.* concession, discount.

redundant *The firm declared a lot of its workers redundant after it lost the big* order. superfluous, too many, unnecessary, unwanted.

reed SEE **water plant**.

reef SEE **geography**.

reel 1 *a reel of film.* spool. 2 *a Scottish reel.* SEE **dance**. 3 *I reeled after that knock on the head.* to rock, to stagger, to totter. 4 *reeling*: dizzy.

refer 1 *I hope dad won't refer to the broken window.* to allude to, to comment on, to mention. 2 *If I can't spell a word I refer to my dictionary.* to consult, to turn to. 3 *If I can't spell a word Mrs Angel refers me to my dictionary.* to direct, to send.

referee adjudicator, arbitrator, judge, umpire. SEE ALSO **sport**.

referendum SEE **poll**.

refine *to refine oil.* to process, to purify, to treat.

refined *Lucy's behaviour was quite refined while she was at auntie's!* cultivated, elegant, dignified, ladylike, polite, (informal) posh, tasteful, well-bred.

reflect 1 *Glass reflects light.* to mirror, to send back. 2 *Give yourself time to reflect before you start your story.* to brood, to consider, to contemplate, to meditate, to ponder, to think.

reflection *a reflection in a mirror.* image, likeness.

reflex camera SEE **photography**.

reform *to reform your behaviour.* to change, to correct, to improve.

refrain 1 *We all sang the refrain.* chorus. 2 *Please refrain from smoking.* to abstain from, to do without.

refresh 1 *Let me refresh your memory.* to jog, to prompt, to stimulate. 2 *The drink refreshed us.* to cool, to invigorate, to quench the thirst, to revive.

refreshments snack. FOR VARIOUS THINGS TO DRINK AND EAT SEE **drink, food**.

refrigerate to chill, to freeze. SEE ALSO **preserve**.

refrigerator SEE **kitchen**.

refuge *The climber found refuge from the blizzard.* asylum, cover, haven, hiding-place, protection, retreat, safety, sanctuary, shelter.

refugee exile, fugitive, outcast.

refund *If the watch doesn't work the shop should refund your money.* to pay back, to repay.

refuse 1 *to refuse an invitation.* to decline, to turn down. **2** *to refuse someone their rights.* to deny, to deprive of.

regain *to regain something you've lost.* to find, to get back, to recover, to retrieve, to win back.

regal *a regal figure.* majestic, royal, stately. SEE ALSO **splendid**.

regard 1 *The policeman regarded us closely.* to contemplate, to eye, to gaze at, to look at, to stare at, to view, to watch. **2** *We regard Tony as our best swimmer.* to consider, to judge, to reckon. **3** *We should have regard for others.* attention, care, concern, consideration, heed, notice, respect, thought.

regarding about, concerning, connected with, involving.

regatta SEE **race**.

regent SEE **royal**.

reggae SEE **music**.

regiment SEE **armed services**.

region *The Arctic is a cold region.* area, district, locality, neighbourhood, territory, vicinity, zone.

register 1 *She keeps our names in a register.* catalogue, directory, index, list. **2** *Grandad registered in the army in 1939.* to enlist, to enrol, to join, to sign on. **3** *The official registered our complaint.* to record, to write down. **4** *The speedometer registered 100 mph.* to indicate, to show.

registry office SEE **wedding**.

regret *I regret being rude.* to be ashamed of, to be sad about, to be sorry for, to repent.

regretful *a regretful smile.* apologetic, penitent, remorseful, repentant, sorry. SEE ALSO **sad**.

regrettable *a regrettable accident.* deplorable, reprehensible, unfortunate. SEE ALSO **bad**.

regular 1 *a regular player.* consistent, dependable, reliable. **2** *regular breathing.* even, rhythmic, steady. **3** *a regular habit.* accustomed, customary, habitual, normal, traditional, usual. **4** *a regular sight.* common, commonplace, everyday, familiar, frequent, ordinary, repeated.

regulate 1 *The police regulate the traffic.* to control, to direct, to govern, to manage, to supervise. **2** *Can you regulate the central heating?* to adjust, to alter, to change, to vary.

regulation *Obey the regulations.* by-law, law, rule.

rehearsal SEE **theatre**.

rehearse *to rehearse a play.* to practise, to prepare.

reign to be king or queen, to govern, to rule.

rein SEE **horse**.

reindeer SEE **animal**.

reinforce 1 *to reinforce a wall.* to fortify, to hold up, to prop up, to strengthen, to toughen. **2** *to reinforce an army.* to assist, to help, to support.

reinforcements SEE **armed services**.

reject 1 *I had no room in my cupboard, so I rejected my old jeans.* to discard, to disown, to eliminate, to renounce, to scrap, to throw away. **2** *We rejected their invitation.* to decline, to dismiss, to refuse, to turn down.

rejoice to be happy, to celebrate, to revel.

relapse *Logan behaved well for a while, but then relapsed again.* to fall back, to return, to slip back.

relate 1 *We related our adventures.* to describe, to narrate, to recount, to report, to tell. **2** *Mrs Angel set us a problem which related to work we did yesterday.* to be relevant, to compare, to connect, to link.

relations SEE **family**.

relationship *The twins have a close relationship.* bond, connection, link, tie.

relatives SEE **family**.

relax 1 *Mum relaxed in front of the TV.* to

be comfortable, to be easy, to feel at home, to rest, to unbend, to unwind. **2** *He relaxed his grip.* to ease off, to loosen, to slacken. **3** *relaxed: a relaxed atmosphere.* casual, comfortable, easygoing, friendly, informal, restful.

relay to broadcast, to pass on, to send out, to transmit, to televise.

relay race SEE **athletics, race**.

release 1 *to release prisoners.* to allow out, to dismiss, to free, to let go, to liberate, to rescue, to save, to set free, to set loose, to unfasten, to untie. **2** *to release a new record.* to distribute, to issue, to make available, to publish, to send out.

relent *He was cross at first, but later he relented.* to be merciful, to show pity.

relentless 1 *a relentless rhythm.* SEE **continual. 2** *a relentless attack.* SEE **cruel.**

relevant *Is your comment relevant to what we are discussing?* connected, linked, related.

reliable *a reliable player.* consistent, constant, dependable, devoted, efficient, faithful, level-headed, loyal, regular, responsible, safe, sound, steady, trustworthy, unchanging.

relic *a relic from the past.* reminder, remnant.

relief *The pills gave some relief from the pain.* aid, assistance, comfort, ease, help, relaxation, respite.

relief map SEE **geography**.

relieve *The medicine relieved the pain.* to calm, to comfort, to console, to ease, to lessen, to soothe.

religion 1 *Which religion do you belong to?* belief, creed, cult, denomination, faith. **2** PEOPLE OF VARIOUS RELIGIONS ARE Buddhist, Christian (SEE **church**), Hindu, Jew (SEE **Jew**), Muhammadan or Muslim (SEE **Islam**), Sikh. SEE ALSO **worship.** !There are many more religions than are give here. **3** LEADERS OR TEACHERS IN VARIOUS RELIGIONS ARE Druid, guru, imam, minister, priest, prophet, rabbi.

religious 1 *a religious ceremony.* divine, holy, sacred. **2** *a religious believer.* committed, dedicated, devout.

relish *Lucy relishes a challenge.* to appreciate, to enjoy, to delight in, to like, to love.

reluctant *I was reluctant to pay £1.* disinclined, hesitant, unwilling.

rely 1 *You can rely on Tony to do his best.* to bank on, to count on, to depend on, to trust. **2** *Dad relies on the car to get to work.* to need.

remain 1 *How much food remained at the end of the party?* to be left, to survive. **2** *The sentry remained at his post.* to carry on, to continue, to endure, to keep on, to linger, to live on, to persist, to stay.

remains 1 *the remains of an animal.* body, carcass, corpse. **2** *the remains of a building.* debris, fragments, rubble, ruins, wreckage. **3** *the remains of the coffee.* dregs.

remark 1 *Logan made a rude remark.* comment, observation, opinion, statement. **2** *He remarked that he was bored.* to comment, to mention, to note, to observe, to say.

remarkable amazing, exceptional, extraordinary, notable, phenomenal, special, surprising, (informal) terrific, (informal) tremendous, uncommon, unusual.

remedy 1 *Mum remedied the fault in the car.* to correct, to cure, to heal, to mend, to put right, to rectify. **2** *Is there any remedy for a cold?* cure, medicine, therapy, treatment.

remember 1 *Do you remember Uncle George?* to recall, to recollect. **2** *It's a good idea to remember your phone number.* to learn, to memorize.

remind *Remind me to buy some potatoes.* ·to jog the memory, to prompt.

remnant *We put the remnants of the bread out for the birds.* fragment, piece, relic, scrap.

remorse *Does Logan show remorse when he's naughty?* grief, guilt, regret, shame.

remorseful apologetic, ashamed,

guilty, penitent, regretful, repentant, sorry.

remote *a remote farmhouse.* desolate, distant, far-away, inaccessible, lonely, outlying, solitary.

remove 1 *The police removed the intruders.* to eject, to evict, to expel, to get rid of, (informal) to kick out, to throw out, to turn out. **2** *Remove your things from the table.* to carry away, to convey, to move, to take away, to transfer, to transport. **3** *He removed the fuse from the bomb.* to detach, to disconnect, to part, to separate, to undo, to unfasten. **4** *Logan had to remove what he wrote on the wall.* to delete, to dispense with, to erase, to get rid of, to wash off, to wipe out. **5** *The dentist removed my tooth.* to draw out, to extract, to pull out, to take out. **6** *The nurse removed the bandage.* to peel off, to strip off, to take off.

rend to rip, to split, to tear.

render 1 *to render a song.* to give, to perform, to recite, to sing. **2** *The shock rendered her speechless.* to make.

rendezvous *Tony and Lucy arranged a rendezvous.* appointment, date, meeting, meeting-place.

renegade deserter, fugitive, outlaw, traitor.

renew 1 *Dad renewed the car tyres.* to change, to replace. **2** *We renewed the paint.* to repair, to restore.

renounce 1 *The duke renounced his title.* to abandon, to abdicate, to give up, to resign. **2** *Don't renounce your friends.* to disown, to forsake, to reject.

renovate *It'll be nice when they renovate the bus station.* to improve, to mend, to modernize, to overhaul, to renew, to repair, to restore.

renown *The actor's renown spread far and wide.* distinction, fame, honour, importance, prestige, reputation.

renowned *He is renowned throughout the world.* eminent, famous, noted, popular, well-known.

rent 1 *Dad forgot to pay the rent for the TV.* instalment, regular payment,

rental. **2** *We rented a caravan for our holiday.* to charter, to hire.

repair 1 *Mum repaired the car.* to fix, to mend, to overhaul, to put right, to rebuild, to rectify, to renovate, to restore, to service. **2** *Tony repaired his jeans.* to darn, to patch, to sew up.

repay *Did they repay you for those bad eggs?* to compensate, to pay back, to recompense, to refund.

repeat 1 *Don't repeat everything I say!* to echo, to quote, to say again. **2** *repeated*: SEE **continual**.

repel 1 *The defenders repelled the attack.* to check, to fend off, to parry, to push away, to repulse, to ward off. **2** *The smell repelled us.* to disgust, to nauseate, to offend, to revolt, to sicken.

repent to be ashamed, to be sorry, to regret.

repentant *Logan was repentant when he saw what he'd done.* apologetic, ashamed, penitent, regretful, remorseful, sorry.

replace 1 *Replace the books on the shelf.* to put back, to restore, to return. **2** *Who is likely to replace the present prime minister?* to come after, to follow, to succeed, to take over from, to substitute. **3** *It's time we replaced those tyres.* to change, to renew.

replica *We saw a replica of a lunar module.* copy, duplicate, imitation, model, reconstruction, reproduction.

reply to answer, to react, to respond, to retort.

report 1 *We reported that we'd been successful.* to announce, to communicate, to declare, to inform, to proclaim, to publish, to reveal, to state. **2** *Report to reception when you arrive.* to announce yourself, to introduce yourself, to make yourself known, to present yourself. **3** *I reported him to the police.* to complain about, to denounce, to inform against, to tell of. **4** *a report in a newspaper.* account, announcement, description, narrative, record, statement, story. 5 *the report of a gun.* bang, blast, explosion, noise.

reporter *a newspaper reporter.* correspondent, journalist. SEE ALSO **job**.

repose *We enjoyed a moment of repose before we went on working.* calm, comfort, ease, peacefulness, relaxation, rest.

reprehensible *It was reprehensible to insult Mrs Angel.* deplorable, immoral, regrettable, shameful, unworthy, wicked. SEE ALSO **bad**.

represent *The paintings represented scenes from history.* to depict, to describe, to illustrate, to paint, to picture, to portray, to show, to stand for, to symbolize.

representation *The statue was a representation of Peter Pan.* figure, image, imitation, likeness, model, picture, statue.

representative 1 *a sales representative.* agent, salesman, traveller. 2 *a government representative.* ambassador, consul, diplomat. 3 *She couldn't come, so she sent a representative.* deputy, stand-in, substitute.

reprieve *They reprieved the prisoner when they found new evidence.* to forgive, to let off, to pardon, to set free, to spare.

reprimand *Mum reprimanded him for being rude.* to censure, to condemn, to criticize, to disapprove of, to rebuke, to reproach, to scold, (informal) to tell off, (informal) to tick off.

reprisal retaliation, revenge, vengeance.

reproach SEE **reprimand**.

reproduce 1 *to reproduce a document.* to copy, to counterfeit, to duplicate, to imitate, to mimic, to photocopy, to print. 2 *Rabbits reproduce quickly.* to breed, to increase, to multiply.

reproduction *It's a reproduction, not the original picture.* copy, duplicate, fake, forgery, imitation, likeness, print, replica.

reptile SOME REPTILES ARE alligator, crocodile, lizard, snake, tortoise, turtle. SEE ALSO **animal**.

republic SEE **country, government**.

repulse *The defenders repulsed the attack.* to drive back, to fend off, to push away, to repel, to resist, to ward off.

repulsive disgusting, hideous, nauseating, odious, offensive, repellent, revolting, ugly, unsightly. SEE ALSO **unpleasant**.

reputation *These cars have a good reputation.* fame, name, prestige, renown.

request 1 *We requested help.* to appeal for, to ask, to beg, to claim, to demand, to entreat, to implore, to invite. 2 *Dad didn't listen to our request.* appeal, entreaty, petition, plea, question.

requiem SEE **church**.

require 1 *We required 3 runs to win.* to be short of, to lack, to need, to want. 2 *The policeman required dad to show his licence.* to command, to compel, to direct, to order.

rescue 1 *Robin Hood rescued the prisoners.* to free, to liberate, to release, to save, to set free. 2 *We managed to rescue our things after the flood.* to recover, to retrieve, to salvage.

research *We did some research into how aeroplanes fly.* inquiry, investigation, searching, study.

resemblance likeness, similarity.

resemble *The twins resemble each other.* to be similar to, to look like, to take after.

resent *Logan resented Lucy's success.* to begrudge, to be jealous of, to envy, to feel bitter about.

resentful bitter, envious, jealous.

reserve 1 *We reserved some of our rations to eat later.* to hold, to keep, to preserve, to save. 2 *We reserved tickets for the play.* to book, to order. 3 *Who are the reserves for Saturday's game?* deputy, stand-in, substitute. 4 *a wild life reserve:* game park, safari park.

reserved *Lucy is not usually quiet and reserved.* bashful, distant, reticent, secretive, self-conscious, shy, stand-offish, timid, withdrawn.

reservoir lake, pond.

reside *to reside in*: to dwell in, to inhabit, to live in, to lodge in, to occupy.

residence SEE **house**.

resident 1 inhabitant, occupant. **2** *a temporary resident*: guest, lodger, visitor.

resign 1 *to resign from your job*. to abdicate, to give up, to leave, to quit, to renounce. **2** *resigned*: *He seemed resigned about his troubles*. calm, patient, philosophical, reasonable.

resist *He made things worse by resisting the police*. to defy, to fight, to oppose, to stand up to, to withstand.

resolute *Tony was resolute about entering the half marathon*. adamant, decided, determined, firm, resolved, undaunted.

resolve *The Brunswicks resolved to have a camping holiday*. to conclude, to decide, to determine, to elect, to opt, to settle.

resort SEE **seaside**.

resound *Our voices resounded in the cave*. to echo, to reverberate.

resourceful *Ask Tony how to do it: he's very resourceful*. clever, creative, enterprising, imaginative, ingenious, inventive.

resources 1 *Lucy and Tony put their resources together to buy a present for Mrs Brunswick*. assets, funds, money, wealth. **2** *Oil and coal are valuable resources*. materials, raw materials.

respect 1 *We stayed silent for a minute as a sign of respect*. admiration, awe, consideration, honour, liking, love, regard, reverence, tribute. **2** *My work isn't perfect in all respects*. aspect, detail, feature, point. **3** *We respected Logan for owning up*. to admire, to honour, to pay homage to, to think well of.

respectable 1 *respectable people*. decent, honest, honourable, law-abiding, worthy. **2** *respectable clothes*. clean, modest, presentable, proper.

respite *It rained without respite*. interval, lull, pause, relief, rest.

resplendent *She was resplendent in all her jewels*. bright, brilliant, dazzling, gleaming, glittering, shining. SEE ALSO **splendid**.

respond *to respond to a question*. to answer, to react, to reply.

responsible 1 *Mrs Angel is responsible for the class*. in charge of. **2** *Who's responsible for the damage?* guilty of. **3** *We need a responsible person to keep the money*. concerned, conscientious, dependable, diligent, dutiful, honest, law-abiding, loyal, reliable, trustworthy.

rest 1 *We had a rest*. break, interlude, interval, lull, pause. **2** *On Mother's Day we give mum the rest she deserves*. comfort, ease, leisure, quiet, relaxation, repose. **3** *Tony made a rest for his telescope*. stand, support. **4** *We rested on the lawn*. to lie, to lounge, to recline, to relax, to sprawl. **5** *Grandad rests in the evening*. to doze, to nod off, to sleep, to snooze, to take a nap. **6** *Rest the ladder against the wall*. to lean, to place, to prop, to stand, to support. **7** *We can't eat all the food: what shall we do with the rest?* extra, remainder, surplus.

restaurant café, cafeteria, canteen, snack-bar.

restless *The class was restless*. agitated, excitable, fidgety, impatient, jittery, jumpy, nervous, unsettled.

restore 1 *I restored what I had borrowed*. to give back, to put back, to return. **2** *They are restoring the old station*. to mend, to renew, to renovate, to repair, to touch up.

restrain *Please restrain your dog*. to check, to control, to curb, to hold back, to keep back, to stop, to subdue.

restrict 1 *The use of cheap tickets is restricted to weekends*. to confine, to keep within, to limit. **2** *The prisoners were restricted in their cells*. to enclose, to shut in.

result 1 *One result of the cold weather is that I have chilblains!* consequence, effect, outcome. **2** *the result of a trial*. decision, judgement, verdict. **3** *the* *result of a game.* score. 4 *What resulted from your interview with the head?* to arise, to come about, to follow, to happen, to occur, to take place, to turn out. 5 *to result in: I hope it doesn't result in tears!* to bring about, to cause, to give rise to, to lead to, to provoke.

resume *We resumed after a break.* to begin again, to carry on, to continue, to proceed.

Resurrection SEE **church**.

retail SEE **sell**.

retain *Please retain your ticket.* to hang on to, to hold, to keep.

retaliate *Logan retaliated because Tony hurt him.* to pay back, to seek retribution, to take revenge.

reticent *a reticent person.* quiet, reserved, shy, timid.

retire 1 *to retire from work.* to give up, to leave, to quit, to resign. 2 *to retire from a fight.* SEE **retreat**.

retort *Logan retorted rudely.* to answer, to react, to reply, to respond.

retreat 1 *The army retreated.* to back away, to fall back, to leave, to move back, to retire, to run away, to withdraw. 2 *The floods retreated.* to ebb, to flow back, to recede. 3 *They made a quick retreat.* escape, flight. 4 *The outlaws found a retreat in the hills.* asylum, hiding-place, refuge, sanctuary, shelter.

retribution *to seek retribution.* justice, punishment, retaliation, revenge, vengeance.

retrieve *Did you retrieve that watch you dropped in the river?* to fetch, to find, to get back, to recover, to regain, to rescue, to salvage, to trace, to track down.

retriever SEE **dog**.

retro-rocket SEE **space**.

return 1 *When are you likely to return?* to come back, to go back, to reappear. 2 *Can you return that money I lent you?* to give back, to repay, to send back, to take back.

reveal 1 *Dad revealed his knobbly knees.* to air, to bare, to display, to expose, to show, to uncover, to unmask. 2 *to reveal the truth.* to announce, to communicate, to declare, to disclose, to divulge, to make known, to produce, to publish.

revel *We revelled in the sunshine.* to be happy, to celebrate, to delight, to enjoy, to love, to rejoice.

revelry celebration, merry-making, orgy, party.

revenge 1 *His heart was set on revenge.* reprisal, retaliation, retribution, vengeance, vindictiveness. 2 *to take revenge:* to retaliate.

revenue SEE **money**.

reverberation echo, rumble, vibration. SEE ALSO **sound**.

revere *Lucy reveres grandad.* to admire, to adore, to honour, to idolize, to praise, to respect, to worship.

reverie *Tony was lost in a reverie.* day-dream, dream, fantasy, meditation, thought.

reverse 1 *What is on the reverse side?* back, contrary, opposite, rear. 2 *What would happen if we reversed the batting order?* to invert, to turn round. 3 *to reverse a car.* to back, to go backwards.

review 1 *Tony wrote a record review for the magazine.* criticism. 2 *We reviewed the evidence.* to consider, to examine, to inspect, to study, to survey. 3 *Tony reviewed a record.* to criticize, to write about.

revise 1 *We revised our articles for the magazine.* to adapt, to alter, to correct, to edit, to improve, to rewrite. 2 *to revise work for an exam.* to go over, to learn, to study.

revive 1 *He revived slowly after being knocked out.* to rally, to recover, to rouse. 2 *A cold drink revived us.* to invigorate, to refresh.

revolt 1 *The people revolted against the dictator.* to disobey, to mutiny, to rebel, to rise up. SEE ALSO **revolution**. 2 *The cruel treatment of the animals revolted us.* to disgust, to nauseate, to repel, to sicken. 3 *revolting:* SEE **unpleasant**.

revolution 1 *The king was killed in a revolution.* mutiny, rebellion, revolt, rising. 2 *The satellite made a revolution of the earth.* circuit, orbit, turn.

revolve *The wheels revolved.* to rotate, to spin, to swivel, to turn, to twirl, to whirl.

revolver SEE **weapon**.

revulsion *a feeling of revulsion.* aversion, disgust, dislike, hatred, loathing.

reward 1 *She received a reward for bravery.* award, decoration, medal, payment, prize. 2 *She was rewarded for her bravery.* to decorate, to honour. 3 *He rewarded us for our hard work.* to compensate, to pay, to recompense.

rewrite to edit, to revise.

rheumatism SEE **illness**.

rhododendron SEE **flower, shrub**.

rhubarb SEE **fruit**.

rhyme SEE **poem**.

rhythm beat, pulse, throb. SEE ALSO **music**.

rhythmic *a rhythmic beat.* regular, repeated, steady.

rib SEE **body**.

ribbon band, braid, strip, tape.

rice SEE **cereal**.

rich 1 *a rich person.* affluent, prosperous, wealthy, well-off, well-to-do. 2 *rich furnishings.* costly, expensive, luxurious, splendid, sumptuous. 3 *riches*: SEE **money**.

rick haystack. SEE ALSO **farm**.

rickety *a rickety old building.* decrepit, dilapidated, frail, ramshackle, ruined, shaky, tumbledown, unsteady.

rickshaw SEE **vehicle**.

ricochet to bounce, to rebound.

rid *to get rid of*: to dispense with, to eject, to evict, to expel, to remove, to throw out.

riddle 1 *Can you solve this riddle?* conundrum, mystery, problem, puzzle, question. 2 *She sifted the soil in a riddle.* sieve. SEE ALSO **garden**.

ride SEE **travel**.

ridge *We had a good view from the top of the ridge.* bank, edge, embankment, hill.

ridicule *It is cruel to ridicule people because of their appearance.* to be sarcastic about, to be satirical about, to jeer at, to laugh at, to make fun of, to mock, to scoff at, to sneer at, to taunt, to tease.

ridiculous *What a ridiculous thing to do!* absurd, amusing, comic, crazy, eccentric, farcical, foolish, funny, grotesque, illogical, irrational, laughable, ludicrous, mad, preposterous, senseless, silly, stupid, unreasonable, weird, zany.

rifle SEE **weapon**.

rift *We noticed a rift in their friendship.* break, crack, split.

rig equipment, gear, kit, tackle.

rigging SEE **vessel**.

right 1 *the right decision.* fair, good, honest, just, lawful, moral, virtuous. 2 *the right answer.* accurate, correct, exact, factual, precise, true. 3 *Is the paint the right colour?* appropriate, apt, fitting, proper, suitable. 4 *Mrs Angel has the right to give orders.* authority, influence, position, power.

right angle SEE **mathematics**.

righteous good, law-abiding, moral, upright, virtuous.

rightful *Who is the rightful owner of this car?* authorized, lawful, legal, legitimate, proper.

rigid 1 *a rigid substance.* firm, hard, inflexible, solid, stiff, unbending, wooden. 2 *a rigid disciplinarian.* harsh, stern, strict, stubborn, unkind, unyielding.

rim *the rim of a cup.* brim, brink, edge.

rind *cheese rind, the rind of an orange.* crust, peel, skin.

ring 1 *Draw a ring.* band, circle, hoop, loop. 2 *a boxing ring.* arena. SEE ALSO **sport**. 3 *The police ringed the area.* to circle, to encircle, to enclose, to surround. 4 *The bell rang.* to chime, to peal, to tinkle, to toll. SEE ALSO **sound**. 5 *I must ring to see how granny is.* to call, to phone, to telephone.

ring road SEE **road**.

rink *an ice-rink.* SEE **sport**.

rinse *Rinse the things in clean water.* to bathe, to clean, to swill, to wash.

riot 1 *The police quelled the riot.* anarchy, commotion, confusion, disorder, disturbance, hubbub, mutiny, pandemonium, revolt, rioting, rumpus, turmoil, unrest, uproar. **2** *Why did the people riot?* to mutiny, to rampage, to rebel, to revolt.

riotous SEE **rowdy**.

rip *Tony ripped his jeans.* to rend, to slit, to split, to tear.

ripe *ripe fruit.* mature, mellow, ready to use.

ripen *These pears need to ripen.* to age, to develop, to mature.

ripple *The wind rippled the surface of the water.* to agitate, to disturb, to make waves, to ruffle.

rise 1 *He rose at 7.30.* to get up. **2** *Prices have risen.* to go up, to grow, to increase. **3** *The balloon rose into the air.* to ascend, to climb, to mount. **4** *My sponge cake didn't rise.* to puff up, to swell. **5** *A cliff rose above us.* to loom, to stand out, to stick up, to tower. **6** *Tony pushed his bike up the rise.* ascent, bank, hill, incline, ramp, slope.

rising SEE **revolution**.

risk 1 *Is there a risk of frost?* chance, danger, possibility. **2** *Mr Brunswick risked a lot of money starting his business.* to dare, to gamble, to venture.

risky *It's risky cycling on icy roads.* chancy, dangerous, hazardous.

risotto, rissole SEE **food**.

rite SEE **ritual**.

ritual *a religious ritual.* ceremony, rite, service.

rival 1 *We beat our rivals from the other school.* adversary, competitor, enemy, opponent, opposition. **2** *The new shop tries to rival the shop down the road.* to compare with, to compete with, to contend with, to contest, to oppose, to struggle with.

rivalry competition, competitiveness.

river stream, tributary. SEE ALSO **geography**.

rivet SEE **fasten**.

road 1 KINDS OF ROAD AND PATH ARE alley, avenue, bypass, causeway, cul-de-sac, drive, footpath, highway, lane, motorway, one-way street, path, pathway, ring road, route, slip-road, street, thoroughfare, towpath, track, trunk road, way. **2** WORDS TO DO WITH ROADS ARE bridge, camber, flyover, foot-bridge, ford, hairpin bend, junction, lamppost, lay-by, level-crossing, roundabout, service area, signpost, traffic lights, underpass, U-turn, viaduct, zebra crossing. **3** SURFACES FOR ROADS AND PATHS ARE asphalt, cobbles, concrete, crazy paving, flagstones, gravel, paving stones, tarmac, tiles.

roam *The sheep roam over the hills.* to ramble, to range, to rove, to stray, to travel, to wander.

roar SEE **sound**.

roast SEE **cook**.

rob 1 *to rob a shop.* to loot, to pilfer, to plunder, to ransack. **2** *to rob someone.* to deprive, to steal from, to take from. **3** SEE **crime**.

robber burglar, highwayman, mugger, pickpocket, shop-lifter, thief. SEE ALSO **criminal**.

robin SEE **bird**.

robot SEE **automatic**.

robust *a robust person.* hardy, healthy, strong, sturdy, tough.

rock 1 boulder, crag, stone. **2** KINDS OF ROCK ARE chalk, clay, flint, granite, gravel, lava, limestone, marble, ore, pumice-stone, sandstone, slate. **3** *a stick of rock.* SEE **sweet**. **4** *I rocked the baby.* to move gently, to sway, to swing. **5** *The ship rocked in the storm.* to lurch, to pitch, to reel, to roll, to shake, to toss, to totter. **6** *Mrs Brunswick collects rock records.* SEE **music**.

rockery SEE **garden**.

rocket SEE **firework, space**.

rock-garden SEE **garden**.

rocking-chair SEE **furniture**.

rocking-horse SEE **toy**.

rod bar, baton, cane, pole, rail, stick, wand.

rodent SEE **animal**.

rodeo SEE **entertainment**.

roe SEE **fish**.

rogue blackguard, knave, rascal, scoundrel, villain. ! These words are rather old-fashioned. SEE ALSO **criminal, ruffian**.

role *a role in a play*. character, part.

roll 1 *a bread roll*. SEE **bread**. 2 *Add your name to the roll*. list, register. 3 *The wheels began to roll*. to revolve, to rotate, to spin, to turn. 4 *Roll up the carpet*. to curl, to twist, to wind. 5 *We rolled the cricket pitch*. to flatten, to level out, to smooth. 6 *The ship rolled in the storm*. to lurch, to pitch, to reel, to sway, to toss, to totter.

roller-skating SEE **sport**.

rolling-pin SEE **kitchen**.

rolling-stock SEE **railway**.

romance SEE **writing**.

romantic *a romantic story*. emotional, nostalgic, sentimental.

romp *We romped in the garden*. to caper, to dance, to frisk, to leap about, to play, to prance, to run about.

rompers SEE **clothes**.

roof 1 SEE **building**. 2 ROOFS ARE MADE OF corrugated iron, slates, thatch, tiles.

rook 1 SEE **bird**. 2 SEE **chess**.

room 1 cell, chamber. SEE ALSO **building, house**. 2 *Give me a bit more room*. freedom, space.

roomy *a roomy car*. large, spacious.

rooster SEE **chicken, male**.

root SEE **plant**.

rope cable, cord, hawser, line. SEE ALSO **fasten**.

rose SEE **flower**.

rosy SEE **colour**.

rot *Wood rots. Iron rots*. to corrode, to decay, to decompose, to disintegrate, to go bad, to perish, to spoil. SEE ALSO **rotten**.

rotor SEE **aircraft**.

rotten 1 *rotten iron, rotten wood*. corroded, decayed, disintegrating.

2 *rotten food*. decomposed, foul, mouldy, perished, putrid, smelly. SEE ALSO **bad**.

rough 1 *a rough surface*. bumpy, irregular, jagged, rugged, uneven. 2 *a rough crowd*. boisterous, disorderly, rowdy. 3 *rough weather*. stormy, turbulent, violent, wild. 4 *rough skin*. bristly, coarse, hairy, harsh, scratchy. 5 *a rough voice*. grating, gruff, hoarse, husky, unpleasant. 6 *rough manners*. bad-tempered, crude, impolite, rude, surly, unfriendly. 7 *rough work*. careless, clumsy, hasty, unfinished, unskilful.

roughly about, approximately, around, close to, nearly.

round 1 *a round shape*. circular, spherical. 2 *a round in a competition*. bout, contest, game. 3 *to round a corner*. to turn. 4 *to round off*: to close, to complete, to conclude, to end, to finish. 5 *to round up*: to assemble, to collect, to gather, to group, to herd, to mass.

roundabout 1 *a roundabout route*. devious, indirect, rambling. 2 SEE **fun-fair**. 3 SEE **road**.

rounders SEE **sport**.

round-shouldered hunchbacked.

rouse 1 *It takes ages to rouse Lucy in the mornings*. to arouse, to awaken, to call, to wake up. 2 *The group roused the audience to a frenzy*. to excite, to incite, to provoke, to stimulate, to stir up.

rout *We completely routed the opposition*. to conquer, to crush, to overwhelm. SEE ALSO **defeat**.

route *Which route shall we take?* course, direction, road, way.

routine *a normal routine*. custom, habit, method, practice, procedure, system, way.

rove *In the safari park the animals rove about freely*. to prowl, to range, to roam, to stray, to wander.

row 1 *Stand in a row*. column, cordon, file, line, queue, rank. 2 *Arrange them in a row*. chain, sequence, series, string. 3 *to row a boat.* to move, to propel.

rowdy *a rowdy crowd.* badly-behaved, boisterous, disorderly, irrepressible, lawless, noisy, obstreperous, riotous, rough, turbulent, undisciplined, unruly, violent, wild.

rowing-boat SEE **vessel**.

royal 1 *a royal palace.* majestic, regal, stately. 2 ROYAL PEOPLE ARE consort, Her or His Majesty, Her or His Royal Highness, king, monarch, prince, princess, queen, regent, sovereign. 3 WORDS TO DO WITH ROYALTY ARE abdication, accession, coronation, crown, throne.

rub 1 *The dog likes you to rub his chest.* to massage, to stroke. SEE ALSO **touch**. 2 *to rub clean*: to polish, to scour, to scrape, to scrub, to wipe. 3 *to rub out*: to blot out, to delete, to erase, to remove, to wipe out.

rubber SEE **material**.

rubbish 1 *Throw away that rubbish.* garbage, junk, litter, (informal) muck, refuse, rubble, scrap, trash, waste. 2 *Don't talk rubbish!* balderdash, bilge, drivel, gibberish, nonsense, tripe, twaddle. !Most of these words are used informally.

rubble *The building collapsed into a pile of rubble.* debris, fragments, remains, ruins, wreckage.

rucksack haversack. SEE ALSO **container**.

rudder SEE **vessel**.

ruddy *a ruddy face.* fresh, flushed, healthy, red, rosy, sunburnt.

rude 1 *rude language, a rude person.* abusive, bad-mannered, bad-tempered, blasphemous, cheeky, coarse, common, crude, discourteous, disparaging, disrespectful, foul, impertinent, impolite, improper, impudent, inconsiderate, indecent, insolent, insulting, loutish, mocking, offensive, saucy, uncomplimentary, uncouth, vulgar. 2 *to be rude to*: to abuse, to insult, to offend, to snub.

rueful *a rueful expression.* dejected,

downcast, down-hearted, regretful, sorrowful. SEE ALSO **sad**.

ruffian desperado, gangster, hooligan, lout, mugger, scoundrel, villain. SEE ALSO **criminal, rogue**.

ruffle *The breeze ruffled the water.* to agitate, to disturb, to ripple, to rumple, to stir.

rug 1 *Wrap yourself in a rug.* blanket. 2 *We put a rug on the floor.* mat. SEE ALSO **floor**.

Rugby WORDS USED IN RUGBY ARE pack, scrum, tackle, touch-down, touch-line, try. SEE ALSO **sport**.

rugged *Ordinary vehicles can't cross this rugged country.* bumpy, irregular, rough, uneven.

ruin 1 *The loss of our money meant the ruin of our plans.* collapse, destruction, downfall, end, fall. 2 *ruins*: debris, remains, rubble, wreckage. 3 *The gale ruined Mrs Brunswick's runner beans.* to demolish, to destroy, to devastate, to flatten, to spoil, to wreck.

rule 1 *Obey the rules.* code, law, regulation. 2 *As a rule we have gravy with meat.* convention, custom, practice, routine. 3 *Who rules the country?* to administer, to command, to control, to direct, to govern, to manage, to run. 4 *Victoria ruled for many years.* to be king or queen, to reign. 5 *The umpire ruled that the batsman was out.* to adjudicate, to decide, to decree, to judge.

ruler 1 VARIOUS RULERS ARE dictator, emperor, empress, king, monarch, president, queen, sultan, tyrant. SEE ALSO **chief**. 2 *Can I borrow your ruler?* SEE **mathematics**.

rum SEE **drink**.

rumble SEE **sound**.

rummage *I rummaged through the cupboard looking for my hat.* to comb, to ransack, to scour, to search.

rummy SEE **cards**.

rumour *The story that Mrs Angel was leaving was only a rumour.* gossip, prattle, scandal.

rump behind, bottom, buttocks, rear.

rumple *Don't rumple the bedclothes.* to agitate, to crease, to crumple, to disturb, to ruffle.

rumpus SEE **commotion.**

run 1 WAYS TO RUN ARE to canter, to dash, to gallop, to jog, to race, to rush, to scamper, to scuttle, to speed, to sprint, to trot. SEE ALSO **move.** 2 *Do the buses run on Sundays?* to go, to operate, to travel. 3 *The car runs well.* to behave, to function, to perform, to work. 4 *The blood ran down his leg.* to dribble, to flow, to gush, to pour, to stream, to trickle. 5 *The government is supposed to run the country.* to administer, to control, to direct, to govern, to look after, to maintain, to manage, to rule, to supervise. 6 *to run away:* SEE **escape.** 7 *to run into:* SEE **collide.** 8 *a run of bad luck.* series, sequence. 9 *a chicken run.* compound, enclosure, pen.

runner bean SEE **vegetable.**

runny *It was so hot that the ice-cream went runny.* creamy, flowing, fluid, liquid, sloppy, smooth, thin, watery, wet.

runway airstrip, landing-strip.

rural rustic. SEE ALSO **country.**

ruse *Logan used a sneaky ruse to trick us.* SEE **trick.**

rush 1 to dash, to gallop, to hasten, to hurry, to run, to scramble, to speed, (informal) to zoom. SEE ALSO **move.** 2 *a rush of water.* cataract, flood, gush, spate. 3 *a rush of people.* panic, stampede. 4 SEE **water plant.**

rusk SEE **food.**

rust *Iron rusts.* to corrode, to rot.

rustic *rustic surroundings.* rural.

rustle SEE **sound.**

rusty *rusty iron.* corroded, rotten.

rut *to stick in a rut.* furrow, groove.

ruthless *a ruthless attack.* SEE **cruel.**

rye SEE **cereal.**

S s

sabbath SEE **church, Jew.**

sabotage damage, destruction.

sabre SEE **weapon.**

saccharine SEE **sweet.**

sack 1 bag, pouch. SEE ALSO **container.** 2 *to sack someone from a job.* to dismiss, to fire.

sacking SEE **cloth.**

sacrament SEE **church.**

sacred *The Bible and the Koran are sacred books.* blessed, consecrated, divine, hallowed, holy, religious.

sacrifice *Lucy sacrificed her weekend to train for the competition.* to give up, to offer up, to surrender.

sacrilegious *I think it's sacrilegious to play about in church.* blasphemous, irreverent, wicked.

sad *a sad expression, a sad story, etc.* careworn, cheerless, crestfallen, dejected, depressed, desolate, despairing, desperate, despondent, disappointed, disconsolate, discontented, discouraged, disgruntled, dismal, dissatisfied, distressed, doleful, down, downcast, down-hearted, dreary, forlorn, gloomy, glum, grave, grieving, grim, guilty, heart-broken, heavy, hopeless, joyless, low, lugubrious, melancholy, miserable, moping, morbid, morose, mournful, pathetic, penitent, pessimistic, pitiful, plaintive, regretful, rueful, sombre, sorrowful, sorry, tearful, touching, tragic, troubled, unhappy, wistful, woeful, wretched.

sadden *The dog's death saddened us.* to depress, to dishearten, to dismay, to grieve.

saddle SEE **horse.**

sadistic SEE **cruel.**

safari SEE **holiday, reserve.**

safe 1 *Are your belongings safe from burglars?* defended, protected, secure. 2 *We got home safe in spite of the storm.* undamaged, unharmed, unscathed. 3 *Is Logan safe with that money?* dependable, reliable, trustworthy. 4 *Is that dog safe?* docile, harmless, innocuous, tame. 5 *a safe aircraft.* airworthy. 6 *a safe ship.* seaworthy.

safeguard *Insurance safeguards us*

against unforeseen disasters. to defend, to guard, to look after, to protect, to shield.

safety protection, security.

safety-belt seat-belt. SEE ALSO **car.**

safety-pin SEE **fasten.**

sag *The rope sags in the middle.* to be limp, to droop, to flop, to slump.

saga SEE **writing.**

sage SEE **herb.**

sail 1 SEE **travel, vessel.** 2 *to sail a boat.* to navigate.

sailor VARIOUS SAILORS ARE able seaman, admiral, boatswain, captain, cox or coxswain, crew, helmsman, mariner, mate, navigator, pilot, rower, seaman.

saint SEE **church.**

saintly blessed, holy, religious. SEE ALSO **good.**

sake *Do it for your own sake.* advantage, benefit, good, welfare.

salad THINGS YOU EAT IN SALAD ARE beetroot, celery, cress, cucumber, lettuce, mustard and cress, onion, potato, tomato, watercress. SEE ALSO **vegetable.**

salary *a salary of £10,000 a year.* earnings, income, pay, wages.

sale KINDS OF SALE ARE auction, bazaar, fair, jumble sale, market.

salesman, saleswoman SEE **job, shopkeeper.**

salmon SEE **fish.**

saloon SEE **vehicle.**

salt SEE **food, taste.**

salute SEE **gesture.**

salvage *They salvaged the wrecked ship.* to recover, to rescue, to retrieve, to save.

same *Lucy wore the same dress as her friend.* corresponding, equal, equivalent, identical, similar.

sample *Show me a sample of your work.* example, illustration, instance, specimen.

sanctuary *The escaping prisoner sought sanctuary in a church.* asylum, haven, refuge, retreat, safety, shelter.

sand grit.

sandal SEE **shoe.**

sand-dune SEE **seaside.**

sandpaper SEE **tool.**

sandwich SEE **food.**

sandy SEE **colour.**

sane *They said he was crazy, but he seems sane to me.* normal, rational, reasonable.

sanitary *You must have sanitary conditions in a hospital.* clean, germ-free, healthy, hygienic, sterilized, unpolluted.

sanitation drainage, drains, lavatories, sewers, WC. SEE ALSO **house.**

sap *The long climb sapped our energy.* to exhaust, to tire, to weaken, to wear out.

sapling SEE **tree.**

sapphire SEE **jewellery.**

sarcastic *Logan's sarcastic jokes hurt Lucy.* disparaging, hurtful, mocking, satirical. SEE ALSO **ridicule.**

sardine SEE **fish.**

sari SEE **clothes.**

satchel bag. SEE ALSO **container.**

satellite 1 moon, planet. SEE ALSO **astronomy.** 2 *a man-made satellite.* SEE **space.**

satin SEE **cloth.**

satire SEE **writing.**

satirical *Logan's satirical comments hurt Lucy.* disparaging, mocking, sarcastic. SEE ALSO **ridicule.**

satisfactory *Mrs Angel said Logan's work was only just satisfactory.* acceptable, adequate, all right, fair, good enough, passable, sufficient, tolerable.

satisfy 1 *Will sandwiches satisfy you?* to content, to make happy, to please. 2 *Will £10 satisfy your needs?* to fulfil, to meet. 3 *to satisfy your thirst.* to quench.

saturate 1 *The rainstorm saturated the ground.* to drench, to soak, to wet. 2 *saturated:* waterlogged.

sauce KINDS OF SAUCE ARE custard, dressing, gravy, ketchup, mayonnaise, mint sauce, salad cream. SEE ALSO food.

saucepan cauldron, pan, pot. SEE ALSO cook, container, kitchen.

saucer SEE crockery.

saucy *a saucy joke.* cheeky, impertinent, impudent, rude.

sauna bath.

saunter SEE walk.

sausage SEE food, meat.

savage 1 *a savage attack.* atrocious, barbaric, beastly, bloodthirsty, bloody, brutal, callous, cold-blooded, cruel, ferocious, fierce, heartless, inhuman, merciless, murderous, pitiless, ruthless, sadistic, uncivilized, unfeeling, vicious, violent. 2 *The explorers were attacked by savages.* barbarian, cannibal, heathen, pagan.
! Nowadays we do not use *savage* to describe people from developing countries.

save 1 *Robin Hood saved the prisoners.* to free, to liberate, to release, to rescue, to set free. 2 *Save something for later.* to hold on to, to keep, to preserve, to reserve, to safeguard, to store up, to take care of. 3 *Have you saved any money?* to deposit, to hoard, to invest, to scrape together, to set aside. 4 *Try to save fuel.* to economize on. 5 *Can they save the wrecked ship?* to recover, to retrieve, to salvage.

savings *Have you got any savings?* capital, funds, investments, riches, wealth.

savoury SEE taste.

saw SEE cut, tool.

saxophone SEE music.

say to comment, to communicate, to convey, to express, to mention, to pronounce, to remark, to speak, to state, to utter. SEE ALSO talk.

saying expression, motto, phrase, proverb, remark, slogan.

scab scar.

scabbard sheath.

scaffold gallows.

scald SEE heat.

scale 1 *a musical scale.* SEE music. 2 *the scale of a map.* proportion, size. 3 *to scale a ladder.* to ascend, to climb, to mount. 4 *the scales of a fish.* SEE fish.

scales *a pair of scales.* balance, weighing-machine.

scalp SEE body, head.

scalpel SEE medicine.

scamp imp, knave, rascal, rogue.

scamper *The dog scampered home.* to dash, to hasten, to hurry, to run, to rush, to scuttle. SEE ALSO move.

scampi SEE food.

scan 1 *The castaway scanned the horizon.* to examine, to eye, to gaze at, to look at, to stare at, to study, to view, to watch. 2 *I scanned the newspaper.* to glance at, to read quickly, to skim.

scandal 1 *It's a scandal that so much food is wasted.* disgrace, embarrassment, notoriety, outrage, sensation, shame. 2 *Logan enjoys a bit of scandal.* gossip, rumour.

scandalous *What a scandalous waste of money!* disgraceful, infamous, notorious, outrageous, shameful, shocking, wicked.

scanty *The provisions were scanty.* inadequate, insufficient, meagre, (informal) measly, scarce, small, sparse, thin.

scar 1 *The wound left a scar.* mark, scab. 2 *The wound scarred his face.* to damage, to deface, to disfigure, to mark, to spoil.

scarce *Vegetables were scarce during the cold weather.* insufficient, rare, scanty, sparse, uncommon.

scarcely barely, hardly.

scare 1 *The explosion scared us.* to alarm, to dismay, to shock, to startle. 2 *Logan's gang tried to scare us.* to bully, to frighten, to intimidate, to make afraid, to menace, to persecute, to terrorize, to threaten.

scarf SEE clothes.

scarlet SEE colour.

scarlet fever SEE illness.

scary (informal) *It was scary in the dark.* creepy, eerie, frightening, ghostly, spooky, uncanny, weird.

scatter 1 *The wind scattered leaves over the road.* to disperse, to shed, to spread, to sprinkle, to throw about. **2** *scattered*: strewn.

scatter-brained absent-minded, careless, disorganized, forgetful, muddled, silly, thoughtless, unsystematic, vague.

scavenger SEE **animal**.

scene 1 *the scene of a crime.* location, place, setting, site. **2** *Logan made a scene because he didn't get a prize.* argument, fuss, quarrel. **3** *a beautiful scene.* landscape, outlook, panorama, picture, view, scenery, sight, spectacle, view, vista.

scenery 1 SEE **scene**. **2** SEE **theatre**.

scenic *a scenic drive.* attractive, beautiful, lovely, picturesque, pretty.

scent 1 *the scent of flowers.* aroma, fragrance, odour, perfume, smell, whiff. **2** SEE **cosmetics**.

sceptical *Mrs Angel was sceptical when Logan said he would do all the clearing up.* disbelieving, doubting, dubious, incredulous, questioning, suspicious, unconvinced.

schedule *a schedule of events.* list, programme, timetable.

scheme 1 *We thought of a scheme to make a lot of money.* conspiracy, design, intrigue, manoeuvre, plan, plot, project, ruse. **2** *The two boys schemed together.* to conspire, to intrigue, to plan, to plot.

scholar SEE **pupil**.

school 1 KINDS OF SCHOOL ARE academy, boarding-school, coeducational school, comprehensive school, high school, infant school, junior school, kindergarten, nursery school, play-group, prep school, primary school, secondary school. **2** WORDS TO DO WITH SCHOOL ARE assembly, audio-visual aids, blackboard, chalk, classroom, cloakroom, desk, display, dormitory, exercise book, SEE **head**, homework, laboratory, lesson, library, monitor, notice-board, peripatetic teacher, playground,

playing-field, playtime, prefect, prep, project, SEE **pupil**, register, satchel, staff, syllabus, SEE **teacher**, textbook, truant, uniform, workcard. **3** SEE **educate**. **4** *a school of whales.* SEE **group**.

schoolchild SEE **pupil**.

schoolteacher SEE **teacher**.

schooner SEE **vessel**.

science VARIOUS SCIENCES ARE anatomy, astronomy, biology, botany, chemistry, electronics, geology, meteorology, physics, psychology, technology, zoology. SEE ALSO **subject**.

science fiction SEE **writing**.

scientific *a scientific investigation.* methodical, organized, systematic.

scientist SEE **job**.

scissors SEE **house**.

scoff SEE **scorn**.

scold *Mrs Angel scolded Logan for being late.* to blame, to censure, to criticize, to rebuke, to reprimand, to reproach, (informal) to tick off.

scone SEE **cake**.

scoop 1 *an ice-cream scoop.* ladle, shovel, spoon. **2** *We scooped out a hole in the sand.* to dig, to gouge, to hollow, to shovel.

scooter SEE **toy, vehicle**.

scope extent, limit, range, reach.

scorch SEE **burn, heat**.

score 1 *What was your score?* mark, result, total. **2** *We scored the polished floor when we moved the piano.* to mark, to scrape, to scratch.

score-board, scorer SEE **sport**.

scorn *They scorned our cooking and bought some chips.* to be contemptuous of, to despise, to disdain, to dislike, to hate, to insult, to jeer at, to laugh at, to look down on, to make fun of, to mock, to ridicule, to scoff at, to sneer at, to taunt.

scoundrel 1 blackguard, knave, rascal, rogue, ruffian, villain. ! These words often sound rather old-fashioned. **2** SEE **rogue, ruffian**.

scour 1 *to scour a saucepan.* to clean, to

polish, to rub, to scrape, to scrub, to wash. **2** *We scoured the house looking for mum's keys.* to comb, to ransack, to rummage through, to search.

scourge 1 crop, lash, whip. **2** SEE **hit**.

scout *You wait here while I scout round.* to get information, to look about.

scowl to frown, to glower. SEE ALSO **expression**.

scraggy *a weak, scraggy animal.* bony, emaciated, gaunt, lean, skinny, thin.

scramble 1 *I scrambled up the cliff.* to clamber, to climb, to crawl. **2** *We scrambled to get some food before it all went.* to fight, to scuffle, to struggle, to tussle. **3** *We scrambled into our places at the last minute.* to dash, to hasten, to rush. **4** *a motor-bike scramble.* SEE **race**.

scrap 1 *a pile of useless scrap.* junk, litter, refuse, rubbish, waste. **2** *a scrap of food.* bit, crumb, fragment, particle, piece, snippet, speck. **3** *Two dogs had a scrap.* SEE **fight**. **4** *We had to scrap our plan when we knew how much it would cost.* to abandon, to discard, to drop, to give up, to throw away.

scrap-book SEE **book**.

scrape 1 *I scraped my knuckles.* to graze, to scratch. **2** *I scraped the mud off my shoes.* to clean, to rub, to scour, to scrub. **3** *I scraped together some money.* to collect, to save. **4** *Logan got into a scrape.* escapade, mischief, prank, trouble.

scratch 1 *Mr Brunswick was mad when Lucy scratched the car.* to damage, to mark, to score, to scrape. **2** *The dog scratched at the door.* to claw. **3** *a scratch on the surface.* groove, line.

scrawl SEE **write**.

scream to cry, to howl, to screech, to shriek, to squeal, to wail, to yell. SEE ALSO **sound**.

scree stones.

screech SEE **sound**.

screen 1 *We closed the screen.* blind, curtain, partition. **2** *Mrs Brunswick planted a bush to screen the manure heap.* to camouflage, to conceal, to cover, to disguise, to hide, to mask, to protect, to shade, to shield.

screw SEE **fasten**.

screwdriver SEE **tool**.

scribble to doodle, to jot. SEE ALSO **write**.

script SEE **writing**.

scripture SEE **church, Jew**.

scroll SEE **book**.

scrounge *The stray cat scrounged for scraps.* to beg, to cadge.

scrub *to scrub the floor.* to brush, to clean, to rub, to scour, to wash.

scruffy *a scruffy appearance.* bedraggled, dirty, dishevelled, scrappy, shabby, tatty, untidy.

scrum SEE **Rugby**.

scrupulous 1 *a scrupulous worker.* diligent, honest. **2** *Tony pays scrupulous attention to detail.* meticulous, painstaking, systematic, thorough. SEE ALSO **careful**.

scrutiny *Mrs Angel subjected Logan's work to close scrutiny.* examination, inspection, investigation.

scuffle SEE **fight**.

scull SEE **vessel**.

scullery SEE **house**.

sculptor SEE **art**.

sculpture carving, figure, image, statue. SEE ALSO **art**.

scum foam, froth.

scurvy SEE **illness**.

scuttle 1 *to scuttle a ship.* to sink. **2** *A crab scuttled away when we moved the stone.* to shuffle, to run. SEE **walk**.

scythe SEE **tool**.

SDP SEE **politics**.

sea 1 ocean. SEE ALSO **geography**. **2** *of* or *on the sea*: marine, nautical, naval, seafaring, seagoing.

seafood SEE **food**.

seagull SEE **bird**.

seal 1 SEE **animal**. **2** *the royal seal.* crest, emblem, sign, stamp, symbol. **3** *to seal a lid.* to fasten, to lock, to secure, to shut. **4** *to seal an envelope.* to close, to stick. **5** *to seal a leak.* to plug, to stop up.

sea-lion SEE **animal**.

seam 1 *Tony sewed up the seam of his jeans.* join, stitching. 2 *a seam of coal.* layer, stratum, thickness.

seaman SEE **sailor**.

seaplane SEE **aircraft**.

search 1 *We searched for a decent snack-bar.* to explore, to hunt, to look, to nose about, to prospect, to seek. 2 *We searched the house for mum's keys.* to comb, to ransack, to rummage through, to scour. 3 *The search took ages.* hunt, look, quest.

searchlight SEE **light**.

sea-shore coast. SEE ALSO **seaside**.

seaside WORDS TO DO WITH THE SEASIDE ARE beach, breaker, breakwater, cliff, coast, dune, esplanade, life-guard, pier, promenade, resort, sand-dune, sands, seashell, seashore, seaweed, skin-diving, sunbathing, sunburn, surf, surf-riding, swimming, tide, water-skiing, wave.

season period. SEE ALSO **time**.

seasoning SEE **food**.

seat KINDS OF SEAT ARE armchair, bench, chair, couch, deck-chair, pouffe, rocking-chair, settee, sofa, stool, throne. SEE ALSO **furniture**.

seat-belt safety-belt. SEE ALSO **vehicle**.

seaweed SEE **seaside, water plant**.

seaworthy *a seaworthy ship.* safe.

secateurs SEE **garden**.

secluded *We were the only people on the secluded beach.* inaccessible, isolated, lonely, private, remote, solitary.

second 1 *The pain only lasted a second.* flash, instant, moment. SEE ALSO **measure, time**. 2 *Tony seconded Lucy in our classroom debate.* to assist, to back, to help, to side with, to support.

secondary school SEE **school**.

second-hand *a second-hand car.* used.

second-rate *We were disappointed by her second-rate performance.* commonplace, mediocre, middling, ordinary, unexciting.

secret 1 *secret information.* confidential, hushed up, intimate, personal, private. 2 *a secret hide-out.* concealed, hidden.

secretary SEE **job**.

secretive *Logan was secretive about where he found the money.* furtive, mysterious, reserved, reticent, shifty, uncommunicative.

section bit, compartment, branch, division, fraction, part, portion, sector, segment.

sector *a sector of a town.* area, district, division, part, section, zone.

secure 1 *Is the house secure against burglars?* defended, protected, safe. 2 *During the storm we remained secure indoors.* snug, unharmed, unscathed. 3 *Is that hook secure?* fast, firm, fixed, immovable, solid, steady, tight, unyielding. 4 SEE **fasten**.

sedate *The procession moved at a sedate pace.* calm, cool, dignified, grave, level-headed, sensible, serious, sober.

sedative sleeping-pill, tranquillizer. SEE ALSO **medicine**.

sediment *sediment at the bottom of a bottle.* deposit, dregs, remains.

seductive *a seductive dress, seductive music, etc.* alluring, appealing, bewitching, captivating, enticing, irresistible, (informal) sexy, tempting. SEE ALSO **attractive**.

see 1 *Did you see anything interesting?* to behold, to discern, to distinguish, to look at, to make out, to notice, to observe, to perceive, to recognize, to sight, to spot, to spy, to witness. SEE ALSO **look**. 2 *Do you see what I mean?* to appreciate, to comprehend, to follow, to grasp, to know, to realize, to understand. 3 *The refugees saw much misery.* to endure, to experience, to go through, to suffer, to undergo. 4 *Guess who I saw in town!* to encounter, to face, to meet, to run into, to visit. 5 *Shall I see you home?* to accompany, to conduct, to escort. 6 *I can't see granny going to a disco.* to conceive, to imagine, to picture, to visualize.

seed pip, stone. SEE ALSO **plant**.

seedling SEE **plant**.

seek to hunt for, to look for, to pursue, to search for.

seem *The weather seems better today.* to appear, to feel, to look.

seep *Water seeped through the crack.* to dribble, to drip, to flow, to leak, to ooze, to run, to trickle.

see-saw SEE **game**.

seethe *She was seething with anger.* SEE **angry**.

segment division, fraction, part, piece, portion, section.

segregate *They segregated the visitors from the home supporters.* to cut off, to isolate, to keep apart, to separate, to set apart.

seize 1 *The police seized a suspect.* to arrest, to capture, to catch, to detain, (informal) to nab, to take prisoner. **2** *I seized the end of the rope.* to clutch, to grab, to grasp, to hold, to pluck, to snatch. **3** *The police seized the stolen property.* to confiscate, to take away.

seldom infrequently, rarely.

select *We selected Lucy as captain.* to appoint, to choose, to decide on, to elect, to nominate, to opt for, to pick, to prefer, to settle on, to vote for.

selection *Make your selection.* choice, pick.

self-catering SEE **holiday**.

self-confident *You need to be self-confident to be a good captain.* assertive, assured, bold, fearless, positive, sure of yourself.

self-conscious *Lucy used to be self-conscious in front of an audience.* bashful, embarrassed, reserved, shy.

self-control *Tony showed great self-control when Logan was teasing him.* calmness, patience, restraint.

self-explanatory *a self-explanatory diagram.* apparent, clear, evident, obvious.

self-important *Logan looked so self-important showing visitors where to park their cars!* arrogant, bumptious, cocky, pompous, stuck-up, vain.

selfish *It's selfish to keep all those sweets to yourself.* grasping, greedy, mean, miserly, stingy, thoughtless, worldly.

self-portrait SEE **picture**.

self-righteous, self-satisfied complacent, pompous, proud, self-important, smug, vain.

sell 1 *What does the shop at the corner sell?* to deal in, to market, to retail, to trade in. **2** PEOPLE WHO SELL THINGS ARE dealer, merchant, retailer, salesman, saleswoman, shopkeeper, stockist, supplier, trader, tradesman. **3** SEE **shop**.

Sellotape SEE **fasten**.

semibreve SEE **music**.

semicircle SEE **shape**.

semicolon SEE **punctuation**.

semi-detached SEE **house**.

semiquaver SEE **music**.

semolina SEE **food**.

send 1 *We sent a parcel to grandad.* to convey, to dispatch, to post, to transmit. **2** *They sent a rocket to the moon.* to launch, to shoot. **3** *to send away*: to banish, to dismiss, to exile, to expel. **4** *to send out*: to belch, to broadcast, to emit. **5** *to send round*: to circulate, to distribute, to issue, to publish.

senile decrepit, infirm, old.

senior *a senior position.* chief, older, superior.

sensation 1 *It was so cold that I had no sensation in my fingers.* awareness, feeling, sense. **2** *It was a sensation when news of the robbery got out.* excitement, outrage, scandal, thrill.

sensational 1 *We won by the sensational score of 13-0.* amazing, exciting, extraordinary, fabulous, fantastic, great, marvellous, spectacular, superb, thrilling, wonderful. ! These words are usually informal. **2** *a sensational murder.* lurid, shocking, startling, violent.

sense 1 YOUR FIVE SENSES ARE hearing, sight, smell, taste, touch. **2** *I had a sense that something awful was happening.* awareness, feeling, sensation. **3** *Haven't you got any sense?*

brains, gumption, intellect,
intelligence, judgement, reason,
reasoning, understanding, wisdom,
wit. **4** *I can't make sense of this.*
meaning, significance. **5** *I sensed that
he was bored.* to be aware, to detect, to
discern, to feel, to perceive, to
realize, to understand.

senseless 1 *It was a senseless thing to
do.* SEE **absurd.** **2** *I was knocked
senseless.* SEE **unconscious.**

sensible 1 *a sensible person.* calm, cool,
level-headed, reasonable,
thoughtful, wise. **2** *a sensible decision.*
advisable, logical, prudent.

sensitive 1 *a sensitive skin.* delicate,
soft, tender. **2** *a sensitive nature.*
emotional, touchy.

sentence 1 SEE **language.** **2** *The
judge sentenced him.* to condemn, to
convict, to pass judgement.

sentiment *What are your sentiments
about experiments on animals?* attitude,
emotion, feeling, opinion, thought,
view.

sentimental *I get sentimental when I
look at old family photographs.*
emotional, nostalgic, romantic, soft-
hearted, tearful, tender.

sentinel, sentry guard, look-out,
watchman.

separate 1 *Keep the mice separate from
the guinea-pigs!* apart, divided,
isolated, segregated. **2** *The infants are
in a separate part of the school.* detached,
different, distinct. **3** *The police
separated the two gangs.* to break up, to
cut off, to detach, to isolate, to part,
to segregate, to set apart, to split.
4 *Our paths separated.* to diverge, to
divide, to fork. **5** *Their parents
separated.* to divorce, to split up.

septic *a septic wound.* festering,
infected, inflamed, poisoned.

sequel *Was there a sequel to the row
Logan had with the head?* consequence,
outcome, result.

sequence *a sequence of events.* SEE
series.

serene *a serene mood.* calm, peaceful,
placid, tranquil, untroubled.

sergeant SEE **rank.**

serial SEE **television.**

series 1 *a series of events.* chain, course,
cycle, line, order, progression, range,
row, sequence, string, succession.
2 *a television series.* SEE **television.**

serious 1 *a serious expression.* dignified,
earnest, grave, sedate, sober,
solemn. **2** *a serious accident, a serious
problem, etc.* appalling, awful,
calamitous, dreadful, frightful,
ghastly, hideous, horrible, nasty,
severe, shocking, terrible, (informal)
terrific, unfortunate, unpleasant,
violent. **3** *a serious worker.* careful,
conscientious, diligent, earnest,
hard-working, sincere.

sermon SEE **church.**

serpent snake.

servant VARIOUS SERVANTS ARE
attendant, butler, chauffeur, cook,
footman, housekeeper, maid, page,
slave, steward, stewardess.

serve 1 *We need volunteers to serve the
community.* to assist, to attend, to
help, to look after, to work for. **2** *to
serve at table.* to wait.

service 1 *Tony did me a service by posting
my letter.* assistance, favour, help. **2** *a
religious service.* ceremony, meeting,
worship. SEE ALSO **church.** **3** *Mr
Brunswick services his own car.* to
maintain, to mend, to overhaul, to
repair.

serviceable *a pair of strong serviceable
shoes.* durable, hard-wearing, lasting,
strong, tough.

service area SEE **road.**

serviette napkin.

session *When does the next session start at
the baths?* period, time.

set 1 *Set the things down on the table.* to
arrange, to deposit, to lay, to leave,
to place, to put, to position, to rest,
to stand. **2** *Mr Brunswick set the
gatepost in concrete.* to embed, to fix.
3 *Has the concrete set?* to harden, to
stiffen. **4** *to set off on a journey.* SEE
depart. **5** *to set off an explosion.* to
detonate, to explode, to let off. **6** *to
set on someone.* SEE **attack.** **7** *to set on*

fire: to ignite, to kindle, to light. 8 *a set of people, a set of tools, etc.* batch, bunch, category, class, collection, group, kind, sort.

set-back *I did well at first, but then I had a set-back.* complication, difficulty, obstacle, problem, snag.

set-square SEE **mathematics**.

settee couch, sofa. SEE ALSO **furniture**.

settle 1 *When did you settle in this country?* to immigrate, to make your home, to move to, to stay. 2 *A robin settled on the fence.* to come to rest, to land, to pause, to rest. 3 *Wait until the dust settles.* to go down, to subside. 4 *Have you settled what to do?* to agree, to choose, to decide, to establish, to fix. 5 *Mum settled the bill.* to pay.

sever *to sever a rope, to sever a pipeline, etc.* SEE **cut**.

severe 1 *a severe ruler.* austere, cruel, hard, harsh, stern, strict. 2 *a severe frost, severe flu, etc.* acute, bad, drastic, extreme, intense, keen, serious, sharp, violent.

sew 1 *Tony sewed up the hole in his jeans.* to darn, to mend, to repair, to stitch, to tack. 2 *sewing*: embroidery, needlework.

sewage waste.

sewers drainage, drains, sanitation.

shabby *shabby clothes.* dowdy, drab, frayed, ragged, scruffy, tattered, tatty, threadbare, unattractive, worn.

shack hovel, hut, shanty. SEE ALSO **house**.

shackles *The prisoners wore shackles on their legs.* bonds, chains, fetters, irons.

shade 1 *We sat in the shade of a tree.* shadow, shelter. 2 *I painted the sky a pale shade of blue.* colour, hue, tinge, tint, tone. 3 *The sun was so bright I had to shade my eyes.* to darken, to mask, to protect, to screen, to shield.

shadow 1 *I won't get a good photo if you stand in shadow.* darkness, shade. 2 *The low sun cast long shadows on the ground.* outline, shape. 3 *The detective shadowed the suspect.* to follow, to hunt, to pursue, to stalk, to tag onto, to tail, to track, to trail.

shady 1 *We sat in a shady spot under a tree.* dark, dim, gloomy, shaded, shadowy. 2 *The man they caught shop-lifting looked a shady character.* disreputable, dubious, suspicious, untrustworthy.

shaft 1 *a wooden shaft.* column, pillar, pole, post, rod. 2 *a mine shaft.* mine, pit, working. 3 *a shaft of light.* beam, ray.

shaggy *a shaggy beard.* bushy, fleecy, hairy, rough, woolly.

shake 1 *I shook with fear!* to quiver, to shiver, to shudder, to tremble. 2 *The earthquake made the buildings shake.* to quake, to sway, to throb, to vibrate, to wobble. 3 *Grandad shook his umbrella.* to brandish, to flourish, to twirl, to wag, to waggle, to wave, to wiggle. 4 *The terrible news shook us.* to alarm, to distress, to frighten, to perturb, to shock, to startle.

shaky *The bench was so shaky we didn't dare sit down.* flimsy, frail, insecure, precarious, ramshackle, rickety, rocky, unsteady, weak, wobbly.

shallow not deep.

sham SEE **pretend**.

shamble SEE **walk**.

shambles 1 slaughterhouse. 2 *Lucy's bedroom is in a shambles.* chaos, confusion, disorder, mess, muddle.

shame 1 *We'll never live down the shame of losing 14-0.* disgrace, dishonour, embarrassment, guilt, humiliation, remorse. 2 *It's a shame to treat a dog so badly!* outrage, pity, scandal.

shameful SEE **bad**.

shameless *Logan is shameless when it comes to keeping the biggest bit for himself.* bold, brazen, impudent, insolent, rude, unashamed.

shampoo SEE **bathroom**.

shandy SEE **drink**.

shanty 1 hovel, hut, shack. SEE ALSO **house**. 2 *a sea shanty.* SEE **sing**.

shape 1 *I saw the shape of a bird against the sky.* figure, form, outline. 2 FLAT SHAPES ARE circle, diamond, ellipse, hexagon, oblong, octagon, oval, pentagon, quadrilateral, rectangle, semicircle, square, triangle. **3** THREE-DIMENSIONAL SHAPES ARE cone, cube, cylinder, hemisphere, prism, pyramid, sphere. **4** *The sculptor shaped the clay.* to carve, to cast, to cut, to form, to mould.

share **1** *We gave everyone a fair share of the food.* allowance, bit, division, fraction, helping, part, piece, portion, quota, ration. **2** *We shared the food equally.* to allot, to deal out, to distribute, to divide, to halve, to split. **3** *If we all share in the work we'll finish quickly.* to be involved, to join, to participate, to take part.

shark SEE **fish**.

sharp **1** *a sharp knife, etc.* cutting, fine, keen, pointed. **2** *a sharp mind.* acute, astute, bright, cute, intelligent, quick, shrewd, smart. SEE ALSO **clever**. **3** *a sharp taste.* acid, sour, tangy, tart. SEE ALSO **taste**. **4** *a sharp drop, a sharp rise.* abrupt, precipitous, steep, sudden. **5** *a sharp frost, a sharp pain, etc.* extreme, intense, serious, severe, violent. **6** *a sharp sound.* high, piercing, shrill. **7** SEE **music**.

sharpen *to sharpen a knife.* to grind.

shatter *The explosion shattered the window. The window shattered.* to break up, to burst, to disintegrate, to explode, to smash, to splinter.

shave SEE **cut**.

shaver SEE **bathroom**.

shawl SEE **clothes**.

sheaf *a sheaf of papers.* bundle, bunch.

shear *to shear sheep.* to clip. SEE ALSO **cut**.

shears SEE **garden, tool**.

sheath scabbard.

shed **1** *a garden shed.* hut, outhouse, shack, shelter. SEE ALSO **building**. **2** *A lorry shed its load.* to discard, to drop, to let fall, to scatter, to spill, to throw off.

sheen *A rub with polish gives the furniture a nice sheen.* brightness, gloss, lustre, polish, shine.

sheep ewe, lamb, ram. SEE ALSO **farm**.

sheepdog SEE **dog**.

sheepish *a sheepish look.* bashful, coy, embarrassed, guilty, self-conscious, shy, timid.

sheer **1** *sheer nonsense.* absolute, complete, pure, total, utter. **2** *a sheer cliff.* precipitous, vertical.

sheet **1** SEE **bedclothes**. **2** *a sheet of paper.* leaf, page. **3** *a sheet of glass.* pane, plate. **4** *a sheet of ice on a pond.* coating, film, layer, skin. **5** *a sheet of water.* area, expanse.

shelf ledge.

shell **1** *an outer shell.* case, covering, crust, exterior, husk, outside, pod. **2** *to fire a shell.* SEE **ammunition**. **3** *They shelled the battleship.* to attack, to bombard, to fire at, to shoot at.

shellfish VARIOUS SHELLFISH ARE barnacle, clam, cockle, crab, limpet, lobster, mussel, oyster, prawn, shrimp, whelk, winkle. SEE ALSO **fish**.

shelter **1** *We sought shelter from the storm.* asylum, cover, haven, protection, refuge, safety, sanctuary. **2** *The fence sheltered us from the wind.* to defend, to guard, to protect, to shield. **3** *Is it wrong to shelter a criminal?* to give asylum to, to give refuge to, to harbour.

shepherd SEE **job**.

sherry SEE **drink**.

shield **1** *The fence acts as a shield against the wind.* defence, guard, protection, safeguard, screen. **2** *Parents try to shield their young from danger.* to defend, to guard, to keep safe, to protect, to safeguard, to shelter. **3** *The umbrella shielded us from the sun.* to cover, to screen, to shade.

shift *Logan refused to shift. Please shift your things.* to budge, to change, to move, to transfer.

shifty *I didn't trust his shifty expression.* crafty, deceitful, furtive, secretive, sly, tricky, untrustworthy, wily.

shin SEE **body, leg**.

shine **1** to gleam, to glimmer, to glow,

to radiate. SEE ALSO light. 2 *shining*:
SEE shiny.

shingle *shingle on the beach.* gravel,
pebbles, stones.

shiny bright, burnished, gleaming,
glossy, polished, shining.

ship 1 SEE vessel. 2 *They ship a lot of
goods to foreign countries.* to carry, to
convey, to export, to ferry, to move,
to transport.

shipshape *We tidied up and made
everything shipshape.* clean, neat,
orderly, tidy, trim.

shipwreck SEE disaster.

shirk *Lucy shirked the washing-up.* to
avoid, to dodge, to evade, to get out
of, to neglect, (informal) to skive.

shirt SEE clothes.

shiver *to shiver with cold.* to quake, to
quaver, to quiver, to shake, to
shudder, to tremble, to vibrate.

shoal *a shoal of fish.* SEE group.

shock 1 *It was a shock to learn that the
head was leaving.* bombshell, surprise.
2 *When the plane crashed we felt the
shock.* blow, collision, impact, jolt.
3 *The garage bill shocked Mr Brunswick.*
to alarm, to amaze, to astound, to
daze, to dismay, to frighten, to scare,
to stagger, to startle, to stun, to
surprise. 4 *The bad language shocked
Aunt Grace.* to appal, to disgust, to
horrify, to offend, to repel, to revolt.
5 *shocking*: SEE outrageous.

shoddy 1 *Don't waste your money on
shoddy goods.* cheap, inferior, nasty,
poor-quality. 2 *Anyone who hands in
shoddy work has to do it again.* careless,
messy, negligent, sloppy, slovenly,
untidy.

shoe KINDS OF SHOE ARE boot,
bootee, brogue, clog, gumboot,
plimsoll, pump, sandal, slipper,
trainer, wellington. SEE ALSO
clothes.

shoemaker cobbler. SEE ALSO job.

shoot 1 *to shoot a gun.* to aim, to
discharge, to fire. 2 *to shoot at*: to
bombard, to shell, to snipe at. SEE
ALSO kill. 3 *He shot out of his chair.* SEE
move. 4 *The plants shoot up in the*

spring. to grow, to spring up, to
sprout. 5 SEE plant.

shooting star SEE astronomy.

shop VARIOUS SHOPS AND
BUSINESSES ARE baker, bank,
barber, betting shop, bookmaker,
book shop, boutique, building
society, butcher, chemist, dairy,
delicatessen, department store, DIY
store, draper, electrician, estate
agent, fishmonger, florist, furniture
store, greengrocer, grocer,
hairdresser, hardware store,
insurance office, ironmonger,
jeweller, launderette, market,
newsagent, off-licence, pawnbroker,
post office, radio and TV shop,
shoemaker, supermarket, tailor,
tobacconist.

shopkeeper 1 merchant, retailer,
salesman, saleswoman, stockist,
supplier, trader, tradesman. SEE
ALSO shop. 2 FOR OTHER JOBS SEE
job.

shop-lifter SEE criminal.

shore bank, beach, coast, sands,
shingle. SEE ALSO seaside.

short 1 *a short book, a short remark.*
brief, compact, concise, terse. 2 *a
short person.* diminutive, little, small,
squat. 3 *a short pause, a short visit.*
cursory, momentary, passing, quick,
temporary, transient. 4 *During the
drought water was short.* deficient,
lacking, scarce, wanting. 5 *He was
short with me when I asked for a loan.*
abrupt, bad-tempered, cross, curt,
grumpy, irritable, snappy, testy.

shortage *There was a shortage of water
during the drought.* deficiency, lack,
scarcity, want.

shortbread SEE cake.

shortcoming *One of Logan's
shortcomings is that he uses bad language.*
defect, fault, failing, imperfection,
vice, weakness.

shorten *We shortened our play because it
was too long.* to abbreviate, to
abridge, to compress, to condense, to
cut short, to reduce, to telescope.

shorthand SEE writing.

shortly *The post should arrive shortly.* directly, presently, soon.

shorts SEE **clothes.**

short-tempered SEE **cross.**

shotgun SEE **weapon.**

shoulder SEE **body, joint.**

shout 1 to bawl, to bellow, to call, to cheer, to cry, to roar, to shriek, to yell. SEE ALSO **sound, talk.** 2 *shouting*: SEE **clamour.**

shove *They shoved me into the water.* to crowd, to hustle, to jostle, to push.

shovel 1 SEE **tool.** 2 *We shovelled the snow off the path.* to dig, to scoop.

show 1 *We showed our work to the parents.* to display, to exhibit, to present, to produce, to reveal. 2 *Tony's knee showed through the hole in his jeans.* to appear, to be seen, to be visible, to emerge, to materialize, to stand out. 3 *She showed me the way to the station.* to direct, to guide, to indicate, to point out. 4 *The photo shows us swimming in the sea.* to depict, to illustrate, to picture, to portray, to represent. 5 *Mrs Angel showed us how they make butter.* to describe, to explain, to instruct, to make clear, to teach, to tell. 6 *The experiment showed that plants need light.* to demonstrate, to prove. 7 *to show off*: to boast, to brag, to crow, to gloat, to swank. 8 *We went to a show at the theatre.* SEE **entertainment, theatre.**

shower 1 SEE **weather.** 2 SEE **bathroom.** 3 *A passing bus showered us with rainwater.* to spatter, to splash, to spray, to sprinkle.

show-jumping SEE **horse.**

showy *You couldn't miss her showy clothes.* bright, conspicuous, flashy, gaudy, lurid, striking.

shred 1 to grate, to tear. SEE ALSO **cut.** 2 *The barbed wire tore her jeans to shreds.* bits, rags, strips, tatters.

shrew SEE **animal.**

shrewd *a shrewd salesman, a shrewd plan.* artful, astute, clever, crafty, cunning, ingenious, intelligent, knowing, sly, wise.

shriek SEE **sound.**

shrill *a shrill voice.* harsh, high, piercing, sharp.

shrimp SEE **shellfish.**

shrink 1 *The river shrank during the drought.* to contract, to decrease, to diminish, to dwindle, to lessen, to reduce, to shrivel. 2 *The dog shrank back when the cat spat at him.* to cower, to cringe, to flinch, to hang back, to quail, to recoil, to wince, to withdraw.

shrivel *The plants shrivelled in the heat.* to droop, to dry up, to shrink, to wilt, to wither.

shroud *Mist shrouded the top of the mountain.* to cloak, to conceal, to cover, to envelop, to hide, to mask, to wrap up.

shrub 1 bush. 2 VARIOUS SHRUBS ARE broom, gorse, heather, lavender, lilac, privet, rhododendron. SEE ALSO **plant.**

shrubbery SEE **garden.**

shrug SEE **gesture.**

shudder *I shuddered when I thought of the monster.* to quake, to quiver, to shake, to tremble.

shuffle 1 *I shuffled upstairs in my slippers.* SEE **walk.** 2 *I shuffled the cards.* to jumble, to mix.

shunter SEE **railway.**

shut 1 *Shut the door.* to close, to fasten, to lock, to replace, to seal, to secure. 2 *to shut in*: to confine, to detain, to enclose, to imprison, to keep in. 3 *to shut out*: to ban, to bar, to exclude, to keep out, to prohibit. 4 *Shut up!* be quiet! be silent! hush! silence!

shutter *Close the shutters.* blind, curtain.

shuttle SEE **space.**

shuttlecock SEE **sport.**

shy *He was too shy to call out.* bashful, coy, modest, nervous, reserved, self-conscious, timid, timorous.

sick 1 *She was away for a week because she was sick.* bedridden, diseased, ill, indisposed, infirm, poorly, queer, unwell. SEE ALSO **illness.** 2 *to be sick*: (informal) to throw up, to vomit.

sicken 1 *The picture of the wounded*

badger sickened us. to disgust, to nauseate, to repel, to revolt. **2** *sickening*: SEE **unpleasant**.

sickly 1 *a sickly child.* delicate, feeble, frail, unhealthy, weak. **2** *a sickly sweet taste.* nasty, nauseating, obnoxious, unpleasant.

side 1 *A cube has six sides.* face, surface. **2** *the side of the road.* edge, margin, verge. **3** *A game of hockey is played by two sides.* team.

sideboard SEE **furniture**.

side-car SEE **vehicle**.

side-show SEE **fun-fair**.

siding SEE **railway**.

siege blockade.

sieve 1 riddle. SEE ALSO **garden**. **2** *Sieve out the lumps.* to filter, to sift, to strain.

sigh SEE **sound**.

sight 1 *the power of sight.* eyesight, vision. SEE ALSO **sense**. **2** *I had a sight of the castle between the trees.* appearance, look, view. **3** *The procession was an impressive sight.* display, scene, spectacle. **4** *The look-out sighted a ship.* to discern, to make out, to notice, to observe, to recognize, to see, to spot.

sightseer *The castle was full of sightseers.* tourist, visitor.

sign 1 *I gave them the sign to begin.* cue, gesture, hint, indication, reminder, signal. **2** *Logan's yawn was a sign that he was bored.* clue, symptom. **3** *The flowers were a sign of our love.* token. **4** *We painted a sign for the sweet stall.* advertisement, notice, placard, poster, publicity. **5** *Do you recognize the British Rail sign?* badge, emblem, symbol. **6** *I signed that I was turning right.* to gesture, to indicate, to signal. **7** *Sign your name.* to autograph, to write. **8** *Our team signed a new goalkeeper.* to enrol, to register, to take on. **9** *He signed on in the army.* to enlist, to join up, to volunteer.

signal 1 *I gave him a clear signal.* cue, gesture, indication, sign. **2** *He signalled that he was turning right.* to gesture, to indicate, to sign.

signal-box SEE **railway**.

signalman SEE **job, railway**.

signature autograph.

significance *What's the significance of wearing a red poppy?* importance, meaning, sense.

significant *a significant amount of rain.* big, considerable, important, sizeable.

signpost SEE **road**.

Sikh SEE **religion**.

silage fodder.

silence to gag, to quieten.

silencer SEE **vehicle**.

silent 1 *a silent engine.* inaudible, noiseless, quiet, soundless. **2** *a silent person.* dumb, mute, reserved, speechless, tongue-tied.

silk SEE **cloth**.

silky *The cat has a silky coat.* sleek, soft, smooth.

sill SEE **building**.

silly *Why did he do such a silly thing?* absurd, crazy, foolish, grotesque, illogical, irrational, laughable, ludicrous, mad, preposterous, ridiculous, senseless, stupid, unreasonable.

silo SEE **building**.

silver SEE **metal, money**.

similar 1 *The twins are similar in their habits.* akin, alike, related. **2** *They are similar to each other.* like, resembling. **3** *They wear similar clothes.* corresponding, matching.

similarity likeness, resemblance.

simmer to boil, to stew. SEE ALSO **cook**.

simple 1 *a simple dress.* austere, plain. **2** *a simple problem.* easy, elementary, uncomplicated. **3** *a simple explanation.* clear, understandable.

sin blasphemy, evil, immorality, sacrilege, vice, wickedness, wrongdoing.

sincere *a sincere opinion, a sincere person.* candid, earnest, frank, genuine, honest, open, real, straightforward, truthful.

sincerity honesty, honour, integrity, truthfulness.

sinful *sinful behaviour.* bad, blasphemous, evil, immoral, sacrilegious, wicked, wrong.

sing 1 to chant, to croon, to hum. 2 SINGERS ARE bass, choir, chorus, contralto, soloist, soprano, tenor, treble, vocalist. 3 KINDS OF MUSIC YOU SING ARE anthem, ballad, blues, calypso, carol, chant, descant, folk-song, hymn, lullaby, opera, pop, reggae, rock, shanty, song, soul, spiritual. 4 SEE **music**.

singe to char, to scorch. SEE ALSO **burn**.

single 1 *There wasn't a single sandwich left!* one, sole, solitary. 2 *a single person.* SEE **unmarried**. 3 *Do you like the song on this new single?* SEE **record**.

single-handed *You can't shift the piano single-handed.* unaided.

singlet SEE **clothes**.

singular 1 SEE **language**. !*Singular* is the opposite of *plural.* 2 *It's a singular sight to see snow so late in the spring.* abnormal, curious, extraordinary, odd, peculiar, remarkable, uncommon, unusual.

sinister *The giant in the pantomime was a sinister character.* evil, forbidding, frightening, menacing, ominous, threatening, villainous.

sink 1 *The sun sinks in the west.* to descend, to drop, to fall, to go down. 2 *to sink a ship.* to scuttle, to submerge, to swamp.

sip *I sipped a little cordial.* to taste. SEE ALSO **drink**.

siren SEE **warning**.

sister 1 *Lucy is Tony's sister.* SEE **family**. 2 *a sister in a hospital.* SEE **medicine**.

sit to be seated, to perch, to rest, to squat.

sitar SEE **music, strings**.

site *a site for a new building.* location, place, position, situation, spot.

sitting-room drawing-room, living-room, lounge. SEE ALSO **house**.

situated *Where is your house situated?* located, placed.

situation 1 *Their house is in a pleasant situation.* location, place, position, site, spot. 2 *We were in an awkward situation when the referee didn't turn up.* circumstances, condition, position.

size amount, area, bulk, capacity, dimensions, extent, largeness, magnitude, volume. SEE ALSO **measure**.

sizeable *sizeable helpings.* considerable, generous. SEE ALSO **big**.

sizzle SEE **sound**.

skate 1 to glide, to skim, to slide. SEE ALSO **move**. 2 *skating*: SEE **sport**.

skeleton bones, frame, framework. SEE ALSO **body**.

sketch 1 description, design, diagram, drawing. SEE ALSO **picture**. 2 *Tony likes to sketch people with crayons.* to depict, to draw, to portray, to represent.

skewer SEE **kitchen**.

skid *I skidded on the ice.* to glide, to slide, to slip.

skiing SEE **sport**.

skilful *a skilful carpenter, a skilful player, etc.* able, accomplished, apt, artful, brilliant, capable, clever, competent, crafty, cunning, deft, experienced, expert, gifted, ingenious, proficient, qualified, shrewd, skilled, smart, talented, trained, versatile.

skill *the skill of a carpenter, the skill of a tennis-player, etc.* ability, accomplishment, aptitude, art, cleverness, craft, gift, handicraft, knack, prowess, talent, workmanship.

skilled SEE **skilful**.

skim 1 *I skimmed over the ice.* to glide, to skate, to slide. SEE ALSO **move**. 2 *I skimmed through the book.* to look through, to read quickly, to scan.

skin 1 FOR OTHER PARTS OF THE BODY SEE **body**. 2 FOR WORDS TO DESCRIBE YOUR SKIN SEE **complexion**. 3 VARIOUS WORDS FOR SKIN ARE coat, coating, exterior, film, husk, outer layer, outside, peel, rind, shell, surface. 4 *an animal's skin.* fur, hide. 5 *to skin an orange.* to peel, to strip.

skin-diving SEE **sport**.

skinny *a skinny person.* emaciated, lanky, scraggy. SEE ALSO **thin**.

skip 1 *The lambs skipped about the field.* to bound, to caper, to dance, to frisk, to hop, to jump, to leap, to prance, to spring. 2 *Logan skips the boring parts of a book.* to forget, to ignore, to leave out, to miss out, to neglect, to overlook.

skipper captain.

skirt SEE **clothes**.

skittles SEE **game**.

skull SEE **body, head**.

skunk SEE **animal**.

sky *The balloon rose into the sky.* air, atmosphere, space, stratosphere.

sky-diving SEE **sport**.

skylark SEE **bird**.

skylight window.

skyscraper SEE **building**.

slab *a slab of chocolate.* block, chunk, hunk, piece.

slack 1 *Logan was dropped from the team because of his slack attitude.* idle, lazy, listless, sluggish. 2 *The tent flapped about because the guy ropes were slack.* loose.

slacken 1 *I slackened the tension in the guy ropes.* to ease off, to loosen, to relax, to release. 2 *The pace of the game slackened in the second half.* to decrease, to lessen, to lower, to reduce.

slacks SEE **clothes**.

slam *to slam a door.* to bang, to shut. SEE ALSO **hit, sound**.

slang SEE **language**.

slant *Lucy's handwriting slants backwards.* to incline, to lean, to slope, to tilt.

slap SEE **hit**.

slapdash *slapdash work.* careless, hasty, messy, shoddy, slovenly, untidy.

slash *to slash with a knife.* to chop. SEE ALSO **cut**.

slate 1 SEE **rock**. 2 *a slate roof.* SEE **roof**.

slaughter 1 *The prisoners were brutally slaughtered.* to annihilate, to massacre, to murder, to slay. SEE ALSO **kill**. 2 *a terrible scene of slaughter.* bloodshed, carnage, killing, massacre, murder.

slaughterhouse shambles. SEE ALSO **building**.

slave 1 SEE **servant**. 2 *We slaved away all day.* to exert yourself, to labour, to toil, to work.

slay to assassinate, (informal) to bump off, to dispatch, to execute, to finish off, to martyr, to massacre, to murder, to put down, to put to death, to slaughter. SEE ALSO **kill**.

sledge sleigh, toboggan.

sledge-hammer SEE **tool**.

sleek *The cat had a sleek coat.* glossy, silky, smooth, soft.

sleep 1 to doze, to nod off, to rest, to slumber, to snooze, to take a nap. 2 *sleeping*: asleep, dormant, hibernating, resting.

sleeper, sleeping-car SEE **railway**.

sleeping-bag SEE **bedclothes**.

sleepy drowsy, tired, weary.

sleet SEE **weather**.

sleeve SEE **clothes**.

sleigh sledge, toboggan.

slender *a slender figure, a slender thread.* fine, lean, narrow, slight, slim, thin, wiry.

slice to carve. SEE ALSO **cut**.

slick *The conjuror was very slick.* artful, clever, cunning, deft, quick, smart, wily.

slide 1 *The toboggan slid over the snow.* to glide, to skate, to skid, to skim, to slip. SEE ALSO **move**. 2 *Dad takes slides with his camera.* transparency. SEE ALSO **photograph**.

slight 1 *a slight improvement.* imperceptible, insignificant, negligible, small, tiny, trivial, unimportant. 2 *a slight figure.* delicate, flimsy, frail, weak. SEE ALSO **slim**.

slim *a slim figure.* fine, lean, narrow, slender, slight, thin, wiry.

slime muck, mud, ooze.

sling 1 *David killed Goliath with his sling.* SEE **weapon**. 2 *Lucy had her broken arm in a sling.* SEE **medicine**. 3 *I slung the rubbish on the tip.* to cast, (informal) to chuck, to fling, to hurl, to lob, to throw, to toss.

slink *The naughty dog slunk into the corner.* to creep, to edge, to slither, to sneak.

slip 1 *I slipped on the ice.* to glide, to skid, to slide. 2 *to slip away:* to abscond, to elope, to escape, to run away. 3 *The detective noticed the suspect's slip.* blunder, error, inaccuracy, miscalculation, mistake. 4 *She wore a slip under her dress.* SEE **underclothes**.

slipper SEE **shoe**.

slippery *Take care: the floor is slippery.* greasy, icy, oily, slithery, smooth.

slip-road SEE **road**.

slit 1 *a slit in your jeans, a slit in a tyre, etc.* breach, break, chink, crack, cut, gap, gash, hole, opening, rift, slot, split, tear, vent. 2 *to slit something with a knife.* SEE **cut**.

slither *The snake slithered away.* to creep, to glide, to slide, to slink, to slip, to worm.

slog SEE **hit**.

slogan *an advertising slogan.* motto, saying.

slop *I slopped my tea into the saucer.* to spatter, to spill, to splash.

slope 1 *It's hard work cycling up the slope.* ascent, bank, hill, incline, ramp, rise. 2 *The beach slopes gently into the sea.* to shelve. 3 *The leaning tower slopes to one side.* to incline, to lean, to slant, to tilt, to tip.

sloppy 1 *a sloppy mixture.* liquid, runny, wet. 2 (informal) *sloppy work.* SEE **slovenly**.

slot *Put a coin in the slot.* groove, slit. SEE ALSO **opening**.

slouch *Don't slouch about in that slovenly way.* to droop, to loaf, to lounge.

slovenly *slovenly work.* careless, hasty, messy, shoddy, slapdash, (informal) sloppy, thoughtless, untidy.

slow 1 *a slow change in the weather.* gradual, moderate, steady, unhurried. 2 *a slow learner.* backward, dense, dim, obtuse, stupid. 3 *a slow worker.* idle, lazy, sluggish. 4 *slow progress.* careful, cautious, deliberate, painstaking. 5 *The bus is slow.* delayed, late. 6 *to be slow:* SEE **dawdle**. 7 *Please slow down!* to brake, to go slower.

slug SEE **insect**. !*Slugs* are not actually insects.

sluggish *Wake up: you're sluggish today!* idle, lazy, listless, slow.

slum SEE **town**.

slumber *Grandad slumbered in his chair.* to doze, to nod off, to rest, to sleep, to snooze, to take a nap.

slump 1 *He slumped unconscious to the ground.* to be limp, to flop, to sag. 2 *Our spirits slumped when we saw how far we had to go.* to decline, to droop, to drop, to sink.

slush, slushy SEE **weather**.

sly *I didn't trust his sly expression.* artful, catty, crafty, cunning, deceitful, devious, furtive, sneaky, tricky, wily.

smack to slap. SEE ALSO **hit**.

small 1 *a small baby.* diminutive, little, minute, (informal) teeny, tiny, undersized, wee. 2 *a small book.* brief, compact, concise, short. 3 *a small TV set.* miniature, portable. 4 *small helpings.* inadequate, meagre, (informal) measly, microscopic, scanty, stingy. 5 *a small problem.* insignificant, minor, negligible, petty, slight, trifling, trivial, unimportant. 6 *small arms:* SEE **weapon**.

smallpox SEE **illness**.

smart 1 *You look smart!* clean, fashionable, neat, (informal) posh, spruce, stylish, tidy, trim. 2 *That was a smart thing to do!* artful, astute, bright, clever, crafty, cute, intelligent, shrewd. 3 *We set off at a smart pace.* brisk, fast, quick, rapid, speedy, swift. 4 *My cut smarts when you* *touch it.* to ache, to be painful, to be sore, to hurt, to sting, to throb.

smash 1 *to smash an egg.* to crumple, to crush, to demolish, to destroy, to shatter, to squash. SEE ALSO **break**. 2 *to smash into a wall.* to bang, to bash, to batter, to bump, to collide, to hammer, to knock, to pound, to ram, to slam, to strike, to thump, to wallop. SEE ALSO **hit**.

smear 1 *a smear of dirt.* mark, smudge, streak. 2 *I smeared fat over the pan.* to rub, to smudge, to spread, to wipe.

smell aroma, fragrance, incense, odour, perfume, reek, scent, stench, stink, whiff. SEE ALSO **sense**.

smile to beam, to grin, to laugh, to smirk. SEE ALSO **expression, laugh**.

smirk SEE **expression, smile**.

smith blacksmith.

smock SEE **clothes**.

smoke 1 *clouds of smoke.* exhaust, fumes, gas, steam, vapour. 2 VARIOUS THINGS WHICH PEOPLE SMOKE ARE cigar, cigarette, (informal) fag, pipe, tobacco. 3 *The fire was smoking.* to smoulder.

smooth 1 *a smooth sea.* calm, even, flat, level, peaceful, placid, quiet, restful, steady. 2 *The cat has a smooth coat.* silky, sleek, soft, velvety. 3 *Mix the ingredients to a smooth mixture.* creamy, runny. 4 *Can we smooth this crumpled paper?* to flatten, to iron, to press.

smother to choke, to stifle, to strangle, to suffocate, to throttle. SEE ALSO **kill**.

smoulder *The ashes were still smouldering.* to smoke. SEE ALSO **burn**.

smudge 1 *I smudged the ink.* to smear, to streak. 2 *I smudged the paper.* to blot, to mark, to stain.

smug *Logan looked so smug when he won that prize!* complacent, pleased, self-righteous, self-satisfied, superior.

smuggler SEE **criminal**.

smuggling SEE **crime**.

snack refreshments. SEE ALSO **meal**.

snack-bar buffet, café, cafeteria.

snag *I'd like to come, but the snag is that I haven't any money.* complication, difficulty, hindrance, obstacle, problem, set-back.

snail SEE **insect**. ! *Snails* are not actually insects.

snake VARIOUS SNAKES ARE adder, boa-constrictor, cobra, grass-snake, python, rattlesnake, viper. SEE ALSO **animal, reptile**.

snap 1 *The dog snapped at me.* to bite, to nip. 2 *She snapped at us angrily.* SEE **talk**. 3 *A twig snapped.* to crack. SEE ALSO **sound**. 4 *holiday snaps.* SEE **photograph**. 5 *a game of snap.* SEE **cards**.

snapshot SEE **photograph**.

snare ambush, booby-trap, trap.

snarl SEE **sound**.

snatch *The muggers snatched her handbag.* to catch, to clutch, to grab, to pluck, to seize, to take.

sneak *I sneaked in without anyone seeing.* to creep, to move stealthily, to prowl, to slink, to stalk, to steal.

sneaky (informal) *It was sneaky to copy Lucy's answer.* crafty, deceitful, devious, furtive, mean, sly, treacherous.

sneer 1 *Some people sneered, but he'd done his best.* to boo, to hiss, to hoot, to jeer, to mock, to ridicule, to scoff, to taunt. SEE ALSO **expression**. 2 *sneering:* contemptuous, scornful.

sneeze SEE **cold, sound**.

sniff SEE **sound**.

snigger *They sniggered at the rude joke.* to chuckle, to giggle, to titter. SEE ALSO **laugh**.

snip SEE **cut**.

snipe *A gunman sniped at them from the roof.* to fire, to shoot.

snippet *We collected every little snippet of information.* fragment, morsel, particle, piece, scrap.

snivel *He started snivelling when the head told him off.* to blubber, to cry, to grizzle, to grovel, to sob, to weep, to whine.

snobbish *Rich people aren't always snobbish.* disdainful, haughty, pompous, posh, presumptuous, superior, (informal) stuck-up.

snooker SEE **game**.

snoop *Don't snoop into my affairs!* to interfere, to intrude, to meddle, to nose about, to pry.

snooze *The dog was snoozing in the sun.* to doze, to nod off, to sleep, to slumber, to take a nap.

snore, snort SEE **sound**.

snout *an animal's snout.* face, nose.

snow SEE **weather**.

snowdrop SEE **bulb, flower**.

snowplough SEE **vehicle**.

snowy SEE **weather**.

snub *He snubbed me by ignoring my question.* to be rude to, to disdain, to insult, to offend, to scorn.

snuff *to snuff a candle.* to extinguish, to put out.

snug *It's nice to be snug in bed on a cold night.* comfortable, cosy, relaxed, safe, secure, soft, warm.

snuggle *The baby snuggled against his mother.* to be comfortable, to cuddle, to huddle, to nestle.

so accordingly, therefore.

soak 1 *The rain soaked us.* to drench, to saturate, to wet thoroughly. 2 *soaked*: sodden, soggy, sopping, wet through. 3 *A sponge soaks up water.* to absorb, to take up.

soap detergent. SEE ALSO **bathroom, wash**.

soar *An eagle soared overhead.* to fly, to glide, to hover, to rise.

sob to blubber, to cry, to gasp, to snivel, to wail, to weep. SEE ALSO **sound**.

sober 1 not drunk. 2 *a sober occasion.* dignified, grave, sedate, serious, solemn.

soccer football. SEE ALSO **sport**.

sociable *a sociable crowd of people.* friendly, hospitable, welcoming.

social 1 *Human beings are supposed to be social creatures.* civilized, friendly, organized. 2 *We organized a social at*

Christmas. ball, dance, disco, gathering, party, reception.

Socialist SEE **politics**.

society 1 *We are all members of society.* civilization, community, nation, the public. 2 *I enjoy the society of my friends.* company. 3 *a secret society.* association, club, group, organization, union.

sock SEE **clothes**.

socket SEE **electricity**.

soda-water SEE **drink**.

sodden *My clothes were sodden after the rainstorm.* drenched, saturated, soaked, soggy, sopping, wet through.

sofa couch, settee. SEE ALSO **furniture**.

soft 1 *soft rubber.* flexible, floppy, limp, pliable, springy, supple. 2 *a soft bed.* comfortable, cosy. 3 *soft material.* silky, sleek, smooth, velvety. 4 *a soft breeze.* delicate, gentle, mild, tender. 5 *soft music.* low, peaceful, quiet, restful. 6 (informal) *a soft teacher.* easygoing, kind, lenient.

soften *Please soften the noise.* to deaden, to quieten, to subdue, to tone down.

soft-hearted *Lucy is soft-hearted where animals are concerned.* emotional, romantic, sentimental, tender. SEE ALSO **kind**.

software SEE **computer**.

soggy 1 *a soggy towel.* drenched, saturated, soaked, sodden, sopping, wet through. 2 *soggy cake.* heavy, stodgy.

soil 1 *I raked the soil before planting the seeds.* earth, ground, loam. 2 *Don't soil your hands with that filthy stuff.* to contaminate, to defile, to make dirty, to stain. 3 *soiled*: SEE **dirty**.

solder SEE **fasten, metal**.

soldier cavalryman, commando, gunner, infantryman, marine, paratrooper, sentry. SEE ALSO **armed services, fighter, rank**.

sole 1 *The weather was so cold that I was the sole person swimming.* one, only, single, solitary. 2 *the soles of your feet.* SEE **foot**. 3 SEE **fish**.

solemn *The funeral was a solemn*

occasion. dignified, earnest, formal, grave, important, sedate, serious, sober, thoughtful.

solicitor SEE **job, law**.

solid 1 *solid rock*. dense, firm, hard, rigid, sound, unyielding. **2** *solid evidence*. physical, real, tangible.

solitary 1 *a solitary person*. alone, friendless, lonely. **2** *a solitary place*. desolate, isolated, remote. **3** *There was a solitary potato in the dish*. one, only, single, sole.

solo *to perform solo*. alone.

soloist SEE **music**.

solution *the solution to a problem*. answer, explanation.

solve *Can you solve a riddle?* to answer, to explain, to work out.

sombre 1 *sombre colours*. cheerless, dark, dismal, drab, dull. **2** *a sombre expression*. gloomy, grave, mournful, serious. SEE ALSO **sad**.

somewhat fairly, moderately, pretty, rather.

son SEE **family**.

song SEE **sing**.

soon presently, quickly.

sooner 1 *I wish you'd come sooner*. before, earlier. **2** *I'd sooner have an apple than sweets*. preferably, rather.

soot dirt, grime.

soothe 1 *Quiet music soothes your nerves*. to appease, to calm, to comfort, to ease, to pacify, to relieve. **2** *soothing*: balmy, gentle, healing, mild, peaceful, pleasant, relaxing.

sophisticated 1 *a sophisticated argument, sophisticated machinery*. advanced, complicated, elaborate, ingenious, intricate, involved, subtle. **2** *sophisticated clothes*. adult, fashionable, grown-up, stylish.

sopping SEE **sodden**.

soprano SEE **sing**.

sorcerer, sorcery SEE **magic**.

sordid *a sordid story, sordid surroundings*. dirty, filthy, foul, (informal) mucky, squalid. SEE ALSO **unpleasant**.

sore 1 *a sore wound*. aching, hurting, inflamed, painful, raw, tender.

2 *They put ointment on his sores*. abscess, boil, inflammation, wound.

sorrow depression, grief, misery, regret, remorse, sadness, unhappiness. SEE ALSO **sad**.

sorry 1 *Logan was sorry for what he did*. apologetic, penitent, regretful, remorseful, repentant. **2** *Lucy was sorry for the girl who came last*. compassionate, merciful, pitying, understanding.

sort 1 *What sort of food do you like?* brand, category, form, group, kind, make, set, type, variety. **2** *What sort of dog is that?* breed, class, species. **3** *We sorted the books in the library*. to arrange, to classify, to group, to put in order. **4** *to sort out: Can you sort out this problem?* to attend to, to cope with, to deal with, to grapple with, to handle, to manage, to tackle.

soufflé SEE **food**.

soul 1 *your immortal soul*. spirit. **2** SEE **music**.

sound 1 *The dog is in a sound condition*. healthy, robust, strong, sturdy, well. **2** *Tony is a sound player*. dependable, reliable, safe, solid, trustworthy. **3** *We couldn't find a flaw in his sound argument*. coherent, convincing, logical, reasonable, sensible. **4** *I heard a sound*. noise. **5** VARIOUS SOUNDS ARE bang, bark, bawl, bay, bellow, blare, bleat, bleep, boo, boom, bray, buzz, cackle, chime, chink, chirp, clang, clank, clap, clash, clatter, click, clink, cluck, coo, crack, crackle, crash, creak, croak, crooning, crowing, crunch, cry, drone, echo, grating, groan, growl, grunt, gurgle, hiccup, hiss, hoot, howl, hum, jabber, jangle, jingle, lowing, miaow, moan, moo, murmur, neigh, patter, peal, ping, plop, pop, purr, quack, rattle, reverberation, ring, roar, rumble, rustle, scream, screech, shout, shriek, sigh, sizzle, slam, snap, snarl, sneeze, sniff, snore, snort, sob, splutter, squawk, squeak, squeal, swish, throb, thud, thunder, tick, tinkle, twang, twitter, wail, warble, whimper, whine, whinny, whistle, whiz, whoop, yap, yell, yelp, yodel. 6 FOR OTHER WORDS TO DO WITH SOUND SEE **music, noise, talk.**

soup broth, stock. SEE ALSO **food.**

sour 1 *sour fruit.* acid, sharp, tangy, tart. SEE ALSO **taste.** 2 *a sour temper.* bad-tempered, bitter, grumpy, peevish, snappy, testy, unpleasant.

source 1 *the source of a rumour.* beginning, cause, origin, starting-point. 2 *the source of a river:* spring.

south SEE **geography.**

souvenir *a souvenir of a holiday.* reminder.

sou'wester mackintosh. SEE ALSO **clothes.**

sovereign SEE **royal.**

sow 1 *to sow seeds.* to plant. 2 SEE **female, pig.**

soya SEE **food.**

space 1 *I need more space.* freedom, room. 2 *Leave an empty space.* area, break, distance, gap, hole, opening, place. 3 *The rocket sped away into space.* emptiness, stratosphere, vacuum. 4 WORDS TO DO WITH TRAVEL IN SPACE ARE blast-off, capsule, extraterrestrial beings, module, orbit, probe, re-entry, retro-rocket, rocket, satellite, spacecraft, spaceship, space shuttle, spacesuit. SEE ALSO **astronomy.**

spacious *a spacious house.* large, roomy, sizeable. SEE ALSO **big.**

spade 1 *a garden spade.* SEE **garden.** 2 *the ace of spades.* SEE **cards.**

spaghetti SEE **food.**

span *The bridge spans the river.* to cross, to pass over, to reach over, to stretch over.

spaniel SEE **dog.**

spank to slap, to smack. SEE ALSO **hit.**

spanner SEE **tool.**

spare 1 *The judge would not spare the violent criminal.* to be merciful to, to forgive, to free, to let off, to pardon, to reprieve, to save. 2 *Can you spare something for our collection?* to afford, to give, to manage, to provide. 3 *a spare tyre.* additional, extra, odd, unused.

sparing *He's sparing with his money.* economical, mean, miserly, stingy, thrifty.

spark *a spark of light.* flash, sparkle. SEE ALSO **light.**

sparking-plug SEE **vehicle.**

sparkle 1 to flash, to spark. SEE ALSO **light.** 2 *sparkling: sparkling drinks.* bubbly, effervescent, fizzy, foaming.

sparkler SEE **firework.**

sparrow SEE **bird.**

sparse *Grass for the cows was sparse during the drought.* inadequate, meagre, scanty, scattered, thin.

spasm *a violent spasm of coughing.* attack, convulsion, fit, seizure.

spasmodic *We've got a spasmodic fault on our TV.* intermittent, occasional, on and off.

spate *a spate of water.* cataract, flood, gush, rush.

spatter *The bus spattered us with water as it went by.* to shower, to slop, to splash, to spray, to sprinkle.

speak 1 *Please speak to me!* to communicate, to express yourself. SEE ALSO **say.** 2 *Can you speak French?* to pronounce, to talk, to utter. 3 *The vicar spoke to us in assembly.* to address, to lecture, to make a speech. 4 SEE **talk.**

spear harpoon, javelin, lance, pike. SEE ALSO **weapon.**

special 1 *A birthday is a special event.* important, infrequent, notable, rare, unusual. 2 *Petrol has a special smell.* characteristic, distinctive, unique. 3 *The baby has a special cup.* individual, particular, personal. 4 *Mr Brunswick has a special tool for cutting glass.* proper, specific, specialized.

specialist *Tony is a specialist on foreign stamps.* authority, expert, professional.

species *a species of animal.* breed, class, race.

specific *I need specific information, not rumours.* definite, detailed, exact, particular, precise.

specimen *Give me a specimen of your*

handwriting. example, illustration, instance, model, sample.

speck *a speck of dirt.* bit, dot, grain, mark, particle, spot.

speckled *a speckled pattern.* blotchy, dotted, mottled, spotty.

spectacle 1 *The fireworks made a colourful spectacle.* display, exhibition, scene, show, sight. 2 *People enjoy the spectacle of a parade.* ceremony, grandeur, pageantry, pomp.

spectacles bifocals, glasses. SEE ALSO optical.

spectacular *a spectacular sunset.* SEE beautiful.

spectator 1 bystander, eyewitness, observer, onlooker, viewer, watcher, witness. 2 *spectators:* audience, crowd.

spectre *The spectre is supposed to appear at midnight.* apparition, ghost, phantom, spirit, (informal) spook.

speech 1 *the power of speech.* speaking. SEE ALSO speak. 2 *to give a speech.* lecture, talk.

speechless dumb, dumbfounded, mute, nonplussed, silent, tongue-tied.

speed 1 *What speed were you going?* pace, quickness, rate, velocity. 2 *He sped along.* to bolt, to career, to dash, to dart, to fly, to gallop, to hasten, to hurry, to hurtle, to race, to run, to rush, to shoot, to streak, to tear, (informal) to zoom. SEE ALSO move.

speed-boat SEE vessel.

speedometer SEE vehicle.

speedway SEE race.

speedy 1 *a speedy journey.* fast, quick, rapid, swift. 2 *a speedy reply.* hasty, immediate, instant, prompt, sudden.

spell 1 *spelling:* SEE language. 2 *We rested for a spell.* interval, period, phase, season, session, stretch, time. 3 *The witch cast a spell.* charm, enchantment. SEE ALSO magic.

spellbound *We were spellbound by the music.* bewitched, captivated, charmed, enchanted, entranced, fascinated.

spend 1 *How much did you spend?* to

invest, to pay. 2 *We spent everything we had.* to consume, to exhaust, to use up, to squander.

sphere ball, globe. SEE ALSO shape.

spice SPICES INCLUDE ginger, pepper. SEE ALSO food.

spicy SEE taste.

spider SEE insect. ! *Spiders* are not proper insects.

spike point, prong.

spiky *a spiky bush.* bristly, prickly, thorny.

spill 1 *Water spilled over the edge.* to brim, to flow, to overflow, to run, to pour, to slop. 2 *The lorry spilled its load.* to drop, to overturn, to scatter, to shed, to tip.

spin *A wheel spins on an axle.* to revolve, to rotate, to swirl, to turn, to twirl, to whirl.

spinach SEE vegetable.

spin-drier SEE house, wash.

spine 1 backbone. SEE ALSO body. 2 *A hedgehog has sharp spines.* bristle, needle, point, spike.

spineless *a spineless coward.* cowardly, faint-hearted, feeble, helpless, timid, unheroic, weak, weedy.

spinster SEE unmarried.

spire SEE church.

spirit 1 soul. 2 *supernatural spirits.* apparition, demon, devil, ghost, imp, phantom, (informal) spook. 3 *The marathon runners had great spirit.* bravery, cheerfulness, confidence, courage, daring, determination, fortitude, heroism, morale, pluck, valour. 4 *spirits:* SEE alcohol.

spirited 1 *a spirited game.* animated, frisky, lively, sprightly, vigorous. 2 *a spirited attempt.* brave, courageous, daring, gallant, intrepid, plucky.

spiritual *negro spirituals.* SEE sing.

spiteful *spiteful remarks.* bitter, catty, hateful, malevolent, malicious, resentful, revengeful, sour, vicious, vindictive.

splash *The dolphin splashed water all over us.* to shower, to slop, to spatter, to spill.

splendid *a splendid banquet, splendid clothes, etc.* admirable, beautiful, brilliant, dazzling, elegant, excellent, first-class, glittering, glorious, gorgeous, grand, great, handsome, imposing, impressive, lavish, luxurious, magnificent, majestic, marvellous, noble, (informal) posh, regal, resplendent, royal, stately, sumptuous, (informal) super, superb, wonderful.

splint SEE **medicine**.

splinter 1 *a splinter of wood.* chip, flake, fragment. 2 *Logan splintered the door when he kicked it.* to chip, to crack, to fracture, to shatter, to smash, to split. SEE ALSO **break**.

split 1 *We split the class into two.* to divide, to separate. 2 *The axe split the log.* to burst, to chop, to crack, to rend, to slice. SEE ALSO **break, cut**. 3 *The roads split here.* to branch, to diverge, to fork. 4 *a split in a plank.* break, crack, slit. SEE ALSO **opening**.

splutter SEE **sound**.

spoil 1 *Don't spoil that nice piece of work.* to blot, to bungle, to damage, to deface, to destroy, to disfigure, to mar, to mess up, to ruin, to stain, to undo, to wreck. 2 *The fruit will spoil if we don't eat it.* to go bad, to perish, to rot. 3 *Grandad spoils us.* to indulge, to make a fuss of, to pamper.

sponge 1 SEE **bathroom**. 2 SEE **cake**. 3 *to sponge down*: to clean, to mop, to rinse, to swill, to wash.

sponsor 1 *Will you sponsor me in a charity race?* to back, to help, to promote, to subsidize, to support. 2 *Our team's sponsor gave us some new equipment.* backer, benefactor, donor, promoter.

spontaneous *a spontaneous performance.* automatic, impromptu, impulsive, involuntary, natural, unplanned, unprepared, unrehearsed.

spook SEE **ghost**.

spooky (informal) *The big house was spooky in the dark.* creepy, eerie, frightening, ghostly, scary, uncanny, weird.

spool *a spool of film.* reel.

spoon SEE **cutlery**.

spoor *an animal's spoor.* footprints, traces, tracks.

sport 1 VARIOUS SPORTS ARE aerobics, angling, SEE **athletics**, badminton, baseball, basketball, billiards, bobsleigh, bowls, boxing, bullfighting, canoeing, climbing, SEE **cricket**, croquet, cross-country, darts, decathlon, discus, fishing, SEE **football**, gliding, golf, gymnastics, hockey, hurdling, ice-hockey, javelin, marathon, martial arts (SEE **martial**), mountaineering, netball, orienteering, pentathlon, (informal) ping-pong, pole-vault, polo, pool, pot-holing, quoits, SEE **race**, rock-climbing, roller-skating, rounders, rowing, SEE **Rugby**, running, sailing, shot, show-jumping, skating, skiing, skin-diving, sky-diving, snooker, soccer, sprinting, squash, surf-riding, swimming (SEE **swim**), table-tennis, tennis, tobogganing, trampolining, volley-ball, water polo, water-skiing, windsurfing, SEE **winter sports**, wrestling, yachting. 2 PLACES WHERE SPORTS TAKE PLACE ARE arena, boxing-ring, circuit, course, court, field, golf-course, grandstand, ground, gymnasium, ice-rink, links, pavilion, pitch, playing-field, race-course, race-track, stadium, stand. 3 WORDS TO DO WITH SPORT ARE ball, bat, club, cue, cup-tie, final, forward, goal, linesman, match, racket, referee, score-board, scorer, semi-final, shuttlecock, touch-judge, umpire. 4 FOR LESS ACTIVE GAMES SEE **game**.

sports car SEE **vehicle**.

spot 1 *a dirty spot.* blemish, blot, blotch, dot, mark, speck, stain. 2 *a spot of water.* bead, blob, drop. 3 VARIOUS SPOTS ON THE SKIN ARE boil, freckle, impetigo, mole, pimple, rash, sty. 4 *a nice spot for a picnic.* location, place, point, position, site, situation. **5** *We spotted a rare bird.* SEE **see**.

spotless clean, hygienic, washed.

spotlight SEE **light**.

spotty *to be spotty*: to have a rash.

spout 1 *Water came out of the spout.* gargoyle, jet, nozzle, outlet. **2** *Water spouted out.* to flow, to gush, to pour, to spurt, to squirt, to stream. **3** (informal) *The head spouted for hours.* SEE **talk**.

sprain *to sprain your ankle.* SEE **wound**.

sprawl *We sprawled on the lawn.* to lean back, to lie, to lounge, to recline, to relax, to slouch, to spread out, to stretch out.

spray 1 *a spray of water.* fountain, shower. **2** *a spray of flowers.* bouquet, bunch, posy. **3** *I accidentally sprayed paint on the carpet.* to scatter, to shower, to spatter, to splash, to sprinkle.

spread 1 *to spread out a map.* to lay out, to open out, to unfold, to unroll. **2** *to spread butter.* to apply. **3** *to spread news.* to disperse, to distribute, to scatter. **4** *to spread out in a line.* to straggle. **5** *What a marvellous spread!* SEE **meal**.

sprightly *Great-granny is sprightly for 90 years old!* animated, brisk, lively, playful, quick-moving, spirited, vivacious.

spring 1 *He sprang over the fence.* to bounce, to bound, to jump, to leap, to pounce, to vault. **2** *Mrs Brunswick's seeds are springing up.* to emerge, to germinate, to grow, to shoot up, to sprout. **3** *This clock is worked by a spring.* coil.

springy bendy, elastic, flexible, floppy, pliable, supple.

sprinkle *We sprinkled water on the plants.* to drip, to scatter, to spatter, to splash, to spray.

sprint SEE **athletics, run**.

sprout *The seeds began to sprout.* to develop, to emerge, to germinate, to grow, to shoot up, to spring up.

spruce 1 *Tony looked spruce in his best clothes.* clean, neat, posh, tidy, trim, well-dressed. **2** *a spruce tree.* SEE **tree**.

spur 1 *Our success spurred us to even greater efforts.* (informal) to egg on, to encourage, to prompt, to stimulate, to urge. **2** SEE **horse**.

spurt *Water spurted out of the leak.* to flow, to gush, to jet, to pour, to spout, to squirt, to stream.

spy 1 informer, (informal) mole, secret agent, tell-tale, undercover agent. **2** *to spy on an enemy.* to inform, to tell tales. **3** *spying*: espionage, intelligence. **4** *We spied a ship in the distance.* SEE **see**.

squabble *We won't get much done if we squabble.* to argue, to fall out, to fight, to quarrel.

squad, squadron SEE **armed services**.

squalid *squalid surroundings.* dirty, filthy, foul, (informal) mucky, sordid, unpleasant.

squall, squally SEE **weather**.

squander *Don't squander your money.* to fritter, to misuse, to use up, to waste.

square SEE **shape, town**.

squash 1 *Don't squash the strawberries!* to compress, to crumple, to crush, to mangle, to mash, to press, to pulp, to smash, to squeeze. **2** *lemon squash.* SEE **drink**. **3** *a game of squash.* SEE **sport**.

squat 1 *a squat figure.* dumpy, plump, podgy, short, stocky. **2** *to squat on the ground.* to crouch, to sit.

squawk, squeak, squeal SEE **sound**.

squeamish *He's squeamish about touching slimy things.* (informal) choosey, fastidious, finicky, prim.

squeeze 1 *He squeezed my hand.* to compress, to clasp, to crush, to grip, to hug, to pinch, to press, to squash, to wring. **2** *They squeezed us into a little room.* to crowd, to push, to shove.

squib SEE **firework**.

squid SEE **fish**.

squint 1 to be cross-eyed. **2** *We squinted through a crack in the door.* to peep, to peer. SEE ALSO **look**.

squirm *The worm squirmed.* to turn, to twist, to wriggle, to writhe.

squirrel SEE **animal**.

squirt *Water squirted out.* to gush, to jet, to spout, to spray, to spurt.

stab *to stab with a dagger.* to jab, to pierce, to stick, to wound. SEE ALSO **cut, kill**.

stabilize to make steady, to settle.

stable 1 *Make sure the tripod is stable.* firm, fixed, solid, sound, steady. **2** *a stable marriage.* continuing, durable, lasting, permanent. **3** *a horse's stable.* SEE **building**.

stack 1 *a stack of books.* heap, mound, pile. **2** *a stack of hay.* rick. **3** *Stack the books on the table.* to accumulate, to collect, to heap, to mass, to pile.

stadium arena. SEE ALSO **sport**.

staff 1 *the staff of a business.* assistants, crew, employees, personnel, workers. **2** *the staff of a school.* caretaker, headteacher, secretary, SEE **teacher**.

stag SEE **deer, male**.

stage 1 *We performed our play on the stage.* platform. SEE ALSO **theatre**. **2** *Logan went through an unsettled stage.* phase, period, time.

stage-coach SEE **vehicle**.

stagger 1 *He staggered after getting a knock on the head.* to falter, to reel, to stumble, to totter. SEE ALSO **walk**. **2** *The price staggered us.* to alarm, to amaze, to astound, to dismay, to shock, to startle, to stun, to surprise.

stagnant *stagnant water.* motionless, stale, static.

stain 1 *The bath is stained with rusty marks.* to blot, to defile, to discolour, to make dirty, to mark, to smudge, to soil, to tarnish. **2** *Mr Brunswick stained the wood an oak colour.* to colour, to dye, to paint, to tint. **3** *What's that stain on your shirt?* blemish, blot, blotch, mark, smear, spot.

stairs escalator, staircase, steps.

stake 1 *a wooden stake.* pole, post, stick. **2** *to put a stake on a horse.* bet, wager.

stale *stale bread, stale news.* dry, old, out-of-date.

stalemate SEE **chess**.

stalk 1 stem, twig. SEE ALSO **plant**.

2 *The lion stalked its prey.* to follow, to hound, to hunt, to pursue, to shadow, to track, to trail. **3** *He stalked up and down.* to prowl, to rove. SEE ALSO **walk**.

stall 1 *a sweet stall.* booth, kiosk, stand. **2** *We sat in the stalls.* SEE **theatre**. **3** *Stop stalling!* to delay, to hang back, to hesitate, to pause, to postpone, to put off, to stop.

stallion SEE **horse, male**.

stammer SEE **talk**.

stamp 1 *Don't stamp on the poor spider!* to crush, to trample, to tread. **2** *to stamp a mark on something.* to brand, to mark, to print. **3** *The king put his stamp on the document.* seal. **4** *I put a stamp on my letter.* postage stamp.

stampede *The cattle stampeded.* to bolt, to career, to dash, to panic, to rush. SEE ALSO **move**.

stand 1 *We stand when a visitor comes in.* to get up, to rise. **2** *A statue stands in the square.* to be, to exist. **3** *I stood my books on a shelf.* to arrange, to deposit, to locate, to place, to position, to put up, to set up, to situate, to station. **4** *The offer I made yesterday still stands.* to be unchanged, to continue, to persist, to remain, to stay. **5** *Mrs Brunswick can't stand people who smoke.* to abide, to bear, to endure, to put up with, to tolerate. **6** *What do these initials stand for?* to be a sign for, to indicate, to mean, to represent, to symbolize. **7** *The church spire stands out.* to be obvious, to be prominent, to show, to stick out. **8** *to stand up to:* to clash with, to confront, to defy, to face up to, to oppose, to resist, to withstand. **9** *to stand up for:* to defend, to help, to protect, to shield, to speak up for, to support. **10** *a stand for a telescope.* base, support, tripod. **11** *a newspaper stand.* booth, kiosk, stall. **12** *a stand for spectators.* SEE **sport**.

standard 1 *a standard procedure, a standard size.* accustomed, common, conventional, customary, everyday, familiar, habitual, normal, ordinary, orthodox, regular, routine, typical, usual. **2** *The regiment flew its standard.*

banner, colours, ensign, flag. 3 *Mrs
Angel wants a high standard of work.*
achievement, grade, level. 4 *By what
standard are you judging us?* ideal,
measurement.

stand-in deputy, reserve, substitute.

stand-offish SEE **unfriendly.**

standpoint *Can you understand my
standpoint?* attitude, belief, opinion,
position, view.

standstill *to come to a standstill.* halt,
stop.

stanza SEE **poem.**

staple SEE **fasten.**

star 1 SEE **astronomy.** 2 *a TV star.*
SEE **entertainment.**

starboard SEE **vessel.** ! *Starboard* is
the opposite of *port.*

stare *What are you staring at?* to
contemplate, to examine, to gape, to
gaze, to study, to watch. SEE ALSO
look.

starfish SEE **fish.**

starlight SEE **light.**

starling SEE **bird.**

start 1 *We start our holiday on Saturday.*
to begin, to commence, to embark
on. 2 *to start a business, to start a process.*
to activate, to create, to found, to
initiate, to introduce, to open, to
originate, to set up. 3 *A loud bang
made me start.* to flinch, to jerk, to
jump, to twitch, to wince.

startle *The explosion startled us.* to
alarm, to frighten, to jolt, to scare, to
shake, to shock, to surprise, to upset.

starvation *to die of starvation.* famine,
hunger, malnutrition.

starve 1 SEE **kill.** 2 *to starve yourself:* to
fast, to go without. 3 *starving:*
emaciated, famished, hungry,
ravenous, underfed.

state 1 *He was in a terrible state!*
condition, fitness, health, situation.
2 *It's important for a state to have a good
government.* nation. SEE ALSO
country. 3 *The head stated that we'd
raised £500.* to announce, to assert, to
comment, to communicate, to
declare, to proclaim, to remark, to
report, to say.

stately *a stately palace.* dignified,
grand, imposing, majestic, noble,
regal, royal. SEE ALSO **splendid.**

statement *The Prime Minister issued an
official statement.* announcement,
comment, communication,
communiqué, declaration, message,
notice, proclamation, report.

statesman SEE **government.**

static motionless, stagnant,
stationary.

station 1 *a railway station.* SEE
railway. 2 *a radio station.* channel,
wavelength. 3 *We stationed a look-out
at the door.* to locate, to place, to
position, to put, to situate, to stand.

stationary *stationary cars.* immobile,
motionless, static, still, unmoving.
! Notice the difference in spelling
between *stationary* and *stationery.*

stationery FOR WRITING MATERIALS
SEE **write.**

statistics data, figures, numbers.

statue carving, figure, image,
sculpture.

status *high status, low status.* class,
level, position, rank, title.

stave SEE **music.**

stay 1 *Stay here.* to carry on, to
continue, to endure, to keep on, to
last, to linger, to live on, to persist, to
remain, to survive, to wait. 2 *Will you
stay with us?* (old-fashioned) to abide,
to be accommodated, to be housed,
to board, to dwell, to live, to lodge,
to reside, to visit.

steady 1 *a steady foundation.* fast, firm,
immovable, secure, solid, stable. 2 *a
steady supply of food.* consistent,
constant, continuous, dependable,
regular, reliable. 3 *a steady rhythm.*
even, invariable, repeated, rhythmic,
unchanging. 4 *a steady friend.*
devoted, faithful, loyal. 5 *Baby is
steady on her feet now.* balanced,
confident, poised. 6 *We steadied the
rocking boat.* to hold, to secure, to
stabilize.

steak SEE **meat.**

steal 1 to loot, (informal) to nick, to
pilfer, (informal) to pinch, to rob, to

sneak, (informal) to swipe, to take.
SEE ALSO **crime**. 2 *I stole quietly
upstairs.* to creep, to move stealthily,
to slink. SEE ALSO **walk**.

stealthy *stealthy movements.* furtive,
quiet, secretive, shifty, sneaky, sly.

steam condensation, smoke, vapour.

steamy 1 *steamy windows.* cloudy,
hazy, misty. 2 *a steamy atmosphere.*
close, damp, humid, moist, muggy.

steam-engine SEE **railway**.

steamer SEE **vessel**.

steam-roller SEE **vehicle**.

steed SEE **horse**.

steel SEE **metal**.

steep *a steep cliff.* abrupt, precipitous,
sharp, sheer, sudden, vertical.

steeple SEE **church**.

steeplechase SEE **horse, race**.

steeplejack SEE **job**.

steer 1 SEE **cattle**. 2 *to steer a vehicle.* to
control, to drive, to guide, to pilot.

steering-wheel SEE **vehicle**.

stem stalk, trunk, twig. SEE ALSO
plant.

stench *the stench of rotting meat.* odour,
reek, smell, stink, whiff.

stencil SEE **art**.

step 1 *I took a step forward.* pace, stride.
2 *I climbed up the steps.* stair, step-
ladder. 3 *Starting at a new school is an
important step.* phase, stage. 4 *Don't
step in the mud!* to trample, to tread.
SEE ALSO **walk**. 5 *The rioters stepped up
the violence.* to escalate, to increase.

stepchild, stepparent SEE **family**.

step-ladder SEE **house**.

stereo SEE **audio equipment**.

sterile 1 *sterile land.* arid, barren, dry,
infertile, lifeless, unproductive.
2 *sterile bandages.* SEE **sterilize**.

sterilize 1 to disinfect, to purify.
2 *sterilized: sterilized bandages.* clean,
disinfected, germ-free, hygienic,
pure, sterile.

stern 1 *The head was stern when he told
Logan off.* austere, forbidding, grim,
hard, harsh, severe, strict. 2 *the stern
of a ship.* SEE **vessel**.

stethoscope SEE **medicine**.

stew 1 *We stewed some apples.* to boil.
SEE ALSO **cook**. 2 *We had stew for
dinner.* goulash, hash, hot-pot. SEE
ALSO **food**.

steward 1 *a steward on a ship.*
attendant, waiter. SEE ALSO
servant. 2 *a steward at a race-course.*
officer, official.

stick 1 *We collected sticks for firewood.*
branch, stalk, twig. 2 OTHER KINDS
OF STICK ARE bar, baton, cane, club,
pole, rod, staff, walking-stick, wand.
3 *A thorn stuck into my tyre.* to jab, to
pierce, to puncture, to stab, to
thrust. 4 *The pages stuck together.* to
adhere, to glue. SEE ALSO **fasten**.
5 *The door stuck.* to jam, to wedge.
6 *Tony stuck at his work.* to continue,
to remain, to stay, to stop. 7 *I hit my
head on a shelf which stuck out.* to jut, to
overhang, to project, to protrude.
8 *The spire sticks up above the other
buildings.* to loom, to rise, to stand
out, to tower.

stickleback SEE **fish**.

sticky *sticky tape.* adhesive, gluey,
gummed, tacky.

stiff 1 *stiff clay.* firm, heavy, solid,
thick, unyielding. 2 *stiff cardboard.*
hard, inflexible, rigid, unbending.
3 *stiff joints.* immovable, paralysed,
tight, wooden. 4 *a stiff task.* difficult,
hard, severe, tough, uphill. 5 *stiff
opposition.* powerful, strong.

stifle 1 to choke, to smother, to
strangle, to suffocate, to throttle. SEE
ALSO **kill**. 2 *We stifled our giggles.* to
deaden, to muffle, to silence, to
suppress. 3 *stifling:* SEE **stuffy**.

still 1 *a still evening.* calm, noiseless,
peaceful, placid, quiet, serene, silent,
tranquil, untroubled. 2 *Keep still!*
immobile, motionless, static,
·stationary, unmoving.

stimulate *Mrs Angel stimulated our
interest.* to arouse, to excite, to incite,
to inspire, to invigorate, to prompt,
to provoke, to rouse, to stir up, to
urge.

stimulus encouragement, incentive,
inspiration.

sting 1 *a wasp sting.* SEE **wound.**
2 *Some insects sting.* to bite, to nip.
3 *These ant bites do sting!* to ache, to
hurt, to throb, to tingle. SEE ALSO
pain.

stingy 1 *a stingy miser.* close, mean,
(informal) mingy, miserly. 2 *stingy
helpings.* inadequate, meagre,
(informal) measly, scanty. SEE ALSO
small.

stink *a nasty stink.* odour, reek, stench,
whiff. SEE ALSO **smell.**

stir 1 *Stir the ingredients thoroughly.* to
agitate, to beat, to mix, to whisk.
2 *Stir yourself!* SEE **move.** 3 *The music
stirred us.* to affect, to arouse, to
excite, to impress, to inspire, to
move, to rouse, to stimulate, to
touch.

stirrup SEE **horse.**

stitch *Tony stitched the hole in his jeans.*
to darn, to mend, to repair, to sew, to
tack.

stoat SEE **animal.**

stock 1 *We keep a stock of crisps.* store,
supply. 2 *We boiled the bones to make
stock.* broth, soup. SEE ALSO **food.**
3 *The farmer bought some new stock.*
animals, livestock. 4 *Our local shop
stocks most things.* to keep, to sell, to
supply.

stockade fence, paling, palisade,
wall.

stock car SEE **race.**

stockist merchant, retailer,
shopkeeper, supplier.

stocks SEE **punishment.**

stocky *a stocky figure.* dumpy, short,
squat, sturdy.

stodgy 1 *a stodgy pudding.* firm, heavy,
lumpy, soggy, solid, starchy. 2 *a
stodgy lecture.* boring, dull, tedious,
uninteresting.

stomach abdomen, belly, (informal)
tummy. SEE ALSO **body.**

stone 1 VARIOUS STONES ARE
boulders, cobbles, gems, gravel,
jewels, pebbles, rocks, scree. SEE
ALSO **jewellery, rock.** 2 *a plum stone.*
pip, seed. 3 *How many stones do*

you weigh? SEE **measure.** 4 *to stone
someone*: SEE **execute.**

stony 1 *a stony beach.* pebbly, rocky,
rough, shingly. 2 *a stony expression.*
cold, hard, heartless, indifferent,
uncaring, unfeeling, unfriendly.

stool SEE **furniture, seat.**

stoop to bend, to bow, to crouch, to
kneel, to lean.

stop 1 *The referee stopped the game. The
music stopped.* to break off, to cease, to
cut off, to discontinue, to end, to
finish, to halt, to terminate. 2 *An
accident stopped the traffic.* to bar, to
block, to check, to curb, to delay, to
hamper, to hinder, to immobilize, to
impede. 3 *Wait for the bus to stop.* to
draw up, to halt, to pull up. 4 *Stop the
thief!* to arrest, to capture, to catch,
to detain, to hold, to seize. 5 *We came
to a stop.* halt, standstill.

stopper *Put the stopper in the bottle.*
bung, cork, plug.

store 1 *a store of supplies.* cache, depot,
reserve, stock, supply. 2 *a grocery
store.* shop, supermarket. SEE ALSO
shop. 3 *We store food in the pantry.* to
accumulate, to keep, to preserve, to
put away, to reserve, to save, to
stock, to stow away.

storey *The building has six storeys.* floor,
level. ! Don't confuse this word with
story.

stork SEE **bird.**

storm 1 KINDS OF STORM ARE
blizzard, cyclone, deluge, gale,
hurricane, rainstorm, tempest,
thunderstorm, tornado, typhoon,
whirlwind. SEE ALSO **weather.**
2 *The army stormed the castle.* to
assault, to attack, to charge, to raid.

story *the story of my life.* account,
narration, narrative, report, tale,
yarn. SEE ALSO **writing.**

stout 1 *stout rope.* sound, strong,
sturdy, thick. 2 *a stout gentleman.*
chubby, fat, heavy, overweight,
plump, portly, stocky, tubby. 3 *a
stout fighter.* bold, brave, courageous,
fearless, gallant, heroic, intrepid,
plucky, spirited, valiant.

stove boiler, cooker, oven. SEE ALSO
fire, kitchen.

stow 1 *We stowed our camping things in
the attic.* to put away, to store. 2 *We
stowed our luggage in the car.* to load, to
pack.

straggle 1 *Some of the runners straggled
behind.* to dawdle, to fall behind, to
lag, to loiter. 2 *straggling*: scattered,
spread out.

straight 1 *a straight line.* direct,
unswerving. 2 *Put the room straight.*
neat, orderly, tidy. 3 *a straight answer.*
SEE **straightforward.**

straightforward 1 *a straightforward
question.* easy, simple, uncomplicated. 2 *a straightforward answer.*
blunt, candid, frank, honest, plain,
straight, truthful.

strain 1 *The sailors strained at the ropes.*
to pull, to stretch, to tighten. 2 *He
strained to escape from the monster's grasp.*
to attempt, to exert yourself, to make
an effort, to strive, to struggle, to try.
3 *Don't strain yourself.* to exhaust, to
tire out, to weaken, to wear out, to
weary. 4 *Lucy strained a muscle during
training.* to damage, to hurt, to injure.
5 *I strained the lumps out of the gravy.* to
filter, to sieve, to sift. 6 *Mum has been
under a lot of strain lately.* anxiety,
difficulty, hardship, pressure, stress,
tension, worry.

strait *the Straits of Gibraltar.* channel.
SEE ALSO **geography.**

strand 1 *a strand of cotton.* fibre,
thread. 2 *The pirates stranded Ben Gunn
on the island.* to abandon, to desert, to
forsake, to maroon. 3 *stranded: a
stranded ship.* aground, helpless.

strange 1 *a strange event.* abnormal,
curious, extraordinary, funny,
irregular, odd, peculiar, queer,
singular, unaccustomed,
uncommon, unnatural, unusual,
weird. 2 *strange behaviour.* (informal)
cranky, eccentric, unconventional,
weird. 3 *a strange problem.* baffling,
inexplicable, insoluble, mysterious,
puzzling. 4 *a strange appearance.* alien,
foreign, new, novel, unfamiliar.

stranger *I'm a stranger here.* alien,
foreigner, outsider, visitor.

strangle to choke, to suffocate, to
throttle. SEE ALSO **kill.**

strap 1 belt. 2 SEE **fasten.**

strategy *We worked out a strategy to beat
the opposition.* manoeuvre, method,
plan, plot, policy, scheme, tactics.

stratum *a stratum of rock.* layer, seam,
thickness.

straw corn, stalks, stubble.

strawberry SEE **fruit.**

stray *It's dangerous to stray in the hills.* to
get lost, to go astray, to range, to
roam, to rove, to wander.

streak 1 *The rocket left a streak of smoke
in the sky.* band, line, stripe. 2 *The rain
streaked the new paint.* to smear, to
smudge. 3 *The cars streaked past.* SEE
move.

stream 1 *We had to cross a stream.*
brook, burn, river. 2 *A stream of water
poured through the hole.* cataract,
current, flood, jet, rush, spate, tide,
torrent. 3 *Water streamed through the
hole.* to flow, to gush, to pour, to
spout, to spurt, to squirt.

streamer banner, flag.

street SEE **road.**

strength 1 *You need good food to build up
your strength.* condition, fitness,
health, vigour. 2 *Have you got the
strength to lift that weight?* energy,
force, might, power.

strengthen 1 *I do exercises to strengthen
my muscles.* to build up, to fortify, to
make stronger, to toughen. 2 *We put
in some stakes to strengthen the fence.* to
prop up, to reinforce, to support.

strenuous 1 *strenuous work.* arduous,
difficult, exhausting, gruelling,
laborious, stiff, tough, uphill.
2 *strenuous efforts.* active, determined,
dynamic, energetic, firm, powerful,
resolute, vigorous.

stress 1 *a time of stress.* anxiety,
difficulty, hardship, pressure, strain,
tension, worry. 2 *The trainer stressed
that we must keep fit.* to assert, to
emphasize, to insist, to underline.

stretch 1 *You can stretch elastic.* to draw

out, to elongate, to lengthen, to pull out. **2** *How far can you stretch your arms?* to extend, to reach, to spread. **3** *a stretch in prison.* period, spell, time. **4** *a stretch of road.* distance, length.

stretcher SEE **medicine**.

strict 1 *strict discipline.* austere, firm, harsh, severe, stern. **2** *a strict rule.* hard, inflexible, unchangeable. **3** *the strict truth.* accurate, correct, exact, precise, right, true.

stride 1 *He strode along the road.* SEE **walk**. **2** *Take two strides forward.* pace, step.

strife *How can we end all strife between nations?* conflict, feud, fighting, hostilities, quarrel, row, unrest, war.

strike 1 *I struck my head.* SEE **hit**. **2** *The employees had a strike.* industrial action, stoppage.

striking *striking colours.* conspicuous, impressive, noticeable, obvious, prominent, showy, unmistakable.

string 1 *We tied it up with string.* cord, line, rope, twine. **2** *a string of coincidences.* chain, progression, row, sequence, series. **3** *stringed*: FOR STRINGED INSTRUMENTS SEE **strings**.

strings MUSICAL INSTRUMENTS WITH STRINGS ARE banjo, cello, double-bass, fiddle, guitar, harp, lute, lyre, sitar, viola, violin, zither. SEE ALSO **music**.

stringy *stringy meat.* tough.

strip 1 *Strip off your clothes.* to peel off, to remove, to take off. **2** *Strip to the waist.* to bare, to expose, to uncover, to undress. **3** *We laid a strip of carpet down the stairs.* band, line, ribbon, stripe.

stripe *Our football shirts have red and white stripes.* band, line, strip.

strive *We strove hard to beat our rivals.* to attempt, to endeavour, to exert yourself, to strain, to struggle, to try hard.

stroke 1 *He scored six with his first stroke.* action, blow, hit, knock, movement. **2** *Uncle went to hospital when he had a stroke.* SEE **illness**. **3** *Stroke the cat.* to

caress, to pat, to pet. SEE ALSO **touch**.

stroll *We strolled round the park.* SEE **walk**.

strong 1 *a strong person.* athletic, beefy, brawny, burly, hardy, hefty, mighty, muscular, sturdy, tough, wiry. **2** *a strong attack.* forceful, powerful, severe, vehement, vigorous, violent. **3** *a strong fortress.* impregnable, invincible, unconquerable. **4** *strong shoes.* durable, robust, sound, well-made. **5** *strong rope.* stout, thick, unbreakable. **6** *a strong smell.* noticeable, obvious, prominent, pronounced, unmistakable. **7** *strong drink.* alcoholic, concentrated, potent, undiluted. **8** *strong evidence.* clear, evident, plain, solid, undisputed. **9** *a strong interest.* eager, earnest, enthusiastic, fervent, keen, zealous.

stronghold castle, citadel, fort, fortress, garrison.

structure construction, edifice, framework. SEE ALSO **building**.

struggle 1 *to struggle to achieve something.* to endeavour, to exert yourself, to make an effort, to strain, to strive, to try, to work hard. **2** *to struggle with an enemy.* to clash, to compete, to conflict, to contend, to fight, to grapple, to oppose, to rival, to wrestle. **3** KINDS OF STRUGGLE ARE battle, bout, brawl, combat, competition, conflict, confrontation, contest, duel, feud, hostilities, quarrel, rivalry, row, scrap, scuffle, squabble, tussle, war. **4** *We struggled through the mud.* to flounder, to wallow.

strut SEE **walk**.

stub *I stubbed my toe.* SEE **hit**.

stubborn *The stubborn animal refused to move.* defiant, disobedient, dogged, inflexible, obstinate, rigid, unmanageable, unyielding, wilful.

stuck-up arrogant, conceited, bumptious, cocky, proud, self-important.

student learner, pupil, scholar, undergraduate.

studio SEE **building**.

studious *a studious pupil.* academic, brainy, intellectual.

study 1 *The jury studied the evidence.* to analyse, to consider, to enquire into, to examine, to investigate, to learn about, to read about, to think about. 2 *to study for an examination.* to learn, to read, (informal) to swot.

stuff 1 *What's that stuff in the jar?* matter, substance. 2 *Lucy bought some stuff to make a skirt.* cloth, fabric, material, textile. 3 *That's my stuff in that drawer.* articles, belongings, possessions, things. 4 *I stuffed everything into a suitcase.* to cram, to fill, to jam, to pack, to squeeze, to tuck.

stuffing SEE **food**.

stuffy *a stuffy room.* airless, close, humid, muggy, oppressive, steamy, stifling, warm.

stumble to blunder, to falter, to hesitate, to stagger, to totter, to trip, to tumble. SEE ALSO **walk**.

stump 1 SEE **cricket**. 2 *The riddle stumped us.* to baffle, to bewilder, to perplex, to puzzle.

stun 1 *The blow stunned him.* to daze, to knock out, to make unconscious, to numb. 2 *The terrible news stunned us.* to amaze, to astonish, to astound, to bewilder, to dumbfound, to shock.

stunt 1 exploit, feat, trick. 2 *stunt man:* SEE **entertainment, job**.

stupendous amazing, exceptional, extraordinary, incredible, miraculous, notable, phenomenal, remarkable, singular, special, unbelievable.

stupid 1 *a stupid decision.* absurd, crazy, foolish, idiotic, irrational, silly, unintelligent. 2 *a stupid person.* dense, dim, dull, obtuse, slow, (informal) thick. 3 SEE **fool**.

sturdy 1 *a sturdy person.* burly, hardy, healthy, hefty, robust, sound, stocky, strong, tough. 2 *a sturdy pair of shoes.* durable, well-made.

stutter to stammer. SEE ALSO **talk**.

sty 1 *a sty for pigs.* SEE **farm**. 2 *a sty on your eyelid.* SEE **spot**.

style *the latest style of dancing.* fashion, manner, method, mode, way.

stylish *stylish clothes.* contemporary, fashionable, modern, (informal) posh, smart, sophisticated, (informal) trendy, up-to-date.

stylus SEE **audio equipment**.

subdue 1 *We subdued the opposition.* to beat, to conquer, to defeat, to master, to overcome. 2 *Subdue your excitement!* to check, to control, to curb, to hold back, to quell, to restrain, to suppress. 3 *subdued: a subdued mood, subdued music.* grave, hushed, peaceful, placid, quiet, soft, solemn, soothing, toned down.

subject 1 *I don't want to hear any more on the subject of the broken window!* affair, issue, matter, theme, topic. 2 SUBJECTS WHICH STUDENTS CAN STUDY ARE anatomy, archaeology, architecture, art, astronomy, biology, botany, business, chemistry, computing, craft, drama, ecology, economics, education, electronics, engineering, English, environment, geography, geology, heraldry, history, languages, Latin, law, literature, mathematics, mechanics, medicine, meteorology, music, ornithology, philosophy, physics, politics, psychology, religious studies, science, scripture, social work, sport, surveying, technology, theology, zoology.

sub-machine-gun SEE **weapon**.

submarine SEE **vessel**.

submerge 1 *The submarine submerged.* to dive, to go under, to subside. 2 *The flood submerged the whole village.* to cover, to drown, to engulf, to flood, to immerse.

submit 1 *The wrestler submitted to his opponent.* to capitulate, to give in, to surrender, to yield. 2 *We submitted to the referee's decision.* to conform to, to keep to, to obey. 3 *Submit your entries* *for the competition by Monday.* to give in, to hand in, to offer, to present.

subordinate *subordinate rank.* inferior, junior, lower.

subscription *a club subscription.* contribution, fee, payment.

subsequent *Tony swam badly in the first race, but subsequent races went better.* following, later, next, succeeding.

subside 1 *The flood gradually subsided.* to decline, to diminish, to dwindle, to go down, to lessen, to melt away, to shrink. 2 *I subsided into a comfortable chair.* to rest, to settle, to sink.

subsidize *Our parents subsidized the cost of our trip.* to aid, to back, to sponsor, to support.

substance material, matter, stuff.

substantial 1 *a substantial door.* strong, well-made. 2 *a substantial amount of money.* big, considerable, large, significant, sizeable.

substitute 1 *They sent on a substitute.* deputy, replacement, reserve, stand-in. 2 *I substituted an apple for the chocolate.* to change, to exchange, to replace, to swop.

subtle 1 *a subtle argument.* clever, ingenious, sophisticated. 2 *a subtle flavour.* delicate, faint, gentle, mild.

subtract *Mrs Angel subtracts marks for carelessness.* to deduct, to take away.

suburb outskirts. SEE ALSO **geography, town**.

subway tunnel, underpass.

succeed 1 *If you work hard you are likely to succeed.* to be successful, to do well, to flourish, to grow, to prosper, to thrive. 2 *Did your plan succeed?* to be effective, to work. 3 *Elizabeth II succeeded George VI.* to come after, to follow, to replace, to take over from.

success 1 *We were pleased with the success of our plan.* accomplishment, achievement, attainment, prosperity. 2 *The plan was a success.* triumph, victory.

successful 1 *a successful business.* flourishing, fruitful, prosperous, well-off. 2 *a successful team.* victorious, winning.

succession *a succession of disasters.* line, progression, sequence, series, string.

successor *the successor to the throne.* heir, replacement, substitute.

sudden 1 *a sudden decision, a sudden rainstorm.* abrupt, hasty, quick, sharp, swift, unexpected. 2 *a sudden illness.* acute.

suds bubbles, foam, froth, lather.

sue to prosecute. SEE ALSO **law**.

suede leather.

suet SEE **fat**.

suffer 1 *to suffer pain.* to bear, to cope with, to endure, to experience, to go through, to put up with, to stand, to tolerate, to undergo. 2 *suffering*: SEE **pain**.

sufficient *Have we got sufficient food?* adequate, enough.

suffix SEE **language**. ! The opposite of *suffix* is *prefix*.

suffocate to choke, to smother, to stifle, to strangle, to throttle. SEE ALSO **kill**.

sugar 1 KINDS OF SUGAR ARE demerara, granulated, icing, lump. 2 OTHER FORMS OF SUGAR ARE sweets, syrup, treacle. SEE ALSO **food, sweet**.

sugar-beet SEE **vegetable**.

sugary SEE **taste**.

suggest 1 *Which brand did the shopkeeper suggest?* to advise, to offer, to propose, to recommend. 2 *The closed curtains suggest they are still in bed.* to hint, to imply, to indicate, to mean.

suicide SEE **kill**.

suit 1 *a suit to wear.* SEE **clothes**. 2 *a suit of cards.* SEE **cards**. 3 *That colour suits you.* to become, to be suitable for, to fit.

suitable *We need a suitable present for granny.* acceptable, appropriate, apt, becoming, convenient, fitting, handy, proper, timely.

suitcase SEE **container**.

suite SEE **furniture**.

suitor lover, sweetheart, wooer.

sulk *Logan sulked because he lost.* to be sulky, to brood, to mope.

sulky *a sulky look.* bad-tempered, cross, disgruntled, moody, sullen.

sullen 1 *a sullen expression.* bad-tempered, moody, sad, sulky. 2 *a sullen sky.* dark, dismal, gloomy, sombre.

sulphur SEE **chemical**.

sultan SEE **ruler**.

sultana SEE **fruit**.

sultry *sultry weather.* close, hot, humid, muggy, oppressive, steamy, stifling, stuffy, warm. SEE ALSO **weather**.

sum 1 *Add up the sum.* amount, number, total, whole. 2 SEE **mathematics**.

summarize *The judge summarized the evidence.* to sum up.

summary outline.

summit *the summit of a mountain.* head, peak, top.

summon *The head summoned Logan to his office.* to call, to send for.

summons SEE **law**.

sumptuous *a sumptuous banquet.* costly, grand, lavish, luxurious, magnificent, rich, splendid, superb.

sun SEE **astronomy**.

sunbathe SEE **seaside**.

sunburn sunstroke, sun-tan.

sundial SEE **clock**.

sun-glasses SEE **glasses**.

sunless *a sunless day.* cloudy, dull, grey, overcast. SEE ALSO **weather**.

sunny *a sunny day.* bright, clear, fine. SEE ALSO **weather**.

sunrise dawn, day-break. SEE ALSO **time**.

sunset dusk, evening, twilight. SEE ALSO **time**.

sunstroke SEE **illness**.

sun-tan sunburn, tan.

super, superb SEE **splendid**.

superficial *a superficial wound.* not deep, shallow, slight, trivial, unimportant.

superfluous *Why not give away your superfluous possessions?* excessive, redundant, unnecessary, unwanted.

superintendent officer, supervisor.

superior 1 *superior quality.* better, greater. 2 *a superior rank.* higher, senior. 3 *a superior attitude.* arrogant, haughty, self-important, smug, snobbish, (informal) stuck-up.

supermarket SEE **shop**.

supernatural 1 *Witches are supposed to have supernatural powers.* magical, miraculous, mysterious, psychic, spiritual. 2 FOR SUPERNATURAL BEINGS SEE **spirit**.

supersonic SEE **aircraft**.

superstar idol, star. SEE ALSO **entertainment**.

supervise *We need an adult to supervise our swimming party.* to administer, to control, to direct, to look after, to manage, to run, to watch over.

supper SEE **meal**.

supple *Gymnasts look so supple.* flexible, graceful, pliable, soft.

supplement *You pay a supplement if you travel first class.* addition, bonus, extra.

supplementary *a supplementary fare.* additional, auxiliary, extra.

supplier SEE **shopkeeper**.

supply 1 *A local firm supplied our new sports equipment.* to contribute, to donate, to equip, to furnish, to give, to provide. 2 *I keep a supply of sweets.* reserve, stock, store. 3 *supplies:* equipment, food, provisions, rations.

support 1 *Those pillars support the roof.* to bear, to carry, to hold up, to prop up. 2 *The lame man supported himself on a crutch.* to lean, to rest. 3 *Tony supported Logan when we were laughing at him.* to aid, to defend, to encourage, to reassure, to speak up for, to stand up for. 4 *Is there any evidence to support your story?* to explain, to justify, to verify. 5 *It costs a lot to support a family.* to feed, to keep, to maintain, to pay for, to provide for. 6 *Which team do you support?* to back, to be interested in, to follow. 7 *Thank you for your support.* aid, assistance, backing, co-operation, help.

supporter *a football supporter.* enthusiast, fan, follower.

suppose 1 *I suppose you want some food?* to assume, to believe, to guess, to imagine, to judge, to presume. **2** *I think Logan sometimes supposes he's brilliant!* to believe, to fancy, to imagine, to maintain, to pretend, to think.

suppress *The soldiers suppressed the rebellion.* to crush, to overcome, to put an end to, to quell, to subdue.

supreme *Lucy's supreme moment was when she won the gold cup.* best, greatest, highest.

sure 1 *He's sure to come.* bound, certain, compelled, obliged, required. **2** *I'm sure I'm right.* assured, confident, convinced, definite, positive. **3** *He's a sure ally.* dependable, faithful, loyal, reliable, safe, steady, trustworthy, undoubted.

surf breakers, waves. SEE **seaside**.

surface 1 *It looks nice on the surface.* coat, covering, crust, exterior, outside, shell, skin. **2** *A cube has six surfaces.* face, side. **3** *The submarine surfaced.* to come up, to emerge.

surf-riding SEE **sport**.

surge *The crowd surged forward.* to move, to push, to rush.

surgeon SEE **job, medicine**.

surgery 1 *They can cure appendicitis by surgery.* operation. **2** *I went to the surgery to see the doctor.* SEE **medicine**.

surly *a surly temper.* bad-tempered, cross, gruff, grumpy, irascible, peevish, rude, sulky, sullen, unfriendly.

surname SEE **name**.

surpass *The success of the jumble sale surpassed our expectations.* to beat, to do better, to exceed, to excel, to outdo, to top.

surplice SEE **clothes**.

surplus *If you've got too many sandwiches, give the surplus to Logan.* excess, extra, remainder.

surprise 1 *The news was a complete surprise.* bombshell, shock. **2** *The news surprised us.* to alarm, to amaze, to astonish, to astound, to dismay, to dumbfound, to shock, to startle, to stun. **3** *We surprised Logan writing rude words on the wall.* to catch, to catch out, to discover, to take unawares. **4** *surprising*: accidental, sudden, unexpected, unforeseen, unplanned.

surrender *After a long fight, they surrendered.* to capitulate, to give in, to submit, to yield.

surround *The police surrounded the warehouse.* to besiege, to encircle, to ring.

surroundings environment.

survey 1 *We did a survey of local sports facilities.* examination, investigation, look, study. **2** *After the fire they surveyed the house to see what damage had been done.* to examine, to inspect, to investigate, to look over, to view.

survive *You can't survive without water.* to carry on, to continue, to endure, to keep going, to last, to live, to persist, to remain.

suspect 1 *I suspect Logan's promises.* to distrust, to doubt, to mistrust. **2** *I suspect that he's lying.* to guess, to imagine, to presume, to suppose, to think.

suspend 1 *We suspended a rope from a branch.* to dangle, to hang, to swing. **2** *We had to suspend the meeting when the bell went.* to adjourn, to break off, to defer, to delay, to interrupt, to postpone, to put off.

suspense *We were full of suspense as we wondered who had first prize.* drama, excitement, tension, uncertainty.

suspension bridge SEE **bridge**.

suspicion *I had a suspicion that she was lying.* distrust, doubt, feeling, misgiving, uncertainty.

suspicious 1 *There's no need to be so suspicious!* disbelieving, distrustful, incredulous, sceptical, unconvinced, wary. **2** *a suspicious character.* disreputable, dubious, shady, unreliable, untrustworthy.

swag (informal) *robbers' swag.* booty, loot, plunder, takings.

swagger SEE **walk**.

swallow 1 SEE **drink, eat.** 2 *The ship was swallowed up in the fog.* to enclose, to engulf. 3 SEE **bird.**

swamp 1 *Don't sink into the swamp!* bog, fen, marsh, quagmire, quicksands. 2 *A tidal wave swamped the town.* to deluge, to engulf, to flood, to inundate, to overwhelm, to submerge.

swan 1 *a young swan:* cygnet. 2 SEE **bird.**

swank to boast, to brag, to crow, to gloat, to show off.

swarm 1 *a swarm of bees.* SEE **group.** 2 *Ants were swarming over the sugar.* to infest, to overrun, to teem.

swarthy *a swarthy skin.* brown, dark, tanned. SEE ALSO **complexion.**

swat *to swat a fly.* SEE **hit.**

sway to rock, to swing.

swear 1 *He swore that he wasn't lying.* to give your word, to pledge, to promise, to take an oath, to testify, to vow. 2 *swearing:* bad language, blasphemy, curses, foul language, obscenity, swear-words.

sweat to perspire.

sweater SEE **clothes.**

swede SEE **vegetable.**

sweep 1 *Sweep the floor.* to brush, to clean. 2 *The bus swept past.* SEE **move.**

sweet 1 SWEET THINGS ARE saccharine, SEE **sugar,** sweets, syrup. 2 VARIOUS SWEETS ARE acid drop, barley sugar, boiled sweet, bull's eye, butterscotch, candy, candy-floss, chewing-gum, chocolate, fruit pastille, fudge, humbug, liquorice, lollipop, marzipan, mint, nougat, peppermint, rock, toffee. 3 *We had jelly as a sweet.* SEE **meal.** 4 SEE **taste.**

sweetcorn SEE **cereal.**

sweetheart beloved, boy-friend, darling, fiancé, fiancée, girl-friend, lover, suitor, wooer.

swell 1 *The balloon swelled as it filled with air.* to billow, to blow up, to bulge, to distend, to enlarge, to grow, to increase, to puff up. 2 *the swell of the ocean.* waves.

swelling *I've got a painful swelling where the wasp stung me.* bulge, hump, knob, lump.

sweltering *a sweltering summer day.* baking, boiling, hot, oppressive, scorching, sizzling, steamy, stifling, sultry. SEE ALSO **weather.**

swerve *The car swerved to avoid the hedgehog.* to change direction, to dodge about, to turn, to veer, to wheel.

swift 1 *a swift journey.* brisk, fast, quick, (informal) nippy, rapid, speedy. 2 SEE **bird.**

swig SEE **drink.**

swill *Swill the plates in clear water.* to bathe, to clean, to rinse, to wash.

swim 1 to bathe, to dive in, to float, to go swimming, to take a dip. 2 VARIOUS SWIMMING STROKES ARE backstroke, breast-stroke, butterfly, crawl. SEE ALSO **sport.**

swimming-bath baths, pool.

swindle *He swindled us by charging too much.* to cheat, to deceive, to defraud, to dupe, to fool, to hoax, to hoodwink, to trick.

swine hog, pig.

swing *to swing to and fro.* to dangle, to flap, to rock, to sway, to swivel, to turn, to wave.

swipe 1 SEE **hit.** 2 (informal) *Logan swiped my sweets.* SEE **steal.**

swirl *The water swirled round.* to eddy, to spin, to twirl, to whirl.

swish SEE **sound.**

switch 1 *a light switch.* SEE **electricity.** 2 *Will you switch places?* to change, to exchange, to replace, to substitute, to swop.

switchboard SEE **telephone.**

swivel *a swivelling chair.* to revolve, to rotate, to swing, to turn.

swoop 1 *The owl swooped down.* to dive, to drop, to fly, to plunge, to pounce. 2 *The police swooped on the thieves' headquarters.* to raid.

swop *I'll swop this book for that record.* to

change, to exchange, to replace, to substitute, to switch.

sword SEE **weapon.**

swot (informal) to learn, to read, to study, to work.

sycamore SEE **tree.**

syllable SEE **language.**

syllabus SEE **school.**

symbol 1 *We designed a symbol for our club.* badge, emblem, sign. **2** *The formula used symbols that I didn't understand.* character, letter.

symbolize *Easter eggs symbolize the renewing of life.* to be a sign for, to communicate, to indicate, to represent, to stand for.

symmetrical balanced, even.

symmetry SEE **mathematics.**

sympathetic benevolent, compassionate, friendly, humane, merciful, pitying, sorry, tolerant, understanding.

sympathize *We sympathized with grandad when his dog died.* to be sorry for, to comfort, to console, to feel for, to pity.

sympathy compassion, consideration, feeling, kindness, mercy, pity, understanding.

symphony SEE **music.**

symptom *Spots are a symptom of measles.* indication, sign.

synagogue SEE **Jew.**

synonym SEE **language.**

synthetic *Nylon is a synthetic material.* artificial, man-made, manufactured, unnatural.

syringe SEE **medicine.**

syrup SEE **food, sugar.**

system 1 *a railway system.* network, organization. **2** *Lucy has a system for her gymnastics training.* method, procedure, process, routine, technique.

systematic orderly, organized, planned, scientific.

T t

tabby SEE **cat.**

table SEE **furniture.**

tablespoon SEE **cutlery.**

tablet 1 *a tablet of soap.* bar, block, chunk, piece, slab. **2** *The doctor prescribed some tablets.* capsule, pellet, pill. SEE ALSO **medicine.**

table-tennis (informal) ping-pong. SEE ALSO **sport.**

tachograph SEE **vehicle.**

tack 1 *to tack down a carpet.* SEE **fasten.** **2** *to tack up the hem of a garment.* to sew, to stitch.

tackle 1 *fishing tackle.* apparatus, equipment, gear, kit, paraphernalia, rig. **2** *a Rugby tackle.* SEE **Rugby. 3** *to tackle a problem.* to attend to, to cope with, to deal with, to grapple with, to handle, to manage, to sort out, to undertake.

tacky *The new paint was still tacky.* gluey, sticky.

tactful *a tactful reminder.* considerate, diplomatic, discreet, polite.

tactics *We planned our tactics for tomorrow's game.* manoeuvre, plan, policy, scheme, strategy.

tactless *It's tactless to say that you don't like the food.* impolite, inconsiderate, insensitive, undiplomatic, unwise.

taffeta SEE **cloth.**

tag *a price tag.* label, sticker, ticket.

tail 1 back, end, rear. **2** *The police tailed our car.* to follow, to pursue, to shadow, to stalk, to track, to trail. **3** *to tail off: Our enthusiasm tailed off when we got tired.* to decline, to lessen, to reduce, to slacken, to subside.

tailor SEE **job.**

take 1 *Take my hand.* to clutch, to grab, to grasp, to hold, to pluck, to seize, to snatch. **2** *The soldiers took prisoners.* to arrest, to capture, to catch, to corner, to detain, to seize. **3** *Who took my pen?* to move, (informal) to nick, to pick up, to pilfer, (informal) to pinch, to remove, to sneak, to steal, (informal) to swipe. **4** *The bus takes* *you to the shopping centre.* to bring, to carry, to convey, to transport. 5 *I took granny round the garden.* to conduct, to guide, to lead. 6 *Take your medicine.* to consume, to have, to swallow, to use. 7 *He wouldn't take any money.* to accept, to receive. 8 *It took a lot of effort to move the piano.* to need, to require, to use up. 9 *to take away*: to deduct, to subtract. 10 *to take in*: SEE **deceive**. 11 *to take place*: to come about, to happen, to occur.

takings *The shopkeeper added up her takings.* income, proceeds, profits. SEE ALSO **money**.

talc, talcum SEE **cosmetics**.

tale *She told us her tale.* account, narrative, story, yarn. SEE ALSO **writing**.

talent *musical talent, etc.* ability, accomplishment, aptitude, genius, gift, know-how, prowess, skill.

talented *a talented musician.* able, accomplished, artistic, brilliant, expert, gifted, intelligent, skilful, skilled, versatile. SEE ALSO **clever**.

talk 1 *Logan talked all through the lesson. Can you talk in French?* to address someone, to communicate, to express yourself, to speak. SEE ALSO **say**. 2 WAYS OF TALKING ARE to babble, to bawl, to bellow, to blurt out, to call out, to chat, to chatter, to croak, to cry, to drone, to exclaim, to gabble, to gossip, to grunt, to harp, to howl, to jabber, to jeer, to lisp, to moan, to mumble, to murmur, to mutter, to prattle, to pray, to preach, to rave, to recite, to roar, to scream, to screech, to shout, to shriek, to snap, to snarl, to speak in an undertone, to splutter, (informal) to spout, to squeal, to stammer, to stutter, to utter, to wail, to whimper, to whine, to whisper, to yell. 3 *I had a nice talk with granny.* chat, conversation, dialogue, discussion. 4 *We heard an interesting talk about engineering.* address, lecture, speech.

talkative 1 chatty, communicative. 2 *a talkative person*: chatterbox.

tall *a tall tower.* high, lofty, towering. SEE ALSO **big**.

talon claw. SEE ALSO **bird**.

tambourine SEE **percussion**.

tame 1 *a tame animal.* docile, domesticated, gentle, meek, obedient, safe. 2 *a tame story.* boring, dull, feeble, tedious, unexciting, uninteresting.

tamper *Don't tamper with the inside of the TV set.* to interfere, to meddle, to play about, to tinker.

tan 1 SEE **colour**. 2 suntan. 3 *tanned*: brown, sunburnt, weather-beaten.

tandem SEE **cycle**.

tangerine SEE **fruit**.

tangible *tangible evidence.* physical, real, solid.

tangle 1 *Don't tangle the guy ropes.* to confuse, to entangle, to muddle, to twist. 2 *tangled*: *tangled hair.* dishevelled, knotted, matted, unkempt.

tangy SEE **taste**.

tank 1 *a water tank.* SEE **container**. 2 *a fish tank*: aquarium. 3 *an army tank.* SEE **vehicle**.

tankard SEE **drink**.

tanker SEE **vessel, vehicle**.

tantalize *The delicious smell tantalized us.* to entice, to tease, to tempt, to torment.

tantrum *Baby had a tantrum when we took her sweets.* hysterics, rage, temper.

tap *I tapped gently on the door.* to knock, to rap. SEE ALSO **hit**.

tap-dancing SEE **dance**.

tape 1 *I tied the parcel with tape.* band, braid, ribbon, strip. SEE ALSO **fasten**. 2 *We recorded our song on tape.* SEE **record**.

tape-measure SEE **tool**.

tape-recorder SEE **audio equipment**.

tapestry SEE **cloth**.

tar SEE **material**.

target *Our target was to raise £100.* aim, goal, objective.

tarmac SEE **road**.

tarnish *The chemicals tarnished the metal.* to blacken, to corrode, to discolour.

tart 1 *Lemons have a tart taste.* acid, sharp, sour, tangy. SEE ALSO **taste.** **2** *jam tarts.* SEE **cake, food.**

tartan SEE **cloth.**

task activity, assignment, chore, duty, errand, job, work.

task-force SEE **armed services.**

taste 1 *Taste a bit of this!* to nibble, to sip, to try. SEE ALSO **drink, eat. 2** *I like the taste of this.* character, flavour, quality. **3** *Can I have a taste?* bit, morsel, piece, titbit. **4** WORDS USED TO DESCRIBE TASTE ARE acid, appetizing, bitter, creamy, delicious, fresh, fruity, hot, luscious, meaty, mellow, peppery, rancid, salt, salty, savoury, sharp, sour, spicy, stale, sugary, sweet, tangy, tart, tasty.

tasteful *tasteful clothes.* attractive, dignified, elegant, fashionable, smart, stylish.

tasty SEE **taste.**

tattered *tattered clothes.* frayed, ragged, tatty, torn, worn out.

tatters rags, shreds.

tattoo 1 *a tattoo on the skin.* SEE **mark. 2** *a military tattoo.* SEE **entertainment.**

tatty *tatty clothes.* frayed, old, patched, ragged, scruffy, shabby, tattered, torn, untidy, worn out.

taunt *They taunted him cruelly when he missed an easy goal.* to boo, to hiss, to hoot at, to jeer at, to laugh at, to mock, to ridicule, to scoff at, to sneer at.

taut *Make sure the rope is taut.* stretched, tense, tight.

tavern bar, inn, pub, public house.

tawdry cheap, fancy, flashy, gaudy, showy.

tawny SEE **colour.**

tax VARIOUS TAXES ARE customs, duty, rates. SEE ALSO **money.**

taxi cab. SEE ALSO **vehicle.**

tea SEE **drink, meal.**

teach to coach, to indoctrinate, to inform, to instruct, to lecture, to train. SEE ALSO **educate.**

teacher VARIOUS TEACHERS ARE coach, guru, headteacher, instructor, lecturer, master, mistress, preacher, professor, schoolmaster, schoolmistress, schoolteacher, trainer, tutor. SEE ALSO **school.**

teak SEE **wood.**

team club, side. SEE ALSO **group.**

teapot SEE **container, crockery.**

tear 1 *Tony tore his jeans.* to rip, to shred, to slit, to split. **2** *The lion tore its prey apart.* to claw, to rend. **3** *We tore home for dinner.* SEE **move. 4** *There's a tear in Tony's jeans.* cut, gash, hole, slit, split. SEE ALSO **opening. 5** *Tony shed a few tears when the dog died.* tear-drop. SEE ALSO **weep.**

tearful SEE **sad.**

tear gas SEE **gas, weapon.**

tease *The cat scratches if you tease her!* (informal) to aggravate, to annoy, to irritate, to laugh at, to make fun of, to pester, to ridicule, to tantalize, to torment, to vex.

teaspoon SEE **cutlery.**

technician SEE **job.**

technique *the technique of a craftsman.* art, craft, dodge, knack, know-how, method, procedure, routine, skill, system, trick, workmanship.

technology SEE **science.**

teddy-bear SEE **toy.**

tedious *a tedious journey.* boring, dreary, dull, long-winded, monotonous, slow, tiresome, tiring, unexciting, uninteresting, wearisome.

teem 1 *The pond teemed with tadpoles.* to be full of, to be infested with, to be overrun by, to swarm with. **2** *The rain teemed down.* to pour. SEE ALSO **weather.**

teenager adolescent, juvenile, youngster, youth.

teeny (informal) *a teeny baby.* SEE **small.**

teetotaller abstainer.

telecommunications SEE **communication.**

telegram cable, wire. SEE ALSO **communication.**

telepathic psychic.

telephone 1 *Telephone us if you can't come.* to call, to dial, to phone, to ring. 2 WORDS TO DO WITH TELEPHONES ARE dial, kiosk, receiver, telegraph pole, telephone-box, switchboard. 3 SEE **communication.**

telephoto lens SEE **photography.**

telescope 1 SEE **optical.** 2 *to telescope things together.* SEE **shorten.**

televise *They televise a lot of snooker these days.* to broadcast, to relay, to send out, to transmit.

television 1 *a television set*: monitor, receiver, (informal) telly, (informal) the box, (informal) the small screen, video. 2 TELEVISION PROGRAMMES ARE cartoon, chat show, comedy, commercial, documentary, drama, film, interview, movie, news, panel game, play, quiz, serial, series, sport. SEE ALSO **entertainment.** 3 SEE **communication.**

tell 1 *Tell us what happened.* to describe, to disclose, to divulge, to explain, to make known, to reveal. 2 *Tell us a story.* to narrate, to recount, to relate. 3 *He told me it would cost less than £10.* to advise, to assure, to inform, to promise. 4 *Mrs Angel told us to stop.* to command, to direct, to instruct, to order. 5 *Can you tell who wrote this?* to discover, to discriminate, to distinguish, to identify, to recognize. 6 (informal) *to tell someone off*: to censure, to condemn, to criticize, to rebuke, to reprimand, to reproach, to scold, (informal) to tick off.

temper 1 *Mum's in a good temper.* disposition, humour, mood, state of mind. 2 *a bad temper*: anger, fury, rage, tantrum. SEE ALSO **angry.**

temperament *a melancholy temperament.* character, disposition, nature, personality.

temperamental *a temperamental*

person. changeable, fickle, inconsistent, irritable, moody, touchy, unpredictable, variable.

temperature 1 SCALES FOR MEASURING TEMPERATURE ARE Celsius, centigrade, Fahrenheit. 2 FOR WORDS TO DO WITH TEMPERATURE SEE **cold, hot, weather.** 3 *to have a temperature*: to be feverish, to have a fever.

tempest cyclone, gale, hurricane, storm, tornado, typhoon, whirlwind. SEE ALSO **weather.**

temple SEE **building, worship.**

tempo *the tempo of a piece of music.* pace, rhythm, speed. SEE ALSO **music.**

temporary 1 *a temporary pause.* brief, momentary, passing, short, transient. 2 *a temporary captain.* acting.

tempt 1 *We tempted the mouse with a bit of cheese.* to bait, to bribe, to coax, to entice, to lure. 2 *tempting*: SEE **attractive.**

tenant *a tenant of a flat.* inhabitant, lodger, occupant, resident.

tend 1 *A shepherd tends sheep.* to attend to, to guard, to look after, to mind, to protect, to watch. 2 *Nurses tend their patients.* to care for, to cherish, to nurse, to treat. 3 *Mr Brunswick tends to fall asleep in the evenings.* to be disposed to, to be inclined to, to be liable to, to have a tendency to.

tendency *Hedgehogs have a tendency to curl up when danger comes.* inclination, instinct, leaning, readiness, trend.

tender 1 *tender plants.* dainty, delicate, fragile. 2 *tender meat.* eatable, edible, not tough. 3 *tender care.* affectionate, compassionate, fond, kind, loving, merciful, soft-hearted, sympathetic, touching. 4 *a tender kiss.* gentle, soft. 5 *a tender wound.* painful, sensitive, sore.

tennis SEE **sport.**

tenor SEE **sing.**

tense 1 *With the scores equal, the competitors were tense.* anxious, edgy, excited, highly-strung, jittery, jumpy, nervous, strained, touchy, (informal) uptight. 2 *The trainer massaged their tense muscles.* stretched, taut, tight.

tension anxiety, suspense.

tent 1 KINDS OF TENT ARE marquee, tepee, wigwam. 2 PARTS OF A TENT ARE canvas, frame, groundsheet, guy rope, pole, tent-peg.

tepid lukewarm, warm.

term 1 *a term in prison.* period, session, spell, stretch. SEE ALSO **time**. 2 *'Offside' is a term used in football.* expression, phrase, saying, word. 3 *We'll surrender if you agree to our terms.* conditions. 4 *The hotel's terms are reasonable.* charges, fees, prices, rates.

terminal 1 SEE **computer, electricity**. 2 *a terminal illness.* deadly, fatal, mortal.

terminate 1 *The head terminated our interview.* to close, to conclude, to end, to finish. 2 *The war terminated when the treaty was signed.* to cease, to stop.

terminus destination. SEE ALSO **railway**.

terrace 1 SEE **garden**. 2 *a terrace house*: SEE **house**.

terrestrial *terrestrial beings.* earthly.

terrible *a terrible accident.* SEE **unpleasant**.

terrier SEE **dog**.

terrific (informal) 1 *It's a terrific size.* SEE **big**. 2 *We had a terrific time.* SEE **good**. 3 *It's a terrific problem.* SEE **serious**. ! *Terrific* once meant *terrifying.* Nowadays its meaning is usually rather vague.

terrify 1 to alarm, to appal, to dismay, to horrify, to make afraid, to petrify, to scare. SEE ALSO **frighten**. 2 *terrifying*: hair-raising, scary.

territory *enemy territory.* area, district, land, region, sector, zone.

terror alarm, dread, fear, fright, horror, panic.

terrorist assassin, gunman, hijacker. SEE ALSO **criminal**.

terrorize *Logan's gang terrorized the*

infants. to bully, to frighten, to intimidate, to persecute, to terrify, to threaten, to torment.

terse *a terse comment.* brief, concise, short.

tessellation SEE **mathematics**.

test 1 *a maths test.* examination, quiz. 2 *a scientific test.* experiment, trial. 3 *a test-match*: SEE **cricket**. 4 *The garage tested the steering.* to check, to examine, to inspect.

testify *The witness testified that she had been attacked.* to declare, to give evidence, to state on oath, to swear.

testimony evidence.

test pilot SEE **job**.

test-tube SEE **container**.

testy *a testy old gentleman.* bad-tempered, cross, disgruntled, grumpy, irascible, irritable, peevish, petulant, short-tempered, snappy.

tether 1 *They kept the goat on a tether.* chain, leash, rope. 2 *The goat was tethered.* to secure, to tie up. SEE ALSO **fasten**.

textbook SEE **book**.

textile fabric, material, stuff. SEE ALSO **cloth**.

texture *I love the texture of velvet.* feel.

thank to acknowledge, to show appreciation, to show gratitude.

thankful *I was thankful to be home.* appreciative, grateful, pleased.

thatch SEE **roof**.

thaw *The snow thawed.* to melt, to soften, to unfreeze. SEE ALSO **weather**.

theatre 1 THEATRICAL ENTERTAINMENTS ARE ballet, comedy, drama, farce, mime, nativity play, opera, pantomime, play. 2 KINDS OF PERFORMANCE ARE dress rehearsal, first night, matinée, première, preview, production, rehearsal, show. 3 PEOPLE WHO WORK IN A THEATRE ARE actor, actress, ballerina, dancer, director, producer, prompter, stage manager, understudy, usher or usherette. 4 PARTS OF A THEATRE ARE balcony, box-office, circle, dressing room, foyer, gallery, stage, stalls. 5 OTHER WORDS TO DO WITH THEATRE ARE costume, curtain, footlights, lighting, make-up, programme, scenery, set, sound-effect, spotlight. 6 SEE ALSO **entertainment**.

theft burglary, pilfering, robbery, shop-lifting, stealing. SEE ALSO **crime**.

theme 1 *the theme of a talk.* issue, matter, subject, topic. 2 *a musical theme.* air, melody, tune. SEE ALSO **music**.

theology SEE **subject**.

theoretical abstract.

theory 1 *I have a theory about how Logan got that money.* argument, assumption, belief, explanation, guess, idea, notion, supposition, view. 2 *Do you understand the theory of how computers work?* laws, principles, rules, science.

therapy *He goes to hospital for therapy.* cure, healing, remedy, treatment. SEE ALSO **medicine**.

therefore accordingly, consequently, so, thus.

Thermos vacuum flask. SEE ALSO **container**.

thick 1 *thick snow.* deep. 2 *a thick book.* fat. 3 *thick rope.* stout, strong, sturdy. 4 *a thick crowd.* dense, impenetrable, solid. 5 *thick mud.* heavy, stiff. 6 (informal) *He must be thick if he doesn't understand!* SEE **stupid**.

thicken *to thicken a sauce.* to concentrate, to condense, to reduce, to stiffen.

thief bandit, burglar, highwayman, mugger, pickpocket, robber, shop-lifter. SEE ALSO **criminal**.

thigh SEE **body, leg**.

thin 1 *a thin figure.* emaciated, lanky, lean, scraggy, skinny, slender, slight, slim, wiry. 2 *a thin line.* fine, narrow. 3 *thin gravy.* runny, watery. 4 *a thin audience.* meagre, scanty, small, sparse. 5 *You need to thin the paint.* to dilute, to water down, to weaken.

thing 1 *What's that thing in your hand?* article, item, object. 2 *I saw a funny thing this morning.* action, affair, deed,

happening, occurrence. 3 *There are some things I want to discuss.* idea, thought.

think 1 *I thought about how to earn some money.* to brood, to consider, to contemplate, to meditate, to ponder, to reflect. 2 *I think he's right.* to accept, to admit, to believe, to conclude, to judge. 3 *I think it's about 12 o'clock.* to assume, to feel, to guess, to presume, to reckon, to suppose. 4 *If you think, you won't make mistakes.* to attend, to concentrate. 5 *to think up: I thought up a clever plan.* to conceive, to concoct, to devise, to imagine, to invent, to make up.

thirst 1 *to have a thirst:* (informal) to be dry, (informal) to be parched. 2 *a thirst for knowledge.* appetite, craving, desire, hunger, itch, longing, love, lust, passion, urge, wish.

thistle SEE **weed**.

thorn *Gorse has sharp thorns.* needle, prickle, spike.

thorny 1 *a thorny bush.* prickly, scratchy, spiky. 2 (informal) *a thorny problem.* SEE **difficult**.

thorough *a thorough piece of work.* attentive, careful, conscientious, diligent, exhaustive, methodical, meticulous, observant, orderly, organized, painstaking, scrupulous, systematic, thoughtful, watchful.

thoroughfare SEE **road**.

thought 1 *Tony was deep in thought.* contemplation, day-dreaming, meditation, reflection, reverie. 2 *I had a sudden thought.* belief, concept, idea, notion, opinion. 3 *It was a nice thought to give granny flowers.* attention, consideration, kindness, thoughtfulness.

thoughtful 1 *It was thoughtful of Lucy to wash up.* attentive, considerate, friendly, good-natured, helpful, obliging, public-spirited, unselfish. SEE ALSO **kind**. 2 *a thoughtful expression.* dreamy, grave, pensive, philosophical, reflective, serious, solemn. 3 *a thoughtful piece of work.* careful, conscientious, diligent, exhaustive, methodical, meticulous, observant, orderly, organized, painstaking, scrupulous, systematic, thorough, watchful.

thoughtless 1 *It was thoughtless to leave the shopping on the bus!* absent-minded, careless, forgetful, inattentive, irresponsible, negligent, scatterbrained. **2** *It was thoughtless to take all the chocolates with Granny's favourite centres!* cruel, heartless, insensitive, selfish, tactless, uncaring, unfeeling.

thrash 1 *Teachers used to thrash naughty children.* to beat, to cane, to flog, to lash, to scourge, to whack, to whip. SEE ALSO **hit**. **2** (informal) *We thrashed them 7-0.* to beat, to conquer, to crush, to overwhelm, to rout, to vanquish. SEE ALSO **defeat**.

thread 1 fibre, hair, strand. **2** THREADS USED IN SEWING AND WEAVING ARE cotton, silk, twine, wool, yarn.

threadbare *threadbare clothes.* frayed, ragged, shabby, tattered, tatty, thin, worn.

threat 1 *to make threats*: SEE **threaten**. **2** *a threat of snow.* danger, risk, warning.

threaten 1 *Logan's gang threatened us.* to bully, to frighten, to intimidate, to make threats, to menace. **2** *An avalanche threatened the town.* to endanger. **3** *threatening: threatening storm-clouds.* forbidding, grim, menacing, ominous, stern, unfriendly.

thrifty *Tony is thrifty with his money.* careful, economical, sparing.

thrill 1 *the thrills of a fun-fair.* excitement, (informal) kicks, sensation, suspense. **2** *The music thrilled us.* to delight, to electrify, to excite, to rouse, to stimulate, to stir. **3** *thrilling*: extraordinary, sensational, spectacular.

thriller SEE **writing**.

thrive 1 *Mrs Brunswick's plants thrive in the greenhouse.* to do well, to flourish, to grow, to prosper, to succeed. **2** *thriving*: prosperous, successful.

throat SEE **body**.

throb 1 *a throb of toothache.* ache, pang, twinge. SEE ALSO **pain**. **2** *the throb of music.* beat, pulse, rhythm.

throne SEE **seat**.

throng *We pushed through the throng.* company, crowd, gathering, horde, mass, multitude, swarm. SEE ALSO **group**.

throttle to choke, to smother, to stifle, to strangle, to suffocate. SEE ALSO **kill**.

throw 1 *to throw a ball, etc.* to bowl, to cast, (informal) to chuck, to fling, to heave, to hurl, to lob, to pelt, to pitch, to sling, to toss. **2** *to throw something away*: to cast off, to discard, to dispose of, to dump, to get rid of, to reject, to scrap, to shed.

thrush SEE **bird**.

thrust 1 *We thrust Logan to the front.* to drive, to force, to propel, to push, to send, to shove. **2** *to thrust with a dagger, etc.* to lunge, to plunge, to poke, to stab.

thud SEE **sound**.

thug delinquent, hooligan, mugger, ruffian, trouble-maker, vandal. SEE ALSO **criminal**.

thumb SEE **body, hand**.

thump *He thumped me in the back.* to bash, to beat, to bump, to butt, to clout, to hammer, to jab, to knock, to poke, to pound, to prod, to punch, to ram, to slog, to smack, to smash, to strike, to swipe, to wallop, to whack. SEE ALSO **hit**.

thunder SEE **sound, weather**.

thunderstruck *I was thunderstruck when she gave me £10.* amazed, astonished, astounded, nonplussed, stunned.

thus accordingly, consequently, so, therefore.

tick 1 *The clock ticks.* SEE **sound**. **2** (informal) *to tick someone off*: to censure, to condemn, to criticize, to rebuke, to reprimand, to reproach, to scold, (informal) to tell off.

ticket *Buy a ticket before you start fishing.* coupon, permit, voucher.

tickle 1 *I giggle if someone tickles me.* SEE **touch**. 2 *My throat tickles when I'm getting a cold.* to itch, to tingle.

ticklish *a ticklish problem.* difficult, (informal) thorny, tricky.

tidal wave SEE **disaster**.

tiddler SEE **fish**.

tiddlywinks SEE **game**.

tide *the tides of the sea.* current, ebb and flow, rise and fall.

tidings (old-fashioned) *good tidings,* information, news.

tidy 1 *Make yourselves tidy before dinner.* neat, presentable, smart, spruce, trim. 2 *Make your room tidy.* orderly, shipshape, spick and span, straight. 3 *tidy in the house:* house-proud.

tie 1 *to tie with string.* to bind, to hitch, to knot, to lash. SEE ALSO **fasten**. 2 *to tie up a boat:* to anchor, to moor. 3 *to tie up an animal:* to secure, to tether. 4 *to tie in a game.* to be equal, to be level, to draw. 5 *I wear a tie at school.* SEE **clothes**.

tiger SEE **animal**.

tight 1 *Make sure the screws are tight.* fast, firm, fixed, immovable, secure. 2 *I need a jar with a tight lid.* airtight, sealed, watertight. 3 *Pull the string tight.* stiff, stretched, taut, tense. 4 *It was a tight crowd in that small room.* close, crammed, crowded. 5 (informal) *He was tight after drinking several beers.* drunk, fuddled, intoxicated.

tights SEE **clothes**.

tile FOR OTHER SURFACES SEE **roof**.

tiller helm. SEE ALSO **vessel**.

tilt *The bike tilts when you go round a bend.* to incline, to lean, to slant, to slope, to tip.

timber KINDS OF TIMBER ARE beam, board, log, lumber, plank, post, tree trunk. SEE ALSO **wood**.

time 1 *What's the best time to call?* date, day, hour, moment, occasion, opportunity. 2 *We spent a long time in the museum.* spell, session, while. 3 *There was a time when Tony was captain.* phase, season, stretch, term. 4 *What was life like in the time of Elizabeth I?* age, era, period. 5 UNITS OF TIME ARE century, day, decade, eternity, fortnight, hour, instant, leap year, lifetime, minute, month, second, week, weekend, year. 6 TIMES OF THE DAY ARE afternoon, bedtime, dusk, evening, midday, midnight, morning, night, nightfall, noon, sunrise, sunset, twilight. 7 DEVICES FOR MEASURING TIME ARE calendar, clock, digital watch, hour-glass, stop-watch, sundial, watch. 8 SPECIAL TIMES OF THE YEAR ARE Advent, autumn, Boxing Day, Christmas, Easter, Good Friday, Hallowe'en, Hogmanay, Lent, midsummer, New Year, Palm Sunday, Passover, Ramadan, St Valentine's Day, spring, summer, Whitsun, winter, Yom Kippur, yuletide.

timely appropriate, apt, fitting, suitable.

timetable *We printed a timetable of events for sports day.* programme, schedule.

timid *Don't be timid — jump in!* bashful, cowardly, coy, faint-hearted, fearful, nervous, reserved, sheepish, shy, timorous, unheroic.

timpani SEE **percussion**.

tin 1 *a tin mine.* SEE **metal**. 2 *a tin of beans.* SEE **container**. 3 *to tin food.* SEE **preserve**.

tinge *The evening sky was tinged with red.* to colour, to dye, to paint, to stain, to tint.

tingle *I still tingle where I sat in the nettles.* to sting, to tickle.

tinker *Never tinker with the inside of a TV set.* to interfere, (informal) to mess about, to tamper.

tinkle SEE **sound**.

tinny *a tinny old car.* cheap, inferior, poor-quality.

tin-opener SEE **kitchen**.

tint *The paint in Lucy's bedroom has a faint tint of pink in it.* colour, dye, hue, shade, stain, tinge, tone.

tiny 1 *a tiny insect, etc.* diminutive, imperceptible, little, microscopic, miniature, minute, (informal) teeny, wee. SEE ALSO **small**. **2** *a tiny wound.* insignificant, minor, negligible, petty, slight, trifling, trivial, unimportant.

tip 1 *the tip of a pencil.* end, point. **2** *the tip of an iceberg.* peak, top. **3** *Mr Brunswick gave us some tips on safety in the water.* advice, clue, hint, suggestion, warning. **4** *We took the rubbish to the tip.* dump, rubbish-heap. **5** *A big wave nearly tipped the boat over.* to capsize, to knock over, to overturn, to topple, to turn over, to upset.

tire 1 *The long game tired us.* to exhaust, to wear out, to weary. **2** *tired*: bored, (informal) done in, drowsy, jaded, listless, sleepy.

tissue 1 handkerchief. **2** SEE **paper**.

tit SEE **bird**.

titbit *Give the dog a few nice titbits.* morsel, piece, taste.

title 1 *the title of a story.* heading, name. **2** *a person's title.* position, rank, status. **3** *a titled person*: aristocrat, lord, nobleman, noblewoman, peer, peeress. **4** *titled*: aristocratic, high-born, noble. **5** TITLES YOU USE WHEN SPEAKING OR WRITING TO PEOPLE ARE Baron, Baroness, Count, Countess, Dame, Dr or Doctor, Duchess, Duke, Earl, Lady, Lord, Master, Miss, Mr, Mrs, Ms, Professor, Rev or Reverend, Sir. SEE ALSO **rank, royal**.

titter to chuckle, to giggle, to snigger. SEE ALSO **laugh**.

TNT SEE **explosive**.

toad SEE **amphibious**.

toadstool fungus, mushroom.

toast SEE **cook, food**.

toaster SEE **kitchen**.

tobacco SEE **smoke**.

tobacconist SEE **shop**.

toboggan sled, sledge.

toddler baby, child, infant. SEE ALSO **person**.

to-do *There was a great to-do when Logan's rats escaped.* bother, confusion, disorder, disturbance, excitement, fuss, turmoil, uproar. SEE ALSO **commotion**.

toe SEE **foot**.

toffee SEE **sweet**.

toil drudgery, effort, exertion, labour, work.

toilet lavatory, (informal) loo, water-closet, WC. SEE ALSO **house**.

token 1 *Please accept these flowers as a token of our love.* indication, mark, reminder, sign. **2** *You can get £1 off if you present this token.* counter, coupon, voucher.

tolerable *The food was just about tolerable.* acceptable, adequate, all right, passable, satisfactory.

tolerant *Grandad is tolerant when we are naughty.* easygoing, forgiving, indulgent, lenient, liberal, patient, sympathetic.

tolerate 1 *I can't tolerate this toothache!* to abide, to bear, to endure, to put up with, to stand. **2** *Mrs Brunswick won't tolerate smoking in the house.* to accept, to allow, to approve of, to permit.

toll 1 *to toll a bell.* SEE **bell**. **2** *We had to pay a toll to cross the bridge.* charge, fee, payment.

tomahawk SEE **weapon**.

tomato SEE **fruit, salad**.

tomb burial place, grave, gravestone, memorial, monument, tombstone.

tom-cat SEE **cat, male**.

tom-tom SEE **percussion**.

ton SEE **measure**.

tone 1 *There was an angry tone in her voice.* expression, note, sound. **2** *We chose some eerie music to set the tone for our play.* atmosphere, feeling, mood. **3** *The paint in Lucy's room has a pink tone.* colour, hue, shade, tinge, tint. **4** *Please tone down the noise!* to lessen, to quieten, to soften, to subdue.

tongs SEE **tool**.

tongue 1 SEE **body, head**. **2** *He spoke a foreign tongue.* language.

tongue-tied *I don't explain things well because I get tongue-tied.* dumb, mute, speechless.

tonic SEE **medicine**.

tonne SEE **measure**.

tonsillitis SEE **illness**.

tonsils SEE **body**.

tool 1 *Mr Brunswick has tools for every job you can think of.* apparatus, contraption, device, gadget, hardware, implement, instrument, invention, machine, utensil.
2 VARIOUS TOOLS ARE axe, bellows, chisel, chopper, clamp, cramp, crowbar, cutter, drill, file, fretsaw, glass-paper, hack-saw, hammer, hatchet, jack, jigsaw, ladder, lever, mallet, oil-can, penknife, pick, pickaxe, pincers, plane, pliers, pocket-knife, sandpaper, saw, screwdriver, shears, shovel, sledgehammer, spanner, tape-measure, tongs, vice, wrench. FOR OTHER TOOLS SEE **house, farm, garden, kitchen**.

tooth 1 SEE **head**. 2 *teeth*: fangs.
3 WORDS TO DO WITH TEETH ARE dental nurse, dental surgery, dentist, denture, extraction, filling, gums, toothache, toothbrush, toothpaste.

top 1 *the top of a mountain.* apex, crown, head, peak, summit, tip. 2 *the top of a jar.* cap, cover, covering, lid. 3 *a spinning top.* SEE **toy**. 4 *Our collection for OXFAM topped last year's record.* to beat, to exceed, to excel, to outdo, to surpass.

topic *a topic for discussion.* issue, matter, subject, theme.

topical *You get topical news on TV.* contemporary, current, recent.

topple 1 *The gale toppled our TV aerial.* to knock down, to overturn, to throw down, to tip over, to upset. 2 *The vase toppled off the mantlepiece.* to fall, to tumble.

topsy-turvy chaotic, confused, disorderly, haphazard, higgledy-piggledy, jumbled, mixed up, muddled, upside-down.

torch SEE **light**.

toreador bullfighter, matador.

torment 1 *The wasps tormented us.* to afflict, to annoy, to bait, to distress, to pester, to vex, to worry. 2 *Logan tormented the infants.* to bully, to hurt, to intimidate, to persecute, to tease, to torture, to victimize. 3 *I hope you never experience the torment of bad sunburn.* agony, anguish, pain, suffering, torture.

tornado SEE **storm**.

torpedo SEE **weapon**.

torrent *a torrent of water.* cataract, deluge, downpour, flood, spate, stream.

torrential *torrential rain.* SEE **weather**.

tortoise SEE **pet, reptile**.

torture 1 to afflict, to be cruel, to cause pain, to hurt, to inflict pain, to torment. 2 agony, pain, suffering.

Tory SEE **politics**.

toss 1 *I tossed a coin in the well.* to bowl, to cast, (informal) to chuck, to fling, to heave, to hurl, to lob, to pitch, to sling, to throw. 2 *The boat tossed about in the storm.* to bob, to pitch, to reel, to rock, to roll, to shake.

total 1 *Dad signed a cheque for the total amount.* complete, entire, full, whole. 2 *Our play was a total disaster.* absolute, perfect, sheer, utter. 3 *Add up the figures and tell me the total.* amount, answer, sum. 4 *Our shopping totalled £37.* to add up to, to amount to, to come to, to make.

totter *We tottered unsteadily off the ship.* to dodder, to falter, to reel, to rock. SEE ALSO **walk**.

touch 1 WAYS TO TOUCH THINGS OR PEOPLE ARE to caress, to contact, to cuddle, to dab, to embrace, to feel, to finger, to fondle, to handle, to kiss, to manipulate, to massage, to nuzzle, to pat, to paw, to pet, to rub, to stroke, to tickle. SEE ALSO **hit**. 2 *The sad story touched us.* to affect, to concern, to move, to stir. 3 *touching: a touching scene.* emotional, moving. 4 *Our speed touched 100 miles an hour.* to reach, to rise to.

touch-down SEE **Rugby**.

touchy *Be careful what you say because he's a bit touchy.* edgy, irritable, jittery, jumpy, nervous, sensitive, snappy, temperamental, tense, (informal) uptight.

tough 1 *tough shoes.* durable, hard-wearing, indestructible, lasting, unbreakable, well-made. 2 *a tough wrestler.* beefy, brawny, burly, hardy, muscular, robust, strong, sturdy, wiry. 3 *tough meat.* hard, gristly, leathery, rubbery. 4 *a tough climb.* arduous, difficult, gruelling, hard, laborious, stiff, strenuous, uphill.

toughen to reinforce, to strengthen.

tour 1 *a coach tour.* excursion, journey, outing, trip. SEE ALSO **travel**. 2 *Our class toured a local factory.* to go round, to visit.

tourist *The cathedral was full of tourists.* holiday-maker, sightseer, tripper, visitor.

tournament *a tennis tournament.* championship, competition, contest, series.

tow *Our car isn't powerful enough to tow a trailer.* to drag, to draw, to haul, to pull.

towel SEE **bathroom**.

tower 1 SEE **building**. 2 *The castle towers above the village.* to loom, to rise, to stand out, to stick up. 3 *towering*: colossal, high, lofty, tall.

town 1 borough, city. SEE ALSO **geography**. 2 PLACES YOU FIND IN A TOWN ARE bank, SEE **building**, café, cinema, college, concert hall, car-park, council-houses, disco, factory, filling-station, garage, ghetto, hotel, SEE **house**, leisure centre, library, museum, night-club, park, police-station, post office, pub, recreation ground, restaurant, SEE **road**, school, SEE **shop**, shopping centre, sports centre, slum, snack bar, square, station, suburb, supermarket, theatre, warehouse.

towpath SEE **road**.

toxic *toxic fumes.* deadly, lethal, poisonous.

toy VARIOUS TOYS ARE ball, doll, SEE **game**, kaleidoscope, kite, rag doll, rattle, rocking-horse, scooter, teddy-bear, top, tricycle, water-pistol. ! Many toys are models of real things, such as *aeroplanes, cars, cooking things, furniture, etc.* Many other toys have special names invented by the manufacturers. So there are lots of toys that are not listed here.

trace 1 *Did mum trace her lost keys?* to discover, to find, to get back, to recover, to retrieve. 2 *The hounds traced the fox across the field.* to follow, to hunt, to pursue, to track down, to trail. 3 *The criminals left no traces.* evidence, mark, sign, track, trail.

track 1 *a cycle track.* SEE **road**. 2 *animal tracks.* footprint, mark, trace, trail. 3 *a railway track.* line, rails. SEE ALSO **railway**. 4 *The hunters tracked the deer.* to chase, to follow, to hound, to hunt, to pursue, to stalk, to tail, to trail. 5 *The police tracked down the stolen property.* to discover, to find, to get back, to recover, to retrieve, to trace.

traction engine SEE **vehicle**.

trade 1 *the clothing trade, the drugs trade, etc.* business, buying and selling, commerce, industry, traffic. 2 *I'm going to train for a trade when I leave school.* calling, employment, occupation, profession, work. FOR VARIOUS TRADES SEE **job**. 3 *Some shops trade on Sundays.* to do business. 4 *to trade in something*: to market, to retail, to sell. 5 *to trade something in*: to exchange, to swop.

trader *Mrs Brunswick would rather support the local traders than go to the supermarket.* dealer, merchant, retailer, salesman, shopkeeper, stockist, supplier, tradesman.

tradition *It's a tradition to have mince pies at Christmas.* convention, custom, habit, practice, routine.

traditional *Our team wore their traditional colours.* accustomed, conventional, customary, established, habitual, orthodox, regular, usual.

traffic 1 *road traffic.* FOR KINDS OF TRAFFIC SEE **vehicle**. 2 *a traffic in drugs.* SEE **trade**.

traffic warden SEE **job**.

tragedy 1 *It was a tragedy when the dog was knocked over.* calamity, catastrophe, disaster, misfortune. **2** *'Romeo and Juliet' is a tragedy by Shakespeare.* SEE **writing**.

tragic *a tragic accident.* awful, calamitous, depressing, dire, disastrous, dreadful, fearful, pathetic, terrible, unfortunate, unlucky. SEE ALSO **sad**.

trail 1 *The hounds followed the trail.* evidence, mark, sign, trace, track. **2** *He trailed an old cart behind him.* to drag, to draw, to haul, to pull, to tow. **3** *They trailed him for miles.* to follow, to hunt, to pursue, to trace, to track down.

trailer SEE **vehicle**.

train 1 SEE **railway**. **2** *Who trains your football team?* to coach, to educate, to instruct, to teach. **3** *Lucy trains every evening.* to exercise, to practise.

trainer 1 coach, instructor, teacher. **2** SEE **shoe**.

traitor *The traitor went over to the other side.* betrayer, deserter, renegade.

tram SEE **travel, vehicle**.

tramp 1 *The tramp had nowhere to live.* beggar, destitute person, homeless person, vagabond, vagrant. **2** *We tramped across the hills.* to hike, to march, to plod, to stride, to trudge. SEE ALSO **walk**.

trample *Tony trampled Mrs Brunswick's flowers.* to crush, to flatten, to stamp on, to tread on, to walk over.

trampolining SEE **sport**.

tramp steamer SEE **vessel**.

trance *to be lost in a trance.* day-dream, hypnotic state, unconsciousness.

tranquil *a tranquil lake.* calm, peaceful, placid, quiet, restful, serene, still, undisturbed, untroubled.

tranquillizer sedative. SEE ALSO **medicine**.

transaction *a business transaction.* deal.

transfer 1 *We transferred our luggage from the bus into the train.* to carry, to convey, to ferry, to take, to

transport. **2** *They transferred Logan into the reserve team.* to change, to move.

transform *Mr Brunswick transformed the attic into a games room.* to adapt, to alter, to change, to convert, to modify, to rebuild, to turn.

transformer SEE **electricity**.

transfusion SEE **medicine**.

transient *Migrating birds are transient visitors to our country.* brief, momentary, passing, temporary.

transistor SEE **radio**.

translate *Can you translate these French words?* to interpret.

transmit 1 *Transmit this message to headquarters.* to convey, to dispatch, to pass on, to send. **2** *The satellite transmits radio signals.* to broadcast, to emit.

transparency SEE **photograph**.

transparent *transparent glass.* clear.

transplant 1 *Mrs Brunswick transplanted some seedlings.* to move, to shift, to transfer. **2** *a heart transplant.* operation, surgery. SEE ALSO **medicine**.

transport 1 *to transport goods.* to carry, to convey, to move, to shift, to ship, to transfer. **2** SEE **travel**.

trap 1 *The gamekeeper set a trap.* ambush, booby-trap, snare. **2** *a pony and trap.* SEE **vehicle**. **3** *to trap an animal, to trap a criminal.* to ambush, to arrest, to capture, to corner, to ensnare.

trapeze SEE **circus**.

trash garbage, junk, litter, refuse, rubbish, waste.

travel 1 VARIOUS WAYS TO TRAVEL ARE to cruise, to cycle, to drive, to fly, to hitch-hike, to journey, to navigate, to paddle, to pedal, to punt, to ride, to row, to sail, to steam, to tour, to trek, to walk. **2** KINDS OF TRAVEL ARE cruise, drive, excursion, expedition, exploration, flight, hike, journey, mission, outing, pilgrimage, ride, safari, sail, tour, trek, trip, visit, voyage, walk. **3** METHODS OF TRANSPORT ARE: SEE **aircraft**, bus, car, coach, SEE **cycle**, horse, lorry, minibus, monorail, (old-fashioned) omnibus, metro, SEE **railway**, ship, taxi, tram, tube, underground, van, SEE **vehicle**, SEE **vessel**. **4** KINDS OF TRAVELLER ARE driver, gipsy, holiday-maker, nomad, passenger, pedestrian, pilgrim, representative, stowaway, tourist, tramp, vagabond, vagrant, wayfarer.

trawler SEE **vessel**.

tray SEE **kitchen**.

treacherous **1** *a treacherous friend.* disloyal, false, sneaky, unfaithful, untrustworthy. **2** *treacherous weather conditions.* dangerous, deceptive, hazardous, misleading, unsafe.

treachery betrayal, disloyalty, treason.

treacle SEE **sugar**.

tread *Logan trod on my foot!* to stamp, to step, to trample, to walk.

treason betrayal, disloyalty, treachery.

treasure **1** *a miser's treasure.* hoard, riches, wealth. **2** *Lucy treasures the brooch granny gave her.* to appreciate, to cherish, to esteem, to love, to prize, to value.

treat **1** *Treat animals kindly.* to behave towards, to care for, to look after. **2** *How would you treat this problem?* to attend to, to deal with, to manage, to tackle. **3** *to treat an illness, to treat a wound.* to cure, to dress, to heal, to nurse, to tend. **4** *They treat milk to kill germs.* to process.

treatment SEE **medicine**.

treaty *a peace treaty.* agreement, alliance, armistice, pact.

treble SEE **sing**.

tree **1** TYPES OF TREE ARE conifer, deciduous, evergreen. **2** VARIOUS TREES ARE ash, beech, birch, cedar, chestnut, cypress, elder, elm, eucalyptus, fir, gum-tree, hawthorn, hazel, holly, horse-chestnut, larch, lime, maple, oak, olive, palm, pine, plane, poplar, spruce, sycamore, willow, yew. **3** *a young tree*: sapling. **4** SEE **plant**.

trek expedition, hike, journey. SEE ALSO **travel, walk**.

trellis SEE **garden**.

tremble **1** *I trembled with fear.* to quake, to quaver, to quiver, to shake, to shiver, to shudder, to vibrate. **2** *The candle flame trembled.* to flicker, to waver.

tremendous **1** *a tremendous explosion.* alarming, appalling, awful, fearful, fearsome, frightening, frightful, horrifying, shocking, terrible, (informal) terrific. **2** (informal) *a tremendous helping of potatoes.* SEE **big**. **3** (informal) *a tremendous party.* SEE **excellent**. **4** (informal) *a tremendous victory.* SEE **remarkable**. ! *Tremendous* originally meant *fearful.* When it is used informally, the meaning is rather vague.

tremor **1** *There was a tremor in his voice.* quiver, shaking, vibration. **2** *an earth tremor*: earthquake.

trench ditch.

trend **1** *There has been a trend towards eating health foods recently.* inclination, leaning, movement, shift, tendency. **2** *What's the latest trend in clothes?* fashion, style, way.

trendy (informal) *trendy clothes, trendy music.* contemporary, fashionable, modern, stylish, up-to-date.

trespass *to trespass on someone's property.* to intrude.

trial **1** *a legal trial.* SEE **law**. **2** *They're doing trials on a new type of spacecraft.* experiment, test. **3** *Every maths lesson is a trial for Logan!* ordeal.

triangle **1** SEE **shape**. **2** *to play the triangle.* SEE **percussion**.

tribe *a tribe of warriors.* clan, family, group, horde, race.

tributary river, stream. SEE ALSO **geography**.

tribute *We paid tribute to her courage.* appreciation, compliment, honour, praise, respect.

trick **1** *a conjuring trick*: illusion, magic. **2** *a nasty trick*: cheat, deceit, deception, fraud, hoax, manoeuvre, pretence, ruse, scheme, stunt, trickery, wile. 3 *I know a trick for opening pop bottles.* dodge, knack, skill, technique. 4 *He tricked us into buying rubbish.* to bluff, to cheat, to deceive, to defraud, to dupe, to fool, to hoax, to hoodwink, (informal) to kid, to mislead, to outwit, to swindle.

trickle *Water trickled out of the crack.* to dribble, to drip, to flow, to leak, to ooze, to run, to seep.

tricky 1 *Watch him — he's a tricky player!* artful, crafty, cunning, deceitful, sly, wily. 2 *Backing the car into the drive is a tricky manoeuvre.* awkward, complicated, delicate, difficult.

tricycle SEE cycle.

trifle SEE food.

trifling *a trifling scratch.* insignificant, minor, negligible, small, trivial, unimportant.

trigger SEE gun.

trim 1 *a trim garden.* neat, orderly, shipshape, tidy. 2 *to trim a hedge.* to clip. SEE ALSO cut.

trio SEE music.

trip 1 *She tripped on the step.* to fall over, to stagger, to stumble, to totter. 2 *a trip to the seaside.* excursion, expedition, journey, outing, visit. SEE ALSO travel.

tripe 1 *tripe and onions.* SEE food. 2 (informal) *She talks a lot of tripe!* SEE nonsense.

triplet SEE family.

tripod *a camera tripod.* support, stand.

triumph 1 *It was a triumph to beat our rival team!* achievement, conquest, success, victory. 2 *We triumphed in the end.* to be victorious, to succeed, to win. SEE ALSO defeat.

trivial *The police thought that losing 10p was a trivial matter.* frivolous, insignificant, minor, negligible, petty, superficial, trifling, unimportant. SEE ALSO small.

troll SEE legend.

trolley, trolley-bus SEE vehicle.

trombone SEE brass.

troop 1 *a troop of circus performers.* band, company, gang, horde. SEE ALSO group. 2 *troops*: SEE armed

services. 3 *We all trooped along the road.* to march, to parade. SEE ALSO walk.

trophy 1 *Lucy won a trophy for gymnastics.* award, cup, medal, prize, reward. 2 *The thieves hid their trophies.* booty, loot.

tropics SEE geography.

trot SEE horse, walk.

trouble 1 *Logan got into trouble.* misbehaviour, misconduct, naughtiness. 2 *The ship was in trouble during the storm.* adversity, difficulty, distress, hardship, misfortune. 3 *What's the trouble?* burden, grief, misery, problem, sadness, sorrow, unhappiness, worry. 4 *Grandad has some trouble with his eyes.* affliction, disease, illness, pain, suffering. 5 *Tony took a lot of trouble with his maths.* care, effort, exertion, labour, struggle, work. 6 *There was trouble in the crowd.* bother, commotion, disorder, disturbance, fighting, fuss, row, turmoil, violence. 7 *Will it trouble you if I open a window?* to annoy, to bother, to concern, to distress, to disturb, to upset, to vex, to worry. 8 *My toothache troubled me.* to afflict, to hurt, to pain, to torment.

trouble-maker culprit, delinquent, hooligan, offender, rascal, ruffian, vandal, wrongdoer.

troublesome 1 *In hot weather, insects can be troublesome.* annoying, inconvenient, irritating. 2 *Logan is a troublesome boy!* badly-behaved, disobedient, naughty, unruly.

trough SEE container.

trousers KINDS OF TROUSERS ARE breeches, dungarees, jeans, jodhpurs, overalls, pants, shorts, slacks, trunks. SEE ALSO clothes.

trousseau SEE wedding.

trout SEE fish.

trowel SEE garden.

truant *to play truant*: (informal) to skive, to stay away. SEE ALSO school.

truce *The two sides agreed on a truce.* armistice, pact, peace, treaty.

truck SEE **railway, vehicle.**

trudge *We trudged home tired out.* to lumber, to plod, to tramp, to trek. SEE ALSO **walk.**

true 1 *a true happening.* actual, authentic, factual, genuine, real. **2** *the true time.* accurate, correct, exact, proper, right. **3** *a true friend.* constant, dependable, faithful, honest, honourable, loyal, reliable, responsible, steady, trustworthy. **4** *Are you the true owner of this car?* authorized, legal, legitimate, rightful, valid.

trumpet SEE **brass.**

truncheon SEE **weapon.**

trundle *A wagon trundled up the road.* to lumber, to lurch.

trunk 1 *a tree trunk.* stem. **2** *a person's trunk.* body. **3** *a clothes trunk.* box, chest. SEE ALSO **container. 4** *trunks*: briefs, shorts. SEE ALSO **clothes. 5** *a trunk road*: SEE **road.**

trust 1 *The team trusts the goalkeeper.* to bank on, to believe in, to be sure of, to count on, to depend on, to have faith in, to rely on. **2** *I trust you are well?* to assume, to expect, to hope, to presume. **3** *The dog has trust in his mistress.* belief, confidence, faith.

trustworthy *a trustworthy friend.* constant, faithful, honest, honourable, loyal, reliable, responsible, safe, steady, true.

truth *Tell the truth.* facts, reality.

truthful *a truthful answer.* accurate, correct, frank, honest, proper, right, sincere, straight, true.

try 1 *Try to do your best.* to aim, to attempt, to endeavour, to exert yourself, to make an effort, to strain, to strive. **2** *Dad tried a new car.* to experiment with, to test. **3** *Logan tries us with his continual chatter.* to annoy, to exasperate, to irritate, to trouble, to upset, to vex, to worry. **4** *Have a try!* attempt, effort, endeavour. **5** *to score a try.* SEE **Rugby.**

T-shirt SEE **clothes.**

tub barrel, bath, butt, cask, drum, pot. SEE ALSO **container.**

tuba SEE **brass.**

tubby *a tubby figure.* chubby, dumpy, fat, overweight, plump, podgy, portly, stout.

tube 1 *a rubber tube.* hose, pipe. **2** *a tube of toothpaste.* SEE **container. 3** *a tube train.* underground. SEE ALSO **travel.**

tuberculosis SEE **illness.**

tubular bells SEE **percussion.**

tuck 1 *Tuck your shirt into your jeans.* to cram, to insert, to push, to shove, to stuff. **2** (informal) *Tuck in to the food!* SEE **eat.**

tuft *a tuft of grass.* bunch, clump.

tug 1 *The tug towed a ship into port.* SEE **vessel. 2** *We tugged a cart behind us.* to drag, to draw, to lug, to tow. **3** *I tugged at the rope.* to jerk, to pull.

tulip SEE **bulb.**

tumble *I tumbled into the water.* to collapse, to drop, to fall, to stumble, to topple.

tumbledown *a tumbledown cottage.* broken down, decrepit, derelict, dilapidated, ramshackle, rickety, ruined.

tumble-drier SEE **house, wash.**

tumbler beaker, glass. SEE ALSO **container, drink.**

tummy (informal) *a pain in the tummy.* abdomen, belly, stomach.

tumult *The crowd went wild, and people were knocked over in the tumult.* bedlam, chaos, commotion, confusion, disorder, disturbance, hubbub, hullabaloo, pandemonium, riot, row, rumpus, turmoil, uproar.

tuna SEE **fish.**

tune air, melody, theme. SEE ALSO **music.**

tuneful catchy, melodious.

tunic SEE **clothes.**

tunnel 1 KINDS OF TUNNEL ARE burrow, hole, mine, passage, shaft, subway, underpass. **2** *Lucy's rabbit tunnelled under the fence.* to burrow, to dig, to excavate.

turban SEE **hat.**

turbine SEE **engine.**

turbot SEE **fish.**

turbulent 1 *a turbulent crowd.* badly-behaved, disorderly, lawless, obstreperous, riotous, rowdy, undisciplined, unruly. **2** *turbulent weather.* rough, stormy, violent, wild, windy. SEE ALSO **weather**.

turf grass, lawn. SEE ALSO **garden**.

turkey SEE **bird, poultry**.

turmoil *There was turmoil in the classroom when Logan's rats escaped.* bedlam, chaos, commotion, confusion, disorder, disturbance, hubbub, hullabaloo, pandemonium, riot, row, rumpus, tumult, upheaval, uproar.

turn 1 *The wheel began to turn.* to revolve, to rotate, to spin, to twirl, to whirl. **2** *The car turned a corner.* to go round. **3** *I turned the wire round a stick.* to bend, to coil, to curl, to loop, to twist, to wind. **4** *Tadpoles turn into frogs.* to become, to change into. **5** *Mr Brunswick turned the attic into a games room.* to change, to convert, to modify, to transform. **6** *The snake turned this way and that.* to squirm, to twist, to wriggle, to writhe. **7** *to turn down: I turned down the invitation.* to decline, to refuse, to reject. **8** *to turn out: How did your party turn out?* to befall, to emerge, to happen, to result. **9** *to turn someone out:* to eject, to evict, to expel, (informal) to kick out, to remove, to throw out. **10** *to turn up:* to appear, to arrive, to come, to materialize. **11** *a turn in the road.* bend, corner, curve, hairpin-bend, junction, twist, U-turn. **12** *It's your turn to play.* chance, opportunity. **13** *I had a nasty turn today.* attack, bout, fit, illness.

turnip SEE **vegetable**.

turnstile entrance, exit, gate.

turntable SEE **audio equipment**.

turquoise SEE **colour**.

turret SEE **building**.

turtle SEE **reptile**.

tussle *The two girls had a friendly tussle.* battle, bout, brawl, clash, combat, conflict, contest, duel, encounter, feud, fight, quarrel, rivalry, row, scrap, scuffle, squabble, strife, struggle.

tutor SEE **teacher**.

twang SEE **sound**.

tweed SEE **cloth**.

twerp ass, blockhead, booby, dope, dunce, fool, halfwit, idiot, ignoramus, imbecile, moron, nitwit. !These words are usually insulting.

twiddle *to twiddle your thumbs.* to fidget with, to fiddle with.

twig branch, stalk, stem, stick.

twilight dusk, evening, gloom, sunset.

twin SEE **family**.

twine *I tied up the parcel with twine.* cord, string, thread.

twinge *Go to the dentist if you felt a twinge in your tooth.* ache, pain, pang, spasm, throb.

twinkle *The lights twinkled in the distance.* to blink, to flicker, to glimmer, to quiver, to tremble, to waver. SEE ALSO **light**.

twirl 1 *The roundabout twirled faster and faster.* to revolve, to rotate, to spin, to turn, to whirl. **2** *She twirled her umbrella.* to brandish, to wave.

twist 1 *I twisted the string round my fingers.* to coil, to curl, to loop, to turn, to wind. **2** *The ropes became twisted.* to entangle, to entwine, to tangle. **3** *The road twisted up the mountain.* to bend, to curve, to zig-zag. **4** *I twisted the lid off the jar.* to jerk, to wrench. **5** *The heat twisted the rails.* to buckle, to crumple, to distort, to warp.

twitch to fidget, to jerk, to jump, to start.

twitter SEE **sound**.

type 1 *Pop songs are a type of music.* class, form, group, kind, set, sort, species, variety. **2** *Mr Brunswick types his business letters.* SEE **write**.

typewriter SEE **write**.

typhoid SEE **illness**.

typhoon cyclone, hurricane, storm, tempest, tornado, whirlwind. SEE ALSO **weather**.

typhus SEE **illness.**
typical 1 *a typical day.* average, normal, ordinary, usual. **2** *a typical Chinese meal.* characteristic, distinctive, particular, special.
tyrannical *The people overthrew their tyrannical ruler.* bossy, cruel, dictatorial, domineering, harsh, oppressive, unjust.
tyrant dictator. SEE ALSO **ruler.**
tyre pneumatic tyre. SEE ALSO **vehicle.**

U u

ugly 1 *an ugly monster.* frightful, ghastly, grisly, grotesque, gruesome, hideous, monstrous, repulsive, unattractive, unsightly. SEE ALSO **unpleasant. 2** *ugly storm-clouds.* dangerous, forbidding, hostile, menacing, ominous, threatening.
ulcer boil, sore. SEE ALSO **illness.**
ultimate *We scored in the ultimate minutes of the game.* closing, concluding, extreme, final, last.
ultimately eventually, finally.
ultimatum *Logan's gang gave us an ultimatum.* final demand.
umpire adjudicator, arbitrator, judge, referee. SEE ALSO **sport.**

un- ! There are many words beginning with the prefix *un-*, and only some of them can be given here. We give full entries for the words you are most likely to need help with, and we tell you where you can look for help with some of the others.

unaccountable SEE **inexplicable.**
unaccustomed SEE **strange.**
unaided single-handed, solo.
unanimous *a unanimous decision.* agreed, united.
unanswerable SEE **insoluble.**
unassuming SEE **modest.**
unauthorized *The train made an unauthorized stop.* abnormal, illegal, irregular, unusual.

unavoidable 1 *an unavoidable accident.* certain, destined, fated, inescapable, inevitable, sure. **2** *an unavoidable payment.* compulsory, necessary, required.
unaware SEE **ignorant.**
unbalanced 1 *an unbalanced load.* asymmetrical, lop-sided, uneven. **2** *an unbalanced mind.* SEE **mad.**
unbearable intolerable.
unbelievable SEE **incredible.**
unbiased SEE **just.**
uncanny SEE **eerie.**
uncaring SEE **careless.**
uncertain SEE **doubtful.**
unchangeable SEE **invariable.**
uncivilized SEE **savage.**
uncle SEE **family.**
unclean SEE **dirty.**
unclothed SEE **naked.**
uncomfortable 1 *an uncomfortable chair.* hard, lumpy. **2** *an uncomfortable feeling.* SEE **uneasy.**
uncommon SEE **rare.**
uncomplimentary SEE **rude.**
unconscious 1 *The boxer was unconscious.* insensible, knocked out, senseless. **2** *I was unconscious of his presence.* unaware. **3** *Blinking is an unconscious action.* automatic, impulsive, involuntary, spontaneous, unthinking, unintentional.
unconventional *unconventional behaviour.* abnormal, (informal) cranky, eccentric, extraordinary, odd, peculiar, queer, singular, strange, unusual, weird, zany.
unconvincing SEE **unlikely.**
uncouth SEE **rude.**
uncover 1 *We were horrified when she uncovered her wound.* to bare, to disclose, to expose, to reveal, to strip, to undress. **2** *The workmen uncovered the foundations of an ancient building.* to come across, to dig up, to discover, to locate, to unearth.
undamaged faultless, in mint condition, perfect.
undaunted SEE **brave, resolute.**

undecided SEE **indefinite**.
undercarriage SEE **aircraft**.
underclothes 1 undergarments,
underwear. **2** VARIOUS
UNDERGARMENTS ARE bra, briefs,
corset, drawers, girdle, knickers,
lingerie, panties, pants, panty-hose,
petticoat, slip, tights, trunks,
underpants, vest. SEE ALSO **clothes**.
underdeveloped backward, slow,
undeveloped.
underdone uncooked.
underfed famished, hungry,
ravenous, starving.
undergarments SEE **underclothes**.
undergo *to undergo an operation*. to
bear, to endure, to experience, to go
through, to put up with, to submit
yourself to, to suffer.
undergraduate student.
underground *an underground railway*:
SEE **travel**.
undergrowth *We forced a way through
the undergrowth*. bushes, plants,
vegetation.
underhand SEE **dishonest**.
underline *Mrs Angel underlined the main
facts*. to emphasize, to stress.
undermine 1 *to undermine a wall*. to
burrow under, to dig under, to
erode, to mine under, to tunnel
under. **2** *to undermine someone's
confidence*. to destroy, to ruin, to
weaken.
underpants SEE **underclothes**.
underpass subway. SEE ALSO **road**.
undersized *an undersized child*.
diminutive, little, minute, small,
(informal) teeny, tiny.
understand 1 *Do you understand what I
mean?* to appreciate, to comprehend,
to follow, to gather, to grasp, to
know, to realize, to see. **2** *Tony
understood the maths at once*. to learn, to
master. **3** *Can you understand this
French?* to decipher, to decode, to
interpret.
understanding 1 *Tony has a good
understanding of maths*. ability,
awareness, grasp, knowledge. SEE
ALSO **intellect**. **2** *The shopkeeper and I*

reached an understanding about the price.
accord, agreement, arrangement,
bargain, consent, contract, deal,
pact, settlement, treaty. **3** *Mrs Angel
showed great understanding when Lucy
was ill*. compassion, consideration,
feeling, kindness, mercy, pity,
sympathy.
undertake 1 *Tony undertook to organize
a collection for OXFAM*. to agree, to
consent, to promise. **2** *Mr Brunswick
undertook the task of building an
extension*. to attend to, to begin, to
cope with, to deal with, to grapple
with, to handle, to manage, to tackle.
undertaker SEE **funeral, job**.
underwear SEE **underclothes**.
underworld hell.
undesirable SEE **unpleasant**.
undeveloped SEE **backward**.
undistinguished SEE **ordinary**.
undo 1 *to undo a fastening, to undo a knot,
etc*. to detach, to disconnect, to
divide, to part, to remove, to
separate, to unfasten, to untie.
2 *Tony undid all Mrs Brunswick's work
in the garden by trampling on the flower
beds*. to destroy, to spoil, to wipe out,
to wreck.
undoubted SEE **sure**.
undress 1 to strip, to uncover
yourself. **2** *undressed*: SEE **naked**.
unearth *The dog unearthed a bone*. to
come across, to dig up, to discover,
to excavate, to locate, to uncover.
unearthly SEE **eerie**.
uneasy *I had an uneasy feeling that I was
being followed*. anxious, apprehensive,
concerned, distressing, fearful,
jittery, nervous, uncomfortable,
worried.
unemployed on the dole, out of
work.
unequal 1 *unequal treatment*. biased,
prejudiced, unjust. **2** *an unequal
contest*. one-sided, uneven, unfair.
uneven 1 *an uneven road*. bumpy,
irregular, rough. **2** *an uneven edge*.
bent, crooked, jagged, wavy. **3** *an
uneven load*. asymmetrical, lop-sided,

unbalanced. 4 *an uneven contest.* one-sided, unequal, unfair.

unexpected *an unexpected meeting.* accidental, sudden, surprising, unforeseen, unplanned.

unfair *an unfair decision, an unfair referee.* biased, one-sided, prejudiced, unjust, unreasonable.

unfaithful 1 disloyal, false, treacherous. 2 *unfaithfulness to your husband or wife*: adultery, infidelity.

unfamiliar SEE **strange**.

unfasten to detach, to disconnect, to divide, to part, to remove, to separate, to undo, to untie.

unfavourable 1 *unfavourable winds.* adverse, contrary, opposing. 2 *unfavourable comments.* attacking, critical, hostile, unfriendly.

unfeeling SEE **callous**.

unfinished imperfect, incomplete.

unfit 1 *A drunkard is unfit to drive a car.* inadequate, incompetent, unsuitable, unsuited. 2 *This stale bread is unfit to eat.* inappropriate, useless.

unforeseen SEE **unexpected**.

unforgettable memorable.

unfortunate SEE **unlucky**.

unfriendly 1 *an unfriendly welcome.* cool, distant, forbidding, indifferent, reserved, stand-offish, unenthusiastic. 2 *unfriendly behaviour.* aggressive, antisocial, disagreeable, hostile, nasty, obnoxious, offensive, rude. 3 SEE ALSO **unkind, unpleasant**.

ungainly SEE **awkward**.

unhappy SEE **sad**.

unhealthy 1 *unhealthy conditions.* dirty, insanitary. 2 *an unhealthy animal.* diseased, feeble, (informal) poorly, sick, unwell. SEE ALSO **ill**.

unhinged SEE **mad**.

unicorn SEE **legend**.

unidentified anonymous, nameless, unnamed, unrecognized.

uniform SEE **clothes**.

unify *The school was unified by our*

determination to raise £100. to bring together, to unite.

unimportant SEE **insignificant**.

uninhabited *an uninhabited house.* deserted, empty, unoccupied, vacant.

uninterested bored. ! This does not mean the same as *disinterested*.

uninterrupted constant, continuous, non-stop.

union 1 *a union of youth clubs.* alliance, association, combination, league. 2 marriage.

unique *The speaking computer is a unique feature of this car.* distinctive, peculiar, singular.

unison SEE **music**.

unit SEE **measure**.

unite 1 *We united the two teams.* to add together, to amalgamate, to bring together, to combine, to couple. 2 *united: a united decision.* unanimous.

universal *It would be wonderful to have universal peace.* general, global, international, widespread.

universe cosmos. SEE ALSO **astronomy**.

university college. SEE ALSO **educate**.

unjust *an unjust decision.* biased, one-sided, prejudiced, unfair, unreasonable, wrongful.

unkempt *an unkempt appearance.* bedraggled, dishevelled, scruffy, tangled, uncombed, untidy.

unkind *We hate unkind treatment of animals.* beastly, brutal, callous, cold-blooded, cruel, hard, harsh, heartless, inconsiderate, inhuman, insensitive, merciless, pitiless, relentless, ruthless, sadistic, savage, stern, thoughtless, uncaring, unfeeling, unfriendly, unsympathetic, vicious. ! People can be *unkind* in many ways, and so there are many other words you can use. SEE **angry, unpleasant**, etc.

unlikely *an unlikely story.* far-fetched, improbable, incredible, unbelievable, unconvincing.

unlimited SEE **boundless**.

unload *We unloaded the cases at the station.* to drop off, to dump, to take off.

unlock SEE **open.**

unlucky *an unlucky mistake.* accidental, calamitous, disastrous, dreadful, tragic, unfortunate, unwelcome.

unmarried 1 single. 2 *an unmarried person*: bachelor, spinster.

unmask SEE **reveal.**

unmistakable SEE **obvious.**

unnatural SEE **artificial.**

unnecessary excessive, extra, redundant, superfluous, surplus, uncalled-for, unwanted.

unoccupied SEE **uninhabited.**

unpleasant abhorrent, abominable, antisocial, appalling, awful, bad-tempered, bitter, coarse, crude, detestable, diabolical, dirty, disagreeable, disgusting, displeasing, distasteful, dreadful, fearful, fearsome, filthy, foul, frightful, ghastly, grisly, gruesome, harsh, hateful, hellish, hideous, horrible, horrid, horrifying, improper, indecent, loathsome, lousy, malevolent, malicious, (informal) mucky, nasty, nauseating, objectionable, obnoxious, odious, offensive, repellent, repulsive, revolting, rude, shocking, sickly, sordid, sour, spiteful, squalid, terrible, ugly, unattractive, uncouth, undesirable, unfriendly, upsetting, vexing, vicious, vile, vulgar. !People and things can be *unpleasant* in many ways, and so there are many other words you can use. SEE **angry, bad, cruel,** etc.

unreal SEE **imaginary.**

unreasonable 1 *It's unreasonable to talk to plants!* SEE **absurd.** 2 *Logan was unreasonable when I asked him to help.* SEE **obstinate.** 3 *They asked an unreasonable price.* SEE **excessive.**

unreliable *unreliable information.* false, inaccurate, misleading.

unrest SEE **riot.**

unruly SEE **disorderly.**

unscathed safe, unharmed.

unscrupulous SEE **dishonest.**

unseen SEE **invisible.**

unselfish SEE **generous.**

unsightly SEE **ugly.**

untidy 1 *untidy work.* careless, disorganized, messy, slapdash, (informal) sloppy, slovenly. 2 *untidy hair.* bedraggled, dishevelled, scruffy, tangled, uncombed, unkempt. 3 *an untidy room.* chaotic, confused, disorderly, jumbled, muddled, topsy-turvy.

untie SEE **undo.**

untold SEE **numerous.**

untrue SEE **false.**

unused *an unused videotape.* blank, clean, in mint condition, new.

unusual SEE **strange.**

unwanted SEE **unnecessary.**

unwell SEE **ill.**

unwieldy SEE **awkward.**

unwilling SEE **reluctant.**

unwise SEE **foolish.**

upbringing *Parents usually look after the upbringing of their children.* education, instruction, teaching, training.

update to modernize.

upgrade to improve, to make better.

upheaval *There was a great upheaval in the house while Mr Brunswick was building the extension.* change, commotion, disruption, disturbance, turmoil.

uphill *an uphill struggle.* arduous, difficult, exhausting, hard, laborious, stiff, strenuous, tough.

uphold *The judge upheld the verdict.* to support, to verify.

upholstery padding.

upkeep *The upkeep of the house is expensive.* maintenance, running.

upright 1 *Human beings walk upright.* erect, vertical. 2 *She is an upright judge.* fair, good, honest, honourable, just, moral, trustworthy.

uproar *There was uproar when Logan kicked the ball into his own goal.* bedlam, chaos, clamour, commotion, confusion, disorder, disturbance, hubbub, hullabaloo, pandemonium, riot, row, rumpus, tumult, turmoil.

uproarious *an uproarious comedy.* SEE **funny**.

uproot *to uproot plants.* to destroy, to dig up, to eliminate, to eradicate, to get rid of, to pull up, to remove.

upset 1 *I upset my tea.* to overturn, to spill, to tip over, to topple. **2** *The thunder upset the animals.* to agitate, to alarm, to bother, to distress, to disturb, to excite, to frighten, to perturb, to scare, to trouble, to worry. **3** *Bad language upsets granny.* to anger, to annoy, to displease, to grieve, to irritate, to offend, to vex. **4** *A sudden rainstorm upset our plans.* to affect, to alter, to change, to disrupt, to interfere with, to interrupt.

upside-down inverted, topsy-turvy.

uptight SEE **tense**.

up-to-date 1 *up-to-date technology.* advanced, current, modern, new, present, recent. **2** *up-to-date clothes.* contemporary, fashionable, stylish, (informal) trendy.

uranium SEE **metal**.

urchin brat, ragamuffin. ! These words are usually insulting. SEE ALSO **child**.

urge 1 *The jockey urged the horse on.* to compel, to drive, to force, to press, to propel, to push, to spur. **2** *Mum urged me to put my money into the bank.* to appeal to, (informal) to egg on, to encourage, to entreat, to invite, to persuade, to plead with, to prompt, to recommend, to stimulate. **3** *I had an urge to giggle.* desire, itch, longing, wish, yearning.

urgent *The car needs urgent repairs.* essential, immediate, important, necessary, pressing.

urn SEE **container**.

use 1 *He used my pen. I used all my strength.* to employ, to exercise, to exploit, to make use of, to utilize, to wield. **2** *Use some polish.* to administer, to apply, to spread. **3** *They say we should use less salt.* to

consume. **4** *How do you use this tool?* to deal with, to manage, to operate, to work. **5** *used:* second-hand.

useful 1 *useful advice.* advantageous, beneficial, constructive, good, helpful, invaluable, positive, profitable, valuable, worthwhile. **2** *a useful tool.* convenient, effective, efficient, handy, powerful, practical, productive. **3** *a useful player.* capable, competent, proficient, successful.

useless 1 *a useless goalkeeper, a useless machine.* (informal) dud, incompetent, ineffective, ineffectual, unhelpful, unusable, worthless. **2** *a useless search.* fruitless, futile, pointless, unsuccessful.

usher, usherette SEE **job, theatre**.

usual 1 *We went by our usual route.* accustomed, conventional, customary, habitual, normal, ordinary, regular, routine, traditional. **2** *It was the usual sort of weather for December.* average, common, everyday, familiar, prevalent, typical, well-known, widespread. **3** *I got the usual reply when I asked for money.* accepted, expected, official, orthodox, standard.

utensil *kitchen utensils.* appliance, device, gadget, implement, instrument, machine, tool. FOR VARIOUS UTENSILS SEE **house, kitchen, tool**.

utilize SEE **use**.

utter 1 *The party was utter chaos!* absolute, complete, perfect, pure, sheer, total, unrestricted. **2** *I didn't utter a word.* to communicate, to express, to pronounce, to speak. SEE ALSO **say, talk**.

V v

vacant 1 *a vacant house.* deserted, empty, uninhabited, unoccupied. **2** *a vacant space.* clear, free, open, unused. **3** *a vacant look.* blank, expressionless.

vacation holiday, leave, time off.

vaccination SEE **medicine**.

vacuum-cleaner SEE **house**.

vacuum flask Thermos.

vagabond, vagrant beggar, destitute person, homeless person, tramp, wanderer, wayfarer. SEE ALSO **travel**.

vague 1 *vague remarks*. ambiguous, broad, confused, general, indefinite, uncertain, unclear, unsure, woolly. 2 *a vague person*. absent-minded, careless, forgetful, inattentive, thoughtless, scatter-brained.

vain 1 *He's vain about his appearance*. arrogant, boastful, cocky, conceited, haughty, proud, self-important, (informal) stuck-up. 2 *They made a vain attempt to rescue her*. fruitless, futile, ineffective, pointless, unsuccessful, useless.

valiant *a valiant struggle*. bold, brave, courageous, daring, fearless, gallant, heroic, intrepid, noble, plucky, spirited, undaunted.

valid *a valid excuse, a valid ticket*. allowed, authorized, genuine, lawful, legal, legitimate, official, permissible, permitted, proper, reasonable, rightful, suitable, usable.

valley KINDS OF VALLEY ARE canyon, chasm, dale, defile, glen, gorge, gully, hollow, pass, ravine, vale. SEE ALSO **geography**.

valour SEE **courage**.

valuable 1 *valuable jewellery*. costly, expensive, precious, priceless. 2 *valuable advice*. advantageous, beneficial, constructive, good, helpful, invaluable, positive, profitable, useful, worthwhile.

value 1 *This old chair may be of value to an antique dealer*. worth. SEE ALSO **price**. 2 *Tony knows the value of keeping fit*. advantage, benefit, importance, merit, significance, usefulness. 3 *Lucy values granny's old brooch*. to appreciate, to care for, to cherish, to esteem, to love, to prize, to treasure.

vampire SEE **legend**.

van SEE **vehicle**.

vandal barbarian, delinquent, hooligan, looter, marauder, raider, ruffian, savage, thug, trouble-maker. SEE ALSO **criminal**.

vanilla SEE **food**.

vanish *The mist vanished when the sun rose*. to clear, to disappear, to dwindle, to evaporate, to fade, to melt away, to pass.

vanity SEE **pride**.

vanquish *to vanquish the opposition*. to beat, to conquer, to crush, to defeat, (informal) to lick, to master, to overcome, to overpower, to overthrow, to overwhelm, to rout, to subdue, to succeed against, to suppress, (informal) to thrash, to triumph over.

vaporize *Petrol vaporizes quickly*. to dry up, to evaporate.

vapour fumes, gas, smoke.

variable *variable weather*. changeable, erratic, fickle, inconsistent, temperamental, unpredictable, unreliable.

variation *a variation from routine*. alteration, change, difference.

variety 1 *I like a bit of variety*. alteration, change, difference, diversity, variation. 2 *We bought a variety of things*. assortment, blend, combination, jumble, mixture. 3 *Mrs Brunswick grows many varieties of flowers*. form, kind, sort, type. 4 *a variety show*: SEE **entertainment**.

various *We made various suggestions*. assorted, contrasting, different, dissimilar, miscellaneous, mixed, varied.

varnish SEE **paint**.

vary *You can vary the temperature by turning the knob*. to adapt, to adjust, to alter, to change, to convert, to modify.

vase SEE **container**.

vast *a vast desert*. broad, enormous, extensive, great, huge, immense, large, wide. SEE ALSO **big**.

vat SEE **container**.

vault 1 *a wine vault*. basement, cellar, crypt. SEE ALSO **building**. 2 *to vault a fence*. to bound over, to clear, to jump, to leap, to spring over.

VDU SEE **computer.**

veal SEE **meat.**

veer *The car veered across the road.* to change direction, to dodge, to swerve, to turn, to wheel.

vegetable VARIOUS VEGETABLES ARE asparagus, beans, beetroot, Brussels sprouts, cabbage, carrot, cauliflower, celery, greens, kale, leek, marrow, onion, parsnip, pea, potato, pumpkin, runner bean, spinach, sugar-beet, swede, tomato, turnip. SEE ALSO **salad.**

vegetarian SEE **food.**

vegetation foliage, greenery, growth, plants, undergrowth, weeds.

vehement *a vehement attack.* eager, excited, fierce, intense, strong, vigorous, violent.

vehicle 1 KINDS OF VEHICLE ARE ambulance, articulated lorry, automobile, bulldozer, bus, cab, car, caravan, carriage, cart, chariot, coach, SEE **cycle,** double-decker, dustcart, estate car, fire-engine, float, go-kart, hearse, horse-box, jeep, juggernaut, lorry, moped, motor car, motor cycle, (old-fashioned) omnibus, panda car, patrol car, pick-up, removal van, rickshaw, saloon, sidecar, sledge, snowplough, sports car, stage-coach, steam-roller, tank, tanker, taxi, traction engine, tractor, trailer, tram, trap, tricycle, trolley, trolley-bus, truck, van, wagon, wheelbarrow, wheelchair. 2 PARTS OF A MOTOR VEHICLE ARE accelerator, axle, bonnet, brake, bumper, carburettor, choke, clutch, cylinder, exhaust, gear, headlight, ignition, milometer, mudguard, piston, plug, radiator, safety belt or seat-belt, sidelight, silencer, sparking-plug, speedometer, starter, steering-wheel, tachograph, tail-light, throttle, tyre, windscreen, windscreen-wiper, wing, wheel.

vein SEE **body.**

velocity *It's hard to imagine the enormous velocity of a spacecraft.* movement, pace, rate, speed.

velvet SEE **cloth.**

vendetta *a vendetta between two families.* dispute, feud, quarrel.

veneer SEE **material.**

venerable *The cathedral is a venerable building.* aged, ancient, old, respected, revered.

vengeance reprisal, retaliation, retribution, revenge.

venison SEE **meat.**

venom poison.

venomous *The adder has a venomous sting.* deadly, lethal, poisonous, toxic.

vent *The smoke escaped through a vent in the roof.* cut, gap, hole, opening, outlet, slit.

ventilate *Ventilate the classroom.* to air, to freshen.

ventriloquist SEE **entertainment.**

venture 1 *I ventured a small wager.* to gamble, to risk. 2 *I wouldn't venture out in this weather.* to dare to go, to risk going.

verandah SEE **building.**

verb SEE **language.**

verdict SEE **law.**

verge 1 *the verge of a road.* border, edge, margin, side. 2 *I think I'm on the verge of a discovery.* brink.

verger SEE **church.**

verify 1 *Tony verified that Lucy's story was accurate.* to confirm, to establish, to prove, to show. 2 *He verified her story.* to support, to uphold.

vermilion SEE **colour.**

vermin pests.

verruca SEE **illness.**

versatile *A versatile footballer plays well in any position.* adaptable, gifted, skilful, talented.

verse SEE **poem.**

version 1 *Logan gave his version of what happened.* account, description, report, story. 2 *We read from a modern version of the Bible.* interpretation, translation. 3 *That car is a new version of the one we used to have.* design, model, type.

versus against.

vertebra SEE **body, joint.**

vertical 1 *a vertical position.* erect, upright. **2** *a vertical drop.* precipitous, sheer. !*Vertical* is the opposite of *horizontal.*

very *I'm very pleased to see you.* enormously, especially, exceedingly, extremely, greatly, most, outstandingly, (informal) terribly, truly.

vessel 1 *There were many vessels in the harbour.* boat, craft, ship. **2** KINDS OF VESSEL ARE aircraft-carrier, barge, battleship, canoe, catamaran, clipper, cruiser, cutter, destroyer, dhow, dinghy, dredger, ferry, frigate, galleon, galley, gondola, gun-boat, house-boat, hovercraft, hydrofoil, hydroplane, ice-breaker, junk, kayak, launch, lifeboat, lightship, liner, merchant ship, motor boat, oil-tanker, paddle-steamer, pedalo, pontoon, power-boat, punt, raft, rowing-boat, schooner, speed-boat, steamer, submarine, tanker, tramp steamer, trawler, tug, warship, whaler. **3** PARTS OF A VESSEL ARE aft, amidships, anchor, boom, bridge, conning tower, crow's nest, deck, fo'c'sle or forecastle, funnel, galley, helm, hull, keel, mast, oar, paddle, poop, port, porthole, propeller, prow, rigging, rudder, sail, scull, starboard, stern, tiller. **4** WAYS TO TRAVEL IN A VESSEL ARE to cruise, to navigate, to paddle, to pilot, to punt, to row, to sail, to steam. **5** *The vessels in the laboratory contained coloured liquids.* FOR VARIOUS CONTAINERS SEE **container**.

vest SEE **underclothes**.

vestry SEE **church**.

vet SEE **job**.

veto *Dad vetoed our plan for a midnight ramble.* to ban, to bar, to forbid, to prohibit.

vex 1 *This cold weather is enough to vex the most patient gardener!* (informal) to aggravate, to anger, to annoy, to bother, to displease, to exasperate, to irritate, to offend, to provoke, to trouble, to try, to upset, to worry. **2** *vexed*: SEE **angry**.

viable *a viable plan.* feasible, possible, practicable, practical, realistic, workable.

viaduct SEE **bridge**.

vibrate *The old bus began to vibrate as it speeded up.* to quake, to quiver, to shake, to shiver, to shudder, to throb, to tremble, to wobble.

vicar SEE **church**.

vicarage SEE **house**.

vice 1 *Don't ever begin to lead a life of vice!* evil, immorality, sin, wickedness, wrongdoing. **2** *Logan's worst vice is his continual chattering.* defect, failing, fault, imperfection, shortcoming, weakness. **3** *Hold the wood in a vice.* SEE **tool**.

vicinity area, district, locality, neighbourhood, region, sector, territory, zone.

vicious 1 *a vicious attack.* barbaric, beastly, bloodthirsty, brutal, callous, cruel, inhuman, merciless, murderous, pitiless, ruthless, sadistic, savage, unfeeling, violent. **2** *a vicious animal.* dangerous, ferocious, fierce, untamed, wild. **3** *a vicious character.* depraved, evil, heartless, immoral, malicious, nasty, spiteful, villainous, vindictive, wicked. SEE ALSO **unpleasant**.

victim 1 *a victim of an accident.* casualty, fatality, injured person, wounded person. **2** *a victim of an illness.* sufferer. **3** *The cat pounced on her victim.* prey.

victimize *Don't victimize the little ones.* to bully, to intimidate, to oppress, to persecute, to terrorize, to torment, to treat unfairly.

victor champion, hero, winner.

victorious *We cheered the victorious team.* successful, triumphant, ·winning.

victory *We celebrated our team's victory.* achievement, conquest, success, triumph, (informal) walk-over, win.

video SEE **record, television**.

view 1 *There's a lovely view from this window.* landscape, outlook, panorama, prospect, scene, scenery, vista. **2** *I had a good view of what happened.* look, sight. **3** *Mrs Brunswick has strong views about smoking.* attitude, belief, conviction, idea, opinion, thought. **4** *We viewed the scene.* to contemplate, to eye, to gaze at, to look at, to observe, to regard, to stare at, to watch.

vigilant *A look-out must be vigilant.* alert, attentive, awake, careful, observant, watchful.

vigorous *a vigorous game, a vigorous player.* active, dynamic, energetic, forceful, lively, spirited, strenuous.

vigour energy, force, liveliness, might, power, strength, vitality, zeal, zest.

vile *a vile crime.* disgusting, filthy, foul, horrible, loathsome, nasty, nauseating, obnoxious, offensive, odious, repulsive, revolting.

villa SEE **house**.

village hamlet, settlement. SEE ALSO **geography**.

villain (informal) baddy, blackguard, knave, rascal, rogue, scoundrel.

villainous SEE **wicked**.

vindictive *There was no need for Logan to be vindictive when Tony beat him.* malicious, revengeful, spiteful, unforgiving, vicious.

vine SEE **climber**.

vinegar SEE **food**.

vinyl SEE **material**.

viola SEE **music, strings**.

violate *to violate a rule.* to break, to defy, to disobey, to disregard, to ignore, to infringe.

violent **1** *a violent attack.* barbaric, brutal, cruel, destructive, ferocious, fierce, murderous, savage, vicious. **2** *a violent wind.* hard, powerful, severe, strong, tempestuous. **3** *violent behaviour.* berserk, desperate, rowdy, turbulent, unruly, vehement, wild. **4** *violent emotions.* burning, intense, passionate, uncontrollable.

violet SEE **colour, flower**.

violin fiddle. SEE ALSO **music, strings**.

viper SEE **snake**.

virile manly, masculine.

virtue **1** *We should respect virtue and hate vice.* decency, goodness, honesty, honour, integrity, morality, nobility, principle, righteousness, sincerity. **2** *The main virtue of our car is that it doesn't use much petrol.* advantage, good point, strength.

virtuoso SEE **music**.

virtuous *virtuous behaviour.* chaste, good, honest, honourable, just, law-abiding, moral, pure, right, trustworthy, upright.

virus (informal) bug, germ, microbe.

visa SEE **document**.

visible *The dog showed visible signs of being cruelly treated.* apparent, clear, conspicuous, evident, noticeable, obvious, perceptible, plain.

vision **1** *The optician said I had good vision.* eyesight, sight. **2** *He claims that he saw a vision.* apparition, ghost, hallucination, illusion, phantom, spirit.

visit *Granny visited us on Sunday.* to call, to come to see, (informal) to drop in, to go to see, to stay.

visitor **1** *We had visitors on Sunday.* callers, company, guests. **2** *The town is full of visitors.* sightseer, tourist, traveller.

vista landscape, outlook, panorama, prospect, scene, scenery, view.

visualize *Can you visualize what it was like here 100 years ago?* to conceive, to dream up, to imagine, to picture, to see.

vital *It is vital to have food.* essential, fundamental, imperative, important, indispensable, necessary.

vitality *Tony's dog is full of vitality.* energy, life, liveliness, sprightliness, vigour, zest.

vitamins SEE **food**.

vivacious SEE **lively**.

vivid **1** *vivid colours.* bright, brilliant, colourful, gay, gleaming, intense, shining, showy. **2** *a vivid description.* clear, lifelike, lively.

vixen SEE **female**.

vocabulary SEE **language**.

vocalist singer. SEE ALSO **sing**.

vodka SEE **drink**.

vogue 1 craze, fashion, style, taste, trend. **2** *in vogue*: fashionable, popular, (informal) trendy.

voice 1 *I recognized her voice.* speech. **2** FOR WORDS TO DO WITH USING YOUR VOICE SEE **sing, talk**.

void SEE **empty**.

volcano SEE **geography**.

vole SEE **animal**.

volley-ball SEE **sport**.

volt SEE **electricity**.

volume 1 *That tank can store a large volume of oil.* amount, bulk, mass, quantity. **2** *What is the volume of that tank?* capacity, dimensions, size. SEE ALSO **measure**. **3** *How many volumes are in the library?* book.

voluntary optional.

volunteer 1 *Tony volunteered to clear up.* to offer. **2** *to volunteer for the army.* SEE **enlist**.

vomit to be sick, (informal) to throw up.

vote 1 *Who did you vote for?* to choose, to elect, to nominate, to opt for, to pick, to select, to settle on. **2** *We had a vote to choose a captain.* ballot, election, poll.

voucher *This voucher gives you £1 off the usual price.* coupon, ticket, token.

vow *Lucy vowed that she was telling the truth.* to give an assurance, to give your word, to guarantee, to pledge, to promise, to swear, to take an oath.

vowel SEE **language**.

voyage SEE **travel**.

vulgar *vulgar language.* coarse, common, crude, foul, impolite, improper, indecent, offensive, rough, rude, uncouth.

vulnerable *Tony's king was vulnerable after he lost his queen.* defenceless, exposed, unguarded, unprotected, weak.

vulture SEE **bird**.

W w

wad *a wad of £5 notes.* bundle, pad.

waddle SEE **walk**.

wade to paddle. SEE ALSO **walk**.

wafer SEE **biscuit**.

wag *A dog wags its tail.* to shake, to waggle, to wave, to wiggle.

wage 1 *wages*: earnings, income, pay, salary. **2** *to wage war.* to carry on, to fight.

wager bet, stake. SEE ALSO **gamble**.

wagon SEE **railway, vehicle**.

wagtail SEE **bird**.

wail to cry, to howl, to moan, to shriek. SEE ALSO **sound**.

waist *She wore a belt round her waist.* middle. SEE ALSO **body**.

wait 1 *Wait there!* to halt, to keep still, to remain, to rest, to stay, to stop. **2** *We waited for the signal.* to delay, to hesitate, to hold back, to pause. **3** *to wait around*: to dally, to linger, to loiter, to lurk. **4** *to wait at table.* to serve.

waiter SEE **job**.

wake *Wake me at 7.30.* to arouse, to awaken, to call, to rouse.

walk VARIOUS WAYS OF WALKING ARE to amble, to crawl, to creep, to dodder, to hike, to hobble, to limp, to lurch, to march, to pace, to pad, to paddle, to plod, to prowl, to ramble, to saunter, to scuttle, to shamble, to shuffle, to slink, to stagger, to stalk, to steal, to step, to stride, to stroll, to strut, to stumble, to swagger, to totter, to tramp, to trample, to trek, to troop, to trot, to trudge, to waddle, to wade.

walker hiker, pedestrian, rambler.

walkie-talkie SEE **communication**.

wall 1 KINDS OF WALL ARE barrier, dam, dike, embankment, fence, paling, palisade, parapet, partition, rampart, stockade. **2** SEE **building**.

wallaby SEE **animal**.

wallet purse. SEE ALSO **container**.

wallflower SEE **flower**.

wallop SEE **hit.**

wallow *The animals wallowed in the mud.* to flounder, to roll about.

wallpaper SEE **paper.**

waltz SEE **dance.**

wan *Lucy looked wan after being ill.* pale, pasty, (informal) poorly, sickly.

wand *a magician's wand.* cane, rod, stick.

wander 1 *The sheep wander about the hills.* to drift, to ramble, to range, to roam, to rove, to stray, to travel. 2 *We wandered off course.* to curve, to swerve, to turn, to twist, to veer, to zigzag.

wane *The light waned as the sun went down.* to decline, to decrease, to diminish, to dwindle, to fade, to fail, to lessen, to weaken.

want 1 *We can't always have what we want.* to desire, to fancy, to hanker after, to long for, to wish for, to yearn for. 2 *The farmers wanted rain after the long drought.* to be short of, to lack, to need, to require.

war KINDS OF ACTION IN WAR ARE ambush, assault, attack, battle, blitz, blockade, bombardment, campaign, counter-attack, hostilities, invasion, manoeuvre, negotiation, operation, retreat, siege, surrender, warfare, withdrawal. FOR WORDS CONNECTED WITH WAR SEE ALSO **armed services, fight, peace, weapon.**

warble SEE **sound.**

warbler SEE **bird.**

ward 1 *a hospital ward.* SEE **medicine.** 2 *to ward off an attack.* to fend off, to parry, to push away, to repel, to repulse.

warden *a traffic warden:* SEE **job.**

warder *a prison warder:* guard, keeper. SEE ALSO **job.**

wardrobe SEE **furniture.**

warehouse depot, store. SEE ALSO **building.**

wares *The saleswoman displayed her wares.* goods, merchandise.

warhead SEE **weapon.**

warlike *warlike tribes.* aggressive, belligerent, hostile, militant, pugnacious.

warm 1 *a warm room, warm weather, etc.* close, sultry. SEE ALSO **hot.** 2 *warm water.* luke-warm, tepid. 3 *a warm welcome.* affectionate, cordial, friendly, genial, kind, loving, warm-hearted.

warn 1 *Mrs Angel warned Logan not to cheat.* to caution, to remind. 2 *The guard warned us that the train would be late.* to alert, to notify.

warning 1 *Was there any warning of trouble?* hint, indication, omen, sign, signal, threat. 2 WARNING SIGNALS ARE alarm, beacon, bell, fire-alarm, fog-horn, gong, red light, siren, whistle.

warp *The floor is uneven because the planks have warped.* to become deformed, to bend, to buckle, to curl, to curve, to distort, to twist.

warrant SEE **document.**

warren *a rabbits' warren.* burrow.

warrior SEE **fighter.**

warship SEE **vessel.**

wart SEE **illness.**

wary *Many animals are wary of strangers.* careful, cautious, distrustful, suspicious, watchful.

wash 1 to bath, to bathe, to clean, to mop, to rinse, to shampoo, to sponge down, to swill, to wipe. 2 THINGS USED IN WASHING YOURSELF ARE bath, flannel, nail-brush, pumice-stone, shampoo, shower, soap, sponge, toothbrush, towel, wash-basin. SEE ALSO **bathroom.** 3 THINGS USED IN WASHING CLOTHES ARE clothes-horse, clothes-line, clothes-peg, detergent, iron, ironing-board, mangle, spin-drier, tumble-drier, washer, washing-machine, wringer.

washing *Hang out the washing.* laundry.

wasp SEE **insect.**

waste 1 *Don't waste time.* to fritter, to misuse, to squander. 2 *He wasted away when his dog died.* to become emaciated, to become thin, to mope, to pine, to weaken. **3** *Nowadays we try to recycle waste.* garbage, junk, litter, refuse, remnants, rubbish, scraps, trash.

wasteful *It's wasteful to throw away good food.* extravagant, prodigal, uneconomical.

watch 1 *Watch what I do.* to attend to, to concentrate on, to heed, to mark, to note, to observe, to take notice of. **2** *We watched the sunset.* to contemplate, to gaze at, to look at, to regard, to stare at. **3** *Will you watch the twins while I pop out for a minute?* to care for, to guard, to keep an eye on, to look after, to mind, to protect, to supervise, to tend. **4** *Who's got a watch?* digital watch, stop-watch. SEE ALSO **clock**.

watchman guard, look-out, night-watchman, sentinel, sentry.

water 1 VARIOUS STRETCHES OF WATER ARE brook, lake, ocean, pond, pool, river, sea, SEE **stream**. **2** *The farmer waters his strawberry fields.* to irrigate, to soak, to sprinkle, to wet. **3** *It's illegal for a farmer to water down the milk.* to dilute, to thin, to weaken.

water-closet lavatory, (informal) loo, toilet, WC. SEE ALSO **house**.

water-colour SEE **paint**.

watercress SEE **salad**.

waterfall *The canoeist negotiated a dangerous waterfall.* cataract, rapids.

watering-can SEE **container, garden**.

water-lily SEE **water plant**.

waterlogged *a waterlogged pitch.* full of water, saturated, soaked.

water-pistol SEE **toy**.

water plant VARIOUS WATER PLANTS ARE reeds, rushes, seaweed, watercress, water-lily.

water polo SEE **sport**.

waterproof watertight.

water-skiing SEE **sport**.

waterway canal, channel, river, stream.

watery 1 *watery eyes.* damp, moist, wet. **2** *watery gravy.* thin, weak.

watt SEE **electricity**.

wave 1 *She waved to me.* SEE **gesture**. **2** *He waved his stick.* to brandish, to flourish, to swing, to twirl. **3** *The trees waved in the wind.* to flap, to move to and fro, to shake, to wag, to waggle, to wiggle. **4** *the waves on the sea.* breaker, ripple, surf, swell. **5** *radio waves.* pulse, vibration.

wavelength *You have to tune your TV to the right wavelength.* channel, station, waveband.

waver 1 *The light from the candle wavered.* to flicker, to quake, to quaver, to quiver, to shake, to shiver, to shudder, to tremble. **2** *I wavered when I saw the fierce dog.* to falter, to hesitate, to pause, to think twice. **3** *Tony's determination never wavered.* to change, to vary.

waxworks SEE **entertainment**.

way 1 SEE **road**. **2** *Which way will you go?* course, direction, route. **3** *Lucy showed Tony the way to mend a fuse.* knack, means, method, procedure, process, system, technique. **4** *Why does Logan dress in that odd way?* fashion, manner, mode, style. **5** *It's our way to have mint sauce with lamb.* custom, habit, practice, routine, tradition.

wayfarer SEE **travel**.

WC SEE **water-closet**.

weak 1 *a weak person.* delicate, feeble, flabby, frail, helpless, ill, listless, poorly, sickly, weedy. **2** *a weak branch.* brittle, flimsy, fragile, rickety, shaky, slight, thin. **3** *a weak leader.* impotent, ineffectual, poor, powerless, spineless. **4** *a weak position.* defenceless, exposed, unguarded, unprotected, vulnerable. **5** *a weak excuse.* lame, unconvincing, unsatisfactory. **6** *weak tea.* diluted, tasteless, thin, watery.

weaken 1 *Logan's absence weakened our team's chances.* to destroy, to erode, to ruin, to undermine. **2** *Our enthusiasm weakened as the day went on.* to decline, to decrease, to diminish, to dwindle, to fade, to flag, to lessen, to reduce, to wane.

weakness *The crash was due to a weakness in the design of the aircraft.* defect, failing, fault, flaw, imperfection.

wealth SEE **money.**

wealthy affluent, prosperous, rich, well off, well-to-do.

weapon 1 *weapons*: armaments. **2** VARIOUS WEAPONS ARE airgun, arrow, artillery, atom bomb, automatic weapon, battering-ram, battle-axe, bayonet, blunderbuss, bomb, boomerang, bow and arrow, cannon, cannonball, catapult, crossbow, cutlass, dagger, foil, grenade, harpoon, H-bomb, incendiary bomb, javelin, lance, land-mine, laser beam, long-bow, machine-gun, mine, missile, mortar, musket, napalm, nuclear weapons, pike, pistol, rapier, revolver, rifle, sabre, shotgun, sling, small arms, spear, sub-machine-gun, sword, tank, tear gas, time bomb, tomahawk, torpedo, truncheon, warhead. SEE ALSO **ammunition.** **3** PLACES WHERE WEAPONS ARE STORED ARE armoury, arsenal, depot, magazine.

wear 1 *Which jeans shall I wear?* to be dressed in, to put on, to wrap up in. FOR THINGS YOU WEAR SEE **clothes.** **2** *to wear away*: to eat away, to erode, to grind down, to rub away. **3** *to wear out*: to exhaust, to tire, to weary. **4** *worn*: *My jumper is worn at the elbows.* frayed, ragged, shabby, tattered, tatty, thin, threadbare.

weary bored, drowsy, exhausted, jaded, sleepy, tired, worn out.

weasel SEE **animal.**

weather 1 VARIOUS FEATURES OF THE WEATHER ARE anticyclone, blizzard, breeze, cloud, cyclone, deluge, depression, dew, downpour, drizzle, drought, fog, frost, gale, hail, haze, heat-wave, hoar-frost, hurricane, ice, lightning, mist, monsoon, rain, rainbow, shower, sleet, slush, snow, squall, storm, sunshine, temperature, tempest, thaw, thunder, tornado, typhoon, whirlwind, wind. **2** USEFUL WORDS TO DESCRIBE WEATHER ARE blustery, bright, brilliant, clear, close, cloudless, cloudy, SEE **cold,** drizzly, dull, fair, fine, foggy, foul, freezing, frosty, grey, hazy, SEE **hot,** icy, misty, oppressive, overcast, rainy, rough, showery, slushy, snowy, squally, stormy, sultry, sunless, sunny, sweltering, teeming, thundery, torrential, turbulent, wet, windy, wintry. **3** OTHER WORDS TO DO WITH WEATHER ARE barometer, climate, forecast, meteorology, outlook, thermometer.

weather-beaten tanned.

weaving SEE **art.**

web mesh, net, network.

wedding 1 marriage. **2** PEOPLE AT A WEDDING ARE best man, bride, bridegroom, bridesmaid, family, groom, guests, page. **3** OTHER WORDS TO DO WITH WEDDINGS ARE confetti, honeymoon, reception, registry office, service, trousseau, wedding-ring. **4** SEE **marriage.**

wedge *Wedge the door open.* to jam, to stick. SEE **fasten.**

wee SEE **small.**

weed SOME GARDEN WEEDS ARE clover, dock, nettle, thistle. SEE ALSO **plant.**

weedy (informal) *You wouldn't expect that weedy boy to be a boxer!* delicate, feeble, frail, helpless, ill, (informal) poorly, sickly, weak.

week SEE **time.**

weep to blubber, to cry, to grizzle, to shed tears, to snivel, to sob, to wail.

weight 1 *What is your weight?* heaviness. SEE **measure.** **2** *This suitcase is a terrible weight.* burden, load.

weighty 1 *a weighty load.* burdensome, heavy, massive, ponderous. **2** *a weighty problem.* grave, important, momentous, serious.

weir dam.

weird 1 *What a weird thing to do!* (informal) cranky, curious, eccentric, funny, odd, peculiar, queer, strange, unconventional, zany. 2 *There was a weird atmosphere in the dungeon.* creepy, eerie, ghostly, (informal) scary, (informal) spooky, uncanny.

welcome 1 *a friendly welcome.* greeting, reception. 2 *She welcomed us at the door.* to greet, to receive. 3 *We had a welcome rest.* SEE **pleasant**. 4 *welcoming:* SEE **friendly**.

weld SEE **fasten**.

welfare *A nurse looks after the welfare of the patients.* happiness, health.

well 1 *You look well.* healthy, hearty, lively, robust, sound, vigorous. 2 *well off:* SEE **wealthy**.

wellington SEE **shoe**.

well-to-do SEE **wealthy**.

west SEE **geography**.

western SEE **film**.

wet 1 *The soil is too wet for gardening.* saturated, soaked, sodden, soggy, waterlogged. 2 *Lucy got wet in the storm.* bedraggled, drenched, dripping, sopping. 3 *The cellar walls were wet.* clammy, damp, dank, moist. 4 *The weather was wet.* drizzly, rainy, showery.

wet-suit SEE **clothes**.

whack SEE **hit**.

whale SEE **animal**.

whaler SEE **vessel**.

wharf *The ship's cargo was unloaded onto the wharf.* dock, landing-stage, jetty, pier, quay.

wheat SEE **cereal**.

wheel 1 KINDS OF WHEEL ARE castor, cog-wheel, spinning-wheel, steering-wheel. 2 PARTS OF A WHEEL ARE axle, hub, rim, spoke, tyre. 3 SEE **vehicle**. 4 *The birds wheeled overhead.* to circle, to move in circles. 5 *He wheeled round when I called.* to change direction, to swerve, to turn, to veer.

wheelbarrow, wheelchair SEE **vehicle**.

wheeze to gasp, to pant, to puff.

whelk SEE **shellfish**.

whiff aroma, fragrance, odour, perfume, scent, smell, stench, stink.

while *I haven't seen granny for a long while.* period, time.

whim impulse.

whimper to cry, to grizzle, to groan, to moan, to wail, to whine. SEE ALSO **sound**.

whine to complain, to cry, to moan, to whimper. SEE ALSO **sound**.

whinny to neigh. SEE ALSO **sound**.

whip 1 *I'd never use a whip on a horse.* crop, lash, scourge. 2 SEE **hit**. 3 *whipping:* SEE **punishment**.

whippet SEE **dog**.

whirl *The roundabout whirled round.* to revolve, to rotate, to spin, to turn, to twirl.

whirlpool eddy.

whirlwind SEE **weather**.

whisk 1 *an egg whisk.* SEE **kitchen**. 2 *Tony whisked some eggs to make an omelette.* to beat, to mix, to stir.

whiskers bristles, hairs, moustache.

whisky SEE **drink**.

whisper SEE **talk**.

whist SEE **cards**.

whistle to blow. SEE ALSO **sound**.

white SEE **colour**.

whiten to bleach, to lighten.

whitewash SEE **paint**.

Whitsun SEE **church**.

whiz SEE **sound**.

whole 1 *She told us the whole story.* complete, entire, full, total, unabridged. 2 *The wolf swallowed the duck whole!* intact, unbroken, undamaged, undivided.

wholesale *The bomb caused wholesale destruction.* extensive, general, global, universal, widespread.

wholesome *wholesome food.* healthy, good, nutritious.

whoop SEE **sound**.

whooping-cough SEE **illness**.

wicked *a wicked deed, a wicked person.* base, blasphemous, evil, foul, immoral, infamous, sinful, sinister,

spiteful, vicious, villainous, wrong.
SEE ALSO **bad, naughty.**

wickerwork SEE **art.**

wicket SEE **cricket.**

wide 1 *a wide river.* broad, expansive.
2 *a wide gap.* extensive, large, open,
spacious, yawning.

widen to enlarge.

widespread *widespread rain.*
extensive, general, universal,
wholesale.

widow, widower SEE **family.**

width breadth.

wield 1 *Lucy wields a cricket bat expertly.*
to handle, to manage. 2 *The
headteacher wields considerable influence.*
to employ, to exercise, to use.

wife SEE **family.**

wig SEE **hat.**

wiggle to fidget, to move restlessly, to
sway, to wag, to waggle.

wigwam tent, tepee.

wild 1 *wild animals.* ferocious, free,
natural, undomesticated, untamed.
2 *wild country.* overgrown, rough,
rugged, uncultivated, uninhabited,
waste. 3 *wild behaviour.* boisterous,
disorderly, excited, lawless, noisy,
obstreperous, reckless, rowdy,
savage, uncivilized, uncontrolled,
undisciplined, unruly. SEE ALSO
mad. 4 *wild weather.* stormy,
turbulent, violent, windy.

wilderness desert, wasteland.

wilful 1 *a wilful character.* determined,
dogged, obstinate, stubborn. 2 *wilful
disobedience.* deliberate, intentional,
premeditated.

will 1 *Have you got the will to succeed?*
desire, determination, resolution,
wish. 2 *She died without leaving a will.*
SEE **document.**

willing 1 *I'm willing to play.* disposed,
eager, inclined, prepared, ready.
2 *She's a willing worker.* cooperative,
helpful, obliging.

willow SEE **tree.**

wilt *Mrs Brunswick's plants wilted in the
drought.* to become limp, to droop, to

flag, to flop, to shrivel, to weaken, to
wither.

wily *Foxes are supposed to be wily
creatures.* artful, astute, clever, crafty,
cunning, furtive, ingenious,
knowing, skilful, sly, tricky.

win 1 *The stronger team won.* to be
victorious, to come first, to succeed,
to triumph. 2 *Tony's performance won a
round of applause.* to deserve, to earn,
to gain, to get, to receive.

wince SEE **expression.**

wind 1 *The wind blew the papers about.*
blast, breeze, draught, gale, gust,
puff, whirlwind. SEE ALSO **weather.**
2 *wind instruments:* SEE **brass,
woodwind.** 3 *The road winds up the
hill.* to bend, to curve, to twist, to
zigzag. 4 *I wound the thread on to a reel.*
to coil, to curl, to loop, to roll, to
turn.

wind-cheater SEE **clothes.**

windmill SEE **building.**

window French window, pane, sash
window, skylight. SEE ALSO
building.

window-box SEE **garden.**

windpipe SEE **body.**

windscreen SEE **vehicle.**

windsurfing SEE **sport.**

windswept *a windswept moor.* bare,
bleak, desolate, exposed, windy.

windy SEE **weather.**

wine SEE **drink.**

wing 1 SEE **aircraft, bird, vehicle.**
2 *They built a new wing onto the hospital.*
annexe, extension.

wink 1 *She winked at me.* SEE ALSO
gesture. 2 *The Christmas tree lights
winked on and off.* to blink, to flash, to
flicker, to twinkle. SEE ALSO **light.**

winkle SEE **shellfish.**

winner champion, conqueror,
medallist, victor.

winnings SEE **money.**

winter sports VARIOUS WINTER
SPORTS ARE bobsleigh, ice-hockey,
skating, skiing, sledging,
tobogganing.

wipe 1 *Wipe the dishes.* to clean, to dry,

to dust, to mop, to polish, to rub, to scour, to sponge, to wash. 2 *Mrs Brunswick tried to wipe out the ants' nest.* SEE **destroy.**

wire 1 *telephone wires.* cable, flex, lead. SEE ALSO **electricity.** 2 *Granny sent a wire to say that she was ill.* telegram.

wireless radio, transistor. SEE ALSO **communication.**

wiry *a wiry figure.* lean, strong, thin, tough.

wise 1 *If you are wise you won't start smoking.* intelligent, knowledgeable, perceptive, prudent, reasonable, sensible, thoughtful. 2 *She made a wise decision.* advisable, appropriate, fair, just, proper, right, sound.

wish 1 *We couldn't have wished for nicer weather.* to desire, to fancy, to hanker after, to long for, to want, to yearn for. 2 *Lucy's secret wish is to be an Olympic gymnast.* ambition, craving, desire, goal, hope, longing, objective.

wistful *Tony looked wistful as he watched his friends go away on holiday.* forlorn, pathetic, sad.

wit 1 *We laughed at the comedian's wit.* cleverness, humour, jokes, quickness. 2 *He didn't have the wit to see that we were only teasing.* brains, intellect, intelligence, reason, sense. 3 *Logan is quite a wit sometimes.* comedian, comic, jester, joker.

witch, witchcraft, witch-doctor SEE **magic.**

withdraw 1 *The general withdrew his troops.* to call back, to recall, to remove, to take away. 2 *The troops withdrew.* to back away, to fall back, to leave, to move back, to retire, to retreat, to run away.

wither *The plants withered in the drought.* to dry, to shrink, to shrivel, to wilt.

withhold *to withhold information from the police.* to conceal, to hold back, to keep back, to keep secret.

withstand *The town withstood a long siege.* to cope with, to endure, to oppose, to resist, to stand up to, to tolerate.

witness 1 *Lucy was a witness of the accident.* bystander, eyewitness, observer, onlooker, spectator. 2 *Call the next witness!* SEE **law.** 3 *Lucy witnessed the accident.* to attend, to behold, to be present at, to observe, to see, to view.

witty *a witty story-teller.* amusing, clever, comic, funny, humorous, quick-witted, sharp-witted.

wizard SEE **magic.**

wobble *The jelly wobbles when you touch the plate.* to be unsteady, to quake, to shake, to sway, to totter, to tremble, to waver.

wobbly *I fell in because one of the stepping-stones was wobbly.* insecure, loose, rocky, shaky, unsteady.

woe distress, grief, misery, sorrow, unhappiness.

woeful SEE **sad.**

wolf SEE **animal.**

woman (old-fashioned) dame, lady. SEE ALSO **person.**

womb SEE **body.**

wonder 1 *We gazed with wonder at the huge spacecraft.* admiration, amazement, awe, respect, reverence. 2 *We wondered at the size of the spacecraft.* to be amazed by, to gape at, to marvel at. 3 *I wondered whether it was time for dinner.* to ask yourself, to be curious about, to question yourself.

woo to court, to make love to.

wood 1 *A carpenter makes things out of wood.* KINDS OF WOOD ARE balsa, beech, cedar, chestnut, ebony, elm, mahogany, oak, pine, rosewood, teak, walnut. SEE ALSO **timber.** 2 *We got lost in the wood.* coppice, copse, forest, grove, jungle, orchard, thicket, trees, woodland.

wood-louse SEE **insect.** ! *Wood-lice* are not proper insects.

woodman SEE **job.**

woodpecker SEE **bird.**

woodwind WOODWIND INSTRUMENTS ARE bassoon, clarinet, flute, oboe, piccolo, recorder. SEE ALSO **music.**

woodwork SEE **art.**

woodworm SEE **insect.**

wool SEE **cloth.**

woolly 1 *a woolly teddy-bear.* downy, fleecy, furry, fuzzy. 2 *woolly ideas.* ambiguous, confused, indefinite, uncertain, unclear, vague.

word *A thesaurus is a book of words.* expression, term. SEE ALSO **language.**

word-processor SEE **computer, write.**

work 1 *Gardening can be hard work.* chore, drudgery, effort, exertion, labour, slavery, toil. 2 *Mum leaves for work at 8.30.* business, employment, job, occupation, profession, trade. FOR VARIOUS KINDS OF WORK SEE **job.** 3 *Mrs Angel set the class some work.* assignment, homework, project, task. 4 *We worked at our maths until dinner.* to be busy, to exert yourself, to labour, to slave, to toil. 5 *How does this machine work?* to act, to function, to go, to operate, to perform, to run. 6 *Did your plan work?* to be effective, to succeed, to thrive. 7 *to work out: Did you work out the answer?* SEE **calculate.**

workmanship *We admired the blacksmith's workmanship.* art, craft, handicraft, skill, technique.

world earth, globe, planet. SEE ALSO **geography.**

worm 1 SEE **insect.** 2 *I wormed my way through the undergrowth.* to crawl, to creep, to slither, to squirm, to wriggle, to writhe.

worn *My shirt was worn at the cuffs.* frayed, ragged, scruffy, shabby, tattered, tatty, threadbare.

worry 1 *Don't worry granny while she's reading.* to annoy, to bother, to disturb, to molest, to pester, to trouble, to upset, to vex. 2 *Don't worry about us: we'll be all right.* to be anxious, to feel uneasy, to fret. 3 *The bad weather is a worry to the farmers.* anxiety, burden, care, concern, problem, trouble.

worsen 1 *Logan worsened the situation by being rude to the referee.* to aggravate, to

make worse. 2 *The referee's temper worsened as the game went on.* to decline, to degenerate, to deteriorate, to get worse.

worship 1 *Lucy worships her grandad.* to adore, to dote on, to idolize, to love, to revere. 2 *to worship God.* to praise. FOR GROUPS WHO WORSHIP IN VARIOUS WAYS SEE **religion.** 3 BUILDINGS WHERE PEOPLE WORSHIP ARE abbey, cathedral, chapel, church, mosque, pagoda, synagogue, temple.

worsted SEE **cloth.**

worth 1 *Is this stamp of any worth?* importance, merit, usefulness, value. 2 *to be worth:* to be priced at, to cost, to have a value of.

worthless *Don't waste money on worthless junk.* frivolous, futile, pointless, trivial, unimportant, useless, valueless.

worthwhile 1 *Our collection for OXFAM raised a worthwhile amount.* biggish, considerable, noticeable, significant, sizeable, substantial, useful, valuable. 2 *Is it worthwhile doing a paper round?* advantageous, beneficial, profitable, rewarding.

worthy *a worthy cause, a worthy winner.* admirable, commendable, creditable, decent, deserving, honest, honourable, praiseworthy, respectable.

wound 1 *The explosion wounded several people.* to cause pain to, to damage, to harm, to hurt, to injure. 2 VARIOUS WAYS OF WOUNDING ARE to bite, to bruise, to burn, to crush, to cut, to fracture, to gore, to graze, to impale, to knife, to make sore, to mangle, to maul, to mutilate, to scratch, to sprain, to strain, to stab, to sting, to torture.

wrap *We wrapped it in a bandage. The mountains were wrapped in mist.* to bind, to cloak, to conceal, to cover, to enclose, to envelop, to hide, to insulate, to lag, to muffle, to shroud, to wind.

wrath anger, exasperation, fury, rage, temper.

wrathful SEE **angry**.

wreath SEE **flower**.

wreck 1 *The ship was wrecked on the rocks*. to break up, to crumple, to crush, to demolish, to destroy, to shatter, to smash. **2** *The storm wrecked our picnic*. to ruin, to spoil.

wreckage bits, debris, pieces, remains, rubble, ruins.

wren SEE **bird**.

wrench 1 SEE **tool**. **2** *I wrenched the lid off*. to force, to jerk, to lever, to prize, to pull, to twist.

wrestle 1 to grapple, to struggle. **2** *wrestling*: SEE **fight, sport**.

wretched 1 *Tony looked wretched when his dog was ill*. SEE **miserable**. **2** *I was suffering from a wretched cold*. SEE **unpleasant**.

wriggle *The snake wriggled away*. to squirm, to twist, to writhe.

wring 1 *He wrung my hand*. to clasp, to grip, to shake. **2** *I wrung the water out of my wet swimming things*. to compress, to crush, to press, to squeeze, to twist.

wrinkle 1 *Tony ironed the wrinkles out of his shirt*. crease, fold, furrow, line, pleat. **2** *Try not to wrinkle the new curtains*. to crease, to crinkle, to crumple.

wrist SEE **body, hand, joint**.

write 1 WAYS OF WRITING ARE to compose, to doodle, to engrave, to inscribe, to jot, to note, to print, to record, to scrawl, to scribble, to type. **2** THINGS YOU WRITE WITH ARE ball-point, chalk, crayon, felt-tip, fountain pen, ink, pen, pencil, typewriter, word-processor. **3** THINGS YOU WRITE ON ARE blackboard, card, exercise book, form, jotter, notepaper, pad, paper, papyrus, parchment, postcard, stationery. **4** SEE **writer, writing**.

writer VARIOUS WRITERS ARE author, bard, composer, correspondent, dramatist, editor, journalist, novelist, playwright, poet, reporter, scriptwriter.

writhe to squirm, to twist, to wriggle.

writing 1 *Can you read this writing?* alphabet, handwriting, hieroglyphics, italics, letters, printing, shorthand. **2** *An author sells his writings to make a living*. literature. **3** VARIOUS WRITINGS ARE article, autobiography, biography, SEE **book**, comedy, diary, editorial, epic, essay, fable, fairy-tale, folk-tale, journalism, legend, letter, lyric, myth, novel, parable, play, SEE **poem**, prose, romance, saga, satire, science fiction, script, SF, sketch, story, tale, thriller, tragedy, verse, yarn.

wrong 1 *Logan got the wrong answer*. false, inaccurate, incorrect, mistaken, untrue. **2** *The umpire made the wrong decision*. improper, inappropriate, incongruous, unfair, unjust, wrongful. **3** *It is wrong to steal*. corrupt, criminal, crooked, deceitful, dishonest, illegal, naughty, reprehensible, unscrupulous. **4** *Cruelty to animals is wrong*. base, evil, immoral, sinful, vicious, villainous, wicked. SEE ALSO **bad**. **5** *The car has gone wrong*. broken down, faulty, out of order, unusable. **6** *We wronged Logan by accusing him unjustly*. to abuse, to be unfair to, to treat unfairly.

wry *a wry smile*. crooked, twisted.

X x

X-ray SEE **medicine**.

xylophone SEE **percussion**.

Y y

yacht SEE **vessel**.

yachting SEE **sport**.

yap SEE **sound**.

yard 1 *There are 36 inches in one yard*. SEE **measure**. **2** *a back yard*. courtyard, enclosure, garden, quadrangle.

yarn 1 SEE **thread.** 2 *She told us an old yarn.* narrative, story, tale.

yashmak SEE **clothes.**

yawn 1 SEE **expression.** 2 *yawning: a yawning hole.* open, wide.

year SEE **time.**

yearn 1 *We yearned for some warmer weather.* to desire, to fancy, to hanker after, to long for, to want, to wish for. 2 *a yearning:* craving, desire, itch, longing, urge, wish.

yeast SEE **food.**

yell to bawl, to bellow, to call, to shout. SEE ALSO **sound, talk.**

yellow SEE **colour.**

yellowhammer SEE **bird.**

yelp SEE **sound.**

yew SEE **tree.**

yield 1 *After a long siege they yielded to the enemy.* to capitulate, to give in, to submit, to surrender. 2 *Our pear tree yielded a huge crop.* to bear, to give, to grow, to produce.

yodel SEE **sound.**

yogurt SEE **food.**

Yom Kippur SEE **Jew, time.**

young 1 *young people, young trees, etc.* growing, undeveloped, youthful. 2 *He seems young for his age.* babyish, childish, immature, infantile. 3 YOUNG PEOPLE ARE adolescent, baby, boy, (insulting) brat, child, girl, infant, juvenile, (informal) kid, lad, lass, (informal) nipper, teenager, toddler, (insulting) urchin, youngster, youth. 4 YOUNG ANIMALS ARE calf, colt, cub, fawn, foal, heifer, kid, kitten, lamb, puppy. 5 YOUNG BIRDS ARE chick, cygnet, duckling, fledgeling, gosling, nestling, pullet. 6 YOUNG PLANTS ARE cutting, sapling, seedling.

youth, youthful SEE **young.**

yule, yuletide Christmas.

Z z

zany *We enjoyed the clowns' zany humour.* absurd, (informal) cranky, crazy, eccentric, ludicrous, mad, odd, preposterous, ridiculous, unconventional, weird.

zeal SEE **zest.**

zealous *There's no need for that traffic warden to be so zealous!* conscientious, diligent, eager, earnest, enthusiastic, keen.

zebra SEE **animal.**

zebra crossing SEE **road.**

Zen SEE **religion.**

zero SEE **nothing.**

zest *Logan finished off the ice-cream with great zest.* eagerness, energy, enjoyment, enthusiasm, liveliness, zeal.

zigzag 1 *a zigzag line.* bendy, crooked, twisting. 2 *The road zigzags up the hill.* to bend, to curve, to twist, to wind.

zinc SEE **metal.**

zip, zip-fastener SEE **fasten.**

zither SEE **music, strings.**

zone area, district, locality, neighbourhood, region, sector, territory, vicinity.

zoo FOR VARIOUS ANIMALS SEE **animal.**

zoology SEE **science.**

zoom (informal) *Lucy zoomed home with her good news.* to dash, to hurry, to hurtle, to rush, to speed. SEE ALSO **move.**

zoom lens SEE **photography.**

Notes

Notes

Notes